A HISTORY OF WESTERN MUSIC

Third Edition • Shorter

Donald Jay Grout

PROFESSOR EMERITUS OF MUSICOLOGY, CORNELL UNIVERSITY

A HISTORY OF
WESTERN MUSIC

Third Edition · Shorter

with *Claude V. Palisca,* YALE UNIVERSITY

 W · W · Norton & Company · New York · London

Music typography by Melvin Wildberger

Library of Congress Cataloging in Publication Data
Grout, Donald Jay.
  A history of western music. Shorter Edition
  Bibliography: p. 484
  Includes index.
  1. Music—History and criticism. I. Title.
ML160.G872 1980   780'.9   80–18420
ISBN 0-393-95142-1

W. W. Norton & Company, Inc., 500 Fifth Avenue, New York, N.Y. 10110

3 4 5 6 7 8 9 0

A. M. D. G.
To my wife, in gratitude and affection

Contents

Preface   xi

I. The State of Music at the End of the Ancient World   1
   The Greek Heritage. The Early Christian Church.

II. Gregorian Chant and Secular Song in the Middle Ages   16
   Gregorian Chant and the Roman Liturgy. Classes, Forms,
   and Types of Gregorian Chant. Later Developments of the
   Chant. Medieval Musical Theory and Practice.
   Nonliturgical and Secular Monody. Medieval Instrumental
   Music and Instruments.

III. The Beginnings of Polyphony and the Music of the
   Thirteenth Century   43
   Historical Background of Early Polyphony. Early Organum.
   Florid Organum. The Rhythmic Modes. Notre Dame
   Organum. Polyphonic Conductus. The Motet. Other Late
   Thirteenth-Century Forms. Summary.

IV. French and Italian Music of the Fourteenth Century   70
   The *Ars Nova* in France. Italian Trecento Music.
   French Music of the Late Fourteenth Century.
   Chromaticism and *Musica Ficta*. Notation. Instruments.
   Summary.

V. Medieval to Renaissance: English Music and the
   Burgundian School in the Fifteenth Century   89
   English Music to the End of the Fifteenth Century. The
   Evolution of Musical Style in the Late Middle Ages. The
   Burgundian School.

VI. The Age of the Renaissance: Ockeghem to Josquin   107
    General Features. The Netherlands Composers. Josquin des
    Prez. Some Contemporaries of Obrecht and Josquin.

VII. New Currents in the Sixteenth Century   130
    The Franco-Flemish Generation of 1520–50. The Rise of
    National Styles. The Rise of Instrumental Music. The
    Madrigal and Related Forms.

VIII. Church Music and Instrumental Music in the
    Late Renaissance   157
    The Music of the Reformation in Germany. Reformation
    Church Music Outside Germany. The Counter-Reformation.
    Instrumental Music of the Later Sixteenth Century. Toward
    the Baroque: The Venetian School. Summary.

IX. Early Baroque Music   181
    General Features of Baroque Music. Early Baroque
    Opera. Vocal Chamber Music. Church Music and Oratorio.
    Instrumental Music.

X. The Mature Baroque: Vocal Music   211
    Opera, Cantata, Song. Church Music and Oratorio.

XI. The Mature Baroque: Instrumental Music   230
    Keyboard Music. Ensemble Music.

XII. The Early Eighteenth Century   248
    Antonio Vivaldi. Jean-Philippe Rameau. Johann Sebastian
    Bach. Bach's Instrumental Music. Bach's Vocal Music.
    George Frideric Handel.

XIII. Sources of Classical Style: The Sonata, Symphony,
    and Opera in the Eighteenth Century   278
    The Background. Instrumental Music: Sonata, Symphony,
    and Concerto. Opera, Song, and Church Music.

XIV. The Late Eighteenth Century   298
    Franz Joseph Haydn. Haydn's Vocal Works. Wolfgang
    Amadeus Mozart. Mozart's Childhood and Early Youth.
    Mozart's First Masterworks. The Vienna Period.

XV. Ludwig van Beethoven (1770–1827)   324
    The Man and His Music. First Style Period. Second Style
    Period. Third Style Period.

XVI. The Nineteenth Century: Romanticism;
Vocal Music   344
  Classicism and Romanticism. Sources and Characteristics of
  the Romantic Style. Choral Music.

XVII. The Nineteenth Century: Instrumental Music   358
  Music for Piano. Chamber Music. Music for
  Orchestra.

XVIII. The Nineteenth Century: Opera and Music
Drama   381
  France. Italy. German Romantic Opera. Richard Wagner:
  The Music Drama.

XIX. The End of an Era   396
  Post-Romanticism. Richard Strauss. Nationalism, Old and
  New: Russia. Other Nations. New Currents in France.
  Peripheries.

XX. The Twentieth Century   425
  Introduction. Musical Styles Related to Folk Idioms. England.
  The United States. Neo-Classicism and Related Movements.
  Hindemith. Messiaen. Stravinsky. Schoenberg and His Fol-
  lowers. After Webern. Conclusion.

Glossary   476

Abbreviations   482

Bibliography   484

Chronology   502

Index   527

Preface

Ten years have passed since this book was last revised, and it now seems time for a third edition—again, not to recast the work entirely, but to include art music of the last decade and results of recent research. This shortened version has been designed for those who prefer or need a more compact presentation of the material. The changes are a matter of compression; no vital aspect of the subject has been slighted.

The history of music is primarily the history of musical style and cannot be grasped except by first-hand knowledge of the music itself. It is therefore essential to become acquainted with the *sound* of the music discussed in this book and to be able to examine it more or less in its entirety. In past editions, the selection of music examples was greatly influenced by the availability of works in standard editions and various anthologies, which were duly listed in the bibliography for each chapter of the book. This procedure inevitably visited great hardship on the student seeking out the sources in disparate volumes and also limited the works available for discussion in the text. Therefore, Professor Claude Palisca of Yale University was asked to participate in the revision and to prepare an abridged version of his two-volume *Norton Anthology of Western Music* (hereafter and forever known as NAWM/S) which could serve as a score resource for this shortened third edition of *A History of Western Music*. The reader will find references to the appropriate pieces in NAWM/S scattered throughout this substantially revised text, since almost all the specific discussions focus on this new repertory. Additional examples are cited in the Bibliography.

An elementary knowledge of musical terms and of harmony has been assumed. The Glossary contains brief definitions of terms not elsewhere defined in this book. The various Appendices to this third edition have been revised and updated; suggestions for further reading in the Bibliography reflect the most recent scholarly advances; and the Chronology has been extended to 1980.

I am especially grateful to all the scholars who have provided expert advice on portions of the book that lay in areas of their special competence and whose help I have acknowledged in the first and second editions.

For the present revised edition I wish to thank Professor William W. Austin, Professor Gaynor Jones, Professor Rey M. Longyear, and Mr. Sidney Cox for valuable suggestions. The following colleagues provided detailed comments on the last edition as a practical teaching tool: Professor William C. Holmes, University of California at Irvine; Professor Steven Ledbetter, formerly of Dartmouth College; Professor K. Marie Stolba, Indiana University-Purdue University at Fort Wayne; and Professor Efrim Fruchtman, Memphis State University. I have carefully considered all their valuable counsels and have heeded many of them. Also my gratitude goes to my able research assistants Mrs. Mary Hunter Parakilas and Mr. Jeffrey Cooper, and to Mr. Michael A. Keller, Music Librarian of Cornell University. Finally, I wish to express my appreciation to Mrs. Claire Brook of W. W. Norton & Company, Inc., for her devoted care in the production of the present edition.

Donald J. Grout
"Cloudbank," Spafford, New York

A HISTORY OF
WESTERN MUSIC

Third Edition · Shorter

I

The State of Music at the
End of the Ancient World

Anyone living in a province of the Roman Empire in the fifth century of the Christian era might have seen roads where people used to travel and now travelled no more, temples and arenas built for throngs and now falling into disuse and ruin, and life everywhere becoming with each generation poorer, more insecure, and more brutish. Rome in the time of her greatness had imposed peace on most of western Europe as well as on considerable parts of Africa and Asia; but Rome had grown weak and unable to defend herself. The barbarians were pouring in from the north and east, and the common civilization of Europe was splintering into fragments which only after many centuries began to coalesce gradually into the modern nations.

The grand events of Rome's decline and fall stand out so luridly in history that it is hard for us even now to realize that, along with the process of destruction, there was quietly going on an opposite process of creation. This came to be centered in the Christian Church, which until the tenth century was the principal—and oftentimes the only—bond of union and channel of culture in Europe. The earliest Christian communities, in spite of three hundred years of sporadic persecution, grew steadily and spread to all parts of the Empire. After his conversion in 312, the Emperor Constantine adopted a policy of toleration and, what is more, made Christianity the religion of the imperial family. In 395 the political unity of the ancient world was formally broken up by the division into Eastern and Western Empires, with capitals at Byzantium and Rome. When after a terrible century of wars and invasions the last Western Emperor finally stepped down from his throne in 476, the foundations of the Papal power were already so firmly laid that the Church was ready to assume the civilizing and unifying mission of Rome.

The Greek Heritage

The history of Western art music properly begins with the music of the Christian Church. But all through the Middle Ages and even to the present time men have continually turned back to Greece and Rome for instruction, for correction, and for inspiration in their several fields of work; this has been true in music —though with some important differences. Roman literature, for example, never ceased to exert influence in the Middle Ages, and this influence became much greater in the fourteenth and fifteenth centuries when more Roman works became known; at the same time, too, the surviving literature of Greece was gradually recovered. But in literature, as well as in some other fields (notably sculpture), medieval or Renaissance artists had the advantage of being able to study and, if they so desired, imitate the models of antiquity. The actual poems or statues were before them. In music this was not so. The Middle Ages did not possess a single example of Greek or Roman music—nor, it may be added, are we today much better off. About a dozen examples—half of them mere fragments—of Greek music have been discovered, nearly all from comparatively late periods, but there is no general agreement as to just how they were meant to sound; there are no authentic remains of ancient Roman music. So we, as well as the men of medieval times, derive nearly all our knowledge of this art in the ancient civilizations at second hand from a few rather vague accounts of performances, but mostly from theoretical treatises and literary descriptions.

There was a special reason for the disappearance of the traditions of Roman musical practice at the beginning of the Middle Ages: most of this music was connected with social occasions on which the early Church looked with horror, or with pagan religious exercises which the Church believed had to be exterminated. Consequently every effort was made not only to keep out of the Church music which would recall such abominations to the minds of the faithful, but, if possible, to blot out the very memory of it. How much may have slipped in and been preserved, and how much may have survived outside the Church over the centuries, no one knows.

Yet there were some features of ancient musical practice that lived on in the Middle Ages if only for the reason that they could hardly have been abolished without abolishing music itself; furthermore, ancient musical theory was the foundation of medieval theory and was part of most philosophical systems. So in order to understand medieval music, we must know something about the music of ancient peoples, and in particular about the musical practice and theory of the Greeks.

Greek mythology ascribed to music a divine origin and named as its inventors and earliest practitioners gods and demigods, such as Apollo, Amphion, and Orpheus. In this dim prehistoric world, music had magic powers: people thought it could heal sickness, purify the body and mind, and work miracles in the realm of nature. Similar powers are attributed to music in the Old Testament: we need only recall the stories of David curing Saul's madness by playing the harp (I Samuel xvi: 14–23), or of the trumpet-blasts and shouting that toppled the walls of Jericho (Joshua vi: 12–20). In the Homeric Age, bards sang heroic poems at banquets (*Odyssey* VIII, 72–82).

Music in ancient Greek life and thought

From earliest times music was an inseparable part of religious ceremonies. In the cult of Apollo the lyre was the characteristic instrument, while in that of Dionysus it was the aulos. Both these instruments probably came into Greece from Asia Minor. The lyre and its larger counterpart, the kithara, were instruments with five to seven strings (later as many as eleven); both were used for solo playing and to accompany the singing or reciting of epic poems. The aulos, a double-pipe reed instrument (not a flute) with a shrill piercing tone, was used in connection with the singing of a certain kind of poetry (the dithyramb) in the worship of Dionysus, out of which it is believed the Greek drama developed. As a conse-

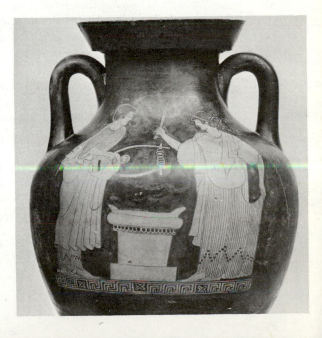

Vase painting of Apollo playing a lyre and Artemis holding an aulos before an altar. The lyre was a loosely constructed instrument with a body made from a tortoise shell or wooden bowl over which was stretched a skin. Two horns or wooden arms projected upward from the bowl and supported a horizontal crosspiece to which strings were attached; the other ends of these arms were fastened to the underside of the sounding bowl after passing over a bridge. The lyre was played by plucking the strings either with the fingers or a plectrum. (Courtesy Metropolitan Museum of Art, Rogers Fund, 1907)

quence, in the great dramas of the classical age—works by Aeschylus, Sophocles, Euripides—choruses and other musical portions were accompanied by, or alternated with, the sounds of the aulos.

From at least as early as the sixth century B.C. both the lyre and the aulos were played as independent solo instruments. There is an account of a musical festival or competition held at the Pythian games in 586 B.C. at which one Sakadas played a composition for the aulos illustrating the combat between Apollo and the dragon —the earliest known piece of program music, and one which remained famous for centuries. Contests of kithara and aulos players, as well as festivals of instrumental and vocal music, became increasingly popular after the fifth century B.C. As instrumental music grew more independent the number of virtuosos multiplied; at the same time the music itself became more complex in every way. In the fourth century Aristotle warned against too much professional training in general music education:

> The right measure will be attained if students of music stop short of the arts which are practised in professional contests, and do not seek to acquire those fantastic marvels of execution which are now the fashion in such contests, and from these have passed into education. Let the young practise even such music as we have prescribed, only until they are able to feel delight in noble melodies and rhythms, and not merely in that common part of music in which every slave or child and even some animals find pleasure.[1]

Sometime after the classical age (about 450 to 325 B.C.) a reaction set in against technical complexities, and by the beginning of the Christian era Greek musical theory, and probably also its practice, had become simplified. Most of our surviving examples of Greek music come from relatively late periods. The chief are: two Delphic hymns to Apollo from about 150 B.C., a *skolion* or drinking song from about the same time or perhaps a little later, and three hymns of Mesomedes of Crete from the second century A.D.

Although we do not know much about Greek music or its history, we can say that in three fundamental respects it was the same kind of music as that of the early Church. In the first place, it was primarily *monophonic,* that is, melody without harmony or counterpoint.

In the second place, as far as we know, musical performances in the most flourishing period of Greek civilization were improvised. The performer was, to a certain extent, also the composer. This does not mean that what he did was completely spontaneous and unpre-

---

[1] Aristotle, *Politics*, VIII, 6, 1341ª 10, tr. B. Jowett in R. McKeon, ed., *The Basic Works of Aristotle*, New York, 1941, 1313. Cf. also Plato, *Laws*, II, 669E, 770A.

pared; he had to keep within the universally accepted rules governing the forms and styles of music suitable for particular occasions, and he probably incorporated in his performance certain traditional musical formulas; but outside these restrictions he had considerable freedom. Improvisation, in this or some similar sense, was characteristic of all ancient peoples. It prevailed also in our Western music up to perhaps the eighth century A.D., and the practice continued to affect musical styles for a long time even after precise musical notations were invented.

Thirdly, Greek music was almost always associated with words or dancing or both; its melody and rhythm were most intimately bound up with the melody and rhythm of poetry, and the music of the religious cults, of the drama, and of the great public contests was performed by singers who accompanied their melody with the movements of prescribed dance patterns.

To say, however, that the music of the early Church resembled Greek music in being monophonic, improvised, and inseparable from a text, is not to assert a historical continuity. No direct historical connection from the one to the other can be demonstrated. It was the theory rather than the practice of the Greeks that affected the music of western Europe in the Middle Ages.

Greek musical theory

Although there is much uncertainty about details, we do know that the ancient world bequeathed to the Middle Ages certain fundamental ideas about music: (1) a conception of music as consisting essentially of pure, unencumbered melodic line; (2) the idea of melody intimately linked with words, especially in matters of rhythm and meter; (3) a tradition of musical performance based essentially on improvisation, without fixed notation, where the performer as it were created the music anew each time, though within communally accepted conventions and making use of certain traditional musical formulas; (4) a philosophy of music which regarded

A Roman matron playing a kithara is depicted in this Roman fresco of the first century A.D. (Courtesy Metropolitan Museum of Art, Rogers Fund, 1903)

the art not as a play of beautiful sounds in a spiritual and social vacuum of art for art's sake, but rather as an orderly system interlocked with the system of nature, and as a force capable of affecting human thought and conduct; (5) a scientifically founded acoustical theory; (6) a system of scale-formation based on tetrachords; and (7) a musical terminology.

Part of this heritage (Nos. 5, 6, and 7) was specifically Greek; the rest was common to most if not all of the ancient world. Knowledge of it and ideas about it were transmitted, albeit incompletely and imperfectly, to the West through various channels: the Christian Church—whose rites and music were taken over in the beginning largely from Jewish sources, though without the Temple accessories of instruments and dancing—the writings of the Church Fathers, and early medieval scholarly treatises which dealt with music along with a multitude of other subjects.

The Early Christian Church

It is impossible for us to know exactly how much, and what, music from Greece or the mixed Oriental-Hellenistic societies around the eastern Mediterranean was taken into the Christian Church during the first two or three centuries of its existence. Certain features of ancient musical life were definitely rejected—for example, the idea of cultivating music purely for enjoyment as an art. Above all, the forms and types of music connected with the great public spectacles such as festivals, competitions, and dramatic performances, as also the music of more intimate convivial occasions, were regarded by many as unsuitable for the Church, not so much from any dislike of music itself as from the need to wean the increasing numbers of converts away from everything associated with their pagan past. This attitude involved at first even a distrust of all instrumental music. Yet the break may not have been complete. Just as early Christian theology was influenced by the philosophy of antiquity, so early Christian music may have taken over something—how much, or what, we cannot tell—from pagan sources.

More important, however, than any such possible external influences was the fact that the worship services of the earliest Christians were closely modelled on the Jewish synagogue services. Like them, they included readings from the holy books, psalms, hymns, prayers, and almsgiving—all elements that remain to this day in the liturgy of the Mass (where they are followed, of course, by the Eucharist, the celebration of the Last Supper). It is a safe assumption that, in music as well as liturgy, the early Church adopted the usual

The Judean heritage

synagogue practices, probably adding certain features taken over from the Temple worship. In both the Jewish and the Christian services, the characteristic styles and forms of the musical portions were adapted to, in fact conditioned by, their liturgical function. We may therefore note here briefly some of the general features of Hebrew music which found a place in early Christian worship and which eventually entered into the various types of Christian chant that developed in later centuries.

Among the Hebrews, psalms were sung in alternation between a soloist and the congregation; in one form of alternation, which later became important in Christian liturgy under the name of *responsorial psalmody,* the leader sang the first line of each psalm verse and the congregation responded by singing the second line. Such a method is particularly appropriate to the psalms, in which many of the verses have two parallel phrases, the second restating or continuing or amplifying the thought expressed in the first:

> Bless the Lord, O my soul,/ and forget not all his benefits:
> Who forgiveth all thine iniquities;/ who healeth all thy diseases.

A related form of singing was *antiphonal psalmody,* in which the two parts of the verse, or alternate verses, were sung in turn by two choruses. Still another usage inherited by the early Church from the Jewish service was the reciting of prescribed passages of Scripture by a soloist, using certain melodic formulas the essential outlines of which could be retained while details were varied to suit the requirements of a particular text.

As the early Church spread through Asia Minor and westward into Africa and Europe, it accumulated musical elements from diverse areas. The monasteries and churches of Syria were important in the development of antiphonal psalmody and for the use of hymns. Both these types of church song seem to have spread from Syria by way of Byzantium to Milan and other Western centers. Hymn singing is the earliest recorded musical activity of the Christian Church (Matt. xxvi:30; Mark xiv:26). Pliny the Younger, about the year 112, reported the Christian custom of singing "a song to Christ as a god" in the province of Bithynia in Asia Minor.[2] It is likely that some of the hymns of the early Church were sung to what would now be called folk melodies, and it is possible that some of these melodies eventually found their way into the official chant repertoire. The oldest surviving example of Christian church music is a hymn of praise to the Trinity, with Greek words and in Greek vocal notation,

---

2 Pliny's phrase "carmen dicere" may mean reciting a poem or incantation, rather than singing.

found on a papyrus at the site of the ancient Egyptian town of Oxyrhynchos and published in 1922.

The Eastern churches, in the absence of a strong central authority, developed different liturgies in the different regions. Although there are no surviving manuscripts of the music used in these Eastern rites during the first few centuries of the Christian era, in recent years comprehensive studies of Jewish and Byzantine music have allowed us to infer a great deal about early Eastern church music.

Byzantium

The city of Byzantium (or Constantinople, now Istanbul) was rebuilt by Constantine and designated in 330 as the capital of his reunited Roman Empire. After the permanent division in 395 it remained the capital of the Eastern Empire for over a thousand years, until its capture by the Turks in 1453. During much of this time Byzantium was the seat of the most powerful government in Europe and the center of a flourishing culture which blended Hellenistic and Oriental elements. The music of the Byzantine Church continued to have some influence in the West until the final schism of the Eastern and Western churches in 1054. Byzantine chant is also the ancestor of the music of the modern Greek Orthodox, the Russian, and other Eastern churches.

The melodies of the Hebrew synagogues and the Byzantine Church (as also those of the Western churches) had been passed along by oral tradition for centuries before being written down. Comparison of the oldest available records and consideration of other evidence have convinced modern scholars that many of the oldest Western chants are constructed according to the method used in Jewish melodies—that is, on the basis of melody-types and including a number of established melodic motives. In a few instances the resemblances between Jewish and Western chants are so close as to suggest either that the latter were taken over from the former or else that both were variants of one common form. Isolated melodic resemblances, however, are less important than the basic similarity of the method and principles of melodic construction used in both Hebrew and Christian chant. From this similarity we can conclude that the earliest Western church music incorporated a great many Jewish elements, either directly from the Hebrew chants or indirectly as the original melodies had been modified in the various early Christian centers in Greece, Syria, Egypt, and other regions of the East. Just how the borrowing occurred, and what the respective contributions from the different centers were, are matters about which we have as yet little accurate knowledge.

Western liturgies

In the West, as in the East, local churches at first were relatively independent. Although they shared, of course, a large area of common practice, yet it is likely that each region of the West received the Eastern heritage in a slightly different form; these original differences combined with particular local conditions to produce several distinct liturgies and bodies of chant between the fifth and the eighth centuries. Eventually all these local versions except one (the Ambrosian) either disappeared or were absorbed into the single uniform practice for which the central authority was Rome. From the ninth to the sixteenth centuries, in theory and increasingly in practice, the liturgy of the Western Church was regulated by the Church of Rome.

The most important Western Church center outside Rome, however, was Milan, a flourishing city with close cultural ties to Byzantium and the East; it was the chief residence of the Western emperors in the fourth century, and later was made the capital of the Lombard Kingdom in northern Italy, which flourished from 568 to 744. The Bishop of Milan from 374 to 397 was St. Ambrose, who first introduced antiphonal psalmody to the West. Owing to the importance of Milan and to the energy and high personal reputation of St. Ambrose, the Milanese liturgy and music exerted a strong influence not only in France and Spain but also at Rome, where antiphonal psalmody was adopted early in the fifth century. The songs of the Milanese rite later came to be known as Ambrosian Chant, though it is doubtful whether any of the music that has come down to us dates from the time of St. Ambrose himself. The Ambrosian liturgy with its complete body of chants has been maintained to some extent at Milan to the present day, in spite of various attempts to suppress it. Many of the chants in their present form are similar to those of the Roman Church, indicating either an interchange or a derivation from a common source.

An important addition to Western church music was the *hymn*. The singing of "hymns, psalms, and spiritual songs" is mentioned by St. Paul (Col. iii: 16; Eph. v: 18–20) and other writers of the first three centuries, but we do not know just what this consisted of. All the surviving hymn texts from these three centuries are Greek; one of them, *O gladsome light*, by an unknown author probably of the third century, is still sung at Vespers in the Greek Church. Hymns were introduced in the West in the fourth century by St. Ambrose, according to an old tradition, though recent scholarship is inclined to credit this innovation to Hilary, Bishop of Poitiers (*ca.* 315–366). Gradually, the meaning of *hymn* had been narrowed to denote a poem in strophic form, all the stanzas of which were intended to be sung to the same melody; the setting was mostly *syllabic* (one note to a syllable), and comparatively simple and tuneful—music originally for the congregation or the individual worshiper rather than for a trained choir or soloist. Many of the earliest hymn melodies were probably taken over from popular secular tunes. As to subject matter, the hymn is limited only by its general purpose of "celebrating Christian truths or events";[3] thus it need not be Scriptural—though there was a considerable struggle before the Church finally admitted non-Biblical hymns. In general, it may be said that hymns, in both form and content, are apt to express personal, individual sentiments, whereas other parts of the liturgy are by comparison more objective, public, and formal.

As the liturgy developed, and especially after the singing of hymns in the service was entrusted to the choir instead of the congregation, many of the earlier tunes were enriched by the addition of ornamental notes; also, new melodies of a sometimes quite ornate character arose. Beside the versified hymns there are a few with prose texts, among which the best known is the *Te Deum laudamus* (*We praise Thee, O God*), written probably in the latter part of the fourth century and sung now to a melody very similar to one which may have been used in the ancient synagogue services and which has been preserved in Jewish tradition.[4] According to legend, at the moment when St. Ambrose baptized St. Augustine the two spontaneously improvised the *Te Deum* in alternate verses. This legend is thought to refer to what was undoubtedly a practice in the early Church, namely the creation of hymns under the inspiration of strong religious feeling, somewhat the way today new phrases of text and new melodic variations spontaneously arise during the enthusiasm of a revival meeting or a folk sing.

In addition to the main outlines of the liturgy, the body of responsorial and antiphonal psalmody, the reciting formulas, and the hymns, one other Jewish element became important in Western church music: the class of songs originally used in the Hebrew synagogue as refrains, for example on the word "amen" or "alleluia." Such refrains were chanted responsively by the congregation after each verse or after the last verse of a psalm, and some of them later developed into independent song types, losing their primitive simple character and becoming more or less elaborate solo melodies. The alleluias were especially noteworthy because of their florid (melismatic) style, in which the last syllable was drawn out in ecstatic melody, soaring phrase after phrase "in gladness of heart outflowing, joy too full to be expressed in words."[5] The alleluia was introduced into the liturgy at Rome before the fourth century and was eventually incorporated in the Mass for every Sunday except during the fasting or penitential seasons.

Another species of Western chant that grew out of the synagogue songs with refrains was the *antiphon*. At first the antiphon,

---

[3] P. Wagner, *Einführung in die gregorianischen Melodien*, Leipzig, 1911, I, 42.
[4] Eric Werner, *The Sacred Bridge*, London and New York, 1959, p. 342.
[5] St. Augustine, "In Psalmum xcix enarratio, sermo ad plebem"; Migne, *Patrologiae cursus completus, Series Latina*, XXXVII, 1272.

a verse or sentence with its own melody, probably was repeated after every verse of a psalm or canticle, like the phrase "for His mercy endureth forever" in Psalm 135/6. In later practice, the refrain was usually sung only at the beginning and end of the psalm; at the present day only the "intonation" or opening phrase of the antiphon is sung first, and the entire antiphon is heard after the psalm. The four *Marian antiphons* (so called, although they are really independent compositions rather than antiphons in the strict liturgical sense) are of comparatively late date, and are especially beautiful melodies (see Example II–1, page 19).

A form akin to the antiphon is the *responsory* or *respond,* a short verse which is sung by a soloist and repeated by the choir before a prayer or short sentence of Scripture, and repeated again by the choir at the end of the reading. The responsory, like the antiphon, was originally repeated by the choir, either wholly or in part, after each single verse of the reading; this early practice survives in a few present-day responsories that contain several verses and are sung at Matins or Nocturns of high feasts. For lesser feasts such *responsoria prolixa* or Long Responsories, however, are sung only before and after the soloist's single short reading.

Although the manner in which the various elements of Eastern chant were adopted by the West during the first three Christian centuries is not altogether clear, one thing is certain: as far as the music is concerned there was no evolution from a simple to a more complex musical style. Many of the chants that were brought from the East were undoubtedly ornate, full of melismatic passages with opportunities for improvisation; and at least some of them may have been based on Oriental scale patterns with chromatic and enharmonic intervals. The course in the West must have been, at first, toward order and relative simplicity, a course made the more imperative by events of the early fourth century.

The dominance of Rome

In 313 Constantine recognized the Christians as entitled to equal rights and protection along with other religions in the Empire; the Church at once emerged from its underground life, and during the fourth century Latin replaced Greek as the official language of the liturgy at Rome. As the prestige of the Roman Emperor declined, that of the Roman Bishop increased, and gradually the predominant authority of Rome in matters of faith and discipline began to be acknowledged.

With ever greater numbers of converts and ever growing riches, the Church began to build large basilicas, and services could no longer be conducted in the comparatively informal manner of early days. From the fifth to the seventh centuries many popes were concerned with revising the liturgy and music, a work in which they were greatly aided by the monks of the Order of St. Benedict (founded in 529). The post of Cantor, or chief solo singer (an institution inherited from the synagogue), was officially established; boy choirs, common at Jerusalem by the beginning of the fifth century, were introduced in the West; by the eighth century there existed at Rome a *Schola Cantorum,* a definite group of singers and teachers entrusted with the training of boys and men as church musicians. In all these steps the original basic distinction between solo and choral singing was retained, and as a consequence, to this day Roman chant preserves a division between the music of responsorial and solo psalmody on the one hand and that of antiphonal psalmody and hymnody on the other—the former being rhythmically flexible and melodically elaborate, the latter by comparison strict and simple.

The culminating reform of the liturgy and chant seems to have been in large part the work of Gregory I (The Great), Pope from 590 to 604. St. Gregory's achievement was so highly regarded that by the middle of the ninth century a legend began to take shape to the effect that he himself had composed all the melodies in use by the Church, under divine inspiration. His actual contribution, though certainly very important, was probably much less than what later medieval tradition ascribed to him; it is simply not believable that so great and so extensive a work could have been accomplished in fourteen years. He recodified the liturgy and reorganized the Schola Cantorum; he assigned particular items of the liturgy to the various services throughout the year in an order that remained essentially untouched until the sixteenth century; he gave impulse to the movement which eventually led to the establishment of a uniform repertoire of chant for use throughout the Church in all countries. Whether St. Gregory actually composed any melodies is a different question.

Nevertheless, the medieval tradition as a whole had a real historical basis. It is therefore appropriate that this whole body of music should be called, as it has been for over a thousand years, Gregorian Chant. It was given also, in the twelfth and thirteenth centuries, the designation *cantus planus (plainsong)* to distinguish it from the *cantus figuralis* or *mensuratus* (figural or measured song), the measured polyphonic music of the Middle Ages.

The Gregorian chants are one of the great treasures of Western civilization. Like Romanesque architecture, they stand as a monument to medieval man's religious faith; they were the source and inspiration of a large proportion of all Western music up to the sixteenth century. They constitute one of the most ancient bodies of song still in use anywhere, and include some of the noblest artistic works ever created in pure melody.

The principal events and tendencies in the history of Western

St. Gregory and scribe. At the moment depicted, the Saint is listening to what the dove (symbolizing the Holy Spirit) is whispering in his ear. The scribe, curious about the intermittent pauses in his master's dictation, has come out from behind the screen to peer at them, still holding his stylus in his hand. Presently, St. Gregory will resume his dictation and the scribe, returning behind the screen, will take it down.

Summary

music to the time of Gregory the Great (making allowance for incomplete knowledge due to the lack of evidence on many points) may be summed up as follows: During the first three centuries of the Christian era the earliest forms of worship and their musical concomitants, taken over from the Hebrew synagogue, were variously modified and expanded in different regions of the East. There was no uniform practice, and individual improvisation seems to have played a certain role. There were three main types of chant: the reciting formulas, the melismatic songs, and the refrains sung by the choir or congregation. The melodies of all these were built up according to the Jewish fashion of combining traditional standard melodic formulas within a given mode. There were three ways of performing: direct (without alternation), responsorial (alternation of soloist and chorus), and antiphonal (alternation of two choruses).

From the fourth to the sixth centuries all this system was assimilated by the Western churches; but the Western trend was toward a uniform practice, which eventually emanated from Rome. Probably the extremes of the inherited chant were modified, the melismatic tunes made somewhat plainer and the simple tunes somewhat more ornate. More and more of the performance was handed over to an officially constituted body of trained singers. The reforms under Gregory I and his successors aimed to organize the whole body of chant in a uniform manner for the entire Western Church, embracing diverse types and practices in one orderly system; concurrently with this change the performance of chants in the service came to be entrusted to a separately constituted body of trained singers. So the first stage of Western music seems to have been one in which an early emphasis on ecstasy and individual liberty was succeeded by emphasis on order and discipline. Thus the Gregorian age may be called the first "classical period" in the history of Western music.

This was the main stream of history—main stream, that is, insofar as recorded history goes. Undoubtedly in those six centuries, as in all times, people sang and played their own music outside the church. But what it was that they sang and played we do not know, for no record of it survives. What little we hear about it comes mainly from incidental references, usually hostile, in clerical writings that are mainly concerned with church matters. We do know, of course, that in later periods the Church continually took over secular music and musical practices, and it is likely that something of this kind occurred during the first Christian centuries—likely, moreover, that the exchange worked in both directions; but as to the extent and manner of it we can do little more than speculate.

During these early centuries, also, the musical theory and philosophy of the ancient world—or as much of it as was accessible after the "time of troubles" and the barbarian invasions—was being gathered up, summarized, modified, and transmitted to the West. Most notable in this work was Martianus Capella in his encyclopedic treatise entitled *The Marriage of Mercury and Philology* (early fifth century) and Anicius Manlius Severinus Boethius (*ca.* 480–524) with

Boethius

his *De institutione musica* (*The Principles of Music;* early sixth century). Boethius was the most influential authority on music in the early Middle Ages and his ideas are quite typical of the period. Like the Pythagoreans and Plato, he regards music as a corollary of arithmetic, thus as exemplifying in sounds the fundamental principles of order and harmony that prevail throughout the universe. His division of the subject is threefold: *musica mundana* ("cosmic" music), referring to the "music of the spheres" and the orderly mathematical relations observable in the behavior of the stars, the planets, and the earth—that is, in the macrocosm; *musica humana,* referring to the ways in which such harmonious relations are imprinted on and exemplified in the soul and body of man—the microcosm; and *musica instrumentalis,* or audible music produced by instruments (including, by implication, the human voice), which exemplifies the same principles of order, particularly in the acoustical ratios of musical intervals. The picture of the cosmos which

Boethius and the other ancient writers drew in their discussions of *musica mundana* and *musica humana* is reflected in the art and literature of the later Middle Ages, notably in the structure of Paradise in the last canto of Dante's *Divine Comedy*. Remnants of the doctrine of *musica humana* survived through the Renaissance and indeed linger on to this day, in the form of astrology.

Translating and summarizing his Greek sources, Boethius emphasizes the influence of music on character and morals. Music thus becomes important as an element in the education of the young and, in its mathematical-theoretical aspects, as an introduction to more advanced philosophical studies; hence music finds a place, along with arithmetic, geometry, and astronomy, in the *quadrivium,* the four higher subjects comprised in the medieval educational system of the seven liberal arts. *De institutione musica* was in use as a textbook at Oxford as late as the eighteenth century.

II

Gregorian Chant and Secular Song in the Middle Ages

Gregorian Chant and the Roman Liturgy

In studying the history of music it is of course necessary to learn certain facts about musical forms and styles in the different historical periods; but it is even more necessary to get to know the music itself. This admonition is the more urgent because, with the change from Latin to the vernacular in the liturgy since the Second Vatican Council of 1962–65 Gregorian Chant has virtually disappeared from the regular services of the Catholic Church. In Europe, it is still in use in some monasteries and for certain services in some of the larger parochial churches; in America, it is cultivated much less. Even though in theory Latin remains the official language and Gregorian Chant the official music of the Church, in practice the traditional chants have been mostly replaced by music thought suitable for the entire congregation to sing: simplified versions of the more familiar Gregorian melodies; new melodies, often of a cheap commercial sort, of little or no musical value; or occasional experiments in more sophisticated popular styles. Even when sung to the authentic melodies, the vernacular speech rhythm alters the musical character of the Chant, while the direct intelligibility of the English words detracts from the objective quality which it possessed with its Latin text.

At present there seems no likely prospect for eventual restoration of Gregorian Chant on any considerable scale. Nevertheless, and regardless of its current practical status, a knowledge of the Chant is both valuable for its own sake and essential for understanding the history of music (not only church music) in the Middle Ages, the Renaissance, and even in later times.

When we hear Gregorian Chant for the first time, we may perhaps have a negative impression of it. We may be struck not so much by what is there as by what is not there. We feel the lack of supporting harmony or accompaniment; or we miss clearly defined time values and regular accents; or we notice that the melodic line sometimes turns strangely and often does not cadence on the expected note; or we are perhaps resentfully conscious that the music makes no attempt to thrill our senses or entangle our emotions. Gregorian Chant consists of single-line melody sung to Latin words by unaccompanied men's voices, in a flexible rhythm articulated by means other than regular accentuation, in a scale system different from our major or minor; and it has an impersonal, objective, other-worldly quality in which sensuous beauty and emotional appeal are largely subordinate to expression of the religious content of the text.

The nature of Gregorian Chant

Gregorian Chant, while beautiful as sheer music, is not meant to be listened to for its own sake; as an adjunct to worship, it is strictly functional music. Consequently, in order to understand the music it is essential to know something of the liturgy within which it has its place. We shall therefore first consider the main outlines of the Catholic Latin liturgy as prescribed since the late sixteenth century, without dwelling on the modifications of detail that are currently in process of adoption, along with the change from Latin to the vernacular, since the Second Vatican Council. What follows, then, is a generalized description (using the present tense for convenience) of what we may call the historically settled form of post-medieval Roman liturgy—which, though not identical in all respects with earlier medieval forms, is close enough to them in essentials to serve our purpose.

The two principal classes of services are the *Office* and the *Mass.* There are eight *Offices,* or *Canonical Hours,* which are celebrated every day at stated times in a regular order, though their public recitation is generally observed only in monasteries and certain cathedral churches: *Matins* (before daybreak), *Lauds* (at sunrise), *Prime, Terce, Sext, Nones* (respectively at about 6 A.M., 9 A.M., noon, and 3 P.M.) *Vespers* (at sunset) and *Compline* (usually immediately after Vespers). The Gregorian music for the Offices is collected in a liturgical book called the *Antiphonale* or *Antiphonal.* The principal features of the Offices are the chanting of psalms with their antiphons, the singing of hymns and canticles, and the chanting of lessons (passages of Scripture) with their responsories. From the musical point of view the most important Offices are Matins, Lauds, and Vespers. Matins includes some of the most

The Roman liturgy

ancient chants of the Church. Vespers has the canticle *Magnificat anima mea Dominum* ("My soul doth magnify the Lord," Luke i:46–55); and inasmuch as this Office is the only one that admitted polyphonic singing from early times, it is especially important to the history of sacred music. A feature of Compline is the singing of the four antiphons of the Blessed Virgin Mary, the so-called "Marian" antiphons, one for each of the main divisions of the Church year:[1] *Alma Redemptoris Mater* ("Sweet Mother of the

[1] The principal seasons of the liturgical year are:
    Advent, starting with the fourth Sunday before Christmas;
    Christmas, including the twelve days to
    Epiphany (January 6th) and following weeks; the
    Pre-Lenten season, beginning nine weeks before Easter;
    Lent, from Ash Wednesday to Easter;
    Eastertide, including Ascension (forty days after Easter) and continuing to
    Pentecost or *Whitsunday,* ten days after Ascension or seven weeks after
      Easter; and
    Trinity, from the first Sunday after Pentecost to the beginning of Advent.
Advent and Lent are sometimes called the "penitential" seasons.

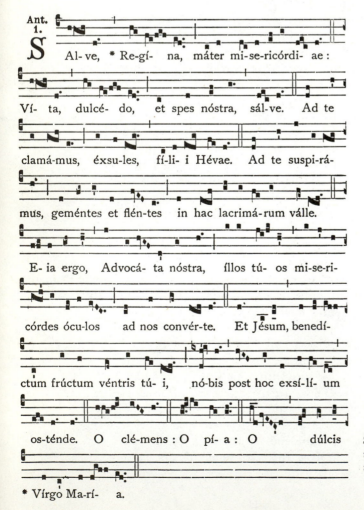

Salve Regina *as it appears in modern Gregorian notation in the* Liber Usualis.

EXAMPLE II–1   Antiphon: *Salve Regina*

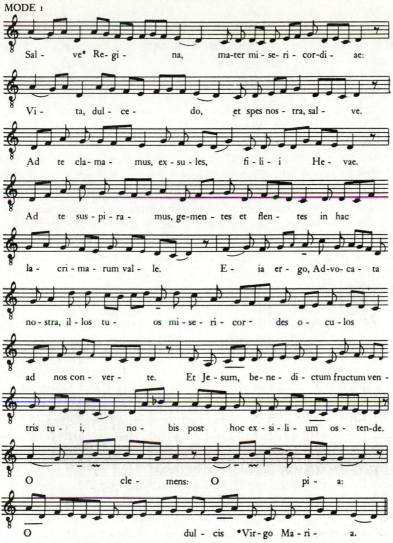

MODE I

Sal - ve* Re- gi - na,   ma-ter mi - se - ri - cor-di - ae:

Vi - ta, dul - ce - do,   et spes nos - tra, sal - ve.

Ad   te cla- ma - mus, ex - su - les,   fi - li - i   He - vae.

Ad   te sus - pi - ra - mus, ge-men - tes et flen - tes in hac

la - cri - ma - rum val - le.   E - ia er - go, Ad-vo-ca - ta

no - stra, il - los tu - os mi - se - ri - cor - des o - cu - los

ad   nos con - ver - te.   Et Je - sum, be - ne - di - ctum fructum ven -

tris tu - i,   no - bis post   hoc ex - si - li - um os - ten-de.

O   cle - mens: O   pi - a:

O   dul - cis *Vir- go Ma - ri - a.

Hail, O Queen, Mother of mercy, our life, our sweetness and our hope! To thee we cry, banished children of Eve; to thee we send up our sighs, mourning and weeping in this vale of tears. Turn then, our Advocate, thine eyes of mercy toward us; and after this our exile, show unto us the blessed fruit of thy womb, Jesus. O clement, O loving, O sweet Virgin Mary.

  * This modern transcription reproduces certain signs that accompany the neumes in the manuscript. The asterisk indicates where the chant alternates between soloist and choir, or between the two halves of the choir. The straight lines under some pairs of notes are extensions of the sign for a slight lengthening of the notes. The small notes correspond to a sign probably indicating a light vocalization of the first ("voiced") consonant in such combinations as *ergo, ventris.* The wavy line represents a sign which probably called for a slight ornamenting of the note, perhaps something like a short trill or mordent.

Redeemer") from Advent to February 1; *Ave Regina caelorum* ("Hail, Queen of the Heavens") from February 2 to Wednesday of Holy Week; *Regina caeli laetare* ("Rejoice, Queen of Heaven") from Easter to Trinity Sunday; and *Salve Regina* ("Hail, O Queen") from Trinity until Advent. (See illustration on page 18 and Example II–1).

The Mass, although its liturgy was developed later than that of the Offices, is the principal service of the Catholic Church. (For a description of a typical, complete Mass, see the Appendix at the end of this chapter.) The word "Mass" comes from the service's closing phrase: *Ite missa est* ("Go, [the congregation] is dismissed"); the service is also known in other Christian churches under the names of the Eucharist, the Liturgy, Holy Communion, and the Lord's Supper. The culminating act of the Mass is the commemoration or re-enactment of the Last Supper (Luke xxii:19–20; I Cor. ii:23–26), the essential parts of the ceremony being the offering and consecration of the bread and wine and the partaking of these by the faithful. Most of that part of the Mass which precedes this was derived originally from the ancient Jewish ritual, to which the specifically Christian Eucharist was added.

In its historically settled form the liturgy of the Mass begins with the *Introit;* originally this was an entire psalm with its antiphon, chanted during the entrance of the priest (the *antiphona ad introitum,* or "antiphon for the entrance"), but later was shortened to only a single verse of the psalm with an antiphon. Immediately after the Introit the choir sings the *Kyrie,* to the Greek words *Kyrie eleison* ("Lord have mercy upon us"), *Christe eleison* ("Christ have mercy upon us"), *Kyrie eleison,* each invocation being sung three times. Next follows (except in the penitential seasons of Advent and Lent) the *Gloria,* begun by the priest with the words *Gloria in excelsis Deo* ("Glory be to God on high") and continued by the choir from *Et in terra pax* ("And on earth peace"). Then come the prayers (*Collects*) and the reading of the *Epistle* for the day, followed by the *Gradual* and *Alleluia,* both sung by a soloist or soloists with responses by the choir. In penitential seasons the Alleluia is replaced by the more solemn *Tract.* After the reading of the *Gospel* comes the *Credo,* begun by the priest *Credo in unum Deum* ("I believe in one God") and continued by the choir from *Patrem omnipotentem* ("the Father Almighty"). This, together with the sermon if any, marks the end of the first main division of the Mass; now follows the Eucharist proper. During the preparation of the bread and wine the *Offertory* is sung. This is followed by various prayers and the *Preface* which leads into the *Sanctus* ("Holy, holy, holy") and *Benedictus* ("Blessed is He that cometh"), both sung by the choir. Then comes the *Canon* or prayer of consecration, followed by the *Pater noster* (the Lord's Prayer) and the *Agnus Dei* ("Lamb of God"). After the bread and wine have been consumed, the choir sings the *Communion,* which is followed by the singing of the priest's *Post-Communion* prayers. The service then concludes with the dismissal formula *Ite missa est* or *Benedicamus Domino* ("Let us bless the Lord"), sung responsively by the priest and choir.

The texts of certain parts of the Mass are invariable; others change according to the season of the year or the dates of particular feasts or commemorations. The variable portions are called the *Proper of the Mass (Proprium missae).* The Collects, Epistle, Gospel, Preface, and the Post-Communion and other prayers are all part of the Proper; the principal musical portions of the Proper are the Introit, Gradual, Alleluia, Tract, Offertory, and Communion. The invariable parts of the service are called the *Ordinary of the Mass (Ordinarium missae),* and include the Kyrie, Gloria, Credo, Sanctus, Benedictus, and Agnus Dei.

The Gregorian music for the Mass, both Proper and Ordinary, is published in a liturgical book, the *Graduale.* The *Liber Usualis,* another book of Gregorian music, contains a selection of the most frequently used chants from both the *Antiphonale* and the *Graduale.* Texts of the Mass and Offices respectively are published in the Missal (*Missale*) and the Breviary (*Breviarium*).

The melodies of Gregorian Chant are preserved in hundreds of manuscripts dating from the ninth century and later. These manuscripts were written at different times and in widely separated areas. Very often the same melody is found in many different manuscripts; and it is remarkable that these manuscripts record the melody in almost identical form—very close, indeed, to the form in which it appears in the present-day liturgical books. How are we to interpret this fact? One possibility, of course, is to say that the melodies must have come from one source and must have been transmitted with great accuracy and fidelity, either by purely oral means or with the help of some early notation of which no specimens have survived. Something of this sort was substantially the interpretation advanced by writers of the eighth and ninth centuries, coupled with statements to the effect that the "one source" was St. Gregory himself. Modern scholarship has shown this interpretation to be untenable without serious modification. How, then, can we account not only for the agreement among the earliest manuscripts but also for the fact that all these manuscripts were written not at Rome nor even in Italy, but at various centers in what are now France, Switzerland, and the western part of Germany—in other words, in the territory of the Frankish kingdom of Charlemagne (742–814)?

It may be remarked that both the systematic writing down of the chant melodies and their ascription to divine inspiration (through St. Gregory) coincide with a determined campaign by the Frankish monarchs to unify their polyglot kingdom. One necessary means to this end was a uniform liturgy and music of the churches, binding on the entire population. Rome, so venerable in the imagination of the Middle Ages, was the natural model, particularly after Charlemagne was crowned there in 800 as head of the Holy Roman Empire. He and his successors undertook to replace the Gallican liturgies in Frankish lands by Roman usages. Great numbers of liturgical-musical "missionaries" travelled between Rome and the north in the late eighth and ninth centuries, and a potent weapon in their propaganda was the legend of St. Gregory and the divinely inspired Chant. Naturally, their efforts met with resistance and a great deal of confusion ensued before unification was finally achieved. Writing down the melodies would then have been one way of assuring that henceforth the chants would be sung everywhere the same.

Just what were the melodies that were brought from Rome to the Frankish lands? No one can answer this question with certainty. The recitation tones, the psalm tones, and some others of the simplest types were very ancient and may have been preserved practically intact from the earliest years; some thirty or forty antiphon melodies may have originated in St. Gregory's time; a great many of the more complex melodies—Tracts, Graduals, Offertories, Alleluias—must have been in use (perhaps in simpler versions) at Rome before being spread to the north; and it may be that some of the early melodies are preserved in the manuscripts of the Old Roman Chant. Whatever the case, we may suspect that in its new home much if not all of this imported music underwent changes before finally being written down in the form in which we find it in the oldest manuscripts. Furthermore, a great many new melodies and new forms of chant grew up in the north after the ninth century. In sum: practically the whole body of the chant as we now know it comes to us from Frankish sources that either incorporate Roman materials to an unknown extent or else represent new music of northern origin. In a strict historical sense, therefore, it is incorrect to call the Chant as a whole "Gregorian." But since the name after all does have some historical justification, and since "Gregorian Chant" is a term well established and consecrated by centuries of use, we may continue to accept it—making a distinction, where necessary, between the Roman or Gregorian heritage and the later Frankish changes and additions.

Classes, Forms, and Types of Gregorian Chant

All chants may be divided into those with *Biblical* and those with *non-Biblical* texts; each of these divisions may be subdivided into chants with *prose* texts and those with *poetical* texts. Examples of Biblical prose texts are the lessons of the Office, and the Epistle and Gospel of the Mass; of Biblical poetical texts, the psalms and canticles. Non-Biblical prose texts include the *Te Deum,* many antiphons, and three of the four Marian antiphons; chants with non-Biblical poetical texts are the hymns and sequences.

Chants may also be classified according to the manner in which they are (or were, in earlier times) sung as *antiphonal* (alternating choirs), *responsorial* (alternating soloist and choir), or *direct* (without alternation).

Still another classification is based on the relation of notes to syllables. Chants in which most or all of the syllables have a single note each are called *syllabic;* those characterized by long melodic passages on a single syllable are called *melismatic.* This distinction is not always clear-cut, since chants that are prevailingly melismatic usually include some syllabic sections or phrases, and many chants otherwise syllabic have occasional short melismas of four or five notes on some syllables. This type of chant is sometimes called *neumatic.*

In general, the melodic outline of a chant reflects the normal modern accentuation of the Latin words by setting the prominent syllables on higher notes or by giving such syllables more notes. But this rule has many exceptions even in a moderately florid chant; and of course it cannot be fully applied in recitative-like chants, where many successive syllables are sung to the same note, or in hymns, where every strophe has to be sung to the same melody. Moreover, in florid chants the melodic accent often has greater importance than the word accent; consequently we may find long melismas on weak syllables, particularly final syllables, as on the final "a" of "alleluia" or the last syllable of words like "Dominus," "exsultemus," or "Kyrie." In such chants the important words and syllables of a phrase are emphasized and made clear by setting them more simply, so that they stand out in contrast to the rich ornamentation of the unstressed syllables. In Gregorian Chant there is seldom any repetition of single words or word-groups in the text; word-painting or similar pointed reflection of single words or images is exceptional. The melody is adapted to the rhythm of the text, to its general mood, and to the liturgical function which a chant fulfills; no attempt is made to adapt the melody to special emotional or pictorial effects. This is not to say that Gregorian Chant is inexpressive, but only that it does not have that quality musicians call *espressivo*.

We shall now examine some of the more important categories of chants used in the Mass and Office, beginning with syllabic and proceeding to melismatic kinds.

Reciting and psalm tones

The chants for the recitation of prayers and readings from the Bible are on the border between speech and song. They consist of a single *reciting note* (usually *a* or *c'*),[2] to which each verse or period of the text is rapidly chanted. This reciting note is also called the *tenor,* or (in later times) the *dominant;* occasionally the upper or lower neighboring note will be introduced to bring out an important accent. The reciting note may be preceded by a two- or three-note introductory formula called the *initium;* at the end of each verse or period there is a short melodic cadence. Similar to these recitation tones, but slightly more complex, are standard formulas called *psalm tones;* there is one tone for each of the eight church modes and an extra one called the *Tonus peregrinus* or "foreign tone." The psalm tones and those for the readings of the Epistle and Gospel are among the oldest chants of the liturgy; they may have been taken over directly from chants of the Hebrew synagogue. Likewise very ancient are the slightly more ornate tones for the Preface and Lord's Prayer. All the psalms are sung antiphonally in the Offices to one or another of the tones. This same general type of melodic formula also occurs in many other chants. A psalm tone consists of the *initium* (used only in the first verse of the psalm), *tenor, mediatio* (semicadence in the middle of the verse), and *terminatio,* or final cadence (see Example II–2). Usually the last verse of a psalm is followed by the *Lesser Doxology* or the *Gloria Patri* ("Glory be to the Father"); in the chant books the closing words of the Doxology are indicated by vowels below the last notes of the music, thus: *euouae.* These vowels are an abbreviation for the last six syllables of the phrase *et in secula sEcUlOrUm, AmEn* ("world without end, Amen").

EXAMPLE II–2   Psalm 109: *Dixit Dominus*

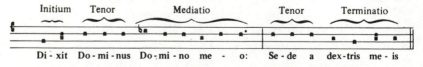

The Lord said unto my Lord: Sit Thou at My right hand.

[2] For an explanation of pitch designations, see Glossary under *Note designation.*

Antiphons are more numerous than any other type of Chant; about 1250 are found in the modern *Antiphonale*. However, many antiphons employ the same melody-type, making only slight variations to accommodate the text, a practice which goes back to the Jewish origins of early Church music.

Moderately ornate forms of antiphonal psalmody are found in the Introit and Communion of the Mass. The Introit as noted above, was originally a complete psalm with its antiphon. In the course of time this part of the service was very much shortened, so that today the Introit consists only of the original antiphon, a single psalm verse with the customary *Gloria Patri,* and the repetition of the antiphon. The tones for the psalm verses in the Mass are slightly more elaborate than the psalm tones of the Office. The Communion coming near the end of the Mass as a counterpart to the Introit at the beginning, is a short chant, often consisting of only one verse of Scripture. In contrast to the Introit, which is apt to be comparatively animated, the Communion usually has the character of a quiet close to the sacred ceremony. **Introit and Communion**

Musically, the most highly developed chants of the Mass are the Graduals, Alleluias, Tracts, and Offertories. The Tract was originally a solo song. The Gradual and Alleluia are responsorial; the Offertory was probably at first an antiphonal chant, but today no trace of the original psalm remains, and what must have been the original antiphon is performed now as a responsorial chant by soloist and choir.

The Tracts are the longest chants in the liturgy, partly because they have long texts and partly because their melodies are extended by the use of melismatic figures. The musical form of the Tracts in both modes is a complex variation of a simple formula very like a psalm tone; each verse of the Tract is divided by a mediatio as in a psalm tone, and the characteristic reciting notes or tenors of psalmody are present. There are certain recurring melodic formulas which are found in many different Tracts, and regularly in the same place—at the mediatio, at the beginning of the second half of the verse, and so on. These features—the construction of so many melodies on only two basic patterns, the form (a psalm recitation ornamented with melismas), and the presence of standard melodic formulas—all suggest that in the Tracts we have a survival, probably in elaborated form, of some of the music from Gregorian or even pre-Gregorian times. **Tracts**

The Graduals were also among the types of chant that came from Rome to the Frankish churches, probably already in a late, highly developed form. Their melodies are more florid than those of the Tracts and their structure is essentially different. A Gradual in the modern chant books is a shortened responsory; it has an introduc- **Graduals** tory refrain or *respond,* followed by a single verse of the psalm. The refrain is begun by a soloist and continued by the choir; the verse is sung by a soloist with the choir joining in on the last phrase.

Alleluias

Alleluias consist of a refrain, on the single word "alleluia," and a verse, followed by repetition of the refrain (see NAWM/S* 9a, *Alleluia Pascha nostrum*). The customary manner of singing is as follows: the soloist (or soloists) sings the word "alleluia"; the chorus repeats this and continues with the *jubilus,* a long melisma on the final "ia" of "alleluia"; the soloist then sings the verse; with the chorus joining on the last phrase, after which the entire "alleluia" with jubilus is sung by the chorus. The "alleluia" is moderately florid; the jubilus is, of course, melismatic. The verse usually combines shorter and longer melismas; very often the last part of the verse repeats part or all of the refrain melody. The Alleluias thus have a design different from that of any other pre-Frankish type of chant: their musical form is outlined by systematic repetition of distinct sections. The repetition of the "alleluia" and jubilus after the verse results in a three-part (*ABA*) pattern; this is subtly modified when melodic phrases from the refrain are incorporated in the verse. Within the general scheme, the melody may be organized by the repetition or echoing of motives, musical rhyme, systematic combination and contrast of melodic curves, and similar devices, all signs of a well-developed sense of musical construction.

Offertories

The Offertories are similar in melodic style to the Graduals. Originally, Offertories were very long chants sung by both congregation and clergy during the ceremony of presentation of bread and wine; when this ceremony was curtailed, the Offertory also was shortened, but curious traces of its original use are evident in the occasional text repetitions.

Chants of the Ordinary

The chants for the Ordinary of the Mass probably were originally quite simple syllabic melodies sung by the congregation; these were replaced, after the ninth century, by other settings. The syllabic style is still maintained in the Gloria and Credo, but the other chants of the Ordinary are now somewhat more ornate. The Kyrie, Sanctus, and Agnus Dei, by the nature of their texts, have three-part sectional arrangements. The Kyrie, for example, suggests the following setting:

A	*Kyrie*	*eleison*
B	*Christe*	*eleison*
A	*Kyrie*	*eleison*

* The acronym NAWM/S which is used throughout this edition, refers to the *Norton Anthology of Western Music,* Shorter Edition by Claude V. Palisca.

Since each exclamation is uttered three times, there may be an *aba* form within each of the three principal sections. More sophisticated versions of the Kyrie may have the pattern *ABC,* with motivic interconnections: parts *A* and *B* may be similar in outline and have identical final phrases (musical rhyme); the last repetition of part *C* may have a different initial phrase or be expanded by repeating the initial phrase, the last section of which will be similar to the first phrase of part *A*. In an analogous fashion, the Agnus Dei may have the form *ABA,* though sometimes the same music is used for all sections:

> *A Agnus Dei . . . miserere nobis* ("Lamb of God . . . have mercy upon us")
> *B Agnus Dei . . . miserere nobis*
> *A Agnus Dei . . . dona nobis pacem* ("Lamb of God . . . grant us peace")

The Sanctus is likewise divided into three sections; a possible distribution of musical materials is as follows:

> *A Sanctus, sanctus, sanctus* ("Holy, holy, holy")
> *B Pleni sunt caeli et terra* ("Heaven and earth are full")
> *B′ Benedictus qui venit* ("Blessed is He that cometh")

Later Developments of the Chant

Between the fifth and the ninth centuries the peoples of western and northern Europe were converted to Christianity and the doctrines and rites of the Roman Church. Gregorian Chant was established in the Frankish Empire before the middle of the ninth century; and from then until near the close of the Middle Ages all important developments in European music took place north of the Alps. The influence of the northern musical spirit had important consequences for Gregorian Chant. The range of expression was enlarged; the melodic line became modified through the introduction of more skips, especially by the interval of a third; and new forms of chant, or forms growing out of chant, were created, chiefly the *trope,* the *sequence,* and the *liturgical drama.*

A *trope* was originally a newly composed addition, usually in neumatic style and with a poetic text, to one of the antiphonal chants of the Proper of the Mass (most often to the Introit, less often to the Offertory and Communion); later, such additions were made also to chants of the Ordinary (especially the Gloria. For an example of a Gloria-trope, see NAWM/S 2). The earliest tropes

Tropes

served as prefaces to the regular chant; at a later stage, tropes are found also in the form of interpolations between the lines of a chant. The custom of troping seems to have originated in northeastern France or the Rhineland in the ninth century—possibly even earlier. An important center of troping was the Monastery of St. Gall, where the monk Tuotilo (d. 915) was distinguished for compositions in this form. Tropes flourished, especially in monastic churches, in the tenth and eleventh centuries; in the twelfth century they gradually disappeared.

Sequences

In the early manuscripts of chants are to be found from time to time certain rather long melodic passages which recur, practically unchanged, in many different contexts: sometimes as a passage in a regular liturgical chant, sometimes included in a separate collection, and in either situation sometimes with words and sometimes without. These are not short melodic formulas such as might be introduced into an improvisational performance, but long, definitely shaped melodies which were evidently widely known and used, either in melismatic form or underlaid with different texts. Such melodies, and similar ones not in the "recurring" category, were typically Frankish creations, though doubtless some of the oldest of them were adapted from Roman models. Long melismas of this sort came to be attached to the Alleluia in the liturgy—at first simply as extensions of the chant but later, in still larger and more elaborate forms, as new additions. Such extensions and additions were given the name *sequentia* or "sequence" (from the Latin *sequor,* to follow), perhaps originally because of their position "following" the Alleluia. When equipped with a text, the proper name for them is *prosa* (diminutive, *prosula*), alluding to the prose form of their texts—though the same word "sequence" is often used loosely for both the texted and untexted versions. Where and how they first arose is hard to say. There is a story that a monk of St. Gall, Notker Balbulus ("the stammerer"; *ca.* 840–912), "invented" the sequence when he began to write words syllabically under certain long melismas as an aid to memorizing the tune. Syllabic prose texts were added to melismatic passages in other chants as well as those of the Alleluia; the so-called "Kyrie tropes," the names of which survive in the modern liturgical books as the titles of certain Masses were at one time *prosulae* consisting of words added syllabically to the melismas of the original chant.

The sequence or *prosa* early became detached from particular liturgical chants and began to blossom forth as an independent form of composition. Hundreds of them appeared all over western Europe from the tenth to the thirteenth centuries and even later. In church, they may have been sung to the accompaniment of organ and bells.

Popular sequences were imitated and adapted to secular uses; there was considerable mutual influence between sequences and contemporary types of semisacred and secular music, both vocal and instrumental, in the late Middle Ages.

In its fully developed independent form the sequence is based on the principle of repetition: each strophe of the text is immediately followed by another with exactly the same number of syllables and the same pattern of accents; these two strophes are sung to the same melodic segment, which is repeated for the second strophe. The only exceptions are the first and last verses, which usually do not have parallels. Although any two paired strophes are identical in length, the length of the next pair may be quite different. The typical sequence pattern may be represented thus: *a bb cc dd . . . n; bb, cc, dd . . .* represent an indefinite number of strophic pairs and *a* and *n* the unpaired verses.

One of the most celebrated sequences is *Victimae paschali laudes* ("Praises to the Paschal Victim"; NAWM/S 1), ascribed to Wipo, chaplain to the Emperor Henry III in the first half of the eleventh century; in it the classical sequence form of paired strophes is plainly evident,[3] as is also the common device of unifying the different melodic segments by similar cadential phrases. The twelfth-century *prosae* of Adam of St. Victor illustrate a later development in which the text was regularly versified and rhymed.

Most sequences were abolished from the Catholic service by the liturgical reforms of the Council of Trent (1545–63), and four only were retained in use: *Victimae paschali laudes,* at Easter; *Veni Sancte Spiritus* ("Come, Holy Ghost"), on Whitsunday; *Lauda Sion* ("Zion, praise") by St. Thomas Aquinas, for the festival of Corpus Christi; and the *Dies irae* ("Day of Wrath"), attributed to Thomas of Celano, dating from the early thirteenth century. A fifth sequence, the *Stabat Mater* ("By the Cross the Mother standing," ascribed to Jacopo da Todi, a Franciscan monk of the thirteenth century), was added to the liturgy in 1727.

Just as in ancient Greece the drama had grown out of religious rites, so in the West the first musical dramas grew out of the liturgy. One of the earliest of these liturgical dramas was based on a tenth-century trope preceding the Introit of the Mass for Easter. The original trope, in dialogue form, represents the three Marys coming to the tomb of Jesus. The angel asks them, "Whom seek ye in the sepulchre?" They reply, "Jesus of Nazareth," to which the angel answers, "He is not here, He is risen as He said; go and proclaim that He has risen from the grave" (Mark xvi:5–7). Contem-

Liturgical dramas

---

[3] One line of one pair in this sequence has been omitted in the modern chant books.

porary accounts indicate not only that this dialogue was sung re-sponsively, but also that the singing was accompanied by appropriate dramatic action.

Similar little scenes were performed in connection with the Christmas liturgy, and on other occasions, and in time the action was expanded to include incidents preceding and following the original scene. As the scope and subject matter of the plays was enlarged and acting grew more realistic, spoken dialogue was intro-duced. Eventually the plays were detached from the regular church service; hymns and songs of a popular nature were introduced in addition to the chants, and the texts became a mixture of Latin and the vernacular. Songs for the congregation to sing were introduced, and probably also trumpet fanfares and other instrumental effects. Different stories from the Bible were dramatized in this way, for example the story of Daniel in the lions' den, of Herod's slaughter of the Innocents, and many others. Many of the Easter plays used the familiar sequence *Victimae paschali laudes,* and the performances often concluded with the singing of the *Te Deum.* The liturgical drama at its height in the twelfth and thirteenth centuries was ex-tremely popular all over western and central Europe, and recent modern revivals of some of these works have had considerable suc-cess. The naive mixture, in the originals, of sacred and secular elements well illustrates the interpenetration of these two areas in late medieval times.

Medieval Musical Theory and Practice

The development of the medieval modal system was a gradual process, not all the stages of which can be clearly traced. In its com-plete form, achieved by the eleventh century, the system recognized eight modes, differentiated according to the position of the tones and semitones in a diatonic octave built on the *finalis* or *final;* in practice this note was usually—not invariably—the last note in the melody. The modes were identified by numbers, and grouped in pairs; the odd-numbered modes were called *authentic* ("original"), and the even-numbered modes *plagal* ("derived"). A plagal mode always had the same final as its corresponding authentic mode. The authentic modal scales were notated as white-key octave scales rising from the notes *D* (mode I), *E* (mode III), *F* (mode V), and *G* (mode VII), with their corresponding plagals a fourth lower (Example II–3). It must be remembered, however, that these notes do not stand for a specific "absolute" pitch—a conception foreign to Gregorian Chant and to the Middle Ages in general—but were chosen simply

The church modes

Guido of Arezzo and Bishop Theobald of Arezzo with the monochord. From a twelfth-century German manuscript.

so that the distinguishing interval patterns could be notated with minimum use of accidentals.

The finals of each mode are shown in Example II–3 as ◖. In addition to the final, there is in each mode a second note, called the *tenor* (as in the psalm tones; see above p. 24) or *dominant* or *reciting tone* (shown in Example II–3 as ●), which sometimes functions as a secondary tonal center. The finals of the corresponding plagal and authentic modes are the same; but the dominants are different. A handy way to identify the dominants is to remember these facts: 1) in the authentic modes the dominant is a fifth above the final; 2) in the plagal modes the dominant is a third below the dominant

EXAMPLE II–3 The Medieval Church Modes

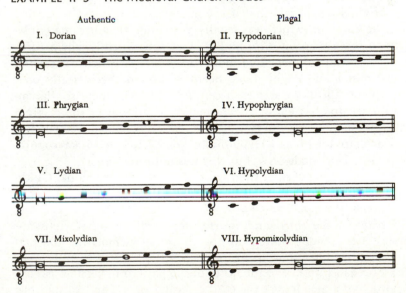

of the corresponding authentic mode; 3) whenever a dominant would fall on the note *B,* it is moved up to *C.*

A mode is identified by its final, its dominant, and its range. A plagal mode differs from its corresponding authentic mode by having a different dominant and a different range: in the authentic modes the entire range lies above the final, whereas in the plagal modes the final is the fourth note from the bottom of the octave. Thus modes I and VIII have the same range, but different finals and dominants.

The only accidental properly used in notating Gregorian Chants is *B♭.* Under certain conditions the *B* was flatted in modes I and II, and also occasionally in modes V and VI; if this was consistently done, these modes became exact facsimiles of the modern natural minor and major scales respectively. Accidentals were necessary, of course, when a modal melody was transposed; if a chant in mode I, for example, were written on *G,* a flat would be required in the signature.

In the tenth century, theorists tried to identify the system of church modes with the ancient Greek keys; because of an understandable vagueness about their meaning, the Greek names were applied to the wrong modes. Although the modern liturgical books do not use the Greek names (preferring a classification by numerals), they are still in general use elsewhere, especially in textbooks on counterpoint. Thus modes I and II are now often called Dorian and Hypodorian, modes III and IV Phrygian and Hypophrygian, modes V and VI Lydian and Hypolydian, and modes VII and VIII Mixolydian and Hypomixolydian.

Why were there no modes on *a, b,* and *c′* in medieval theory? The original reason was that if the modes on *d, e,* and *f* were sung with the flatted *b* (which was legally available), they became equivalent to the modes on *a, b,* and *c′,* and consequently, these three modes were superfluous. The modes on *a* and *c,* which correspond to our minor and major, have been recognized theoretically only since the middle of the sixteenth century: the Swiss theorist Glarean in 1547 set up a system of twelve modes by adding to the original eight, two modes on *a* and two on *c,* respectively named Aeolian and Hypoaeolian, Ionian and Hypoionian. Some later theorists recognize also a "Locrian" mode on *b,* but this was not often used.

The hexachord system

For the teaching of sight singing an eleventh-century monk, Guido of Arezzo, perfected a method which had as its basis the memorizing of six tones in the pattern *C–D–E–F–G–A;* in this pattern a semitone falls between the third and fourth steps and all other steps are whole tones. Guido pointed out, as an aid to memorizing the pattern, that in a familiar hymn, *Ut queant laxis,* each of the six phrases began with one of the notes of the pattern in regular ascending order—the first phrase on *C,* the second on *D,* and so on. (See

EXAMPLE II–4   Hymn: *Ut queant laxis*

Ut que-ant la - xis *re*-so-na-re fi-bris   *Mi* - ra ge-sto-rum *fa*-mu-li tu-o - rum,

Sol - ve pol-lu - ti   *La* - bi - i re - a-tum, San - cte Jo - an-nes.

That thy servants may freely sing forth the wonders of thy deeds,
remove all stain of guilt from their unclean lips, O Saint John.

Example II–4.) The initial syllables of the words of these six phrases
became the names of the notes: *ut, re, mi, fa, sol, la.* We still learn
them this way today, except that we say *do* for *ut* and add a *ti*
above *la.* The semitone, it will be noticed, is always the interval
mi–fa.

This *hexachord,* or pattern of six notes, could be found at different places in the scale: beginning on C, on G, or (by flatting
the B) on F. The hexachord on G used the B-natural, for which
the sign was ♮ , "square b" (*b quadrum*); the F hexachord used
the B–flat, which had the sign ♭ , "round b" (*b rotundum*). Although these signs are obviously the models for our ♮, ♯, and ♭, their
original purpose was not the same as that of the modern accidentals;
originally they served to indicate the syllables *mi* and *fa.* Because the
square form of the B was called "hard" and the rounded form
"soft," the G and F hexachords were called respectively the "hard"
(*durum*) and "soft" (*molle*) hexachords; the one on C was called
the "natural" hexachord. The whole of the musical space within
which medieval composers worked and with which medieval theorists were concerned extended from G (which was written as
the Greek letter Γ, and called *gamma*) to e″; within this range
every note was named not only by its letter, but also according to

EXAMPLE II–5   The System of Hexachords

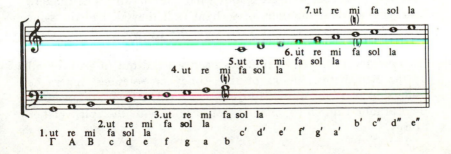

7. ut   re   mi   fa   sol   la
        (♮)
6. ut   re   mi   fa   sol   la
5. ut   re   mi   fa   sol   la
4. ut   re   mi   fa   sol   la
        (♮)
3. ut   re   mi   fa   sol   la
2. ut   re   mi   fa   sol   la
1. ut   re   mi   fa   sol   la
Γ   A   B   c   d   e   f   g   a   b   c′   d′   e′   f′   g′   a′   b′   c″   d″   e″

the position it occupied within the hexachord or hexachords to which it belonged. Thus gamma, which was the first note of its hexachord, was called *gamma ut* (whence our word *gamut*); e″, as the top note of its hexachord, was *e la*. Middle c′, which belonged to three different hexachords, was *c sol fa ut* (see Example II–5). Both the Greek and the medieval note names were retained by theorists until well into the sixteenth century, but only the medieval names were in practical use.

Notation

One task that occupied the theorists of the Middle Ages was that of developing an adequate musical notation. Beginning sometime before the middle of the ninth century, signs (*neumes*) were placed above the words to indicate an ascending melodic line (╱), a descending one (╲), or a combination of the two (╱╲). These neumes probably were derived from grammatical accent marks like those still used in modern French and Italian. Eventually, a more precise way to notate a melody was required, and by the tenth century scribes were placing neumes at varying heights above the text to indicate more exactly the course of the melody; these are called *heighted neumes*. Sometimes dots were added to the solid lines to indicate the relationship of the individual notes within the neume, and thus make clearer what intervals the neume represented. A decisive advance was made when a scribe drew a horizontal red line to represent the pitch *f*, and grouped the neumes about this line; in time a second line, usually yellow, was drawn for *c′*. By the eleventh century Guido of Arezzo was describing a four-line staff then in use, on which letters indicated the lines for *f*, *c′* and sometimes *g′*— letters which eventually evolved into our modern clef signs.

This invention of the staff made it possible to notate precisely the relative pitch of the notes of a melody, and freed music from its hitherto exclusive dependence on oral transmission. It was an event as crucial for the history of Western music as the invention of writing was for the history of language. The staff notation with neumes was still imperfect, however; it conveyed the pitch of the notes, but did not indicate their relative durations. Signs showing rhythm do exist in many medieval manuscripts, but modern scholars have not been able to agree about what they meant. The modern practice is to treat the notes of a chant as if they all had the same basic value; notes are grouped rhythmically in twos or threes, these groups being in turn flexibly combined into larger rhythmic units. This method of interpretation has been worked out in great detail by the Benedictine monks of the Abbey of Solesmes under the leadership of Dom André Mocquereau, and has been approved by the Catholic Church as being in conformity with the spirit of her liturgy.

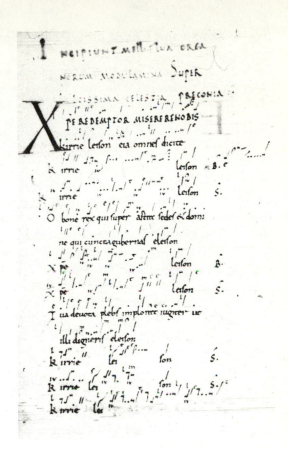

Two pages from the Winchester Troper Manuscript (eleventh century) Cambridge, Corpus Christi 473. On the left (f55) is the chant, a "troped Kyrie," that is, a Kyrie with insertions; on the right (f135) is the added organal part intended to be sung with the chant. The melody of the chant is that of the "ad libitum" Kyrie No. vi (Te Christe Rex supplices) in the modern liturgical books (see Liber Usualis, *p. 78)*

Nonliturgical and Secular Monody

The oldest preserved specimens of secular music are songs with Latin texts. The earliest of these form the repertoire of *Goliard songs* from the eleventh and twelfth centuries. The Goliards—named after a probably mythical patron, Bishop Golias—were students or footloose clerics who migrated from one school to another in the days before the founding of the great resident universities.

Early secular forms

Another kind of monophonic song written in the period from the eleventh to the thirteenth century is the *conductus*. Conductus are outstanding illustrations of how vague the dividing line was between sacred and secular music in the Middle Ages. They originally may have been sung at moments when an actor in a liturgical drama or a celebrant in the Mass or some other service was formally "conducted" in procession from one place to another. Their texts were metrical verses, like the texts of sequences of the same period; but their connection with the liturgy was so tenuous that by the end of the twelfth century the term *conductus* was applied to any non-liturgical Latin song, generally of a serious character, with a metrical text, on either a sacred or a secular subject. One important feature of the conductus was that, as a rule, its melody was newly composed, instead of being borrowed or adapted from Gregorian Chant or some other source.

The characteristic aspects of the secular spirit of the Middle Ages are, of course, most clearly reflected in the songs with vernacular texts. One of the earliest known types of vernacular song was the *chanson de geste* or "song of deeds"—an epic narrative poem recounting the deeds of national heroes, sung to simple melodic formulas, a single one of which might serve unchanged for each line throughout long sections of the poem. The poems were transmitted orally and not reduced to writing until a comparatively late date; virtually none of the music has been preserved. The most famous of the *chansons de geste* is the *Song of Roland,* the national epic of France, which dates from about the second half of the eleventh century, though the events it relates belong to the age of Charlemagne.

Jongleurs

The people who sang the *chansons de geste* and other secular songs in the Middle Ages were the *jongleurs* or *ménestrels* ("minstrels"), a class of professional musicians who first appear about the tenth century.

The minstrels, as a class, were neither poets nor composers in exactly the sense we give to those terms. They sang, played, and danced to songs composed by others or taken from the common domain of popular music, no doubt altering them or making up their own versions as they went along. Their professional traditions and skill played a part in an important development of secular music in western Europe—that body of song commonly known today as the music of the troubadours and the trouvères.

Troubadours and trouvères

These two words mean the same thing: finders or inventors; the term *troubadour* was used in the south of France, *trouvère* in the north. In the Middle Ages the words apparently were applied to anyone who wrote or composed anything; modern usage which restricts them to two particular groups of musicians is therefore historically inaccurate. Troubadours were poet-composers who flourished in Provence, the region now comprising southern France; they wrote in Provençal, the *langue d'oc.* Their art, taking its original inspiration from the neighboring Hispano-Mauresque culture of the

Iberian peninsula, spread quickly northward, especially to the provinces of Champagne and Artois. Here the trouvères, active throughout the thirteenth century, wrote in the *langue d'oïl,* the dialect of medieval French that became modern French.

Neither troubadours nor trouvères constituted a well-defined group. Both they and their art flourished in generally aristocratic circles (there were even kings among their number), but an artist of lower birth might be accepted into a higher social class on the ground of his talent. Many of the poet-composers not only created their songs but sang them as well. Alternatively, they could entrust the performance to a minstrel. Where the extant versions differ from one manuscript to another, they may represent versions of different scribes—or, perhaps, various renditions of the same song by different minstrels who had learned it by rote and afterward dealt with it in their own way, as happens whenever music is transmitted orally for some time before being written down. The songs are preserved in collections (*chansonniers*), some of which have been published in modern edition with facsimiles. Altogether, about 2600 troubadour poems and over 260 melodies have been preserved, and about 4000 trouvère poems and 1400 melodies.

The poetic and musical substance of the troubadour and trouvère songs is often not profound, but the formal structures employed show great variety and ingenuity. There are simple ballads and ballads in dramatic style, some of which require or suggest two or more characters. Some of the dramatic ballads evidently were intended to be mimed; many obviously call for dancing. Often there is a refrain which, at least in the older examples, must have been sung by a chorus. In addition, and especially in the south, they wrote love songs—the subject par excellence for troubadour song. There are songs on political and moral topics, and songs whose texts are debates or arguments, frequently on an abstruse point of chivalric or courtly love.

A favorite genre was the *pastourelle,* one of the class of dramatic ballads. The text of a pastourelle always tells the following story: a knight makes love to a shepherdess who usually, after due resistance, succumbs; alternatively, the shepherdess screams for help, whereupon her brother or lover rushes in and drives the knight away, not without blows given and received. In the earliest pastourelles, all the narration was monologue; it was a natural step, however, to make the text a dialogue between the knight and the shepherdess. Later, the dialogue came to be acted as well as sung; if one or two episodes were added, and if the rescuing shepherd appeared with a group of rustic companions, and the performance were decked out with incidental songs and dances, the result was a little musical play. One such play, in fact, is the famous *Jeu de Robin et de Marion,* written by Adam de la Halle, the last and the greatest of all trouvères, about 1284. It is uncertain whether all the songs in this work were written by Adam himself or whether they were popular chansons incorporated in the play. A few of them have polyphonic settings. Typical of the tuneful songs is that sung by Marion with choral refrains at the opening of the *Jeu, Robins m'aime* (NAWM/S 4). It is a monophonic rondeau in the form *ABaabAB* (using separate letters for each musical phrase, capitals for choral, lower case for solo performance).

Techniques of troubadour and trouvère melodies

The melodic settings of both troubadour and trouvère songs were generally syllabic with occasional short melismatic figures; it is probable that in performance melodic ornaments were added and that the melody was varied from stanza to stanza. The range is narrow, frequently no more than a sixth and hardly ever more than an octave. The modes seem to be chiefly the first and seventh, with their plagals; certain notes in these modes were probably altered chromatically by the singers in such a way as to make them almost equivalent to the modern minor and major. For example, *Baros, de mon dan covit* (NAWM/S 3), approaches F major if the Bs are flatted, but this would alter the character of the song. There is some uncertainty about the rhythm of the songs, especially with regard to the oldest extant melodies, which are notated in a way that does not indicate the relative time values of the notes. In trouvère songs the phrases are almost always clear cut, fairly short (three, four, or five measures in a modern transcription in ¾ time), and with a definite, easily retained melodic profile. The troubadour melodies are less sectional and often suggest a freer rhythmic treatment.

The repetition, variation, and contrast of short, distinctive musi-

Adam de la Halle, also called the Hunchback of Arras, was born in Arras about 1237 and died at Naples about 1287. Gifted as both poet and composer, he is depicted here in a miniature from the Chansonnier d'Arras.

cal phrases naturally produce a more or less distinct formal pattern. Many of the troubadour and trouvère melodies repeat the opening phrase or section before proceeding in a free style. But on the whole the melodies in the original manuscript sources do not fall so neatly into categories as the designations in some modern collections suggest. Many of the trouvère songs have *refrains*, recurring lines or pairs of lines in the text which usually also involve the recurrence of the corresponding musical phrase.

The art of the troubadours was the model for a German school of knightly poet-musicians, the *Minnesinger*. The love (*Minne*) of which they sang in their *Minnelieder* was even more abstract than troubadour love, and sometimes had a distinctly religious tinge. The music is correspondingly more sober; some of the melodies are in the ecclesiastical modes, while others veer toward major tonality. As nearly as can be inferred from the rhythm of the texts, the majority of the tunes were sung in triple meter. Strophic songs were also very common, as in France. The melodies, however, tended toward tighter organization through melodic phrase repetition. For example in Prince Wizlau von Rügen's *We ich han gedacht* (NAWM/S 5) the *Weise* or melodic pattern for singing the ten-line stanzas has a musical form that is even more repetitive than the rhyme scheme:

Minnesinger

Rhyme *a a b | c c b | d e e d*
Melody *A A B | A A B | C A A B*

In France toward the end of the thirteenth century the art of the trouvères came to be carried on more and more by cultured middle-class citizens instead of predominantly by nobles as in earlier times. A similar movement took place in Germany in the course of the fourteenth, fifteenth, and sixteenth centuries; the eventual successors of the Minnesinger were the *Meistersinger,* stolid tradesmen and artisans of German cities, whose lives and organization have been portrayed by Wagner in his opera *The Mastersingers of Nuremberg*. Hans Sachs, the hero of this opera, was an historical figure, a Meistersinger who lived in the sixteenth century. Some fine examples of Sachs's art have survived, one of the most beautiful being *Nachdem David war redlich* (NAWM/S 6), a commentary on the strife between David and Saul in I Samuel xvii ff. It is in a form common in the Minnelied that was taken over by the Meistersinger; in German it is called a *Bar—AAB*—in which the same melodic phrase, *A,* is repeated for a stanza's first two units of text (called *Stollen*), and the remainder, *B* (called *Abgesang*), is longer and has new melodic material. Though there are masterpieces such as this, the art of the Meistersinger was so hedged about by rigid rules that their music seems stiff and inexpressive in comparison with that of the Minnesinger. The Meistersingers' guild had a long history, and was finally dissolved only in the nineteenth century.

Meistersinger

Hans Sachs

Other kinds of song

In addition to monophonic secular songs, there were also in the Middle Ages many monophonic religious songs not intended for use in church. These songs were expressions of individual piety; they had vernacular texts and were written in a melodic idiom that seems to be derived about equally from church plainchant and popular folk song. The few surviving English songs of the thirteenth century show a variety of moods and suggest a much more extensive musical life than is now possible to reconstruct. Spanish monophonic songs include a large number of *cantigas,* songs of praise to the Virgin; these have been preserved in a large late-thirteenth-century collection, and resemble in many ways the music of the troubadours. Contemporary Italian monophonic songs were the *laude;* they were sung by processions of penitents, and have music of a vigorous, popular character.

Medieval Instrumental Music and Instruments

Dances in the Middle Ages were accompanied not only by songs but by instrumental music as well. The *estampie,* of which several English and Continental examples exist from the thirteenth and fourteenth centuries, was a dance piece, sometimes monophonic and sometimes polyphonic, in several sections (*puncta* or *partes*), each of which was repeated (compare the sequence); the first statement ended with an "open" (*ouvert*), or incomplete, cadence; the repetition ended with a "closed" (*clos*), or full, cadence. Usually the same open and closed endings were used throughout an estampie, and the sections preceding the endings are also similar. Derived from the French estampie are the *istanpite* in a fourteenth-century Italian manuscript, which display a somewhat more complex variant of the same form. For example, the istanpita entitled *Palamento* (NAWM/S 7) has five *partes,* the first three sharing the same music for all but the first fifteen or twenty measures, the fourth and fifth *partes* having dissimilar long *ouvert* and *clos* endings.

Estampies happen to be the earliest known examples of an instrumental repertoire that doubtless goes back far beyond the thirteenth century. It is unlikely that the early Middle Ages had any instrumental music other than that associated with singing or dancing, but it would be completely incorrect to think that the music of this period was exclusively vocal.

The oldest characteristically medieval instrument was the *harp,* which was imported to the Continent from Ireland and Britain some time before the ninth century. The principal bowed instrument of medieval times was the *vielle* or *Fiedel,* which had many

King David holds his harp while musicians below play the bell chimes, recorder, vielle, and positive organ. A miniature from a late eleventh-century Bible.

different names and a great variety of shapes and sizes; it is the prototype of the viol of the Renaissance and the modern violin. The thirteenth-century vielle had five strings, one of them usually a drone. This is the instrument with which jongleurs are most often depicted, and with which they probably accompanied their singing and recitations. Another stringed instrument was the *organistrum;* described in a tenth-century treatise, it was a three-stringed vielle played by a revolving wheel turned by a crank, the strings being stopped by a set of rods instead of by the fingers. In the early Middle Ages, the organistrum was apparently a large instrument requiring two players, and was used in churches; after the thirteenth century it degenerated into a smaller form, from which the modern hurdy-gurdy is descended.

An instrument that appears frequently in the Middle Ages is the *psaltery,* a type of zither played either by plucking, or more often by striking, the strings—the remote ancestor of the harpsichord and clavichord. The *lute* was known as early as the ninth century, having been brought into Spain by the Arab conquerors; but it did not come into common use in other countries much before the Renaissance. There were *flutes,* both the recorder and the transverse types, and *shawms,* reed instruments of the oboe variety. *Trumpets* and *horns* were used only by the nobility; the universal folk instrument was the *bagpipe. Drums* came into use by the twelfth century, chiefly to beat time for singing and dancing.

In the Middle Ages there were, in addition to the great organs in churches, two smaller types, the *portative* and the *positive.* The portative organ was small enough to be carried (*portatum*), perhaps suspended by a strap around the neck of the player; it had a single rank of pipes, and the keys or "slides" were played by the right hand while the left worked the bellows. The positive organ also could be carried but had to be placed (*positum*) on a table to be played and required an assistant for the bellows.

III

The Beginnings of Polyphony
and the Music of the
Thirteenth Century

Historical Background of Early Polyphony

The eleventh century is of crucial importance in Western history. The years 1000–1100 A.D. witnessed a revival of economic life throughout western Europe, an increase in population, reclamation of wastelands, and the beginning of modern cities; the Norman conquest of England, important strides toward the recovery of Spain from the Muslims, the First Crusade; a revival of culture, with the first translations from Greek and Arabic, the beginnings of the universities and scholastic philosophy, and the rise of Romanesque architecture. The cultural independence of the West was marked by the growth of vernacular literature and symbolized by the final schism between the Western and Eastern Churches in 1054.

The eleventh century was equally crucial in the history of music. During this time certain changes were beginning—changes which, when eventually worked out, would result in giving to Western music many of its basic characteristics, those features which distinguish it from other musics of the world. Those changes may be summarized as follows:

(1) *Composition* slowly replaced improvisation as a way of creating musical works. Improvisation, in one form or another, is the normal way in most musical cultures and was probably the exclusive

way in the West up to about the ninth century. Gradually the idea arose of composing a melody once for all instead of improvising it anew each time on traditional melodic pattern-structures; and thenceforward a piece of music could be said to "exist," in the way in which we ordinarily think of it now, apart from any particular performance.

(2) A composed piece could be taught and transmitted orally, and might be subject to alterations in the course of transmission. But the *invention of musical notation* made it possible to write music down in a definitive form, which could be learned from the score. The score, in other words, was a set of directions which could be executed whether or not the composer was present. Thus composition and performance became separate acts instead of being combined in one person as before, and the performer's function became that of a mediator between composer and audience.

(3) Music began to be more consciously structured and made subject to certain *principles of order*—for example, the theory of the eight modes, or the rules governing rhythm and consonance; such principles were eventually formulated into systems and set forth in treatises.

(4) *Polyphony* began to replace monophony. Of course, polyphony as such is not exclusively Western; but it is our music which, more than any other, has specialized in this technique. We have developed polyphonic composition to a unique degree and, it must be admitted, at the expense of rhythmic and melodic subtleties that are characteristic of the music of other highly civilized peoples, India and China for example.

Early Organum

There are good reasons to believe that polyphony existed in Europe long before it was first unmistakably described. It was probably used chiefly in nonliturgical sacred music; it may have been employed also in folk music, and probably consisted of melodic doubling at the third, fourth, or fifth, along with a more or less systematic practice of heterophony—that is, by performing the same melody simultaneously in ornamented and unornamented form. Needless to say, there are no surviving documents of this supposed early European polyphony; but the first clear description of music in more than one voice, dated about the end of the ninth century, manifestly refers to something already being practiced, and is not a proposal of something new. In this treatise, *Musica enchiriadis* ("Handbook of Music") and in a contemporary commentary on it, the *Scholia enchiriadis,* two distinct kinds of "singing together" are described,

EXAMPLE III–1   Parallel Organum

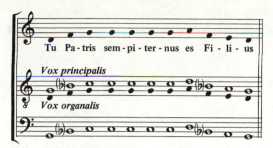

Tu Pa-tris sem-pi-ter-nus es Fi-li-us

Vox principalis

Vox organalis

Thou art the everlasting Son of the Father.

(Facsimile of original in Apel, *Notation of Polyphonic Music,* p. 205.)

both being designated by the name *organum* (pronounced or'-gan-um). In one species of this early organum, a plainsong melody in one voice, the *vox principalis,* is duplicated at a fifth or a fourth below by a second voice, the *vox organalis;* either voice or both may be further duplicated at the octave and at other intervals, as shown in Example III–1.

In another kind of early organum the two voices start at the unison; the *vox principalis* moves upward until it forms the interval of a fourth with the *vox organalis,* whereupon both proceed in parallel fourths until they come together again on a unison at the cadence (Example III–2). Duplication of the voices is possible in this as in the first type.

EXAMPLE III–2   Organum with Parallel Fourths

Rex cae-li do-mi-ne ma-ris un-di-so-ni
Vox principalis

Vox organalis

King of Heaven, Lord of the wave-sounding sea.

(Facsimile of original in Parrish, *Notation of Medieval Music,* plate XXa.)

Despite the fact that no theorist in the tenth century and only one in the eleventh so much as mentions organum, during this time it was undoubtedly being sung—improvised—and the idea of two simultaneous distinct voices seems to have gradually caught on. Organum in its first stage—where the added voice simply duplicates the original at a fixed interval—was hardly susceptible of development, and its mention in the theory books may have been no more than an attempt to account theoretically for certain examples of its use in contemporary musical practice. Extant musical examples of the eleventh century show important progress toward melodic independence and equal importance of the two voices: contrary and oblique motion become regular features. These are illustrated in Example III–3.

EXAMPLE III–3   Eleventh-century Organum

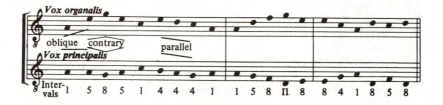

As a rule the *vox organalis* sings above the *vox principalis,* though the parts frequently cross; and rudimentary rhythmic diversity is shown by the *vox organalis* occasionally singing two notes against one of the *vox principalis.* In all eleventh-century organa the consonant intervals are the unison, octave, fourth, and fifth; all others occur only incidentally and are treated as dissonances requiring resolution. The rhythm is that of plainsong, on which the pieces are always based.

By the end of the eleventh century, polyphony had developed to a point where composers were able to combine two *melodically* independent lines by using oblique and contrary motion. Harmonic intervals had been stabilized by the invention of precise pitch notation on a staff. Two other essentials had still to be achieved: the ability to combine two or more *rhythmically* independent melodies; and a precise method of notating rhythm.

The development of notation was hastened by the growth of polyphony. As long as there was only one melody, a certain leeway in pitch and rhythm could be allowed; but when two or more melodies were to be played or sung together from a score, not only the pitches had to be made clear but also some means had to be devised to show the rhythmic relationships.

Florid Organum

A new type of organum appears early in the twelfth century. Examples are preserved in one manuscript at the monastery of Santiago de Compostela in the northwest corner of Spain and in three manuscripts from the Abbey of St. Martial at Limoges in south-central France. In this kind (called variously "florid," "melismatic," "Aquitanian," or "St. Martial" organum), the original plainchant melody (played or sung) lies always in the lower voice; but

A page from a St. Martial manuscript showing the organum Lux descendit. *(Courtesy of the British Library)*

each note is prolonged so as to allow the upper (solo) voice to sing phrases of varying length against it. It is not always clear from the notation whether the upper voice was sung in a free non-rhythmic manner or was subject to definite rhythmic patterns. In either case, it is obvious that this new kind of organum not only greatly increased the length of pieces but also deprived the lower voice of its original character as a definite tune, making it in effect rather a series of single notes, like "drones," with melodic elaborations above —a device common in some eastern European folk singing as well as in many non-Western musical systems. Clearly it was a style that could have originated, and probably did, in improvisation; the versions in the manuscripts may have actually been taken down in the first place from improvised performances. The lower voice, because it sustained or held the principal melody, came to be called the *tenor*, from the Latin *tenere*, "to hold"; and this word was used to designate the lowest part of a polyphonic composition until after the middle of the fifteenth century.

The term *organum* properly refers only to the style in which the lower voice holds long notes; when both parts came to move in similar measured rhythm, as happened later in the twelfth and early thirteenth centuries, the usual medieval term was *discant*. Since florid organum was at first applied in a two-voice texture, one designation for it was *organum duplum vel purum* ("double or pure organum"). By extension, *organum* has also come to have other meanings: it is sometimes used as a general term to denote all polyphonic music based on Gregorian Chant up to about the middle of the thirteenth century; it is used (like the modern word *sonata*) as the name of a *type* of composition, so that we can speak of "an organum" or "the organa" of a composer; and finally *organum* is the Latin word for any musical instrument, and also refers particularly to the organ. It is necessary not to confuse these different meanings; for example, when contemporaries called a certain composer "*optimus organista,*" they were not calling him an "excellent organist," but an "excellent composer of organa," that is, of compositions like the ones now being discussed.

The texts of the St. Martial organa consist mainly of *Benedicamus Domino* tropes and rhyming, scanning, accentual Latin poems called *versus.* As a rule the two voices of a trope setting have the same words; occasionally the lower voice carries the original plainsong text, while the upper voice sings the melody to the words of a trope. The versus, on the other hand, are newly composed texts, so some of this polyphony is the earliest not based on chant. The versus *Senescente mundano filio,* like most of the repertory, consists of a mixture of note-against-note and florid organal writing. Although the two voices are similar in range and both active, the lower one has a sharper melodic focus and was therefore probably conceived first, while the upper is more ornamental. Decided preference is given to contrary motion, and when parallel intervals appear they tend to be thirds and sixths, which are also admitted quite freely

EXAMPLE III–4   Versus: *Senescente mundano filio*

Prepare the guest chambers worthy of the deserving. A fitting companion fills the palaces. The Bridegroom enters the hall through the doors.

Source: Bibliothèque nationale, 3549, fol. 153, transcribed by Sarah Ann Fuller, *Aquitanian Polyphony of the Eleventh and Twelfth Centuries,* III, 33–34. Diss. University of California, Berkeley, 1969.

otherwise, though fifths, octaves, and unisons almost always begin and close the lines. Seconds and sevenths may be appoggiatura-like ornaments, but the points at which the voices come together is not altogether certain, since the notation is indefinite with respect to rhythm. One of the outstanding traits of the St. Martial organa is the use of melodic sequences both in parallel and contrary motion, as in Example III–4 (the entire piece is in **NAWM/S 8**).

The most typical style of organum in the St. Martial repertory is that in which the upper part has many notes to one in the lower part, that is, melismatic or florid organum. This kind of organum could have been sung from a notation that did not specify the relative time values of the notes in the two voices. The two parts were written one above the other—*score notation*—fairly well-aligned vertically, and with vertical lines on the staff to mark off the phrases; two singers, or one soloist and a small group, could not easily go astray. But in pieces whose rhythmic structure was more complicated—for example, if one or both melodies were laid out in regular rhythmic patterns formed by longer and shorter tones of definite relative time values—some way had to be found of distinguishing between long and short notes and indicating their relative durations.

The Rhythmic Modes

The system which eleventh- and twelfth-century composers devised for the notation of rhythm proved adequate for all polyphonic music until well into the thirteenth century. It was based on a fundamentally different principle from that of our notation: instead of showing fixed relative durations by means of different note signs, it indicated different *rhythmic patterns* by means of certain combinations of single notes and especially of note-groups. By about 1250, these patterns were codified as the six rhythmic modes, identified as a rule simply by number:

$$\text{I.} \; \quad\quad \text{IV.}$$
$$\text{II.} \quad\quad \text{V.}$$
$$\text{III.} \quad\quad \text{VI.}$$

Theoretically, according to the system, a melody in Mode I should consist of an indefinite number of repetitions of the pattern ♩ ♪, each phrase ending with a rest which replaced the second note of the pattern, thus:

♩ ♪♩ ♪|♩ ♪♩ ⅞|♩ ♪♩ ♪| *etc.*

In practice, however, the rhythm of such a melody would be more flexible than such a scheme shows. Either of the notes ♩ ♪ could be broken into shorter units, or the two notes of the pattern could be combined into one, and various other means for variety were available; also, a melody in Mode I might be sung over a tenor which held long notes not strictly measured, or which might be organized in the pattern of Mode V:

The required rhythmic mode was indicated to the singer by the choice and order of the notes. *Ligatures,* compound signs derived from the compound Gregorian neumes, denoting a group of two, three, or more tones, were one important means of conveying this information. For example, if a melody were notated as in Example III–5a—a single three-note ligature followed by a series of two-note ligatures—a singer would sing it in a rhythm that can be expressed in the modern notation of Example III–5b; in other words, the

EXAMPLE III–5   Use of Ligatures to Indicate a Rhythmic Mode

particular series of ligatures in Example III–5a signaled to the singer that he was to use the first rhythmic mode. The other rhythmic modes could be shown in equivalent ways. Departures from the prevailing rhythmic pattern, change of mode, or repeated tones (which could not be indicated in a ligature) necessitated modifications of the notation which are too complex and lengthy to be described in detail here.

Notre Dame Organum

It must not be supposed that the system of rhythmic modes was invented at one stroke, or that the system was invented first and the music written to conform to it. The opposite is true: the system and its notation were developed gradually during the twelfth and early thirteenth centuries to fill the needs of a school of polyphonic composers who were active at Paris, Beauvais, Sens, and other centers in the north-central part of France. Two composers of this school—the first composers of polyphony whose names are known to us—were Leonin, who lived in the third quarter of the twelfth century, and Perotin, who lived perhaps in the last part of the twelfth century and the first part of the thirteenth (1183?–1238?). Both men apparently were choirmasters at the Church of Notre Dame (predecessor to the cathedral now known by that name). Their compositions, together with those of their anonymous French contemporaries, are known collectively as the music of the Notre Dame school.

Three principal styles or types of composition are represented in the music of the Notre Dame school and the later thirteenth century: organum, conductus, and motet. Leonin wrote a cycle of two-part Graduals, Alleluias, and responsories for the entire church year, called the *Magnus liber organi (The Great Book of Organum)*. The *Magnus liber* no longer exists in its original form, but its contents have survived in various manuscripts at Florence, Wolfenbüttel, Madrid, and elsewhere; some of them are available in modern editions or facsimiles.

Leonin

Leonin's organa are set to the soloistic portions of the responsorial chants of the Mass and Office. The Alleluia is such a chant, and that for Easter Mass—*Alleluia Pascha nostrum*—was elaborated not only by him but also later composers, making it an ideal example for tracing the layers of polyphonic embellishment bestowed upon this category of chant. A comparison of Leonin's setting (NAWM/S 9b) with the original chant (NAWM/S 9a) makes it evident that the choral sections were left in simple plainsong, while the soloistic sections were amplified polyphonically. The formal and sonorous contrast already present in the responsorial performance is thus magnified. Further contrast is built into the polyphonic sections through differentiated styles of setting. The first section, the intonation "Alleluia" (Example III–6), looks at first like the older melismatic or florid organum: the plainsong melody is stretched out into indefinite unmeasured long notes to form the tenor. Above the long notes of the tenor, a solo voice sings textless melismatic phrases, broken at irregular intervals by cadences and rests.

The exact note values of this upper voice (called the *duplum*) in a modern transcription are not to be taken too literally. The inter-

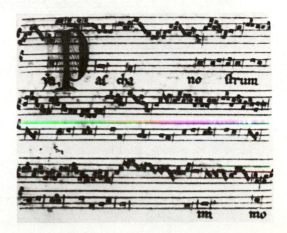

Duplum of Leonin's Alleluia Pascha nostrum *from the Biblioteca Medicea-Laurenziana, Florence (MS Pluteus 29.1, fol. 109r)*

pretation of some details of modal notation is not absolutely certain; besides, the desired effect seems to be one of expressive improvisation over a series of slowly changing "drone" notes.

After a choral unison chanting of the word "Alleluia," the soloistic two-voice texture is resumed with the psalm verse. But be-

EXAMPLE III–6   *Organum Duplum:* First Section of *Alleluia Pascha nostrum,* Leonin

Source: Florence, Biblioteca Medicea-Laurenziana, MS Pluteus 29.1, fol. 109r.

The original notation is shown in the illustration on page 51. The only two single note signs are the *longa or long* ▀ and the *brevis or breve* ■ ; ligatures of various shapes are combinations of longs and breves. In this kind of notation, neither the long nor the breve has a fixed duration; their time value depends on the context, on their position in the pattern. Brackets in the transcription indicate either ligatures in the original or a stepwise descending group of small diamond-shaped notes called *conjunctura* or *currentes* attached to a single long. Currentes attached to a ligature are shown by slurs. The sign ♪ stands for a *plica,* a short upward or downward dash affixed to a single note or to the final note of a ligature. Originally a sign for an ornamental or passing tone, the plica is used in modal notation to divide a longer note into two shorter ones; it takes its time value from the note to which it is attached.

ginning with the word "nostrum" a quite different style is heard (Example III–7). The tenor now sings in strictly measured rhythm; the upper voice, which moves in still faster notes, likewise takes on a more distinctly rhythmic character. Both parts sing in notes of definitely measured duration, in contrast to the more flexible rhythm of the previous section. As has already been mentioned, the style in which all the parts are in measured rhythm came to be called discant; it did not exclude occasional short melismas, particularly at cadential points, but for the most part the two voices moved according to the rhythmic modes.

EXAMPLE III–7   Beginning of Verse from *Alleluia Pascha nostrum* including Clausula on "nostrum," Leonin

This version of the clausula on "nostrum" may be compared to that in the manuscript known to scholars as W₂ (Wolfenbüttel, Herzog August Bibliothek, Helmstad.1099) in NAWM/S 9b.

The choice of whether to use organal or discant style was not a matter of caprice. It was based on the general principle that in those portions of the original chant which were syllabic or only slightly florid—in other words, in the portions where there were comparatively few notes to a syllable—the organal style with long sustained tones in the tenor was appropriate; but in those portions where the original chant was itself highly melismatic, it was necessary for the tenor to move along more quickly in order not to lengthen the whole piece unduly. Such sections, built over the more melismatic portions of the chant and written in discant style, were called *clausulae*. Each clausula was kept distinct, with a definite final cadence. In the Florentine source from which Examples III–6 and 7 are taken this Alleluia has three clausulas: on "nostrum," as we saw; on "latus" of the word "immolatus"; and on "lu" of the final "Alleluia." Between these clausulae there are contrasting sections in organal style. After the last discant section the chorus finishes the piece with the concluding few phrases of the plainsong Alleluia on which the organum is based.

One of the distinctive features of the Leonin style was the juxtaposition of old and new elements, passages of organum of the florid type alternating and contrasting with the livelier rhythmic discant clausulae. As the thirteenth century went on, *organum purum* was gradually abandoned in favor of discant; in the course of this development, clausulae first became quasi-independent pieces, and eventually evolved into a new form, the *motet*.

The work of Perotin and his contemporaries may be regarded as a continuation of that done by Leonin's generation. The basic formal structure of the organum—an alternation of unison chant with polyphonic sections—remained unchanged by Perotin, but within the polyphonic sections there was a continuing tendency toward greater rhythmic precision. Not only were the older rhap-

Perotin organum

sodic portions of the florid organa often replaced with discant
clausulae; many of the older clausulae were replaced with other,
so-called *substitute clausulae,* movements in definite and stylized
patterns. Such a substitute clausula, perhaps by Perotin, is that found
in the Florence manuscript for the "nostrum" melisma (NAWM/S
9d). The composer reversed the two components of the rhythmic
pattern (converting ♩. ♩. 𝄾 ♩. ♩. 𝄾 to ♩. ♩. ♩. 𝄾 ♩. ♩. 𝄾) and in the upper
part he adopted the third rhythmic mode in place of the first. As
in the original clausula the tenor melody is repeated twice (see
Example III–7, where the two statements are marked I and II),
but in the substitute clausula the repetition does not start on the
first note of the rhythmic pattern. The tenor of Perotin's organum
was characteristically laid out in a series of reiterated identical
rhythmic motives, corresponding usually to the fifth or third rhythmic mode; these tenors, in modern transcription, give the effect of
distinct binary grouping in two, or multiples of two, measures—see
Example III–8. Moreover, the tenor melody, which in Perotin's
style was typically in shorter notes than the tenors of Leonin, often
had to be repeated wholly or in part in order to bring a section
out to the length the composer desired. Both these kinds of
repetition—of rhythmic motive and of melody—were also part of
the formal structure of the later thirteenth-century motet. Nos. 7
and 8 of Example III–8, where the tenor is laid out in identical
repeated rhythmic patterns, actually foreshadow the technique of
the fourteenth-century "isorhythmic" motet which we shall study
in the next chapter (see pages 70–88).

One important innovation made by Perotin and his contemporaries was the expansion of organum from two voices to three or
four voices. Since the second voice was called the duplum, by analogy
the third and fourth were called respectively the *triplum* and
quadruplum. These same terms also designated the composition as
a whole; a three-voice organum was called an *organum triplum,* or
simply *triplum,* and a four-voice organum a *quadruplum.* The
three-voice organum, or triplum, became standard in the Perotin
period and remained in favor for a long time. Two fairly distinct
styles are usually present in a long organum triplum, either intermingled or alternated. Most tripla begin with long-held notes of
the chant in the tenor, and two voices moving above in measured
phrases. This style corresponds to the sustained-note portions of
Leonin organum, differing only in the more regular rhythmic
quality of the upper voices. In a typical Perotin organum, an opening section of this sort will be followed by one or more discant sections in which the tenor is also measured, though it moves less
rapidly than the upper voices. As the composition proceeds, sections
in sustained-tone style blend and alternate with sections in discant

EXAMPLE III–8   Tenors on "Domino" from *Haec dies*

1. Gregorian (*Graduale*, p. 241)

2. Two-voice clausula (Leonin, W1, fol. 27')

3. Two-voice clausula (Perotin? W1, fol. 46')

4. Three-voice clausula (Perotin? W1, fol. 81)

5. Motet (W2, fols. 126–127: cf. Los Huelgas ms. 131)

6. Motet (Montpellier ms. 190)

7. Motet (Montpellier ms. 193)

8. Motet (Montpellier ms. 221)

style; the latter as a rule correspond to the melismatic parts of the original chant, and the sections in sustained-tone style to the more syllabic parts of the chant.

The sustained-note sections, which sometimes involve as many as a hundred or more measures of a modern transcription in 6/8 time over one unchanging tenor tone, form great blocks of fundamentally static harmony, markedly different from the quick-moving harmonic rhythm of the discant sections. Yet even the latter do not have the quality of harmonic movement to which we are accustomed in music of the eighteenth and nineteenth centuries, organized

1) e′ in original   2) c′ in original

around clearly related tonal centers and working with dominant-tonic relationships; one cannot properly speak of chord *progressions* in Perotin, but only of chord *successions*.

The musical shape of a Perotin organum is defined by the design of the Gregorian Chant on which the piece is built, much as the plan of a Gothic cathedral is defined by the form of the Cross; in both arts the basic sacred symbol has almost unlimited possibilities for expansion and enrichment, depending on the creative fantasy of the artist. A melody used in this way as the basis of a polyphonic composition was later called a *cantus firmus* or "fixed song"; if the melody was taken from some already existing source, that fact might be indicated by calling it a *cantus prius factus,* or "song previously made."

Polyphonic Conductus

The tripla and quadrupla of Perotin and his generation are the summit of purely ecclesiastical polyphony in the early thirteenth century. The conductus, of which there are numerous examples up to about 1250, developed from quasi-liturgical sources such as the hymn and the sequence, but was extended to include secular words. Its texts were like those of the eleventh- and twelfth-century monophonic conductus and the St. Martial versus: they were metrical Latin poems, hardly ever liturgical, though often on sacred themes; if they were secular, they dealt seriously with moral questions or historical events.

The polyphonic conductus written by Perotin and by other composers of the Notre Dame era had a less complex musical style than

Characteristics of the conductus

organum. The music of the polyphonic conductus was written in two, three, or four voices which, as in organum, were held within a comparatively narrow range, crossing and recrossing, and were organized harmonically around the consonances of the octave, fourth, and fifth.

As usual with music of this period, the basis of the rhythm was a triple division of the beat; but typically in conductus the voices moved in nearly the same rhythm, so that the effect was—to use a modern term—chordal, in contrast to the greater rhythmic variety of the voices in organum. This thirteenth-century chordal manner of writing is often referred to as "conductus style," and sometimes was used in compositions other than conductus: for instance, two-part or three-part settings of hymns, sequences, ballads, and rondeaux were written in this style throughout the twelfth and thirteenth centuries, as were also some early thirteenth-century motets.

The Motet

Leonin, as we have seen, had introduced into his organa distinct sections (*clausulae*) in discant style. The idea evidently fascinated composers of the next generation—so much so that Perotin and others produced hundreds of discant clausulae, many of them designed as alternates or substitutes for those of Leonin and other earlier composers. These "substitute clausulae" were interchangeable; as many as five or ten might be written using the same tenor, and from these a choirmaster could select any one for a particular occasion. Presumably, the added upper voice or voices originally had no words; but sometime before the middle of the century words began to be fitted to them—usually tropes or paraphrases, in rhymed Latin verse, of the tenor text. Eventually, the clausulae cut loose from the larger organa in which they had been imbedded and began life on their own as separate compositions—in much the same way that the sequence, after starting out as an appendage to the Alleluia, later became independent. Probably because of the addition of words, the newly autonomous substitute clausulae were called *motets*. The term comes from the French *mot*, meaning "word," and was first applied to French texts that were added to the duplum of a clausula. By extension, "motet" came to signify the composition as a whole. The Latin form *motetus* is customarily used to designate the second voice (the original duplum) of a motet; when there are more than two voices, the third and fourth have the same names (triplum, quadruplum) as in organum.

Origins and general features

The earliest type of motet, based on the substitute clausula with Latin texts supplied for the upper voices, was soon modified in various ways. (1) It was a natural step to discard the original upper voices, and instead of putting words to one or more pre-existing melodies, to keep only the tenor and write one or more new melodies to go with it. This practice gave the composers much more freedom in the selection of texts, since they were able to set to music the words of any poem instead of having to choose or write one that would fit a given musical line; and as a further consequence, they had much greater possibilities for variety of rhythm and phrasing in the melodies. (2) Motets were written to be sung outside the church services, in secular surroundings; the upper voices of these motets were given a secular text, usually in the vernacular. Motets with French words in the upper voices still used a plainsong melody as *cantus firmus;* but as the *cantus firmus* served no liturgical function, there was no point in singing the original Latin text, so probably these tenors were played on instruments. (3) It had become customary before 1250 to use texts that were different in words, though related in meaning, for the two upper voices in a three-voice motet. Both texts might be in Latin, or both in French, or (rarely) one in Latin and the other in French. This kind of three-part motet with different texts (not necessarily in different languages) in the upper voices became standard in the second half of the thirteenth century.

Both the original and the substitute clausulae of the organum *Alleluia Pascha nostrum* (NAWM/S 9b) in the *Magnus liber* were reworked as motets by adding texts in Latin, French, or both. For example, the clausula on *latus* (NAWM/S 9f), through the setting of a Latin text *Ave Maria, Fons letitie* to the duplum, became a motet in honor of the Virgin. The brevity of the phrases of the duplum obliged the poet to invent rhyming endings for every second line. One of the substitute clausulae on *nostrum* (NAWM/S 9d), slightly revised, and with the addition of a third part or triplum, became the motet *Salve salus hominum—O radians stella preceteris—Nostrum* (NAWM/S 9e). The two poetic texts are unrelated to the Alleluia verse but complement each other in that they are addressed to the Virgin. They are set to the music rather than the contrary, so their line lengths are irregular, and the rhyme scheme is extremely simple, alternating two syllables, "is" and "ia" in the duplum, "um" and "ie" in the triplum. The third rhythmic mode of the triplum matches that of the duplum, but the lengths of the phrases are so calculated that they do not rest at the same time. This motet was also converted to secular uses by the substitution of a French text for each of the upper parts, namely *Qui d'amors veut bien—Qui longuement porroit—Nostrum* (NAWM/S 9g). As in the Latin motet, the two texts reinforce each other and each uses only two different rhyming syllables.

In the French motets—that is, motets with French words in both motetus and triplum—there was, naturally, seldom any connection between the texts of the upper voices and the Gregorian tenor, which functioned simply as a convenient, traditional, instrumentally performed *cantus firmus*. The two French texts were almost always love songs. The triplum was usually merry, and the motetus complaining, and both poems were usually in the style of the contemporary trouvère works, as in Example III–9.

EXAMPLE III–9   Motet: *Pucelete—Je languis—Domino*

Triplum: *The fair maid, pretty, polite, and pleasing, the delightful one whom I desire so much, makes me joyful, gay, and loving. No nightingale in May sings so gaily. I shall love with all my heart my sweetheart, the fair brunette. Fair friend, who hast held my life in thy command so long, I cry you mercy, sighing.*
Motetus: *I languish with the sickness of love; I had rather that this kill me than any other illness; such death is very pleasant. Relieve me, sweet friend, of this sickness lest love kill me.*

Such admixture of sacred and secular elements in a motet must be understood from the medieval point of view, which recognized no such gulf between those two realms as exists in modern thought.

A motet was not one piece, but many, like a garment that serves different purposes according to the weather or the occasion.

In early motets, the motetus and triplum were essentially alike in character: they intertwined in a moderately lively movement with similar slight modifications of a basic rhythmic mode, but remained practically indistinguishable as far as melodic style was concerned. In the later period, composers often sought to introduce distinctions in style not only between the upper voices and the tenor, but also between the two upper voices themselves. This kind of later motet is sometimes called *Franconian*, after Franco of Cologne, a composer and theorist who was active from about 1250 to 1280. The triplum had a longer text than the motetus, and was given a rather fast-moving melody with many short notes in short phrases of narrow range; against this triplum, the motetus sang a comparatively broad, long-breathed, lyrical melody. A charming example of a Franconian style motet is *Pucelete—Je languis—Domino* (Example III–9). Each voice in this motet is in a different rhythmic mode. The tenor is in the fifth mode; the motetus moves for the most part in the ♩ ♩ pattern of the second mode; the triplum moves in a version of the sixth mode, with the first note broken into two shorter ones (♩ ♩ ♩ = ♫ ♩ ♪).

The musical contrast between the two upper voices in this piece is supported by the texts. The triplum is a chatty description of a lady's attractions, and the motetus a conventional plaint by her despairing lover. The tenor text, *Domino,* simply refers to the source of this melody (the setting of the word "Domino" in the chant *Benedicamus Domino*—see *Liber Usualis,* p. 124) and has nothing to do with either motetus or triplum, since this part would have been played rather than sung.

Another development in the rhythm used in motets involved the tenor. In the middle thirteenth century, one of the most conspicuous traits of the motet was the tenor's rigid rhythmic scheme; indeed, much of the effect of freedom and freshness in the unsymmetrically phrased triplum depended on its contrast with the more regularly laid out motetus and especially with the persistence of a strongly marked and unvarying tenor motive. Toward the end of the thirteenth century, however, even the tenor was sometimes written in a more flexible style approaching that of the other two parts. *Pucelete —Je languis—Domino* is an early example of the use of a freer tenor; the (instrumental) lowest voice, with its diversified phrasing and quiet movement, is assimilated into the texture, instead of standing out in aggressive isolation after the fashion of the earlier motet tenor.

The two tendencies just described—the one toward greater diversity and the other toward greater homogeneity of texture— were to a certain extent contradictory. By the late thirteenth cen-

The Franconian motet

tury, they were not ordinarily found together in the same composition. Rather, the trend at this time was toward the emergence of two distinct types of motets: one with a fast, speech-like triplum, a slower motetus, and a Gregorian (though instrumentally performed) tenor in a strict rhythmic pattern; and the other, usually on a French secular tenor, in which all voices proceeded in more nearly equal rhythm, although the triplum was frequently most important melodically.

The first type of motet is often called *Petronian*, after Petrus de Cruce (Pierre de la Croix), one of the few identifiable thirteenth-century composers, who was active from about 1270 to 1300. He wrote motets in which the triplum attained an unprecedented speed in comparison with the lower voices, the long notes being broken up into shorter and shorter values. A motet in this style, though not attributed to Petrus, is *Aucun vont—Amor qui cor—Kyrie* (Example III–10; the entire piece is in NAWM/S 10). The triplum

EXAMPLE III–10   Motet: *Aucun vont—Amor qui cor—Kyrie*

Triplum: *Some, through envy, often speak ill of love; but there is no life so good as loving loyally. For from loving comes all courtesy, all honor . . .*
Duplum: *Love that wounds the human heart, that carnal affection generates [can never, or rarely, be without vice] . . .*

Source: Hoppin, *Anthology of Medieval Music*, No. 54.

breaks away from the rhythmic modes with from two to six semibreves in the time of one breve. To enable the singer of the triplum
to fit in so many notes, the speed of the breve had to be reduced.
Originally the breve was a "short" note as the name implies, perhaps about M.M. 132 in the mid-thirteenth century; by the end of
the century it came to signify a duration close to half that, and
this in turn led eventually, as the process of metrical "inflation"
continued in the fourteenth century, to the semibreve becoming the
new unit of the beat. As in the polytextual motets in a single language, the two texts here complement each other, but in this case
the Latin text ascetically tempers the effusive praise of love in the
French text.

Changes in the rhythmic structure of the motet in the course of
the thirteenth century were more extensive than changes in its
harmonic vocabulary. In 1300, as in 1200, the fifth and octave were
the accepted correct consonances for strong beats. The fourth had
come more and more to be treated as a dissonance. Thirds were beginning to achieve theoretical status as consonances, though they
were not actually being used much more often at the end of the
century than they had been at the beginning. The harmonic rhythm
of a motet was, at least after the middle of the century, that of the
tenor part; that is to say, each note of the tenor carried its own
chord, so that in works in the style of Petrus de Cruce, where the
tenor notes were extremely long in comparison with those of the
triplum, a characteristic contrast existed between a rapid melodic
movement and long-drawn-out harmonic changes. After 1250, cadences began to be written more often in forms that were to remain
standard for the next two centuries; these are given in Example
III–11.

EXAMPLE III–11   Cadence Forms

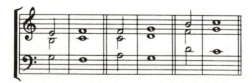

**Notation
in the
thirteenth
century**

Progress in rhythm in the thirteenth century was accompanied
by changes in notation. As has been explained, the rhythmic organization of music in the first half of the century was based on the
rhythmic modes, in which no note sign had a fixed value and the
chief means of indicating a mode as well as variants within the
modal pattern were the meter of the words or the use of ligatures.
But now the rise of the motet created difficulties. Modal notation
could still be used for the tenors, where either there were no words

or else each single syllable was stretched out under a long melisma. But the texts of the upper voices of motets were often not in any regular meters; moreover, these texts were usually set syllabically, that is, with one syllable to one note. Ligatures were useless here because of the unbreakable rule that a ligature could never carry more than one syllable. It was necessary somehow to stabilize the relative durational values of the written notes so that a performer could easily tell what rhythm was demanded.

Various ways to approach this ideal were proposed, but the codification of a practicable system was in a work attributed to Franco of Cologne. In the *Ars cantus mensurabilis* (*The Art of Mensurable Music*), written probably about 1280, rules were established for the values of single notes, ligatures, and rests. This system of notation remained in use through the first quarter of the fourteenth century and many of its features survived until the middle of the sixteenth century.

The Franconian notation, like that of rhythmic modes, was based on the principle of ternary grouping. There were four single-note signs: the double long: ▜ ; the long: ▜ ; the breve: ■ ; and the semibreve: ◆ . The basic time unit, the *tempus* (plural, *tempora*), was the breve. A double long always had the value of two longs; a long might be perfect (three *tempora*) or imperfect (two *tempora*); a breve normally had one *tempus*, but might under certain conditions have two, in which case it was called an *altered* breve; similarly the semibreve might be either *lesser* (1/3 of a *tempus*) or *greater* (2/3 of a *tempus*). Three *tempora* constituted a *perfection*, equivalent to a modern measure of three beats. Obviously, this system does not provide for what we call ties across a barline; the pattern must be completed within a perfection.

The main principles governing the relationships of the long and the breve are indicated in the following table, where the perfect long is transcribed as a dotted half-note:

▜ ▜ = 𝅗𝅥. | 𝅗𝅥.

▜ ■ ▜ = 𝅗𝅥 𝅗𝅥 | 𝅗𝅥.   (First long imperfect)

▜ ■ ■ ▜ = 𝅗𝅥. | 𝅗𝅥 𝅗𝅥 | 𝅗𝅥.   (Second breve altered)

▜ ■ ■ ■ ▜ = 𝅗𝅥. | 𝅗𝅥 𝅗𝅥 𝅗𝅥 | 𝅗𝅥.

▜ ■ ■ ■ ■ ▜ = 𝅗𝅥 𝅗𝅥 | 𝅗𝅥 𝅗𝅥 𝅗𝅥 | 𝅗𝅥.   (First long imperfect)

▜ ■ ■ ■ ■ ■ ▜ = 𝅗𝅥 𝅗𝅥 | 𝅗𝅥 𝅗𝅥 𝅗𝅥 | 𝅗𝅥 𝅗𝅥   (Both longs imperfect)

▜ ■ ■ ■ ■ ■ ■ ▜ = 𝅗𝅥 𝅗𝅥 | 𝅗𝅥 𝅗𝅥 𝅗𝅥 | 𝅗𝅥 𝅗𝅥 | 𝅗𝅥.   (First long imperfect, last breve altered)

Any of these relationships could be changed by introducing a dot, which indicated a division between two perfections; for example:

♩· ■ ♩ = ♩· | ♩ ♩   (Second long imperfect)

♩ ■ ■ ♩ = ♩ ♩ | ♩ ♩   (Both longs imperfect)

♩ ■ ■ ■ ♩ = ♩ ♩ | ♩ ♩ | ♩·   (First long imperfect, third breve altered)

♩ ■ ■ ■ ♩ = ♩· | ♩ ♩ | ♩ ♩   (Second breve altered, second long imperfect)

Similar principles regulated the relations of the semibreve to the breve. In addition, signs were established for rests and rules given on how to recognize notes in ligatures as longs, breves, or semibreves.

The Franconian system allowed the breve to be divided into not more than three semibreves. When Petrus de Cruce began writing music in which four or more notes were to be sung within the time value of one breve, he simply used as many semibreves as he needed for the syllables of the text, sometimes indicating their grouping by dots. Thus, although values shorter than a lesser semibreve were actually in use by the end of the thirteenth century, there were at first no specific notational signs to represent them. Eventually, of course, a scheme of organization, with appropriate notation, was set up to apply to these groups of four or more semibreves.

One further notational change came about as a result of the evolution of thirteenth-century motet style. The earliest motets were

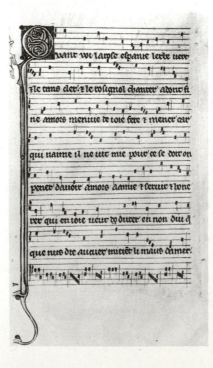

written in score, like the clausulae from which they were derived. As the upper voices acquired longer texts, and as each syllable had to have a separate note-sign, composers and scribes soon found that these voices took a great deal more room on the page than did the tenor, which had fewer notes and which, being melismatic, could be written in the compressed modal notation of ligatures. To write all the parts in score would mean that there would be long vacant stretches on the tenor staff, a waste of space and costly parchment (see Example III– 9). Since the upper voices sang different texts, it was natural to separate them; and so in a three-voice motet, the triplum and the motetus came to be written either on facing pages or in separate columns on the same page, with the tenor on a single staff extending across the bottom. This arrangement may be seen in the illustrations on page 66 and below, which show the motet *En non Diu—Quant voi—Eius in oriente* in the original notation of the Montpellier and Bamberg Codices.[1] The writings of the voices in different places on the same or facing pages is called *choirbook* format, and was the usual way of notating polyphonic compositions after 1230 until the sixteenth century.

Other Late Thirteenth-Century Forms

The word *cantilena* was used in a loose sense by some late medieval writers to designate a whole class of secular songs, both monophonic

[1] This piece is transcribed in MM, No. 10.

(Left) *Two facing pages of the motet* En non Diu—Quant voi—Eius in oriente *as it appears in the Montpellier manuscript.*
(Right) *The same motet as it appears in the Bamberg Codex.*

and polyphonic. As a rule, polyphonic songs of this nature have a single text, with the voice parts moving in uniform phrases and the chief melodic interest in the upper line or lines. Cantilena is defined in a more restricted sense in a treatise written at Paris about 1300 by Johannes de Grocheo, in which he describes the various forms and types of music currently in use. Under polyphonic music Johannes mentions, along with motet, organum, and conductus, a kind of "cut-up song" called *hocket*. (The word, properly descriptive of a technique rather than of a form, is thought to be derived from the Latin *ochetus,* literally "hiccup.") In hocket, the flow of melody is interrupted by the insertion of rests, generally in such a way that the missing notes are supplied by another voice so that the melody is divided between the voices (compare Webern's orchestration of the Ricercare from Bach's *Musical Offering;* the device also occurs in the music of some non-Western peoples). Passages in hocket occur occasionally in secular conductus and motets of the late thirteenth century and more frequently in the early fourteenth century. Pieces in which hocketing was used extensively were themselves called hockets. Such compositions might be either vocal or instrumental. A fast tempo is implied in an instrumental hocket; indeed, theorists distinguished three tempos: slow for motets in which the breve in the triplum was subdivided into many shorter notes (the Petrus de Cruce style motets); moderate for those in which there were not more than three semibreves in a breve (the Franconian motets); and fast, for hockets.

Hocket

Summary

The period from the middle of the twelfth to the end of the thirteenth century may be regarded as a distinct epoch in the history of music. It is commonly known under the name of *ars antiqua* —the "old art" or manner of composing, so called by modern scholars in contrast to the *ars nova* or "new art" of the fourteenth century—and is chiefly remarkable for the rapid growth of polyphony and the rise of three types of polyphonic composition: organum and conductus in the Notre Dame period, to about 1250, and the motet in the second half of the thirteenth century. All this activity centered around Paris, so that for one hundred and fifty years all western European polyphonic music was dominated by French composers. The principal technical achievements of these years were the codification of the rhythmic modal system and the invention of a new kind of notation for measured rhythm—both examples of the growing tendency to make explicit the rational principles underlying the art of musical composition and to give the composer more control over the way in which his works were to be performed.

The late thirteenth-century motet became, as it were, a microcosm of the cultural life of its time. The structure of the motet, with its motley concourse of love songs, dance tunes, popular refrains, and sacred hymns, all held together in a rigid formal mold based on Gregorian plainsong, is analogous to the structure of Dante's *Divine Comedy*, which likewise encompasses and organizes a universe of secular and sacred ideas within a rigid theological framework. By the end of the thirteenth century, however, this neatly closed medieval universe was beginning to dissolve, to lose both its inner coherence and its power to dominate events. Signs of the dissolution appeared in the motet as in a mirror: gradual weakening of the authority of the rhythmic modes, relegation of the Gregorian tenor to a purely formal function, exaltation of the triplum to the status of a solo voice against the accompanying lower parts. The road was open to a new musical style, a new way of composing.

IV

French and Italian Music of the Fourteenth Century

The *Ars Nova* in France

Musical background

Ars nova—the "new art" or "new technique"—was the title of a treatise written about 1316–18 by the French composer and poet Philippe de Vitry, Bishop of Meaux (1291–1361). The term was so apt that it has come to be used to denote the musical style which prevailed in France through the first half of the fourteenth century. Musicians of the time were quite conscious of striking out a new path. The chief technical points at issue were (1) acceptance in princi- by that of another French work, Jean de Muris's *Ars novae musicae* (*The Art of the New Music*, 1319). On the opposite side was a Flemish theorist, Jacob of Liège, who in his encyclopedic *Speculum musicae* (*The Mirror of Music, ca.* 1330) vigorously defended the "old art" of the late thirteenth century as against the innovations of the "moderns."

The chief technical points at issue were (1) acceptance in principle of the modern duple or imperfect division of the long, breve (and, eventually, semibreve) into two equal parts, as well as the traditional triple or perfect division into three equal (or two unequal) parts; and (2) the use of four or more semibreves as equivalent to a breve—already begun in the motets of Petrus de Cruce—and, eventually, of still smaller values.

It is typical for the fourteenth century that composers produced far more secular than sacred music. The motet, which had begun as a sacred form, had been to a great extent secularized before the end of the thirteenth century, and this trend continued. The earliest fourteenth-century musical document from France is a beautifully decorated manuscript, dating from 1316, of a satirical poem, the *Roman de Fauvel*. In one of the manuscripts of this work are interpolated about 130 pieces of music, constituting in effect an anthology of the music of the thirteenth and early fourteenth centuries. Most of the *Fauvel* pieces are monophonic, but the collection includes also 33 polyphonic motets. Among these, along with other examples of late thirteenth-century style, are several that introduce the new duple division of the breve. Many of the texts are denunciations of the clergy, and there are many allusions to contemporary political events. Such allusions were characteristic of the motet in the fourteenth century, as they had been of the conductus in an earlier period; and the motet in the fourteenth century came to be used as the typical form of composition for the musical celebration of important ceremonial occasions both ecclesiastical and secular, a function it retained through the first half of the fifteenth century.

Five of the three-part motets in the *Roman de Fauvel* are by Philippe de Vitry, who appears to have been one of the outstanding poets and composers of his time. His motet tenors are often laid out in segments of identical rhythm, on the same principle we have already encountered in some motets of the late thirteenth century (see Examples III–8 and 9); as in some earlier motets also, the rhythmic formula may be varied after a certain number of repetitions. But now, all this takes place on a much larger scale than before: the tenor is longer, the rhythms are more complex, and the whole line moves so slowly, so ponderously, under the faster notes of the upper voices that it is no longer recognizable as a melody, but functions rather as a foundation on which the piece is constructed.

As the fourteenth century went on, theorists and composers—largely under the influence of de Vitry—evidently began to think of such a motet tenor as being constituted by two distinct elements: the set of intervals, which they called the *color;* and the pattern of rhythm, called the *talea* (a "cutting" or segment). *Color* and *talea* might be joined in various ways: for example, if the two were of the same length, the *color* might be repeated with the *talea* in halved (or otherwise diminished) note values; or the *color* might consist of three *taleae,* and might then be repeated with the *taleae* in diminished values; or again, *color* and *talea* might be of such differing lengths that their endings did not coincide, so that some repetitions of the *color* would begin in the midst of a *talea*. Motets having a tenor constructed in some such way as these just described are called *isorhythmic* ("same rhythm") motets. In some instances the upper voices as well as the tenor may be written isorhythmically (or "isometrically"), and the technique was also occasionally applied to compositions in other forms.

The isorhythmic motet

The basic idea of isorhythm was not new in the fourteenth century; but during this period and on into the fifteenth century it came to be applied in ever more extended and complex ways. Isorhythm was a way of giving unity to long compositions which had no other effective means of formal organization. True, the interlocked repetitions of *color* or *talea*, extending over long stretches of the music, might be anything but obvious to the ear. Yet the isorhythmic structure, even if not immediately perceived, does have the effect of imposing a coherent form on the entire piece; and the very fact of the structure's being concealed—of its existing, as it were, at least partially in the realm of abstraction and contemplation rather than as something capable of being fully grasped by the sense of hearing—would have pleased a medieval musician.

Guillaume de Machaut

The leading composer of the *ars nova* in France was Guillaume de Machaut (*ca.* 1300–77), whose works include examples of most of the forms that were current in his time, and show him as a composer of mingled conservative and progressive tendencies.

Most of Machaut's 23 motets were based on the traditional pattern: an instrumental liturgical tenor and different texts in the two upper voices. They continue the contemporary trends toward greater secularity, greater length, and much greater rhythmic complexity. Isorhythmic structure sometimes involves the upper parts

A miniature depicting a charivari; from the Roman de Fauvel, *an early fourteenth-century musical manuscript. Fauvel was a symbolic horse or ass whose name was made up from the first letters of Flaterie, Avarice, Vilanie, Variété, Envie, and Lascheté. (After Gérold)*

Guillaume de Machaut in his study. Amour is presenting to him his three children Doux Penser, Plaisance, and Espérance. A miniature by the Maître aux Bouqueteaux in a manuscript of Machaut's works.

as well as the tenor. Considerable use is made of hocket in these motets, but the only work of Machaut's specifically called a "hocket" is an apparently instrumental three-part motet-like piece with an isorhythmic tenor whose melody came from the Gregorian melisma on the word "David" in an Alleluia verse.

Machaut's monophonic songs may be regarded as continuing the trouvère tradition in France. They comprise nineteen *lais,* a twelfth-century form similar to that of the sequence, and about twenty-five songs which he called *chansons balladées,* though the more common name for them is *virelai.* Characteristic of the virelai is the form *Abba . . . ,* in which *A* stands for the refrain, *b* the first part of the stanza (which is repeated) and *a* the last part of the stanza (which uses the same melody as the refrain). If there are several stanzas the refrain *A* may be repeated after each.

Machaut also wrote a few polyphonic virelais, with an accompanying instrumental tenor part below the vocal solo; in these he occasionally introduced the device of a musical rhyme between the endings of the two melodic sections.

It was in his polyphonic virelais, rondeaux, and ballades—the so-called "formes fixes"—that Machaut showed most clearly the progressive tendencies of the *ars nova.* The rondeau, like the virelai, made use of only two musical phrases, combined typically in the pattern *ABaAabAB* (capital letters indicate the refrain of the text). The rondeau form had great attraction for poets and musicians of the late Middle Ages. Machaut's rondeaux have a highly sophisticated musical content, and one of them is an often cited example of ingenuity. Its enigmatic tenor text—"Ma fin est mon commencement et mon commencement ma fin" ("My end is my beginning and my beginning my end")—means that the melody of the tenor is that of the topmost voice sung backward; the melody of the contratenor also illustrates the text, because its second half is the reverse of its first half.

One of Machaut's most important achievements was the development of the "ballade" or "cantilena" style. This style is exemplified in his polyphonic virelais and rondeaux, as well as in the forty-one *ballades notées,* so called to distinguish them from his poetic ballades without music. Machaut's ballades, whose form was in part a heritage from the trouvères, normally consisted of three or four stanzas, each sung to the same music and each ending with a refrain. Within each stanza the first two lines (or first two pairs of lines) had the same music, although often with different endings; the remaining lines within each stanza, together with the refrain, had a different melody, the ending of which might correspond to the ending of the first section. The formula for the ballade is thus similar to that of the Bar of the Minnesinger; it may be diagrammed *aabC,* in which *C* stands for the refrain.

Machaut wrote ballades with two, three, and four parts and for various combinations of voices with instruments; but his typical settings were for high tenor solo or duet with two lower instrumental parts. Those for two voices, each with its own text, are called *double ballades. Quant Theseus—Ne quier veoir* (NAWM/S 13) is such a work, but unlike the other ballades, which were based on poems of his own, the first text here is by Thomas Paien, to which Machaut added a second poem as a response in friendly competition. It can be dated through the amorous correspondence between Machaut and a young woman poetess, Peronne, for he sent it to her on November 3, 1363, saying "I have listened to it several times and it pleases me right well." The two vocal parts are in the same range and frequently exchange melodic material, and in one place there is even a moment of imitation (measures 44–45). They also share the text of the refrain, "Je voy asses, puis que je voy ma dame" ("I see enough, since I see my lady"). By contrast with the complex subliminal architecture of the isorhythmic motets, the ballades bare their form on the sensuous surface. Despite the bitextuality, all verses begin and come to cadences together, and this coherence is enhanced by Machaut's having imitated the rhymes used in his model, which in turn permits the long simultaneous melismas to be sung to the same penultimate syllables. Although the form of the music is *a* (open ending) *a* (closed ending) *b C*, the last eleven measures of the refrain (*C*) are almost identical to the end of *a*. This economy of material is typical of Machaut. The lower parts are filler voices, supplying missing beats through syncopations, or, where the voice line is syncopated, downbeats add a harmonic bass and reinforcement. Having four parts does not make the cadences fuller, however, for all are built up of the perfect consonances of fifth and octave except for the cadence that precedes the refrain, which contains a third in its final chord.

The most famous musical composition of the fourteenth century is Machaut's *Messe de Notre Dame* (*Mass of Our Lady*), a four-part setting of the Ordinary of the Mass together with the dismissal formula *Ite, missa est*. This was not the first polyphonic setting of the Ordinary; there had been a half-dozen more or less complete earlier cycles. But Machaut's is important because of its spacious dimensions and four-part texture (unusual at the time), because it is clearly planned as a musical whole, and because it is by any standard a first-rate work. In the twelfth and thirteenth centuries composers of polyphonic music had been chiefly interested in texts from the Proper of the Mass, for example the Graduals and Alleluias in Leonin's and Perotin's organa; they sometimes set parts of the Ordinary too, but when these pieces were performed together in one service, their selection and combination were fortuitous. No one seemed to care whether the Kyrie, Gloria, Credo, Sanctus, and Agnus Dei were in the same mode or based on the same thematic material or musically unified in any particular way. This attitude prevailed until about the second quarter of the fifteenth century; although fourteenth- and early fifteenth-century composers did write music for the Ordinary, they did not as a rule attempt to relate the different movements musically. In the manuscripts the different parts of the Mass were usually separated, all the Glorias being placed together, followed by all the Credos, and so on; the choirmaster could choose from these collections what he considered appropriate individual items for the complete Ordinary to be performed. Machaut's *Messe de Notre Dame,* therefore, insofar as he seemed to regard the five divisions of the Ordinary as one musical composition rather than separate pieces, was exceptional not only for its time but for the next seventy-five years as well. The means by which musical unity is achieved in this work are not easy to define; the relationship between movements is based on similarity of mood and general style rather than obvious thematic interconnections.

Machaut's *Messe de Notre Dame*

The Kyrie, Sanctus, Agnus Dei, and *Ite, missa est* are based on Gregorian tenors and are wholly or partly isorhythmic. In the Agnus (NAWM/S.14), isorhythmic organization begins at the words "qui tollis," that is, after the intonation of each Agnus (Agnus III repeats Agnus I). The plainchant used is an earlier form of Mass XVII as numbered in the *Liber Usualis* (p. 60). Both the Gloria and the Credo, probably because of the length of their texts, are given a straight conductus-like setting in syllabic style; their extraordinarily austere music, full of parallel progressions, strange dissonances, chromatic chords, and abrupt pauses, is organized in a free strophic form, a series of musical "stanzas" articulated by conspicuous similar cadences.

It is impossible to tell with certainty just how Machaut's Mass was meant to be performed. All the voice parts may have been doubled by instruments. It seems likely that the contratenor part, in view of its general melodic style and the fact that in some of the manuscript sources it has no text, was played rather than sung; in the isorhythmic movements, at least, the tenor part also may have been played on or doubled by an instrument. In the Gloria and Credo there are numerous short interludes, always for tenor and contratenor, that are almost certainly instrumental. But what instruments were used, and to what extent, we cannot say. Nor do we know for what occasion the work was written, despite a persistent but unfounded legend that it was for the coronation of the French King Charles V in 1364; whatever the occasion, it must have been one of unusual solemnity and magnificence.

Machaut was a typical fourteenth-century composer in that his sacred compositions formed only a small proportion of his total output. The relative decline in the production of sacred music in this period was due partially to the weakened prestige of the Church and to the ever increasing secularization of the arts. In addition, the Church itself had become critical of the use of elaborate musical settings in the service. From the twelfth century on, there had been numerous ecclesiastical pronouncements against complicated music and against displays of virtuosity by the singers. The burden of these complaints was twofold: it was objected, first, that such practices distracted the minds of the congregation and tended to turn the Mass into a mere concert; and second, that the words of the liturgy were obscured and the liturgical melodies made unrecognizable. One effect of this official attitude apparently was to discourage the composition of polyphonic church music in Italy. Composition of motets and Mass sections meanwhile continued to develop mainly in France. Sometimes a particular section in a Mass would be written in the style of a motet with an instrumental tenor, sometimes as a choral conductus-like movement with text in all the voices. In addition to these two styles, both of which had been used by Machaut, composers of the later fourteenth and early fifteenth centuries wrote Masses and hymns in cantilena style—that is, for solo voice, usually with two accompanying instrumental parts. A few Masses and hymns made use of a liturgical *cantus firmus;* for example, a Gregorian Kyrie might be adapted as the tenor of a polyphonic Kyrie in motet style, or a Gregorian hymn, more or less ornamented, might appear as the upper voice in a ballade-like setting of the same text.

Italian Trecento Music

Italian music in the fourteenth century (the "trecento") has a history different from that of French music in the same period. The Italians at this time seemed allergic to erudite styles of composition. They had no use for the *cantus firmus* technique and were but little interested in the structural complexities of the motet. The Italian spirit expressed itself rather in spontaneous, flowing melodies and comparatively simple textures. Very few actual examples of Italian polyphony have been preserved which can be dated earlier than about 1330. After that date, however, the stream flows more abundantly. Three types of secular Italian composition are represented: *madrigal, caccia,* and *ballata.* The fourteenth-century madrigal, one of the first polyphonic genres to be cultivated in Italy, has many traits that suggest some historical connection with the French thirteenth-century polyphonic conductus. Madrigals were usually written for two voices; their texts were idyllic, pastoral, amatory, or satirical poems of two or three three-line stanzas. The stanzas were all set to the same music; at the end of the stanzas an additional pair of lines, called the *ritornello,* was set to different music with a different meter. Jacopo da Bologna's *Fenice fù* (NAWM/S 11) is a fine example of the genre. As in most madrigals, the two voices have the same text, and here it is very obvious that both parts were meant to be sung, for they enter separately except at the beginning of the ritornello. In two places (measures 12–15, 45–46) they are in imitation, and in one short passage they indulge in a hocket-like alternation. Otherwise the upper voice is the more florid one, having extended mellifluous runs on the last accented syllable of each line.

The caccia is another form which may have owed something to foreign examples. The Italian caccia, which seems to have flourished chiefly from 1345 to 1370, was canonic, for two equal voices at the unison; but it usually also had a free supporting instrumental part in slower movement below. Its poetic form was irregular, though many cacce, like madrigals, had a ritornello, which was not always in canonic style. Both the French and Italian words have the same meaning: "hunt" or "chase." As the name of a type of composition, they have also a punning sense, alluding to the canon (Latin *fuga,* "flight") and also, in the case of the caccia, to the subject matter of the text, which typically described a hunt or some other scene of animation, such as a fishing party, a bustling market-place, a party of girls gathering flowers, a fire, or a battle. Vivid realistic details—shouts, bird songs, horn calls, exclamations, dialogue—all are brought out with spirit and humor in the music, often with the aid of hocket and echo effects.

Composers in the fourteenth century had what seems to us a strange attitude toward the use of imitation as a technique. They either wrote strict canons or eschewed systematic imitation almost entirely. Canons are found sporadically in Italian madrigals and ballate; but continuous systematic free imitation, pervading all the voices of a composition, does not come into general use before the last part of the fifteenth century.

The ballata

The polyphonic ballata, the third type of Italian secular fourteenth-century music, flourished later than the madrigal and caccia, and showed some influence of the French ballade style. Originally the word ballata signified a song to accompany dancing (Italian *ballare,* to dance); the thirteenth-century ballate (of which no musical examples have survived) were monophonic dance songs with choral refrains. In Boccaccio's *Decameron* the ballata or "ballatetta" is still associated with dancing. A few early fourteenth-century monophonic ballate have been preserved, but most of the examples in the manuscripts are for two or three voices, and date after 1365. These purely lyrical, stylized, polyphonic ballate resemble in form the French virelai. A typical ballata form is that of *Non avrà ma' pietà* (NAWM/S 12) of Francesco Landini (1325–97). A two-line refrain (*ripresa*) is sung both before and after a six-line stanza. The first two pairs of lines in the stanza, which were called *piedi,* have their own musical phrase, while the last pair, the *volta,* uses the same music as the refrain. A melisma on the first as well as the penultimate syllable of a line is characteristic of the Italian style. The end of every line, and often of the first word and of the caesura, is marked by a cadence, usually of the type that has become known as the "Landini" cadence, in which the movement from sixth to octave is ornamented by a lower auxiliary leaping up a third in the upper part (see measures 3–4, 5–6, 10–11 of Example IV–1, which shows the first line of the ripresa).

Francesco Landini

Landini was the leading composer of ballate and the foremost Italian musician of the fourteenth century. Blind from boyhood as a result of smallpox, Landini nevertheless became a well-educated man, an esteemed poet (like Machaut and de Vitry), and a master of the theory and practice of music; a virtuoso on many instruments, he was especially known for his skill at the organetto, a small portative organ, which he played "as readily as though he had the use of his eyes, with a touch of such rapidity (yet always observing the measure), with such skill and sweetness that beyond all doubt

EXAMPLE IV–1   Ballata: *Non avrà ma' pietà*, Francesco Landini

She will never have pity, this lady of mine . . . Perhaps by her will
be extinguished [the flames] . . .

Source: *Polyphonic Music of the Fourteenth Century,* ed. Leo Schrade (Paris,
1958), IV, 144.

he excelled beyond comparison all organists who can possibly be
remembered."[1]

Landini's extant works comprise about 90 two-part and 50 three-
part ballate, besides a couple of cacce and a dozen madrigals. The
two-part ballate are evidently early works; their style in general
resembles that of the madrigals, save that the melodic line is more
ornate. Many of the three-part ballate are, like the French ballades,
for solo voice with two accompanying parts.

It should be stressed that there was no uniform, fixed way of **Performance**
performing this or indeed any other music of the fourteenth century. The fact that one part lacks a text is not conclusive evidence
for regarding it as instrumental, since another manuscript may show
the same part furnished with words; and conversely, the presence of
a text does not always imply exclusively vocal performance. We
may suppose, however, that the tenor parts of Landini's ballate and
Machaut's ballades, with their long notes, frequent wide skips, and

[1] From an account by a fourteenth century Florentine chronicler, Filippo
Villani (*Le Vite d'uomini illustri fiorentini,* ed. G. Mazzuchelli, Florence, 1847,
p. 46.)

customary notation with many ligatures (which precludes syllabic rendition of a text, since it was a rule that only one syllable might be sung to a ligature), were conceived as primarily instrumental. The contratenor parts were evidently composed after the superius (the highest part) and tenor, with the purpose of completing the harmonic sonority. For the contratenor, again, we may often suppose an instrumental rendition; but many contratenors are equally suitable for singing, and many are furnished with texts. The superius is always vocal in character, and often quite florid. But this part also could have been played; the description quoted above of Landini's rapid manner of playing the organetto suggests a style of playing to which the superius parts of his madrigals and some of his ballate would be quite adaptable. Furthermore, we must keep in mind the likelihood of instrumental doubling (perhaps with added embellishments) of a sung melody and also the possibility of alternation of instrument and voice; for example, the florid melismas at the beginning and end of a madrigal may have been played and the rest of the part sung, and both conceivably by the same performer. Finally, evidence exists that vocal pieces were sometimes played entirely instrumentally, with added embellishments in the melodic line.

French Music of the Late Fourteenth Century

It is a paradox typical of the time that the Papal Court at Avignon was apparently a more important center for secular than for sacred music. Here and at other courts in southern France a brilliant chivalric society flourished, providing a congenial environment for the work of many late fourteenth-century French and Italian composers. Their music consisted chiefly of ballades, virelais, and rondeaux for solo voice with supporting instrumental tenor and contratenor parts. Most of the texts probably were written by the composers themselves. Some of the ballades include reference to contemporary events and personages, but the majority of all the pieces are love songs. Many of them are works of refined beauty, with sensitive melodies and delicately colored harmonies, examples of aristocratic art in the best sense of the word. Their musical style is matched by the visual appearance of some pages in the manuscripts, with their fanciful decorations, ingenious complications of notation, and occasional caprices such as the writing of a love song in the shape of a heart (see illustration on facing page) or a canon in the shape of a circle.[2]

---

[2] See facsimiles of both in MGG II, plate 55; color facsimiles of other pages from the famous Chantilly manuscript of the late fourteenth century are in MGG I, plate 28; II, plate 34; Apel, *Notation*, facsimile 83, p. 413.

Belle bonne, *the splendid "Musical Heart" by Baude Cordier from the Chantilly Codex*, ca. 1400.

One feature of French secular music of this period is a remarkable rhythmic flexibility. The solo melody in particular exhibits the most subtle nuances: the beat is subdivided in many different ways, and the line of the phrase is broken by pauses in hocket, or held in suspense through long-continued syncopation—as though the composers had tried to capture and fix in notation the free, rubato-like delivery of a singer.

Rhythmic complexity penetrates the very texture of all this late fourteenth-century French music: voices move in contrasting meters and in contrasted groupings within the beat; harmonies are refracted and purposely blurred through suspensions and syncopations. No doubt sometimes the fascination of the technique caused it to be carried to extremes that degenerated into mannerism; but, properly used, it was an indispensable element of the style. Example IV–2 (the two lowest staves are merely a reduction of the parts, not an accompaniment) shows a typical phrase from a rondeau by Anthonello da Caserta, a late fourteenth-century Italian composer who may be said to have excelled the French at their own game. Here the synco-

Rhythm

pation gives the effect of a delayed entrance by the soloist; the rhythmic subtlety of the passage is of an order not to be matched in any other music before the twentieth century, yet everything falls logically into place. Noteworthy is the delightful effect of the sixth at measure 2, the coquettish hesitation between B♭ and B♮ after the first rest in the solo part, and the way in which the contra-tenor sounds now above, now below the tenor, so that the real bass of the harmony is in first one then the other of these voices, and is sometimes revealed in one by the cessation of the other. We may imagine the sheer variety of sonorities resulting from these two lower parts being played on instruments of contrasting timbres—say a trombone for the tenor and an alto oboe or a viol for the con-tratenor, with a recorder doubling the voice in the superius.

Since most of the phrase quoted in Example IV–2 is a melisma, the text has been omitted.[3] Accidentals below or above the notes are not in the original. The so-called "partial signatures"—different signatures in different voices—were common in the fourteenth and fifteenth centuries.

The sophisticated music of the southern French courts was de-signed for auditors of exceptional cultivation and performers of pro-fessional skill. Its formidable rhythmic and notational complexities began to go out of fashion by the end of the fourteenth century. Meanwhile, contemporary with developments in the south, in the latter part of the century a simpler type of secular polyphony existed in northern France, cultivated by guilds of musicians who were in a sense heirs of the trouvère tradition. Their poems had a popular character: instead of the polished sentiments of courtly love, they

[3] The entire composition may be found in Apel's *French Secular Music of the Late Fourteenth Century*, No. 29.

EXAMPLE IV–2   Rondeau: Portion of *Dame gentil,* Anthonello da Caserta

Vous [estes tout mon bien]

The sharp near the end of line one in the original above belongs with the *B*, not the *C*; it signifies that the note is *mi*, that is, *B*-natural. (Ms. Modena, Bib. Estense, L. 568, fol. 38v., *ca.* 1410)

offered realistic scenes of the hunt and the marketplace, sometimes introducing imitations of bird songs. The music had a corresponding liveliness and freshness, with vigorous straightforward rhythms like those of folk song. It is probable that this simpler art flourished more widely than the few examples preserved in fourteenth-century manuscripts would suggest. Whether it had any influence on composers in the south of France is doubtful.

Chromaticism and *Musica Ficta*

A special flavor is imparted to much fourteenth-century music, both French and Italian, by the use of chromatically altered notes. Chromatic alteration was common at cadences in which otherwise there would have been a whole step between the seventh note of the modal scale and its upward resolution to the final, as for instance at a cadence on *D*, illustrated in Example IV–3a and b. This species of chromatic alteration was enjoined by a rule that the interval of a third contracting to a unison must be made minor, and a sixth expanding to an octave must be made major. As a rule in cadences of the type shown in Example IV–3b, *both* the upper two notes of a penultimate three-note chord would be raised, thus making what we have called a double leading tone—Example IV–3c. Cadences on *G* and *C* were altered similarly to those on *D*. Cadences on *E*, however, were a special case, since the outer interval of the penultimate chord was already a major sixth so that no chromatic alteration was required—see Example IV–3d.

EXAMPLE IV–3 Chromatic Alteration at Cadences

a. Strict modal forms   **b.** Chromatically   **c.** Form with   **d.** Modal (Phrygian)
                              altered forms   double lead-   cadence on E
                                                     ing tones

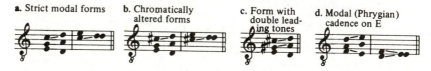

Elsewhere than at cadences, chromatic alteration was used in order to avoid sounding a diminished fifth or an augmented fourth above the lowest note of a chord, and especially to avoid in a melody the tritone interval *F–B♮*, which later came to be called *diabolus in musica,* the devil in music. Chromatics might also be introduced to make a smoother melodic line, or for no other reason than *causa pulchritudinis,* simply because they sounded well—literally, "for the sake of beauty"; but for this, of course, no rules could be given.

Since in this way notes might be introduced that were not provided for in the Guidonian system (see page 32), the result was called *musica ficta* or *musica falsa*—"fictitious" or "false music." Manuscripts of the fourteenth and early fifteenth centuries, especially the Italian ones, are relatively well supplied with accidentals, but after 1450 they largely disappear; and it is still not certain whether this reflected a real change in the sound—a reversion to the purity of the diatonic modes—or whether (as is more likely) it was simply a matter of notation, and the performers continued to apply chromatic alterations as before. In view of these uncertain factors a careful modern editor will not insert any accidentals in this music that are not found in the original sources, but will indicate, usually above or below the staff, those that he believes were applied by the performers.

Notation

Obviously, anything like a detailed description of fourteenth-century notation is beyond the scope of this book.[4] We shall try to indicate only some of the main principles that guided Italian and French musicians in working out a notation for the new alternative duple or triple subdivision of longer notes, the introduction of many new short note values, and the greater rhythmic flexibility which marked music of the latter part of the century.

The basis of the Italian system was described by Marchetto da Padua in his *Pomerium* of 1318.[5] Briefly, the method consisted of dividing semibreves into groups set off by dots, supplemented by certain letter signs to indicate the various combinations possible in duple and triple subdivisions and by newly invented note forms to mark exceptions to the general rules of grouping and to express shorter note values. This kind of notation, particularly convenient as it was for florid melodic lines, served well for Italian music until the latter part of the century; by then it began to be supplemented and was eventually replaced by the French system, which had proved itself better adapted to the musical style of that time.

The French system was an extension of Franconian principles. The long, the breve, and the semibreve could each be divided into either two or three notes of the next smaller value. The division of the long was called *mood,* that of the breve *time,* and that of the semibreve *prolation;* division was *perfect* if it was triple, *imperfect* if duple. Two new note forms were introduced to indicate values shorter than the semibreve: the *minim* ♩, one-half or one-third of a semibreve; and the *semiminim* ♪, one-half of a minim. The framework of the system thus was as follows:

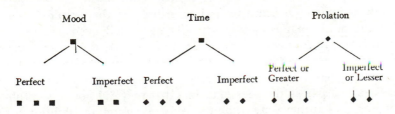

4 For further information see W. Apel, *The Notation of Polyphonic Music 900–1600.*

5 This section is translated in SR, 160–71 (= SRA, 160–71).

Eventually the original signs for perfect and imperfect mood were dropped and simplified signs for time and prolation were combined: a circle indicated perfect time and a half-circle imperfect time; a dot inside the circle or half-circle indicated greater prolation, and the absence of a dot lesser prolation, thus:

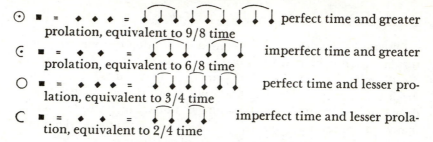

These were the "four prolations," as they were called, of late medieval music theory.

The half-circle C, has come down to us as the modern sign for 4/4 time. Our ₵ , with its corresponding designation "alla breve," is a relic of the late medieval and Renaissance system of "proportions" whereby the unit of movement (the "beat") could be transferred from the normal note values to other note values in an indicated ratio—in this case, in the ratio 1 : 2, thus transferring the beat from the usual semibreve to the breve.

About 1425 all the forms pictured above began to be written as "white" notes, that is with black outlines unfilled (◖ ◻ ◇ ◊);[6] the semiminim became ♩ , and shorter notes were devised *ad libitum* by adding flags to the semiminim (♪ ♫ ♬ etc.). These are essentially the forms of present-day notes; the change from diamond-shaped to rounded heads took place toward the end of the sixteenth century.

Instruments

A full and accurate account of instrumental music in the fourteenth and fifteenth centuries is impossible, for the simple reason that the music manuscripts practically never tell even whether a given part is instrumental or vocal, let alone specify the instruments. If composers had had in mind some particular combination of voices and instruments, there was no reason why they should not have marked it clearly on the page. The fact that they did not do so probably means that they were content to rely on custom or tradition for

---

6 This change may have come about as one consequence of the contemporary shift from parchment to paper: filling in black notes on rough-surfaced paper with the crude pens of the time would have increased the chance of spattered ink and a ruined page.

the manner of performing their music, and did not feel that specific directions were needed.

We know from pictorial and literary sources that the most usual way of performing polyphonic music in the fourteenth and early fifteenth centuries was with a small vocal and instrumental ensemble, normally with only one voice or one instrument to a part. There is also some evidence to suggest that, in pieces in cantilena style, the solo voice part was simultaneously played on an instrument which added embellishments, thus making heterophony. We can be fairly sure that certain parts, such as the Latin tenors in isorhythmic motets and the textless tenors in Landini's three-part ballate, were instrumental rather than vocal. But beyond a few general principles like these we can discern no uniform rules; apparently performances varied according to circumstances, depending on what singers or players happened to be at hand, or on the taste or caprice of the performers.

For out-of-doors music, for dancing, and for especially festive or solemn ceremonies, larger ensembles and louder instruments were employed; the fourteenth-century distinction betwen "high" (*haut*) and "low" (*bas*) instruments referred not to pitch, but to loudness. The low instruments most used in this century were harps, vielles, lutes, psalteries, portative organs, and flutes; among the high instruments were shawms, horns, trumpets, and sackbuts (trombones). Percussion instruments, including small bells and cymbals, were common in ensembles of all kinds. The prevailing quality of tone was clear, bright, or shrill; instruments, if one may judge from the art of the time, were grouped not in families of homogeneous timbre (like a string quartet, for example), but in contrasting colors, such as viol, lute, harp, and trombone; or viol, lute, psaltery, flute, and drum. Crescendo and diminuendo were probably unknown. Although polyphonic vocal music was probably never sung unaccompanied in this period, motets and other vocal pieces were sometimes performed with instruments alone. There was also, of course, a large repertoire of instrumental dance music, but as these pieces were generally either improvised or played from memory, not many written examples have been preserved.

The earliest keyboard instruments of the clavichord and harpsichord type were invented in the fourteenth century, but do not seem to have come into common use until the fifteenth century. In addition to the portative organ or organetto, there were positive organs; and large organs were being installed in an increasing number of churches. A pedal keyboard was added to organs in Germany toward the end of the fourteenth century. A mechanism of stops enabling the player to select different ranks of pipes at will, and the addition of a second keyboard, were achievements of the early fifteenth century.

Summary

One of the most striking characteristics of the fourteenth century was the massive transfer of emphasis from sacred to secular composition. Corresponding to this shift of interest, and partly as a consequence of it, we see innovations in general musical style. Most obvious among these is the greater diversity and freedom of rhythm, carried by some late composers to almost fantastic extremes. Throughout the fourteenth century there is also a growing sense of harmonic organization, a definite planning of progressions to center about certain tonal areas. The "imperfect" consonances—thirds and, to a lesser degree, sixths—begin to occur more often on strong beats, though the final sonority is still always a unison, octave, or empty fifth. Passages of parallel thirds and sixths appear, while parallel fifths and octaves become rarer. Chromatic alteration by means of *musica ficta* helps to stabilize cadential points and give more flexibility to the melodic line. The range of voices is slowly extended upward. The abstract linear style of the thirteenth-century motet loses its dominance, though it continues to exist alongside the more melodic-harmonic idiom of cantilena texture; and in connection with the latter there is a growing search for sensuous attractiveness. In France, the motet continues as a special form of composition, no longer mainly liturgical but becoming more political and ceremonial in function as well as more intricate in structure. New forms of composition are developed. Some, like the caccia and (possibly) the madrigal, seem to derive rather closely from popular musical practice; some, like the ballata and other songs with refrains, go back to the thirteenth century and, more remotely, to popular models. The sophisticated types, the "formes fixes," which likewise continue an earlier tradition, are literary as well as musical in conception: the virelai; the ballade; and the rondeau, which was increasing in favor toward the end of the century and beginning to branch out into more complex types.

By the year 1400 the two formerly distinct musical styles of France and Italy had begun to merge. As we shall see in the next chapter, this incipient international style was to be augmented in the fifteenth century by streams from other sources, chiefly England and the Netherlands area.

V

Medieval to Renaissance: English Music and the Burgundian School in the Fifteenth Century

English Music to the End of the Fifteenth Century

English music, like that of northern Europe generally, had been characterized from earliest times by a rather close connection with folk style and, by contrast with Continental developments, a certain disinclination to carry abstract theories to extremes in practice. Thus there had always been a tendency in English music toward major tonality (as opposed to the modal system), toward greater harmonic unity (as opposed to the independent lines, divergent texts, and harmonic dissonances of the French motet), toward greater fullness of sound, and toward a freer use of thirds and sixths than in the music of the Continent. It was in the writings of English theorists around 1300 that the third was first recognized as a consonant interval, and a twelfth-century example of parallel thirds occurs in a *Hymn to St. Magnus,* patron saint of the Orkney Islands. The practice of writing in parallel thirds or parallel sixths was common in English polyphonic compositions of the thirteenth century.

General features

89

The works of the Notre Dame school were known in the British Isles, as we gather from the fact that one of the principal source manuscripts of this repertoire, Wolfenbüttel 677 (called W_1), was probably copied in England or Scotland; it contains, in addition to Notre Dame compositions, many works once thought to be of British origin. These pieces consist for the most part of two-voice tropes and sequences; they are similar to the syllabic conductus, but with the upper voice slightly more melismatic than the tenor, which is usually a liturgical or quasi-liturgical melody, often freely paraphrased.

Three-part conductus and motets were composed in England in the thirteenth century and were also known on the Continent; for instance, the presumably English motet *Alle psallite—Alleluia* is found in the Montpellier Codex. One of the most characteristic techniques in the English motet is the *rondellus,* which exploits voice exchange (sometimes referred to as *Stimmtausch*) as a method of composition. One of the Worcester fragments has a motet for three voices *Fulget coelestis curia—O Petre flos—Roma gaudet* which relies upon this method. Example V–1 shows the original statement and one of the interchanges of the first half. Normally in a rondellus the voices exchange texts along with the music, but in this motet only the outer voices exchange texts. Since the three voices are in the same range, the listener hears a threefold repetition of each half. The fresh, folklike quality of all the melodic lines and the harmonious blending of the voices are other English traits, such as may also be heard in the famous *Sumer is icumen in.* This belongs to the category known as *rota,* essentially a round or canon. The piece, of English origin, dating from about 1240, shows many traits characteristic of English medieval music, especially its full chordal texture, its free use of thirds as consonances, and its distinct major tonality. Below the four-part canon two tenors sing a *pes* ("foot," i.e., a repeated bass motive) with continuous interchange of the voices.

It must be remembered in connection with English medieval church music that the basic repertoire of chant was that of the Sarum rite, the melodies of which differ to some extent from those of the Roman rite which we find in the *Liber Usualis* and other modern chant books. Not only English, but also many Continental composers in the fifteenth century, used the Sarum rather than the Roman versions of plainchant as *cantus firmi* in their compositions.

Fourteenth century

The conductus and some of the conductus-like tropes of the Ordinary exhibit a new stylistic feature, one that had begun to appear as early as the thirteenth century and was to be of great importance in the music of the early fifteenth century: the melodic line is accompanied by two other voices in generally parallel motion, in such a way as to produce, from time to time, successions of chords that

EXAMPLE V–1   Rondellus: *Fulget coelestis curia—O Petre flos—Roma gaudet*

Heaven's court shines forth, with Peter sitting as guard under the Prince of Heaven. Rome delights in such a bishop.
O Peter, flower of the apostles, shepherd of the heavenly court, nourish your sheep sweetly, leading them to higher things.
Rome delights in such a bishop, granted by divine gift.

Source: Luther Dittmer, ed., *The Worcester Fragments.* Copyright by Hänssler-Verlag/American Institute of Musicology. Used by permission only. All rights reserved.

would be described in modern terms as first-inversion triads or sixth chords. This kind of writing reflects the English national predilection for thirds and sixths and for full, harmonious sounds. It may have originated in the same frequent practice of voice-exchange in thirteenth-century English music that led to such forms as the rondellus. It was recognized in theory and practice by the establishment of rules for "discanting," that is, for singing an unnotated part against a *cantus firmus,* the added part moving note-against-note in equal rhythm with the given melody and always forming consonances with it. By the late thirteenth century, the rules for discanting forbade consecutive perfect fifths and octaves, but allowed a limited number of consecutive parallel thirds or sixths. One consequence was the rise of a peculiarly English sonority, marked by a generally homophonic texture (in contrast to the cantilena and motet textures of Continental music) and permeated to an extraordinary degree with the sound of the "softer" harmonic intervals of the third and sixth—including the sound of that particular combination which we call the $\frac{6}{3}$ chord.

Fauxbourdon   English music was becoming known on the Continent in the early part of the fifteenth century. Perhaps due to the English example, the sound of sixth-chord progressions so fascinated Continental composers that from about 1420 to 1450 this manner of writing affected every form of composition. The usual name for it is *fauxbourdon*—a term whose exact significance and etymology are still in dispute. In the strict sense, a *fauxbourdon* was a composition written in two voices which progressed in parallel sixths with octaves interspersed and always with an octave at the end of the phrase; to these written parts an unnotated third part was added in performance, moving constantly at a fourth below the treble. The actual sound of fauxbourdon, then, was like that of the passages of $\frac{6}{3}$ chords in English works; the difference in principle was that in fauxbourdon the principal melody was in the treble, whereas in English compositions that used a *cantus prius factus* this usually was heard in the middle or the lowest voice.

The important practical consequence of this device was not the production of such pieces of these, but the emergence, around the middle of the century, of a new style of three-part writing. In this style the principal melodic line is in the upper voice, so that in this respect it resembles the cantilena of the fourteenth century; but there are important differences. In the older cantilena style the two lower voices stood as it were apart, holding to a slower rhythm and serving as a more or less neutral background for the melody. Now, by contrast, the top voice and the tenor are coupled as if in a duet; these two voices—and eventually the contratenor as well—become more nearly equal in importance, in melodic quality, and in rhythm (though the treble may be enlivened by ornamental tones); and all three are assimilated in what is, by comparison with the previous century, a more consonant sound and a more harmonious progression of sonorities within the phrase. This new style exercised a strong influence on all types of composition.

The chief collection of English music of the early part of the fifteenth century is the Old Hall manuscript. It contains 147 compositions dating from about 1350 to 1420, of which approximately four-fifths are settings of various sections of the Ordinary of the Mass and the remainder are motets, hymns, and sequences. Most of the Mass settings are in the chordal "discant" style, modified in some instances by greater melodic activity in the top voice; they often incorporate plainchant melodies in one of the inner voices. Thus, one Sanctus by Leonel Power[1] has a four-part setting with a liturgical *cantus firmus* in the tenor voice, which often lies above the contratenor. This type of setting, with the plainsong melody in the next-to-lowest voice of a four-part texture not only allows greater freedom of harmonic treatment on the composer's part but also is historically important as a forerunner of the manner of using a plainsong tenor in the Masses of the late fifteenth and early sixteenth centuries. Other Mass sections in the Old Hall manuscript are in cantilena style, with the principal melody in the treble; in still others, a plainsong melody appears now in one voice, now in another, as a "migrant" *cantus firmus*. About one-seventh of the compositions in this collection, including both Masses and settings of other texts, are in the style of the isorhythmic motet. Among the composers named in the Old Hall manuscript is one "Roy Henry," probably King Henry IV of England, who reigned from 1399 to 1413.

The Old Hall manuscript

There was in the first half of the fifteenth century a considerable number of English composers whose works are found in Continental manuscripts of the period, and through whom the characteristic features of English musical style became known. Their influence is attested by a French poem of about 1440 which speaks of the *"contenance angloise"* (English countenance, or qualities) which contributed to making contemporary Continental music so "joyous and bright" with "marvelous pleasantness." Allusion is made particularly to the leading English composer of the time, John Dunstable (*ca.* 1385–1453). Part of Dunstable's life was probably spent in the service of the English Duke of Bedford, Regent of France from 1422 to 1435 and commander of the English armies that fought against Joan of Arc; the extensive English possessions and claims in France in this period partly explain the presence of Dunstable and many other English composers on the Continent as well as the spread of their music.

John Dunstable

Dunstable's compositions, of which about sixty are known, include examples of all the principal types and styles of polyphony that existed in his lifetime: isorhythmic motets, sections of the Ordinary of the Mass, secular songs, and three-part settings of miscellaneous liturgical texts. His twelve isorhythmic motets testify to the

---

[1] *The Old Hall Manuscript*, I, 2, ed. A. Hughes and M. Bent (American Institute of Musicology, 1969; CMM 46), pp. 357–60.

continued vitality of this ancient and venerable form of composition in the early fifteenth century. His most celebrated motet, a four-part setting that combines the hymn *Veni Creator Spiritus* and the sequence *Veni Sancte Spiritus,* is not only a splendid example of isorhythmic structure, but also a thoroughly impressive piece of music, embodying the English preference for full-bodied sonority with complete triads. Some of the sections of the Ordinary of the Mass, which comprise about one-third of Dunstable's known works, are also constructed on a liturgical melody set forth isorhythmically in the tenor. Only a few secular songs are attributed to Dunstable; of these, *O rosa bella* and *Puisque m'amour* are excellent examples of the expressive lyrical melodies and clear harmonic outlines of the English music of their time.

Dunstable's three-part sacred works

Most numerous and most important historically among Dunstable's works are the three-part sacred pieces—settings of antiphons, hymns, and other liturgical or Biblical texts. These are composed in various ways: some have a *cantus firmus* in the tenor part; others have a florid treble line and a borrowed melody in the middle voice, which moves for the most part in thirds and sixths above the tenor; others have an ornamented liturgical melody in the treble (see Example V–2); and still others are freely composed, without borrowed thematic material. A piece of this last type is the antiphon *Quam pulchra es* (NAWM/S 15), a work that we shall analyze in some detail, since it not only exemplifies Dunstable's style but also illustrates some important historical developments.

In *Quam pulchra es* the three voices are similar in character and of nearly equal importance; much of the time they move in the same rhythm and usually pronounce the same syllables together: the musical texture is that of conductus, and the short melisma at the end of the word "alleluia" is in accordance with the ornamented conductus style. A composition like this one was not limited by a

EXAMPLE V–2   Treble of Motet: *Regina caeli laetare,* John Dunstable

cantus firmus, nor by any prescribed scheme of structure, as in an isorhythmic motet, nor by any prescribed pattern of repetitions or sections, as in the *formes fixes* like the virelai or rondeau. The form of the music, therefore, was a matter for the composer's free choice, limited only insofar as he might wish to follow any suggestions of a formal outline that were implicit in the text. In this instance Dunstable has divided the piece into two sections. Section one (measures 1–38) comprises, in shortened form, verses 6, 7, 5, 4, and 11 of Chapter vii of *The Song of Solomon;* section two, beginning with "et videamus," is on verse 12, with an added "alleluia." The longer first section is punctuated near the end by the held notes on the word "veni" ("come"); its pattern of subdivision is $9 + 9 + 11 + 8$ measures, with cadences on *C, C, D,* and *G.* The second section subdivides, though less neatly, into $(4 + 3) + (6 + 3) + 4$ measures, with cadences on *F, D, C, D,* and *C.* The musical subdivisions of the first section correspond to the modern division of the text into verses; those of section two are less distinct, just as the subdivisions of the text are less clearly marked than in section one, but the "alleluia" is definitely set off by its melisma and the livelier melodic and harmonic rhythm as the final cadence is approached.

Not only is the musical form in its main outlines determined by the text; the outline of many phrases also is molded to the rhythm of the words, as may be noted in the declamation by repeated notes of "statúra túa assimiláta est," "mála Púnica," and "íbi dábo tíbi." Other details to be noted are: the conspicuous melodic intervals of a third in the topmost voice, and the occasional outlining of a triad in the melody (for example, measures 1–5, 43, 55); and the use of fauxbourdon style, particularly at the approach to a cadence (as in measures 12–15).

Among English musicians on the Continent after Dunstable may be mentioned Walter Frye (fl. 1450), composer of Masses, motets, and chansons; and John Hothby (d. 1487), who worked at Lucca and elsewhere in Italy for a great part of his life. Meanwhile, development of English music at home continued. One form that was especially cultivated was the *votive antiphon,* a sacred composition in honor of some particular saint or, most often, of the Virgin Mary. A large collection of such pieces, in elaborate polyphonic settings for five to nine voices, is preserved in a choirbook from the late fifteenth century at Eton College. The full sonority of these works, the alternation of larger and smaller voice-groups, and the large-scale division into sections of perfect, then imperfect time, are characteristic of votive antiphon and Mass composition in England through the first half of the sixteenth century.

Another form of English composition that flourished in the fifteenth century was the *carol.* Originally the carol, like the rondeau

Votive antiphons

The carol

and ballata, was a monophonic dance song with alternating solo and chorus portions. By the fifteenth century it had become stylized as a setting, in two or three (sometimes four) parts, of a religious poem in popular style, often on a subject of the Incarnation, and sometimes written in a mixture of English and Latin rhyming verses. In form the carol consisted of a number of stanzas all sung to the same music, and a *burden* or refrain with its own musical phrase, which was sung at the beginning and then repeated after every stanza. The carols were not folk songs, but their fresh, angular melodies and lively triple rhythms give them a distinctly popular character and an unmistakably English quality.

The Evolution of Musical Style in the Late Middle Ages

Dunstable's *Quam pulchra es* represents a trend in musical composition which had become continuously stronger throughout the fourteenth century. The history of musical style can be regarded from one point of view as a continual contest between the *contrapuntal* and the *harmonic* principles, that is, between independence of melodic lines on the one hand and unity of harmonic effect on the other. The general line of evolution in the late Middle Ages was away from the contrapuntal and toward the harmonic principle. The thirteenth-century motet had been primarily contrapuntal in style; emphasis was on the independent melodic lines, with comparatively little attention being given to the harmonies. During the fourteenth century the trend was in the direction of a growing feeling for the importance of harmonic organization and for the sensuous effect of harmonic combinations. Sharp dissonant clashes between melodic lines began to be avoided; the cantilena style, with one principal melody supported by subordinate lower parts, was a step in the direction of harmonic, as opposed to contrapuntal, organization of music; the rise of fauxbourdon, and the gradual penetration into all types of composition of the sonority of sixth chords, was still another step toward the dominance of the harmonic principle.

From another point of view, we may summarize the course of musical evolution from 1225 to 1425 as a movement from the *motet* principle to the *conductus* principle: from the French Gothic motet with its stylized liturgical *cantus firmus*, highly independent melodic lines, multiple texts, rigidly logical abstract structure, and relative indifference to harmonic progression or suavity of effect, to the secularized style of the mid-fifteenth century with its fusion of

French, Italian, and English qualities. In this new international style, a liturgical *cantus firmus* is either altogether absent or, if present, is incorporated into the musical ensemble without dominating it; dissonance is at a minimum; the form is determined either by the musical device of repeated and contrasted sections or by the literary form of the single text; and the harmonies, enriched by the employment of thirds and sixths as consonant intervals, begin to assume significance in the shaping of the phrase and of the work as a whole. Dunstable's *Quam pulchra es* is an example of this new style, which had favorable soil for growth in fourteenth-century England because English composers had continued to cultivate the conductus and conductus-like style of composition after these had largely fallen out of use on the Continent.

Quam pulchra es is classified in the standard edition of Dunstable's works as a "motet." This word, which we have hitherto used to denote the French form of the thirteenth century and the isorhythmic form of the fourteenth and early fifteenth centuries, had begun in the fourteenth century to take on a broader meaning being applied also to settings of liturgical or even secular texts in the newer musical style of the time. This broader meaning of the term has prevailed up to the present day: a motet, in this usage, means almost any polyphonic composition on a Latin text other than the Ordinary of the Mass, and thus includes such diverse forms as antiphons, responsories, and other texts from the Proper and the Office. From the sixteenth century onward, the word was also applied to sacred compositions in languages other than Latin. This usage, though regrettable in some respects, is so widely accepted that we shall have to retain it, remembering however that within the general class "motet" there are many different subclasses which must sometimes be distinguished. In particular, special categories are usually made of the *Magnificat* canticle and the *Lamentations*.

The fifteenth-century motet

The Burgundian School

The Dukes of Burgundy, although feudal vassals of the Kings of France, were virtually their equals in power. During the second half of the fourteenth century and the early years of the fifteenth, by means of a series of political marriages and a course of diplomacy that took full advantage of their Kings' distress in the Hundred Years' Wars, they acquired possession of territories comprising most of what are today Holland, Belgium, northeastern France, Luxembourg, and Lorraine; these they added to their original fiefs, the medieval Duchy and County of Burgundy in east central France, and ruled over the whole as virtually independent sovereigns until 1477.

Though their nominal capital was Dijon, they had no fixed principal city of residence but sojourned from time to time at various places in their dominions. The main orbit of the peripatetic Burgundian court after the middle of the century was around Lille, Bruges, Ghent, and especially Brussels, an area comprising modern Belgium and the northeastern corner of France. Most of the leading northern composers of the late fifteenth century came from this general region and many of them were connected in one way or another with the Burgundian court.

All the Dukes of Burgundy were active patrons of art and music. Like most great nobles, they maintained a *chapel*, with an accessory corps of composers, singers, and instrumentalists who furnished music for church services, probably also contributed to the secular entertainment of the court, and accompanied their master on his journeys.

The court and chapel of Philip the Good, ruler of Burgundy from 1419 to 1467, were the most resplendent in Europe, and his influence as a patron of music was so extensive that the name "Burgundian" has been given both to the style of music and the composers who flourished during his reign. The term, of course, does not connote nationality. The Burgundian chapel, numbering fifteen to twenty-seven musicians, in the early part of the century was recruited chiefly from Paris; later, it was made up of musicians from England and various parts of the Continent, but most numerous were those from the Franco-Belgian region. In addition to his chapel, Philip the Good maintained a band of minstrels—trumpeters, viellists, lutenists, harpists, organists—which included Frenchmen, Italians, Germans, and Portuguese. The cosmopolitan atmosphere of such a fifteenth-century court was accentuated by numerous visits from foreign musicians and by the fact that the members of the

Guillaume Dufay (ca. 1400–1474) and Gilles Binchois (ca. 1400–1460), the leading Burgundian composers, are shown together in this miniature from Le Champion des Dames. *(Bettmann Archive)*

A fête champêtre *at the court of Duke Philip the Good (1396–1467) of Burgundy. The musicians, ever present on these occasions, serenade the Duke's party, which is at the center. Hunters are chasing game in the background. This painting, dated 1430–31, is ascribed to Jan Van Eyck.*

chapel themselves were continually on the move, migrating from one service to another in response to "better offers." Under such circumstances a musical style could not be other than international; the prestige of the Burgundian court was such that the kind of music cultivated there influenced other European musical centers, such as the chapels of the Pope at Rome, the Emperor in Germany, the kings of France and England, and the various Italian courts, as well as cathedral choirs—the more so because many of the musicians in these other places either had been at one time, or hoped some day to be, in the service of the Duke of Burgundy himself.

**Guillaume
Dufay**

Guillaume Dufay is commonly named as one of the chief figures of the Burgundian School, although he was perhaps never a regular member of the ducal chapel. Dufay was born about 1400 in the Burgundian province of Hainaut (the present Franco-Belgian border region). He travelled much, and was a welcome guest at many European courts. Already before his death in 1474, and for a generation after, he was celebrated as one of the greatest composers of his time and the teacher of many famous musicians.[2]

The principal types of composition of the Burgundian School were Masses, Magnificats, motets, and secular chansons with French texts. The prevailing combination of voices was the same as in the French ballade and the Italian ballata: tenor and contratenor both moving within the range *c* to *g'*, and a treble or discantus normally not exceeding the compass of a tenth (*a* to *c''* or *c'* to *e''*). As in the fourteenth century, the intention was for each line in performance to have a distinct timbre and the whole a transparent texture, with predominance of the discantus as the principal melody. The style in general may be regarded as a combination of the homophonic suavity of fauxbourdon with a certain amount of melodic freedom and contrapuntal independence, including occasional points of imitation. The typical discantus line flows in warmly expressive lyrical phrases, breaking into graceful melismas at the approach to important cadences.

The Burgundian cadence formula was still for the most part that of the fourteenth century (Example III–11), and the "Landini" embellishment figure was very common (Example IV–1); but along with this older type of cadence, another began to appear which was in effect a dominant–tonic progression and which, in three-part writing, nearly always involved crossing of the two lower voices; see Example V–3a and b.

The feeling for chord progressions of this character became more marked throughout the fifteenth century; and after about 1460 the normal cadence formula was one that would be described in modern terminology as V–I. It must be understood, however, that the composers did not think of such progressions with the implications attached to the modern terms we are using to describe them. Music theorists until after the middle of the sixteenth century did not even recognize the triad as an entity, still less any tonal-functional chord progressions. Their unit was not the chord, but the interval between a pair of voices. Thus in Example V–3a and b the bass, and in V–3c and d the bass and alto, are to be thought of as "added" parts which fill out the vertical sonorities and accommodate themselves to the

---

[2] See Craig Wright, "Dufay at Cambrai: Discoveries and Revisions," in JAMS, XXVIII (Summer, 1975), 175–229.

EXAMPLE V-3 Cadential Formulas

a. Dufay, *Motet* b. Binchois, *Rondeau*

c. Dufay, *Mass* d. Dufay, *Mass*

intervallic progressions of the essential soprano-tenor framework—
which here (as in the cadential formulas of Examples III–11 and
IV–3) is moving by rule to a perfect interval (the octave) from the
next preceding imperfect interval (the sixth).

The great majority of the compositions of the Burgundian School
were in some form of triple meter, with frequent cross rhythms resulting from the combination of the patterns ♩ ♩ ♩ and ♫♫ ♫♫;
see Example V–3b and d. Duple meter was used principally in subdivisions of longer works as a means of contrast.

In the fifteenth century, *chanson* was a general term for any
polyphonic setting of a secular poem in French. The Burgundian
chansons were, in effect, accompanied solo songs. Their texts—nearly
always love poems—were most often in the pattern of the rondeau,
sometimes the traditional form with a two-line refrain, sometimes
an expanded form such as the *rondeau quatrain* or *cinquain*, which
had four- and five-line stanzas and refrains respectively. The chansons were the most characteristic products of the Burgundian
School. An example of the *rondeau cinquain* is Dufay's *Adieu ces
bons vins de Lannoys* (Farewell, *these good wines of Lannoys;*
NAWM/S 23), which has been dated 1426. It follows the normal
form of *ABaAabAB.* One distinctive feature is the occasional shift
from a triple division of the measure—3/4 in the modern transcription—to 6/8 in one of the parts. The tenor must be an instrumental
part, as there are not enough notes for the syllables of the text.

Another outstanding master was Gilles Binchois (c. 1400–60)
whose chansons excel in the expression of a tender melancholy, just
touched with sensuous longing. The moving charm of the melodies,
the clear, bright-colored sound of the ensemble, and the miniature
proportions of the whole contrive to suggest to our minds the pic-

**The
Burgundian
chanson**

ture of a visionary world, remote yet strangely familiar, standing at the threshold between the Middle Ages and the Renaissance. So strong was the spell of this Burgundian musical style that the tradition of it lingered in Europe long after the Duchy of Burgundy had ceased to exist as an independent political power.

Burgundian motets

In their church music the Burgundian composers at first developed no distinctive sacred style, but wrote both motets and Masses in the manner of the chanson, with a freely melodic solo treble coupled with a tenor and supported by a contratenor part in the usual three-voice texture. The treble might be newly composed, but in many cases it was an embellished version of a chant (for example, Dufay's *Alma Redemptoris Mater*). This use of a liturgical *cantus firmus* was fundamentally different from the way such a theme was used in the tenor of the old thirteenth- and fourteenth-century motet. There the liturgical melody was no more than a mystical base for the structure: as long as it was present, no matter how distorted in rhythm and regardless of whether any hearer could recognize it, its purpose was fulfilled. In Burgundian motets, on the contrary, the Gregorian melodies were meant to be recognized; they were not only a symbolic link with tradition, but also a concrete, musically expressive part of the composition. The influence of fauxbourdon style on the Burgundian motet may be recognized in the prevailing homophonic texture and relatively frequent sixth chords of Dufay's *Alma Redemptoris Mater,* his *Veni Creator Spiritus,* and, in a simpler form quite close to strict fauxbourdon, some of his other hymn settings, for example, *Conditor alme siderum (Creator of the propitious stars;* NAWM/S 16). Here the plainchant is in the cantus part, while the tenor harmonizes it mainly in sixths and octaves. As in English discant, an improvised middle voice fills in the harmony. It was customary for the verses of the hymn to be sung alternately in plainchant and fauxbourdon.

Burgundian Masses

It was in settings of the Mass that composers of the Burgundian period first developed a specifically sacred musical style, and moreover began an evolution which by the end of the century made this form the principal vehicle for the thought and effort of composers. We have already noted the increased number of polyphonic settings of the Mass in the late fourteenth and early fifteenth centuries. Previous to about 1420 the various sections of the Ordinary were composed as separate pieces (Machaut's Mass and a few others excepted), though occasionally such separate items might be brought together by a compiler into a unified cycle. A central achievement of the fifteenth century was to establish as regular practice the polyphonic setting of the Ordinary as a musically unified whole. At first only a pair of sections (for example, Gloria and Credo) would be brought into perceptible musical relationship; gradually the practice was extended to all five divisions of the Ordinary. The motive for this development was the desire of musicians to give coherence to a large and complex musical form; moreover, similar cyclical groupings of the plainsong chants of the Ordinary had existed as early as the beginning of the fourteenth century.

Of course a certain feeling of musical unity resulted simply when all five parts of the Ordinary were composed in the same general style, which on the Continent in the early fifteenth century was usually that of the ballade or chanson. If in addition each movement took an appropriate chant from the *Graduale* for a *cantus firmus* (which would usually appear in ornamented form in the treble), the impression of unity was strengthened—but by liturgical association rather than by musical resemblance, since the plainsong melodies were not necessarily thematically related. (A Mass using Gregorian themes in this way is called a *missa choralis* or *Plainsong Mass*.) The most practical way of achieving a definite, perceptible musical interconnection of the various sections of a Mass was to use the same thematic material in each. At first the connection consisted only in beginning each movement with the same melodic motive, usually in the treble (a Mass that uses this device is sometimes called a *motto Mass*); but this technique—which the Englishman John Hothby at Lucca had also used in his settings of the *Magnificat*—was soon superseded by or combined with another, namely the use of the same *cantus firmus* in every movement. The resulting cyclical musical form is known as a *cantus firmus Mass* or *Tenor Mass*. The earliest cyclical Masses of this kind were written by English composers, but the form was quickly adopted on the Continent and by the second half of the fifteenth century had become the customary one.

The tradition of the medieval motet suggested the placing of the borrowed melody in the tenor; but the new conception of music in the fifteenth century required that the lowest voice be free to function as a foundation for the desired harmonic progressions, particularly at cadences. To use as the lowest voice a given melodic line which could not be essentially modified would have limited the composer's freedom and possibly have led to harmonic monotony. This difficulty was resolved by making the tenor the next-to-lowest voice, placing below it a part at first called *contratenor bassus* ("low contratenor"), later simply *bassus*; placing above the tenor a second contratenor called *contratenor altus* ("high contratenor"), later *altus;* and retaining in the highest position the treble part, called variously the *cantus* ("melody"), *discantus* ("discant"), or *superius* ("highest" part). These four voice parts came into being about the middle of the fifteenth century, and this distribution has remained, with few interruptions, the standard one to our own day.

Another heritage from the medieval motet was the custom of writing the tenor of a *cantus firmus* Mass in longer notes than the

EXAMPLE V–4   *L'homme armé*

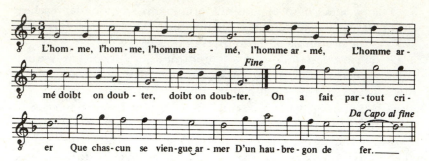

The armed man is to be feared; everywhere it has been proclaimed that everyone should arm himself with an iron coat of mail.

other parts and in isorhythmic fashion—either imposing a certain rhythmic pattern on a given plainsong melody and repeating it with the same pattern, or keeping the original rhythm of a given secular tune and altering the successive appearances of the melody by making them now faster, now slower, in relation to the other voices. Thus, as in the isorhythmic motet, the identity of the borrowed tune might be quite thoroughly disguised, the more so that it lay now in an inner voice and not in the lowest one as in the fourteenth century; nonetheless its regulative power in unifying the five divisions of the Mass was undeniable. The melodies used as *cantus firmi* were taken from the chants of the Proper or the Office, or else from a secular source, most often the tenor part of a chanson; in neither case did they have any liturgical connection with the Ordinary of the Mass. The name of the borrowed melody was given to the Mass for which it served as a *cantus firmus* as in Dufay's Mass *Se la face ay pale* (*If my face is pale*), which is based on the composer's own chanson, or such as the favorite song *L'homme armé* (*The armed man*), on which nearly every composer of the late fifteenth and sixteenth centuries wrote at least one Mass. Numerous arrangements of the latter survive, none of them the original. One by Robert Morton (NAWM/S 30) takes the more usual three-part version and adds a bass, obviously for a fuller effect in instrumental performance. The melody of the song (Example V–4) is in the tenor. A section of the Agnus Dei I from Dufay's Mass on *L'homme armé* is in Example V–5. It is obvious that the words of the Mass do not fit the tenor well, and this may be taken as a sign that it was performed by one or more instruments. This is also true of the bass, which at one point (measures 14–15) pre-imitates the tenor. The two upper voices are easier to sing to a text, but here too the manuscripts are vague about the placement of the syllables, which was left to the singers to determine. The rhythmic complication of the alto and bass at measures 22–23 is notable.

EXAMPLE V–5   Agnus Dei I from the Mass *L'homme armé*, Guillaume
Dufay

Lamb of God that takest away the sins of the world, have mercy [on us].

Another example of Dufay's *cantus firmus* technique may be found in his Mass *Se la face ay pale*. In the Gloria and Credo the tune is heard three times, first in long note values, then in somewhat shorter note values, and finally at nearly the same speed as the other voices, so that at this third hearing the melody becomes for the first time easily recognizable.

Dufay's four-part *cantus firmus* Masses are late works, dating for the most part after 1450. It is clear that in such compositions as these we are no longer dealing with typically Burgundian music in the style of the chansons and chanson-like motets and Masses of the earlier part of the century. Some of the new features in the *cantus firmus* Masses of Dufay are indicative of a "learned" musical style which rose to a dominating position after 1450, and which in some respects seemed to signalize a revival of medieval ideals of church music. On the whole, however, the course of development after about 1430 tended to emphasize those features which were to differentiate the musical style of the Renaissance from that of the late Middle Ages: control of dissonance, predominantly consonant sonorities including sixth chords, equal importance of voices, melodic and rhythmic congruity of lines, four-part texture, and occasional use of imitation. From this point of view it would not be unreasonable to classify Dufay and Binchois, and in some respects Dunstable also, as early Renaissance composers.

VI

The Age of the Renaissance: Ockeghem to Josquin

General Features

The period from about 1450 to 1600 in the history of music is now generally known as "the Renaissance," a term which, like "Gothic" for the late Middle Ages or "Baroque" for the seventeenth and early eighteenth centuries, has been borrowed from art history. Its literal meaning is "rebirth," and many writers and artists of the fifteenth and sixteenth centuries hailed the achievements of their own time as a revival of the glories of Greece and Rome, a revival stimulated in part by discoveries of many ancient works of art and literature. No comparable discoveries of ancient music were made, so there could be no literal "rebirth" in the same sense as in the other fields. The essentials of Greek musical theory had been handed down by Boethius, but few read him directly in the Middle Ages; Renaissance theorists diligently studied such of the ancient treatises as were available and sought to apply their teachings to the contemporary musical scene. Descriptions of the marvelous effects of ancient music led to some attempts in the sixteenth century to discover the lost secret of its power in the hope of reviving its glories. Projected revival of the chromatic and enharmonic genera of Greek music by the theorist Vicentino (1555), as well as later experiments that led eventually to opera, were among the consequences of the eager Renaissance interest in the music of antiquity.

Also to be considered is the more general meaning of Renaissance as a rebirth of the human spirit, a revival of standards of culture.

Renaissance men were convinced that theirs was an age both different from and better than immediately preceding times: "The world is coming to its senses as if awaking out of a deep sleep," Erasmus said. The whole temper of the age was optimistic and buoyant.

Historical events

Of course it is impossible to date precisely any such momentous and far-reaching change in human attitudes, habits, and institutions as is implied in the idea of the Renaissance. From our own vantage point in time, we can see that certain historical and cultural events of the late fifteenth and early sixteenth centuries appear to signal the end of the Middle Ages and the beginning of the modern era. In 1453, the year of Dunstable's death, the Turks captured Constantinople, the capital and last stronghold of the eastern Roman Empire, thereby severing the last visible link with the world of antiquity; many Byzantine scholars fled to Italy, where their presence stimulated the study of the Greek language and of ancient Greek literature and philosophy. The invention of printing from movable type was made at about the same time. The rediscovery of America by Columbus in 1492 was followed by other voyages of discovery and the eventual colonization of the western hemisphere. Finally, the two great universal medieval institutions—the Catholic Church and the Holy Roman Empire—were both splintered. The Reformation begun by Martin Luther in 1517 divided the Church into Catholic and Protestant branches. As for the Empire, its authority had long since become a mere shadow, and its territory, now embracing approximately the extent of modern Germany, Austria, and a portion of the Netherlands, comprised merely one state in the European community.

Music printing

One of the most important factors in the growth of music during the Renaissance was the rise of music printing. The first collection of polyphonic music printed from movable type was brought out in 1501 by Ottaviano de' Petrucci at Venice. By 1523 Petrucci had published fifty-nine volumes (including reprints) of vocal and instrumental music. Music printing in France began in 1528, in Germany about 1534, and in the Netherlands in 1538. Most published ensemble music in the sixteenth century was printed in the form of partbooks—one small volume, usually of oblong format, for each voice or part, so that a complete set was requisite for performances.

The application of the art of printing to music was obviously an event of far-reaching consequence. Instead of a few precious manuscripts laboriously copied by hand and liable to all kinds of errors and variants, a plentiful supply of new music was now made possible—not exactly at a low price, but still less costly than equivalent manuscripts, and of uniform accuracy. Furthermore, the existence of printed copies meant that now many more works of music would be preserved for performance and study by later generations.

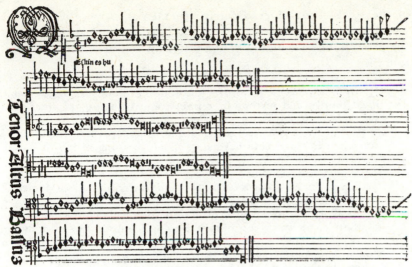

A page from Harmonice Musices Odhecaton, *a collection of 96 part-songs by Franco-Netherlandish composers, the first such book to be printed from movable type. Ottaviano de' Petrucci (1466–1539) published it at Venice in 1501. Petrucci's editions are highly prized for their neat presswork.*

Insofar as it is possible to define a Renaissance musical style, the following general features may be noted:

The characteristic "ideal" sound was that of four or more voice lines of similar character in a homogeneous tone color, instead of three more or less dissimilar lines in contrasting timbres as in the Middle Ages and early Renaissance. Composers began to write all the voice-parts simultaneously instead of successively as before. The lines were of equal importance in that all shared equally in presenting the musical motives in a texture of imitative counterpoint, although the two outer voices had special functions in defining tonal centers. The units of vertical sonority were the combinations we call the triad and the $\frac{6}{3}$ chord—conceived, however, not as such but rather in terms of intervallic relationships and progressing according to the requirements of melodic movement and harmonic consonance within a modal framework.[1] The bass was gradually given the function of a harmonic foundation, even when it was imitating the other voices.

By the end of the fifteenth century some "rules" for *musica ficta*—that is, for the performers' application of accidentals not specified

Renaissance musical style

---

[1] A brief compendium of sixteenth-century theory relating to these matters may be read in the selections from Glarean's *Dodecachordon* (1547) and Zarlino's *Istitutioni* (1558) printed in SR 219–55 (SRRe, 29–65); see also Zarlino, *The Art of Counterpoint*, trans. Guy A. Marco and Claude V. Palisca (New Haven, 1968; New York, 1976); E. E. Lowinsky, ed., *The Medici Codex of 1518* (Chicago, 1968, 3 vols.); Andrew Hughes, *Manuscript Accidentals*, MSD 27 (1972).

**Musica
ficta**

in the score—had achieved fairly general currency. These rules, which were given further currency by printed treatises at the end of the fifteenth and beginning of the sixteenth centuries included the following:

(1) In direct melodic leaps of a fourth or a fifth, or melodically out-lined fourths and (except in certain contexts) fifths, the intervals should be perfect.

(2) Except in certain contexts, "Una nota supra la semper est canendum fa" (one note beyond la should be sung as fa)—that is, when the melody proceeds upward only a single step from la, that step should be a semitone.

(3) Except in certain contexts, harmonic intervals of the fourth, fifth, and octave should be perfect.

(4) (a) When the two voices of a third proceed stepwise outward to a fifth, or the two voices of a sixth stepwise outward to an octave, the imperfect interval (that is, the third or sixth) should be major. Similarly, when the two voices of a third proceed inward to a unison, the third should be minor.

(b) Especially in suspension-cadences, the sixth immediately pre-ceding the octave should be major.

(5) If the final harmony of a piece contains a third, it should be major.

(6) Some theorists also say that in certain circumstances the middle note of each of the following melodic groups should be raised a semi-tone: *A–G–A, D–C–D, G–F–G.*

There is no general agreement on the order of priority in the application of these rules in cases where two or more of them would conflict. Conventions governing their application doubtless varied from place to place and from time to time.

The presence of explicit accidentals in manuscripts and prints of the period can be used to support the idea that the rules they seem to illustrate were current, or, on the other side of the argument, that they were not self-evident. Undoubtedly, there was a growing tend-ency in the first half of the sixteenth century for composers to make intended accidentals explicit.[2]

Rhythm

With regard to rhythm, two distinct tendencies were apparent in the Renaissance: (1) the music might move with fluid rhythm either in a contrapuntal texture with systematic free imitation involving all the voices, or in a freely improvisatory style, as in certain types of lute and keyboard pieces; or, (2) the movement might be by strongly marked rhythmic patterns in a predominantly chordal texture, as in instrumental dance pieces and certain kinds of secular vocal compositions. These two tendencies represent two different tradi-tions; they interact to some extent in the sixteenth century, but on the whole they remain differentiated.

Renaissance music became both more closely united with words

---

[2] Arthur Mendel, "Towards objective criteria for establishing chronology and authenticity," in *Josquin des Prez*, Edward E. Lowinsky, ed. (London, 1976) 297–308.

and more independent of words. On the one hand there was a constant and successful effort throughout the sixteenth century to make the texts in vocal music more easily understandable and to make the music immediately and strikingly express the images and especially the feelings suggested by the text; at the same time the rise of instrumental music bears witness to the urge to create musical forms which should be complete and satisfying as purely musical entities, not needing the support of words.

Music and words

Finally, although the older cantilena texture of a solo voice with instrumental accompaniment was not entirely dropped during the Renaissance, for a long time it was neglected. The fundamental nature of most Renaissance music suggests general equality of the voices, yet many pieces in contrapuntal style were actually performed by a vocal soloist with instruments playing the other parts. Also, a certain number of pieces were frankly written as solos with accompaniment; but it was not until near the end of the sixteenth century that this particular type of composition rose to special prominence.

Texture

For convenience we may distinguish two main overlapping periods in the history of Renaissance music. Until well into the sixteenth century the prevailing style was international, relatively uniform, and largely dictated by composers from northern France and the Lowlands. As the sixteenth century progressed, diverse national styles arose; and after about 1550, the progress of music was marked by the growing dominance of those styles and by new departures that foreshadowed the Baroque era.

Title page of Silvestro di Ganassi's Fontegara, 1535. *A recorder consort and two singers are shown performing from printed partbooks.*

In this and the next two chapters we shall divide the complex history of Renaissance music in the following way: the present chapter will deal with the principal composers and musical forms from the late fifteenth century to about 1520. Chapter VII will be concerned with the Catholic church music of the period from 1520 to 1550, with the beginnings of national styles and of instrumental music, and the flowering of the madrigal and related forms in the middle and late sixteenth century. In Chapter VIII we shall follow the growth of sacred music in the Lutheran and other Protestant churches in the sixteenth century, the Catholic church music of the latter half of the sixteenth century, the instrumental music of the same period, and the rise of the Venetian school, the immediate predecessor of the Baroque.

The Netherlands Composers

The period between 1450 and 1550 in the history of music has been called "the age of the Netherlanders." Other terms used or advocated include "Flemish," "Franco–Flemish," "Franco–Belgian," "Franco–Netherlandish," or simply "Northern." The choice is of little consequence, and we shall use any or all of the above names as may be most convenient. The essential thing to remember is that they all designate not race or nationality, but either (a) a certain geographical area or (b) a certain musical style which, however modified from composer to composer or from generation to generation, retains permanent common features that appear in most of the music written in Europe up to about 1570.

The dominance of the Northerners, which had begun early in the fifteenth century, is vividly illustrated in the careers of their chief composers and performers between 1450 and 1550: most of these men passed a large part of their lives in the service of the Emperor (service which might take them to Spain, Germany, Bohemia, or Austria), the King of France, the Pope, or one of the Italian courts. In Italy, the courts or cities of Naples, Florence, Ferrara, Modena, Mantua, Milan, and Venice were the chief centers for the diffusion of the art of the Netherlanders. Their music was regarded as the proper style for cultivated composers, and musicians of all countries willingly learned from them.

The period after the middle of the fifteenth century is represented by the later works of Dufay and the compositions of Johannes Ockeghem. As is true of many other Netherlands composers, the exact date (1420?) and place of Ockeghem's birth are unknown. We first hear of him as a singer in the choir of the Cathedral at Antwerp in 1443. In 1452 he entered the chapel of the King of France, and in 1465 was made its leader (*maître de chapelle*), which

Johannes Ockeghem

post he held until his death in 1497. He was celebrated not only as a composer but also as the teacher of many of the leading Nether- landers of the next generation. A miniature in a French manuscript of about 1530 shows Ockeghem and eight other singers of his chapel singing a Gloria from a large manuscript choirbook on a lectern (see p. 115), in the usual fashion of the time.

Ockeghem does not seem to have been an exceptionally prolific composer. His known works comprise about twelve Masses, ten motets, and some twenty chansons. The relatively large number of Masses reflects the fact that in the second half of the fifteenth cen- tury this was the principal form of composition, in which the composer was expected to demonstrate most fully his skill and imagination. Most of Ockeghem's Masses are similar in general sonority to Dufay's, and Ockeghem's *Caput* Mass (Agnus Dei in NAWM/S 21) may be compared to the anonymous Mass, once at- tributed to Dufay, on the same subject (NAWM/S 20). Four voices of essentially like character interact in a contrapuntal texture of in- dependent melodic lines. However, the bass, which before 1450 rarely sang below *c,* is now extended downward to *G* or *F,* and sometimes as much as a fourth lower in special combinations of low voices; otherwise the ranges normally are the same as in the early part of the century. Example VI–1 shows the ranges used; the com-

Ockeghem's style

EXAMPLE VI–1 Normal Ranges of Voice Parts in the Late Fifteenth Century

pass of the superius corresponds to that of the modern alto; the tenor and contratenor (the "tenor altus") are in nearly the same range, and frequently cross each other in the part-writing. The re- sult, as compared with Burgundian style, is a fuller, thicker texture, a darker and at the same time a more homogeneous sound. This effect is reinforced by the character of Ockeghem's melodic lines, which are spun out in long-breathed phrases, in an extremely flexible rhythmic flow much like that of melismatic plainchant, with infrequent cadences and few rests (see Example VI–2).

Ockeghem's harmonic vocabulary is by no means oriented toward the modern tonal system. In fact, the sound of his church music is more austerely modal, and thus closer to the spirit of Gregorian Chant, than that of the Burgundians. This is one sign of a general tendency on the part of composers in the second half of the fifteenth century to create a style of church music different from that of secular music, instead of, as in the earlier period, writing Masses and

EXAMPLE VI–2 Agnus Dei from the *Missa caput,* Johannes Ockeghem

motets in a style practically indistinguishable from that of the chanson.

In general, Ockeghem did not rely heavily on imitation in his Masses; there are many imitative passages, but these seldom involve all the voices, and the technique is used only incidentally, as in the Agnus I at measures 27–30 in the three upper parts. By contrast Obrecht begins each of his three Agnus settings on the *Caput* subject with imitative entries (see NAWM/S 22). One class of compositions, however, the *canons,* are a conspicuous exception to this general rule. Ockeghem, in common with his contemporaries, took delight in writing music in which the audible structure was supported by another, concealed structure of a theoretically rigid nature; it was the same propensity as that which led medieval composers to write isorhythmic motets, partly for sheer pleasure in the exercise of technical virtuosity, and partly as a public demonstration of professional skill. With the Netherlanders these displays of technique took the form of canons.

The method of writing canon is to derive one or more additional voices from a single given voice. The additional voices may be written out by the composer, or they may be sung from the notes of the given voice, modified according to certain directions. The

The Netherlands Canon

Johannes Ockeghem and the singers of his chapel.

additional voice may be derived in various ways. For example, the second voice may start at a certain number of beats or measures after the original one; the second voice may be an inversion of the first—that is, move always by the same intervals but in the opposite direction; or the derived voice may be the original voice backward —called a *retrograde* canon, or *cancrizans* ("crab") canon.

Another possibility is to make the two voices move at different rates of speed; canons of this sort are sometimes called *mensuration* canons, and they may be notated by prefixing two or more different mensuration signs (see pp. 85–86) to a single written melody. In a mensuration canon the ratio between the two voices may be simple augmentation (second voice moving in note values twice as long as the first), simple diminution (second voice in values half as long), or some more complex ratio. Of course, any of the devices just described may be used in combination. Furthermore, in any instance the derived voice need not be at the same pitch as the original one, but may reproduce its melody at some chosen interval above or below. A composition may also involve *double canon*, that is, two canons (or even more) being sung or played simultaneously. Two or more voices may proceed in canon while other voices move in independent lines. All in all, it is evident that considerable complication is possible.

An example of canonic writing is Ockeghem's *Missa prolationum*, every movement of which is constructed as a double mensuration canon making use of various intervals and various combinations of time signatures. Example VI–3 shows the beginning of the second Kyrie from this Mass. Each of the two parts in the original notation has two mensuration signatures— ○ and ◖ in the superius, ☉ and ◖

EXAMPLE VI-3   Kyrie II from the *Missa prolationum*, Ockeghem

in the contra—and two C clefs, one with each signature. In the transcription (Example VI-3b) the two top voices represent the superius and the lower voices the contra, with appropriate reduction of the original note values.

The importance of these and similar flights of virtuosity can easily be exaggerated. It is less important to know that Ockeghem wrote canons than to realize, by listening to his music, that in the comparatively few compositions where he does use such artifices, they are most artfully hidden; they do not in the least inhibit his ability to communicate through the music, even to listeners untutored in the "science" of musical composition. But when the underlying scheme of the work is known, one must admire all the more the smooth melodic lines, the harmonious proportions, and the apparent ease with which the music moves despite the formidable technical problem which the composer has set himself.

In the fifteenth and sixteenth centuries, Masses without a *cantus firmus* took their titles from the mode in which they were written (for example, *Missa quinti toni,* "Mass in Mode V") or from some peculiarity of structure. A Mass having neither a *cantus firmus* nor any other identifying peculiarity, or one whose source the composer did not wish to indicate, was often called a *Missa sine nomine,* "without a name."

The essential quality of Ockeghem's church music is difficult to describe. The low range, the nonpulsatile rhythms, the prevailing texture of nonimitative counterpoint, the seemingly random harmonic progressions, and especially the long-breathed, winding melodies, unarticulated either by regular cadences or melodic sequences —all combine to produce an effect of vastness and mystery, a suggestion of inward rapture rising from the contemplation of thoughts embodied in the sacred text.

One important change in the manner of performing church music had come about gradually during the first half of the fifteenth century. All through the Middle Ages polyphony had been sung by solo voices, the chorus being used only for unison plainchant. But in the Old Hall manuscript, and in some English and Italian manuscripts of the 1420s and '30s, we begin to find unequivocal directions for certain passages to be rendered by several singers on a part, that is, by a chorus (not necessarily a large group) instead of by an ensemble of soloists. By the middle of the century, choral performance of church music—alternating with duets or trios for solo voices—seems to have been the rule. (For most secular vocal music throughout the Renaissance, however, solo voices remained the normal medium.) Choruses were not large by modern standards. An ensemble of thirty singers was exceptional; eight or twelve was a more usual size. The customary manner of performance was from a single large choirbook placed on a lectern, with the music written large enough so that all the singers could read from the same open pages (see illustration, p. 115). Apparently in the few churches where the choir was sufficiently skilled, performances were *a cappella;* but instrumental doubling or replacement of human voices was probably common, and on especially festive occasions instruments might always be brought in.

Ockeghem's Masses show an extreme reaction against the Burgundian chanson-style Mass and motet of the early fifteenth century; a more even balance between mystic withdrawal on the one hand and articulate expressiveness on the other was restored in the next generation of Franco–Flemish church composers, many of

Ockeghem's church music

whom directly or indirectly were pupils of Ockeghem. The three most eminent figures of this generation were Jacob Obrecht, Henricus Isaac, and Josquin des Prez, all born around the middle of the century—Obrecht near Rotterdam, Isaac perhaps at Bruges, and Josquin somewhere in the territory of Hainaut. All received their earliest musical training and experience in the Netherlands. All travelled widely, working in various courts and churches in different countries of Europe. The careers of these three composers, like those of most of their contemporaries, well illustrate the lively continual interchange in musical matters that went on in the fifteenth and sixteenth centuries between northern and southern Europe, between the Franco–Belgian centers and those of Italy and (somewhat later) Spain. It is natural, therefore, that we should find in their music a diversity, a mixture, and to some extent a fusion, of northern and southern elements: the serious tone, the leaning toward rigid structure, the intricate polyphony, the smoothly flowing rhythms of the Netherlands; the more spontaneous mood, simpler homophonic texture, more distinct rhythms, and more clearly articulated phrases of the Italian style.

Few details are known of the life of Jacob Obrecht (*ca.* 1452–1505). His works include some two dozen Masses, about an equal number of motets, and a number of chansons and instrumental pieces. Most of his Masses are built on *cantus firmi,* either secular songs or liturgical Gregorian melodies; but there is much variety in the treatment of these borrowed themes. His Masses and motets differ from those of Ockeghem first of all by reason of the more spontaneous, impulsive quality of his musical imagination.

The opening of the Agnus Dei of his *Missa caput* (Example VI–4; NAWM/S 21 is the entire movement) may be compared to the sample from Ockeghem's Mass on the same subject (Example VI–2). Like Ockeghem, Obrecht begins with a pair of voices in quite strict, if not exact, imitation. Obrecht's melody is typically Netherlandish in its smoothly vocal curves and its richly melismatic character; but unlike the long, winding, rapt, unbroken line of Ockeghem, Obrecht's melody is organized into relatively short though perfectly proportioned phrases with periodical cadences, supported always by clear and appropriate harmonies.

The chanson

Although polyphonic church music, especially settings of the Ordinary of the Mass, had achieved greater prestige in the second half of the fifteenth century than at any time in the previous two hundred years, there was no lack of secular composition in this period. The miniature proportions typical of the early Burgundian school were being expanded into larger musical forms; late Burgundian chansons of 1460–80 show a gradually increasing use of imitative counterpoint, involving at first only the superius and tenor voices, later all

EXAMPLE VI–4   Agnus Dei from the *Missa caput*, Jacob Obrecht

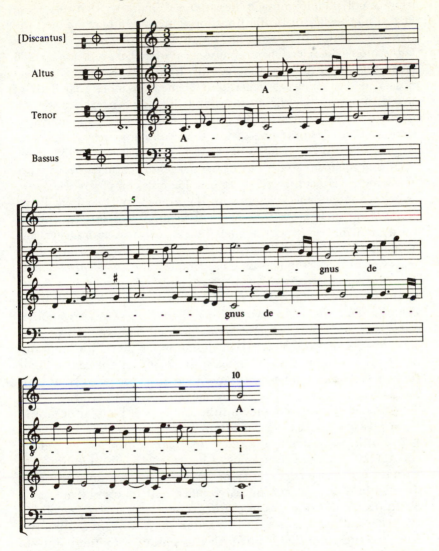

three. Binchois's *Filles à marier* has a sustained tenor and contratenor (possibly instrumental) supporting two soprano voices written in free imitation and a vivacious syllabic style. Most of Ockeghem's chansons, as well as those of his hardly less famous contemporary Antoine Busnois (d. 1492), made use of the traditional *formes fixes* of courtly poetry.

The chanson in the generation of Obrecht, Isaac, and Josquin may be studied in one of the most famous of all music anthologies, the *Harmonice Musices Odhecaton A,* which was published by Petrucci at Venice in 1501 (see facsimile, p. 109). The title means

The
Odhecaton

"One hundred songs [actually there are only ninety-six] of harmonic [that is, polyphonic] music"; the letter "A" indicates that this is the first of a series of such collections, of which the other volumes, the *Canti B* and *Canti C*, were in fact issued in 1502 and 1504. The *Odhecaton* is a selection of chansons written between about 1470 and 1500; it includes pieces ranging from late Burgundian composers to the "modern" generation. Somewhat more than half of the chansons are for three voices, and these in general are written in the older styles. Among the composers represented in the collection are Isaac, Josquin, and two of their contemporaries, Alexander Agricola (*ca.* 1446–1506) and Loyset Compère (*ca.* 1455–1518).

During the first two decades of the sixteenth century various types of chanson were cultivated by Franco-Flemish composers who were associated more or less closely with the French royal court at Paris. Some of these chansons were entirely original compositions; others incorporated already existing melodies. By contrast with Ockeghem, Josquin virtually abandoned the *formes fixes;* rather, many of his texts are strophic, though some are simple four- or five-line poems. In *Mille regretz* (NAWM/S 24), for example, every voice is essential to the conception, for this is no longer an accompanied song but a composition in which a pair of voices sometimes answers another pair, as in the words "et paine douloureuse" (Example VI–5, measures 20–24), or two voices are in imitation, as the cantus and alto on "brief mes jours definer" (measures 27–30), or the entire choir repeats the same phrase twice and then tacks on a coda on this same text at the end. All voices are meant to be sung.

Sometimes Josquin adopted a tune and text of popular origin. In *Faulte d'argent* he set the melody in strict canon at the lower fifth between the contratenor and the *quinta pars* ("fifth part"); around this the other three voices weave a network of close imitation, but without ever sacrificing clarity of texture. Another favorite procedure of Josquin, and also of his younger contemporary Antoine de Fevin (*ca.* 1470–1511), was to place a similarly borrowed melody in the tenor and enclose it with two outer voices which echo motives from the tune in a lighthearted play of imitative counterpoint—an adaptation of the *cantus firmus* technique. Still another method was to use separate motives from a given melody in a free four-part polyphonic texture. Again, the tune, or a paraphrased version of it, might be heard in the highest voice. In all these and other ways composers in the period 1500–1520 aimed to blend popular elements with the courtly and contrapuntal tradition of the chanson.

Josquin des Prez

Throughout the history of Western music, periods of exceptionally intense creative activity have occurred, during which the curve of

EXAMPLE VI–5 Chanson: *Mille regretz*, Josquin des Prez

I feel so much sadness and painful distress that soon my days will seem to decline.

© 1964 by the President and Fellows of Harvard College. Reprinted by permission.

musical production rises to a notable peak. The early sixteenth century was such a period. Out of the extraordinarily large number of first-rank composers living around 1500, one, Josquin des Prez, must be counted among the greatest of all time. Few musicians have enjoyed higher renown while they lived, or exercised more profound and lasting influence on those who came after them. Josquin was hailed by contemporaries as "the best of the composers of our time," the "Father of Musicians." "He is the master of the notes," said Martin Luther. "They must do as he wills; as for the other composers, they have to do as the notes will."

Josquin was born about 1440 in the province of Hainaut, the present Franco-Belgian border region. From 1473 to at least 1479, and probably longer, he was a member of the ducal chapel of the Sforza family in Milan, and perhaps remained under the patronage of Cardinal Ascanio Sforza until the latter's death in 1505. From 1486 to 1494 we hear of him from time to time at the Papal chapel in Rome; from 1501 to 1503 he apparently was in France, perhaps at

Josquin's career

the court of Louis XII. In 1503 he was appointed *maestro di cappella* at the court of Ferrara, but in the next year he left Italy for France. Toward the end of his life he returned to his natal region and died at Condé-sur-l'Escaut in 1521. His compositions were published in large numbers of sixteenth-century printed collections, and also occur in many of the manuscripts of the time. They include altogether about eighteen Masses, one hundred motets, and seventy chansons and other secular vocal works.

The high proportion of motets in Josquin's output is noteworthy. In his day the Mass was still the traditional vehicle by which a composer was expected to demonstrate mastery of his craft; but because of its liturgical formality, unvarying text, and established musical conventions, the Mass offered little opportunity for experimentation. The motets were freer; they could be written for a wide range of texts, all relatively unfamiliar and hence suggesting interesting new possibilities for word-music relationships. In the sixteenth century, therefore, the motet, rather than the Mass, came to be the most progressive form of sacred composition.

Josquin's Masses

Josquin's Masses illustrate many of the techniques and devices that were commonly used in the sixteenth century. The theme of the Mass *Hercules dux Ferrariae* offers an example of what the sixteenth century called a *soggetto cavato,* a "subject [or theme] carved out" of a word or sentence by letting each vowel indicate a corresponding syllable of the hexachord, thus:

Hercules, or Ercole I, Duke of Ferrara from 1471 to 1505, from whose name this theme was derived, was a patron for whom Josquin wrote at least two other works in addition to this Mass.

Parody Masses

Josquin's Mass *Malheur me bat* is an instance of a procedure that became more common later in the sixteenth century. This Mass is based on a chanson by Ockeghem; but instead of only a single voice, all the voices of the chanson are employed at one time or another and subjected to free fantasy and expansion. A Mass which thus takes over not merely a single voice, but several—including the characteristic motives, progressions, or even the general structure and the musical substance—of some pre-existing chanson, Mass, or motet, is called a *parody Mass.* (This somewhat unfortunate term, of nineteenth-century German coinage, refers only to a method of composition and has no pejorative meaning; an alternative term is *derived Mass*.) The extent of borrowing can vary tremendously; more important, so can the degree of originality in treatment of the borrowed material. One extreme consists merely in putting new words under old music, a procedure sometimes called "parody" but better denoted by the word *contrafactum*. A *cantus firmus* Mass with a borrowed tune in the tenor part exemplifies the typical fifteenth-century method; in an extension of this practice, motives from the given melody may be heard in other voices besides the tenor. The decisive step toward the parody Mass is taken when the chosen model is no longer a single melodic line but a whole texture of contrapuntal voices. Foreshadowings, isolated instances of the new technique, appear sporadically in Mass music from the fourteenth century on; the trend accelerates greatly in the early sixteenth century. The full-fledged parody Mass—in this state perhaps better termed a *paraphrase Mass*—not only borrows musical material to a significant extent but also makes something new out of it, especially by means of combining borrowed motives in an original contrapuntal structure with systematic imitation among all the voices, and finally replaces the *cantus firmus* Mass as the dominant form by about 1540.

In Josquin's Mass *Faysans regres* there is a fascinating mixture of motives from secular and sacred sources. This Mass takes its theme from the second part of a rondeau by Walter Frye, an English composer of the mid-fifteenth century who was perhaps associated with the Burgundian court. (The same theme was used in a chanson by Alexander Agricola, published in Petrucci's *Canti C* of 1504.) Josquin, taking over only a single phrase of the melody, constructs the tenor of his Mass from beginning to end on nothing but this four-note motive, transposed to different scale degrees and subjected to a myriad of rhythmic variations; in the Agnus Dei it is combined with another motive (in the altus) from the first part of the original chanson. In addition, in the Kyrie, Gloria, and Credo, Josquin introduces appropriate Gregorian melodies. The superius uses only these liturgical motives and figures derived from them; the melodic material of the altus comes chiefly from the superius, and that of the bassus from either the superius or the tenor. Example VI–6 shows how expertly Josquin worked.

Hearing Italian popular music, such as frottole, or laude, must have made Josquin particularly aware of the potential of simple chordal harmony. A motet that is in part modeled on this style, apparently dating from Josquin's early years, is *Tu solus, qui facis mirabilia* (NAWM/S 17). Sections of four-part declamatory homorhythmic music alternate with episodes in which pairs of voices imitate each other. The chordal sections use a technique resembling

EXAMPLE VI–6 Kyrie I from the Mass, *Faysans regres*, Josquin

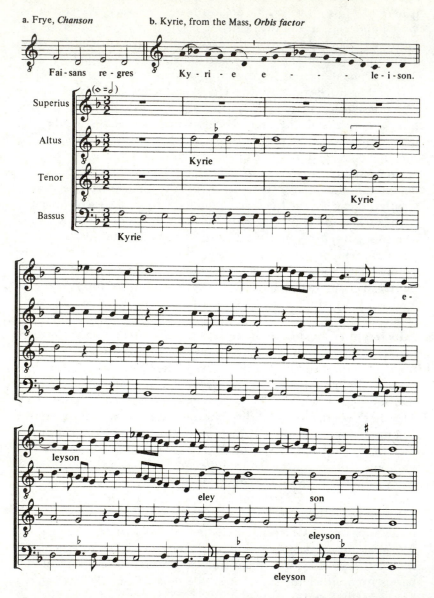

a. Frye, *Chanson*   b. Kyrie, from the Mass, *Orbis factor*

what was later to be known as *falsobordone*,[3] a procedure for improvising harmonizations of the psalm recitation formulas. What we

[3] *Falsobordone* and *fauxbourdon* were two methods of improvising polyphony on a plainchant that, if linked by a cognate term, appeared to stem from different traditions. *Falsobordone*, consisting mainly of root-triads harmonizing a recitation tone in the treble, was applied particularly in Italy and Spain to the psalms, Magnificats and Lamentations, while *fauxbourdon*, a French technique in which the chant was accompanied by sixths and thirds spreading out to octaves and fifths at cadences, was applied particularly to hymns.

call root-position chords are used exclusively, or, as it would have
been expressed then, each chord contains both the third and the
fifth to the bass. In some manuscripts certain sequences of such
chords have fermatas above them, indicating flexible durations. At
other times Josquin has carefully followed the accentuation and
rhythm of speech, as in the passage quoted in Example VI–7. The
division of the choir into voice pairs at the words "Ad te solum
confugimus, in te solum confidimus" is an exceptionally fine use of
this common device, suggested here naturally by the parallelism of
the words.

EXAMPLE VI–7   Motet: *Tu solus, qui facis mirabilia,* Josquin

In you alone we seek refuge, in you alone we place our trust

There was more to setting texts meaningfully, however, than
getting the word accents and rhythms right, and making them audible, as Josquin realized more and more in the course of his career.
In his late motets he drew on every resource then available to a
composer to bring home the message of the text.

"Suiting the music to the meaning of the words, expressing the
power of each different emotion, making the things of the text so
vivid that they seem to stand actually before our eyes . . ."—these
words are from a famous description of the music of a later Franco-
Netherlandish composer,[4] but they apply equally well to Josquin.
The author adds: "This kind of music is called *musica reservata.*"
This strange term (literally, "reserved music") seems to have come
into use shortly after the middle of the sixteenth century to denote
the advanced or "new" style of those composers who, motivated by
a desire to give strong and detailed reflection of the words, intro-

**Musica
reservata**

---

[4] Wolfgang Boetticher, *Orlando di Lasso,* I, 240. The passage refers to the
Penitential Psalms of Orlando di Lasso, which were written about 1560 and published in 1584. The author was Samuel Quickelberg, a Dutch scholar and
physician residing at the court of Munich; the date of his description is 1565.

duced chromaticism, harmonic freedom, ornaments, and contrasts of rhythm and texture in their music to a degree hitherto unknown. There is also, perhaps, the implication that such music was "reserved" for a particular patron's chambers. The expression *musica reservata* occurs occasionally in other writings of the late sixteenth and early seventeenth centuries with various meanings that are not clearly explained. Insofar as it refers to vivid musical expression of moods and images suggested by the text, one may justly call Josquin its originator, or at least its precursor.

One of the most eloquent of his motets is *Absalon fili mi* (*O My Son Absalom;* David's lament in II Samuel xviii: 33 is one of the sources of the text), believed to have been written for Pope Alexander VI in mourning for the murder of his son Juan Borgia in 1497. Toward the end it has an extraordinary passage of tone-painting on the words "but go down weeping to the grave" (Example VI–8). Here the voices descend not only melodically but also harmonically, taking the music through the circle of fifths from $B\flat$ to $G\flat$. This

EXAMPLE VI–8   Motet: *Absalon fili mi,* Josquin

But let me descend to hell, weeping.

shows Josquin as a bold experimenter, for the early sixteenth century as a rule never went in this direction beyond $E\flat$, and even that note occurred only rarely.

Josquin had by this time attained a consummate mastery of the fugal technique, which he demonstrated in the beautiful motet for four voices, *Ave Maria*, dating from about the same year. Each phrase of text has its own musical motive, which is first presented in imitation by each voice in turn; the musical sentence thus initiated comes eventually to a cadence, and a similar sentence, on the next phrase of the text and with its own musical motive, begins. But the cadences are concealed by overlapping, so that while some of the voices are still finishing one sentence, others are begining the next, and the music continues without obvious division into sections. This was the basic plan of a sixteenth-century motet. However, the plan was subject to various modifications in order to avoid the danger of monotony arising from the same kind of texture too long continued and in order to achieve clear formal outlines and proportioned structure in the work as a whole.

Some of the means that Josquin used to attain this balance and formal articulation were: (1) the repetition of phrases, either literally or with added voices; or—frequent with Josquin and not uncommon with other composers of the time—with contrasting pairs of voices; (2) division of the work into large sections, set off by simultaneous cadencing of all voices and by the introduction of changes in meter and tempo; (3) a rounded three-part form, resulting from the similarity of sections one and three and their contrast with section two; (4) a purposive approach to cadences: the cadence of one part may be signalized by a long preparation on the dominant with threefold repetition of the bass motive and the coming together of all voices in a chordal ensemble at the end; or by a similar piling-up of voices and a marked quickening of the harmonic pulse as well as of the movement of the individual voice-parts and increasing use of dissonances. This "drive to the cadence" was characteristic of all Netherlands polyphony between 1480 and 1530.

Motet structure

Josquin was a composer of the period of transition between medieval and modern times, as Monteverdi was between the Renaissance and Baroque, Handel between the Baroque and Classical periods, and Beethoven between the Classical and Romantic. Josquin and Beethoven resemble each other in many ways. In both, the strong impulse of personal utterance struggled against the limits of the musical language of their time. Both were tormented by the creative process, and worked slowly and with numerous revisions. Both had a sense of humor; both, because of their independent attitude, had trouble with their patrons. Both, in their best works, achieved that combination of intensity and order, individuality and universality, which is the mark of genius. It may be added that both annoyed fastidious critics for the same reasons: "He lacked moderation, and the judgment that comes from sound learning, so that he did not always properly curb the violent impulses of his imagination." This was said by the Swiss theorist Glarean[5] about Josquin, whom he nevertheless admired above all other composers.

Some Contemporaries of Obrecht and Josquin

Henricus Isaac

A general history of music must, for lack of space, renounce all hope of doing justice to the many excellent composers of the early sixteenth century who were contemporary with Obrecht and Josquin. Henricus Isaac (*ca.* 1450–1517), a Netherlander by birth, was a prolific composer in all the forms current in his time; he absorbed into his own style musical influences from Italy, France, Germany, and the Netherlands, so that his output is more fully international in character than that of any other composer of his generation. He wrote a large number of songs with French, German, and Italian texts, and many other short chanson-like pieces which, since they occur without words in the sources, are usually regarded as having been composed for instrumental ensembles. During his first sojourn at Florence, Isaac undoubtedly composed music for some of the *canti carnascialeschi,* "carnival songs" which were sung in gay processions and pageants that marked the Florentine holiday seasons. The simple chordal declamatory style of these mainly anonymous part songs influenced Isaac's settings of German popular songs such as *Innsbruck, ich muss dich lassen.* The melody of this perennial favorite was later adapted to sacred words and became widely known as the chorale *O Welt, ich muss dich lassen (O world, I now must leave thee).*

Isaac's sacred compositions include some thirty settings of the Ordinary of the Mass and a cycle of motets based on the liturgical texts and melodies of the Proper of the Mass (including many sequences) for a large portion of the church year. This monumental cycle of motets, comparable to the *Magnus liber* of Leonin and Perotin, was commissioned by the church at Constance; it was completed by Isaac's pupil Ludwig Senfl, and is known as the *Choralis Constantinus.* Its musical style is representative of the Netherlands practice of Isaac's time: a prevalent texture of imitative counterpoint is clarified by repetitions and melodic sequences, and it is often evident that Isaac took particular care to emphasize important

---

5 Dodecachordon, 1547, III, xxiv.

or dramatic words. Many of the melodic lines, especially in the altus and bassus voices, have a rather unvocal character which is not uncommon in the works of this period, and which may or may not indicate that the composer had instrumental performance in mind.

One of the foremost Franco-Netherlandish composers of the early sixteenth century was Pierre de la Rue (*ca.* 1460–1518), whose numerous Masses and motets still await a comprehensive modern edition. The supreme example of his technical skill is the Mass *Ave Sanctissima*. This is a parody Mass based on a motet which is perhaps by la Rue himself although it is also attributed to another Franco-Flemish composer, Philippe Verdelot (d. *ca.* 1545). La Rue's *Ave Sanctissima* is for six voices, and is written entirely in canon: from three notated voices three others are derived by canonic imitation at the fourth above, at various distances in each movement. The miracle, however, is not the technique but the music itself, for within this rigid and extremely difficult technical framework la Rue created one of the most beautiful settings ever made of the Mass.

Pierre de la Rue

Another important contemporary of Obrecht and Josquin was the Franco-Netherlander Jean Mouton (1459–1522). Mouton held several positions in France before beginning his long period of service in the royal chapel under two kings, Louis XII and Francis I. Described by the theorist Glarean as one of the "emulators" of Josquin, Mouton wrote Masses and motets that are remarkable for their smooth-flowing melodic lines and skillful use of various unifying devices. He was highly esteemed in Italy as well as in France, and is of particular historical interest also as a teacher of Adrian Willaert (*ca.* 1490–1562), a Netherlander who was to become the leading early figure in the rise of the Venetian school (see below, pages 177ff.).

Jean Mouton

VII

New Currents in the Sixteenth Century

The Franco-Flemish Generation of 1520–1550

The thirty years between 1520 and 1550 witnessed a constantly growing diversity of musical expression. In every country new types and forms of vocal music began gradually to modify the dominant cosmopolitan style of the Netherlands; the amount and importance of instrumental music also increased. The generation of Netherlanders after Josquin was not unaffected by these changes. Those who lived abroad, especially those in Italy and southern Germany, were naturally influenced by acquaintance with the musical idioms of their adopted homes.

Nicolas
Gombert

The Netherlands motet style of the period 1520–50 is found in the works of Nicolas Gombert (*ca*. 1500–*ca*. 1556), supposedly a pupil of Josquin, who as an official of the chapel of the Emperor Charles V accompanied the court on numerous voyages and worked at Vienna, Madrid, and Brussels. His motet *Super flumina Babilonis* exemplifies this motet style: a continuous series of imitative sentences with interlocking cadences, save for a single short contrasting section in triple meter and fauxbourdon harmonies; a generally smooth and uniform texture, without many rests, with all dissonances carefully prepared and resolved—quite undramatic in effect as compared with many of the works of Josquin, though not without a sensitive feeling for the rhythm and general mood of the text. The

130

majority of Gombert's 169 motets are divided into two approximately equal parts or sections; in some instances these are thematically connected by making the closing portions identical in both text and music.

Another important Netherlands composer of this period was Jacob Clement or, in Latinized form, Jacobus Clemens (*ca.* 1510–*ca.* 1556); he was called "Clemens non Papa," probably to distinguish him from a poet named Jacobus Papa who lived in the same city of Ypres. All but one of Clemens's Masses are of the parody type. His motets are similar in style to Gombert's, though the phrases are somewhat more clearly distinguished, and the melodic motives more carefully shaped to the sense of the words.

Jacobus Clemens

The most notable Netherlander in Italy during this period was Adrian Willaert. Born around 1490 in Flanders, he studied composition with Mouton at Paris. After holding various positions in Rome, Ferrara, and Milan, Willaert was appointed director of music in St. Mark's church at Venice in 1527. Here he remained until his death in 1562, conducting, composing, and training many eminent pupils, through whom his fame and influence spread all over Italy. Willaert, representing the tradition of Josquin, Mouton, and other composers associated with the French Court, must be regarded as one of the principal founders of the Venetian school and a pioneer of new tendencies that were to become increasingly important in the second half of the century.

Adrian Willaert

In Willaert's sacred compositions, which are the bulk of his work, the text determines every dimension of the musical form. He was one of the first to insist that syllables be printed carefully under notes. For example, in the antiphon *O crux, splendidior* (NAWM/S 18) for First Vespers on the feast of the Finding of the Holy Cross, the sections of the music are carefully laid out according to the accentuation, rhetoric, and punctuation of the text. Among the precepts he observed was never to allow a rest to interrupt a word or thought within a vocal line, never to make a cadence in a voice before a unit of text has been completed, and to delay a strong cadence until the end of a principal period in the text. Although *O crux* is based throughout on the plainchant antiphon, no one voice monopolizes it as in the older *cantus firmus* procedure, nor does it appear in canon in two voices, as in some of Willaert's earlier motets; rather in this work, published in 1550, the chant fragments are sources of subject-matter for imitative development which is extremely free.

How to preserve modality in polyphony, where it tends to be undermined by *musica ficta,* was a problem faced by the composers of the early Renaissance, who clung to the modes as a link to the Christian tradition and as a path to the effects they were said to have had in antiquity. But few succeeded as Willaert did to capture the essence of a mode. In *O crux* he adopted Mode I of the chant but transposed it down a fifth by means of a flat. He gave prominence in the initial melodies of all the voices to the "species" of fifth and fourth characteristic of Mode I, namely the rising fifth *G–D,* which in this key has the species tone–semitone–tone–tone, and the fourth *D–G,* tone–semitone–tone (Example VII–1). He fur-

EXAMPLE VII–1   Opening of Motet *O crux, splendidior,* Willaert

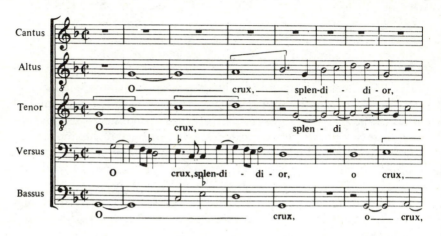

O cross, shining more brightly than all the stars, renowned throughout the world

ther saw to it that each of the perfect cadences—those referred to above as marking major points of punctuation—closed on G. It was with good reason that his pupil, Zarlino, considered Willaert to have reached the zenith, the standard of perfection, in the manner of composition that Zarlino deemed the only proper one for sacred music.

The Rise of National Styles

ITALY

Although Franco-Netherlandish composers were scattered all over Western Europe in the early sixteenth century, and their idiom was a common international musical language, each country also had its own distinctive music which was certainly better known and probably better enjoyed by most people than the learned art of the northerners. Gradually in the course of the sixteenth century these various national idioms rose to prominence and eventually caused the Netherlands style to be modified in varying degrees. The process was most clearly marked in Italy. When Petrucci started to print music at Venice in 1501, he began with chansons, Masses, and motets; but then, from 1504 to 1514, he published no fewer than eleven collections of strophic Italian songs, set syllabically to music in four parts, having marked rhythmic patterns, simple diatonic harmonies, and a definitely homophonic style with the melody in the upper voice. These songs were called *frottole* (singular, *frottola*), a generic term which embraces many sub-types. **The frottola**

The religious counterpart of the frottola was the polyphonic *lauda* (pl. *laude*), a popular nonliturgical devotional song. The texts were sometimes in Italian, sometimes in Latin; these were set to four-part music, the melodies being often taken from secular songs. **The lauda**

Although French composers of Masses and motets in the early sixteenth century continued to write in a slightly modified version of the international style of the Netherlands, chanson composers in this period and during the long reign of Francis I (1515–47) developed a type of chanson that was more distinctively national in both poetry and music. Such works appeared in the publications of the first French music printer, Pierre Attaingnant, who between 1528 and 1552 brought out in Paris more than fifty collections of chansons, about 1,500 pieces altogether. **FRANCE**

Typical chansons of the earliest Attaingnant collections resembled in many respects the Italian frottola and the *canti carnascialeschi*. They were light, fast, strongly rhythmic songs for four voices, syllabic, with many repeated notes, predominantly in duple meter with occasional passages in triple meter, and predominantly homophonic with the principal melody in the highest voice, but not excluding short points of imitation. They had distinct short sections, which as a rule were repeated so as to form an easily grasped pattern, such as *aabc* or *abca*. The texts covered a considerable range of verse forms and subjects, a favorite topic being some amatory situation that might allow the poet occasion for all sorts of pleasant comments and equivocal allusions. Not all the texts, however, were frivolous. The beginning of one of these chansons, by Claudin de Sermisy (*ca.* 1490–1562), is illustrated in Example VII–2 (for the entire song, see NAWM/S 25). **The new French chanson**

The two principal composers of chansons in the first Attaingnant collections were Sermisy and Clément Janequin (*ca.* 1485–*ca.* 1560). Janequin was particularly celebrated for his descriptive chansons in free form, songs not unlike the Italian fourteenth-century caccia, introducing imitations of bird calls, street cries, and the like. The most famous of Janequin's descriptive chansons was one entitled *La Guerre,* traditionally supposed to have been written about the Battle of Marignan (1515); it is the ancestor of innumerable "battle" pieces in the sixteenth century and afterward. The leading composer of chansons at Paris after Sermisy and Janequin was Pierre Certon

EXAMPLE VII–2 Chanson: *Vivray je tousjours en soucy,*
Claudin de Sermisy

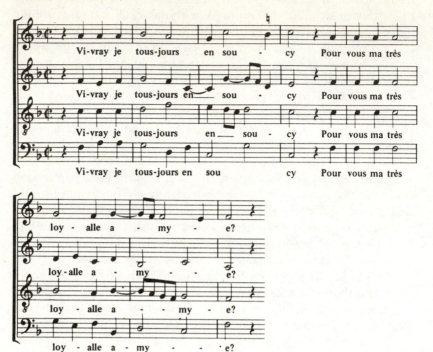

Shall I live ever in worry for you, my very faithful love?

(*ca.* 1510–72), whose works ably continue the style founded by Sermisy.

GERMANY A distinctive type of German polyphonic *Lied* (song) came into existence during the fifteenth century. Composers skillfully combined German melodic material with a conservative method of setting and a contrapuntal technique derived from the Netherlands. The first real masters of the polyphonic Lied were Isaac and his contemporary Heinrich Finck (1445–1527).

Another excellent composer of Lieder was Paul Hofhaimer (1459–1537), court organist of the Emperor Maximilian. With Ludwig Senfl, the Lied reached artistic perfection; some of his Lieder are, in all respects except the language of the text, full-fledged motets of the Netherlands type, and most beautiful examples of that style.[3] Senfl also wrote many shorter songs on folklike tenor tunes, filled with picturesque or humorous touches, yet always exhibiting a certain earthy, serious quality that seems inseparable from the German musical feeling.

Spanish sacred polyphony, like that of all continental Europe in the late fifteenth and early sixteenth centuries, was strongly under

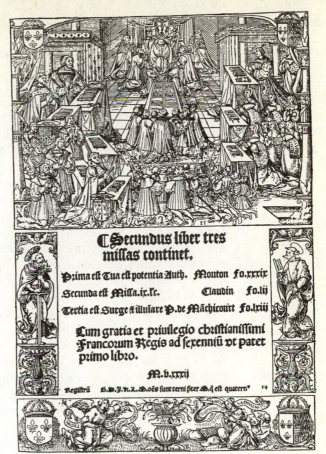

Title page for the second of seven volumes of Masses published by Attaingnant in 1532; it contains works by Mouton, Claudin (de Sermisy), and Pierre de Manchicourt. The scene shows a mass at the court of the King of France, Francis I.

SPAIN

the influence of the Netherlands style. Gombert, Manchicourt, Crécquillon, and other Netherlanders worked from time to time in Spain, and Spanish manuscripts of the period include many works by Franco–Flemish masters. Within its basic framework of Netherlands technique, however, Spanish sacred music was marked by a particular sobriety of melody and moderation in the use of contrapuntal artifices, together with a passionate intensity in the expression of religious emotion. These qualities may be heard in the motet *Emendemus in melius* (*Let us Amend*) by Cristóbal de Morales (*ca.* 1500–53), the most eminent Spanish composer of the early sixteenth century and one who had acquired fame in Italy during his residence at Rome from 1535 to 1545 as a member of the Papal chapel.

Morales was one of a large number of Spanish composers in the sixteenth century; some of these men worked entirely in their own country, while others, like Morales and Victoria, were closely associated with the music of the church at Rome. As in Germany and Italy, so also in Spain: after the middle of the sixteenth century the traditional Netherlands technique was gradually absorbed into a new style of both sacred and secular music, a style determined in large part by national characteristics.

EASTERN EUROPE

To varying degrees and at varying intervals of time, the eastern countries of Europe participated in the general musical developments of the late medieval and Renaissance periods. As far as Catholic church music was concerned, there was a common basis in Gregorian Chant, examples of which are found in Eastern manuscripts from as early as the eleventh and twelfth centuries. Everywhere, elements of foreign origin intermingled with native popular traditions; melodies of sequences, tropes, and liturgical dramas were adapted to vernacular texts. By the sixteenth century Polish and Bohemian composers were writing chansons, Masses, and motets as well as music for lute, organ, and instrumental ensembles. Polish organ tablatures are particularly important in this period. The leading composers of Catholic church music were Wacław of Szamotuł (*ca.* 1520–*ca.* 1567) in Poland, and in Bohemia, Jacobus Gallus and Jan Trajan Turnovský, sometimes called the "Bohemian Palestrina."

ENGLAND

The greatest English musician of the early sixteenth century was John Taverner (*ca.* 1495–1545), a man whose career included four years as choirmaster in an Oxford college, a short term of imprisonment for heresy, and an active part in the suppression of the monasteries as an agent of Thomas Cromwell in 1538–39. Taverner's *Western Wynde* Mass is one of three on this tune by English composers of the sixteenth century; all three are peculiar in that they treat the *cantus firmus* not in any of the conventional ways, but rather as a series of variations, in a manner similar to English keyboard variations of the later part of the century. In some of his shorter sacred works, Taverner makes use of a simple chordal style, with antiphonal choral effects.

Toward the middle of the century the leading English composer was Thomas Tallis (*ca.* 1505–85), whose musical production bridges early and late sixteenth-century English styles and whose career reflects the religious upheavals and bewildering political changes that affected English church music in this period. His late works include two sets of *Lamentations* which are among the most eloquent of all settings of these verses from the prophet Jeremiah, texts which first attracted the attention of composers shortly after the middle of the fifteenth century and which in the sixteenth century formed a distinct type of church composition.

The Rise of Instrumental Music

Although the period from 1450 to 1550 was primarily an era of vocal polyphony so far as written music is concerned, the same hundred years witnessed a growth of interest in instrumental music on the part of serious composers and the beginnings of independent styles and forms of writing for instruments. As we have already seen, instruments took part with voices in the performance of every type of polyphonic music in the Middle Ages, although we cannot be certain of the extent or the exact manner of the participation. Moreover, a great deal of music was performed purely instrumentally, including on occasion many of the compositions we customarily regard as at least partly vocal; medieval manuscripts, which include keyboard arrangements and elaborations of cantilenas and motets, undoubtedly represent only a fraction of the music that was transcribed in this way; and in addition independent instrumental music, in the form of dances, fanfares, and the like, has not come down to us apparently for the reason that it was always either played from memory or improvised. So the seeming increase in instrumental music after 1450 is to a considerable degree an ilusion; it means only that now more of this music began to be written down and that consequently we are in a position to know something definite about it. The fact that it was written down at all reflects an improvement in the status of instrumental musicians, who, in the Middle Ages, had been regarded for the most part with contempt or condescension. Even so, the written and printed documents do not by any means preserve all the instrumental music of the Renaissance, since there was still a great deal of improvisation; and much of the notated instrumental (as well as some of the vocal) music of this period was elaborated in performance by improvised embellishments.

One sign of the sixteenth century's growing regard for instrumental music was the publication of books which describe instruments or give instructions for playing them. The first such publication was in 1511; others followed in increasing numbers throughout the century. It is significant that from the outset most of these books were written not in Latin but in the vernacular; they were addressed not to theorists, but to practicing musicians. From them we can learn some of the problems of pitch, temperament, and tuning in this period, and can observe the importance that was attached to improvising ornaments on a given melodic line.

In Sebastian Virdung's *Musica getutscht und ausgezogen* (*A Summary of [the science of] Music in German*) of 1511, and much more fully in the second volume of Michael Praetorius's *Syntagma musicum* (*Treatise of Music*) of 1618, there are descriptions and woodcuts of the various instruments in use during the sixteenth century. Two things are of particular interest: the extraordinary number and variety of wind instruments, and the fact that all instruments were built in sets or families, so that one uniform timbre was available throughout the entire range from bass to soprano.

Instruments

This is in keeping with the Renaissance ideal of a homogeneous sound mass; the "chest" or "consort"—the complete set—of three to eight recorders or viols, for example, corresponded to the complete "family" of voices ranging from bass to soprano.

Besides recorders, the principal wind instruments were the shawms (double-reed instruments), cromornes (or krummhorns, also

A plate from Michael Praetorius's Syntagma musicum, *showing sets of Renaissance horns: trombones (Nos. 1, 2, 3, and 4); cornetts (Nos. 5, 6, and 7, curved; Nos. 8 and 9, straight); trumpets (Nos. 10, 11, and 12); and (No. 13) a crook by the use of which a horn player could achieve extra tones.*

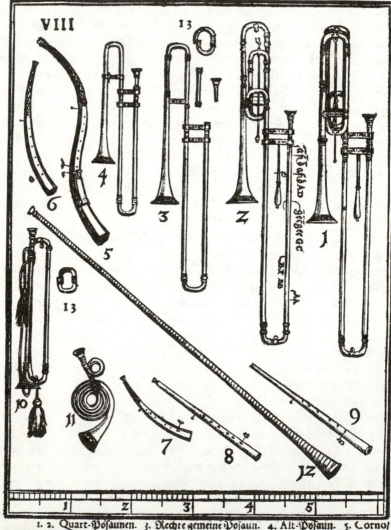

1. 2. Quart-Pofaunen. 3. Rechte gemeine Pofaun. 4. Alt-Pofaun. 5. Corno/ Groß Tenor-Cornet. 6. Recht Chor Zinck. 7. Klein Discant Zinck/so ein Quint höher. 8. Gerader Zinck mit ein Mundstück. 9. Still Zinck. 10. Trommet. 11. Jäger Trommet. 12. Hölzern Trommet. 13. Krumbbügel auff ein ganz Thon.

with a double reed, but softer than the shawm), and cornetts (made of wood or ivory, with cup-shaped mouthpieces); the trumpets and trombones were softer in tone than their modern counterparts. The viols differed in many details of construction from the present-day violin family of bowed instruments: the neck was fretted, there were six strings tuned a fourth apart with a major third in the middle (as *A-d-g-b-e'-a'*), and the tone was more delicate, finer, less *espressivo*—because without vibrato—than that of modern instruments of the violin type.

Another indication of the Renaissance ideal was the rise to prominence of solo instruments which could by themselves cover the entire compass of tones with a uniform sonority. The tone of the organ began to be varied by the addition of solo stops and stops of softer sound, which could be combined with the unvariable principals and mixtures of the medieval instrument. By about 1500 the large church organ was similar in essentials to the instrument as we know it today, although the pedal keyboard was employed in Germany and the Netherlands long before it was adopted in other countries. The medieval portative organ did not survive beyond the fifteenth century, but the sixteenth century had small positive organs, including the regal, which had reed pipes of a delicately strident tone.

There were two types of clavier instruments, the clavichord and the harpsichord. In the clavichord, the tone was produced by a metal tangent which struck the string and remained in contact with it; the tone was delicate, but within narrow limits its volume could be controlled by the performer and a slight vibrato could be imparted. Instruments of the harpsichord type were built in different shapes and sizes, and were known under various names (virginal, spinet, clavecin, clavicembalo, among others); in all these the sound was produced by a quill plucking the string. The tone was more robust than that of the clavichord, but could scarcely be shaded by varying the pressure on the key; different timbres and degrees of loudness were possible only by a special mechanism of stops. The clavichord was essentially a solo instrument for use in small rooms; the harpsichord was used for both solo and ensemble playing.

By far the most popular household solo instrument of the Renaissance was the lute. Lutes had been known in Europe for over five hundred years; before the end of the sixteenth century they were being built in various sizes, often of costly materials and with exquisite workmanship. A Spanish type of lute, the *vihuela de mano*, had a guitar-like body; but the standard lute was pear-shaped. It had one single and five double strings, tuned *G-c-f-a-d'-g'*; the neck was fretted and the pegbox turned back at a right angle. The usual method of playing was to pluck the strings with the fingers. Chords,

The lute

melodies, runs and ornaments of all kinds, eventually even contrapuntal pieces, could be performed on the lute; it was used as a solo instrument to accompany singing, and in ensembles, and a skilled player could produce a great variety of effects. A special kind of notation was used for lutenists, called *tablature,* the principle of which was to show, not the pitch of each sound, but the point at which the finger had to stop the strings in order to produce the required pitch. (See illustrations on pages 155 and 208). Tabulatures were also devised for viols and keyboard instruments.

Instrumental forms: the ricercar

The adaptation of vocal pieces to instrumental performance led naturally to certain species of instrumental compositions which, while not necessarily derived from any particular vocal piece, were obviously patterned on vocal prototypes. Such were the imitative *ricercar* and the *canzona,* instrumental counterparts respectively of the motet and chanson. The word *ricercar* comes from an Italian verb meaning both "to seek" or "search out," and "to attempt" or "try." Both of these meanings are reflected in the different types of instrumental pieces which in the first half of the sixteenth century are called ricercari. The earliest ones are improvisatory in character with sporadic bits of imitation; later ones achieve clearer form by means of some repetition of phrases and balanced passages of paired imitation. By 1540, ricercari appear which consist of a succession of themes without marked individuality or contrast, each developed in imitation and interlocked with the next by overlapping the cadence—in effect, a textless imitative motet. Ricercari of this kind were usually intended for ensemble playing, but they were written also for keyboard instruments and for the lute; they differ from strict vocal style simply by freer voice leading and by the addition on the printed pages of typically instrumental embellishments. However, the same name ricercare continued to be applied both to motet-like pieces of this kind and also the improvisatory type, as well as to pieces in a mixture of those two styles.

Canzona

Canzona is the Italian word for "chanson." An instrumental canzona in Italy was called a *canzon da sonar* ("chanson to be played") or *canzona alla francese* ("chanson in the French style"). Canzonas were written for both ensembles and solo instruments. The development of the canzona as an independent instrumental form in the second half of the sixteenth century had important historical consequences.

Dance music

Social dancing was more widespread and more highly regarded in the Renaissance than it had ever been in Western history. A considerable part of the instrumental music of the sixteenth century, therefore, consists of dance pieces for lute, keyboard, or ensembles; these are no longer improvised, as they were in the late Middle Ages, but are written out in tablatures or partbooks, and appear in printed collections issued by Petrucci, Attaingnant, and other pub-

An early sixteenth-century court scene. In the foreground, four couples dance "the great ball," a ceremonious pavane, while musicians accompany them on flute, trumpets, and drums.

lishers. As befits their purpose, these pieces usually have clearly marked and quite regular rhythmic patterns, and are divided into distinct sections. There is little or no contrapuntal interplay of lines, though the principal melody may be highly ornamented or colored. Commonly the dances were grouped in pairs or threes, and these groups are the historical precursors of the instrumental dance suite of later times. A favorite combination was a slow dance in duple meter followed by a fast one in triple meter on the same tune, the second dance thus constituting a variation of the first. One instance of this kind of pairing of dances is the combination, frequently found in French publications of the sixteenth century, of *pavane* and *gaillarde*. Similarly paired dances are found in Polish tablatures of the same period (See Example VII–3).

The dance pieces of the early sixteenth century owed little to vocal models, and in them, therefore, the characteristics of instrumental style could be freely developed. Much dance music, of course, in the sixteenth century as in later ages, became detached from its original purpose and developed into stylized pieces which retained the characteristic rhythms and general outlines of dances but which were obviously not intended for actual dancing—any more than the waltzes of Chopin were intended for ballroom waltzing.

The growth of instrumental style was related to the widespread practice of improvisation in the Renaissance. The peculiarly instrumental traits in the earliest written or printed instrumental music of the sixteenth century undoubtedly were for the most part only the

EXAMPLE VII–3 *Czayner Thancz* from the Tablature of John of Lublin

Improvisatory pieces

spelling out in notation of procedures that were already common in practice. Compositions in improvisatory style, not based on any given *cantus firmus* but unfolding freely, often in a somewhat rambling fashion, with varying textures and without continued adherence to a definite meter or form, are found among the earliest specimens of music for solo players (this style being obviously unsuited to ensembles). Such pieces appeared under various names: prelude or *preambulum, fantasia,* or *ricercare.* The fantasias of Luis Milán (*ca.* 1500–*ca.* 1561) in his *Libro de musica de vihuela de mano intitulado El Maestro* (Valencia, 1536) give us an idea of the improvisations that lutanists played before accompanying themselves or a singer in a lute song, such as those in his collections—*villancicos, sonetos,* and *romances.* Each of the fantasias is in a given mode—

no. 11, for example, is in Modes I and II (NAWM/S 31)—and the purpose was to set the tonality of the vocal piece that was to follow.

One other new form of composition, the *theme and variations*, probably began with the Spanish lute and keyboard composers in the first half of the sixteenth century. Here, as in other instrumental forms, the works of the great Spanish organist and composer Antonio de Cabezón (1510–1566) were outstanding. A form related to the theme with variations was the composition on a short ostinato pattern, the prototype of the later chaconne and passacaglia.

Variations

The Madrigal and Related Forms

The Italian madrigal of the sixteenth century had practically nothing in common with the madrigal of the fourteenth century but the name. The *trecento* madrigal was a strophic song with a refrain (ritornello); the early sixteenth-century madrigal as a rule made no use of a refrain or any other feature of the old *formes fixes* with their patterned repetitions of musical and textual phrases. It was a through-composed setting of a short poem, constructed as a series of (usually) overlapping sections, some contrapuntal and some homophonic, each based on a single phrase of the text. Most of the works in the first period of the madrigal production, from about 1520 to 1550, were set for four voices; after the middle of the century five voices became the rule, although six-part settings were not infrequent and the number might even rise occasionally to eight or ten. The word "voices" is to be taken literally: the madrigal was a piece of vocal chamber music intended for performance with one singer to a part; as always in the sixteenth century, however, instrumental doubling or substitution was possible and doubtless common.

Although essentially similar in form to the motet, the madrigal was usually more varied and vivid. Of course it was not subject to the restrictions of style that prevailed in church music; and the free atmosphere of the secular surroundings in which madrigals were sung encouraged experimentation. Consequently, madrigal composers developed pictorial and expressive writing to an extraordinary degree, and particularly experimented with harmonic boldness. Moreover, some madrigals of the second half of the century show the Renaissance *a cappella* ideal of equal voices being transformed into the Baroque ideal of dominating solo parts against a firm harmonic bass and chordal background. In these respects, the madrigal was the most progressive form of composition in the late sixteenth century, as the motet had been in the earlier part of the century and the Mass before that.

Most madrigal texts were sentimental or erotic in subject matter, with scenes and allusions borrowed from pastoral poetry. Usually

the text ended with an epigrammatic climax in the last line or
two. Madrigals were sung in all sorts of courtly social gatherings;
in Italy they were sung especially at meetings of the academies,
societies organized in the fifteenth and sixteenth centuries in many
cities for the study and discussion of literary, scientific, or artistic
matters. The output of madrigals and similar polyphonic songs in
Italy was enormous: some two thousand collections (counting reprints and new editions) were published between 1530 and 1600,
and the flood of production continued well into the seventeenth
century.

The leading early composers of Italian madrigals were Philippe
Verdelot (*ca.* 1480–1545), a Franco-Fleming who worked at Florence
and Rome; Costanzo Festa (*ca.* 1490–1545) of Rome, one of the few
Italians in the Papal chapel in the early sixteenth century and one
of the first Italian composers to offer serious competition to the
Netherlanders; Adrian Willaert at Venice; and Jacob Arcadelt (*ca.*
1505–*ca.* 1568), a northerner who for a time was head of the Pope's
chapel and later became a member of the Royal chapel at Paris. All
the composers wrote chansons as well as madrigals, and there was

EXAMPLE VII–4   Madrigal: *Ahime, dov'è 'l bel viso,* Jacob Arcadelt

*My dear treasure, the greatest good. Alas, who keeps it from me, who
hides it from me?*

probably a good deal of mutual influence between the two forms. Arcadelt's madrigal *Ahime, dov'è 'l bel viso* of around 1538 (NAWM/S 26) illustrates two aspects of this genre in an early stage. On the one hand, the homophonic motion, the square rhythms, and the strict adherence to the form of the verse ally it to the chanson and frottola. On the other hand, it is full of subtle expressive touches. The emotion-laden words "mio caro thesoro" (my dear treasure; Example VII–4), are heightened by turning from a C-major to a sustained B♭-major chord, which is outside the mode of the piece and causes a cross-relation with the previous harmony. At measure 25 the passage on the phrase "Oimè chi me'l ritiene" (Alas, who keeps it from me) is set to a plaintive series of parallel sixth-chords and at the same time introduces imitation.

Important innovations in the madrigal were made with the publication in 1542 of the first book of five-part madrigals by Cipriano de Rore (1516–65). Rore was a Netherlander who worked in Italy chiefly at Ferrara and Parma, although he also for a short time held the post of music director at St. Mark's in Venice as successor to his master Willaert. Rore's publications included five books of madrigals

Cipriano de Rore

EXAMPLE VII–5   Madrigal: *Datemi pace,* Cipriano de Rore

Give me peace, O my jarring thoughts
[the memory] which would destroy all that remains of me

for five voices and three books for four voices; these and other works were issued repeatedly in new printings and editions throughout the second half of the sixteenth century.

Rore's settings matched in refinement and imagery the verses of his preferred poet, Petrarch. *Datemi pace,* from the second book of madrigals for four voices of 1557, subjects every detail of the music to the sense and feeling of the sonnet. The antithesis in the first line between the sought-for peace and the painful thoughts that break into it is reflected in the contrast between the serene root-position harmonies and cheerful triple rhythms of the first half of the line, "Datemi pace" (Give me peace), and the staggered rhythms, the bleak chords of the 6th and $^6_4$, and the archaic fauxbourdon-like cadence of the second half of the line, "o duri miei pensieri" (O my jarring thoughts: Example VII–5a; the entire madrigal is in NAWM/S 27).

One result of composers' efforts to depict vividly the emotions of the text was their use of venturesome harmonic progressions, such as juxtaposition of chords whose roots are a major third apart (see Example VII–6) or sudden transitory modulations that touch distant points of the tonal spectrum (as in Example VII–5b), where within a few measures the harmony wanders far from the central G into B major and F major.

Netherlands madrigalists

Among the many northern composers who shared in the development of the Italian madrigal after the middle of the century, three in particular must be mentioned: Orlando di Lasso, Philippe de Monte, and Giaches de Wert. Orlando di Lasso (1532–94) is most important as a church composer, but his was a universal genius equally at home with the madrigal, the chanson, and the Lied. Philippe de Monte (1521–1603), like Lasso, was prodigiously productive in both the sacred and secular fields; he began writing madrigals in his youth in Italy and continued uninterruptedly through the many years of his service under the Habsburg Emperors in Vienna and Prague. He published thirty-two collections of secular madrigals, in addition to three or four books of *madrigali spirituali*. Giaches de Wert (1535–96), though Netherlandish by birth, spent nearly his entire life in Italy; he further developed the style of madrigal composition begun by Rore and his late quasi-dramatic madrigals apparently exercised an important influence on Monteverdi.

Luca Marenzio

The leading madrigalists toward the end of the century were Italians. Luca Marenzio (1553–99) was a composer of remarkable artistry and technique, in whose works contrasting feelings and visual details were depicted with utmost virtuosity. As was typical of madrigal composers of the late sixteenth century, Marenzio mainly used pastoral poetry as his texts. One of the most celebrated of his madrigals is a setting of a Petrarchan sonnet in which the mood of the opening lines:

Solo e pensoso i più deserti campi	Alone, thought-sick, I pace where none has been,
Vo misurando a passi tardi e lenti	Roaming the desert with dull steps and slow [1]

is suggested by means of a slow chromatic scale in the topmost voice, rising without a break from *g'* to *a''* and returning to *d''*, while the other voices form a background of expressively drooping figures for the first line and all but come to a dragging halt for the second—a masterpiece of sensitive musical imagery, harmonic refinement, and skilful contrapuntal writing.

[1] *The Sonnets of Petrarch,* Joseph Auslander, tr., 1931. Quoted by permission of the publishers, Longman, Green and Co.

EXAMPLE VII–6 Madrigal: *"Io parto" e non più dissi,* Carlo Gesualdo

Hence I remain in suffering. May I not cease [to languish in painful laments.]

Carlo Gesualdo

The height of chromaticism in the Italian madrigal was reached not in the works of Marenzio but in those of Carlo Gesualdo, Prince of Venosa (*ca.* 1560–1613), a picturesque character who was both "musician and murderer," as his biographer puts it. In some of his later madrigals Gesualdo carries chromatic harmony to a point that almost suggests Wagner. Chromaticism was for Gesualdo no mere affectation of antiquity but a deeply moving response to the text, as in Example VII–6 (see the entire madrigal in NAWM/S 28).

For the lover's exclamation "Dunque ai dolori resto" (Hence I remain in suffering), Gesualdo combined melodic half-step motion with the ambiguous successions of chords whose roots are a third apart. He fragments the poetic line, yet achieves continuity by avoiding conventional cadences.

Claudio Monteverdi

The musician who served as a transition figure from the sixteenth century to the seventeenth—that is, from the Renaissance to Baroque —was Claudio Monteverdi (1567–1643), one of the principal composers in the history of Western music. Monteverdi was born at Cremona and received his earliest training from Marc' Antonio Ingegneri, head of the music in the cathedral of that city. In 1590 Monteverdi entered the service of Vincenzo Gonzaga, Duke of Mantua, and in 1602 became master of the ducal chapel. From 1613 until his death in 1643 he was choirmaster at St. Mark's in Venice.

The works of Monteverdi with which we are concerned at present are the first five books of madrigals, published respectively in 1587, 1590, 1592, 1603, and 1606. In these madrigals Monteverdi, without going to such extremes as Gesualdo, demonstrated his mastery of the madrigal technique of the late sixteenth century, with its smooth combination of homophonic and contrapuntal part-writing, its faithful reflection of the text, and its freedom in the use of expressive harmonies and dissonances. But there were certain features —not altogether absent in the music of his contemporaries—which showed that Monteverdi was moving swiftly and with remarkable assurance toward the new style of the seventeenth century. For example, many of the musical motives are not melodic but declamatory, in the manner of recitative; the texture often departs from the Renaissance ideal of equal voices and becomes a duet over a harmonically supporting bass; and certain formal practices characteristic of the Baroque are foreshadowed. An example of the flexible, animated, vivid, and variegated style of Monteverdi's sixteenth-century madrigals, rich in musical invention, humorous and sensitive, audacious yet perfectly logical in harmonies, is the five-voice madrigal *Cruda Amarilli* (Example VII–7; the entire madrigal is in NAWM/S 32). Although many of Monteverdi's dissonances may be rationalized as embellishments, their real motivation was to convey through harmony, rather than through the graphic images

EXAMPLE VII–7 Madrigal: *Cruda Amarilli,* Claudio Monteverdi

Cruel Amaryllis, who with your name, to love alas, [bitterly you teach . . .]

of some earlier madrigals, the meaning and feeling of the poet's message.

The madrigal was not the only type of Italian secular polyphony in the sixteenth century. Among the lighter varieties of song was the *canzon villanesca* (peasant song) or *villanella,* which first appeared around Naples in the 1540s and flourished chiefly in the Neapolitan area. The villanella was a three-voice, strophic, lively little piece in homophonic style, in which composers often deliberately used parallel fifths—originally to suggest its supposedly rustic character, later perhaps to caricature the suave correctness of the madrigals, which were often parodied in both the words and music of the villanella. Neither the villanella nor any of the other lighter types of Italian song are to be regarded as distinctively popular or nationalistic; they were written by the same Italians and

Other Italian secular vocal forms

Netherlanders who composed serious madrigals, and were meant for the same sophisticated audiences. In the course of time the villanella became like the madrigal and gradually lost its own identity.

By the end of the sixteenth century the most important lighter forms of Italian vocal polyphony were the *canzonetta* ("little song") and the *balletto*. These two forms are similar; they are written in a neat, vivacious, homophonic style, with clear major-minor harmonies and distinct, evenly phrased sections which are often repeated. Balletti, as the name suggests, were intended for dancing as well as singing or playing; a "fa-la-la" refrain is one of their characteristics. The leading composer of canzonette and balletti was Giacomo Gastoldi (d. 1622). Both forms were popular in Italy, and were imitated by German and English composers.

GERMANY

Orlando di Lasso

Chief among the international composers in Germany in the sixteenth century was Orlando di Lasso, who entered the service of Duke Albrecht V of Bavaria in 1556 or 1557, became head of the ducal chapel in 1560, and remained in that post at Munich until his death in 1594. Among the vast number of Lasso's compositions were seven collections of German Lieder. The Lied *Ich armer Mann* has somewhat uncouth verses which Lasso matched with appropriate music (see Example VII–8). Lasso's setting no longer surrounds a familiar tune in the tenor by a web of counterpoint, as was done in earlier German Lieder; instead, he sets the text in the manner of a madrigal, with all the parts having equal importance in the variegated interplay of motives, bits of imitation, echoes, and mock-pathetic melismas at the phrase "muss ich im hader stahn" (I must always be bickering).

A fruitful union of Italian sweetness with German seriousness was achieved in the music of the greatest German composer of the late sixteenth century, Hans Leo Hassler. Born at Nuremberg in 1564, Hassler was studying in 1584 with Andrea Gabrieli at Venice; from 1585 until his death in 1612 he held various positions at Augsburg, Nuremberg, Ulm, and Dresden. His works comprise instrumental ensemble and keyboard pieces, canzonets and madrigals with Italian texts, German Lieder, Latin motets and Masses, and settings of Lutheran chorales. The two Lieder *Ach Schatz* and *Ach, süsse Seel'*[2] are good examples of Hassler's music, and show his suave melodic lines, sure harmonic structure, and clearly articulated form with its varied repetitions and balanced echoing of motives. Hassler's work stands nearly at the end of the age of German Renaissance polyphony for equal voices. The only notable German composers in this style after Hassler were Johann Hermann Schein (1586–1630) and Heinrich Schütz (1585–1672); but their Lieder and

---

[2] See HAM, No. 165 for *Ach Schatz,* and GMB, No. 152 for *Ach, süsse Seel'.*

madrigals in Italian style were youthful works, and both men were
more important for the Baroque than for the Renaissance.

EXAMPLE VII–8   Lied: *Ich armer Mann*, Orlando di Lasso

*I, poor man, what have I done? I have taken a wife. [It would be
better if I had never done it; how often I have rued it you may well
imagine:] all day long I am being scolded and nagged, [at bedtime
and at table].*

FRANCE

In France and the Netherlands the chanson continued to flourish in the second half of the sixteenth century. The old polyphonic tradition remained alive longest in the north, as may be seen from two books of chansons published by the Dutch composer Jan Sweelinck (1562–1621) in 1594 and 1612. In France, however, the tradition was modified by a lively interest in the Italian madrigal, the effects of which on French music were particularly evident in the period from 1560 to 1575. One of the principal mediators of the Netherlandish-Italian influence in France was Orlando di Lasso, whose powerful musical personality impressed itself on the chanson as on every other type of vocal composition in the later sixteenth century. Many of Lasso's chansons with French texts are written in a tight polyphonic texture with close imitations and sudden changes of pace in tense, delightfully humorous settings; others are in the homophonic style of the Parisian chanson, with varied rhythms which seem to spring spontaneously from each nuance and accent of the text. An example of a homophonic chanson, which also illustrates Lasso's gift for penetrating to the essential qualities of a style, is *Bon jour, mon coeur*.

Other chanson composers in France in the latter part of the sixteenth century were Claude Le Jeune (1528–1600), Guillaume Costeley (1531–1606), and Jacques Mauduit (1557–1627). Many of Le Jeune's chansons are serious polyphonic works in several sections for five or more voices, and have other points of similarity to the Italian madrigals of the Rore period. The later Italian madrigal experiments (for example, those of Marenzio and Gesualdo) were not favorably received in France; on the other hand, the villanella and balletto had many French imitators.

Musique mesurée

Along with the polyphonic chanson, a different type of chanson appeared in France about 1550. These new chansons were strictly homophonic, short, strophic, often with a refrain, and usually performed as a solo with lute accompaniment. They were at first called *vaudevilles*, a word whose etymology and precise meaning are obscure; later this type of song was known as an *air* or *air de cour* (court tune). The forms taken by these compositions in homophonic style with a musical meter bound to the meter of the text reflected the experiments of some poets and composers who in 1570 formed an *Académie de Poésie et de Musique* (Academy of Poetry and Music) under the patronage of King Charles IX. The poet Jean-Antoine de Baïf wrote strophic French verses in ancient classical meters (*vers mesurés à l'antique*), substituting for the modern accentual principle the ancient Latin usage of long and short syllables; and composers (Le Jeune, Mauduit, and others) set these verses to music for voices, strictly observing the rule of a long note for each long syllable and a note half as long for each short syllable.

The variety of verse patterns thus produced a corresponding variety of musical rhythms in which duple and triple groupings freely alternated. This *measured music (musique mesurée)*, as it was called, was too artificial a creation to endure for long, but it did serve to introduce nonregular rhythms into the later *air de cour,* a feature which remained characteristic of this form as it was developed by a school of French composers in the first half of the seventeenth century; and after about 1580, the *air de cour* was the predominant type of French vocal music.

The golden age of secular song in England came later than in the Continental countries. In 1588 (incidentally, the year of the Spanish Armada), Nicholas Yonge published at London *Musica transalpina,* a collection of Italian madrigals in English translation. Four more anthologies of Italian madrigals appeared in the next decade; these publications gave impetus to the rise of the English madrigal school which flourished in the last decade of the sixteenth century and continued, with decreasing momentum, in the early years of the seventeenth century. The leading composers were Thomas Morley (1557–1602), Thomas Weelkes (*ca.* 1575–1623), and John Wilbye (1574–1638). Morley, earliest and most prolific of the three, specialized in lighter types of madrigal and in the related forms of the *ballett* and *canzonet.* Balletts were derived from the like-named Italian form, especially the balletti of Gastoldi. They are songs mainly homophonic in texture with the tune in the topmost voice, in dance-like meter (as the name suggests), with distinct sections set off by full cadences and with repetitions resulting in formal patterns such as *AABB* or the like, and with two or three strophes sung to the same music. There is a refrain, often sung to the syllables *fa-la,* whence the pieces were sometimes called *fa-la's.*

ENGLAND

Such a madrigal is Weelkes's *O Care, thou wilt despatch me* (NAWM/S 29). Particularly notable is the opening, with its learned imitations in both direct and contrary motion and the chain of suspensions to convey the poet's complaint (Example VII–9). Weelkes's harmony is as intense and wry as Marenzio's or Gesualdo's, but the overall effect is one of suave vocality and broadly sweeping momentum.

The English madrigal

The English madrigal differs from its Italian prototype basically in the greater attention it gives to the overall musical structure, in its "preoccupation with purely musical devices, a reluctance to follow the Italians in splitting up compositions mercurially at the whim of the text. The English madrigalist is first of all a musician; his Italian colleague is often more of a dramatist."[3] Madrigals, balletts, and canzonets were all written primarily for unac-

[3] Joseph Kerman, *The Elizabethan Madrigal,* 254

EXAMPLE VII–9 Madrigal: *O Care, thou wilt despatch me,*
Thomas Weelkes

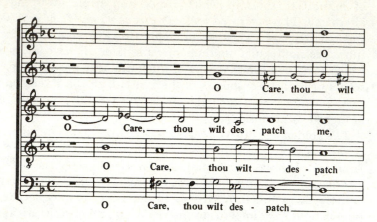

companied solo voices, though many of the published collections of
partbooks indicate on the title page that the music is "apt for voices
and viols," presumably in any available combination. Ability to
read a part, either vocally or instrumentally in such pieces, seems to
have been expected of educated persons in Elizabethan England.

A comprehensive idea of the English madrigal may be obtained
from *The Triumphes of Oriana,* a collection of twenty-five madrigals
by different composers, edited and published by Thomas Morley in
1601 after the model of a similar Italian anthology called *Il trionfo
di Dori* published in 1592. Each of the madrigals in Morley's collection presumably acclaims Queen Elizabeth I (*reg.* 1558–1603), and
each madrigal ends with the words "Long live fair Oriana," a name
from the conventional vocabulary of pastoral poetry often applied
to Elizabeth.

A large proportion of English madrigal texts are pastoral poems,
for the most part anonymous. An example of a madrigal with a

pastoral text is Wilbye's *Stay Corydon thou swain* from his *Second Set of Madrigals* of 1609. He wittily takes up the pictorial suggestions in the text, such as "flying," "light and shadow like," "swiftly," "follow," and renders them with appropriate musical figures.

The expressive and pictorial traits in the music of the madrigals are combined with accurate, nimble declamation of the English texts. The accents of the words are maintained independently in each voice (to appreciate this feature fully, remember that the barlines of modern editions did not exist in the original), so that the ensembles produce sparkling counterpoints of endless rhythmic vitality. Moreover, with all the sharpness of detail, the long line of the music is never obscured.

The solo song with accompaniment for lute and viol, popular on the continent since the early part of the sixteenth century, was taken

John Dowland's song, What if I never speed, *for solo voice with lute accompaniment in tablature (left), and in an optional arrangement for voices (right). This song appeared in Dowland's* The third and last booke of songs and aires. Newly composed to sing to the lute. *(By permission of the British Library)*

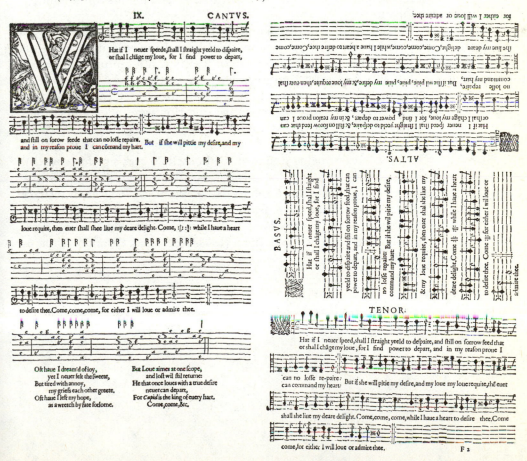

Lute songs

up in England as early as 1589, but its most flourishing period came at and after the turn of the century—coinciding thus with the decline of the madrigal. The leading composers in this field were John Dowland (1562–1626) and Thomas Campion (1567–1620). The poetry of the English ayres is considerably better than that of the madrigals. The music as a rule lacks the madrigalesque pictorial touches and the mood is uniformly lyrical, but the ayres—especially those of Dowland—are remarkable for sensitive text-declamation and melodic subtlety. The lute accompaniments, while always carefully subordinated to the voice, have a certain amount of rhythmic and melodic independence. The voice and lute parts are usually printed on the same page in vertical alignment, evidently so the singer could accompany himself. In some collections the songs are printed both this way and in an alternative version with the lute part written out for three voices and the staffs so arranged on the page that singers or players sitting around a table could all read their parts from the same book (see illustration on page 155). These vocal and instrumental versions rarely differ except in slight details. The alternative four-part version might be performed with either voices or instruments or both; some of these versions are quite similar to madrigals.

Along with the madrigal and the ayre, both of which were more or less indebted to foreign examples, there continued a native English tradition which in the latter half of the sixteenth century manifested itself in the form of *consort songs,* that is, solo songs or duets with accompaniment of a consort of viols and, at a later stage, the addition of a chorus. Likewise in the native tradition were polyphonic songs for either vocal or mixed vocal-instrumental performance, on texts ranging over a great variety of subjects from secular to sacred (the latter, however, being designed for household use, not for church). These are frequently called "madrigals," but they are really a distinct species. They maintain a relatively conservative, somewhat abstract style, concentrating on musical qualities and avoiding the detailed text-painting characteristic of the madrigal. The outstanding composers here were William Byrd (1543–1623) and Orlando Gibbons (1583–1625).

VIII

Church Music and Instrumental Music in the Late Renaissance

The Music of the Reformation in Germany

When Martin Luther posted his ninety-five theses on the church door at Wittenberg in 1517, he had no intention of initiating a movement that would result in the formation of organized Protestant churches completely separate from Rome. Even after the break was irreparable, the Lutheran church still retained much of the traditional Catholic liturgy, along with a considerable use of Latin in the services; and similarly, much Catholic music, both plainsong and polyphony, was kept, sometimes with the original Latin text, sometimes with the original text translated into German, or sometimes with new German texts adapted to the old melodies (called *contrafacta* or *parodies*).

Martin Luther

The position of music in the Lutheran church, especially in the sixteenth century, reflected Luther's own convictions on this subject. He was a lover of music, a singer, a composer of some skill, and a great admirer of Netherlands polyphony and of the works of Josquin des Prez in particular; he published as early as 1526 a *German Mass* (*Deudsche Messe*), which followed the main outlines of the Roman Mass, but with many changes of detail: the Gloria was omitted; new recitation tones were used, adapted to the natural cadence of the German language; several parts of the Proper were omitted or condensed; and for the remainder, as well as for most of the Ordinary, German hymns were substituted. But Luther never intended either this formula or any other to prevail uniformly in the Lutheran churches, and almost every imaginable combination and compromise between the Roman usage and the new ideas could be found somewhere in Germany sometime in the sixteenth century. Latin Masses and motets continued to be sung, and Latin remained in the liturgy at some places even into the eighteenth century: at Leipzig in Bach's time, for example, considerable portions of the services were still sung in Latin.

The Lutheran Chorale

The most distinctive and important musical contribution of the Lutheran church was the strophic congregational hymn called in German a *Choral* or *Kirchenlied* (church song) and in English a *chorale*. Since most people today are acquainted with these hymns chiefly in four-part harmonized settings, it must be pointed out that the chorale, like plainsong and folk song, consists essentially of only two elements, a text and a tune; but—also like plainsong and folk song—the chorale lends itself to enrichment through harmony and counterpoint and can be expanded into large musical forms. As most Catholic church music in the sixteenth century was an outgrowth of plainsong, so much Lutheran church music of the seventeenth and eighteenth centuries was an outgrowth of the chorale.

For a long time the demand for suitable songs in the Lutheran church far exceeded the supply. Luther himself wrote many chorale texts, for example, the well-known *Ein' feste Burg* (*A mighty fortress*); it has never been definitely established that Luther wrote the melody of this chorale (first printed in 1529), though the music is generally ascribed to him. Many chorale tunes were newly composed, but even more were made up entirely or partly from songs already existing. Thus the Gregorian hymn *Veni Redemptor gentium* became *Nun komm' der Heiden Heiland* (*Come, Saviour of the nations*); familiar nonliturgical spiritual songs were taken over, for example, the mixed Latin-German Christmas hymn *In dulci jubilo* or the German Easter song *Christ lag in Todesbanden* (*Christ lay in death's dark prison*), later rearranged by Luther on the model of the Easter sequence *Victimae paschali laudes*.

Contrafacta

A particularly important class of chorales were the *contrafacta* or *parodies* of secular songs, in which the given melody was retained but the text was either replaced by completely new words or else altered so as to give it a properly spiritual meaning. The adaptation of secular songs and secular polyphonic compositions for church purposes was common in the sixteenth century, as we have already seen in the history of the Mass. Perhaps the most famous and certainly one of the most beautiful of the contrafacta was *O Welt, ich muss dich lassen* (*O world, I now must leave thee*), adapted from Isaac's Lied, *Innsbruck, I now must leave thee*. A later and somewhat startling example was the tune from Hassler's Lied *Mein Gmüth ist mir verwirret* (*My peace of mind is shattered* [by a tender maiden's charms]), which in about 1600 was set to the sacred words *Herzlich thut mich verlangen* (*My heart is filled with longing*) and later to *O Haupt voll Blut und Wunden* (*O sacred head now wounded*). The transfiguration of the opening phrase of this song from Hassler's original version into two of the settings in Bach's *Passion according to St. Matthew* is shown in Example VIII–1.

Lutheran composers early began to write polyphonic settings for chorales. In 1524 Luther's principal musical collaborator, Johann Walter (1496–1570), published a volume of 38 German chorale settings together with five Latin motets; this collection was expanded, with a larger proportion of Latin motets, in subsequent editions, of which the fifth and last appeared in 1551. A more important collection of 123 polyphonic chorale arrangements and motets was issued at Wittenberg in 1544 by Georg Rhaw (1488–1548), the leading music publisher of Lutheran Germany. Unlike Walter's work, this was a compilation of pieces by all the leading German and Swiss-

Polyphonic chorale settings

EXAMPLE VIII–1

a. Hans Leo Hassler, *Mein Gmüth ist mir verwirret*

Mein G'müth ist mir ver-wir - ret, das macht ein Jungk-frau zart, bin hart
gantz und gar ver - ir - ret, mein Herz das kränkt sich

[*etc.*]

b. J. S. Bach, *Passion according to St. Matthew*

Be - fiehl du dei - ne We - ge und was dein Her - ze kränkt
Der al - ler-treu - sten Pfle - ge dess, der den Him - mel lenkt;

c. J. S. Bach, *Passion according to St. Matthew*

Wenn ich ein-mal soll schei - den, so schei-de nicht von mir!
Wenn ich den Tod soll lei - den, so tritt du dann her - für!

[*etc.*]

German composers of the first half of the sixteenth century, including Ludwig Senfl, Thomas Stoltzer (*ca.* 1475–1526), Benedictus Ducis (*ca.* 1490–1544), Sixtus Dietrich (*ca.* 1490–1548), Arnold von Bruck (*ca.* 1470–1554), and a Netherlander, Lupus Hellinck (*ca.* 1495–1541). The chorale settings in these and other sixteenth-century collections naturally varied considerably in style; some used the older technique of the German Lied, with the plain chorale tune in long notes in the tenor, surrounded by three or more parts in free-flowing polyphony, with independent motives and little use of imitation; others were like the Franco-Flemish motets, with each phrase of the chorale being developed imitatively through all the voices; still others were in a simple, almost chordal style. Through the first half of the century there was a general trend toward this last style of simplified writing, and also toward placing the tune in the soprano instead of in the tenor.

In the last third of the century a gradual change took place; more and more frequently chorales began to be published in *cantional* style, that is, in plainly chordal, hymn-like, rhythmically straightforward settings with the tune in the topmost voice. The chief composers of cantional settings in the early seventeenth century were H. L. Hassler (1608), Michael Praetorius (1571–1621), and Johann Hermann Schein (1627).

The chorale motet

By the end of the sixteenth century many Lutheran regions of Germany had returned to the Catholic faith, and the line between Protestant northeast and Catholic southwest was fixed substantially as it has remained to this day. With this definitive separation, a new and distinctive kind of Lutheran polyphonic church music emerged. Composers began to use the traditional melodies as the basic material for free artistic creation, to which they added individual interpretation and pictorial details. These new settings were called *chorale motets.*

Composers of chorale motets could, and did, break away altogether from the traditional chorale tunes, though they still used melodic material related to the chorale or Lied style. The appearance of these motets confirmed the division which has existed ever since in Protestant church music between simple congregational hymns and more elaborate music for a trained choir. The leading composers of German motets at the turn of the sixteenth century were Hassler, Johannes Eccard (1553–1611), Leonhard Lechner (*ca.* 1550–1606), and Michael Praetorius. Their work established the Lutheran church music style in Germany and opened the road to a development that culminated over a hundred years later in J. S. Bach.

Reformation Church Music Outside Germany

The effect that the Reformation had on music in France, the Netherlands, and Switzerland was quite different from developments in Germany. Jean Calvin (1509–64) and other leaders of the reformed Protestant sects opposed much more strongly than did Luther the retention of elements of Catholic liturgy and ceremonial. To a general distrust of the allurements of art in services of worship was added a particular prohibition of the singing of texts not found in the Bible. As a consequence, the only notable musical productions of the Calvinist churches were the Psalters, rhymed metrical translations of the Book of Psalms, set to melodies either newly composed or, in many cases, of popular origin or adapted from plainchant. The principal French Psalter was published in 1562, with psalm texts translated by Clément Marot and Théodore de Bèze set to melodies selected or composed by Loys Bourgeois (*ca.* 1510–*ca.* 1561).

The principal French composers of polyphonic Psalm settings were Claude Goudimel (*ca.* 1505–72) and Claude Le Jeune; the most important Netherlands composer was J. P. Sweelinck. Translations of the French Psalter appeared in Germany, Holland, England, and Scotland, and many of the French tunes were taken over by the Reformed churches in those countries. In Germany many Psalter melodies were adapted as chorales (see Example VIII–2a). In Holland the translation of 1566 replaced an earlier Dutch Psalter, the *Souterliedekens* of 1540, the melodies of which had been taken from contemporary popular songs and were later given three-part settings by Clemens non Papa.

The French model also influenced the most important English Psalter of the sixteenth century, that of Sternhold and Hopkins (1562), and was even more influential for the Scottish Psalter of 1564. A combination of the English and the French-Dutch traditions, embodied in the Psalter brought out by Henry Ainsworth at Amsterdam in 1612 for the use of the English Separatists in Holland, was brought to New England by the Pilgrims in 1620, and remained in use many years after the appearance of the first American Psalter, the *Bay Psalm Book* of 1640.

The French Psalter melodies on the whole are suave, intimate, and somewhat austere in comparison with the forthright, vigorous quality of most of the German chorales. Since the Calvinist churches discouraged musical elaboration, the Psalter tunes were seldom expanded into larger forms of vocal and instrumental music, as were the Lutheran chorales; and consequently they are much less conspicuous in the general history of music. Yet as devotional music

The Psalter

they are excellent; their melodic line, which prevailingly moves by step, has something of the quality of plainsong, and the phrases are organized in a rich variety of rhythmic patterns. It is surprising that so few of the melodies from the French Psalter of 1562 are found in modern hymnals: the best-known example is the tune sung originally to Psalm 134, used in the English Psalters for Psalm 100 and hence known as "Old Hundredth" (Example VIII–2b).

A Pre-Reformation movement in Bohemia led by Jan Hus (1373–1415) resulted in the effectual banishment of polyphonic music and instruments from the church until the middle of the sixteenth century. In 1561, a group known as the Czech Brethren published a hymnbook with texts in the Czech language and melodies borrowed

EXAMPLE VIII–2 Melodies from the French Psalter of 1562, with some Later Adaptations.

a.   Psalm 36

Du ma-lin le mes-chant vou-loir   Parle en mon coeur et me fait voir

Qu'il n'a de Dieu la crain - te   [etc.]

The transgression of the wicked saith within my heart that there is no fear of God [before his eyes].

Bach: *Chorale Prelude*

b.   Psalm 134

Or sus, ser-vi-teurs du Sei-gneur,   Vous qui de nuit en Son hon-neur [etc.]

Arise ye servants of the Lord, which by night [stand] in the house of the Lord.

Presbyterian Hymnal

All peo-ple that on earth do dwell, Sing to the Lord with cheer-ful voice
[etc.]

from Gregorian Chant, secular songs, or French Calvinist Psalms in four-part settings. The Czech Brethren, later called the Moravian Brethren, emigrated to America in the early eighteenth century where their settlements—especially the one at Bethlehem, Pennsylvania—became important centers of music.

The Church in England was formally separated from the Roman Catholic communion in 1534 and by the middle of the century the English liturgy of the Book of Common Prayer was adopted. Music was required to be written in a simple homophonic style so that the words could be clearly understood. Fortunately, the more extreme demands were later modified so far as to allow for some counterpoint; some of the Latin motets of Tallis and Byrd remained favorites in English translation. Still, the end result of the changes in language and liturgy was the rise of a new body of English church music. Tye and Tallis contributed to it, although their output in this field was neither so extensive nor so important as in that of Latin church composition. William Byrd, though a Roman Catholic, wrote five Services and about sixty anthems for Anglican use; some of this music is equal in quality to his Latin motets and Masses. Orlando Gibbons is often called the father of Anglican church music; his works, despite the fact that they derive their technique from the Latin tradition, are thoroughly English in spirit. Thomas Weelkes and Thomas Tomkins (1572–1656) should also be mentioned among the early composers of English church music.

The principal forms of Anglican music are the *Service* and the *anthem*. A complete Service consists of the music for the unvarying portions of Morning and Evening Prayer (corresponding respectively to the Roman Matins and Vespers) and of that for Holy Communion, which corresponds to the Roman Mass but which had a less important place in the Anglican musical scheme—often only the Kyrie and the Creed were composed. A Service is either a "Great Service" or a "Short Service"; these terms refer not to the number of items composed but to the style of the music used, the former being contrapuntal and melismatic, the latter chordal and syllabic. One of the finest examples of Anglican church music is the *Great Service* of Byrd.

The English anthem corresponds to the Latin motet. There are two types of anthems. One, which later came to be called a "full" anthem, was for chorus throughout, usually in contrapuntal style and (ideally, though not always in practice) unaccompanied; an example is Tomkins's *When David Heard* [1], an extraordinarily moving and beautiful setting of this emotional text. The "verse" anthem was for one or more solo voices with organ or viol accompaniment, and with brief alternating passages for chorus. This type, which

[1] HAM, No. 169.

certainly originated from the consort song, was most popular in England during the seventeenth century.

The Counter-Reformation

The Council of Trent

From 1545 to 1563, with numerous intermissions and interruptions, a Council was held at Trent in northern Italy to formulate and give official sanction to measures for purging the Church of abuses and laxities. With respect to Church music the final pronouncement of the Council of Trent on these matters was extremely general, however; it merely stated that everything "impure or lascivious" must be avoided in order "that the House of God may rightly be called a house of prayer." The implementation of this directive was left to the diocesan bishops, and a special commission of cardinals was appointed to oversee its enforcement in Rome. The Council touched on no technical points whatever: neither polyphony nor the parodying of secular models was specifically forbidden.

Palestrina

The essential effect of the Council's decrees was to recognize and sanction stylistic tendencies in church music which were already established, particularly at Rome, by the middle of the century. The consequence was a style of composition whose greatest representative was Giovanni Pierluigi da Palestrina (1525/6–94).

By far the greatest part of Palestrina's work was sacred: he wrote 102 Masses, about 450 motets and other liturgical compositions, and 56 spiritual madrigals with Italian texts. His 83 secular madrigals are not particularly outstanding examples of their kind, and in later life he "blushed and grieved" to have written music for profane love poems.

The Palestrinian style

No other composer before Bach is so well known by name as Palestrina, and no other composer's technique has been subjected to more minute scrutiny. He has been called "the Prince of Music" and his works the "absolute perfection" of church style. It is generally recognized that, better than any other composer, he captured the essence of the sober, conservative aspect of the Counter-Reformation in a polyphony of utter purity, detached from any secular suggestion. The Palestrina style is exemplified most clearly in his Masses; its objective, coolly impersonal quality is most appropriate to the formal and ritualistic texts of the Ordinary. The basis of his style is, of course, the Franco-Flemish imitative counterpoint; voice parts flow in continuous rhythm, with a new melodic motive for each phrase of the text. Palestrina's most important predecessors at Rome had been Festa, Arcadelt, and Morales, all of whom had adhered in their church music to the conservative, anti-secular, strictly liturgical principles which were typical of the Roman school and which are so fundamental in Palestrina's works.

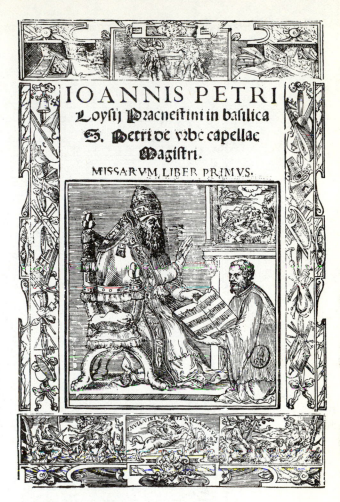

IOANNIS PETRI
Loyſij Praeneſtini in baſilica
S. Petri de vrbe capellae
Magiſtri.
MISSARVM, LIBER PRIMVS.

Title page of the first published work by Palestrina (Valerio & Luigi Dorico, Rome, 1554); the engraving shows the composer presenting the music to Pope Julius III.

A significant reflection of Palestrina's churchly attitude is the fact that of his 102 Masses no fewer than 79 are built on themes from Gregorian Chant; this figure includes those parodied on motets or similar pieces which themselves were based on plainsong, such as the Mass *Veni sponsa Christi*. This matter is more than one of mere statistics. Gregorian Chant is the very earth out of which Palestrina's music grows, the only background against which his music can be properly heard and understood. Palestrina not only uses melodic substance from the chant; its essential spirit and its technical procedures he takes up and transfigures in his polyphony.

For example, take the melodic line of any individual voice-part of a typical piece such as the first Agnus Dei from the famous *Mass of Pope Marcellus* (Example VIII–3)[2]: long-breathed, flexibly articulated in rhythmic measures of varying length; prevailingly

2 The entire piece may be found in the Norton Critical Score edited by Lewis Lockwood.

EXAMPLE VIII–3 Agnus Dei I from the *Pope Marcellus Mass,*
Giovanni Pierluigi da Palestrina

stepwise, with few repeated notes, moving for the most part within the range of a ninth, easily singable, the few skips greater than a third never dramatically exploited but smoothed over by returning to a note within the interval of the skip—in all, an even, natural, elegant curve of sound.

Purity of line is matched by purity of harmony. Characteristic of Palestrina is the complete—one might say, studied—avoidance of chromaticism, that new expressive resource which was being so thoroughly explored by the more progressive contemporary composers. Even in his secular madrigals Palestrina was conservative in this respect; the more so in his sacred works, and above all in the Masses, where the peculiarly intense, personal, carnal quality of chromatic harmonies would have been for him an unthinkable secular intrusion. Only the essential alterations required by the rules of *musica ficta* are tolerated.

Palestrina's harmony

The diatonic character of the harmony and especially the discreet handling of dissonance give Palestrina's music a consistent serenity and transparency not matched by any other composer's.

The rhythm of Palestrina's music, like that of all sixteenth-century polyphony, is compounded of the rhythms of the various voices plus a collective rhythm resulting from the harmonic and contrapuntal combination of the lines. Example VIII–4 represents the first seven measures of Example VIII–3 but with each voice barred in accordance with its own natural rhythm; this example shows graphically how independent the individual lines are. However, the collective rhythm, heard when all the voices are sounding, gives the impression of a fairly regular succession of 2/2 or 4/4 "measures," set off not by stress accents but mostly by the changes of harmony and the plac-

EXAMPLE VIII–4 Rhythms in Agnus Dei I from the *Pope Marcellus Mass,* Palestrina

ing of suspensions on strong beats. This gently marked regularity of rhythm is characteristic of the Palestrina style.

This same Agnus Dei also illustrates how Palestrina unifies a composition by purely musical means. Externally, the movement resembles a typical motet by Gombert: each phrase of the text has its own musical motive, and the contrapuntal development of each motive is merged with that of the next by means of a cadence at which the voices overlap, some stopping, others continuing. But in Palestrina's work the connection between motives is more than one of mere succession; an organic unity is achieved in part through the harmonic organization and in part through systematic repetition.

Palestrina's style was the first in the history of Western music to be consciously preserved, isolated, and imitated as a model in later ages when composers quite naturally were writing altogether different kinds of music. His great and venerable art is the expression of medieval mysticism in an intentionally restricted, and in some respects archaic, Renaissance musical vocabulary.

Contemporaries of Palestrina

Some contemporaries of Palestrina whose musical style was related to his must be only briefly mentioned. Giovanni Maria Nanino (*ca.* 1545–1607), Palestrina's pupil and his successor at Santa Maria Maggiore and later director of the Papal Chapel, is to be counted among the foremost composers of the Roman school. Felice Anerio (1560–1614) was a pupil of Nanino who in 1594 succeeded Palestrina as official composer to the Papal Chapel. Giovanni Animuccia (*ca.* 1500–71) was Palestrina's predecessor at St. Peter's. He is noted chiefly for his laude written for the Congregation of the Oratory at Rome. This Congregation grew out of meetings organized by a priest (later canonized), Filippo Neri, for religious lectures and spiritual exercises, which were followed by the singing of laude; the name came from the original place of meeting, the "oratory" (prayer chapel) of one of the Roman churches. The laude and similar devotional songs—Palestrina himself contributed a few pieces to this repertory—later were occasionally given in the form of dialogues or otherwise dramatized.

Victoria

Next to Palestrina, however, the most important composer of the Roman school was the Spaniard Tomás Luis de Victoria (*ca.* 1549–1611). As the career of Morales indicated, there was a close connection between Spanish and Roman composers throughout the sixteenth century. Victoria came to Rome in 1565, probably studied with Palestrina, and followed him as teacher at the Seminary in 1571; returning to Spain about 1595, he became chaplain to the Empress Maria, for whose funeral services he wrote a famous Requiem Mass in 1603. His compositions are exclusively sacred. Though his style is like that of Palestrina, Victoria often infuses his music with a mystical intensity, a quality which makes it both thoroughly personal and typically Spanish. A good example of his work is the motet *O vos omnes*[3]: instead of the gentle, even rhythm of Palestrina, the lines are broken as if into sobbing ejaculations; arresting vivid phrases with repeated notes ("attendite"—behold) give way to cries of lamentation underlined by poignant dissonances ("sicut dolor meus"—like unto My sorrow). Palestrina's art may be compared to that of Raphael; Victoria's, with its passionate religious fervor, is like that of his contemporary, El Greco. Even in his more conventional motets this fervent spirit is always immanent in Victoria's music.

The last of the illustrious line of sixteenth-century Franco-Flemish composers were Philippe de Monte and Orlando di Lasso. Unlike Palestrina and Victoria, a large part of their work was secular. Nevertheless, Monte produced 38 Masses and over 300 motets in which he demonstrated his mastery of contrapuntal technique and his faithfulness to the Netherlands musical tradition, although not without some more modern touches.

Orlando di Lasso ranks with Palestrina among the great composers of sacred music in the late sixteenth century. But whereas Palestrina was above all the master of the Mass, Lasso's chief glory is his motets. His settings of the penitential psalms[4] (about 1560), though perhaps the best known of his church works, are not fully representative. In both his career and his compositions, Lasso was one of the most cosmopolitan figures in the history of music. By the age of twenty-four he had already published books of madrigals, chansons and motets, and his total production eventually amounted to over 2000 works. The principal collection of his motets, the *Magnum opus musicum (Great Work of Music)* was published in 1604, ten years after his death. In contrast to Palestrina's considered, restrained, and classic nature, Lasso had an impulsive, emotional, and dynamic temperament. In his motets both the over-all form and the details are generated from a pictorial, dramatic approach to the text. The distinctive technical features of his musical style seem to be an outgrowth of this attitude: the melodic movement is frequently by leap; phrases are uneven in length; texture is freely varied to suit the emotional or pictorial suggestions in the words; the harmonic rhythm is often rapid and irregular; and the expressive values of harmonic combinations are exploited.

In the latter years of his life, under the influence of the spirit of the Counter-Reformation, Lasso devoted himself wholly to setting sacred texts, particularly spiritual madrigals, renouncing the "gay" and "festive" songs of his youth for music of "more substance and energy." However, one cannot properly speak of a "Lasso style"; the

Orlando di Lasso

[3] HAM No. 149.
[4] Psalms 6, 32, 38, 51, 102, 130, 143 in the King James version of the Bible; 6, 31, 37, 50, 101, 129, 142 of the Vulgate.

man is too versatile for that. Netherlands counterpoint, Italian harmony, Venetian opulence, French vivacity, German gravity, all are to be found in his work, which more fully than that of any other sixteenth-century composer sums up the achievements of an epoch and in many ways looks forward to the age of the Baroque.

The last of the great Catholic Church composers of the sixteenth century was William Byrd of England (1543–1623). His works include English polyphonic songs, keyboard pieces, and music for the Anglican Church; undoubtedly his best vocal compositions are his Latin Masses and motets. In view of the contemporary religious situation in England, it is not surprising that Byrd wrote only three Masses (respectively for three, four, and five voices); yet these are beyond doubt the finest settings of the Mass written by an English composer.

Byrd seems to have been the first English composer to absorb Continental imitative techniques to a point where they are used imaginatively and without any sense of constraint. The texture of his music is pervaded by the same essentially English quality of vocality that we have already noticed in the music of Tallis. An excellent example of Byrd's style may be studied in *Laudate pueri dominum* (NAWM/S 19), a nonliturgical setting of a text compiled from Psalms 113, 121, and 125, published in his *Cantiones sacrae* of 1575. It illutrates particularly well the formal structure of a late sixteenth-century motet, being divided (at "sit nomen," "auxilium," "benefac") into four interlocking fugal sections. Within each section Byrd preserves thematic unity by setting more than' one text to the same or slightly modified subject. So, in the superbly

EXAMPLE VIII–5 Motet: *Laudate pueri dominum*, William Byrd

Do good, O Lord, to those who are good and true.

climactic final section, "Benefac, Domine bonis" and "et rectis corde" are set to the same subject, which is expansively developed over forty-five measures (see Example VIII–5).

Instrumental Music of the Later Sixteenth Century

Late sixteenth-century instrumental music can best be surveyed by dividing it into four classes: compositions derived from vocal models, dances, improvisatory pieces, and variations. This classification is of course imperfect, since the categories are not of the same order; they relate respectively to source, function, style, and form of compositions. Consequently, any given work may belong to more than one class, as, for example, a dance in the form of variations. It is therefore essential to regard these four classes not as so many pigeon-holes but rather as *basic principles of procedure* which are operative in the composition of instrumental music in the late sixteenth century, and one or another of which usually can be regarded as the *main* principle in any actual work of that period.

Of the compositions derived from vocal models a large number are nothing more than transcriptions of madrigals, chansons, or motets, decorated by turns, trills, runs, and other embellishments. Many instrumental compositions are based on *cantus firmi* of vocal origin; others make use of a favorite *cantus firmus* consisting of the six notes of the hexachord (*ut, re, mi, fa, sol, la*), around which

Compositions derived from vocal models

Student Collegium musicum. *In this engraving by Crispyn de Passe the Elder (1564–1637), a group of students is shown singing and playing. Among the instruments are a violin, a lute, a harpsichord, and a string bass. The presence of both ladies and wine indicate that music was not the only order of business!*

English composers wrote many ingenious counterpoints. One celebrated "hexachord fancy" by John Bull (*ca.* 1562–1628) takes the hexachord through all twelve keys in turn. Since Bull's "fancy" appears in the Fitzwilliam Virginal Book as a keyboard piece, it has been suggested that some approximation to equal temperament must have been known in England by the end of the sixteenth century; however, the keyboard version we have may be only a condensed score of a fantasy for four viols.

The canzona   Keyboard and ensemble ricercari in the manner of vocal motets were composed throughout the sixteenth century, but more importantly historically was the development of the canzona. Originally, the canzona was an instrumental composition with the same general style as the French chanson—that is, light, fast-moving, strongly rhythmic, and with a fairly simple contrapuntal texture. The composers of instrumental canzonas took over these characteristics from the chanson, as well as the typical opening rhythmic figure ♩ ♩♩│♩ or ♩ ♫│♩, which occurs in nearly all canzonas. More lively and entertaining than the sober and somewhat abstruse ricercar, the canzona became in the late sixteenth century the leading form of contrapuntal instrumental music. The earliest Italian examples (apart from mere transcriptions) were for organ; about 1580, Italian composers began to write ensemble canzonas as well. The organ canzonas were the forerunners of the fugue; these two terms were used synonymously in Germany as early as 1607. The ensemble canzonas, on the other hand, eventually developed into the *sonata da chiesa* (church sonata) of the seventeenth century.

The essential step in this development was the division of the

canzona into a number of more or less distinct sections. Many of
the earliest canzonas had a single theme, or perhaps several themes
very similar in character, treated contrapuntally in one continuous
and unchanging movement. Others, however, introduced themes
of somewhat contrasting character, each theme in turn going
through its contrapuntal working-out and then yielding to the
next. Since the themes themselves were noticeably different from
each other in melodic outline and rhythm, the piece as a whole
began to take on the aspect of a series of contrasting sections—
even though the divisions between sections were usually concealed
by overlapping of the cadences. Example VIII–6 shows the four

EXAMPLE VIII–6   Themes from a Canzona, Jean de Macque

themes in a canzona of this type written by the Netherlander Jean de Macque (*ca.* 1550–1614).

A further stage in the direction of independent sections is illustrated in Example VIII–7, themes from an instrumental piece by the Venetian composer Andrea Gabrieli (*ca.* 1520–86). Although it was called ricercare, it is of the canzona type, an indication of the

EXAMPLE VIII–7   Themes from a Ricercare, Andrea Gabrieli

looseness of terminology in this period. The themes are more contrasting than those in de Macque's canzona, and moreover the second section of the piece is set off from the others by being written in a predominantly homophonic style. The opening section is repeated in its entirety after section four.

This composition of Gabrieli's thus illustrates also an important structural principle—repetition. Of course, the ideas of contrast and repetition were not new; both are basic in musical composition, and both appear in Western music from its earliest beginnings. But before the sixteenth century the use of repetition and contrast was dictated largely by liturgical requirements, or by the poetic form of the text, or by the nature of a dance pattern. In independent instrumental pieces, such as the canzonas, the decision to use these devices is made for purely musical reasons: to give coherence and variety to polyphony intended only to be listened to, without the distractions or support of ritual, dancing, or text. This new approach embodied in the late sixteenth-century canzona, and in similar contemporary forms with other names—capriccio, ricercare, fantasia, fancy, and the like—was important, for in it was implicit the later development of independent instrumental music.

Dance pieces In the latter half of the sixteenth century, dance music for lute, keyboard instruments, and ensembles was published in increasing amounts. Some dances were simple arrangements of tunes for popular use, but the majority seem to have been written for social occasions in the homes of the bourgeoisie or the courts of the aristocracy. The tendency already present in the early sixteenth century to group dances in pairs or threes continued, as did the writing of stylized dance music. The favorite pairs of dances in the late sixteenth century were the *pavane* (*padovano, paduana*) and *galliard;* or the *passamezzo* and *saltarello.* In either pair the first dance was slow and stately and in duple time, and the second dance was a more lively movement in triple time, usually on the same melody or a variation thereof. The second dance is sometimes called in German sources the *proportio* or *proportz,* a name surviving from the terminology of fifteenth-century notation.

The chief form of keyboard music in improvisatory style in the latter half of the century was the *toccata.* This word comes from the Italian verb *toccare* (to touch), and carries the suggestion of an organist improvising at the keyboard. The toccata was a specialty of the Venetian organ composers. Claudio Merulo (1533–1604), publishing at the very end of the century, was the first to introduce to this form a ricercare-like middle section developed by imitation. Most sixteenth-century toccatas were simply in one movement, in straight improvisatory style. Various names were used for pieces of this sort: *fantasia, intonazione, prelude,* and others.

Improvisatory pieces

A rather different kind of improvisatory writing is found in some keyboard pieces toward the end of the sixteenth century, pieces in which the composer seems to wander dreamily through

EXAMPLE VIII–8   *Consonanze stravaganti,* de Macque

* *So in original; delete* a?
† *So in original; delete* d?

a maze of strange harmonies, as an organist might when quietly improvising. Example VIII–8 shows a passage from a work of this sort, appropriately entitled *Consonanze stravaganti (Roving Harmonies)*, by Jean de Macque. The peculiar chromaticism of this example is reminiscent of Gesualdo, with whom de Macque was associated for a time at Naples. The style is a forerunner of the beautiful chromatic toccatas of the seventeenth-century Roman organist Frescobaldi.

English keyboard music

The extraordinary flowering of the variation form in the late sixteenth century was due primarily to a school of English keyboard composers called the *virginalists* from the name used at the time for all plucked keyboard instruments. The leading composer in this group was William Byrd; important among his colleagues were Orlando Gibbons and Thomas Tomkins. Of the many manuscript collections of keyboard music which were made in England in this period, the most comprehensive is the *Fitzwilliam Virginal Book,* a manuscript compiled about 1620, which contains nearly 300 compositions written in the late sixteenth and early seventeenth centuries. Among these pieces are madrigal transcriptions, contrapuntal fantasias, dances, preludes, descriptive pieces, and many sets of variations.

Most of the variations in the *Fitzwilliam Virginal Book* are on slow dance tunes (as Bull's *Spanish Paven*) or familiar songs (as Munday's *Goe from my window*). Many folk tunes of the time also served as subjects for variation.

The tunes used as the basis for the variations as a rule were short, simple, and song-like, regular in phrasing, with a clear binary or ternary pattern set off by distinct cadences. The variations follow in uninterrupted sequence, sometimes a half-dozen of them, sometimes as many as twenty or even more. Each variation preserves the structure of the theme: the same articulations, the same cadences, the same harmonic plan. Sometimes the melody is presented intact throughout an entire set of variations, passing occasionally from one voice to another. More often, in some of the variations the melody is broken up by figuration, so that its original profile is only suggested. Sometimes this decorative figuration is derived from some phrase of the melody itself, but as a rule it is freely invented. Some of the passage work, particularly in the variations by Bull, has a high order of virtuosity, if not always important musical content; evidently fast scale-playing and similar feats of technical skill had the same fascination for composers and players then as in the nineteenth century.

In most English virginal music, however, mere technical display is not a prominent feature. Each variation commonly makes use of one main type of figuration; and sometimes the two halves of a variation, or two successive variations, will be paired by the use

A seventeenth-century double spinet or virginal, with an ornamental and painted case, made by Ludovicus Grovvelus of Flanders. The right-hand instrument can be removed from the case and used as a portable virginal. (Courtesy Metropolitan Museum of Art, the Crosby Brown Collection of Musical Instruments, 1889)

of the same figure in the right hand for one and in the left hand for the other, as in the third and fourth variations of Bull's *Spanish Paven*. Apart from such pairing, the only comprehensive plan in most sets of variations was to increase the animation as the work progressed—although with intermittent quieter interludes. Changes of meter were sometimes introduced, and once in a while a composer would show off his learning by writing a variation using two or three different meters simultaneously. Quite often the last variation was slower, a broadened restatement of the theme with fuller sonority and richer harmonization. The technique may be studied with pleasure in the charming little set of variations by Farnaby on *Loth to depart* and in Munday's *Goe from my window*.

Toward the Baroque:
The Venetian School

In the sixteenth century, Venice was (next to Rome) the most important city of the Italian peninsula. The heart and center of Venetian musical culture was the great eleventh-century church of

Social conditions in Venice

Saint Mark. Most of the exalted civic ceremonies of Venice took place in this church and in the vast *piazza* which it faced. Thus most Venetian music was conceived as a manifestation of the majesty of both State and Church, and was designed to be heard on solemn and festive occasions when that majesty was publicly displayed with every possible array of sound and pageantry.

Music in the church of Saint Mark was supervised by officials of the State, and no pains or expense were spared to keep it worthy of Venice's high traditions. The position of choirmaster was the most coveted musical post in all Italy. There were two organs, and the organists, chosen after stringent examination, were always renowned artists. Choirmasters in the sixteenth century were Willaert, Rore, Zarlino, and Baldassare Donati; organists included Jacques Buus, Annibale Padovano, Claudio Merulo, Andrea Gabrieli, and his nephew, Giovanni Gabrieli (*ca.* 1557–1612). All these men were not merely conductors and players, but famous composers as well; and it will be seen that as the century went on the northerners (Willaert, Rore, Buus) were succeeded by native Italians.

Many Venetian composers of the sixteenth century contributed notably to the madrigal, and Venice produced the best organ music of all Italy. Venetian music was characteristically of full, rich texture, homophonic rather than contrapuntal, varied and colorful in sonority. In the motets, massive chordal harmonies were the rule, rather than the intricate polyphonic lines of the Netherlanders.

Venetian polychoric motets

From the time of Willaert, and even before that, the Venetian church composers had often written for double chorus, the two separate choirs which in Saint Mark's were placed with the organs on opposite sides of the church. The use of such *cori spezzati* (divided choirs) was not original with Venice or peculiar to it (Palestrina's *Stabat Mater,* for example, is written for double chorus); but the practice was congenial to, and further encouraged, the homophonic type of choral writing and the broad rhythmic organization which the Venetian composers preferred. Moreover, Venice was not committed, as was Rome, to the ideal of *a cappella* performance. Not only the organ, but many other instruments as well—trombones, cornetts, viols—sounded with the voices. In the hands of Giovanni Gabrieli, the greatest of the Venetian masters, the motet was expanded to unheard-of proportions: two, three, four, even five choruses were employed, each with a different combination of high and low voices, each intermingled with instruments of diverse timbres, answering one another antiphonally, alternating with solo voices, and joining for massive sonorous climaxes. An example is Gabrieli's motet *In ecclesiis*. In such works a new principle of composition was established, namely the contrast and opposition of sonorities; this principle became a basic factor in the *concertato* style of the Baroque period.

The famous *Sonata pian' e forte* of Gabrieli is essentially nothing else than a double-chorus Venetian motet for instruments. This composition owes its prominent place in music history books less to its intrinsic musical worth than to the fact that it is one of the first instrumental ensemble pieces printed which designates particular instruments for each part: the first orchestra consists of a cornett and three trombones, the second of a viol (*"violino"*) and three trombones.

Instrumental music

Another innovation in Gabrieli's sonata was the indication, both in the title and in the score itself, of *"pian[o]"* and *"forte"*; the former rubric is used when each orchestra is playing alone and the latter when both are playing together. This is one of the earliest instances of dynamic markings in music. As for the term *sonata*, it was used occasionally in the sixteenth century in a very general way for almost any kind of ensemble instrumental composition, and implied nothing about form. The only connection of the sixteenth-century "sonatas" with the sonata of the Baroque and Classical periods is nominal.

Venetian influence

The Venetian school, everywhere admired as the most progressive in Italy, exercised wide influence in the late sixteenth and early seventeenth centuries. Pupils and followers of Gabrieli were numerous in northern Italy and were scattered all over Germany, Austria, and Scandinavia. The most famous of his direct pupils was the German Heinrich Schütz. A notable proponent of Venetian style in northern Germany was Hieronymus Praetorius (1560–1629) of Hamburg. Jacob Handl (1550–91), a Slovenian by birth—known also by the Latin form of his name, Jacobus Gallus—worked at Olmütz and Prague; most of his works, particularly his motets for double chorus, show a close affinity with Venetian style. The motets of Hans Leo Hassler, a German pupil of Andrea Gabrieli, are prevailingly polychoric, with typical Venetian fullness of sound and richness of harmony. In Poland, the polychoric style was cultivated by Mikolaj Zielenski (d. 1615) and many others.

Summary

This discussion of music in the second half of the sixteenth century has many times overstepped the arbitrary boundary of the year 1600 which we set as the limit of the Renaissance period. The reason, of course, is that changes in musical style occur gradually, in complex ways, and at different times in different places. Development of the English madrigal school, for example, continued in the seventeenth century, but it has been dealt with in this section because the style of the English madrigal is more closely allied to Renaissance music than to Baroque. Certainly, late Renaissance traits persisted well into the seventeenth century; and many features of the early Baroque began to be manifest long before the end of the sixteenth.

To speak of "traits" or "features" of Renaissance or Baroque music, however, implies that there are certain characteristics by which we can identify a given piece as at least predominantly one or the other, regardless of the exact date of its composition. In discussing Renaissance music, we listed five general features; let us now see how each of these was affected by the changes that took place between 1450 and 1600.

Texture

The characteristic texture of similar contrapuntal voice parts was still the rule in the work of Palestrina, Lasso, Byrd, and Gabrieli, at the end of the sixteenth century, as it had been in the music of Ockeghem and Josquin. This texture, more than any other single feature, separates Renaissance music from Baroque. On the other hand, homophony, both in its pure form as familiar style and as a centripetal tendency curbing the independence of contrapuntal lines, had begun to invade all forms of polyphonic writing. Its dominance in the Venetian school is one sign of the approaching Baroque. The outlines of major-minor tonality were already taking shape in much of the music of Palestrina, Lasso, Byrd, Dowland, and Gabrieli.

Rhythm

Rhythm, supported by systematic harmonic progressions within the sixteenth-century tonal system, had become comparatively steady and predictable by the end of the century, even in the contrapuntal style of Palestrina and in such apparently free compositions as the Venetian organ toccatas. The barline in the modern editions of Palestrina, Gabrieli, and Byrd is no longer the intrusion it sometimes seems to be in modern editions of Ockeghem and Josquin. The Baroque begins with a conspicuous revolt against rhythmic regularity; but it ends by embracing this regularity completely, within the framework of the eighteenth-century tonal system.

Music and words

Musica reservata, the pictorial and expressive touches in the madrigal, Gesualdo's chromatic aberrations, and the splendorous sonorities of the Venetian massed choruses, are all signs of the sixteenth-century drive toward vivid outward expression in music. The Baroque carries this drive to still greater lengths, and embodies it in the new forms of cantata and opera. With the rise of pure instrumental forms (the ricercare, canzona, and toccata), Renaissance music had already begun to transcend words; this line of development also continues without a break through the Baroque and beyond. Finally: whereas the solo songs of the Renaissance were lyrical pieces, hardly different in style from madrigals, one of the chief innovations of the Baroque was the discovery that the solo song could be used as a vehicle for dramatic expression. The violent states of feeling expressed by Gesualdo and Gabrieli in an ensemble of voices are by the Baroque composers expressed in a solo with instrumental accompaniment.

IX

Early Baroque Music

General Features of Baroque Music

The music of the Baroque era (roughly 1600–1750) was dominated largely by Italian ideas. Independent national styles flourished for a time in France, Germany, and England during the seventeenth century, but by 1750 the music of Europe had become, in effect, an international language with Italian roots.

Despite continuous change, certain musical features remained constant throughout the Baroque era. One of these was a distinction drawn between various styles of composition. Monteverdi, for example, in 1605 distinguished between a *prima prattica* and a *seconda prattica,* or first and second "practices." By the first, he meant the style of vocal polyphony derived from the Netherlanders; by the second he meant the style of the modern Italians. The basis of the distinction for Monteverdi was that in the first practice music dominated the text, whereas in the second practice the text dominated the music; hence it followed that in the new style the old rules might be modified and, in particular, dissonances might be used freely to make the music conform to the expression of feeling in the text. Others called the two practices *stile antico* and *stile moderno* (old and modern style), or *stylus gravis* and *stylus luxurians* (severe and ornamented style); this last designation implied the use of fast notes, unusual skips, and a well-marked melody, as well as dissonances.

Another characteristic of Baroque music was that composers began to be attracted by the idea of writing music specifically for a

The two practices

181

Idiomatic writing

particular medium, such as the violin or the solo voice, rather than music that might be either sung or played or performed by almost any combination of voices and instruments, as could many pieces composed in the sixteenth century. While the violin family began to replace the older viols in Italy, and composers there were developing an idiomatic violin style, the French began cultivating the viol, which became the most respected bowed instrument in France during the last decades of the seventeenth century; wind instruments were technically improved and came to be used for their specific color and capabilities; an idiomatic style for keyboard music arose; indications for dynamics began to appear; and the art of singing, promoted by famous teachers and virtuosi, advanced very rapidly in the seventeenth century. Instrumental and vocal styles began to be differentiated.

The affections

One trait common to all Baroque composers was the effort they made to express, or rather represent, a wide range of ideas and feelings with the utmost vividness and vehemence by means of music. Composers, continuing certain tendencies already evident in the late sixteenth-century madrigal, struggled to find musical means for the expression of *affections* or states of the soul, such as rage, excitement, grandeur, heroism, lofty contemplation, wonder, or mystic exaltation, and to intensify these musical effects by means of violent contrasts. In Baroque architecture, sculpture, and painting the normal forms of objects were sometimes distorted, as though past the natural limits of the medium, to reflect the passionate intensity of the artist's thought; in Baroque music, also, the limits of the old order of consonance and dissonance, of regular and equable rhythmic flow, were being broken down. In the seventeenth century this was an important stimulus both to the development of music itself and also to its increasing relative importance.

The music of the Baroque was not primarily written to express the feelings of an individual artist, but to represent the affections; these were conveyed by means of a systematic, regulated vocabulary, a common repertory of musical *figures* or devices. Such figures included the comparatively simple, obvious pictorial touches common in Renaissance vocal music, but went beyond these into much greater detail. The musical figures of the seventeenth century were systematized in contemporary theoretical treatises on the analogy of the figures or special devices of language used in rhetoric, and were given corresponding names. Thus the Baroque composers, from Monteverdi to Bach, consistently used particular devices of melody, rhythm, harmony, texture, and so on—even figures that might violate the ordinary rules of composition—to illustrate and enforce the literal or implied meaning of words or passages in a text. Their musical language, consequently, has a far more specific vocabulary than we ordinarily expect, and we need to be aware of this if we are to understand what they are saying. They used the same vocabulary in instrumental as well as vocal music, with similar implied meanings.

Diversity of styles and idioms, together with the effort made to represent vividly and precisely objects, ideas, and feelings, brought into Baroque music factors that were somewhat incompatible. Baroque music shows conflict and tension between the centrifugal forces of freedom of expression and the centripetal forces of discipline and order in a musical composition. This tension, always latent in any work of art, was eventually made overt and consciously exploited by Baroque musicians; and this acknowledged dualism is the most important single principle which distinguishes between the music of this period and that of the Renaissance. The dualism is apparent in the existence of Monteverdi's two "practices." It is also evident in the two ways the Baroque treated rhythm: (1) regular metrical barline rhythm on the one hand; and (2) free unmetrical rhythm, used in recitative or improvisatory solo instrumental pieces, on the other.

Dualism: Rhythm

Regular dance rhythms were, of course, known in the Renaissance; but not until the seventeenth century did most music begin to be written and heard in *measures*—definite patterns of strong and weak beats. At first these patterns were not regularly recurring; the use of a single time signature corresponding to a regular succession of harmonic and accentual patterns, set off by barlines at regular intervals, was common only after 1650. By the late Baroque, it had become customary for a composer to establish a distinctive rhythmic pattern at the beginning of a composition or movement, and to hold predominantly to this basic pattern throughout; the piece thus represented a single "basic affection," and made only sparing use of contrasting material.

Along with strictly measured rhythm, Baroque composers also used an irregular, inconstant, flexible rhythm in writing instrumental toccatas and vocal recitatives. Obviously the two rhythms could not be used simultaneously; but they were frequently used successively for deliberate contrast, as in the customary pairing of toccata and fugue or recitative and aria.

The basic sound ideal of the Renaissance was a polyphony of independent voices; the sound ideal of the Baroque was a firm bass and a florid treble, held together by unobtrusive harmony. The idea of a musical texture consisting of a single melody supported by accompanying harmonies was not in itself new; something like it had been used in the cantilena style of the fourteenth century, in the Burgundian chanson, in the early frottola, in the sixteenth-century lute songs, and in the Elizabethan ayre. The ideas that were new in the Baroque were the emphasis on the bass, the isolation of the bass and treble as the two essential lines of the texture, and the

Sound ideal: the basso continuo

seeming indifference to the inner voice lines. This indifference was perfectly pictured in a system of notation used during the Baroque, called the *thoroughbass* or *basso continuo:* the composer wrote out the melody and the bass; the bass was played on one or more *fundament* or *continuo* instruments (clavier, organ, lute), usually reinforced by a sustaining instrument such as a bass gamba or violoncello or bassoon; and above the bass notes the keyboard or lute player filled in the required chords, which were not otherwise written out. If these chords were other than common triads in root position, or if non-harmonic tones (such as suspensions) or added accidentals were to be played, the composer could so indicate by little figures or signs placed above or below the bass notes.

The *realization*—the actual playing—of such a *figured bass* varied according to the nature of the composition and the taste and skill of the player, who had a good deal of room for improvisation within the framework set by the composer: he might play simple chords, introduce passing tones, or incorporate melodic motives in imitation of the treble or bass parts. (A modern edition of compositions with a figured bass usually indicates in smaller notes the editor's conception of a proper realization: see the piece by Caccini and its realization on the preceding pages.) The realization of the basso continuo was not always essential: that is to say, many pieces were provided with a continuo even though all the notes necessary for the full harmony were already present in the notated melodic vocal or instrumental parts. In motets or madrigals for four or five voices, for example, the continuo instrument actually did no more than double or support the voices. But for solos and duets the continuo was usually necessary to complete the harmonies as well as to produce a fuller sonority.

A portion of Sfogava con le stelle *by Giulio Caccini, as printed in* Le nuove musiche, *a collection published in Florence in 1602.*

It might seem that the Baroque basso continuo implied a total rejection of the kind of counterpoint written in the sixteenth century and earlier. As a matter of fact, this was true when the continuo was used alone as accompaniment to a solo, unless the composer chose to give the bass line itself some melodic significance, for the thoroughbass *was* a radical departure from all previous methods of writing music. But it must be remembered that a firm bass and florid treble was not the only kind of musical texture in the Baroque. For a long time, composers continued to write unaccompanied motets and madrigals (though they sometimes tried to give them a "modern" look by adding a basso continuo); some instrumental ensemble pieces, as well as all solo keyboard and lute music, made no use of the basso continuo; most important, even in ensembles where the continuo was used, counterpoint did not disappear. But the new counterpoint of the seventeenth century was different from that of the Renaissance. It was still a blending of different melodic lines, but the lines all had to fit into the regulative framework of a

The new counterpoint

A modern edition of the same portion of Caccini's Sfogava con le stelle, *with the basso continuo realized by a modern scholar, Dr. Carol MacClintock, as published in her book* The Solo Song, 1580–1730 *(New York, 1972).*

series of harmonic chord progressions explicitly defined and sounded by the continuo: it was, in short, a harmonically governed counterpoint, whose melodies were subordinated to the harmonic scheme. Within the harmonies thus defined, composers eventually were able to use dissonance quite freely, just because the underlying harmonies were so clear.

The major-minor system

Gradually, music came to be organized in the system of major-minor tonality familiar to us in the music of the eighteenth and nineteenth centuries: all the harmonies of a composition organized in relation to a triad on the key note or tonic supported primarily by triads on its dominant and subdominant with other chords secondary to these, and with temporary modulations to other keys allowed without sacrificing the supremacy of the principal key. This particular tonal organization had long been foreshadowed in music of the Renaissance, especially that written in the latter half of the sixteenth century. Rameau's *Treatise on Harmony* (1722) completed the theoretical formulation of the system, but it had existed in practice for at least forty years before.

The basso continuo was important in the later stages of this theoretical development because it emphasized the harmonic progressions by isolating them, as it were, in a special notation different from the notation of the melodic lines. The basso continuo was the road over which music travelled from counterpoint to homophony, from a linear-melodic to a chordal-harmonic structure. After the middle of the eighteenth century, when the system of harmonic relationships had become so firmly established that there was no further need to make it explicit by continually sounding the basic chord progressions, the basso continuo gradually disappeared.

Early Baroque Opera

Monody

Various experiments in combining music with drama were made in the sixteenth century, but the creation of genuine opera had to await the discovery of a style of solo singing suitable for dramatic expression. That style came into being as a by-product of the Renaissance veneration for classical antiquity; it was announced as a rediscovery of ancient Greek solo song and was later given an appropriate Greek name: *monody*. In monody, the vocal line aimed chiefly to intensify the natural accents of speech: the accompaniment consisted of a few simple, inconspicuous chords. The earliest surviving compositions in the Florentine monodic style are some songs written by Caccini in the 1590s and published in 1602 under the title of *Le nuove musiche (The New Music)*.[1]

---

[1] The excellent new edition of this collection of solo madrigals and airs, together with a translation of the preface by H. Wiley Hitchcock (Madison, Wisc., 1970), should be consulted.

The monodic style quickly made its way into all kinds of music, both secular and sacred, in the early years of the seventeenth century. It was the one thing needed to make opera possible, for it provided a medium by which both dialogue and exposition could be conveyed in music clearly, quickly, and with all the necessary freedom and flexibility for truly dramatic expression. In 1600, Caccini and Jacopo Peri (1561–1633) jointly set to music a pastoral-mythological drama, *Euridice,* by Ottavio Rinuccini (1562–1621), which was publicly performed in that year at Florence. In the following year each composer published a version of his own, and these two are the earliest surviving complete operas.

The first opera

Euridice was the well-known myth of Orpheus and Eurydice, treated in the currently fashionable manner of the pastoral and modified so as to have a happy ending. Of the two settings of Rinuccini's pastoral, Caccini's is more melodious and lyrical, not unlike the madrigals and airs of his *Nuove musiche*. Peri's is more dramatic; he not only realized a style that is between speech and song but he varied his approach according to the demands of the dramatic situation. Three examples from his *Euridice* will illustrate three styles of monody found in this work (NAWM/S 33a, b, c). Only one of them is truly new. The Prologue (33a) is modeled on the strophic aria for singing verses as practiced throughout the sixteenth century. Tirsi's song (33b) is also a kind of aria, markedly rhythmic and tuneful. Finally, Dafne's speech (33c) is a true example of the new recitative. The chords specified by the basso continuo and its figures have no rhythmic profile or formal plan and are there only to support the voice's recitation, which is free to imitate the rhythms of speech, and while it begins with a note consonant with the harmony it may wander away from it on syllables that are not sustained in speech. Thus Peri devised an idiom that answered to the demands of dramatic poetry. Although he and his associates knew that they had not brought back Greek music, they nevertheless realized a speech-song analogous to what they believed was employed in the ancient theatre, one that was compatible with modern practice.

Monteverdi's *Orfeo,* produced in Mantua in 1607, is clearly patterned both in its subject matter and its mixture of styles on the Florentine *Euridice* operas. Rinuccini's little pastoral was expanded by the poet Alessandro Striggio into a five-act drama, and Monteverdi, already an experienced composer of madrigals and church music, drew upon a rich palette of vocal and instrumental resources. The representation of emotions is stronger and more varied; the harmonies are more expressive; the recitatives no longer depend solely on the words for continuity but are organized into perceptible musical forms. Moreover, Monteverdi introduced many solo airs, duets, madrigal-like ensembles, and dances, which together make up

Claudio Monteverdi

Beginning of Orfeo's aria Possente spirto, *from Act III of Monteverdi's* Orfeo.

quite a large proportion of the work and furnish a needed contrast to the recitative.

It is instructive to consider three sections from *Orfeo* that are more or less analogous to those discussed above from *Euridice:* the Prologue, Orfeo's song, and the messenger's narration of Euridice's death (NAWM/S 34a, b, c). It is immediately obvious that the proportions are very much expanded. Whereas the Prologue is patterned on the air for singing poetry, Monteverdi writes out each strophe, varying the melody while leaving the harmony intact, another technique practiced in the sixteenth century in the improvised singing of poetry. It should be mentioned that Orfeo's famous aria in Act III, *Possente spirto,* is based on the same procedure, but the composer furnished a different ornamentation of the melodic formula for each strophe under the melodic formula itself (see the facsimile above). It probably surpasses in artfulness what a singer could have improvised, but is a valuable witness to the art of vocal ornamentation.

Orfeo's strophic canzonet, *Vi ricorda o boschi ombrosi* (34b), is not unlike Peri's aria for Tirsi in spirit, but the ritornello is worked out in five-part counterpoint. As in Peri's work, the most modern style is reserved for dramatic dialogue and impassioned speeches. The Messenger's speech, *In un fiorito prato* (NAWM/S 34c), imitates the recitative style developed by Peri, but the harmonic movement and melodic contour is more broadly conceived. In Orfeo's lament, which follows, the recitative attains a new height of lyricism that leaves the first monodic experiments far behind.

Monteverdi's treatment of the orchestra in *Orfeo* is especially interesting. Florentine operas had used only a few lutes or similar instruments for accompaniment; in conformity with the monodic ideal, these were placed behind the scenery and kept as inconspicuous as possible. Monteverdi's orchestra in *Orfeo,* on the other hand, numbered about forty instruments (never used all at one time, however), including flutes, cornetts, trumpets, trombones, a complete family of strings, and several different continuo instruments. In many places the composer, in order to make the dramatic situation more vivid, specified exactly which instruments were to play. Furthermore, the score contains twenty-six brief orchestral numbers; these include an introductory "toccata" (a short fanfare-like movement twice repeated) and several ritornellos.

Apparently little progress was made in opera during the twenty years after Monteverdi's *Orfeo,* for the next important school of composers is found at Rome in the 1630s. Here, as might be expected, operas were written on sacred subjects and ensembles held a prominent place. The most important early Roman opera was *Sant' Alessio* (1632), based on the life of the fifth-century Saint Alexis, with music by Stefano Landi (*ca.* 1590–*ca.* 1655). Roman composers also produced a number of pastoral operas and, strangely enough, it was at Rome that the comic opera began its independent career; the first writer of comic opera librettos was a nobleman of the church, Giulio Rospigliosi, who later became Pope Clement IX.

Roman composers of opera

In the music of the Roman operas the separation of solo singing into two clearly defined types, recitative and aria, becomes more marked than ever. The monodic declamation of Monteverdi's *Orfeo* (and this remained true also of his later operas) was semimelodic; in Landi's work, and still more in the Roman comic operas, this original semimelodic recitative became a rather dry, quick movement with many repeated notes, lacking definite musical contour and supported by thin and musically insignificant harmonies in the continuo—became, in short, more like the recitative in the Italian operas of Mozart and Rossini, a mere vehicle for the rapid delivery of words. Melody and all other elements of musical interest gradually were concentrated in the songs or arias, which now began to assume rather definite shapes: strophic arias, arias over a ground bass, and (most often) arias in a loose two-part form with the sections framed by orchestral ritornellos. The many concerted vocal pieces in the Roman operas are derived from the madrigal tradition, modified of course by the presence of a continuo and by the more regular rhythm of the seventeenth century.

The chief later Roman opera composer was Luigi Rossi (1597–1653). His *Orfeo* (Paris, 1647), on a libretto by Francesco Buti, is based on the same subject as the earlier operas of Peri, Caccini, and Monteverdi. This work illustrates the change that had come over the opera libretto during the first half of the seventeenth century. The antique simplicity of the myth is almost totally buried under a mass of irrelevant incidents and characters, spectacular scenic effects, and incongruous comic episodes. The intrusion of the comic, the grotesque, and the merely sensational into a supposedly serious drama was a common practice of Italian librettists during most of the seventeenth century. It was an indication that the integrity of the drama was no longer of first importance, as it had been with the early Florentines and Monteverdi, and that the ancient Greek and Roman myths had come to be regarded merely as conventional material to be elaborated upon in any way that promised to provide entertainment and offer good opportunities to the composer and singers. The decline of the libretto coincided with the development of an imposing style of theatre music. Rossi's *Orfeo* is, in effect, a succession of beautiful arias and ensembles well calculated to make the hearer forgive its faults as a drama.

In part, the deterioration of the opera libretto and the changes in the character of the music were the consequences of presenting **Venetian opera** in public performance rather than to private audiences. This step was taken when the first public opera house was opened at Venice in 1637. Before many years Venice had become the operatic capital of Italy, a position she retained until the end of the seventeenth century. Venetian composers, or composers trained in the Venetian school, were also responsible for the spread of Italian opera to the cities of southern Germany in this period.

Monteverdi wrote his two last operas for Venice: *Il ritorno d'Ulisse* (*Ulysses' Homecoming*) and *L'incoronazione di Poppea* (*The Coronation of Poppea*), performed respectively in 1641 and 1642. *Poppea* is in many respects Monteverdi's operatic masterpiece. It lacks the varied orchestral colors and the large instrumental and scenic apparatus of *Orfeo*, but excels in the depiction of human character and passions through music, being in this respect far in advance of any other seventeenth-century opera.

One of the leading Venetian opera composers was Monteverdi's pupil, Pier Francesco Cavalli (1602–76). The steady demand for new works at Venice is reflected in the quantity of Cavalli's output. Of his forty-one operas, the most celebrated was *Giasone* (1649), a full-blown score with scenes in which arias and recitatives alternate, though the two styles are always kept carefully distinct. Three other Cavalli operas, *Egisto* (1643), *Ormindo* (1644), and *Calisto* (1651),

"The Palace of Paris," a sumptuous scene for the first act of Antonio Cesti's Il pomo d'oro. This typically Baroque setting was designed by Ludovico Burnacini, an important seventeenth-century theatre architect.

have been recently revived, with alterations and additions that would probably have astonished the composer. Cavalli's recitative lacks the variety and psychological shadings of Monteverdi's, but it is still rich in dramatic and pathetic touches. The arias are much more developed and are true set pieces. One of the most famous is the lament of Climene in *Egisto* (NAWM/S 35); it must have contributed to solidify the *topos* of the ground-bass lament, of which it is an exemplary specimen.

The operas of Antonio Cesti (1623–69) are more polished but less forceful in style than those of Cavalli; Cesti excels in lyrical arias and duets. His most famous opera is *Il pomo d'oro* (*The Golden Apple*), which was performed at Vienna in 1667 on the occasion of the wedding of Emperor Leopold I. As a festival opera, it was staged without regard to expense and therefore includes many features that were not common at Venice, such as an unusually large orchestra and many choruses. *Il pomo d'oro* was remarkable also for its lavish scenic effects.

By the middle of the seventeenth century Italian opera had assumed the main outlines of form it was to maintain without essential change for the next two hundred years. The principal features of this form were: (1) concentration upon solo singing with (for a long time) comparative neglect of ensembles and of instrumental music; (2) separation of recitative and aria; and (3) introduction of distinctive styles and patterns for the arias. This development was accompanied by a complete reversal in the relation of text and music: the Florentines had considered music accessory to poetry; the Venetians treated the libretto as hardly more than a conventional scaffolding for the musical structure.

Vocal Chamber Music

At the opening of the seventeenth century composers were confronted with two disturbing new problems. The first involved monody: could the rhythmic flexibility and the lifelike dramatic power of the solo recitative be absorbed into a system of vocal music based on counterpoint of several equally important parts? If so, what means of formal coherence could be devised? Then there was the basso continuo: within the bare texture of a supporting bass and one or two high voices could any resources be found to equal the ample sonority of the older contrapuntal music? The way in which composers of the early seventeenth century effected their reconciliation can perhaps be more clearly understood by regarding it as a process of gradual enrichment and formal stabilization of the monodic style. Many different means were employed, of which two were of particular importance: (1) the use of the bass, as well as the entire harmonic structure, to give formal coherence to a composition; and (2) the use of the *concertato* principle to supply variety of texture and contrapuntal interest.

The bass as a unifying force

In the many collections of monodies that were published during the early part of the seventeenth century one of the most important means of obtaining unity was to keep the same bass for every stanza of the text while varying the melody of the solo part at each repetition of the bass pattern. Such an arrangement is called *strophic variation.* The bass might not be identical in every repetition, but its outline was maintained so that the same succession of harmonies occurred in every strophe. This is the scheme, for example, of most of the coloratura aria *Possente spirto* from the third act of Monteverdi's *Orfeo;* in simpler form, it also occurs in the strophic arias of Caccini's *Nuove musiche.*

For such songs the bass might be freely invented, in which case it was usually a mere series of notes without any particular melodic shape. There were, however, traditional bass patterns or *grounds,* many of them inherited from sixteenth-century dances or improvisatory practices, which composers might use instead of inventing a bass of their own. These traditional bass grounds were quite short and with easily recognizable outlines. If they were not long enough to accommodate an entire stanza of poetry, they were repeated over and over again, either unchanged (*ostinato bass*), transposed, or varied by rhythmic and melodic elaboration of the essential few notes. These repeated bass patterns of one kind or another served as unifying devices in hundreds of compositions, both instrumental and vocal, of the Baroque period. One favorite was the *romanesca* bass, the essential outline of which is given in Example IX–1.

EXAMPLE IX–1   Outline of *romanesca* bass.

A particularly important class of *ostinato* patterns appears in pieces called *chaconne* (*ciacona*) or *passacaglia* (*passecaille*). Both evidently arose in Spain sometime late in the sixteenth century as frameworks for improvisation. Characteristic of both as we find them in the works of seventeenth-century composers is the continuous repetition of a four-bar formula in triple meter and slow tempo. The formula may be: (1) a series of harmonies, either simply I–IV–V–I or with additional or different harmonies between the first I and the final V–I; or (2) a melodic figure decending stepwise

EXAMPLE IX–2   Descending tetrachord figures (sometimes called "Passacaglia Bass")

a. Major diatonic form

b. Minor diatonic form

c. Chromatic form

d. Chromatic form, extended (Purcell, *Dido and Aeneas*, 1689)

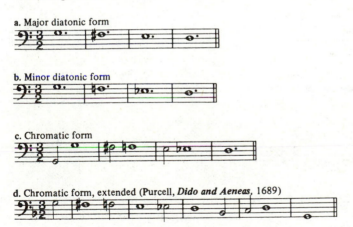

through the tetrachord from tonic to dominant (see Example IX–2). This figure will appear most often or most prominently in the bass, but it may also migrate to other voices and may be melodically varied. Around the middle of the seventeenth century, a keyboard piece built on a repeated series of harmonies—formula (1) above—would probably be called a chaconne, while one featuring the descending melodic tetrachord would be more likely to be called a passacaglia. Both obviously belong to the general category of *variation*. The nomenclature, however, was never fully consistent; by the

end of the century, not only were the formulas themselves sometimes expanded, but also any distinction that might have existed
between the terms "chaconne" and "passacaglia" had vanished—as
may be seen from the titles of pieces from which Examples IX–3a–d
are taken.

A widespread development of the early seventeenth century was
the rise of the *concertato* style. This adjective comes from the same
root as *concert* and *concerto;* it connotes not only "sounding together"—as in a "consort" of instruments—and the common meaning of the Italian verb *concertare* (to reach agreement), but also
some idea of competition or emulation, as in the Latin *concertare*
(to contend or dispute).[2] The *concertato* style, then, is one in which
different musical elements are engaged not always in uniform array,
as in counterpoint or monody, but in a manner which deliberately
emphasizes the contrast of one voice or instrument against another,
or of one group against another, or of a group against a solo. The

**The
concertato
style**

EXAMPLE IX–3   Bass Patterns

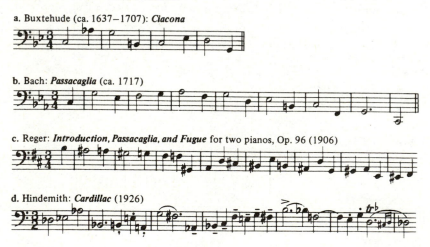

a. Buxtehude (ca. 1637–1707): *Ciacona*

b. Bach: *Passacaglia* (ca. 1717)

c. Reger: *Introduction, Passacaglia, and Fugue* for two pianos, Op. 96 (1906)

d. Hindemith: *Cardillac* (1926)

origins of the *concertato* style of the Baroque lie in the polychoral
works of the Venetian school and in the many polyphonic madrigals
of the late sixteenth and early seventeenth centuries in which two
or three voices, or a solo voice, are brought into prominence against
the background of the ensemble.

The growth of the *concertato* style, along with other developments, can be followed in the fifth, sixth, seventh, and eighth books
of Monteverdi's madrigals, published respectively in 1605, 1614,

---

[2] There may also be in the word "concerto" some echo of the Latin *conserere,*
meaning to unite for contest, as in the expression *conserere manum* = to join in
close combat, hand-to-hand fighting. Insufficiently rehearsed performances of
concertos may make this etymology seem quite plausible.

1621, and 1638. It is fascinating to observe the greatest composer of his time succeed in fusing the heterogeneous musical elements of the early seventeenth century into an eloquent language, firm in structure, varied in color, alternately joyous and sad, robust and tender, warlike and peaceful, responsive to every suggestion of the text.

All these madrigals, beginning with the last six of Book V, have a basso continuo, and many call for other instruments as well. Solos, duets, and trios are set off against the vocal ensemble; there are instrumental introductions and recurring instrumental interludes (ritornellos). The seventh book is entitled *Concerto* and is described as consisting of "madrigals and other kinds of songs." Book VIII, *Madrigals of War and Love,* is especially noteworthy for the variety of forms and types, including madrigals for five voices; solos, duets, and trios with continuo; and large works for chorus, soloists, and orchestra. Among the finest compositions in this volume is the madrigal *Hor che'l ciel e la terra* (*Now that heaven and earth*) for six voices, two violins, and continuo, a masterpiece of moods and sonorities, of abundantly varied harmonies and vivid dramatic contrasts.

In the eighth book also are two *balli* (semidramatic ballets) and another work in the *genere rappresentativo* or theatre style, the *Combattimento di Tancredi e Clorinda* (*The Combat of Tancred and Clorinda*), which had been performed at Venice in 1624. The instruments (string quartet with bass gamba and continuo), in addition to accompanying the voices, play interludes in which various parts of the action are imitated or suggested: the galloping of horses, the clash of swords, the excitement of combat. For such purposes Monteverdi invented a kind of music which he called the *stile concitato* or "excited style"; one device prominent in the *stile concitato* was the rapid reiteration of a single note, either with quickly spoken syllables in the voice or instrumentally as a string tremolo in rhythm.

The complex Baroque musical style thus was achieved by the interaction of diverse elements. Monody and madrigal were combined; formal articulation was approached through the organization of the bass and the harmonies and through systematic use of ritornellos; texture was varied by use of the *concertato* style. As a result, the representational and pictorial power of music was enlarged and intensified. All these developments coincided with a reaction, especially strong after 1630, against considering the text the only or chief unifying factor in serious vocal composition; the innate requirements of the music became more important to composers as they began to discard the original concept of music as merely a transparent veil for text. The gradual separation of recitative and aria left the composer free to write aria melody unhampered by the necessity of following

Forms of vocal solo music

every nuance of the text; and arias began to unfold in graceful, smoothly flowing phrases supported by simple harmonies, most often in slow triple meter with a persistent single rhythmic motive (see NAWM/S 35). This *bel canto* style of vocal writing was a creation of Italian composers; it was imitated in all countries and was influential in both vocal and instrumental music throughout the Baroque and after.

Italian vocal chamber music in the first half of the seventeenth century was published in collections of madrigals, arias, dialogues, duets, and the like. The form that eventually came to engage the chief attention of Italian composers was the *cantata* (literally, a piece "to be sung"). This word, like its counterpart, *sonata,* has been used to designate many different types of composition. In a collection published before 1620 it was applied to arias in the form of strophic variations. Neither that form nor any other was consistently followed by cantata composers during the next two or three decades. Toward the middle of the century *cantata* came to mean a composition usually for solo voice with continuo accompaniment, in several sections which often intermingled recitatives and arias, on a lyrical or sometimes quasi-dramatic text. Yet the Roman, Luigi Rossi, the first eminent master of this particular type of cantata, also wrote others which had simpler forms—either plain strophic songs, strophic variations, arias with ostinato bass, or arias in an *ABA* pattern. Other leading Italian cantata composers of the mid-seventeenth century were Giacomo Carissimi (1605–74)—whose chief field, however, was the sacred oratorio—and the opera composer Antonio Cesti.

Church Music and Oratorio

Sacred music was affected as soon and almost as strongly as secular music by the innovations of the late sixteenth and early seventeenth centuries. Monody, the basso continuo, and the *stile concertato* were all applied to sacred texts. There was, of course, some opposition to the new styles, and indeed, in the Roman Catholic Church, Renaissance polyphony of the Palestrina type was never completely abandoned. Thus throughout the seventeenth century two distinct styles, one conservative (*stile antico*) and one progressive (*stile moderno*), were opposed. Many times both tendencies were manifest in one and the same composer: Monteverdi, for example, wrote in either *stile antico* or *stile moderno* with equal mastery and occasionally alternated the two in the same composition. Before the middle of the seventeenth century, Palestrina had become the supreme model for the conservative style. All composers were trained to write counterpoint based on Palestrina's practice, though in the course of time the details were modified: a basso continuo was often added, rhythms became more regular, and the older modes gave way to the major-minor system.

The conservative Roman counterpoint, although invaluable for study and discipline, was less important in actual early seventeenth-century composition than the style, stemming from the polychoric works of Giovanni Gabrieli and the Venetian school, which is today called the "colossal Baroque." Many composers in this period wrote sacred music for huge aggregations of singers and players, but the master of this style, and one of the major figures in seventeenth-century Catholic church music, was Orazio Benevoli (1605–72). His festival Mass written for the consecration of the cathedral at Salzburg in 1628 calls for two eight-part choruses with soloists; each chorus is associated with three different instrumental combinations and each has its own basso continuo; there is, in addition, a third basso continuo for the whole ensemble. This formidable score takes up fifty-three staves. Benevoli's later works, written mostly for St. Peter's in Rome during the 1640s, give a more adequate idea of his true stature than does the somewhat unwieldy Salzburg Mass; these later works include Psalms, motets, and Masses for three, four, or more choruses, which are provided with a figured bass for the organ but which may equally well be sung unaccompanied. The choruses were stationed at separate places on different levels within the ample basilica of St. Peter's, so that the listeners felt they were enveloped in music from all directions—a truly grandiose and typically Baroque conception.

One of the first composers to adopt the _stile moderno_ in church music was Lodovico Viadana (1560–1627), who in 1602 published a collection called _Cento concerti ecclesiastici_ (_One Hundred Church Concertos_) for solo voice, or various combinations of solo voices, with basso continuo. _O Domine Jesu Christe_ from this collection (NAWM/S 40) is a good example of how Viadana feigned a complex texture in a single voice by having it imitate itself at different pitch levels. This reduction of the polyphonic idiom to a few voices was of great practical significance: it allowed a work to be performed, if necessary, with a small number of singers, and so eliminated the necessity for doubling or replacing vocal parts by instruments as had often been done in the sixteenth century.

Settings of sacred texts in monodic or in _concertato_ style became common during the first half of the seventeenth century. The _stile concertato_—in the form of solos, duets, dialogues, trios, choruses, and diverse small or large combinations of voices and instruments—was applied to both motets and Masses. In this field as in others Monteverdi was a notable pioneer. His _Vespers_ of 1610 is a magnificent setting of a complete liturgical Office incorporating traditional Gregorian Chants as _cantus firmi_ but making use of all the new musical resources of the time—recitative, aria, and all varieties

The Baroque polychoric style

Other styles in church music

of solo, choral, and instrumental groupings—in a unified artistic whole. That the original print of 1610 also included a Mass *In illo tempore,* parodied on a motet of Gombert and written in strict Flemish contrapuntal style, is an illustration of the contrast between *stile antico* and *stile moderno* typical of the early seventeenth century.

The sacred compositions of Monteverdi's Venetian period are for the most part in the *concertato* style, but treated in a completely free and sometimes operatic manner. One stirring Gloria for seven voices *concertate* with two violins and four viols or trombones (?1631) is a brilliant example of a personal, nonliturgical musical treatment of a liturgical text.

One of Monteverdi's contemporaries particularly notable for his sacred compositions in the new style is Alessandro Grandi (*ca.* 1577–1630), who exerted a strong influence on Schütz when he made his second visit to Venice in 1628–29. The solo motet *O quam tu pulchra es* of around 1625 (NAWM/S 41), on a text from the *Song of Songs,* a source very popular for musical setting at this time, shows how a composer could without breaking his stride incorporate into a single composition elements from theatrical recitative, solo madrigal, and *bel canto* aria.

Not only the monodic and *concertato* styles but also the specific dramatic methods of opera were turned to sacred uses. In 1600 Emilio de' Cavalieri (*ca.* 1550–1602) produced on the stage at Rome a morality play with music—in effect, a sacred opera with allegorical characters—entitled *La rappresentazione di anima e di corpo* (*The Representation of the Soul and Body*). This work incorporated verses from an earlier lauda and like the laude was intended as part of an informal devotional religious service at the oratory of S. Filippo Neri.

Oratorios

Apparently this first experiment with sacred opera was not considered successful enough to be imitated; but during the first three or four decades of the century a number of semidramatic dialogues on sacred themes were produced, as well as similar works involving solos and choruses with orchestra and continuo; these compositions combined elements of narrative, dramatic dialogue, and meditation or exhortation, and were not usually intended for stage performance. Toward the middle of the century, works of this kind were called *oratorios,* though the word did not at first have any very precise connotation as to musical genre. The libretto of an oratorio might be in Latin (*oratorio latino*) or Italian (*oratorio volgare*). The principal master of the oratorio in the mid-seventeenth century was Giacomo Carissimi at Rome.

The oratorio was thus distinguished from the contemporary opera by its sacred subject matter, by the presence of the *testo* or narrator, by the use of the chorus for dramatic, narrative, and meditative purposes, and by the fact that oratorios were seldom if ever meant to be staged. Action was narrated or suggested, not presented. Both oratorio and opera used monodic recitative, arias, duets, and instrumental preludes and ritornellos.

In Austria and the Catholic southern cities of Germany, sacred music during the Baroque remained wholly under Italian influence. Italian composers were particularly active at Munich, Salzburg, Prague, and Vienna. Composers in the Lutheran central and northern regions began early in the seventeenth century to utilize the new monodic and *concertato* techniques, sometimes with chorale tunes as melodic material, but often also without reference to traditional melodies.

The new styles in Lutheran music

The new methods were best adapted to compositions for a small number of performers. An important collection of such pieces was published in 1618 and 1626 at Leipzig by J. H. Schein, entitled *Opella nova* [literally, *New Little Works*] *Geistliche Konzerte . . . auff jetzo gebräuchliche Italiänische Invention* (*Sacred Concertos in the Nowadays Customary Italian Manner*). In many respects the pieces are like Lutheran counterparts of some of Monteverdi's *concertato* madrigals. The collection consists chiefly of duets and a few solos on chorale texts; however, Schein does not always use chorale melodies. When he does he treats them with freedom, inserting vocal embellishments, breaking up the phrases and dividing them between the voices. These sacred concertos of Schein were followed by a long series of similar works by Lutheran composers of the seventeenth century.

The greatest German composer of the middle seventeenth century, and one of the most important musical figures of the Baroque, was Heinrich Schütz (1585–1672). After beginning university studies, Schütz was sent to Venice, where he studied with Giovanni Gabrieli from 1609 to 1612 and brought out his first published work, a collection of five-part Italian madrigals. From 1617 to the end of his life, Schütz was Master of the Chapel of the Elector of Saxony at Dresden, although during the disturbed times of the Thirty Years' War he spent several years as Court Conductor in Copenhagen. Schütz renewed his acquaintance with Italian music when he went to Venice in 1628.

Heinrich Schütz

As far as is known, Schütz wrote no independent instrumental music. He is reputed to have composed the first German opera, as well as several ballets and other stage works, but the music of all these has been lost; our knowledge of him consequently rests almost entirely on his church compositions, which we possess in considerable quantity and variety, dating from 1619 to the latest years of his life. The simplest of these works are plain four-part harmonic settings of a German translation of the Psalter (1628). Contrasting with the Calvinist plainness of the Psalm settings are the Latin motets of the

Cantiones sacrae (1625); in these motets a basically conservative Catholic contrapuntal style is enlivened by harmonic novelties and by traits derived from the madrigal, such as the musical representation of sleep and waking at the beginning of *Ego dormio et cor meum vigilat (I sleep, and my heart waketh;* Example IX–4).

Venetian magnificence and color appear frequently in Schütz: for example, in the *Psalmen Davids* (1619) for multiple choruses, soloists, and *concertato* instruments, where the massive colorful sonority of the colossal Baroque is combined with sensitive treatment of the German texts. Indeed, the fusion of Italian and German styles, begun by Hassler and others toward the end of the sixteenth century, was carried to completion by Schütz, who thus established the fundamental characteristics of German music for the remainder of the Baroque age. Only one significant element of the fully developed Lutheran Baroque style was lacking in his works: he seldom made use of traditional chorale melodies, although he set many chorale texts.

In 1636 and 1639, during years when war had sadly reduced the Electoral Chapel, Schütz published his *Kleine geistliche Konzerte*

EXAMPLE IX–4 *Ego dormio,* Heinrich Schütz

I sleep, and my heart waketh.

(*Little Sacred Concertos*), motets for one to five solo voices with organ accompaniment. The year 1636 also saw the publication of the *Musikalische Exequien* (funeral music for Schütz's friend and patron Prince Heinrich Posthumus von Reuss), for soloists and choruses in various combinations with accompaniment of basso continuo. Another collection of German motets, written in a severe contrapuntal style, was the *Geistliche Chormusik* (*Spiritual Choral Music*) of 1648. Most important of Schütz's *concertato* motets are the *Symphoniae sacrae* (*Sacred Symphonies*), which were published in three series in 1629, 1647, and 1650. The first two of these are for various small combinations of voices and instruments, up to a total of five or six parts with continuo. The *Symphoniae sacrae* of 1629 betray the strong influence of the music of Monteverdi and Grandi. *O quam tu pulchra es* (NAWM/S 42) from that collection has approximately the same text as Grandi's, but if it consists of the same ingredients—recitative, aria, and solo madrigal styles—it deploys them quite differently. Schütz sets the apostrophe to the beloved, "O how fair you are . . . ," as a refrain, a kind of ritornello, with two violins, in triple-time aria style, while the individual parts of her body are eulogized in recitative, arioso, or madrigal style. The madrigalistic sections abound in word painting, and the recitative shows how well Schütz assimilated the bold dissonance practices of his Venetian colleagues.

The last part of the *Symphoniae sacrae*, published after the end of the Thirty Years' War when the full musical resources of the Dresden chapel were again available, calls for as many as six solo voices and two instrumental parts with continuo, supplemented by a full choral and instrumental ensemble. Many of these works are broadly laid out as dramatically conceived "scenes," sometimes with a closing chorus of pious reflection or exhortation; they thus approach the plant of the later church cantata.

Schütz's compositions of the oratorio type include his most famous work, *The Seven Last Words* (?1645). Here the narrative portions are set as solo recitative (in two instances, for chorus) over a basso continuo, while the words of Jesus, in free and highly expressive monody, are always accompanied by continuo and strings. There is a short introductory chorus and sinfonia; after the seventh Word the sinfonia is repeated, followed by another short closing chorus. The quality of this music seems to sum up in itself a quiet yet deeply felt piety, a personal, ardent, yet infinitely respectful devotion before the figure of the Saviour.

The *Christmas Oratorio* (1664) is on a larger scale. The narrative portions are given in rather rapid recitative over a continuo, while the "scenes" are treated separately with arias, choruses, and instrumental accompaniment in *concertato* style. Schütz's three Passions, written toward the end of his life, are by comparison austere, hieratical works: narrative and dialogue are both in a style of un-accompanied recitative which, in spirit although not in technical details, is like Gregorian Chant. The *turba* (crowd), that is, the chorus that represents the disciples, the priests, and other groups, is given motet-like unaccompanied settings. Schütz's *Seven Last Words*, oratorios, and Passions are the most significant examples of Lutheran music in these quasi-dramatic forms before J. S. Bach.

Instrumental Music

In the early seventeenth century, vocal music had to assimilate the new technique of monody, which brought about profound changes from the style of the sixteenth century; but instrumental music for the most part had only to continue along the paths that had already been well marked out before the end of the Renaissance. The transference of the monodic principle to instrumental music, as for example in sonatas for solo violin with continuo, was not complicated by consideration of a text. The basso continuo was easily adapted to instrumental ensembles; moreover, there was a small but steady production throughout the Baroque of ensemble pieces in imitative counterpoint which dispensed with the continuo or admitted it only optionally; while for solo keyboard and lute music, of course, the question of continuo did not arise at all.

Instrumental music in the first half of the seventeenth century was gradually becoming the equal, in both quantity and content, of vocal music. Forms were still far from being standardized, however, and designations were still confused and inconsistent. Nevertheless, certain basic ways of proceeding, resulting in certain general types of composition, may be distinguished in instrumental music of this period:

1. The ricercare type: pieces in continuous (that is, nonsectional) imitative counterpoint. These were called *ricercare, fantasia, fancy, capriccio, fuga, verset,* and other names; for the most part, these eventually coalesce into the fugue.

2. The canzona type: pieces in discontinuous (that is, sectional) imitative counterpoint, sometimes with admixture of other styles. These pieces lead to the Baroque *sonata da chiesa,* the most important line of development in seventeenth-century instrumental music.

3. Pieces based on a given melody or bass: principally the *theme and variations* (or *partita*), the *passacaglia* or *chaconne,* the *chorale partita,* and the *chorale prelude.*

4. Dances and other pieces in more or less stylized dance rhythms, either strung loosely together or more closely integrated: the *suite.*

5. Pieces in improvisatory style for solo keyboard instrument or lute: called *toccata, fantasia,* or *prelude.*

These classifications are useful as an introduction to a somewhat complex field; but it must be remembered that the categories are neither exhaustive nor mutually exclusive. For example, the procedure of varying a given theme is found not only in compositions specifically called "variations" but often in ricercari, canzonas, and dance suites as well; toccatas may include short ricercare-like sections; canzonas may have interludes in improvisatory style; in short, the various types interact and interlock in many ways.

In its purest form the seventeenth-century ricercare is a fairly short, serious composition for organ or clavier in which one theme is continuously developed in imitation. One example is the *Ricercar dopo il Credo*[3] by Girolamo Frescobaldi (1583–1643), who was organist of St. Peter's in Rome from 1608 until his death. Frescobaldi published it in 1635 in a collection of organ pieces called *Fiori musicali (Musical Flowers)* intended for use in the church service. This ricercare was part of the music for the *Missa della Madonna (Mass of the Blessed Virgin;* No. IX in the *Liber Usualis,* p. 40); as the title says, it was to be played "after the Credo." The piece is remarkable for the skillful handling of the chromatic lines and the subtle use of shifting harmonies and dissonances, producing the typically Baroque effect of quiet intensity that characterizes much of Frescobaldi's organ music.

Ricercare

On a larger scale than the simple ricercare, and with a more complex formal organization, is a type of early seventeenth-century keyboard composition usually called a *fantasia.* The leading fantasia composers in this period were the Amsterdam organist Jan Pieterszoon Sweelinck (1562–1621) and his German pupils, Samuel Scheidt (1587–1654) of Halle and Heinrich Scheidemann (*ca.* 1596–1663) of Hamburg. The *Fantasia a 4* (NAWM/S 51) is quite typical of Sweelinck's work in this genre. After a fugal exposition in the third mode (transposed down a fifth), the subject, which remains relatively unchanged although stated at times in augmentation or diminution, is combined in successive sections with different countersubjects and toccata-like figurations. Although there are numerous accidentals and chromatic progressions, the music never departs from the chosen modal focus. As with other pieces of the improvisatory type, its function must have been to set and explore a mode or key in preparation for some other music.

Fantasia

Titles like ricercare, fantasia, fancy, capriccio, sonata, sinfonia, and canzona were applied to polyphonic instrumental compositions in the early seventeenth century rather indiscriminately. In general it may be said that the ricercare and fantasia were built on a theme or themes of sustained legato character. The tendency was to develop the themes in such pieces in continuous imitative counter-

[3] MM, No. 34.

point, as in the fugue; and, as has already been mentioned, *fuga* was the name used for pieces of this sort in Germany from the earliest years of the seventeenth century. The canzona, on the other hand, had livelier, more markedly rhythmic melodic material and composers tended to emphasize division of this material into sections.

Consort (ensemble) music for viols flourished in England from the early decades of the seventeenth century when the works of Alfonso Ferrabosco the Younger (d. 1628) and John Coprario (Cooper; d. 1626) were popular. The fancies of John Jenkins (1592–1678), the leading composer in this field in the mid-seventeenth century, illustrate both the ricercare and the canzona: his early five-part contrapuntal fancies for viols and organ have ricercare-like melodic subjects, though often more than one subject is presented and there is a suggestion of sectional division; and his later three-part fancies for two violins and bass are like Italian trio sonatas in their light texture, tuneful themes, and division into sections of contrasting styles. In still other works Jenkins uses the term *fancy* for an introductory movement in imitative counterpoint followed by one or more dances or "ayres."

The contrapuntal fantasia for strings without basso continuo, the leading form of early seventeenth-century English chamber music, was cultivated even after the Restoration. The principal later composers were Matthew Locke (*ca.* 1630–77) and Henry Purcell (*ca.* 1659–95), whose fantasias for viols, written about 1680, are the last important examples of the species.

Canzona

The continuous, monothematic ricercare gradually evolved toward the fugue; the multisectional canzona evolved toward the Baroque sonata. As in the sixteenth century, canzonas were written both for keyboard instruments and ensembles. There are several approaches to the canzona in the seventeenth century. One is to build several contrasting sections each on a different theme in fugal imitation, much like a vocal chanson, rounding off the whole with a cadenza-like flourish. Another type, called the *variation canzona,* uses transformations of a single theme in successive sections, as in the keyboard canzona of G. M. Trabaci (*ca.* 1580–1647) illustrated in Example IX–5. A similar structure is used in many of the keyboard canzonas by Frescobaldi and in those of his most distinguished German pupil, the Viennese organist Johann Jakob Froberger (1616–67). Some keyboard canzonas, however, and the majority of ensemble canzonas, dispensed with the variation technique and were cast in thematically unrelated sections—sometimes with many short periods only a few measures long, put together like a patchwork; and sometimes with fewer but longer sections, one or more of which might be repeated either literally or in varied form after intervening material and thereby serve as an element of unity.

EXAMPLE IX–5   Keyboard Canzona, G. M. Trabaci

Ensemble canzonas of this kind were written by Tarquinio Merula (b. *ca.* 1600).

Merula himself called these pieces *canzonas*. A later composer would probably have called them *sonatas*. This term, the vaguest of all designations for instrumental pieces at the beginning of the seventeenth century, gradually came to mean compositions whose form was like that of the canzona but with special features. Pieces called sonatas in the early seventeenth century were often for one or two melody instruments, usually violins, with a basso continuo; whereas the true ensemble canzona was traditionally written with four parts which could almost always be played just as well without a continuo. Moreover, sonatas were frequently written for a particular instrument and hence took advantage of the idiomatic possibilities of that instrument; they were likely to have a somewhat

Sonata

free and expressive character, whereas the typical canzona had more of the formal, abstract quality of instrumental polyphony in the Renaissance tradition.

By the middle of the seventeenth century the canzona and the sonata had thoroughly merged, and the term *sonata* gradually replaced *canzona;* sometimes the name was expanded to *sonata da chiesa,* since many of such pieces were intended for use "in church." Sonatas were written for many different combinations of instruments; a common medium was two violins with continuo. The texture of two treble melodic parts, vocal or instrumental, above a basso continuo had a particular attraction for composers throughout the seventeenth century. Sonatas of this type are usually called *trio sonatas.*

Variations

The seventeenth century has been called "the age of the variation" because the variation principle permeates so many of the instrumental forms of the period. In a more specific sense, the *theme and variations* is the continuation of a favorite type of keyboard composition of the late Renaissance. Three techniques were used in such pieces:

1) The melody could be repeated with little or no change, although it might be transferred from one voice to another and surrounded with different contrapuntal material in each variation. This type is sometimes called the *cantus firmus variation.* The leading seventeenth-century composers were, in addition to the English virginalists, Sweelinck and Scheidt.

2) The melody itself could be ornamented differently for each variation; as a rule it remained in the topmost voice, with the underlying harmonies essentially unchanged. One of the leading composers of this type of variation was the Hamburg organist Jan Adam Reinken (1623–1722). Incidentally, it should be noted that the word *partite* (divisions) was used in the early seventeenth century to designate sets of variations; only later did it come to be applied to sets or suites of dances.

3) In a third type of variation, the bass or the harmonic structure, not the melody, is the constant factor. Often, as in the case of the *romanesca,* a treble tune is also associated with the bass, but it is usually obscured by figuration. An early example is the set of *partite* by Frescobaldi on the *Aria di Ruggiero* (NAWM/S 52). Like the *romanesca, Ruggiero* was an air or tune for singing *ottave rime;* indeed it received its name from the stanza in Ariosto's *Orlando furioso* once sung to it, "Ruggier, qual sempre fui, tal sempre voglio" (Canto 44, stanza 61). The bass and harmony of the air are clearly the fixed elements in Frescobaldi's twelve *partite,* and only in the *Sesta Parte* is the melody at all prominent.

An important class of Baroque organ compositions from middle and northern Germany were works based on chorale melodies.

These pieces were produced in large numbers and in a great variety of forms after the middle of the seventeenth century, but there are examples already in the works of Sweelinck and Scheidt. In 1624, Scheidt published a large collection of compositions for the organ under the title *Tabulatura nova*—new, because instead of the old-fashioned German organ tablature, Scheidt adopted the modern Italian practice of writing out each voice on a separate staff. Among the chorale compositions of the *Tabulatura nova* are a notable fantasia on the melody *Ich ruf' zu dir* (*I call to Thee*) and several sets of variations on other chorale tunes. There are also shorter organ settings of plainsong melodies, many variations on secular songs, and several monumental fantasias. The works of Scheidt, and his influence as a teacher, were the foundation of a remarkable development of North German organ music in the Baroque era.

Dance music in the seventeenth century continued to be produced in ever greater quantity and variety. Notable is the appearance in German collections at this time of numerous pieces called *Polnischer Tanz* (*Polish Dance*), *Polacca,* and the like—evidence of the extent to which the folk-based music of Poland was coming to be known in western Europe. Dance music was important not only in itself but also because dance rhythms began to permeate other music, both vocal and instrumental, sacred and secular. The characteristic rhythm of the sarabande, for example, and the lively movement of the gigue appear in many compositions that are not called dances at all. As in the sixteenth century, dances were written both for solo instruments and for ensembles.

Dance music

The early seventeenth century is especially remarkable for the production in Germany of *suites* of dances for instrumental groups, commonly a set or consort of viols, although with the usual understanding that other instruments, such as violins or cornetts, might be substituted. The stimulus for the suites seems to have come largely from English composers living in Germany; probably it was the English influence also that led the Germans to extend the technique of thematic variation—already established in the pavane-galliard combination of the sixteenth century—to all the dances of a suite. One of the most important collections of dances was J. H. Schein's *Banchetto musicale* (*Musical Banquet*), published at Leipzig in 1617.

Suites

The conception of the suite as a musical entity, as one composition in several movements rather than a mere succession of short pieces each in a certain mood and rhythm, was a German contribution. In France, the great achievement of the early and middle seventeenth century was to establish a characteristic idiom and style for the individual dances. This achievement was a reflection of the fact that most French suites were not written for an ensemble

French lute and keyboard music

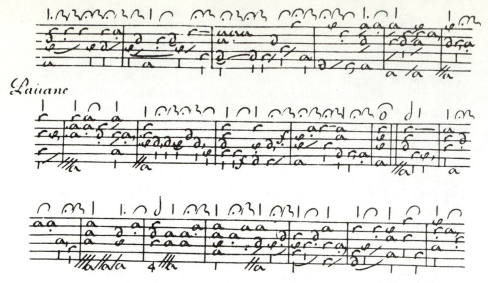

A page of Gaultier's La Rhétorique des dieux.

but for a solo instrument—first the lute and later the clavecin (the French term for harpsichord) or the viole (the French term for viola da gamba). Lute music flourished in France during the early seventeenth century, culminating in the work of Denis Gaultier (*ca.* 1600–72). A manuscript collection of Gaultier's compositions entitled *La Rhétorique des dieux* (*The Rhetoric of the Gods*) contains twelve sets (one in each mode) of highly stylized dances. Each set includes an allemande, courante, and sarabande, with other dances added apparently at random; each suite is thus actually a little anthology of short character pieces, many of which were given fanciful titles.

Since the lute was incapable of sustained tone, it was necessary to sketch in the melody, bass, and harmony by sounding the appropriate tones now in one register, now in another, leaving it to the imagination of the hearer to supply the implied continuity of the various lines. This was the *style brisé* or broken style which other French composers adapted to the harpsichord, together with certain features of the variation technique derived from the English virginalists; they also systematically developed the use of little ornaments (*agréments*), sometimes indicated by stenographic signs on the page and sometimes left to the discretion of the player. The French lute style was the source not only of important developments in keyboard music but also of the entire French style of composition in the late seventeenth and early eighteenth centuries. This was also the period when the viol flourished as a solo instrument.

The earliest important composer in the new keyboard idiom was Jacques Champion de Chambonnières (*ca.* 1602–72), the first of a long and brilliant line of French clavecinists among whom Louis Couperin (1626–61) and Jean Henri d'Anglebert (*ca.* 1628–91) should be especially mentioned. The new style was carried to Germany by Froberger, who established the allemande, courante, and sarabande as standard components of dance suites. In Froberger's manuscripts the suites end with a slow dance, the sarabande; in a later, posthumous publication of the suites in 1693, they were revised so as to end with a lively gigue. The fusion of genre pieces and dance rhythms in the mid-seventeenth century keyboard suite is well illustrated in one of Froberger's most famous compositions, a lament (*tombeau*) on the death of the Emperor Ferdinand IV; this piece, in the pattern and rhythm of an allemande, forms the first movement of a suite.

A different kind of improvisatory composition, already foreshadowed by some Italian keyboard works of the late sixteenth century, occurs in some of the toccatas of Frescobaldi. In contrast to the imposing objective grandeur and virtuosity of the Venetian school, these toccatas are in a reserved, subjective, mystical vein, with sustained harmonies and extraordinary original chord progressions. These works, exemplified by the well-known *Toccata for the Elevation* from the *Missa delli apostoli* (*Mass of the Apostles;* No. IV in the *Liber Usualis,* p. 25) in the *Fiori musicali,* are the very essence of improvisatory style, although they utterly renounce technical display. **Improvisatory compositions**

Other keyboard toccatas of Frescobaldi's, however, are related to the Venetian type: they allow scope for virtuosity and in form are a long series of loosely connected sections with great luxuriance of musical ideas. The various sections of these toccatas, the composer states, may be played separately, and the piece may be ended

A seventeenth-century Italian harpsichord in an elaborately sculptured Baroque case. (Courtesy Metropolitan Museum of Art, Crosby Brown Collection of Musical Instruments, 1889)

at any appropriate cadence if the player so desires; moreover, Frescobaldi indicates that the tempo is not to be subject to a regular beat but may be modified according to the sense of the music, especially by retarding at cadences.

More solidly formed though less exuberant toccatas were written by Froberger; in these, the free improvisatory passages provide a framework for systematically developed sections in the contrapuntal style of a fantasia. Froberger's pieces were the model for the later Baroque merging of toccata and fugue, such as occurs in the works of Buxtehude, or their coupling, as in the familiar *Toccata and Fugue in D minor* of Bach.

X

The Mature Baroque:
Vocal Music

Opera, Cantata, Song

In the second half of the seventeenth century, opera spread through
Italy and outward to other countries. The principal Italian center
was Venice, whose opera houses were famous all over Europe.

The Venetian opera of this period, although by later standards
dramatically ridiculous, was scenically and musically splendid. The
plots were a jumble of improbable characters and situations, an
irrational mixture of serious and comic scenes, and served mainly
as pretexts for striking stage effects, pleasant melodies, and beautiful solo singing. Vocal virtuosity had not yet reached the dizzying
heights it attained in the eighteenth century, but the way was being prepared. The chorus had practically disappeared, the orchestra
had little to do except accompany, and the recitatives were of only
slight musical interest: the aria reigned supreme. Composers of the
new aria did not entirely disregard the text, but they considered it
merely a starting point; they were chiefly interested in the musical
construction, the material for which they drew from the rhythms
and melodies of popular music—that is, music familiar to the people
in general. Motives imitated from trumpet figures were used for
martial or vehement arias, often being expanded into brilliant
coloratura passages. An example is the aria *Vittrici schieri* (*Victorious hosts*) from the opera *Adelaide* (1672) by M. A. Sartorio (*ca.*
1620–*ca.* 1685). The coloratura had not yet become—as it had by the

Italian opera

**Agostini and
Sartorio**

end of the century with some composers—an arbitrary vocal adornment for display of virtuosity; it was still serving a definite expressive function.

Sartorio was one of the last of the Venetians who continued the heroic style of opera established by Monteverdi and Cavalli. In the works of Sartorio's follower Giovanni Legrenzi (1626–90) a milder, more genial temper prevails. The aria *Ti lascio l'alma impegno* (*I leave my soul imprisoned with thee*) from Legrenzi's *Giustino* (Venice, 1683) shows the combination of graceful nobility of melodic line and natural contrapuntal and constructive skill which is typical of Italian music in the late seventeenth century.

In addition to Sartorio and Legrenzi, the most important Italian opera composers of the late seventeenth and early eighteenth centuries were Francesco Provenzale of Naples (1627–1704), Alessandro Stradella (1644–82), Carlo Pallavicino (1630–88), Agostino Steffani (1654–1728), and Alessandro Scarlatti (1660–1725).

Steffani

Pallavicino and Steffani were two of the many Italian composers who in the late seventeenth and early eighteenth centuries carried Italian opera to the eagerly receptive German courts. Pallavicino worked chiefly in Dresden, Steffani at Munich and Hanover.

In his later works Steffani wrote amply proportioned arias and accompaniments of rich *concertato* texture; he nearly always managed to maintain an equal balance between form and emotional content in his music. One of the best Italian opera composers of his time, his works are important not only for themselves but also historically; they illustrate the transition from the style of the middle Baroque to that of the late Baroque, and they exerted influence on eighteenth-century composers, especially Keiser and Handel.

The Neapolitan style

In Italy even before the end of the seventeenth century there were distinct tendencies in opera toward stylization of musical language and forms, and toward a simple musical texture with concentration on the single melodic line of the solo voice, supported by ingratiating harmonies. The eventual result was a style of opera which was more concerned with elegance and external effectiveness than with dramatic strength and truth; but the dramatic weaknesses were often redeemed by the beauty of the music. This new style, which became dominant in the eighteenth century, was apparently developed in its early stages principally at Naples, and hence is often called the *Neapolitan* style.

Another notable feature of eighteenth-century Italian opera was the emergence of two distinct types of recitative. One type—which later was given the name *recitativo secco* (dry recitative) and was accompanied only with the harpsichord and a sustaining bass instrument—was used chiefly to get through long stretches of dialogue or monologue as quickly as possible with a minimum of musical interference. The second type—*recitativo accompagnato, obbligato,* or *stromentato* ([orchestrally] accompanied recitative)—was used for especially tense dramatic situations; the rapid changes of emotion in the dialogue were reinforced by the orchestra, which both accompanied the singer and punctuated his phrases by brief instrumental outbursts. There was also a type of melody which was neither so rhythmically free as the recitative nor so regular as the aria, but stood somewhere between the two; this kind of melody is called *arioso*, that is, "aria-like."

The transition from the seventeenth-century Baroque opera to the newer style is evident in the works of Alessandro Scarlatti, who has generally been regarded as the principal founder of the Neapolitan school. In many of his later works, notably in *Mitridate* (Venice, 1707), *Tigrane* (Naples, 1715), and *Griselda* (Rome, 1721), the broad dramatic conception of the arias and the importance of the orchestra evidence Scarlatti's devotion to a serious musical ideal. The *da capo aria* becomes in the hands of Scarlatti the perfect vehicle for sustaining a lyrical moment through a musical design that expresses a single reigning affection, with sometimes a subordinate related sentiment. This is clearly evident in the aria that opens Act II of *Griselda, Mi rivedi, o selva ombrosa (You see me again, O shady wood;* NAWM/S 38).

By the beginning of the eighteenth century, Italian opera had been accepted by nearly every country in western Europe save France. Although a few Italian operas had been played at Paris toward the middle of the seventeenth century, the French for a long time would neither accept the Italian opera nor create one of their own. However, in the 1670s a national French opera was finally achieved

Opera in France

A contemporary engraving of a performance of Lully's Alceste *given in the candle-lit marble courtyard at Versailles. The orchestra can be seen seated in enclosures on both sides at the front of the stage; the royal personages directly face the singers.*

Jean-Baptiste Lully

under the august patronage of Louis XIV. With special features that distinguished it from the Italian form, it remained essentially unchanged until past the middle of the eighteenth century. Tentative experiments in French opera were made by Robert Cambert (*ca.* 1628–77) beginning in 1659; but the first important composer was Jean-Baptiste Lully (1632–87), who succeeded in blending elements from the ballet and the drama in a form which he called a *tragédie lyrique* (tragedy in music).

Lully was an Italian who came to Paris at an early age, and who by astute business management and the favor of the king made himself virtually the musical dictator of France. His music is most immediately attractive to modern ears in the massive spectacular choruses and in the rhythmical dances of the ballet scenes, for example the Chaconne from *Roland*. Dances from Lully's ballets and operas eventually became widely popular in arrangements as independent instrumental suites, and many composers in the late seventeenth and early eighteenth centuries wrote dance suites in imitation of Lully's.

An important contribution of Lully was the treatment of recitative. Devising musical declamation for French words was by no means a simple task, since neither the rapid *recitativo secco* nor the quasi-melodic *arioso* of Italian opera was suitable to the rhythms and accents of the French tongue. Lully solved the problem by studying the style of declamation used in the French theatre and imitating it as closely as possible. Leaving nothing to the discretion of the singers, he notated his recitative in exact detail. The result, in the best instances, is an effect of genuine power, due not so much to the qualities of the melodic line or the harmony as to the way in which the music follows precisely the changing dramatic inflections and pauses of the text.

One of the most impressive scenes of recitative is the first part of the monologue in *Armide*, Act II, scene 5, in which Armide stands over her captive warrior, the sleeping Renaud, with a knife, prevented by her love for him from plunging it into his breast. (The entire scene is in NAWM/S 36b). Armide sings in an unmetrical rhythm, that is, measures of four quarters are interspersed with measures of three. Each line is generally followed by a rest, as are sometimes caesuras within a line. Rests are also used dramatically, as in the passage where Armide hesitates: "Let's get it done . . . I tremble . . . let us avenge ourselves . . . I sigh!" Despite the lack of regular meter, Lully's recitative is more melodious than the Italian and the line is more determined by the harmonic movement. In the aria that follows in the graceful rhythm of a minuet Armide calls upon her demons to transform themselves into zephyrs and transport her and Renaud to some remote desert, where her shame and weakness would not be observed.

EXAMPLE X–1   Air, *Bois épais* from *Amadis,* Jean-Baptiste Lully

Thick forest, redouble your shadows: you cannot be dark enough, you cannot sufficiently conceal my unhappy love.

Another kind of air, less rooted in the dramatic action but of greater musical interest, is the poetical depiction of a quiet scene and of the contemplative feelings aroused by it. An example is *Bois épais* from the opera *Amadis* (1684; Example X–1). Musical mood-paintings of this kind—serious, restrained, elegantly proportioned, full of aristocratic yet sensuous charm—were much admired and frequently imitated by later composers.

Even before he began to write operas Lully had established the musical form of the *ouverture,* the "French overture." In the late seventeenth and early eighteenth centuries, instrumental pieces in this form not only introduced operas and other large composite works, but also appeared as independent compositions and sometimes constituted the opening movement of a suite, sonata, or concerto. The overture to *Armide* is a good example (NAWM/S 36a). It has two parts. The first section is homophonic in style, slow in movement, majestic, with persistent dotted rhythm and motives that rush toward the downbeat. The second section starts with a semblance of fugal imitation and is comparatively fast-moving, without sacrificing a certain grave and serious character. Then there is a return to the slow tempo of the beginning with some reminiscences of its music. Each of the two sections is marked to be repeated. Some later opera overtures and other instrumental

The ouverture

pieces begin in this way, then continue with a number of additional movements. The original aim of the *ouverture* was to create a festive atmosphere for the opera that was to follow; Venetian overtures of the early seventeenth century had served the same purpose. By the end of the century, the Italian opera composers were beginning to write overtures, which they called *sinfonie,* of quite a different type (see page 238ff.), but the French remained faithful to their traditional form.

Lully's influence extended beyond the field of opera. The rich five-part texture of his orchestration and his use of the woodwinds—both for supporting the strings and in contrasting passages or movements for a trio of solo wind instruments (usually two oboes and bassoon)—found many imitators in France and Germany. In the latter country it was Georg Muffat (*ca.* 1645–1740) who first introduced Lully's style of composition and the French manner of orchestral playing.

English opera

John Blow

Opera in England—or what was there known as opera—had a short career in the second half of the seventeenth century. *Venus and Adonis* (1684 or 1685) by John Blow (1649–1708) is an unpretentious pastoral opera, containing some charming and even moving music, in which the influences of the Italian cantata as well as of both the native English and the fashionable French styles of the period are discernible. The overture and prologue are obviously modeled on those of French opera; many of the airs and recitatives adapt the emotionally expressive curves of Italian *bel canto* to English words; other songs have more purely English rhythms and melodic outlines. The final threnodic chorus *Mourn for thy servant* is typically English in its simple, truthful interpretation of the text, its grave rhythms, flawless declamation, lucid part-writing, and frequent harmonic audacities.

Henry Purcell

Henry Purcell, the finest English musical genius after William Byrd and the last great English composer before the twentieth century, was a pupil of Blow; he served as organist of Westminster Abbey from 1679 and held other posts in the official musical establishments of London. In addition to many odes for chorus and orchestra, cantatas, songs, catches, anthems, Services, fancies, chamber sonatas, and keyboard works, he wrote incidental music for 49 plays, the largest and most important part of this theatre music being composed during the last five years of his life.

His *Dido and Aeneas* (1689) is a masterpiece of opera in miniature; the orchestra consists of strings and continuo, there are only four principal roles, and the three acts, including dances and choruses, take only about an hour to perform. The music shows that Purcell was able to incorporate in his own style both the achievements of the English school of the seventeenth century and the influences on that school from Continental sources. The overture is of the French type, and the homophonic choruses in dance rhythms suggest, although they surpass in tunefulness, the choruses of Lully. The minuet rhythm $\frac{3}{4}$ ♩ ♩ | ♩ ♫ | ♩ ♩ | ♩ of the chorus *Fear no danger to ensue,* beginning in alternate iambics and trochees ∪ — | — ∪ | ∪ — | — , is especially reminiscent of French models. The closing chorus *With drooping wings* must certainly have been suggested to Purcell by the final chorus in Blow's *Venus and Adonis;* equally perfect in workmanship, it has a larger scale and a profounder depth of elegiac sorrow, the sentiment being supported by the musical suggestion of "drooping" and the impressive pauses after the word "never." The recitatives are neither the rapid chatter of the Italian *recitativo secco* nor the stylized rhythms of French operatic recitative, but free plastic melodies flexibly molded to the accents, pace, and emotions of the English text. Three of the arias are built entirely over a ground bass; the last of these—and one of the greatest arias in all opera—is Dido's lament *When I am laid in earth.* In its perfect adaptation of technique to expression this song is one of the landmarks of seventeenth-century music.

Apart from *Dido and Aeneas,* Purcell's output of dramatic music was all incidental music for plays. For most of the plays for which he wrote music he wrote only a few pieces and most of these few pieces were short ones. There are four or five plays, however, in which the musical portions are so extensive as to make them in effect operas within the seventeenth-century English meaning of the word —that is, dramas in spoken dialogue but with overtures, entr'actes, and long ballets or other musical scenes. Purcell's principal "operas" of this sort were *Dioclesian* (1690), *King Arthur* (1691), *The Fairy Queen* (1692; an adaptation of Shakespeare's *Midsummer Night's Dream*), *The Indian Queen* (1695), and *The Tempest* (1695).

Unfortunately for English music, no composer appeared after Purcell who had sufficient stature to maintain the national tradition against the preference for Italian opera at the beginning of the eighteenth century. For two hundred years English opera remained a stepchild while English audiences lavished their enthusiasm on the productions of Italian, French, or German composers.

Despite the prevailing fashion for Italian opera at the German courts in the seventeenth century, a few cities supported German companies and gave operas in German by native composers. The **German** most important center was the northern free city of Hamburg, **opera** where the first public opera house in Europe outside Venice was opened in 1678. The Hamburg opera existed until 1738, by which time the changed public taste would no longer support native opera on any considerable scale. During these sixty years, however, a number of German opera composers were active, and a national school of opera arose. Many librettos of German operas in this period were translated or imitated from the Venetian poets, and the music of the German composers was influenced by both Venetian and French models.

The foremost early German opera composer was Reinhard Keiser (1674–1739), who wrote over 100 works for the Hamburg stage between 1696 and 1734. Keiser's operas at their best represent a union of Italian and German qualities. In subject matter and general plan the librettos are like those of the Venetian operas, and the virtuoso arias even surpass their Italian counterparts in vigor and brilliance. The slower melodies, though lacking the suave perfection of the Italian *bel canto,* are serious and sometimes profoundly expressive; the harmonies are well organized in broad, clear structures. Keiser was no slave to the current Italian fashion of casting practically every aria in the da capo form; when he uses this pattern it is often with modifications, and in addition he introduces free arioso melodies not bound strictly to any rhythmic or formal scheme, as well as songs in purely German style. His accompaniments are of special interest, for Keiser shared the preference of most German Baroque composers for a comparatively full polyphonic texture in contrast to the Italian tendency to concentrate everything in the melody. Thus his arias abound in interesting basses and varied combinations of orchestral instruments which "concertize" or "compete" with the voice in independent melodic figures.

Reinhard Keiser *(marginal note)*

Along with opera, the other important Italian form of vocal composition in the second half of the seventeenth century was the cantata. After the early years of the century, the cantata had developed from monody with strophic variation to a form consisting of many short contrasting sections; in the second half of the century it finally settled into a more clearly defined pattern of alternating recitatives and arias—normally two or three of each—for solo voice with continuo accompaniment, on a text usually of amatory character in the form of a dramatic narrative or soliloquy, the whole taking perhaps ten to fifteen minutes to perform. Thus in both its literary and its musical aspects the cantata resembled a detached scene from an opera; it differed from opera chiefly in that both poetry and music were on a more intimate scale. Designed for performance in a room, without stage scenery or costumes, and for smaller and more discriminating audiences than those of the opera houses, the cantata always kept a certain elegance and refinement of workmanship that would have been out of place in opera. Because of its intimate character, also, it offered more opportunity than opera for experimental musical effects.

The cantata *(marginal note)*

Practically all the Italian opera composers of the seventeenth century were prolific composers of cantatas. In quantity as well as in quality the years from 1650 to about 1720 were astoundingly productive ones in Italy; but as is true of the operas, only a tiny fraction of these works is accessible in modern editions.

The most noted cantata composers after Carissimi, L. Rossi, and Cesti were Legrenzi and Stradella. A climax was reached toward the end of the century with the more than six hundred cantatas of Alessandro Scarlatti. His cantata *Lascia, deh lascia (Cease, O Cease)* has many characteristics typical of the form. It begins with a short section of arioso, that is, a melody in slow tempo not so highly organized in form nor so regular in rhythmic pattern as an aria, with an expressive character midway between aria and recitative. (See Example X–2a.) The ensuing recitative is typical of the mature style of Scarlatti in its wide harmonic range: notice the modulation to the remote key of E♭ minor at the words "inganni mortali" (deceptions of mortal life; Example X–2b). Then follows a full da capo aria with long, supple melodic phrases over a bass in stately eighth-note rhythm, organized partly by the help of sequences and containing likewise some unusual harmonic progressions and chromatics expressive of the word "tormentar" (Example X–2c).

Alessandro Scarlatti

EXAMPLE X–2   Cantata: *Lascia, deh lascia,* Alessandro Scarlatti

a.

a. *Cease, O cease to torment me.*

b.

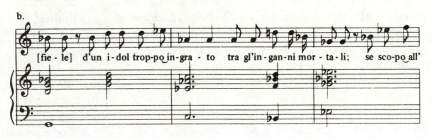

b. . . . *[bitterness] of an adored one too ungrateful, among the deceptions of mortal life; if it is the purpose of the wrath of adverse fate [only to make me die] . . .*

c. Enough, cruel Love; torment me no more.

A second brief recitative, leading in rapid succession through various keys from F major to B minor, introduces a second da capo aria in E minor, the key of the opening movement. Although the middle sections of both arias end in the dominant minor, the general tendency of the modulations throughout is toward the subdominant. The mood of tender melancholy, the elegant melodic lines, and the refinement of the harmonic workmanship are thoroughly characteristic of Scarlatti.

Song in other countries

The Italian chamber cantata was imitated or adapted in other countries, though to a lesser extent than Italian opera. In France Marc-Antoine Charpentier (1634–1704), a pupil of Carissimi, composed both secular cantatas and sacred oratorios in the Italian style. Italian influence remained strong on most of the French cantata composers of the early eighteenth century; thus Louis Nicolas Clérambault (1676–1749), who published five books of cantatas between 1710 and 1726, alternated recitatives in the manner of Lully with arias in Italian style, sometimes even with Italian words. In France there was also a modest but steady production throughout the seventeenth century of *airs* of various types, some attaching to the older tradition of courtly vocal music and others of a more popular cast.

The situation in Germany was similar; Keiser, Telemann, and others in the early eighteenth century wrote cantatas on Italian as well as on German texts. Among the many seventeenth-century German composers of solo songs the most notable was Adam Krieger (1634–66) of Dresden, a pupil of Scheidt; his *Neue Arien* (*New Airs*), published in 1667 and 1676, were for the most part strophic melodies in a charmingly simple popular style with short five-part orchestral ritornellos, though occasionally he approached the form of the cantata with through-composed texts in contrasting movements. The use of orchestral accompaniments and ritornellos with solo songs was more common in Germany than in other countries, and many German composers also wrote songs and arias on sacred texts. Toward the end of the seventeenth century in Germany the song as a type of independent composition practically disappeared, being absorbed into composite forms—the opera or the cantata. Occasional songs in collections around the turn of the century are similar in style, if not in form, to opera arias.

England was comparatively remote from Italian influence during much of the seventeenth century. There were some attempts to imitate the new monodic recitative during the Commonwealth, and after the Restoration English musicians became acquainted with the work of Carissimi and Stradella; but the best song productions of English composers owed little to foreign models. In this genre as in all others the outstanding composer was Henry Purcell.

Church Music and Oratorio

The separation, so characteristic of the Baroque era, between conservative or "strict" style and progressive or "free" style is nowhere more vividly illustrated than in the music of the Roman Catholic Church during the later seventeenth and early eighteenth centuries. Hundreds of Masses and other liturgical compositions were written in the manner of the Roman school of Palestrina, many of them employing the Renaissance techniques of parody and *cantus firmus*. Frequently such works included canons and other learned contrapuntal artifices; they were sung by unaccompanied voices, or with instruments merely doubling the vocal parts. Their composers for the most part were men like Scarlatti, who were equally at home with the up-to-date musical language of the opera and cantata. A famous late example of this conservative church music was the *Missa di San Carlo*, known also as the *Missa canonica*, of Johann Josef Fux (1660–1741), composed at Vienna in 1716, every movement of which is built on elaborate but strictly canonic development of original themes. Fux mentions in his dedicatory letter that he composed this Mass particularly to revive the "taste and dignity of ancient music." But works of the old *a cappella* type, though considerable in quantity and interesting because they reflect the continued vitality of the Palestrina tradition, are less important for the history of church music than compositions in more progressive style.

South German church music in this period was the product of a union of Italian and German characteristics, and sums up many of the principal stylistic achievements of the Baroque. The Mass and other liturgical texts were set to music on a magnificent festive scale with choruses and solo ensemble sections freely intermingled, supported by full orchestral accompaniment as well as orchestral preludes and ritornellos. Especially elaborate choruses were written for the *Amen* of the Gloria and Credo in the Mass. Sequential repetitions became a common constructive device within a clearly outlined harmonic major-minor system.

In the Masses of Antonio Caldara (1670–1736), perhaps a pupil of Legrenzi, there are not only solo or ensemble sections within predominantly choral movements but also independent, self-contained solo arias and duets with concertizing instruments and orchestral ritornellos; these Masses thus have somewhat the aspect of a series of separate musical numbers, like an opera—although the operatic recitative was never used in liturgical compositions, and the full da capo aria form appeared but seldom.

Pergolesi and Hasse

The originators of the peculiarly plaintive early eighteenth-century chromaticism, which of course affected the melody as well as the harmony, were Italian—the north Italian composers Legrenzi and Antonio Lotti (*ca.* 1667–1740), and especially the Neapolitan Giovanni Battista Pergolesi (1710–36). Pergolesi's *Stabat Mater* exemplifies the fragile texture, the admirably balanced phrasing, and the lyrically sentimental tone of much Italian religious music of the eighteenth century. Italian style predominates in the music of Johann Adolf Hasse (1699–1783), a German who studied and lived many years in Italy and who in addition to some 100 operas also wrote many oratorios, Masses, and other church compositions.

Oratorio and motet

The oratorio, although on sacred subjects, had a poetic rather than a Biblical text; moreover, it was not bound by the conventional limitations of purely liturgical music, being intended rather for performance in what might be called sacred concerts, and thus often serving as a substitute for opera during Lent or at other seasons when the theatres were closed. After Carissimi's time, the Latin oratorio with choruses was largely abandoned in favor of the *oratorio volgare* (that is, oratorio with Italian words). Practically all composers of Italian opera in the Baroque also wrote oratorios, and as a rule there was little if any difference in musical style between the two. The chorus was retained to a slight extent in the oratorio, but most of the oratorio music was written as solos and duets, as in opera. The close connection between the two forms is suggested by the fact that most of the oratorios in the Catholic centers of South Germany in this period were, like the operas, on Italian texts.

The favorite church composer of the early eighteenth century at Paris was Michel-Richard Delalande or de Làlande (1657–1726), some of whose motets for chorus and orchestra are worthy examples of the grand style in ecclesiastical music of this period. Another eminent name in this field is that of François Couperin (1668–1733); his *Leçons de ténèbres* (1714), on texts from the Offices of Matins and Lauds for Holy Week for one or two solo voices with accompaniment in a spare *concertato* style, are uniquely impressive works.

The principal forms of Anglican Church music after the Restoration were the same as those of the early part of the century, namely anthems and Services. Among the many English church composers, John Blow and Henry Purcell were outstanding. Since Charles II favored solo singing and orchestral accompaniments, many anthems of the verse type were produced, such as Pelham Humfrey's (1647–74) *Hear o heav'ns* (NAWM/S 43). The solo lines are in a kind of French measured recitative applied to a very rhetorical style, full of sighing appoggiaturas and plaintive chromaticisms. This is combined with an English love for augmented and diminished intervals used melodically, in cross relations, and in harmony. A rich expressive style results.

Anglican church music

Anthems for coronation ceremonies were, of course, especially elaborate works; examples are Purcell's *My heart is inditing* or the splendid coronation anthems of Blow. Not a few of the composers of English Restoration verse anthems descended to triviality in their efforts to mimic the attractions of theatre music. A more even level of musical excellence was maintained in the less pretentious "cathedral" or "full" anthems for chorus without soloists, of which Purcell's earlier four-part *Thou knowest, Lord, the secrets of our hearts* is a beautiful example. Some of the best of Purcell's sacred music is in his settings of nonliturgical texts, pieces for one or more solo voices usually in a rhapsodic arioso style with continuo accompaniment, evidently designed for private devotional use.

The Baroque era, particularly the period from 1650 to 1750, was the Golden Age of Lutheran music. Its development was affected by two conflicting tendencies within the church. The Orthodox party, holding to established dogma and public institutional forms of worship, favored using all available resources of choral and instrumental music in the services. Opposed to Orthodoxy was the widespread movement known as Pietism, which emphasized the freedom of the individual believer; Pietists distrusted formality and high art in worship, and preferred the expression of personal feelings of devotion in music of more simple character.

Lutheran church music

The enormous increase in production of devotional songs in the latter part of the seventeenth century was accompanied by a general decline in both poetic and musical quality. Many of the Pietistic texts expressed self-centered and sentimental religious attitudes in extravagantly emotional language, while attempts to give the music a simple folklike quality too often resulted only in mediocrity. Not until after 1700 did the opposing currents of Pietism and Orthodoxy arrive at a mutually beneficial union. In the meantime developments of importance took place in Orthodox centers where the environment was favorable and the material resources adequate for the maintenance of high artistic standards.

Concerted church music

Three distinct musical-textual elements were involved in these developments: the concerted style, with Biblical text, as established in Germany by Schein, Scheidt, Schütz, and other composers of the early and middle seventeenth century; the solo aria, with strophic non-Biblical text; and the chorale, with its own text and the tune which, as *cantus firmus*, might be treated in various ways. Combinations of these elements resulted in three basic types of composition: 1) the "concerto-aria" cantata, consisting of arias only (or arias and choruses), treated in *concertato* style; 2) the "concerto-chorale" cantata, consisting of chorales only, treated in *concertato* style; and 3) the "chorale-aria" cantata, consisting of both chorales and arias, the former either in simple harmonic settings or in *concertato* style.

EXAMPLE X–3 Chorus from Cantata: *Wenn der Herr die Gafangenen*

The following few examples must suffice to show something of the wide range and variety of production in the late seventeenth and early eighteenth centuries.

Schütz's tradition of concerted music for chorus, solo voices, and orchestra without reference to chorale melodies may be illustrated by a chorus, *Die mit Tränen säen* (*They that sow in tears*) from a larger work by his pupil the Hamburg organist Matthias Weckmann (1619–74). Weckmann's treatment of the words "They that sow in tears shall reap in joy" is typically Baroque in the contrast between the two opposite moods suggested by the text (Example X–3).

More subjective in mood, and showing some influence of Pietist sentiment, were the influential *Dialogues between God and a Believing Soul* by Andreas Hammerschmidt (1612–75), published in 1645 (Example X–4). This work is remarkable for the skillful use of a trombone obbligato in the tenor register.

One of the principal Lutheran composers of the late seventeenth century was Dietrich Buxtehude (*ca.* 1637–1707), Tunder's son-in-law and his successor at Lübeck. Although the majority of Buxtehude's works were of the free *concertato* type, he also wrote *chorale variations,* a form in which each stanza of a chorale in turn serves as a basis for elaboration by voices and instruments. His *Wachet auf* is written this way; its form consists of a short festive instrumental prelude or *sinfonia,* the outline of which seems to have been suggested by the first two phrases of the chorale melody; a first stanza of the chorale for soprano voice and orchestra (strings, bassoon, continuo), in 3/2 and 4/4 time, each phrase slightly ornamented in the voice and the vocal phrases separated by brief orchestral interludes, the whole being considerably extended by repetition of the last half of the chorale tune; a second stanza, bass voice with orchestra, treated similarly to the first stanza, but in brisk 3/4 rhythm; a third stanza, for two sopranos and bass, in 3/2, which is more compact,

EXAMPLE X–4   Dialogue: *Wende dich, Herr,* Andreas Hammerschmidt

Alto: *Turn thee, O Lord, and be merciful unto me.*
Bass: *Is not Ephraim my dear son and my beloved child? Because I remember well [what I have said to him]* . . .

with short points of imitation on several of the chorale phrases, and which broadens out at the end to a sonorous climax. All movements are in the same key, D major, so that contrast is achieved mainly through change of texture and rhythm.

The variation form, so common in the Baroque period, is frequently found in chorale-based concerted compositions of the late seventeenth century. When a chorale melody was not used, composers felt free to employ a more flexible arrangement, alternating short solo arioso sections with ensemble and choral parts. Toward the end of the century a somewhat standardized pattern of concerted church music developed, consisting of a motet-like opening chorus on a Bible verse, a solo movement or movements (aria or arioso) and a final chorus setting a stanza of a chorale. Free *concertato* without chorale prevails in the vocal works of Johann Pachelbel (1653–1706), most famous of a long line of composers working at or in the vicinity of Nuremberg. Like many of the composers in southern Germany, where Venetian influence remained powerful, Pachelbel frequently wrote for double chorus.

Until the end of the seventeenth century the texts of Lutheran compositions had consisted chiefly of passages from the Bible or the church liturgy, together with verses taken from or modelled on chorales. In 1700, Erdmann Neumeister (1671–1756) of Hamburg, an Orthodox theologian but a poet of decidedly Pietist leanings, introduced a new kind of sacred poetry for musical setting, in a form which he designated by the Italian term "cantata." Neumeister (and, after him, several other Lutheran poets of the early eighteenth century) wrote cycles of cantatas, intended to be used systematically throughout the church year. The characteristic feature of these church cantatas was the employment, in connection with the prescribed Biblical passages or hymns, of original poetic insertions which sought to expound the given scriptural text and to bring its meaning home to the individual worshipper through devout meditations of a subjective character. Each of the added poetic texts was designed to be composed either as an arioso or else as an aria, usually in da capo form and frequently with an introductory recitative. Neumeister and his imitators favored the free fancy of the composer by writing their poetry in the so-called "madrigal" style, that is in lines of unequal length with the rhymes irregularly placed; many of Bach's cantata texts and the arias in the *St. Matthew Passion* are in this madrigal style.

The Lutheran church cantata

The widespread acceptance of this new cantata type was of cardinal importance for Lutheran church music. Its poetic scheme reconciled Orthodox and Pietistic tendencies in a satisfactory blend of objective and subjective, formal and emotional elements; its musical scheme incorporated all the great traditions of the past—the chorale, the solo song, the concerted style—and added to these the dramatically powerful elements of operatic recitative and aria. Strictly speaking, the designation "cantata" is applicable only to compositions of the sort described above; concerted church compositions of the seventeenth and early eighteenth centuries in Lutheran Germany usually had no particular designations (though terms like "Kantate," "Konzert," and "Geistliches Konzert," or even simply "die Musik" were applied to them in various instances). However, as in the case of the word "motet," a somewhat loose practice now exists of applying "cantata" indiscriminately to nearly all types of concerted Lutheran church music of the Baroque period, both before and after Neumeister's innovations.

J. S. Bach was the greatest master of the church cantata. His most important immediate forerunners were Johann Philipp Krieger of Weissenfels (1649–1725), who also composed operas; Johann Kuhnau (1660–1722), Bach's predecessor at Leipzig; and Friedrich Wilhelm Zachow (1663–1712) of Halle. Zachow's cantatas have a great variety of forms: recitatives and da capo arias are intermingled with choruses, which sometimes make use of chorale melodies. The writing for both solo and chorus is brilliant in sonority and strong in rhythm; instruments are prominently used in *concertato* fashion. His works point directly and unmistakably to the cantatas of Bach, with which they have many characteristics in common.

Among the contemporaries of Bach notable for their church compositions should be mentioned Christoph Graupner (1683–1760) of Darmstadt; Johann Mattheson (1681–1764) of Hamburg, who wrote Passions and oratorios, and was also important as a scholar and essayist; and Georg Philipp Telemann (1681–1767), who worked at Leipzig, Eisenach, Frankfurt, and Hamburg. Telemann's immense production included 40 operas, 12 complete cycles of cantatas and motets (about 3000 pieces altogether), 44 Passions, and a large number of oratorios and other church compositions as well as hundreds of orchestral and chamber works.

The Passion

Among the forms of church music in Lutheran Germany was the *historia,* a musical setting based on some Biblical narrative, for example the story of Christmas or of Easter. The most important type of *historia,* however, was the *Passion.* Plainsong settings of the Gospel accounts of the suffering and death of Christ had existed since early medieval times. After about the twelfth century it was customary to have the story recited in semidramatic form, with one priest singing the narrative portions, another the words of Christ, and a third the words of the crowd (*turba*), all with appropriate contrasts of range and tempo. (The Passion was still sung in this way in some Catholic churches up to quite recent times.) After the late fifteenth century, composers made polyphonic settings of the *turba* portions in motet style, contrasting with the plainsong solo parts; this type of setting was known as the "dramatic" or "scenic"

Passion. Johann Walter adapted the dramatic Passion to Lutheran use with German text in his *St. Matthew Passion* of 1550, and his example was followed by many subsequent Lutheran composers, including Heinrich Schütz. Often, however, the entire text would be set as a series of polyphonic motets—called the *motet Passion.*

The rise of the concerted style in the late seventeenth century led to a new type of Passion which approximated the form of the oratorio and hence is called the *oratorio Passion;* this setting employs recitatives, arias, ensembles, choruses, and instrumental pieces, all of which lend themselves to a dramatic presentation, as in opera. Schütz's *Seven Last Words* was an early approach to this kind of musical treatment, although its text is a composite of all four Gospels instead of being taken, as was customary in the Passion, from one Gospel exclusively.

In the second half of the seventeenth century the Gospel text was expanded by the addition of, first, poetic meditations on the events of the story, which were inserted at appropriate points and set to music usually as a solo aria, sometimes with a preceding recitative; and second, by chorales traditionally associated with the story of the Passion, which were usually sung by the choir or congregation.

XI

The Mature Baroque: Instrumental Music

Up to now instrumental music has been discussed on the basis of musical forms derived from compositional procedures: the ricercare and other fugal forms; the canzona and sonata; variations and other pieces based on a *cantus firmus;* dances and the suite; the toccata and related improvisatory forms. By the late seventeenth century, however, there seems to have been a growing feeling that there was a style not only of performance, but also of composition, appropriate to each type of instrument, rather than a general instrumental (as opposed to vocal) style; and this led naturally to a different type of treatment for each instrument or each category of instruments. Therefore, it will be appropriate to deal with instrumental composition in this period on the basis of medium of performance: music for a keyboard instrument (organ, harpsichord, or clavichord); and music for an ensemble of instruments, whether a small (chamber) group or one of larger size.

The principal types of compositions associated with each of these media are:

Keyboard: toccata (prelude, fantasia) and fugue; arrangements of Lutheran chorales or other liturgical material (chorale prelude, verset, etc.); variations; passacaglia and chaconne; suite; sonata (after 1700).

Ensemble: sonata (*sonata da chiesa*), sinfonia, and related forms; suite (*sonata da camera*) and related forms; concerto.

230

Keyboard Music

Three principal species of organ compositions were cultivated in the late Baroque in northern Germany: the *toccata,* the *fugue,* and the *organ chorale.* Each of these designations stands for a general class of compositions, and, as usual in this period, the nomenclature is unstable.

The toccata was originally and always remained essentially a style of music which aimed to suggest the effect of an improvised performance. To this end it used many devices: irregular or free rhythm in contrast with a propulsive unceasing drive of sixteenth-notes; phrases deliberately kept indistinct or wilfully irregular; sudden sharp changes of texture. But mostly the effect of improvisation was maintained by means of a contrived uncertainty in the harmonic flow of the music: by quick erratic changes of direction or (at the opposite extreme) a slow-paced movement involving long, harmonically inert stretches marked usually by extended pedal points. The naturally capricious, exuberant character of toccatas was often intensified by making them vehicles for displaying a performer's skill at the keyboard and on the organ pedals; the demand made for virtuosity in playing the pedals was a feature that especially distinguished the German composers from all other organ composers of the time.

The toccata

Toccatas best exhibit the outthrusting, fantastic, dramatic aspects of the Baroque spirit in music. It was equally characteristic of the Baroque, however, to discipline the freedom of the toccata, and in the most drastic manner, by yoking it with the ricercare in a union of musical opposites. Composers early began to incorporate in their toccatas well-defined sections of imitative counterpoint which contrasted with the otherwise prevailing rhapsodic style. The desire for clearly articulated and symmetrical phrases became stronger as the seventeenth century wore on; and even in short toccatas without fugal interludes some measure of order was brought into the rhapsodic flow of sound by means of the two most common crystallizing devices of late Baroque music, the melodic sequence and sequential imitation. The Toccata in E minor by Pachelbel is a good example of this usage.

Works which illustrate on a grand scale the Baroque conflict between impulse and order are the monumental organ compositions of the north German masters of the seventeenth century, above all those by Buxtehude. Buxtehude's toccatas are made up of sections in free style which alternate regularly with as long or longer sections of imitative counterpoint. They have a wonderful sense of movement and climax, with great variety in the figuration, and they take full advantage of the idiomatic qualities of the organ. Yet the soaring fantasy of the composer is held in balance by the architectural plan of the whole work. The opening is always in free improvisatory style, ending with a solid cadence; then follows a fugue, on a subject of salient melodic outline and with well-marked rhythm, fully developed in counterpoint; this merges at length gradually into a second toccata-like section, shorter than the first, and again leading to a cadence. At this point the composition may close; but as a rule Buxtehude goes on to a second and sometimes a third fugue, with brief interludes and a closing climactic section in toccata style. When there is more than one fugue, the subjects in the majority of cases are variants of a basic musical idea (see Example XI–1, the three fugue subjects from Toccata No. 1).

Keyboard pieces like the one described above were called in the seventeenth century "toccata," "prelude," or some similar name, even though they included fugal sections. In keyboard music, the simple coupling of two contrasted movements, a prelude in free or homophonic style and a fugue in contrapuntal style, is found only in the late Baroque; most seventeenth-century compositions called "Prelude and Fugue" by later editors show a relationship to the simpler Buxtehude type of toccata, that is, a toccata with one comparatively long fugal section in the middle.

Fugues were also written as independent pieces. By the end of the seventeenth century the fugue had almost entirely replaced the

EXAMPLE XI–1   Varied Forms of a Fugal Subject, Dietrich Buxtehude

old ricercare. The essential differences between the two are apparent in the late seventeenth-century works by Johann Krieger (1651–1735) brother of Johann Philipp. The fugue subject has a more definite melodic character and a livelier rhythm than the ricercare subject; the ricercare develops in a placid, abstract manner without much variety or any marked climax, but the fugue drives ahead energetically to its close; the fugue has some short episodes (passages where the subject is not being heard in any voice) which are set off by a little lightening of the texture and sometimes also by the use of sequences; whereas the ricercare has fewer such passages and those few not sequential nor in any way different in texture from the rest of the piece. Moreover, the fugue has a tonal organization with a clear dominant-tonic relationship, while the conservative ricercare tends to stay closer to the old modal system. The final perfection of the fugue, as well as of all the other large musical forms characteristic of the late Baroque, was inseparable from the full development of the major-minor system of tonality with its hierarchy of keys, which made possible a systematic use of key relationships in the musical design of long movements.

The fugue

Corollary to this development was the gradual extension of the system of *equal temperament* to the tuning of keyboard instruments. In this tuning, the octave is divided into twelve exactly equal semitones, so that an instrument sounds equally in tune in any one of the twelve keys. Formulated by many theorists after the early sixteenth century, and apparently in actual use for lutes, viols, and other fretted instruments during the sixteenth and seventeenth centuries, the system or some practical approximation to it began to be generally applied to keyboard instruments on the Continent by the early years of the eighteenth century.

Equal temperament

The other principal class of organ composition of the late seventeenth and early eighteenth centuries comprises works based on a chorale melody. Organ composers in the seventeenth century used the chorale in three fundamental ways: as a theme for variations, as a subject for a fantasia, or as a melody to be presented with appropriate embellishment and accompaniment. These three ways of treating a chorale melody gave rise to three distinct types of composition: the *chorale partita,* the *chorale fantasia,* and the *chorale prelude.* The chorale partita, a set of variations on a chorale tune, was initiated early in the century by Sweelinck and Scheidt, and was continued, although with modifications in the technique, by later organ composers to the time of Bach and after. Buxtehude's *Danket dem Herrn, denn er ist sehr freundlich (Thank the Lord, for he is very kind;* NAWM/S 48) shows one of the many ways a chorale may be made the subject of a set of variations. The chorale fantasia, also dating from the early part of the century, gradually

Chorale compositions

moved away from the severe contrapuntal style of the fantasias of Scheidt. At the hands of Reinken, Buxtehude, and other north German composers, the form became extended. The treatment of the material became freer; each phrase of the chorale was worked out in turn and a great variety of figuration and texture was introduced, always with emphasis on brilliant virtuoso effects.

The chorale prelude

Chorale prelude, a term often loosely applied to any organ composition based on a chorale melody, will be used here in a somewhat more restricted sense to denote relatively short pieces in which the entire melody is presented once in readily recognizable form. This form of the chorale prelude did not appear until after the middle of the seventeenth century. As the name implies, such pieces probably originated as functional liturgical music: the organist played through the tune, with accompaniment and ornaments *ad libitum,* as a prelude to the singing of the chorale by the congregation or choir; later on, when pieces in this same general style were written down, they were called "chorale preludes" whether or not they were intended to serve the original liturgical purpose. Naturally, many varieties of treatment are found: (1) Each phrase of the melody in turn may serve as the subject of a short fugal development, the whole piece thus taking on the form of a chain of fughettas. This form has an obvious resemblance to the chorale fantasia, but is more concise and more consistent in style. (2) In one particular type of chorale prelude, chiefly associated with the name of Pachelbel, the first phrase receives a fairly extended fugal treatment, after which this and all the following phrases in turn appear, usually in the top voice, in long notes with relatively little ornamentation; each such appearance is preceded by a short anticipatory imitative development of its characteristic melodic motive in short notes (that is, in diminution) in the other voices. Sometimes the opening fugal development is shortened and the first phrase introduced in the same manner as the ones following. (3) More numerous are chorale preludes in which the relation between melody and accompaniment is less exact. The accompaniment, while still borrowing many of its motives from the chorale tune, is treated much more freely and with greater variety from phrase to phrase; the melody, which usually begins at once without any introductory imitative material, is ornamented in an imaginative, unstereotyped manner, and sometimes extended in a long melismatic phrase at the final cadence. The masters of this subjective and often highly poetic form of the chorale prelude were Buxtehude and Georg Böhm. (4) Finally, there are chorale preludes in which the melody, usually unornamented, is accompanied, in one or more of the lower voices, by a continuous rhythmic figure not related motivically to the melody itself. This type is not common in the seventeenth century, but is often found in Bach.

A distinctive French Baroque school of organ music produced

some attractive settings of popular airs and pieces resembling the overtures and expressive recitatives of French opera, as well as more learned, contrapuntal works and antiphonal "dialogues" for the three or four divisions of a large organ. This music has the typically French ornaments (*agréments*); many pieces were designed to exploit particular color possibilities on the organ, and the stops were often specified. Among the finest French organ music of this age are the "Masses" (versets and interludes to be played in the Mass) of François Couperin, which include specimens of all the distinctive types mentioned above. Couperin's noble organ music is one of the glories of the Baroque era in France, as was Buxtehude's in Germany.

The term *clavier* (i.e. keyboard) is used to denote both the clavichord and the harpsichord. It is not always possible in the Baroque period, especially in Germany, to tell which of the two a composer intends in a given piece; sometimes it is even uncertain whether a clavier or an organ is the desired instrument. Though all the types of composition described in the preceding section were also used in clavier music, the two important forms of clavier music were the *theme and variations* and the *suite*. **Clavier music**

As has already been mentioned, variation of a given musical subject was one of the most widely used techniques in Baroque composition. This basic arrangement of a theme (air, dance, chorale, or the like) followed by a series of variations goes back to the early history of instrumental music. No essential change occurred in the late Baroque, although there was a tendency to abandon the earlier *cantus firmus* type of variation, except in chorale partitas. Many composers after 1650 preferred to write an original song-like melody (often called an *aria*) for the theme rather than borrow a familiar tune as earlier composers had commonly done. **Theme and variations**

A large proportion of the clavier music of the late seventeenth and early eighteenth centuries is in the form of the *suite*. Two distinct varieties existed. In France, the *ordres* of François Couperin published between 1713 and 1730 consist each of a loose aggregation of many—sometimes as many as 20 or more—miniature pieces. Most of these are in dance rhythms, such as courante, sarabande, gigue, and so on, highly stylized and refined. Their transparent texture and delicate melodic lines decorated with many embellishments, as well as their conciseness and humor, are typical of French music of the time of the Regency. Most of them carry fanciful titles; for example, *La Visionaire* (*The Dreamer*), *La Misterieuse* (*The Mysterious One*), *La Muse victorieuse* (*The Victorious Muse*) are the titles of a few of the pieces in the Twenty-fifth Ordre (they are in NAWM/S 53) from Couperin's fourth book for clavecin published in 1730. **The suite**

A stately movement in triple rhythm that was made popular by

Lully's music for the stage is that of the passacaglia and chaconne. Both the chaconne and the related form of the ground or ground bass (in which there is a repeated bass melodic pattern as well as a repeated harmonic pattern) were applied not only to keyboard music but to instrumental and vocal ensemble works as well. All sorts of refinements of the basic scheme were possible. The *Passacaille ou Chaconne* from Couperin's first Suite for Viols (1728) maintains for 199 measures the regular 4 + 4-measure phrasing with only an occasional slight shortening or lengthening at cadences, but with numerous variations and alterations in the pattern (see Example XI–2).

EXAMPLE XI–2 *Passacaille ou Chaconne* from Suite No. 1 for Viols, François Couperin

The lower line of music is for the second viol, together with the harpsichord realizing the basso continuo. In his two suites for "basse de viole," Couperin did not use the agrément signs that were typical of music for that instrument; instead he notated the agréments in the same manner as for his Pièces de clavecin. According to his Explication, they are to be interpreted as follows:

pincé-simple   tremblement   port de voix pincé-simple   port de voix tremblement   aspiration

Since each ornament begins on the beat and takes its time value from the note to which it is attached, the upper line of parts a and b of this example would be played approximately as follows:

The dotted sixteenths in part c should be slightly over-dotted, but not to the full extent of a double dot.

In Germany before the end of the seventeenth century the clavier suite (or *partita*, as it was also called) had assumed a definite order of four dances: allemande, courante, sarabande, and gigue. To these might be added an introductory movement or one or more optional dances placed either after the gigue or before or after the sarabande. The added dances as well as the general style of the writing reveal a continuing French influence on German clavier composers of this period.

The keyboard sonata

The sonata, which in the Baroque period was primarily a type of composition for instrumental ensemble, was first transferred to the clavier by Kuhnau in 1692. His *Frische Klavierfrüchte* (*Fresh Clavier-fruits*), published in 1696, consists entirely of sonatas. More interesting than these rather experimental pieces are the six sonatas Kuhnau published in 1700, which represent in music stories from the Old Testament, with titles such as "Saul's Madness Cured by Music," "The Combat between David and Goliath," or "Hezekiah's Illness and Recovery." These Biblical sonatas are attractive and well-constructed pieces, as well as amusing musical renditions of the stories.

Ensemble Music

By the beginning of the eighteenth century Italian musical pre-eminence had been challenged by the achievements of the French clavecinists and the north German organists; but in the realm of instrumental chamber music, as in the opera and cantata, the Italians reigned as undisputed masters and teachers of Europe. The age of the great violin makers of Cremona—Niccolò Amati (1596–1684), Antonio Stradivari (1644–1737), and Giuseppe Bartolomeo Guarneri (1698–1744)—was also the age of great string music in Italy.

The word "sonata" appears fairly regularly on the title pages of Italian musical publications throughout the seventeenth century. In the earlier decades the term (like the parallel word, *sinfonia*) chiefly

Violin made of maple, pine, and ebony by Antonio Stradivari (1644–1737) of Cremona. (Courtesy Metropolitan Museum of Art, Bequest of Annie Bolton Matthews Bryant, 1934)

denoted instrumental preludes or interludes in predominantly vocal works; after 1630, though the earlier usage continued, *sonata* and *sinfonia* were used more and more often to designate separate instrumental compositions. The early stages of the emergence of the sonata from the canzona have been sketched in Chapter IX.

The
ensemble
sonata

In the most general sense, the independent instrumental sonata of the Baroque period is a composition for a small group of instruments —usually two to four—having a basso continuo and consisting of several sections or movements in contrasting tempos and textures. Within this general scheme, of course, there may be any amount of diversity. Two main types or classes of sonatas begin to be clearly distinguished after about 1660: the *sonata da chiesa* (the church sonata, usually designated simply as "sonata"), the movements of which are not obviously in dance rhythms and do not bear the names of dances; and the *sonata da camera* (chamber sonata), which is a suite of stylized dances. So goes the definition, but in practice the two types do not always appear unmixed: many church sonatas end with one or more dance movements (not always so designated), while many chamber sonatas have an opening movement which is not a dance. The most common instrumentation after 1670 for both church and chamber sonatas is two treble instruments (usually violins) and bass, the harmonies to be completed by the continuo player. A sonata written in this way is called a *trio sonata,* even though for performance it requires four players (since the basso continuo line is doubled on a violoncello or similar instrument while the harpsichordist or organist fills in the implied harmonies). The texture exemplified in the trio sonata—two high melody lines over a bass—is fundamental to many other types of Baroque music, and persists even beyond the Baroque era.

Less numerous than trio sonatas in the seventeenth century, although more numerous after 1700, are sonatas for solo violin (or flute or gamba) with continuo (the so-called *solo sonata*). Larger groups, up to six or eight instrumental parts with continuo, are also used in the Baroque, and there are a few sonatas (or like pieces under a different designation) for a single stringed instrument without accompaniment.

With respect to its external form, the evolution of the canzona-sonata in the seventeenth century may be summarized as a progressive reduction in the number of movements and a progressive increase in the length of each movement. The order of the movements did not become standard until toward the end of the seventeenth century.

It is significant that the trio sonata, not the solo sonata, was especially favored by Italian composers of this era. The instrumentation of the trio sonata made possible an ideal balance of lyrical melody and limpid polyphony. The two high singing violins could interweave their contrapuntal patterns (in which the distant bass as well might join), but the texture, held together by the unobtrusive harmonies of the harpsichord, was sufficiently open so that there was no danger of obscuring the lines or making the sonority too thick. Also, the solo sonata was always prone to excesses of virtuosic display; but the trio sonata subordinated the individual to the ensemble in a regulated disposition of forces which directed attention to the substance rather than to the outward show of the music.

The perfect examples of the serene, classical phase of Baroque musical art are the violin sonatas of Arcangelo Corelli (1653–1713). His works include trio sonatas, solo sonatas, and concertos.

Arcangelo Corelli

In his trio sonatas Corelli summed up the achievements of Italian chamber music in the late seventeenth century; in his solo sonatas and concertos he initiated developments that were followed for the next fifty years and more. He was exceptional among Italian composers of his time in that he apparently wrote no vocal music whatever; he transferred the national genius for song to the violin, the instrument that most nearly approaches the expressive lyric quality of the human voice.

Corelli's trio sonatas

A fundamental technical device in all of Corelli's music is the sequence. It is no coincidence that Corelli, the first major Baroque composer to make extensive and systematic use of this means of construction, was also the first to write music in which we hear the full realization of the major-minor tonality practically free from any trace of modality. The sequence, whether carried out diatonically within one key or modulated downward in the circle of fifths, is one of the most powerful agents in establishing tonality. Corelli's modulations within a movement—most often to the dominant and (in minor keys) the relative major—are always logical and clear; he established the principles of tonal architecture which were elaborated and extended by Handel, Vivaldi, Bach, and all other composers of the next generation. Corelli's music is almost completely diatonic; chromaticism is limited virtually to a few diminished sevenths or an occasional flatted second (Neapolitan sixth) at a cadence.

Many of Corelli's trio church sonatas consist of four movements in the order slow–fast–slow–fast, analogous to the order of the four movements in many cantatas of this period. The same order of movements was often used by other composers of the late seventeenth and early eighteenth centuries, so that some music historians regard it as "the" type of Baroque sonata—an over-simplified view, as there are so many exceptions to the general rule. Corelli's chamber sonatas, both trio and solo, usually begin with a *preludio,* which is followed by two or three of the conventional dances of the suite in the normal order; but the final gigue may be replaced by a gavotte.

It is typical of the seventeenth century that in the majority of

Title page of the second violin part of Corelli's Opus 3: "Trio sonatas, [for] two violins, violone or archlute, with bass for the organ." The first edition, Rome 1689.

Corelli's trio sonatas, all movements are in the same key. This is not true of his later works: all the solo sonatas that are in major keys (eight out of eleven) have one slow movement in the relative minor, and all the concerti grossi have a slow movement in a contrasting key. In general, there are no contrasting or "secondary" themes within a movement. The subject of the whole musical discourse to come is stated at once in a complete sentence with a definite cadence; from then on the music unfolds in a continuous expansion of this subject, with sequential treatment, brief modulations cadencing in nearby keys, and fascinating subtleties of phraseology (see NAWM/S 46). This steady unfolding or "spinning out" (the Germans call it *Fortspinnung*) of a single theme is highly characteristic of the late Baroque.

Corelli's solo sonatas have the same order and character of movements as the corresponding types of trio sonatas, though in his solo sonatas an additional fast movement of contrasting texture is always coupled with one or the other of the regular two. Naturally, the solo sonatas have a larger proportion of homophonic movements than do the trio sonatas. Corelli's most conspicuous innovation, however, is the technical treatment of the violin. Although the third position is never exceeded, there are difficult double and triple stops, fast runs, arpeggios, cadenzas, and étude-like movements in *moto perpetuo.*

Corelli's solo sonatas

All in all, these solo sonatas give us a comprehensive idea of what Corelli expected in the way of technique from his students. His teaching was the foundation of most of the violin schools of the eighteenth century; it was as influential on later generations of players as his music was on later generations of composers. Some of his contemporaries and many of his followers surpassed him in *bravura,* but none in the understanding of the *cantabile* qualities of his instrument nor in the good taste with which he avoided mere displays of virtuosity unjustified by musical content.

Improvisation in Baroque musical performance

Performers in the Baroque era were always expected to add notes to those the composer had written. The realization of a figured bass, for example, was worked out by the player. Vocal and instrumental solo melodic lines were dependent on performers' skill, taste, and experience for their proper completion by means of ornaments. Ornaments probably always originated in improvisation; and although they might at some later stage be partially or wholly written out, or else indicated by special signs (as in Example XI–2), still they always kept a certain coloring of spontaneity. For us, the word *ornamentation* is liable to carry misleading connotations, to suggest something unessential, superfluous, a mere optional adjunct to the melody. This was not the Baroque view. The ornaments were not merely decorative; they had a definite expressive function as means of conveying affections. Moreover, some of the more common ornaments—especially the trill and the appoggiatura—incidentally added a spice of dissonance, of which the notated version of the music gives no hint.

In general, there were two ways of ornamenting a given melodic line: (1) small melodic formulas (such as trills, turns, appoggiaturas, mordents) attached to one or two of the written notes. These were sometimes, though not always, indicated by special signs; and (2) longer ornaments, which included the smaller formulas and also scales, runs, leaps, arpeggios, and the like, by means of which the notes of a melody were broken down into a multitude of smaller notes to produce a free and elaborate paraphrase of the written line. The longer ornamentation (called *division, diminution, figuration, graces,* and other names) was, of course, most appropriate to melodies in slow tempo. Graces for the slow movements of Corelli's solo sonatas have been preserved from an eighteenth-century edition, one of the few instances in Italian compositions where such ordinarily improvised decorations were written out. Whether or not the graces as we now have them are Corelli's own, they undoubtedly represent the general character of such melodic embellishments as practiced in the late Baroque.

Still another species of ornamentation, common in late Baroque opera and found also in some of the instrumental music of Corelli and his contemporaries, was the *cadenza,* an elaborate extension of the six-four chord of a final cadence. The cadenza at the end of the second movement of Corelli's solo sonata Opus 5, No. 3 is a foreshadowing of the long cadenzas in the concertos of the Classical and Romantic periods.

Performers in the Baroque thus had the liberty to add to the composer's written score; they were equally free to subtract from it or change it in various other ways. Arias were omitted from operas, or different arias substituted, practically at the whim of the singers. Frescobaldi permitted organists to dismember his toccatas or end them at any point they pleased. Composers of variations, suites, and sonatas took it for granted that the players would omit movements *ad libitum*. Very many title pages of instrumental ensemble music collections allow not only for different kinds of instruments, but also for an optional number of them: for example, sonatas were issued for violin and basso continuo with an additional violin or two "if desired."

Ensemble sonatas outside Italy

The Italian trio sonatas were imitated or adapted by composers in all countries. Purcell in his two sets of trio sonatas published in 1683 and 1697 "endeavor'd a just imitation of the most fam'd Italian masters"; some traces of French influence may be discerned in his rhythms and melodies, but many passages are profoundly English and Purcellian. Handel's trio sonatas are mostly in the same four-movement form and general style as those of Corelli.

The earliest as well as the most important trio sonatas in France were those of Couperin. Some of these works were composed probably as early as 1692, although not published until many years later. A collection of 1726, entitled *Les Nations: Sonades et Suites de Simphonies en Trio,* contains four ordres, each consisting of a *sonata da chiesa* (the *sonade*) in several movements followed by a suite of dances (the *suite de simphonies*). The style, though obviously influenced in the *sonades* by that of Corelli and the other Italians, is distinguished throughout by the same refinement of melody and the same exquisite taste in ornaments that mark Couperin's clavecin pieces.

The solo violin sonata had always been a prime vehicle for experiments in special bowings, multiple stops, and all kinds of difficult passage work. This early Baroque tradition lived on in Germany in the works of Johann Jakob Walther (1650–1717?), whose collection of twelve sonatas published in 1676 under the tile *Scherzi* outdid in these respects anything previously known. Likewise a virtuoso player, but a composer of broader interests, was Heinrich Ignaz Franz Biber (1644–1704). Although Biber composed church music and instrumental ensemble works, he is remembered chiefly for his fifteen violin sonatas composed around 1675, which represent for the most part meditations on episodes in the life of Christ. These ingenuous examples of Baroque program music make considerable

The solo sonata

use of *scordatura,* unusual tunings of the violin strings to facilitate the playing of particular chords. Biber's passacaglia for unaccompanied solo violin which is appended to the collection of Biblical sonatas is perhaps the most important precursor of Bach's great Chaconne in D minor. Most German violin composers after Biber and Walther came under the influence of the Italian schools and developed a cosmopolitan style on that foundation.

A famous pupil of Corelli was Francesco Geminiani (1687–1762), who had a long career as virtuoso and composer in London. He published there, in 1751, *The Art of Playing on the Violin,* a method which undoubtedly embodies the principles of technique and interpretation that were taught by Corelli and the other Italian masters of the early eighteenth century. Geminiani's solo sonatas and concerti grossi are founded on the style of Corelli, which is intermingled with progressive traits. Most celebrated of all the Italian virtuosi was Giuseppe Tartini (1692–1770); but his solo sonatas and concertos are predominantly in the pre-Classical style of the mid-eighteenth century.

Works for larger ensembles

The trio and solo instrumentations, although they were the most common, were not the only sonorities to be employed for sonatas (or similar pieces under whatever name) in the Baroque period. In Italy, from the days of Giovanni Gabrieli on through the first half of the seventeenth century, there was a steady production of canzonas, dance suites, sonatas, and sinfonias for groups of three or more melody instruments in addition to a basso continuo.

The sonata and more especially the suite for an ensemble of instruments had a particularly long life in Germany. The most notable (though not the most typical) works in this form after Schein's *Banchetto musicale* were the chamber sonatas of Johann Rosenmüller (*ca.* 1620–84), published in 1670.

Orchestral music

Toward the end of the seventeenth century a generally recognized distinction of style began to be made between *chamber* music and *orchestral* music—that is, between ensemble music with only one instrument to a part and ensemble music with more than one instrument playing the same part. In a large proportion of seventeenth-century ensemble works it is not clear if composers had any preference in this regard; the choice could depend on circumstances. For instance, a trio *sonata da chiesa,* though presumably conceived for two solo violins, might be played in church by an orchestral ensemble if the size of the auditorium made it desirable or if the occasion were festive. Conversely, neither the designation "sinfonia" nor the presence of three, four, or more melodic parts above the bass necessarily called for an orchestral rather than a chamber group of players. When parts were to be reinforced the usual procedure in the seventeenth century was to increase the number of chord-playing instruments for the continuo and add more melody instruments on the soprano line. Beyond the use of the basso continuo and the predominance of the stringed instruments, there was no common standard that regulated either the makeup of an ensemble or the number of instruments to a part.

Opera houses of course maintained orchestras; consequently the opera overture in both Italy and France, as well as the numerous dances that formed an indispensable part of French opera, were always conceived as specifically orchestral music, and were written in a style suited to orchestral rather than chamber performance. The most famous orchestra in Europe was that of the Paris Opéra, which under the severe regime of Lully had been brought to a pitch of technical perfection hitherto unknown for so large a group of instrumental performers.

German disciples of Lully introduced French standards of playing, along with the French musical style, into their own country. One result was a new type of *orchestral suite* which flourished in Germany from about 1690 to 1740. The dances of these suites, patterned after those of Lully's ballets and operas, did not appear in any standard number or order. From the fact that they were always introduced by a pair of movements in the form of a French overture, the word *ouverture* soon came to be used as a designation for the suite. Among the early collections of orchestral suites was Georg Muffat's *Florilegium* (1695 and 1698), the second part of which included an essay with much information about the French system of bowing, the playing of the *agréments,* and other matters. Another important collection was J. K. F. Fischer's (*ca.* 1665–1746) *Journal de Printemps* (1695). *Ouverture* suites were written also by Fux, Telemann, and a host of other German composers, including J. S. Bach.

The orchestral suite

A new kind of orchestral composition, the *concerto,* appeared in the last two decades of the seventeenth century, and became the most important type of Baroque orchestral music after 1700. The concerto was the synthesis in purely instrumental music of four fundamental Baroque practices: the *concertato* principle; the texture of a firm bass and a florid treble; musical organization based on the major-minor key system; and the building of a long work out of separate autonomous movements.

The concerto

Three different kinds of concertos were being written around 1700. One, the orchestral concerto (also called concerto-sinfonia, *concerto-ripieno,* or *concerto a quattro*), was simply an orchestral work of several movements in a style that emphasized the first violin part and the bass, and that usually avoided the more complex contrapuntal texture characteristic of the sonata and sinfonia. More numerous and important at this time were the other two types, the *concerto grosso* (grand concerto) and the *solo concerto,* both of which systematically contrasted sonorities: in the concerto grosso, a small group of solo instruments, in the solo concerto a single instrument, were set against the main mass of orchestral sound. The "orchestra" was almost always a string orchestra, usually divided into first and second violins, viola, violoncello, and violone, with basso continuo. The solo instruments also were usually strings: in the solo concerto, a violin; in the concerto grosso, as a rule two violins and continuo— though other solo string or wind instruments might be added or substituted. *Concerto grosso* originally signified the "large consort," that is, the orchestra, as opposed to the *concertino* or "little consort," the group of solo instruments. Later, the term *concerto grosso* was applied to the composition which used these opposed groups. In both the solo concerto and the concerto grosso, the usual designation for full orchestra is *tutti* (all) or *ripieno* (full).

The concerti grossi of Corelli, which are among the earliest examples of the form, employ the principle of solo-tutti contrast; but Corelli did not differentiate in style between the solos and the tutti portions, and these concertos are in effect merely church sonatas or chamber sonatas divided between a small and a larger group of instruments, although the comparative prominence of the first violin part occasionally suggests the texture of the later solo concerto.

Giuseppe Torelli

The composer who contributed most to the development of the concerto around the turn of the century was Giuseppe Torelli (1658–1709), the leading figure in the last years of the Bologna school. A significant stage of evolution is apparent in the violin concertos from Torelli's last publication (1709), a collection of six concerti grossi and six solo concertos. Most are in three movements (fast–slow–fast), an arrangement which became general with later concerto composers. The Allegros as a rule are in fugal style, while the middle movement is made up of two similar Adagios framing a brief Allegro. Torelli's vigorous, dynamic Allegro themes are characteristic of the early eighteenth century. Equally significant is the distinction in style between the tutti and the solo passages: the latter blossom forth with lively, diversified, idiomatic figuration, contrasting brightly with the solid thematic quality of the ripieno.

Also important is the form of Torelli's Allegro movements: each begins with a complete exposition of the theme by the full orchestra; alternating with solo episodes, the material of this tutti exposition recurs once or twice, slightly modified and in different keys; the movement is rounded off and brought to a close with a final tonic tutti practically identical with the opening one. A tutti which recurs in this way in a concerto is called a *ritornello;* this structure is typical for all first and last movements of late Baroque concertos. The form is something like that of the rondeau, with the important exception that in a concerto all the ritornellos except the first and last are in different keys. The concerto therefore combines the principle of recurrence with the equally important principle of key relationship. An outline of the structure of the finale of Torelli's Opus 8, No. 8 illustrates the scheme:

Ritornello I: Theme, C minor (10 measures) with sequential extension and cadence in the dominant minor (6 measures).

Solo I: 9½ measures with prominent sequential patterns, beginning in the dominant minor and modulating to the relative major.

Ritornello II: 8 measures, similar to Ritornello I, in the relative major, modulating to the subdominant.

Solo II: 12 measures, modulating to the tonic and concluding with four nonthematic measures of dominant preparation for:

Ritornello III: same as Ritornello I but cadencing in the tonic and with the last four measures repeated *piano* by way of coda.

The achievements of Torelli in the realm of the concerto were matched and extended by other Italian composers. The greatest master of the Italian concerto of the late Baroque was Antonio Vivaldi, whose works we shall study in the following chapter.

XII

The Early Eighteenth Century

The overlapping of style periods had seldom if ever been so extensive as in the first half of the eighteenth century. All around the late Baroque masters a new style of music was growing up. We have already discussed the first half of the eighteenth century under its aspect as a late stage of the Baroque; in the chapter that follows this one, we shall discuss it as an early stage of the Classical era. But the composers working during these years were not consciously, or at any rate not primarily, concerned with either the historical past or the possible historical future; they were living in the present. In this chapter we shall try to achieve a fuller understanding of the music of the first half of the eighteenth century by surveying the life and works of its four most important composers: Vivaldi, Rameau, Bach, and Handel.

All these four composers were· successful and eminent in their own time; all wrote music which, by virtue of its craftsmanship, integrity, and imaginative content, is still significant today. All came to terms with the contemporary conflict between contrapuntal and homophonic styles; all were competent in both instrumental and vocal composition. All were aware of the new currents·in musical thought, though none was a deliberate revolutionary in his own music. All worked within the established forms and styles of the late Baroque, and their originality consisted chiefly in doing the accepted things in a uniquely excellent way. Bach brought to consummation all forms of late Baroque music except opera. Vivaldi, Rameau, and Handel excelled in opera; Vivaldi, in addition, was a prolific master of the Italian Baroque concerto; Handel created—out of Baroque elements—a new kind of oratorio; and Rameau, in his theoretical writings, developed a new conception of harmony and tonality that proved valid not only for the music of his own time but also for that of many succeeding generations.

Antonio Vivaldi

Antonio Vivaldi (1678–1741), son of one of the leading violinists of St. Mark's chapel, was educated both for music (under Legrenzi) and for the priesthood. He began his priestly duties in 1703, but because of ill health was excused from active service a year later and thenceforward devoted himself wholly to music. From 1704 to 1740 Vivaldi was continually employed as conductor, composer, teacher, and general superintendent of music at the Conservatory of the Pietà in Venice, with frequent leaves of absence to compose and conduct operas and concerts in other Italian cities and elsewhere in Europe.

Vivaldi's career

The conservatories of eighteenth-century Naples and Venice were pious institutions founded originally to shelter orphans and illegitimate children—of whom there must have been a formidable number, if we are to believe some of the tales told by travellers.[1] Instruction was efficiently organized and pursued without stinting either energy or expense. The resulting throng of enthusiastic young amateurs, their natural emulation spurred by special rewards in privileges and stimulated always by the presence of a few outstandingly gifted individuals, must have provided a highly favorable environment for any composer. Vivaldi was expected to furnish new oratorios and concertos for every recurring festival at the Pietà. For these, he wrote concertos, the form of instrumental music commonly used at church festival services. About 450 concertos of his are extant, in addition to 23 sinfonias, 75 solo or trio sonatas, 49 operas, and many cantatas, motets, and oratorios.

Vivaldi's vocal works

As an opera composer, Vivaldi was certainly successful in his day; during the years in which he was writing operas (1713–39) the theatres of Venice staged more works of his than of any other composer, and his fame was by no means limited to his own city and country. The few accessible specimens of his church music show that in this realm also Vivaldi was a composer of real stature. The fact that many solo and choral passages in his works sound as though they might have been written by Handel proves merely that both composers used the international musical language of the early eighteenth century.

Vivaldi's instrumental works, and especially the concertos, are perennially attractive because of the freshness of their melodies,

---

[1] Thus Edward Wright, *Some Observations Made in Travelling through Italy* [etc.], London, 1730, I, 79 reports that the Pietà sometimes held as many as six thousand girls. It has been reliably estimated that this would have required a campus twice the size of Vassar.

Musicians singing in St. Mark's, Venice, 1766. A drawing by Antonio Canal, known as Canaletto. (Kunsthalle, Hamburg)

Vivaldi's concertos

their rhythmic verve, their skilful treatment of solo and orchestral color, and the clarity of their form. Many of the sonatas, as well as some of the early concertos, are in the late seventeenth-century contrapuntal style of Corelli. However, in his first published collection of concertos (Opus 3, *ca.* 1712) Vivaldi already showed that he was fully aware of the modern trends toward distinct musical form, vigorous rhythm, and idiomatic solo writing exemplified by Torelli.

About two-thirds of Vivaldi's concertos are for one solo instrument with orchestra—usually, of course, a violin, but with a considerable number also for other instruments. The usual orchestra at the Pietà probably consisted of twenty to twenty-five stringed instruments, with harpsichord or organ for the continuo; this is always the basic group, though in many of his concertos he also calls for flutes, oboes, bassoons, or horns, any of which may be used either as solo instruments or in ensemble combinations. The exact size and makeup of Vivaldi's orchestra varied, of course, depending on the players that might be available on a particular occasion. Vivaldi's writing is always remarkable for the variety of color he achieves with different groupings of the solo and orchestral strings; the familiar *Primavera* (*Spring*) concerto—first of a group of four concertos in Opus 8 (1725) representing programmatically the four seasons—is but one of many examples of his extraordinary instinct for effective sonorities in this medium.

Most of Vivaldi's concertos are in the usual eighteenth-century pattern of three movements: an Allegro; a slow movement in the same key or a closely related one (relative minor, dominant, or subdominant); and a final Allegro somewhat shorter and sprightlier than the first. Though a few movements are found in the older fugal style, the texture is typically more homophonic than contrapuntal —but homophonic in the late Baroque sense, with much incidental use of counterpoint and with particular emphasis on the two outer voices. Typical of the late Baroque, also, is Vivaldi's constant use of sequential patterns.

The formal scheme of the individual movements of Vivaldi's concertos is the same as in Torelli's works: ritornellos for the full or-

A page from one of Vivaldi's manuscripts—a tutti section from the finale of the Concerto in A for solo violin and four-part string ensemble.

chestra, alternating with episodes for the soloist (or soloists). Vivaldi differs from earlier composers not by virtue of any innovation in the general plan of the concerto but because his musical ideas are more spontaneous, his formal structures more clearly delineated, his harmonies more assured, his textures more varied, and his rhythms more impelling. Moreover, he establishes between solo and tutti a certain dramatic tension; he does not merely give the soloist contrasting idiomatic figuration (which Torelli had already done) but makes him stand out as a dominating musical personality against the ensemble as the solo singer does against the orchestra in opera—a relationship inherent in the ritornello aria, but one which Vivaldi first brought to full realization in a purely instrumental medium. "The tutti announces the propositions that are to be debated in the course of the movement; and the arguments which these provoke give rise to a musical contest between soloist and orchestra, ending in a reconciliation or synthesis of emotions and ideas."[2]

Vivaldi was the first composer to give the slow movement of a concerto equal importance with the two Allegros. His slow movement is usually a long-breathed expressive cantabile melody, like an adagio operatic aria or arioso, to which the performer was of course expected to add his own embellishments. The slow movements of the later concertos are particularly interesting because of their forward-looking style. For example, the Largo of Opus 9, No. 2, for solo violin (NAWM/S 47) exhibits many features of the pre-Classic style: balanced phrases, frequent half-cadences clarifying the structure, trills, triplets, and feminine cadences with appoggiaturas. Like most of Vivaldi's slow movements, it is lightly scored, only the violoncellos and the continuo playing with the solo violin. In his program music, such as the widely admired *Seasons* concertos and a dozen or so others of similar cast, Vivaldi shared the half-serious, half-playful attitude of the eighteenth century toward the naïve realism implied in such musical depictions.

Vivaldi's influence

Vivaldi's influence on instrumental music in the middle and later eighteenth century was equal to that of Corelli a generation earlier. Vivaldi was one of the most important figures in the transition from late Baroque to early Classical style; the assured economy of his writing for string orchestra was a revelation; his dramatic conception of the role of the soloist was accepted and developed in the Classical concerto; above all, the concise themes, the clarity of form, the rhythmic vitality, the impelling logical continuity in the flow of musical ideas, all qualities so characteristic of Vivaldi, were transmitted to many other composers, and especially directly to

2 C. R. Brijon, *Réflexions sur la musique et sur la vraie manière de l'exécuter sur le violon*, Paris, 1763, 2–3; paraphrased from the quotation in Pincherle, *Vivaldi*, I, 163.

J. S. Bach. Bach copied at least ten of Vivaldi's concertos, arranging six of them for harpsichord, three for organ, and one (originally for four violins) for four harpsichords and string orchestra. Vivaldi's influence is apparent both in the general scheme and in the details of many of Bach's original concertos, as well as in those of his German contemporaries. Finally, Vivaldi, more than any other single composer, through his concertos impressed on the eighteenth century the idea of an instrumental sound in which the effect of solo-tutti contrast was important, an idea that prevails not only in concertos of the period but in much of the other orchestral music and keyboard music as well.

Jean-Philippe Rameau

Jean-Philippe Rameau (1683–1764), the foremost French musician of the eighteenth century, had a career unlike that of any other eminent composer in history. Practically unknown until the age of forty, he attracted attention first as a theorist and only afterward as a composer. He produced most of the musical works on which his fame depends between the ages of fifty and fifty-six. Attacked then as an innovator, he was assailed twenty years later even more severely as a reactionary; in favor with the French Court and reasonably prosperous during the later years of his life, he remained always a solitary, strict, and unsociable person, but a conscientious and intelligent artist.

Throughout his life, Rameau was interested in the theory or, as it was called at that time, the "science" of music. In his numerous writings he sought to derive the fundamental principles of harmony from the laws of acoustics and formulated certain ideas which not only clarified musical practice of his time but also remained influential in music theory for the next two hundred years. Rameau considered the chord the primal element in music—not the single tone, not melodic lines or intervals. The major triad he eventually derived from the overtone series; he had more difficulty in accounting for the minor triad on "natural principles," though he did establish the so-called melodic minor scale. He posited the building of chords by thirds (upward and downward), whereby the triad was expanded to a chord of the seventh or ninth. Rameau's recognition of the identity of a chord through all its inversions was an important insight, as was also the corollary idea of the *basse fondamentale*, or, as we would say, the root-progressions in a succession of harmonies. Moreover, Rameau established the three chords of the tonic, dominant, and subdominant as the pillars of tonality, and related other chords to these, thereby formulating the notion of functional harmony; he also stated the conception that modulation might result

Rameau's theoretical works

from the change of function of a chord (in modern terminology, a pivot chord). Less significant were his theory of the derivation of all melody from harmony (expressed or implied) and his views on the peculiar quality of specific keys.

Rameau's musical style

The entire development of French opera after Lully had been toward increasing the already large proportion of decorative elements—scenic spectacle and ballet, with descriptive orchestral music, dances, choruses, and songs. More and more the drama, even in works called *tragédies lyriques,* had deteriorated in both importance and quality, and eventually opera-ballet had frankly come to be nothing but ballet and spectacle on a huge scale with only the thinnest thread, or none at all, of continuity between the various scenes. Rameau's "heroic ballet" *Les Indes galantes (The Gallant Indies,* 1735) is a finished example of an opera-ballet: each of its four *entrées* or acts has a self-contained plot, and each takes place in a different quarter of the globe, thus giving opportunity for a variety of decorations and dances which gratified the early eighteenth-century French public's interest in exotic scenes and peoples. Rameau's music, especially in the *entrée* of the Incas, is far more dramatic than the libretto would lead one to expect.

As far as musical features are concerned, Rameau's theatre works are obviously similar to Lully's. Both show the same minute interest in appropriate declamation and exact rhythmic notation in recitatives; both intermingle recitative with more formally melodic aria sections, choruses, or instrumental interludes; both follow the tradition of introducing frequent long *divertissement* scenes; and (in Rameau's early operas) the form of the overture is the same. But within this general frame, Rameau introduced many changes, so that in reality the resemblance between his music and Lully's is superficial rather than substantial.

Perhaps the most notable contrast is in the nature of the melodic lines. Rameau the composer constantly put into practice the doctrine of Rameau the theorist that all melody is rooted in harmony. Many of his melodic phrases are plainly triadic and none leave room for any uncertainty as to the harmonic progressions that must underlie them. Moreover, the harmony is of the eighteenth-century sort, with an orderly relationship, within the major-minor tonal system, of dominants, subdominants, and all secondary chords and modulations. Rameau uses purely harmonic means for expressive purposes in a way that is completely lacking in Lully's style. Rameau's harmonies are for the most part diatonic, but on occasion he uses chromatic and enharmonic modulations most effectively: in the trio of the Fates in the fifth scene of Act II of *Hippolyte et Aricie* (Example XII–1) he modulates rapidly by a descending chromatic sequence through five keys in as many measures, underlining the import of the words "Où cours-tu, malheureux? Tremble, frémis

EXAMPLE XII–1   Modulations in *Hippolyte et Aricie,* Jean-Philippe
Rameau

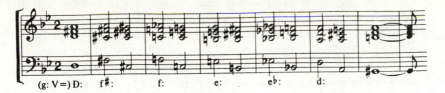

(g: V=) D: f♯:   f: e: e♭:   d:

d'effroi!" (Where dost thou flee, miserable one? Tremble, shudder
with terror!)

In his treatment of form also Rameau was an innovator. Even
when he maintained Lully's pattern of the French *ouverture,* as
he did in *Castor et Pollux* (1737) and *Les Indes galantes,* the second
movement, particularly, was expanded and deepened. Some of the
formal plans of the overtures are evidently experimental and in his
last works Rameau freely adapted the three-movement form of the
Italian sinfonia. Quite often his overture introduces a theme that
is used later in the opera, and occasionally (as in *Zoroastre*) the
overture becomes a kind of symphonic poem, depicting the course
of the drama to follow.

As with Lully and other French composers, Rameau used less
contrasting melodic styles for recitative and aria than did the Italian
composers of this period. Rameau's vocal airs, despite their variety
of dimensions and types, can for the most part be classified into
two basic formal patterns: the relatively short two-part form *AB;*
and the longer form with repetition after contrast, either *ABA*
as in the Italian da capo aria or with more than one repetition as
in the usual French rondeau. Nearly always, whatever their form
or size, Rameau's airs preserve a certain coolness and restraint in
contrast to the intensity and abandon of the early Italian opera aria.
Elegance, picturesqueness, piquant rhythms, fullness of harmony,
and melodic ornamentation by means of *agréments* are their outstanding traits.

This is not to say that Rameau's music lacks dramatic force;
the opening scenes of Act I of *Castor et Pollux* and the monologue,
Ah! faut-il in Act IV, Scene 1 of *Hippolyte et Aricie* (NAWM/S 37)
have a grandeur not surpassed in eighteenth-century French opera.
However, the most powerful effects in his operas are achieved by
the joint use of solo and chorus. Choruses, which remained prominent in French opera long after they had passed out of use in Italy,
are numerous throughout Rameau's works. The invocation to the
sun (*Brilliant soleil*) in Act II of *Les Indes galantes* is an excellent
example of the effectiveness of his predominantly homophonic
choral writing.

On the whole, Rameau's most original contributions were made in the instrumental portions of his operas—the overtures, the dances, and the descriptive symphonies that accompany the stage action. In all these, his invention is inexhaustible; themes, rhythms, and harmonies have an incisive individuality and an inimitable pictorial quality. The French valued music especially for its depictive powers and Rameau was their leading tone-painter. His musical pictures range from graceful miniatures to broad representations of thunder (*Hippolyte,* Act I), tempest (*Les Surprises de l'Amour* [1757], Act III), or earthquake (*Indes galantes,* Act II). The pictorial quality of his music is often enhanced by novel orchestration. Rameau's use of the bassoons and horns, and in general the independence of the woodwinds in his later scores, are in accordance with the most advanced orchestral practice of his time.

Rameau's clavecin pieces have the fine texture, the rhythmic vivacity, elegance of detail, and picturesque humor that appeared also in the works of Couperin. In his third and last collection (*Nouvelle Suites de Pièces de clavecin, ca.* 1736), Rameau experimented with virtuoso effects in somewhat the same manner as Domenico Scarlatti. Rameau's only publication of instrumental ensemble music was a collection of trio sonatas entitled *Pièces de clavecin en concerts* (1741); in these, the harpsichord is not treated simply as accompaniment but shares equally with the other instruments in the presentation and working out of the thematic material.

Summary

The work of Rameau may be summed up under three aspects. In the heroic, grand style of his early operas and opera-ballets, he is a representative figure of the late Baroque, comparable to Bach and Handel. His heroic qualities are always accompanied, and sometimes supplanted, by the characteristic French traits of clarity, grace, moderation, and elegance, and by a constant striving toward the picturesque; in these respects he may be compared with his contemporary, Watteau. Finally, and equally typical of his country, he is a *philosophe* as well as a composer, an analyst as well as a creator; and in this respect he may be compared to his contemporary, Voltaire. These three aspects cannot be separated if we are to understand Rameau's achievements fully. He was one of the most complex as well as one of the most fecund musical personalities of the eighteenth century.

Johann Sebastian Bach

Bach's career

The uneventful external career of Johann Sebastian Bach (1685–1750) was similar to that of many successful musical functionaries of his time in Lutheran Germany. Bach served as organist at Arnstadt

(1703–07) and Mühlhausen (1707–08); as court organist and later Concertmaster in the chapel of the Duke of Weimar (1708–17); as Music Director at the court of a prince in Cöthen (1717–23); and finally as Cantor of St. Thomas's school and Music Director in Leipzig (1723–50), a position of considerable importance in the Lutheran world. He enjoyed some reputation in Protestant Germany as an organ virtuoso and writer of learned contrapuntal works, but there were at least a half-dozen contemporary composers who were more widely known in Europe. He regarded himself as a conscientious craftsman doing a job to the best of his ability for the satisfaction of his superiors, for the pleasure and edification of his fellowmen, and to the glory of God. Doubtless he would have been astonished if he had been told that two hundred years after his death his music would be performed and studied everywhere and his name more deeply venerated by musicians than that of any other composer.

Bach's Instrumental Music

Bach was trained as a violinist and organist, and organ music first attracted his interest as a composer. As a youth he visited Hamburg to hear the organists there, and while he was at Arnstadt he made a journey on foot to Lübeck, where he was so fascinated by the music of Buxtehude that he overstayed his leave and was duly reproved by his superiors.

Bach's organ works

Bach's earliest organ compositions include chorale preludes, several sets of variations (partitas) on chorales, and some toccatas and fantasias which in their length, diffuseness, and exuberance of ideas recall the toccatas of Buxtehude. Then, while he was at the court of Weimar, Bach became interested in the music of Italian composers, and with his usual diligence set about copying their scores and making arrangements of their works; thus he arranged several of Vivaldi's concertos for organ or harpsichord, writing out the ornaments, occasionally strengthening the counterpoint, and sometimes adding inner voices. He also wrote fugues on subjects by Corelli and Legrenzi. The natural consequence of these studies was an important change in Bach's own style: from the Italians, especially Vivaldi, he learned to write more concise themes, to clarify and tighten the harmonic scheme, and above all to develop subjects by a continuous rhythmic flow into lucid, grandly proportioned formal structures. These qualities were combined with his own prolific imagination and his profound mastery of contrapuntal technique to make the style which we consider typically "Bachian," and which is in reality a fusion of Italian and German characteristics.

As has already been noted, one of the characteristic large musical structures of the late Baroque was the combination of a prelude

Bach's preludes and fugues

(or toccata, fantasia) and a fugue. Most of Bach's important compositions in this form date from the Weimar period, though a few were written at Cöthen and Leipzig. Perfectly idiomatic to the instrument, technically difficult but never parading empty virtuosity, Bach's preludes and fugues sum up all the striving of the Baroque toward pure, balanced tonal architecture on a monumental scale.

The Toccata in D minor (?1709; BWV 565) [3] is an example of the form established by Buxtehude, in which the fugue is interspersed with sections of free fantasia. The Passacaglia in C minor (?1717; BWV 582) serves as prelude to a double fugue, one of whose subjects is identical with the first half of the passacaglia theme. Some of the preludes are extensive compositions in two or three movements; that of the great Fantasia and Fugue in G minor (Cöthen, 1720; BWV 542) glorifies the Baroque conception of a richly colored, passionately expressive fantasia or toccata with contrapuntal interludes. The infusion of elements of the Italian concerto is evident in a number of the toccatas and fugues, particularly in the Prelude and Fugue in A Minor (BWV 543; NAWM/S 50).

From the later years of Bach's life comes the gigantic Prelude in E♭ major, and the Fugue ("St. Anne's") in the same key (BWV 552), published in 1739; these two are respectively the opening and closing sections of Part III of the *Clavier Übung* (literally, *Keyboard Practice,* an overall title that Bach used for four different collections of his keyboard pieces). The central portion of Part III of the *Clavier Übung* is a series of chorale preludes on the hymns of the Lutheran Catechism and Mass (Kyrie and Gloria, the so-called *missa brevis*). In symbolic recognition of the dogma of the Trinity, Bach writes for conclusion a triple fugue with a key signature of three flats; each of the three sections of the fugue has its own subject. The multisectional fugue goes back to the practice of Buxtehude and other earlier masters; Bach had used it in his early Toccata in E major (BWV 566).

Bach's trio sonatas

Less spectacular than the preludes and fugues, but equally important, are the six Trio Sonatas (BWV 525–530) which, according to Forkel, Bach wrote at Leipzig for his eldest son Wilhelm Friedemann. These works show the way Bach adapted the Italian ensemble trio sonata as a piece for a solo performer. They are written in a contrapuntal texture of three equal independent voices, one for each manual and one for the pedals, but the order of movements (mostly fast–slow–fast) and the general character of the themes show the influence of their Italian prototypes.

---

[3] BWV stands for *Thematisch-systematisches Verzeichnis der musikalischen Werke von Johann Sebastian Bach* (*Thematic-Systematic List of the Musical Works of J. S. Bach*), Wolfgang Schmieder, ed., Leipzig, 1950. The abbreviation S. (for Schmieder) is sometimes used instead of BWV for referring to Bach's works.

Bach, as an organist and a devout Lutheran, was naturally concerned with the chorale. Among the approximately 170 chorale settings which he made for the organ, all types known to the Baroque are represented; moreover, as with other forms of composition, Bach brought the organ chorale to a summit of artistic perfection. Short chorale preludes comprise the collection called the *Orgelbüchlein* (*Little Organ Book*), which Bach compiled at Weimar and during his first years at Cöthen. The arrangement and intention of this collection illustrate several things essential for an understanding of Bach. He originally planned to include settings for the chorale melodies required by the liturgy for the entire church year, 164 in all, though he actually completed only 45. However, the plan is characteristic of Bach's desire to fulfil thoroughly the potentialities of a given undertaking, to realize all the suggestions inherent in any musical situation. This is the reason that in the maturity of his life his compositions often are devoted to single aspects of one large unified design—for example, the complete circle of keys in *The Well-Tempered Clavier,* the cycle of catechism chorales in the *Clavier Übung,* the systematic order of the *Goldberg Variations,* the exhaustive working out of a single subject in *A Musical Offering,* or the exemplification of all types of fugue in *The Art of Fugue.*

Bach's chorale preludes

All the numbers of the *Orgelbüchlein* are chorale preludes in which the tune is heard once through, generally in the soprano, in complete, continuous, and readily recognizable form; a few treat the melody in canon, and three present it with fairly elaborate *agréments.* Quite often the accompanying voices are not derived from motives of the chorale melody but each is constructed throughout on a single independent motive. In some instances the accompaniment exemplifies the practice—common to many composers of the Baroque, especially notable in Schütz, and carried out by Bach with surpassing poetic ingenuity—of recognizing, by means of pictorial or symbolic motives, the visual images or underlying ideas of the text of the chorale. Thus in *Durch Adams Fall ist ganz verderbt* (*Through Adam's fall all is spoiled;* NAWM/S 49), the idea of *fall* is depicted by a jagged falling motive in the pedals, while the tortuous chromatic lines of the inner voices suggest at once the ideas of sin and sorrow and the sinuous writhing of the serpent (Example XII–2).

Similar pictorial or symbolic suggestions abound in Bach's organ chorales, as well as, of course, in his vocal works; however, he never uses pictorial devices as mere superficial adornments, but always as a way to present the inner, musical significance of a passage. One of the finest examples of the poetic transfiguration of an external suggestion is the final cadence of the chorale prelude *O Mensch, bewein' dein' Sünde gross* (*O man, bewail thy grievous sin*) from

EXAMPLE XII–2   Chorale Prelude: *Durch Adams Fall*, J. S. Bach

the *Orgelbüchlein,* in which the long-drawn-out *adagissimo* reflects the word *lange* (long) in the closing phrase of the chorale text (see illustration, page 265).

Three collections of organ chorales were compiled during Bach's Leipzig period. The six *Schübler* chorales (BWV 645–650) are transcriptions of movements from cantatas. The *Eighteen Chorales* (BWV 651–668) that Bach collected and revised between 1747 and 1749 were composed at earlier periods of his life; they include all varieties of organ chorale settings: variations, fugues, fantasias, trios, and extended chorale preludes of various types. The catechism chorales in Part III of the *Clavier Übung* (BWV 669–689) are grouped in pairs, a longer setting requiring the organ pedals and a shorter one (usually fugal) for manuals only. This pairing has been sometimes regarded as a symbolic reference to the "longer" and "shorter" catechisms, but more probably the aim was only to offer prospective buyers the alternative of using either one or the other setting depending on what instrument was available.

Bach's clavier music

Bach's music for the clavier, like that for the organ, includes masterpieces in every form known to the late Baroque: preludes, fantasies, and toccatas; fugues and other pieces in fugal style; dance suites; and variations. In addition there are early sonatas and capriccios, miscellaneous short works (including many teaching pieces), and clavier concertos with orchestra. A large proportion of Bach's clavier music was written at Cöthen, although many important works were produced in the Leipzig period. In general, the clavier compositions—which were not bound, like the organ works, to a local German tradition or to a liturgy—show prominently the cosmopolitan or international features of Bach's style, the intermingling of Italian, French, and German characteristics.

The best known of Bach's clavier works is the famous set of preludes and fugues called *The Well-Tempered Clavier.* Part I was completed at Cöthen in 1722, and Part II was collected at Leipzig around 1740. Each part consists of twenty-four preludes and fugues, one prelude and one fugue in each of the twelve major and minor keys. Part I is more unified in style and purpose than Part II, which includes compositions from many different periods of Bach's life. In addition to demonstrating the possibility, with the then novel tempered tuning, of using all the keys, Bach had particular didactic intentions in Part I. In most of the preludes a single specific technical task is given the player; thus they might be called, in the terminology of a later age, *études,* for which some of Bach's little preludes (BWV 933–943) as well as all the two-part inventions and the three-part sinfonias may be regarded as preliminary studies. The teaching aims of *The Well-Tempered Clavier* go beyond mere technique, however, for the preludes exemplify different types of keyboard composition of the late Baroque. The fugues, wonderfully varied in subjects, texture, form, and treatment, constitute a compendium of all the possibilities of concentrated, monothematic fugal writing. The ancient ricercare is represented (Book I, No. 4 in C♯ minor), as well as the use of inversion, canon, and augmentation (No. 8, E♭ minor), virtuosity in a fugue with a da capo ending (No. 3, C♯ major), and many other styles. In Part II, the Fugue in D major (No. 5) may be mentioned as a superlative example of concentrated abstract musical structure using the simplest materials, while the Prelude and Fugue in F♯ minor (No. 14) is outstanding for beauty of themes and proportions. As in the organ fugues, each subject in Bach's clavier figures is a clearly defined musical personality, of which the entire fugue is to be a logical development and projection.

The Well-Tempered Clavier

Bach's clavier suites show the influence of French and Italian as well as of German models. There are three sets of six suites each: the *French* and *English Suites,* composed at Cöthen, and the six Partitas published separately between 1726 and 1730 and then collected in 1731 as Part I of the *Clavier Übung.* Part II of the *Clavier Übung* also contains a large Partita in B minor, entitled "Overture in the French style for a harpsichord with two manuals."

Bach's suites

The designations *French* and *English* for the suites composed at Cöthen are not Bach's own, and have no descriptive significance. The suites in both sets consist of the standard four dance movements (allemande, courante, sarabande, gigue) with additional short movements between the sarabande and gigue; each of the *English* suites opens with a prelude.

In one clavier work Bach summarized another characteristic species of Baroque keyboard music, the theme and variations. The *Aria with* (thirty) *Different Variations,* published (probably) in 1742 as Part IV of the *Clavier Übung* and generally known as the *Goldberg Variations,* is organized in the monumentally complete fashion of many of the compositions from the latter part of Bach's life. The theme is a sarabande in two balanced sections, the essential bass and harmonic structure of which are preserved in all thirty variations. The form of the whole, therefore, is that of a chaconne or passacaglia.

Goldberg Variations

Mm. 21 (2d half)–24 (1st half), in Bach's autograph

Mm. 21–26, in Carl Czerny's edition

Mm. 22–24, in Hans Bischoff's edition

This passage from the first Prelude in Book I of Bach's The Well-Tempered Clavier *is shown in Bach's autograph manuscript and in two editions. Carl Czerny's edition (first published in the 1830s), evidently based on a copy made after Bach's death, incorporates an inauthentic extra measure after measure 22; elsewhere, Czerny adds phrasings, tempo and dynamic markings not present in Bach's manuscript (e.g. the dimin. in m. 21). Bischoff's edition (1883) attempts to give as accurate as possible a reproduction of the source—an ideal that, while not entirely unproblematic in practice, has generally been adhered to by modern scholars.*

The variations are grouped by threes, the last of each group being a canon, with the canons at successive intervals from the unison to the ninth. The thirtieth and last variation, however, is a *quodlibet*, a mixture of two popular song melodies combined in counterpoint above the fundamental bass; and after this the theme is repeated da capo. The noncanonic variations are of many different types, including inventions, fughettas, a French *ouverture*, ornamental slow arias, and, at regular intervals, sparkling *bravura* pieces for two keyboards. The diverse moods and styles in these variations are unified by means of the recurring bass and harmonies and also by the symmetrical order in which the movements are arranged; the entirety is a perfectly organized structure of magnificent proportions.

Bach wrote six sonatas and partitas for violin alone (BWV 1001–1006), six suites for violoncello alone (BWV 1007–1012), and a sonata for solo flute (BWV 1013). In these works he demonstrated his ability to create the illusion of a harmonic and contrapuntal texture by means of multiple stops or single melodic lines which outline or suggest an interplay of independent voices—a technique going back to the lute composers of the Renaissance and related to the style of the French lutenists and clavecinists of the middle and late Baroque. The chaconne from Bach's solo violin Partita in D minor is one of the most famous works in this form.

Works for solo violin and violoncello

In the ensemble forms of chamber music Bach's chief compositions include sonatas for violin and harpsichord (BWV 1014–1019), for viola da gamba and harpsichord (BWV 1027–1029), and for flute and harpsichord (BWV 1030–1035). Most of these works have four movements in slow–fast–slow–fast order, like the *sonata da chiesa;* and moreover, most of them are actually trio sonatas, since often the right-hand part of the harpsichord is written as a single melodic line which forms a duet in counterpoint with the melody of the other instrument.

Ensemble sonatas

The amalgamation of Italian and German styles is most fully exemplified in Bach's six concertos composed at Cöthen and dedicated to the Margrave of Brandenburg in 1721 (BWV 1046–1051). In these, Bach adopted the usual three-movement, fast–slow–fast order of the Italian concertos; the triadic themes, the steadily driving rhythms, and the ritornello form of the Allegro movements are also of Italian derivation. But Bach, as usual, transfigured all these elements, and in addition provided his concertos with such wealth of counterpoint and such variety of instrumental color as to make them unique in the literature of this form.

Concertos

The four *Ouvertures* or orchestral suites (BWV 1066–1069) are likewise masterly examples of this favorite type of Baroque composition, and contain some of Bach's most exuberant and attractive music. The third and fourth suites, which have trumpets and drums added to the strings and winds, were undoubtedly intended for performance out-of-doors. The piece popularly known as *Air for the G String* is an arrangement of the slow movement of the third suite.

Bach's orchestral suites

Bach also wrote two concertos for solo violin (and one for two violins) with orchestra, and was probably the first composer to write (or arrange) concertos for harpsichord. There are seven concertos for solo harpsichord with orchestra, three for two harpsichords, two for three harpsichords, and one for four harpsichords, this last an arrangement of a Vivaldi concerto for four violins. Most if not all

Works for solo violin and violoncello

of the harpsichord concertos, in fact, are arrangements of violin compositions by Bach himself or by other composers.

Other works

Two late instrumental works of Bach are in a class by themselves: *Musikalisches Opfer* (*A Musical Offering*) and *Die Kunst der Fuge* (*The Art of Fugue*). The former is based on a theme proposed by Frederick the Great of Prussia on which Bach improvised when he was visiting that monarch at Potsdam in 1747. On returning to Leipzig, Bach wrote out and revised his improvisations, dedicating the finished work to the king. It contains a three- and a six-part ricercar for keyboard and a trio sonata in four movements for flute (King Frederick's instrument), violin, and continuo, together with ten canons. *The Art of Fugue*, composed in 1749–50 and apparently left unfinished at Bach's death, is a systematic demonstration and summary of all types of fugal writing: it consists of eighteen canons and fugues in strictest style, all based on the same subject or one of its transformations, and arranged in a general order of increasing complexity, in the course of which the most difficult and abstruse contrapuntal devices are handled with masterful ease.

Bach's Vocal Music

Bach at Leipzig

In 1723, Leipzig was a flourishing commercial city with about 30,000 inhabitants, noted as a center of printing and publishing, and the seat of an ancient university. There were five churches in Leipzig in addition to the university chapels; most important were the churches of St. Nicholas and St. Thomas, in which Bach was responsible for the music.

St. Thomas's school was an ancient foundation which took in both day and boarding pupils. It provided fifty-five scholarships for boys and youths who were obliged in return to sing or play in the services of four Leipzig churches as well as to fulfill other musical duties, and who consequently were chosen on the basis of musical as well as general scholastic ability. As Cantor of the school Bach ranked third in the academic hierarchy. His duties included four hours of teaching each day (he had to teach Latin as well as music), and also preparing music for the church services.

Bach's church cantatas

Altogether, the Leipzig churches required 58 cantatas each year, in addition to Passion music for Good Friday, Magnificats at Vespers for three festivals, an annual cantata for the installation of the City Council, and occasional music such as funeral motets and wedding cantatas for which the Cantor received an extra fee. Bach undertook to provide new works for the church services from his own pen as frequently as possible. No generalized description can possibly suggest the infinite variety, the wealth of musical invention, technical

Bach's manuscript of the closing measures of the chorale prelude, O Mensch, bewein'.

mastery, and religious devotion in Bach's cantatas. Two or three examples will serve as introduction to this vast treasure of music.

Of the cantatas composed in Weimar, No. 61,[4] *Nun komm, der Heiden Heiland (Come, Gentiles' Savior)* of 1614 (NAWM/S 44), merits particularly close study. The text, by Erdmann Neumeister, combines chorale verses, newly invented metrical poetry, and prose from the Bible. The opening movement is based on the text and melody of the chorale *Nun komm, der Heiden Heiland*, upon which Bach wrote an elaborate variation in the style and form of a French overture. The choice of this genre is significant, because Bach was preoccupied at this time with the assimilation of foreign styles into his work and because it was written for the opening—i.e., *ouverture*—of the church year, the first Sunday of Advent. The juxtaposition of this secular from with an elaboration of a Lutheran

Cantata No. 61

4 The numbering of the Bach cantatas follows the Bach Gesellschaft edition, which is also that of BWV. The order is not chronological.

hymn is full of youthful ingenuity and completely convincing as a work of art. The first recitative, on a stanza of uneven line-lengths announcing the coming of the Savior, borrows a technique from Italian opera— the *cavata*. This is the drawing (*cavare*) from the last line or lines of a recitative the text for a short aria passage. The first real aria, on a more formal iambic stanza, is a *siciliano*— another operatic genre, based on a folk dance—and uses a repetition *dal segno,* that is, a da capo that omits the first ritornello. Bach converts the welcoming of Christ to his church into a pastoral love song. The next recitative, composed on a prose text from Revelation iii:20, "Behold, I stand at the door and knock," frames the words of Christ in five-part strings playing pizzicato to depict the knocking at the door. For the aria that follows Neumeister wrote a trochaic poem that voices the sentiment of the worshipper who, having heard Christ's knocking, opens her heart to him. It is in the intimate medium of a continuo aria with da capo. The final movement is a motet-like elaboration of the *Abgesang* from the chorale *Wie schön leuchtet der Morgenstern* on the last lines of its last stanza, "Come, you beautiful Crown of Joy," the crown being suggested in a wreath of violin figuration posed above the voices.

Cantatas No. 4 and No. 80

Bach used chorale melodies in a multitude of different ways in his cantatas. Cantata No. 4, *Christ lag in Todesbanden (Christ lay in death's dark prison),* refashioned from an earlier version and sung at Leipzig in 1724, is exceptional in that it goes back to the old form of chorale variations. A more usual scheme in the Leipzig cantatas is that used in No. 80, *Ein' feste Burg (A mighty fortress),* composed in 1715 and later (in 1724?) revised. The opening chorus in D major is a towering fantasia on the melody and words of the first stanza of the chorale. The vocal lines, freely adapted from the chorale tune, introduce each phrase in turn fugally, leading to a simple climactic statement of the phrase by the trumpet[5] in its high "clarino" register, answered in strict canon by the bass instruments. In this way the melody, phrase by phrase, is expanded into a vast architectural structure of 223 measures. The next number is a duet, also in D, for soprano and bass. The soprano sings the words of the second chorale stanza to an ornate version of the tune while the bass, in an even more ornate but completely independent line, has a separate text appropriately commenting on that of the soprano; they are accompanied by a steady vigorous sixteenth-note figure in the strings *unisono* and the continuo bass moving in eighth notes. The texture is one of four independent contrapuntal parts, of which the highest, the soprano solo, is doubled and further embellished by the oboe. Then follow a recitative and arioso for bass and an aria

---

[5] It is now believed that the trumpet parts to this cantata were added after Bach's death by his son Friedemann.

(B minor) for soprano, both on inserted poetic texts. The third stanza of the chorale is set in the form of a chorale prelude, the tune being proclaimed by the chorus in unison while each phrase is introduced and accompanied by the full orchestra in an energetic 6/8 rhythm. A recitative-arioso for tenor and a quietly moving duet for tenor and alto (G major) follow, and the cantata is concluded by the fourth and final stanza of the chorale, now in a straightforward four-part harmonic setting for full chorus (in which the congregation also may have joined) with instruments doubling the vocal parts.

Bach's secular cantatas, most of which he titled "dramma per musica," were composed for various occasions, and not infrequently he used some of the same music for a sacred text: eleven numbers of the *Christmas Oratorio,* for example, appear also in secular cantatas, six of them in *Hercules auf dem Scheidewege* (*Hercules at the Crossroads;* BWV 213). Among the best of the "musical dramas" are *Phoebus and Pan* (BWV 201) and *Schleicht, spielende Wellen* (*Glide gently, ye waters;* BWV 206) which was written to celebrate the birthday of Augustus III in 1733; the *Coffee Cantata* and the burlesque *Peasant Cantata* (BWV 211 and 212) are delightful specimens of Bach's lighter music.

Bach's secular cantatas

The word *motet* at Leipzig in Bach's time signified a composition for chorus, generally in contrapuntal style, without obbligato instrumental parts, and with a Biblical or chorale text. The motets sung in the Leipzig churches were relatively short, and were used as musical introductions to the service; apparently they were chosen from a traditional repertoire of old works, and the Cantor was not expected to furnish new motets. The six surviving motets of Bach (BWV 225–230) were written either for particular occasions (such as funerals) or perhaps for special church services. They are long works, and four of them are for double chorus. The voice parts are always complete in themselves, but undoubtedly in Bach's time they were sung with instrumental doubling—as was also, for example, the opening chorus of Cantata No. 38, which is in motet style. Many of the motets incorporate chorale melodies; the five-voice *Jesu meine Freude* (*Jesus, my joy*) uses the chorale in six of its eleven movements.

Bach's motets

The great Magnificat (BWV 243), for five-part chorus and orchestra, is one of Bach's most melodious works, more Italian in style than most of his church music. The *Christmas Oratorio* (BWV 248), produced at Leipzig in 1734, is in reality a set of six cantatas for the festivals of the Christmas and Epiphany season. The Biblical narratives (Luke ii:1–21; Matt. ii:1–12) are presented in recitative; appropriate arias and chorales are added to reflect or comment on the various episodes of the story. The designation of "oratorio" is justified by reason of the narrative element, which is not present in the usual cantata.

The culmination of Bach's work as a church musician was reached in his settings of the Passion according to St. John and St. Matthew. These two works, essentially similar in structure, are the crowning examples of the north German tradition of Gospel Passion settings in oratorio style. For the *St. John Passion,* in addition to the Gospel story (St. John xviii and xix, with interpolations from St. Matthew) and fourteen chorales, Bach also borrowed words, with some alterations, for added lyrical numbers from the popular Passion poem of B. H. Brockes, adding some verses of his own. Bach's musical setting, which was, probably, first performed at Leipzig in 1724, was subjected later to numerous revisions.

The *St. Matthew Passion,* for double chorus, soloists, double orchestra, and two organs, first performed in 1729 (or possibly 1727), is a drama of epic grandeur, the most noble and inspired treatment of its subject in the whole range of music. The text is from St. Matthew's Gospel, chapters xxvi and xxvii; this is narrated in tenor solo recitative and choruses, and the narration is interspersed with chorales, a duet, and numerous arias, most of which are preceded by arioso recitatives. The "Passion Chorale" (see Example VIII–1) appears five times, in different keys and in four different four-part harmonizations. The author of the added recitatives and arias was C. F. Henrici (1700–64; pseudonym, Picander), a Leipzig poet who also provided many of Bach's cantata texts. As in the St. John Passion, the chorus sometimes participates in the action and sometimes, like the chorus in Greek drama, is an articulate spectator introducing or reflecting upon the events of the narrative. The opening and closing choruses of Part I are huge chorale fantasias; in the first, the chorale melody is given to a special ripieno choir of soprano voices.

Nearly every phrase of the *St. Matthew Passion* affords examples of Bach's genius for merging pictorial musical figures with expressive effects. Of the many beautiful passages in this masterpiece of music, four may be singled out for special mention: the alto recitative *Ah, Golgotha;* the soprano aria *In Love my Saviour now is dying;* the last setting of the Passion Chorale, after Jesus's death on the Cross; and the stupendous three measures of chorus on the words *Truly this was the Son of God.*

The *Passion According to St. Matthew* is the apotheosis of Lutheran church music: in it the chorale, the *concertato* style, the recitative, the arioso, and the da capo aria are united under the ruling majesty of the central religious theme. All these elements, save the chorale, are equally characteristic of Baroque opera. The dramatic, theatrical qualities of both the *St. Matthew* and the *St. John Passions* are obvious. While it is true that Bach never wrote an opera, nevertheless the language, the forms, and the spirit of opera are fully present in the Passions.

The *Mass in B minor* is, necessarily, more general in content and more contemplative in viewpoint than the Passions, and hence less dramatic in detail. Choruses (mostly in five parts) take a far larger proportion of the work than they do in the Passions. The Kyrie and Gloria were presented in 1733 to Frederick Augustus, the Catholic King of Poland and Elector of Saxony, together with Bach's petition for an honorary appointment to the Electoral Chapel—a petition which was not granted until three years later. The remaining movements—some newly composed, others adapted—date from various periods in Bach's life; the work was not completed before 1747 or 1749. Bach probably never heard it performed in its entirety, though parts were sung at Leipzig, where an abbreviated form of the Latin Mass still had a place in the liturgy.

The *Mass in B minor*

Several numbers of the B-minor Mass are rearrangements from cantatas, for example, the *Gratias agimus* and the *Dona nobis pacem* (both of which use the same music) from the first chorus of Cantata No. 29. The brilliant Vivace e Allegro section of the Credo's *Et expecto resurrectionem* (*And I await the resurrection;* NAWM/S 45b) is a reworking of the chorus *Jauchzet, ihr erfreuten Stimmen* (*Shout, you joyful voices*) from Cantata No. 120, in which some of the purely instrumental music of the cantata chorus is ingeniously made to accompany a choral fugue. The *Crucifixus* is perhaps the most wonderful example in all music of the use of an ostinato bass. The music was written originally in 1714, to different words, as the opening chorus of Cantata No. 12. Bach altered the original ending to depict Christ's descent into the grave by the low register of the voices and, at the same time, by a modulation to G major, to suggest the hope of the resurrection, which bursts forth in the next chorus like a dance of joy.

This Mass is not liturgical music; it is too long and too elaborate to be used in any ordinary church service. It is rather a work which, like Beethoven's *Missa solemnis,* transcends denominational limits and rises to the height of a universal statement of Christian faith. Bach symbolized the continuity of the Christian tradition by using Gregorian *cantus firmi* in the Credo and in the *Confiteor* choruses. The latter (NAWM/S 45a), one of Bach's last compositions, is written in *stile antico.* Bach returns to the *alle breve* time signature and fugal procedures of that style, but he adds a modern touch: a quasi-ostinato basso continuo accompaniment.

Burial and resurrection might serve in some degree to describe the history of Bach's music. Works published, or prepared by Bach for publication, during his lifetime include the *Clavier Übung,* the *Schübler* chorales, the variations on *Vom Himmel hoch,* the *Musical Offering,* and *The Art of Fugue.* Changed musical taste in the later eighteenth century led to a general neglect of Bach, but the eclipse was far from total. Although no complete large work of his was published between 1752 and 1800, some of the preludes and fugues

Summary

from *The Well-Tempered Clavier* appeared in print and the whole collection circulated in innumerable manuscript copies. Haydn owned a copy of the *Mass in B minor.* Mozart knew *The Art of Fugue* and studied the motets on a visit to Leipzig in 1789. Citations from Bach's works are frequent in the musical literature of the time, and the important periodical, the *Allgemeine musikalische Zeitung,* opened its first issue (1798) with a Bach portrait. The full discovery of Bach, however, was the work of the nineteenth century. It was marked by the publication of the first important biography (by J. N. Forkel) in 1802; by Zelter's revival of the *St. Matthew Passion* and its performance at Berlin under Mendelssohn's direction in 1829; and by the foundation, in 1850, of the Bach society, whose collected edition of Bach's works was completed by 1900.

We can begin to understand the central position Bach has in the history of music when we realize, first, that he absorbed into his music the multiplicity of styles and forms current in the early eighteenth century and developed hitherto unsuspected potentialities in every one; and second, that in his music the opposed principles of harmony and counterpoint, melody and polyphony, are maintained in a tense but satisfying equilibrium found in no other composer. The continuing vitality of his music is not, of course, due to its historical significance as a summation of the late Baroque, but to the qualities of the music itself: the concentrated and individual themes, the copious musical invention, the balance between harmonic and contrapuntal forces, the strength of rhythm, the clarity of form, the grandeur of proportion, the imaginative use of pictorial and symbolic figures, the intensity of expression always controlled by a ruling architectural idea, and the technical perfection of every detail.

George Frideric Handel

Handel's career

Handel (1685–1759) was a typically international composer of the eighteenth century. As a boy in his native town of Halle, he became an accomplished organist and harpsichordist, studied violin and oboe, received a thorough grounding in counterpoint, and became familiar with the music of contemporary German and Italian composers by the usual and effective method of copying their scores. After a year at the University he went to Hamburg, where his first opera, *Almira,* was performed in 1705. From some time in 1706 until the middle of 1710 Handel was in Italy, where he was soon recognized as one of the coming young composers and where he associated with the leading patrons and musicians of Rome, Florence, Naples, and Venice. In 1710 he was appointed Music Director at the Electoral Court of Hanover. From 1712, Handel lived in London where he had a long and generally prosperous career; he became a naturalized British subject in 1726.

Oratorios and operas form the most important part of Handel's work, although he also wrote for keyboard instruments and for ensembles both vocal and instrumental. His keyboard works include three sets of concertos for harpsichord or organ, two collections of suites for harpsichord published respectively in 1720 and 1733, and a number of miscellaneous pieces. The suites contain not only the usual dance movements but also specimens of most of the keyboard forms of the time. The popular set of variations called *The Harmonious Blacksmith* (the title was bestowed in the nineteenth century) is the air (with variations) from the fifth Suite of the first collection. Handel composed 19 solo sonatas and an equal number of trio sonatas, for various chamber music combinations. In most of these the dominant influence is obviously that of Corelli, but the sophistication of the harmonies and the smooth, easy assurance of the musical movement (particularly in the Allegros) mark a later stage of the Italian style.

Handel's suites and sonatas

The most significant of Handel's instrumental works are those for full orchestra, including the overtures to his operas and oratorios, the two suites known as the *Fireworks Music* (1749) and the *Water Music* (?1717), and above all the concertos. There are six concertos for woodwinds and strings, usually called the "oboe concertos," and twelve *Grand Concertos* Opus 6, composed in 1739.

Handel's concertos

On the whole, the concertos of Opus 6 show a combination of retrospective and modern elements, with the former predominating. The ruling conception is the same as that in Corelli's work, namely, a *sonata da chiesa* for full orchestra. The framework is the usual order of four movements (slow–fast–slow–fast), with one of the Allegros fugal; but this scheme is usually expanded by an additional movement or two, which may be in dance rhythm. The common designation of *concerto grosso* does not strictly suit these works, since as a rule the solo parts are not markedly set off from the tuttis: in fact, in a majority of the movements the concertino strings either merely play throughout in unison with the ripieno or else appear by themselves only for brief trio-like interludes; and when there are extended passages for the solo violins, these usually differ neither in thematic material nor in style from the tutti passages. Only rarely and, as it were, incidentally, does Handel imitate Vivaldi in giving decorative figuration to a solo violin (as in Nos. 3, 6, and 11). Moreover, the serious, dignified bearing and the prevailingly full contrapuntal texture of this music are less characteristic of the 1730s than of the earlier part of the century when Handel was forming his style in Italy. But, conservative or no, the concertos are fascinating music, original and abundantly varied.

To the general public, Handel has long been known almost

Handel's operas

exclusively as a composer of oratorios; nonetheless, for thirty-five years of his life his principal occupation was composing and conducting operas—and his operas contain as large a proportion of memorable music as do his oratorios. He was no revolutionist, like Monteverdi or Wagner; his achievement was simply that in an age when opera was the main concern of ambitious musicians, Handel excelled all his contemporaries. His operas were heard not only in London but also quite frequently in Germany and Italy during his lifetime. Today, after a long period of neglect, they are beginning to come back into favor.

The subjects of these operas are the usual ones of the time: tales of magic and marvelous adventure, or, more often, episodes from the lives of heroes of antiquity, freely adapted to get the maximum number of intense dramatic situations. The musical scheme is likewise that of the early eighteenth century: development of the action in *recitativo secco,* interrupted periodically by solo da capo arias. Each aria is intended to give musical expression to a single specific mood or affection, so that the opera as a whole consists of a series of arias strung like pearls on the thread of the plot.

These operas· were written so that every singer had arias that favorably displayed the scope of his vocal and histrionic powers; furthermore, the arias had to be distributed according to the importance of each member of the cast. Within the limits of these requirements the composer might work with as much freedom as he chose or as his inventive powers allowed. Handel, like most eighteenth-century composers, could turn out an opera any time that would be good enough to satisfy expectations and enjoy the usual brief success; but he could also on occasion create a masterpiece like *Ottone,* which teems with beautiful melodic writing. His scores are remarkable for the wide variety of aria types, a variety that eludes strict classification. Arias range from brilliant virtuoso coloratura effects to sustained, sublimely expressive pathetic songs, such as the *Cara sposa* in *Rinaldo* or *Aure, deh per pietà* in *Giulio Cesare* (NAWM/S 39); arias of Baroque grandeur with rich contrapuntal accompaniments alternate with simple folk-like melodies or arias *all'unisono,* in which the strings play in unison with the voice throughout; still other songs are in dance rhythms. The pastoral scenes are especially noteworthy examples of eighteenth-century musical nature painting. Not all of Handel's arias are in da capo form, and occasionally he presented two contrasted affections in the same aria.

Transcending all mastery of technique is Handel's power of incarnating in music the essence of a mood or affection with overwhelming poetic depth and suggestiveness. This is a quality that cannot be adequately analyzed or described in words, but can only be sensed from the experience of the music itself. It is because of this power that some of the personages in Handel's operas loom as figures of heroic grandeur, like the great characters in the tragedies of Corneille and Racine.

Beginning in the 1730s Handel, finding his kind of opera no longer very popular, turned his energy increasingly to composing oratorios. These works, of which there are twenty-six in all, laid the foundation of Handel's long-continued influence on English musical life. Among his principal oratorios are _Saul, Israel in Egypt_ (both 1739), _Messiah_ (1742), _Judas Maccabaeus_ (1747), and _Jephtha_ (1751).

Handel's oratorios

The Italian Baroque oratorio was hardly anything other than an opera on a sacred subject, presented in concert instead of on the stage. This conception is an essential element of Handel's oratorios. Most of the arias in these works differ in no important respects—neither in form, musical style, nature of the musical ideas, nor technique of expressing the affections—from the arias in his operas. As in the operas also, the mood of each aria is usually prepared, and the aria introduced, by a preceding recitative. But there are alterations and additions which transform the oratorios into something different from the conventional eighteenth-century opera.

Fundamental is the fact that Handel's oratorio librettos were in English. The Italian used in opera undoubtedly had snob appeal for London listeners, most of whom, if pressed, could hardly have translated a dozen words of that language without help. The use of English was gratifying to the middle class; it also meant that at least some of the absurdities and conceits which were part of the tissue of the usual opera libretto must be renounced, since they could no longer be decently concealed under the cloak of a foreign tongue. Even more important, a new kind of subject matter had to be found. Classical mythology and ancient history were all very well for upper-class audiences who, whatever the actual state of their education, felt obliged to pretend some acquaintance with such matters.

The entire storehouse of both history and mythology known to middle-class Protestant England in the eighteenth century was the Bible, or, more accurately, the Old Testament, including the apocryphal books. All of Handel's sacred oratorios, and especially his most popular ones, were based on Old Testament stories (even _Messiah_ has more text from the Old than from the New Testament, except in its third part). Moreover, such subjects as _Saul, Israel in Egypt, Judas Maccabaeus_, and _Joshua_ had an additional appeal based on something besides familiarity with the ancient sacred narratives: it was impossible for English audiences in an era of prosperity and expanding empire not to feel a kinship with the chosen people of old whose heroes triumphed by the special favor of Jehovah. Handel more than once was chosen to be the official musical spokesman on occasions of national moment. But even where there was no immediate connection with a particular occasion, many of Handel's oratorios struck a responsive patriotic note with the British public.

The oratorios are not to be regarded as church music. They are intended for the concert hall, and are much closer to the theatre than to the church service. Not all are even on sacred subjects: some, like *Semele* and *Hercules* (1744), are mythological; others, like *Alexander's Feast*, the *Ode for St. Cecilia's Day* (1739), and Handel's last composition, *The Triumph of Time and Truth* (1757), are allegorical. The arrangement of the libretto varies: *Susanna* (1748), *Theodora* (1749), and *Joseph* (1743) are practically straight operas; most of the Biblical oratorios stay close to the original narrative, but the Biblical text was rewritten in recitatives (sometimes prose, sometimes rhymed verse), arias, and choruses; *Israel in Egypt*, on the other hand, tells the story of the exodus of the Israelites entirely in the words of scripture. *Messiah* also has a purely Scriptural text, but is the least typical of all Handel's oratorios in that it tells no story; it is a series of contemplations of the Christian idea of redemption, starting with Old Testament prophecies and going through the life of Christ to His final triumph.

Beyond question the most important innovation in the oratorios was Handel's use of the chorus. To be sure, the chorus had had its place in the Italian oratorios of Carissimi, and Handel's early training had made him familiar with the Lutheran choral music of Germany as well as with the characteristic combination of the chorus with orchestra and soloists in the southern German Catholic centers; but the English choral tradition impressed him most profoundly. His conquest of this English musical idiom was fully achieved in the *Chandos* anthems, written for the Duke of Chandos between 1718 and 1720—masterpieces of Anglican Baroque church music from which the composer frequently borrowed in his later works.

Handel's choral style

The monumental character of Handel's choral style was particularly appropriate to oratorios in which emphasis is on communal rather than individual expression as in the opera aria. Handel often used choruses in the oratorios where in opera an aria would appear —that is, as appropriate commentary or reflection on a situation that has arisen in the course of the action. Inevitably the collective nature of the choral group tends to endue such places with a certain impersonality, a quality akin to the choruses of Greek drama: one of the best of many examples from the Handel oratorios is the chorus *How dark, O Lord, are Thy decrees* in *Jephtha*. Handel's chorus also participates in the action, for instance in *Judas Maccabaeus;* is an element in incidental scenes, as in *Solomon;* or even narrates, as in *Israel in Egypt*, where the choral recitative *He sent a thick darkness* is remarkable equally for its unusual form, its strange modulations, and its pictorial writing.

Handel's autograph manuscript of I know that my Redeemer liveth *from* Messiah. *(The Royal Music Library, British Library)*

Pictorial and affective musical symbolism is one of the most conspicuous and endearing features of Handel's choral writing. Of course word painting and descriptive figures—the musical language of the affections—were universal in the Baroque, but Handel often used these devices in especially felicitous ways. Many examples may be found in *Israel in Egypt:* the somewhat literal representation of frogs, flies, lice, hail, and the other plagues of Egypt is amusing rather than impressive; but the profound and moving symbolism of *The people shall hear* lifts this chorus to an eminence hardly equalled elsewhere even by Handel himself. In *Messiah* there is a half-playful use of word painting, the appositeness of which is surprising in view of the fact that the music, up to the last few measures, was adapted from a rather frivolous Italian duet of Handel's composed shortly before. The chorus in *Messiah* sings: "All we like sheep have *gone astray* [diverging melodic lines]; we have *turned* [a rapidly twisting, turning figure that never gets away from its starting point] every one *to his own way*" [stubborn insistence on a single repeated note]; but the point is revealed suddenly, with incomparable dramatic force, at the solemn coda: "and the Lord hath laid on Him the iniquity of us all." A parallel though less striking dramatic contrast is heard in the chorus *For unto us a child is born.* This music is taken from another part of the same Italian duet; the carefree roulades that celebrate the birth of the Redeemer lead up to the mighty Handelian hammerstrokes on the words "Wonderful, Counsellor, the Mighty God."

Passages such as these reveal Handel the dramatist, the unerring master of grandiose effects. He is one of the great composers who know how to write well for a chorus. His style is simpler than Bach's, less finely chiseled, less subjective, less consistently contrapuntal. He alternates passages in open fugal texture with solid blocks of harmony, sets a melodic line in sustained notes against one in quicker rhythm. Everything is planned so as to lie well within the most effective range of the voices; at points where he designs the maximum fullness of choral sound, especially, Handel brings the four parts tightly together, the basses and tenors high, the sopranos and altos in the middle register. This grouping is often used in the characteristically Handelian closing cadences: an allegro chorus climaxing on an inconclusive chord; a tense moment of silence; and then the final cadential chords in three or four splendid sonorous adagio harmonies, in which the chorus, in one great outburst of sound, gathers up the whole meaning of everything that has come before.

Handel's borrowings

Handel, like most eighteenth-century composers, occasionally incorporated in his compositions themes, sections, or even whole movements from other works, sometimes literally but more often with changes and improvements. Most of his borrowings were from his own earlier works, but a considerable number were from other composers; three duets and eleven of the 28 choruses of *Israel in Egypt,* for example, were taken in whole or in part from the music of others, while four choruses were arrangements from earlier works by Handel himself. Further borrowings, although not on such an extensive scale, have been traced in many of Handel's compositions written after 1737. It has been conjectured that he resorted to this as a means of overcoming the inertia that sometimes afflicted him when he was beginning a new work, particularly after 1737, when he had suffered a paralytic stroke and nervous collapse. However that may be, Handel is not to be criticized as a modern composer might be for plagiarism. Borrowing, transcribing, adapting, rearranging, parodying (in the same sense as in the Parody Mass of the sixteenth century) was a universal and accepted practice in the Baroque. When Handel borrowed, he more often than not repaid with interest, clothing the borrowed material with new beauty and preserving it for generations that otherwise would scarcely have known of its existence. [6]

[6] Apropos the question of originality in art are these words of William Ivins. He is speaking particularly of drawing, but his conclusions are equally relevant to music: " 'Originality' in art is very much like originality in sin, for we should always bear in mind that 'original sin' is the sin, or at least the kind of sin, about which we poor mortals can do nothing at all. We have it simply because we are descended from Adam and Eve. In the same way, draughtsmen who are original are so no matter how much they may attempt to copy or emulate something that someone else has done before them. . . . 'Copies' and imitations made by men who have this ineradicable quality of originality are infinitely more original than

Handel's greatness and historical significance rest on two achievements: his contribution to the musical treasure of the late Baroque and his anticipation of many elements that became important in the new style of the mid-eighteenth century. As a choral composer in the grand style he is without peer. He is a consummate master, not only in choral music but in all fields, of the basic Baroque principle of contrast. At the same time, Handel's emphasis on melody and harmony, as compared to the more strictly contrapuntal style of Bach, links him with the progressive elements of his time. His deliberate appeal to a middle-class audience in the oratorios was one of the first manifestations of a social change which continued throughout the latter half of the century, and which had far-reaching effects on music. In some details it might be said that Handel anticipated even the Romantics—the descriptive music of the pastoral scenes in *Giulio Cesare;* the dramatic scene-painting in the "Witch of Endor" episode in *Saul;* the use of clarinets in *Tamerlano* (antedating Rameau by twenty-five years); or the four horns in *Giulio Cesare.* The vast intellect of this lord of music seems to have embraced both past and future in one superb and comprehensive grasp.

Summary

'original drawings' made by men who lack it . . . The best way to find out how much originality a man has is to see what he can do with another man's idea. I believe it is something of this kind that explains why the great masters—the most original men, that is—have always come out of long lineages of other great artists, on whose shoulders and triumphs they stand." William M. Ivins, Jr., "Some Disconnected Notes about Drawing," *Harper's Magazine,* December, 1949, 84–85. Quoted by permission of the publishers. See also F. B. Zimmerman, "Musical Borrowings in the English Baroque," MQ 52 (1966), 483–95.

XIII

Sources of Classical Style: The Sonata, Symphony, and Opera in the Eighteenth Century

The Background

Aspects of eighteenth-century life

Four aspects of eighteenth-century life and thought are especially important for understanding the music of this period. In .the first place, the eighteenth century was a *cosmopolitan* age. National differences were minimized in comparison with the common humanity of men. Quantz, writing at Berlin in 1752, postulates as the ideal musical style one made up of the best features of the music of all nations: "A music that is accepted and recognized as good not by one country only . . . but by many peoples . . . must, provided it is based as well on reason and sound feeling, be beyond all dispute the best."[1] Chabanon, in 1785, declared "Today there is but one music in all of Europe . . . this universal language of our continent."[2]

---

[1] J. J. Quantz, *Versuch*, XVIII, in SR, 597–98 (SRC, 23–24).
[2] Michel Paul Gui de Chabanon, *De la musique considerée en elle-même et dans ses rapports* [etc.], Paris, 1785, p. 97.

278

The Enlightenment was *humanitarian* as well as cosmopolitan. Rulers not only patronized arts and letters but also busied themselves with programs of social reform. Humanitarian ideals, longings for universal human brotherhood spread over Europe. Mozart's *Magic Flute,* Schiller's *Ode to Joy,* and Beethoven's Ninth Symphony were among the outgrowths of the eighteenth-century humanitarian movement.

With the rise of a numerous middle class to a position of influence, the eighteenth century witnessed the first steps in a process of *popularization* of art and learning. A new market was appearing for the productions of writers and artists, and not only the subject matter but also the manner of presentation had to be shaped to the new demands. The popularizing trend found powerful support with the growth of the "back to nature" movement and the exaltation of sentiment in literature and the arts.

Music was affected along with everything else. Patronage was on the wane and the modern musical public was coming into being. Public concerts designed for mixed audiences began to rival the older private concerts and academies. Music printing increased enormously; the bulk of the publication was directed at amateurs, and much music was issued in periodicals. An amateur public naturally demanded and bought music that was easy to understand and to play, and the same public was interested in reading about and discussing music. Musical journalism began; after the middle of the century magazines sprang up which were devoted to musical

Concert at Vauxhall Gardens *(1786), by Thomas Rowlandson. Opened in 1736, this popular place of amusement in London offered concerts every summer. Among its "resident composers" was Thomas Augustine Arne. (Prints Division, New York Public Library, Astor, Lenox, and Tilden Foundations)*

news, reviews, and criticism. The first histories of music were written and the first collection of medieval musical treatises published.

Finally, the Enlightenment was a *prosaic* age. Its best literature was prose, and it valued in all the arts the virtues of good prose writing: clarity, animation, good taste, proportion, and elegance. Rational rather than poetic, the age had little liking for Baroque mysticism, gravity, massiveness, grandeur, and passion, and its critical temper inhibited great poetry in large forms. Early eighteenth-century esthetics held that the task of music, like that of the other arts, was to imitate nature, to offer to the listener pleasant sounding images of reality; music was an imitative, hence a decorative art, "an innocent luxury," as Dr. Burney called it.

Moreover, music of the Enlightenment was supposed to meet the listener on his own ground, and not compel him to make an effort to understand what was going on. It overwhelmingly favored the major mode. It must please (by agreeable sounds and rational structure) and move (by imitating feelings), but not too often astonish (by excessive elaboration) and never puzzle (by too great complexity). Music, as "the art of pleasing by the succession and combination of agreeable sounds,"[3] must eschew contrapuntal complexities, which could only be appreciated by the few learned in such abstruse matters. Quantz felt that "the old composers were too much absorbed with musical 'tricks' [contrapuntal devices] and carried them too far, so that they neglected the essential thing in music, which is to move and please."[4] Such opinions were shared by most critics in the 1780s, and the expressive qualities of eighteenth-century music were often sentimental and childlike, bound up as they were with this artificial striving for naturalness. [5]

The ideal eighteenth-century music The ideal music of the middle and later eighteenth century, then, might be described as follows: its language should be universal, not limited by national boundaries; it should be noble as well as entertaining; it should be expressive within the bounds of decorum; it should be "natural," in the sense of being free of needless technical complications and capable of immediately pleasing any normally sensitive listener. The music that most fully realized these ideals was written in the Classical period, approximately the years 1770 to 1800, and its masters were Gluck, Haydn, Mozart, and the young Beethoven.

Because Gluck, and more especially Haydn and Mozart, over-

---

[3] Burney, "Essay on Musical Criticism," introducing Book III of his *General History of Music.*

[4] Quantz, *op. cit.,* Introduction, §16.

[5] On the sixty-odd distinct meanings attached to the words "nature" and "natural" by different writers from the seventeenth to the nineteenth centuries, see references in the index of Arthur O. Lovejoy's *Essays in the History of Ideas,* New York, 1955.

shadow their predecessors and contemporaries in much the same way that Bach and Handel overshadow theirs, it is easy to fall into the error of viewing the late seventeenth-century composers merely as the forerunners of Bach and Handel, and the mid-eighteenth century composers merely as the forerunners of Gluck, Haydn, and Mozart. It is especially easy in the latter instance because comparatively little is known about early eighteenth-century opera or the origins of the Classical symphony. The fallacy of this "mere forerunner" conception is undoubtedly due to a confused notion that progress occurs when old things are superseded by new; we are prone to imagine that in the same way that the automobile superseded the horse and buggy, the symphonies of Mozart superseded those of Stamitz. To deny this is not to deny that Mozart was a greater composer than Stamitz, but only to assert that the idea of progress is not the only possible way to approach a comparison of the two.

Instrumental Music:
Sonata, Symphony, and Concerto

Two general styles or manners can be distinguished within the so-called pre-Classical period beginning around 1720: the *rococo* and the *expressive*. The former was cultivated especially in France, and the French term *style galant* (gallant style) is often used as a synonym for rococo. The expressive style, which arose somewhat later and was chiefly associated with German composers, is often designated by the equivalent German phrase *empfindsamer Stil* (literally, sensitive style). Both may be regarded as outgrowths of the Baroque tendency to concentrate all musical interest in the two outer voices; but in these newer styles the bass loses all vestiges of leadership and contrapuntal independence, and becomes simply an underpinning for the melody, while the inner voices are mere harmonic fillers.

Rococo and expressive styles

The rococo or *galant* style arose in courtly, aristocratic circles; it was elegant, playful, easy, witty, polished, and ornate. *Rococo* originally described the elaborately ornamental decoration of interiors and furnishings fashionable in France during the age of the Regency; *galant* was a catchword of the same period, applied to everything that was thought to be modern, smart, chic, smooth, easy, and sophisticated. The rococo is Baroque decorativeness without grandeur. The expressive style, on the other hand, was an affair of the middle class; it was the *style bourgeois*. Instead of being ornate, it is sometimes ostentatiously plain. It domesticates the Baroque affections, turning them into sentiments of the individual soul. The ease and elegance of the rococo, as well as some of its decorative charm, were combined with the expressive quality of the *style bourgeois* in most compositions by the middle of the eighteenth century, and both styles are completely absorbed into the music of the Classical period.

New concepts of melody and harmony

The change from Baroque to the new kind of eighteenth-century music included among other things a change in the conception of melody and melodic development. The new composers of the eighteenth century, while retaining the late Baroque method of constructing a movement on the basis of related keys, gradually abandoned the older idea of the one basic affection and began to introduce contrasts between the various parts of a movement or even within the theme or themes themselves. Moreover, instead of the Baroque continuity and spinning-out technique, the melodies came to be articulated into distinct phrases, typically two or four measures in length (but also frequently three, five, or six measures), resulting in a periodic structure and thereby raising the problem of how to achieve continuity under this new condition.

The harmonic vocabulary and tonal system of the middle and late eighteenth century were substantially the same as those of the late Baroque, but the harmonic rhythm of most of the new music is slower and the harmonic progressions less weighty than in the older style. A great deal of bustling activity goes on over relatively slow-moving and conventional harmonies, and important harmonic changes almost always coincide with the strong accents indicated by the barlines. The subordination of the bass and harmonies to the role of mere accompaniment to the melody is symbolized by one of

Chamber Music in a Garden Salon *(1769), by Daniel Nikolaus Chodowiecki; an engraving for a 1770 textbook.*

the most widely used devices of mid-eighteenth-century keyboard music, the *Alberti bass,* named for the Italian composer Domenico Alberti (*ca.* 1710–40). This device consists in breaking each of the underlying chords into a simple pattern of short notes incessantly repeated, thus producing a discreet undulation in the background which sets off the melody to advantage. The Alberti bass was extremely useful; it was not disdained by Haydn, Mozart, and Beethoven, and lasted well into the nineteenth century.

The chief Italian keyboard composer of the eighteenth century, and one of the most original geniuses in the history of music, was Domenico Scarlatti (1685–1757). Son of the famous Alessandro Scarlatti, born in the same year as Bach and Handel, Domenico Scarlatti produced no works of lasting importance before his first collection of harpsichord sonatas (called on the title page *essercizi* —exercises or diversions) which was published in 1738. In 1720 or 1721 Scarlatti left Italy to enter the service of the King of Portugal. When his pupil the Infanta of Portugal was married to Prince Ferdinand of Spain in 1729, Scarlatti followed her to Madrid, where he remained for the rest of his life in the service of the Spanish courts and where he composed most of his 555 sonatas.

Domenico Scarlatti

Scarlatti's music is idiomatic for the harpsichord as Chopin's or Debussy's is for the piano. Every imaginable shading of harpsichord sonority, every resource of harpsichord technique, may be found in the sonatas. Some are virtuoso pieces of formidable difficulty, others quiet pastorale-like movements; variegated moods, reminiscences of popular song and of Italian, Portuguese, and Spanish dance rhythms pervade them. A basic two-voice homophonic texture is alternately filled and thinned, sometimes with sudden contrasts of key or texture but always with an infallible ear for the shape of the phrase and the right sound on the instrument. Rhythmic vitality is combined with an exuberant flow of thematic invention.

All the Scarlatti sonatas are organized by means of tonal relationships into the standard late Baroque and early Classical binary pattern used for dance pieces and other types of composition: two sections, each repeated, the first cadencing in the dominant or relative major (rarely some other key), the second modulating further afield and then returning to the tonic. This is the basic scheme which underlies much instrumental and solo vocal music in the eighteenth century. In Scarlatti's sonatas the closing part of the first section invariably returns, but in the tonic key, at the end of section two.

The one-movement sonata written around 1749 and identified as K.119 (K. for Ralph Kirkpatrick's index of the sonatas) or Longo 415 (the number in A. Longo's complete edition of the sonatas) exhibits many of these points (NAWM/S 54). It is in two sections, each repeated. After a brilliant opening, several ideas are announced, each immediately restated. This repetition, so characteristic of pre-

Classical music, seems to derive from the habit of reiterating phrases in comic opera, thereby making the most of witty and clever lines. In this work it has a similar function, for many of these attractive ideas do not return and the initial repetition allows us to savor and grasp them better.

The Classical Sonata

The Classical sonata (likewise the symphony and most kinds of chamber music), as found in Haydn, Mozart, and Beethoven, is a composition in three or four (sometimes two) movements of contrasting mood and tempo. Typically the first movement, and often the slow movement and the finale, exemplify what is known as *sonata form* or *first-movement form,* the essential outlines of which are: [6] (1) division into two distinct sections, the first being usually and the second not always repeated; (2) in the first section, establishment of a tonic, modulation to the dominant (or relative major), and close on a cadence in the new key; (3) beginning with the second section, further modulations with increasing tension to a point not more than halfway through this section, at which comes (4) a strongly marked return to the tonic, coinciding with a recognizable (not necessarily literal) restatement of the opening material of section one and constituting the principal climax of the movement; then (5) continuation in the tonic with "reinterpretation" of the material from section one—especially that material which had there been heard in the dominant—and proceeding to a final resolution on the tonic.

The above outline of sonata form is partially represented in the well-known "textbook" definition, which posits: (1) an *exposition* (usually repeated), incorporating a first theme or group of themes in the tonic, a second more lyrical theme in the dominant or relative major, and a closing theme also in the dominant or relative major— the different themes being connected by appropriate transitions or bridge passages; (2) a *development* section, in which motives or themes from the exposition are presented in new aspects or combinations, and in the course of which modulations may be made to relatively remote keys; (3) a *recapitulation,* where the material of the exposition is restated in the original order but with all themes now in the tonic; following the recapitulation there may be a *coda.*

The textbook definition is an abstraction, made by dwelling exclusively on the key scheme and the melodic-thematic elements of sonata form. So understood, it will fit a good many sonata movements of the late Classical period and the nineteenth century; but there are many more (including most of Haydn's) which it will fit only awkwardly if at all. For example: many other elements besides "themes" are important for defining a form; themes them-

---

[6] For this outline of sonata form, I am much indebted to the excellent book of Charles Rosen, *The Classical Style: Haydn, Mozart, Beethoven,* New York, 1971.

selves are not always melodies of definite contour; there may be no "second theme," or if there is one it may not differ in character from the "first theme"; new themes may be introduced anywhere; development may occur in any part of the movement, including the coda; or there may be no coda. A sonata that brings back the opening material in the dominant at the start of the second section (as many early Classical sonatas do) instead of recapitulating it in the tonic further on, or one that altogether avoids any formal restatement of the opening material (as most of Scarlatti's do) is not on such account to be thought imperfect or "primitive." Many different composers in the eighteenth century, with different kinds of musical ideas, made use of a common, loosely defined pattern, modifying or expanding or adding to it as their own inventiveness and the nature of their musical material required.

Both keyboard sonatas and orchestral compositions of similar form of the early part of the eighteenth century were influenced by the Italian opera overture (*sinfonia*), which about 1700 assumed a structure of three movements in the order fast–slow–fast, that is, an Allegro, a short lyrical Andante, and a finale in the rhythm of some dance, such as a minuet or a gigue. Inasmuch as such overtures as a rule had no thematic or other connection with the opera to follow, they could be played as independent pieces in concerts. Hence it was natural, around 1730, for Italian composers to begin to write concert symphonies using the general plan of the opera overtures—though the earliest such symphonies are equally if not more indebted to the tradition of the late Baroque concerto and trio sonata for details of structure, texture, and thematic style. One of the first symphonists was G. B. Sammartini (1701–75) of Milan. Composers in Germany, Austria, and France soon followed the lead of the Italians, so that from about 1740 the symphony gradually replaced the concerto as the leading form of concerted instrumental music.

Pre-Classical symphonies and chamber music

The entrance of the expressive style (*empfindsamer Stil*) into instrumental music toward the middle of the century, though not exclusively the achievement of German composers, may be most clearly illustrated in their works.

The *emfindsamer Stil*

One of the most influential composers of his generation was Carl Philipp Emanuel Bach (1714–88), son of the great Johann Sebastian Bach. Trained in music by his father, he was in service at the court of Frederick the Great in Berlin from 1740 to 1768 and then became music director of the five principal churches in Hamburg. His compositions include oratorios, songs, symphonies, and chamber music, but most numerous and important are his works for clavier. In 1742 he published a set of six sonatas (the *Prussian* sonatas) and in 1744 another set of six (the *Württemberg* sonatas). These sonatas, especially those of 1742, were quite new in style, and exerted a strong influence on later composers. Bach's favorite keyboard instrument

C. P. E. Bach

was not the harpsichord but the softer, more intimate clavichord, with its capacity for delicate dynamic shadings. The clavichord enjoyed a spell of renewed popularity in Germany around the middle of the eighteenth century before both it and the harpsichord were gradually supplanted by the pianoforte; the last five sets of Emanuel Bach's sonatas (1780–87) were written for the pianoforte.

The principal technical characteristics of the *empfindsamer Stil*, of which C. P. E. Bach was one of the leading exponents, may be observed in the second movement, Poco Adagio, of the fourth of the *Sonaten . . . für Kenner und Liebhaber* (*Sonatas for Connoisseurs and Amateurs*), (Example XIII–1; the entire movement is in

EXAMPLE XIII–1   Sonata, W. 55/4: [7] Poco Adagio, C. P. E. Bach

[7] The numbering used for C. P. E. Bach's sonatas follows Alfred Wotquenne, *Thematisches Verzeichnis der Werke von Carl Philipp Emanuel Bach*, Leipzig, 1905.

NAWM/S 55). It begins with a kind of melodic sigh, a singing motive ending in an appoggiatura that resolves on a weak beat, followed by a rest, and all this decorated with mordents, Scotch snaps, and trills; in short, with *galanterie,* as they were called. The multiplicity of rhythmic patterns, nervously, constantly changing—short dotted figures, triplets, asymmetrical runs of five and thirteen notes—gives the music a restless, effervescent quality. Measures 6 to 10, making up the transition to the relative major tonal area, illustrate the marriage of sentimentality and *galanterie* so typical of Bach's style. Thus, ornamentation serves and is not a mere accessory to expression.

Ornamentation was not by any means precluded in the ideal of simplicity or naturalness as understood by the eighteenth century, but composers did endeavor to keep the ornaments within proportion and to assimilate them into the entire expressive content of a passage. The expressive style often exploited the element of surprise, with abrupt shifts of harmony, strange modulations, unusual turns of melody, expectant pauses, changes of texture, sudden *sforzando* accents, and the like. The subjective, emotional qualities of the *Empfindsamkeit* reached a climax during the 1760s and 1770s; the style is sometimes described by the same term *Sturm und Drang*—storm and stress—which is applied to German literature of the same period. The Classical composers later brought this emotionalism under control by imposing unity of content and form. The entire development will be traced in the discussion of Haydn, in the following chapter.

Movements in sonata form in Emanuel Bach's works often do not have two distinct themes; even when two themes are present, there is seldom a real contrast in character between them. As is usual with the north German composers, Bach's ruling ideal is unity of mood and material; consequently, themes usually begin to be developed as soon as they have been stated; and the section immediately after the double bar, the development section of the standard Classical symphony, is relatively short. In this concept of thematic unity within sonata form, as well as in his general musical language, Bach is closer to Haydn than to Mozart. Most of his sonatas have three movements—Allegro (or Allegretto), Andante, Allegro—though in some of the later ones the Andante was shortened to a mere bridge between the two fast movements. Some of Bach's most ingenious and charming music is found in the rondos which alternate with the sonatas and fantasias of the last five sets of the *Sonatas for Connoisseurs* published from 1780 to 1787.

Not the least of his contributions to music was Bach's *Essay on the True Art of Playing Keyboard Instruments* (1753–62), the most important treatise on ornamentation in the middle eighteenth century and a work which, like Quantz's essay on flute playing, includes much information about the musical thought and practice of the period.

The principal German centers of symphonic composition from 1740 onward were Mannheim, Vienna, and Berlin. The founder of the Mannheim school was Johann Stamitz (1717–57); under his leadership the Mannheim orchestra became renowned all over Europe for its virtuosity (Burney called it "an army of generals"), for its hitherto unknown dynamic range from the softest *pianissimo* to the loudest *fortissimo,* and for the thrilling sound of its crescendo. The growing use of crescendo and diminuendo around the middle of the century was one symptom of a trend toward attaining variety within a movement by means of gradual transitions; Baroque movements had either kept to a uniform dynamic level or else introduced distinct contrasts, as in the concerto. The same desire for flexibility of musical effects was responsible for the eventual replacement of the harpsichord by the pianoforte.

German symphonic composers

Stamitz was one of the first composers to introduce a contrasting theme in the dominant section, sometimes lyrical, sometimes graceful or playful, as opposed to the dynamic and energetic opening section. The Allegro assai (NAWM/S 58) of the *Sinfonia a 8* known as *La Melodia Germanica,* No. 3, from the mid-1750s, has a quiet graceful second subject that provides a pleasant relief after the rather military and busy tonic section. The first thematic group actually contains three elements, the first featuring heavy chords and unisons, the second a tuneful soft violin motive that begins after a characteristic "sighing" rest, and the third a horn call. Besides an Andante slow movement this symphony includes both a minuet and a Prestissimo, comprising the set of four movements that became standard in most of Haydn's symphonies.

The Vienna school is of especial interest because it was the immediate background of the work of Haydn, Mozart, and Beethoven. Georg Matthias Monn (1717–50) was one of the earliest of the Viennese composers, but a more important figure was Fux's pupil Georg Christoph Wagenseil (1715–77). In his music, as also in that of the later Austrian composers Florian Leopold Gassmann (1729–74) and Michael Haydn (1737–1806), we find the pleasant, typically Viennese lyricism and good humor that is such an important feature in Mozart's style. The Viennese composers for the most part favored contrasting theme-groups in their movements in sonata form.

The principal symphonists of the Berlin or north German school were grouped around the person of Frederick the Great, who was himself a composer; two of its chief members were Johann Gottlieb Graun (1703–71) and C. P. E. Bach. The north Germans were conservative, in that they held consistently to three-movement structure for the symphony and were chary of introducing sharp thematic contrasts within a movement. On the other hand, it was they chiefly who initiated the technique of thematic development in a dynamic, organically unified, serious, and quasi-dramatic style, and at the same time enriched symphonic texture with contrapuntal elements.

Paris became an important center of composition and publication toward the middle of the eighteenth century; a considerable number of German and other foreign composers lived there. Works of the French school included symphonies and, particularly after 1770, a form known as the *symphonie concertante,* that is, a symphonic work employing two or more solo instruments in addition to the regular orchestra. One of the most noted composers of symphonies in France was a Belgian, François Joseph Gossec (1734–1829). Particularly important in his work were the marches and cantatas written for public ceremonies of the new republic, such as his *Marche lugubre* (NAWM/S 60), for a celebration to commemorate the defense of the new regime. Pieces such as this must have been in Beethoven's mind when he composed the Funeral March for his Third Symphony, the "Eroica" (NAWM/S 61).

In the last quarter of the eighteenth century the symphony and other forms of ensemble music gradually discarded the basso continuo as all the essential voices were taken over by the melody instruments. With the final disappearance of the harpsichord from the symphony orchestra, toward the end of the century, the responsibility of conducting the group fell on the leader of the violins.

The eighteenth-century symphony orchestra was much smaller than the orchestra of today. In 1756 the Mannheim orchestra consisted of twenty violins, four each of violas, violoncellos, and double-basses, two each of flutes, oboes, and bassoons, four horns, one trumpet, and two kettledrums; but this was an exceptionally large group. Haydn's orchestra from 1760 to 1785 rarely had more than twenty-five players, including strings, flute, two oboes, two bassoons, two horns, and a harpsichord, with trumpets and kettledrums occasionally added. Even in the 1790s the orchestras at Vienna normally had not more than thirty-five players.

The symphony orchestra

In the symphonies of the middle eighteenth century the usual orchestration gave all the essential musical material to the strings, and used the winds only for doubling, reinforcing, and filling in the harmonies. Sometimes in performance woodwinds and brasses might be added to the orchestra even though the composer had written no parts for them. Later in the century the wind instruments came to be entrusted with more important and more independent material.

The types of chamber music in the 1770s and 1780s included the sonata for clavier and violin, with the violin usually in a subsidiary role; but the principal medium eventually became the string quartet. A distinguished composer of chamber music was Luigi Boccherini

Chamber music

(1743–1805), whose output includes about 140 string quintets, 100 string quartets, and 65 string trios, besides other chamber and orchestral music. The composer before Haydn who enhanced the independence of the four string parts to forge a true string-quartet style was Franz Xaver Richter (1709–89). Particularly noteworthy is the second of the Opus 5 quartets which has a Fugato as fourth movement (NAWM/S 56) that amalgamates strict fugue with sonata form. The string quartet reaches an early maturity in this fine work.

A different type of music, designed primarily for out-of-doors or for informal occasions, was the Viennese serenade, which like the divertimento, cassation, and notturno was an intermediate form between the Baroque orchestral suite and the Classical symphony; it consisted usually of five or more movements, many of them in dance rhythms, but in no regularly prescribed order. Such pieces were written for wind instruments alone, or strings alone, or a combination of the two; they kept a certain popular flavor in their tunes and rhythms, and were not without influence on the style of the Viennese Classical symphony. Historically, they were important because they accustomed composers to the sound of ensemble music without basso continuo, the elimination of which was an essential step in the evolution of the Classical string quartet.

Opera, Song, and Church Music

As with the sonata and symphony, so with the opera: new forms and styles were emerging from and gradually supplanting the old during the first quarter of the eighteenth century. The French *tragédie lyrique* was resistant to change in this period, and the general style of Venetian Baroque opera maintained itself for a long while in Germany; but a strong progressive current was emanating from Italy. The new Italian opera that eventually dominated the stages of Europe in the eighteenth century was a product of the same forces that were reshaping all other forms of music in the age of the Enlightenment. It aimed to be clear, simple, rational, faithful to nature, of universal appeal, and capable of giving pleasure to its audiences without causing them undue mental fatigue. The artificialities which it soon acquired, and for which it was roundly condemned by critics in the latter part of the century, were in part merely outmoded conventions of an earlier period and in part accidental accretions.

The aria   The musical interest of the Italian opera was centered in the arias, which were created by eighteenth-century composers in astounding profusion and variety. The most common form in the earlier part of the century was the da capo aria, a basic scheme that permitted infinite variation in detail. After about the middle of the century it became more common to write arias in a single movement, usually an expanded version of the first part of a da capo aria, with a key-scheme like that of the sonata and with orchestral ritornellos as in a concerto.

Concentration upon the aria as almost the only significant musical ingredient in opera opened the way to abuses. The scheme of regularly alternating recitatives and arias came to be treated too rigidly. Singers, including the famed Italian *castrati* (male sopranos and altos), made arbitrary demands on the poets and composers, compelling them to alter, add, and substitute arias without respect for dramatic or musical propriety. Moreover, the melodic embellishments and cadenzas which the singers added at will were all too often mere tasteless displays of vocal acrobatics. A famous satire on the opera and everything connected with it, entitled *Il teatro alla moda* (*The Fashionable Theatre*), was published anonymously by Benedetto Marcello (1686–1739) in 1720, but not until about 1745 did Italian composers attempt any important reforms. The beginning of operatic reform coincided with the rise of the expressive style, and, like that style, was a sign of the growing influence of middle-class ideas on the narrowly aristocratic standards of the early part of the century.

Some of the other composers who wrote in this idiom were Handel in his late operas such as *Alcina* and *Serse,* Pergolesi, Giovanni Bononcini, Karl Heinrich Graun (1704–59), Domingo Terradellas (1713–51), a Spaniard who studied and worked in Naples, Nicola Porpora (1686–1768), and a German, Johann Adolph Hasse (1699–1783). Hasse was for most of his life director of music and opera at the court of the Elector of Saxony in Dresden, but he spent many years in Italy, married an Italian wife (a celebrated soprano, Faustina Bordoni), and became thoroughly Italian in his musical style. His music is the perfect complement to the poetry of Pietro Metastasio (1698–1782); the great majority of his eighty operas are on Metastasio librettos, some of which he set two and even three times. He was the most popular and successful opera composer of Europe around the middle of the century.

When certain Italian composers began seriously to try to bring the opera into harmony with changing ideals of music and drama, their efforts were directed toward making the entire design more "natural"—that is, more flexible in structure, more deeply expressive in content, less laden with coloratura, and more varied in other musical resources. The da capo aria was not abandoned but it was modified, and other forms were used as well; arias and recitatives were alternated more flexibly so as to carry on the action more rapidly and realistically; greater use was made of accompanied recitative; the orchestra became more important both for its own sake and for adding harmonic depth to accompaniments; choruses,

Beginnings of opera reform

long disused in Italian opera, reappeared; and there was a general stiffening of resistance to the arbitrary demands of the solo singers.

Christoph Willibald Gluck

The consummation of the international style of opera was the work of Christoph Willibald Gluck (1714–87). Born in Bohemia, Gluck studied under Sammartini in Italy, visited London, toured in Germany as conductor of an opera troupe, became court composer to the Emperor at Vienna, and triumphed in Paris under the patronage of Marie Antoinette. He began by writing operas in the conventional Italian style, but was strongly affected by the movement of reform in the 1750s. Spurred on by the more radical ideas of the time, he collaborated with the poet Raniero Calzabigi (1714–95) to produce at Vienna *Orfeo ed Euridice* in 1762 and *Alceste* in 1767. In a dedicatory preface to the latter work Gluck summarized his aims: to remove the abuses that had hitherto deformed Italian opera, "to confine music to its proper function of serving the poetry for the expression and the situations of the plot" without regard either to the outworn conventions of the da capo aria or the desire of singers to show off their skill in ornamental variation; furthermore, to make the overture an integral part of the opera, to adapt the orchestra to the dramatic requirements, and to lessen the contrast between aria and recitative. "I believed that my

A stage setting for Gluck's Alceste, *as produced in Paris in 1776; drawing by François-Joseph Bélanger.*

greatest effort should be directed to seeking a beautiful simplicity . . . and there is no accepted rule that I have not thought should be gladly sacrificed in favor of effectiveness."

The beautiful simplicity which Gluck professed to seek is exemplified in the celebrated aria *Che farò senza Euridice? (What shall I do without Euridice?)* from *Orfeo,* and in other airs, choruses, and dances of the same work. *Alceste* is a more monumental opera, in contrast to the prevailingly pastoral and elegiac tone of *Orfeo.* In both, the music is plastically molded to the drama, with recitatives, arias, and choruses intermingled in large unified scenes. One of the most impressive such scenes is the first in Act II of *Orfeo* (NAWM/S 63), which takes place in the cavernous spaces of the underworld, obscured by thick dark smoke and illuminated only by flames.

Gluck achieved his mature style in *Orfeo* and *Alceste,* assimilating Italian melodic grace, German seriousness, and the stately magnificence of the French *tragédie lyrique.* He was ready for the climax of his career, which was ushered in with the production of *Iphigénie en Aulide (Iphigenia in Aulis)* at Paris in 1774. Revised versions of *Orfeo* and *Alceste* (both with French texts) swiftly followed. In a mischievously instigated rivalry with the popular Neapolitan composer Niccolò Piccinni (1728–1800), Gluck composed in 1777 a five-act opera, *Armide,* on the same libretto of Quinault that Lully had set in 1686. Gluck's masterpiece, *Iphigénie en Tauride (Iphigenia in Tauris),* was produced in 1779. It is a work of large proportions, having an excellent balance of dramatic and musical interest, and utilizing all the resources of opera—orchestra, ballet, solo and choral singing—to produce a total effect of Classical tragic grandeur.

Gluck's operas were models for the works of his immediate followers at Paris, and his influence on the form and spirit of opera was transmitted to the nineteenth century through such composers as his erstwhile rival Piccinni, Luigi Cherubini (1760–1842), Gasparo Spontini (1774–1851), and Hector Berlioz (1803–69) in *Les Troyens.*

Comic opera

The term *comic opera* denotes works that are lighter in style than serious opera; they present familiar scenes and characters rather than heroic or mythological material, and require relatively modest performing resources. Comic opera took different forms in different countries, although everywhere it represented an artistic revolt against the *opera seria,* the "serious" or tragic Italian opera. Comic opera librettos were always in the national tongue, and the music likewise tended to accentuate the national musical idiom. From humble beginnings the comic opera grew steadily in importance after 1760, and before the end of the century many of its characteristic features had been absorbed into the main stream of operatic composition. Its historical significance was twofold: it responded to the universal demand for naturalness in the latter half of the eighteenth century, and it was the principal early channel of the movement toward musical nationalism which became prominent in the Romantic period.

ITALY

An important type of Italian comic opera was the *intermezzo,* so called because it originated in the custom of presenting short comic musical *intermezzi* between the acts of a serious opera. An early master was Pergolesi, whose *La serva padrona (The Maid as Mistress,* 1733) is still popular. Written for only bass and soprano (there is a third character who is mute) with a string orchestra, the music is a paragon of the nimble, spirited comic style at which Italian composers surpass the rest of the world.

One of the achievements of Italian comic opera was its exploitation of the possibilities of the bass voice, either in straight comedy or in burlesque of other styles. In the comic operas of Nicola Logroscino (1698–*ca.* 1765) and Baldassare Galuppi (1706–85) another feature appeared, the *ensemble finale:* for the ending of an act all the characters are gradually brought on to the stage while the action continues with growing animation until it reaches a climax in which every singer in the cast takes part. These ensemble finales were unlike anything in the serious opera, and in writing them composers were forced to follow the rapidly changing action of the scene without losing coherence in the musical form. The challenge was well met by two Neapolitan composers, Piccinni and Giovanni Paisiello (1740–1816), but complete success in this difficult task was reserved for Mozart.

Meanwhile, beginning about the middle of the century, largely owing to the Italian dramatist Carlo Goldoni (1707–93), a refinement of the comic opera libretto took place; plots of a serious, sentimental, or pathetic character began to appear, as well as the traditional comic ones. Conforming to this change, the older designation *opera buffa* was replaced by *dramma giocoso*—literally a jocular but more accurately a pleasant or cheerful, that is a non-tragic, drama. An example of this new type was Piccinni's *La buona figliuola (The Good Girl)* of 1760, adapted by Goldoni from Richardson's novel *Pamela* which had appeared twenty years before. Paisiello's *Barbiere di Siviglia (The Barber of Seville;* 1782), from Beaumarchais's drama, was a semiserious treatment of current political issues, while his *Nina* (1789) had an out-and-out sentimental plot. Another famous work in this vein was Domenico Cimarosa's (1749–1801) *Matrimonio Segreto (The Secret Marriage),* which was performed at Vienna in 1792. All in all, the *opera buffa* came a long way, both dramatically and musically, in the course of the century; Mozart made good use of its mingled heritage of comic, serious, and sentimental drama and live, flexible, and widely acceptable musical style.

The national French form of light opera was known as *opéra comique.* It began around 1710 as a lowly form of popular entertainment, and until the middle of the century relied almost entirely on popular tunes (*vaudevilles*), or simple melodies in imitation of such tunes, for its music. The visit of the Italian buffonists to Paris in 1752 stimulated the production of *opéras comiques* in which original airs (called *ariettes*) in a mixed Italian-French style were introduced along with the old vaudevilles; gradually the ariettes replaced the vaudevilles until by the end of the 1760s the latter were completely discarded and the entire score was newly composed.

FRANCE

The French *opéra comique*, like all the national forms of light opera except the Italian, used spoken dialogue instead of recitative. Following the general European trend in the second half of the century, the *opéra comique* took on a romantic tinge, and some of the librettos furthermore dealt quite boldly with the burning social issues that were agitating France during the pre-Revolutionary years. The principal composers were François André Danican-Philidor (1726–95; also famous as a chess master), Pierre-Alexandre Monsigny (1729–1817), and above all the Belgian-born André Ernest Modeste Grétry (1741–1813), whose *Richard Coeur-de-Lion (Richard the Lion-Hearted;* 1784) was a forerunner of numerous "rescue" operas around the turn of the century—Beethoven's *Fidelio* was one—in which the hero, after lying for two and a half acts in imminent danger of death, is finally saved through the devoted heroism of a friend. Grétry's music in his fifty or more operas is never profound, but it is melodious, singable, and quite effective, with occasional moments of moving dramatic expression. The *opéra comique,* with its alternation of spoken dialogue and musical numbers, was extremely popular in France. It flourished through the Revolution and the Napoleonic era and took on even greater musical significance during the Romantic period.

The English *ballad opera* rose to popularity after the extraordinary success of *The Beggar's Opera* at London in 1728. This piece broadly satirized the fashionable Italian opera; its music, like that of the early *opéra comique,* consisted for the most part of popular tunes —ballads—with a few numbers parodied from familiar operatic airs. The immense popularity of ballad operas in the 1730s was one sign of a general reaction in England against foreign opera, that "exotic and irrational entertainment," as Dr. Johnson called it—a reaction which had among its consequences that of turning Handel's energies from opera to oratorio in the latter part of his life. The only notable composer of English opera in the eighteenth century was Thomas Augustine Arne; many comic operas on sentimental or romantic subjects were produced by him and lesser composers throughout the century.

ENGLAND

In Germany a form of comic opera called the *Singspiel* arose about the middle of the eighteenth century. The first singspiels were adaptations of English ballad operas, but the librettists soon turned

GERMANY

The Lied

for their material to translations or arrangements of French comic operas, for which the German composers provided new music in a familiar and appealing national melodic vein. Many of the eighteenth-century singspiel tunes found their way into German song collections and thus in the course of time have become practically folk songs. The principal early singspiel composer was Johann Adam Hiller (1728–1804) of Leipzig. In northern Germany, the singspiel developed along Romantic lines, its history eventually merging with that of early nineteenth-century German Romantic opera. In the south, particularly at Vienna, the fashion was for farcical subjects and treatment, with lively music in popular style, influenced to some extent by the idioms of the Italian comic opera. A typical Viennese singspiel composer was Karl Ditters von Dittersdorf (1739–99), who was also notable for his instrumental music. The German singspiel was as important as the Italian *dramma giocoso* in the historical background of Mozart's works for the theatre.

Solo songs, cantatas, and other types of secular vocal music outside opera were produced in every country during the eighteenth century, but special artistic importance attaches to the rise of the new German *Lied*. The principal center of song composition after the middle of the century was Berlin, with J. J. Quantz (1697–1773), K. H. Graun, and C. P. E. Bach the chief composers. The professed ideals of the Berlin school required that Lieder should be in strophic form with melodies in a natural, expressive style like folk song, having but one note to a syllable; only the simplest possible accompaniments, held completely subordinate to the vocal line, were permitted. These principles, which were in accord with the philosophy of the expressive style, were generally accepted in the eighteenth century; but their effect eventually was to impose artificial restrictions on the Lied, and composers of imagination gradually transcended them, particularly in the direction of making the form more varied and giving more significance to the accompaniment.

Over 750 collections of Lieder with keyboard accompaniment were published in Germany during the second half of the century, and this figure does not include the numerous singspiels of the same period, which consist for the most part of songs exactly similar to Lieder. Practically all composers of singspiels, in fact, also wrote Lieder in large quantities. The production continued steadily into the nineteenth century; when Schubert began composing songs in 1811 he was entering into a long and rich tradition, which his own work carried to new heights.

Church music

The secular, individualistic temper of the eighteenth century had the effect of bringing sacred music into conformity with the style of secular music, particularly that of the theatre. A few composers in the Catholic countries ably carried on the ancient tradition of

Palestrina or the polychoric style of Benevoli; but the dominant trend was to introduce into the church the musical idioms and forms of opera, with orchestral accompaniment, da capo arias, and accompanied recitatives. The list of the leading eighteenth-century Italian church composers is almost identical with the list of leading opera composers of the same period. Even more than the Mass and motet, the oratorio in Italy grew to be almost indistinguishable from opera. At the same time some composers, particularly in northern Italy and southern Germany and Austria, effected a compromise between conservative and modern elements, and this mixed style—influenced also by the instrumental symphonic forms of the Classical period—was the background of the sacred compositions of Haydn and Mozart.

Lutheran church music rapidly declined in quality and importance after the death of J. S. Bach. The principal achievements of the north German composers were in the half-sacred, half-secular form of the oratorio; oratorios written after 1750 show some reaction against the excesses of operatic style. The best oratorios of this period were those of C. P. E. Bach. Karl Heinrich Graun's *Der Tod Jesu* (*The Death of Jesus*), a mediocre work which was first performed at Berlin in 1755, remained popular in Germany up to the end of the nineteenth century.

In England, the overpowering influence of Handel operated to discourage originality, and the generally low level of church music is relieved only by the works of a few composers such as Maurice Greene (1695–1775) and Samuel Wesley (1766–1837). Wesley, incidentally, was one of the first musicians of his time to recognize the greatness of J. S. Bach and did much to stimulate performance of Bach's organ music in England. The latter half of the eighteenth century was not by any means a period of musical stagnation in England; there was an active concert life, and much intelligent appreciation of foreign musicians, notably Haydn, who wrote several of his finest symphonies for London audiences.

XIV

*The Late Eighteenth
Century*

Franz Joseph Haydn

Franz Joseph Haydn (1732–1809) was born at Rohrau, a little town
in the eastern part of Austria near the Hungarian border. The year
1761 was momentous in Haydn's life: he was taken into the service
of Prince Paul Anton Esterházy, head of one of the wealthiest and
most powerful Hungarian noble families, a man devoted to music
and a bountiful patron of the art.

In the service of Paul Anton and his brother Nicholas, called "the
Magnificent," who succeeded to the title in 1762, Haydn passed
nearly thirty years under circumstances well-nigh ideal for his
development as a composer. Although the estate at Eszterháza was
isolated, the constant stream of distinguished guests and artists,
together with occasional trips to Vienna, enabled Haydn to keep
abreast of current developments in the world of music. He had the
inestimable advantages of a devoted, highly skilled band of singers
and players and an intelligent patron whose requirements, it is true,
were burdensome, but whose understanding and enthusiasm were
at most times an inspiration. As Haydn once said, "My prince was
pleased with all my work, I was commended, and as conductor of
an orchestra I could make experiments, observe what strengthened
and what weakened an effect and thereupon improve, substitute,
omit, and try new things; I was cut off from the world, there was

The Castle at Esterháza. Engraving by János Beckeny after Szabó. (Hungarian National Museum, Budapest)

no one around to mislead and harass me, and so I was forced to become original."

Haydn's contract with Prince Paul Anton Esterházy forbade him to sell or give away any of his compositions; but this provision was later relaxed, and as Haydn's fame spread in the 1770s and '80s he filled many commissions from publishers and individuals all over Europe. He remained at Eszterháza until the death of Prince Nicholas in 1790, when he moved to Vienna and settled in his own house. Then followed two strenuous but productive and profitable seasons in London (January, 1791 to July, 1792 and February, 1794 to August, 1795), mostly under the management of the impresario Johann Peter Salomon. Here Haydn conducted concerts and wrote a multitude of new works, including the twelve *London* symphonies. Returning home, he resumed his service with the Esterházy family, living now, however, most of the time in Vienna.

The new prince, Nicholas II, cared less for Haydn's music than for the glory that accrued to himself from having such a famous man in his employ; since Haydn's other duties were by now nominal, he was able to devote himself to the composition of quartets and his last two oratorios, *The Creation* and *The Seasons*. Haydn's last work was the String Quartet Op. 103, begun probably in 1802, but of which he completed (in 1803) only two movements.

It is impossible to determine exactly how many compositions Haydn wrote. Publishers in the eighteenth century (and later) brought out many compositions which they falsely attributed to Haydn because they knew his name would attract buyers. Some 150 such false attributions of symphonies and 60–70 of string quartets have been detected. The task of establishing a corpus of authentic Haydn works is still engaging the efforts of scholars. Provisionally, the list of his authenticated compositions includes 106 symphonies and 68 string quartets; numerous overtures, concertos, divertimentos, serenades, baryton trios, string trios, piano trios, and other chamber works; 60 piano sonatas; songs, arias, cantatas, Masses and other settings of liturgical texts; between 20 and 25 operas (of which only 15 are extant), and 4 oratorios. Most important are the symphonies and quartets, for Haydn was above all an instrumental composer and the symphonies and quartets are his finest achievements in this field.

Haydn's symphonies

Very many of Haydn's earliest symphonies are in the pre-Classical three-movement form derived from the Italian opera overture (*sinfonia*); these consist typically of an allegro followed by an andante in the parallel minor or subdominant key, ending with a minuet or a rapid gigue-like movement in 3/8 or 6/8 (examples: Nos. 9, 19).[1] Other Symphonies from the early period recall the Baroque *sonata da chiesa* in that they begin with a slow movement and continue with (usually) three other movements in the same key, the typical order being andante–allegro–minuet–presto (examples: Nos. 21, 22). Soon, however, the normal type becomes that represented by Symphony No. 3, in G major, which apparently was written not later than 1762. It has the standard Classical division into four movements—I. Allegro; II. Andante moderato; III. Minuet and Trio; IV. Allegro—departing from the usual pattern only in that the slow movement is in the parallel minor key instead of the more common subdominant or dominant.

Minuet and Trio is a movement found in almost every Classical symphony. The Minuet itself is always in a two-part ||: a :||: a' (a) :|| form; the Trio has a similar form and is usually in the same key as the Minuet (possibly with change of mode), but is shorter and has lighter orchestration; after the Trio the Minuet returns da capo without repeats, thus making a three-part *ABA* form for the movement as a whole. Haydn's minuets with their trios contain some of his most charming music. It is remarkable what a wealth of musical ideas, what happy traits of harmonic invention and instrumental color he was able to infuse into this modest form; he said once that he wished someone would write "a really new minuet," but he himself succeeded admirably in doing so nearly every time he wrote one.

Occasional concerto-like use of solo instruments, the Corelli-like adagio passages with chains of suspensions, and the constant underlying tendency toward compromise between pre-Classical articulated phrasing and Baroque *Fortspinnung*—all are ways in which Haydn, even from his earliest works, was enriching the language of the Classical symphony by the fusion of new and old elements. His orchestration retains another Baroque feature, the employment of the

---

[1] Numbering is according to the catalogue in Appendix I of H. C. Robbins Landon's *Symphonies of Joseph Haydn* and A. van Hoboken's *Thematisches-bibliographisches Werkverzeichnis*. (The numberings of the symphonies do not always represent the true chronological order.)

harpsichord and the doubling of the bass line (by the bassoon along with the violoncellos and double basses) for a basso continuo. The harpsichord is an essential instrument in Haydn's symphonies until about 1770, and it or the piano was used even in his later ones in eighteenth-century performances, since at that time the orchestra was usually conducted from the keyboard instrument. Even the *London* symphonies were conducted in this way.

Of all the four movements, it was the finale which eventually came to be the crowning glory of a Haydn symphony. The Classical symphony generally aims to get through its more serious business in the first two movements. The Minuet provides relaxation, since it is shorter than either of the two preceding movements, is written in a more popular style, and has a form easy for the listener to follow. But the Minuet does not make a satisfactory closing movement: it is too short to balance the preceding two, and moreover, the spirit of relaxation which it induces needs to be balanced by a further climax of tension and release. Haydn soon came to realize that the 3/8 or 6/8 Presto finales of his earliest symphonies were inadequate to accomplish this, as well as being too light in form and content to produce a satisfying unity of effect in the symphony as a whole. He therefore developed a new type of closing movement which begins to make its appearance in the late 1760s: an Allegro or Presto in 2/4 or ¢, in sonata or rondo form or a combination of the two, shorter than the first movement, compact, swiftly moving, overflowing with high spirits and nimble gaiety, abounding in little whimsical tricks of silence and all sorts of impish surprises. The first of his sonata-rondo finales occurs in No. 77 (see NAWM/S 59).

In general, Haydn's symphonies after 1765 progress toward more serious and meaningful musical content (No. 35) and more subtle use of form (finale of No. 38). The symphonies in minor keys (Nos. 26, 39, and 49, all from 1768) have an intensity of feeling that is a harbinger of the music written in the years 1770–72, the first great culmination of Haydn's style. No. 26 (*Passio et lamentatio*) incorporates a melody from an old plainsong Passion drama as thematic material in the first movement and a liturgical chant from the *Lamentations* in the second.

The works of 1771–72 show Haydn as a composer of ripe technique and fervent imagination, with a quality analogous to the type of emotion expressed in the literary monument of the *Sturm und Drang*. As representative symphonies from these years we may take Nos. 44, 45, and 47. All are on a larger scale than the symphonies of the previous decade. Themes are more broadly laid out, those of the fast movements often beginning with a bold unison proclamation followed immediately by a contrasting idea, with the whole theme then restated. Development sections, which use motives from the

The symphonies of 1771–74

themes, become more propulsive and dramatic. Dramatic also are the unexpected changes from *forte* to *piano,* the crescendos and *sforzati* that are a part of this style. Counterpoint appears, not as a foreign element contrasting with homophonic texture, but as a natural concomitant of the musical ideas. The harmonic palette is richer than in the early symphonies; modulations range more widely and the harmonic arches are broader.

The slow movements have a romantically expressive warmth. Symphony No. 44, in E minor, known as the *Trauersinfonie (Symphony of Mourning),* has one of the most beautiful Adagios in all Haydn's works. Most of the slow movements are in sonata form, but with such leisurely, freely drawn out progression of the thought that a listener is hardly conscious of the structure. The slow movement of No. 47, however, is a theme with variations, a favored form for slow movements in Haydn's later works; the first period of the theme is constructed in double counterpoint at the octave, so that the last period of the theme (and of each of the four variations) is the same as the first but with the melody and the bass interchanged. Another contrapuntal device is exhibited in the Minuet of No. 44, which is in canon at the octave. The Minuet of No. 47 is written *al rovescio* —that is, the second section of the Minuet, and also of the Trio, is the first section played backward.

The quartets of 1760–81

Haydn's string quartets[2] of the time around 1770 testify as strongly as do the symphonies to his arrival at full artistic stature. Many, if not all the earliest quartets once attributed to him are spurious. With Op. 9 (*ca.* 1770) we come into the definite Haydn style. The dramatic opening movement of No. 4 of this group, in D minor, reveals a new mood of seriousness, as well as some measures of genuine motivic development after the double bar. The proportions of this movement—two repeated sections of nearly equal length— clearly illustrate the relationship of Classical sonata form to the Baroque suite movements; the recapitulation is so condensed (nineteen measures as against thirty-four of the exposition) that this and the development section together are only seven measures longer than the exposition.

[2] Haydn's string quartets are identified by the familiar Opus numbers, which correspond to the numbering in Group III of van Hoboken's catalogue as follows:

"Opus"	Hoboken	"Opus"	Hoboken
3	13–18	50	44–49
9	19–24	54, 55	57–62
17	25–30	64	63–68
20	31–36	71, 74	69–74
33	37–42	76	75–80
42	43	77	81–82
		103	83

Henry Fuseli, The Nightmare *(ca. 1790–1). Friend and teacher of William Blake, Fuseli rejected the gay elegance of the* style galant *and turned his attention to the macabre and fantastic subjects that characterized the* Sturm und Drang *in art. (Freies Deutsches Hochstift/Frankfurter Goethe-Museum)*

In the Quartets Opp. 17 and 20, composed respectively in 1771 and 1772, Haydn achieved a union of all stylistic elements and a perfect adaptation of form to expressive musical content. These works definitely established both Haydn's contemporary fame and his historical position as founder of the Classical string quartet. Rhythms are more varied than in the previous quartets; themes are expanded, developments become more organic, and all the forms are treated with assurance and finesse. The four instruments have individuality and equality; particularly in Op. 20, the violoncello begins to be used as a melodic and solo instrument. The texture is free from any suspicion of dependence on a basso continuo; at the same time, counterpoint rises to importance. Everywhere in these quartets contrapuntal writing enriches the texture, as in the symphonies of this same period. Movements in sonata form approach the full three-part structure, with development sections enlarged so that all three parts—exposition, development, and recapitulation—are more nearly equal in length than they are in the quartets of Op. 9; moreover, development of the announced themes is spread over the entire movement, a procedure typical of Haydn's later works in sonata form. One of Haydn's favorite "effects" makes its appearance in the first movement of Op. 20, No. 1: the opening theme pops up, in the tonic key, in the midst of the development section, as though the recapitulation had already begun—but this is a deception, for the theme is only a starting point for further development and the real recapitulation comes later. This device, sometimes called a *fausse reprise* or false recapitulation, may be regarded historically as a vestige of the Baroque concerto form.

Haydn's piano sonatas follow in general the same lines of style development as the symphonies and quartets. Notable among the sonatas of the late 1760s are Nos. 19 (30)[3] in D major and 46 (31) in A♭, both evidencing the influence of C. P. E. Bach on Haydn at this time; the great sonata in C minor, No. 20 (33), composed in 1771, is a tempestuous work very characteristic of Haydn's so-called romantic period.

The symphonies of 1774–88

Immediately after 1772 Haydn entered into a new period of craftsmanship—emerging, as it seems, from a critical phase in his development as a composer. The rather striking change is most evident, perhaps, in the symphonies Nos. 54 and 57, both composed in 1774: the minor keys, the passionate accents, the experiments in form and expression of the preceding period now give way to a smooth, assured, and brilliant exploitation of orchestral resources in works of predominantly cheerful, robust character. Symphony No. 56 (1774) is one of Haydn's twenty symphonies in C major. All but the very earliest of the symphonies written in that key form a special group, many of them possibly having been composed for particular celebrations at Eszterháza. They are generally festive in spirit, and require the addition of trumpets and drums to the normal Haydn orchestra.[4]

Symphony No. 73 (*ca.* 1781) is typical of the smooth craftsmanship of this period; its rollicking 6/8 finale, taken over from an opera *La fedeltà premiata* (*Fidelity Rewarded*), is entitled *La Chasse*. With No. 77 of 1782 Haydn introduced a new kind of finale (Mozart, it should be noted, used it years before): the sonata rondo (NAWM/S 59), in which the serious tone of the rest of the symphony is maintained but combined with the rondo, then enjoying great popularity.

The six quartets of Op. 33, known as the *Russian* quartets, were composed in 1781. These quartets are on the whole lighter in mood than those of 1772, less romantic, but more witty and popular. Only the first movements are in sonata form; the finales (except that of No. 1) are either rondos or variations. The Minuets, although entitled "scherzo" or "scherzando" (whence the alternative name *Gli Scherzi* for this set), are not essentially different from Haydn's other minuets except that they require a slightly faster tempo in performance. The finest of this group is No. 3, in C major, known as the *Bird* quartet from the trills in the trio of the Minuet.

The piano sonatas Nos. 21–26 (36–41), a set of six written in 1773 and dedicated to Prince Esterházy, show a general relaxation and lightening of style comparable to that in the symphonies and quar-

---

[3] The sonatas are numbered according to van Hoboken's catalogue and (in parentheses) the excellent three-volume edition by Christa Landon, Universal Edition 13337–39.

[4] The most important C-major symphonies are Nos. 48, 50, 56, 69, 82, 90, and 97. See Forewords to pocket score editions by H. C. Robbins Landon (Universal Edition).

tets of the same period. Most interesting from the middle and late
'70s are the two sonatas No. 32 (47) and 34 (53), respectively in B
and E minor.

The six *Paris* symphonies (No. 82–87) of 1785 and the five next
following (Nos. 88 to 92) of 1787–88 introduce the culmination of
Haydn's symphonic achievements. All the works of this period have
ample dimensions, incorporating significant and expressive musical
ideas in a complex but thoroughly unified structure and making
always appropriate use of many different and ingenious technical
resources. One feature[5] of the first movements of these symphonies
is the slow introduction, themes of which are sometimes related to
those of the following Allegro. Haydn still avoids or at least mini-
mizes contrasting subjects in movements in sonata form; thematic
development, instead, pervades all parts of the movement. Many of
the slow movements have a quiet introspective coda featuring the
woodwind instruments and using colorful chromatic harmonies (as
in No. 92). The wind instruments are prominent also in the trios of
the minuets; indeed, Haydn gives to the winds in all his symphonies
much more responsibility than the average listener is likely to
realize, for the large size of the string section in a modern symphony
orchestra tends to overwhelm the sound of the flutes, oboes, and
bassoons and thus destroy the balance of timbres that the composer
intended.

The finales of Symphonies Nos. 82–92 are either in sonata form
or, more characteristically, sonata-rondo form. Unlike Haydn's
earlier finales, these make great use of contrapuntal texture and
contrapuntal devices—for example, the canon in the last movement
of No. 88. By such means Haydn perfected closing movements that
at the same time had popular appeal and sufficient weight to balance
the rest of the symphony; the finale of No. 88 is a particularly fine
example.

The quartets of the late 1780s are on an equally high level of
inspiration with the symphonies. The opus numbers are 42 (one
quartet, 1785), 50 (the six *Prussian* quartets, 1787), 54, 55 (three
each, 1788) and 64 (six quartets, 1790). Technique and forms are
like those of the symphonies of the same period, except that the first
movements do not have a slow introduction. Many of the slow
movements have the form of theme and variations, and among these
we find some special types: the Andante of Op. 50, No. 4 is a set of
double variations, using two themes in alternation, one in major
and the other in minor, so that the pattern becomes *A* (in major)
B (in minor) *A'B'A''*. In the slow movements of Op. 54, No. 3 and
Op. 64, No. 6, the variation technique is combined with a broad
lyric three-part form (*ABA'*); similar patterns emerge in Nos. 3 and
4 of Op. 64, except that in these the *B* section is either a variant of,

The quartets of the 1780s

5 Already anticipated in some earlier symphonies, e.g. Nos. 6, 7, 53, 64.

or clearly derived from, *A*. The slow movement of Op. 55, No. 2 (in this instance the first movement of the quartet) is a full set of double variations, alternately minor and major, with a coda. The double variation form was frequently employed by Haydn in his later works, as in the Andante of Symphony No. 103 (*Drum Roll*) and the beautiful pianoforte Variations in F minor, composed in 1793.

The *London* symphonies

The invitation from Salomon in 1790 to compose and conduct six, and later six more, symphonies for the cosmopolitan and exacting audiences of London spurred him to supreme efforts. Everything he had learned in forty years of experience went into them. While there are no radical departures from his previous works, all the elements are brought together on a grander scale, with more brilliant orchestration, more daring conceptions of harmony, and an intensified rhythmic drive. Some very characteristic examples of folk-song-like melodies among the themes of the *London* symphonies (for example, the first, second, and fourth movements of No. 103; finale of No. 104) evidence Haydn's desire to make the basis of appeal in these works as broad as possible. He always aimed to please both the ordinary music lover and the expert; and it is one of the measures of his greatness that he succeeded.

The orchestra of the *London* symphonies includes trumpets and timpani, which (contrary to Haydn's earlier practice) are used in most of the slow movements as well as in the others. Clarinets make their appearance in all but No. 102 of the second set of *London* symphonies. Woodwinds are treated even more independently than hitherto, and the whole sound of the orchestra achieves a new spaciousness and brilliance.

Even more striking than the orchestration, however, is the expanded harmonic range of the *London* symphonies and other works of the same period. Between the various movements, or between Minuet and Trio, the mediant relationship is sometimes exploited instead of the conventional dominant or subdominant; examples occur in Symphonies 99 and 104, and similar contrasts of tonality may be found in the three quartets of Op. 74, which were composed in 1793. An illustration of Haydn's expansion of the harmonic frontiers, a foretaste of Romantic harmony, is found in the Adagio, entitled *Fantasia,* of the Quartet Op. 76, No. 6 (1797), which begins in B major and wanders through C♯ minor, E major and minor, G major, B♭ major and minor, back to B major (Example XIV–1), then through C♯ minor, G♯ minor, and A♭ major, finally settling down in B major for the second half of the movement.

Harmonic imagination is an important factor also in the slow introductions to the first movements of Haydn's *London* symphonies. These opening sections have a portentous quality, a purposive dramatic suspense which prepares the listener for the Allegro to follow; they are either in the tonic minor of the Allegro (as in Symphony No.

104). The first movements in sonata form usually have two distinct themes, but the second one is apt to appear only toward the close of the exposition as a closing element, while the function of the "text-book" second theme is taken over by a varied repetition, in the dominant, of the first theme. The slow movements are either in the form of theme and variations (Nos. 94, 95, 97, 103) or in a free adaptation of sonata form; one common feature is a contrasting minor section. The minuets are no longer courtly dances, but rather allegro symphonic movements in minuet-and-trio pattern; like the corresponding movements of the late quartets, they are already scherzos in everything but name. Some of the finales are in sonata form with two themes, but the favored pattern is the sonata-rondo— a general formal concept that admits the utmost variety and in- genuity in actual practice.

Some of the quartets of Haydn's last period have already been mentioned. Altogether they include Opp. 71, 74 (three each, 1793), 76 (six, 1797), 77 (two, 1799, of which the second is probably Haydn's greatest work in this form), and the two-movement torso, Op. 103 (1803). Of the relatively familiar late quartets, a few details should be mentioned: the interesting modifications of sonata form in the first movement of Op. 77, No. 1 and the wonderful coda of

The last quartets

EXAMPLE XIV–1   Adagio (_Fantasia_), Quartet Op. 76, No. 6, Haydn

the slow movement; the lovely variations on Haydn's own melody, the Austrian national hymn, in the slow movement of Op. 76, No. 3; the romantic character of the Largo (in F♯ major) of Op. 76, No. 5; and the apotheosis of the Haydn finale in all these quartets, especially perhaps in Op. 76, Nos. 4 and 5 and Op. 77, No. 1.

We have said nothing about Haydn's other chamber music or his concertos because the essential steps in the evolution of his style as well as the best illustrations of his genius are to be found in the symphonies, sonatas, and quartets. Among the late Haydn sonatas, special attention should be called to No. 49 (59) in E♭, which was composed in 1789–90; all three movements are of full Classical dimensions, and the Adagio, Haydn himself declared, has "deep significance." From the London period there are three sonatas, Nos. 50–52 (60–62), dating from 1794–95, of which the one in E♭ is the best; its slow movement is in the remote key of E major (prepared for by a passage in that key in the development of the first movement), and has an almost Romantic quality with its Chopinesque ornaments.

Haydn's Vocal Works

Few people since the eighteenth century have ever heard a Haydn opera, but they were very successful in their day. Opera occupied a large part of Haydn's time and energy at Eszterháza. Besides his own works, he arranged, prepared, and conducted some 75 operas by other composers there between 1769 and 1790; Eszterháza was, in fact, despite its remote situation, an international center for opera fully comparable in importance to Vienna in this period.[6] Haydn himself wrote six little German operas for marionettes and at least fifteen regular Italian operas. Most of the latter were of the *dramma giocoso* variety, with music abounding in the frank humor and high spirits characteristic of the composer. Haydn also wrote three serious operas, the most famous of which was the "heroic drama" *Armida* (1784), remarkable for its dramatic accompanied recitatives and arias on a grand scale. Still, he must have come eventually to realize that his future as a composer lay elsewhere. In 1787, he declined a commission to compose an opera for Prague on the ground that he was not familiar with the conditions there and that in any event "scarcely any man could stand comparison with the great Mozart"—who by that time had written *Figaro* and *Don Giovanni*.

Haydn's songs for solo voice with clavier accompaniment, espe-

[6] Dénes Bartha, "Haydn's Opera Repertory at Eszterháza Palace" in W. W. Austin, ed., *New Looks at Italian Opera*, Ithaca, 1968, pp. 172–219.

cially the twelve to English words which he composed in 1794, are an unpretentious but valuable portion of his work. In addition to original songs, Haydn, with the help of his pupils, arranged about 450 Scottish and Welsh airs for various English publishers.

Of Haydn's church music written before the 1790s, two works deserve special mention. The *Mass of Mariazell* of 1782 combines Baroque and newer style elements: the Kyrie is in a kind of sonata form with slow introduction; there is an exciting fugue at the end of the Gloria, and the *Incarnatus* and *Crucifixus* portions of the Credo are particularly impressive. About 1786 Haydn wrote on commission for the Cathedral of Cadiz an introduction and seven orchestral "sonatas," all adagios lasting about ten minutes each, with a concluding "earthquake" movement. These pieces were written to serve as instrumental interludes between short sermons on the Seven Last Words of Christ on the Cross, and in the original version each "sonata" was preceded by a baritone recitative declaiming the Word in question. To compose seven adagios in succession, and to maintain throughout a single basic mood yet offer sufficient variety to avoid monotony was, as Haydn remarked, "no easy matter"; but the work was so successful that one year later the composer arranged the *Seven Last Words* for string quartet, and in 1799 published another rearrangement of the whole work as an oratorio with a suitable Passion text.

Haydn's church music

Haydn's last six Masses, composed between 1796 and 1802, show the influence of his preoccupation with the symphony at that time. All are on the large scale of festival Masses, using orchestra, chorus, and four solo vocalists. What is new is the leading position given to the orchestra, and the pervasion of the entire work by symphonic style and even by symphonic principles of form. Probably the best known of Haydn's late Masses is the *Missa in angustiis,* known also as the *Lord Nelson* or *Imperial* Mass, in D minor, composed in 1798. Among the many impressive features of this work, the beautiful setting of the *Incarnatus* and the electrifying close of the *Benedictus* are moments of particularly high inspiration.

One important consequence of Haydn's sojourn in London was that he became acquainted with Handel's oratorios. The results of this discovery are apparent in all the choral parts of Haydn's late Masses, and above all in his oratorios *The Creation* (1798) and *The Seasons* (1801).

The text of *The Creation* is based on the book of Genesis and Milton's *Paradise Lost;* that of *The Seasons* is distantly related to James Thomson's poem of the same name, which had been published between 1726 and 1730. A large part of the charm of both works consists in their naïve and loving depiction of Nature and of man's innocent joy in the simple "natural" life. The various instrumental introductions and interludes are among the finest examples of late eighteenth-century program music. The *Depiction of Chaos* at the beginning of *The Creation* introduces Romantic harmonies that foreshadow Wagner, while the transition in the following recitative and chorus, climaxed by the superb choral outburst on the C-major chord at the words "and there was light," is one of Haydn's great strokes of genius. The choruses *The Heavens are telling,* and *Achieved is the glorious work* from *The Creation* and the chorus *But who shall dare these gates to pass?* at the end of *The Seasons* have a Handelian breadth and power. These two oratorios are among the most extraordinary instances in history of a composer's manifestation, at an advanced age, of unimpaired youthful freshness and vigor.

Summary

In forming an estimate of Haydn's historical position, it is necessary to avoid extremes. In the first place, he is not the naïve, amiable composer of pretty tunes that the nickname "Papa Haydn" has unfortunately connoted to so many generations; nor, on the other hand, is he a devout mystic like Bach, or a heaven-storming Titan like Beethoven. Least of all is he a mere forerunner of Beethoven or of Romanticism. His achievement was original and complete. His personal development was long and laborious, marked by emotional and stylistic crises of which the severest was that of 1770–72. He assimilated the past, enriching the spare mid-century style with elements of the late Baroque, absorbing the Romantic impulses of the *Empfindsamkeit* and the "storm-and-stress" movements, fusing all finally in that singular blend of sophistication and second naïveté which is the special quality of his compositions after 1790. The perfected Classical style of the late eighteenth century owes more to Haydn than to anyone else. His art is characterized by the union of sophistication with honest craftsmanship, humility, purity of intention, and a never-failing spiritual contact with the life of the common people from whom he had sprung.

Wolfgang Amadeus Mozart

Mozart (1756–91) was born in Salzburg, a city then situated within the territory of Bavaria (now in western Austria). Salzburg was the seat of an archbishopric, one of the numerous quasi-independent political units of the German Empire; it had a long musical tradition and in Mozart's time was a lively provincial center of the arts. His father, Leopold Mozart, was a member of the archbishop's chapel and later became its assistant director; he was a composer of some ability and reputation, and the author of a celebrated treatise on violin playing. From earliest childhood Wolfgang showed such a prodigious talent for music that his father dropped all other ambitions and devoted himself to educating the boy—and to exhibiting his accomplishments in a series of journeys that eventually took them to France, England, Holland, and Italy, as well as to Vienna and the principal cities of Germany.

Young Mozart was thus on tour and on show over half of his time between the ages of six and fifteen. By 1762 he was a virtuoso on the clavier, and soon became a good organist and violinist as well. His public performances as a child included not only the playing of prepared pieces, but also reading concertos at sight and improvising variations, fugues, and fantasias. Meanwhile he was composing: he produced his first minuets at the age of six, his first symphony just before his ninth birthday, his first oratorio at eleven, and his first opera at twelve. His more than 600 compositions are listed and numbered in the thematic catalogue first compiled by L. von Köchel in 1862 and periodically since brought up to date in new editions incorporating the results of modern research; the Köchel or "K." numbers are universally used to identify a Mozart composition.

Thanks to his father's excellent teaching, and even more to the many trips made during his formative years, young Mozart was brought into contact with every kind of music that was being written or heard in contemporary western Europe. He absorbed all that was congenial to him with uncanny aptitude. He imitated, but in imitating he improved on his models; and the ideas that influenced him not only were echoed in his immediate productions but also continued to grow in his mind, sometimes bearing fruit many years later. His work thus came to be a synthesis of national styles, a mirror in which was reflected the music of a whole age, illumined by his own transcendent genius. In this particular cosmopolitan quality Mozart differs from Haydn, whose background was more exclusively Austrian.

Mozart's own musical style is related to a trait which we may call *absolute musicality*. This expression requires some qualification. A good deal of the music of Beethoven, as well as that of some Romantic composers like Berlioz and Chopin, is in a sense autobiographical. Mozart's music is much less so. It is hard to find in it any specific traces of all the hardships and disappointments which he underwent during his life, particularly in his last ten years. It is even harder to draw from it any definite conclusions about his attitude toward Nature, or toward the greatest historical event of his time, the French Revolution (to which he never alludes in any surviving document), or toward the widely prevalent new ideas associated with that movement. All these influences were undeniably there, but Mozart's music reflects them only as sublimated, transformed into measured Classic beauty. Like all great artists, but to a greater degree than with many composers, Mozart lived his real life in the inner world of his music, to which his everyday existence often seems only a troubled and shadowy parallel.

Mozart did not have to struggle with composing. He had been trained systematically and thoroughly from infancy, and he learned instantaneously from each new musical impression. Haydn always found composition a labor, and he was always experimenting with the machinery. He set himself to compose at regular hours; when ideas did not come at once he prayed for them, and when they came he worked them out with conscious and unremitting industry. One cannot imagine Mozart having to pray for musical ideas: they were always superabundantly there. Usually he worked them out first in his mind, with intense and joyous concentration, complete to the last detail. Writing them down then consisted only in transferring to music paper a structure which was already, so to speak, before his eyes; hence he could laugh and joke and carry on conversation while "composing." There is a touch of the miraculous, something both childlike and godlike, about all this; and although recent research has revealed in some cases more of labor and revision in Mozart's creative processes than used to be thought, nevertheless the aura of miracle remains. It was perhaps this that made him, rather than Haydn, the musical hero of the early Romantic generation.

One monumental study of Mozart distinguishes in his life and work no fewer than thirty-five style periods. For our purposes a broader and simpler division will suffice: (1) childhood and early youth, to 1774; (2) the period of the first masterworks, 1774–81; and (3) the years in Vienna, 1781–91.

Mozart's Childhood and Early Youth

The first period may be considered Mozart's apprentice and journeyman years. During all this time he was under the tutelage of his father—completely as far as practical affairs were concerned, and to a considerable extent also in musical matters. Another early influence was that of Johann Christian Bach (1735–82), the youngest of the sons of Johann Sebastian; the spirit of Italian music and especially the Italian style in opera, to which Mozart was first introduced by Bach, became a fundamental and permanent factor in his work.

A visit to Vienna in 1768 led, among other things, to the composition by the precocious twelve-year-old of an Italian *opera buffa*, *La finta semplice* (*The Pretended Simpleton;* not performed until the next year at Salzburg) and the attractive German singspiel *Bastien und Bastienne.* The years 1770 to 1773 were largely occupied with travels in Italy, from which Mozart returned more thoroughly italianized than ever and profoundly discontented with his limited prospects in Salzburg. The chief events in these years were the production of two *opere serie* at Milan in 1770 and 1772, and some studies in counterpoint with Padre Giambattista Martini (1706–84) at Bologna. Mozart's first string quartets also date from these Italian years. The influence of the Italian symphonists—for example, Sammartini—on Mozart may be discerned in his symphonies written from 1770 to 1773, especially K. 81, 95, 112, 132, 162, and 182; but a new influence, that of Joseph Haydn, becomes apparent in some other symphonies of this period, particularly K. 133 (composed in July, 1772). Another sojourn at Vienna in the summer of 1773 brought Mozart a renewed understanding and feeling for the characteristic qualities of southern German music; from this time onward Haydn's works became an increasingly important factor in Mozart's creative life, and after 1781, their influence was reinforced by personal friendship with the older composer.

Haydn expressed an enlightened view and at the same time uttered a profound judgment of Mozart's genius when he said to Leopold Mozart: "Before God and as an honest man I tell you that your son is the greatest composer known to me either in person or by name. He has taste and, what is more, the most profound knowledge of composition." Those were the two essentials: taste, the instinct for what is appropriate, the awareness of limits; and knowledge, the technique to say what one has to say fully, clearly, and persuasively.

Mozart's First Masterworks

Late in 1773 and early in 1774, Mozart composed two symphonies which were his first masterworks in this form. The one in G minor (K. 183) is a product of the mood of *Sturm und Drang* which was finding expression in the contemporary symphonies of Haydn. It is remarkable not only for its intense, serious quality but also for its thematic unity and for the expansion of the entire form as compared with Mozart's earlier symphonies. Similar dimensions and formal characteristics are found in the A-major Symphony (K. 201), the mood of which is robust and cheerful; the finale has a particularly long and well worked out development section. On the whole, Mozart was much less adventurous than Haydn in the matter of formal experiments. His themes seldom give the impression, as Haydn's sometimes do, of having been invented with a view chiefly to their possibilities for motivic development; on the contrary, a theme of Mozart usually is complete in itself, and his invention is so profuse that sometimes he will dispense with a formal development section altogether and in its place write a completely new theme (as in the first movement of the String Quartet K. 428). Again unlike Haydn, Mozart nearly always has a contrasting, lyrical second theme (or themes) in his allegro movements in sonata form, though he is apt to conclude the exposition with a reminiscence of the opening subject; and, once more unlike Haydn, he seldom surprises the listener by making extensive changes in the order or treatment of his materials in the recapitulation.

Piano and violin sonatas

From 1774 to 1781, Mozart lived chiefly at Salzburg, where he became more and more impatient with the narrowness of provincial life and the lack of musical opportunities. In a fruitless attempt to better himself he undertook, in September, 1777, in company with his mother, another journey, this time to Munich, Augsburg, Mannheim, and Paris. All his hopes for a good position in Germany came to nothing, and prospects for a successful career at Paris likewise ended in failure. The stay in Paris was further saddened by his mother's death in July, 1778, and Mozart returned to Salzburg early in 1779 more discontented than ever. Nonetheless, he was steadily growing in stature as a composer. Among the important works of this period are the piano sonatas K. 279–284 (Salzburg and Munich, 1774–75), K. 309 and 311 (Mannheim, 1777–78), K. 310 and 330–333 (Paris, 1778), and several sets of variations for piano, including those on the French air *Ah, vous dirais-je maman* (K. 265; Paris, 1778). The variations were probably intended for pupils, but the sonatas were played by Mozart himself as part of his concert repertoire. His custom in the earlier years had been to improvise such pieces as needed, so that few very early Mozart solo piano compositions have survived.

The sonatas K. 279–284 were undoubtedly designed to be published together: there is one in each of the major tonalities in the circle of fifths from D to Eb, and the six works show a wide variety of form and content. The two Mannheim sonatas have brilliant and showy Allegros and tender and graceful Andantes. The Paris sonatas are among Mozart's best-known compositions in this form: the tragic A-minor sonata (K. 310), its light counterpart in C major (K. 330), the A-major sonata with the variations and the *rondo alla turca* (K. 331), and two of the most characteristically Mozartean sonatas, those in F major and Bb major (K. 332 and 333).

Of the chamber music from this middle period we may mention the Flute Quartet in D major (K. 285), composed in December, 1777, an excellent example of the light, charming Mozart style; and the Oboe Quartet (K. 370), an equally representative but more serious work dating from the early part of 1781.

Most of Mozart's music was composed either on commission or for a particular occasion; even in those works that do not seem to have been intended for an immediate performance, he had in mind a definite type of potential performer or audience, and considered their preferences. Like all his contemporaries, he was a "commercial composer" in that he not merely hoped but expected as a matter of course that his music would be performed, that it would please, and that he would make money from it. There are, of course, some compositions of his that have little significance outside their immediate social or commercial occasion—for instance, the many sets of dances that he turned out for balls at Vienna during the last four years of his life. But there are other works which, though produced only with the modest aim of furnishing background music or light entertainment for some ephemeral occasion, have greater musical importance than their original purpose deserved.

Of this sort are the pieces, dating for the most part from the 1770s and early 1780s, which Mozart composed for garden parties, serenades, weddings, birthdays, or home concerts for his friends and **Serenades** patrons, and which he called usually either serenade or divertimento. The most familiar of Mozart's serenades is *Eine kleine Nachtmusik* (K. 525), a work in five movements written originally for string quartet but now usually played by a small ensemble of strings; it was composed in 1787 but for what occasion (if any) is not known. Elements of the concerto appear in the three Salzburg

Mozart's autograph manuscript of the first page of the Serenade in Bb, K. 361. (Library of Congress)

serenades in D (K. 203, 204, 320), each of which has interpolated two or three movements where the solo violin is featured. The *Haffner Serenade* of 1776 is the clearest example of the concerto-symphonic style, and the *Haffner Symphony* (1782) was originally written as a serenade with an introductory and closing march and an additional Minuet between the Allegro and the Andante.

Violin concertos

Among the notable compositions of Mozart's second period are the violin concertos K. 216, 218, and 219, in G, D, and A respectively, all from the year 1775, the piano concerto in E♭, K. 271 (1777) with its romantic slow movement in C minor, and the expressive Symphonie Concertante, K. 364 in E♭, for solo violin and viola with orchestra. The violin concertos are works of great beauty; nowhere is the Mozartean blend of crystalline clarity with sensuously luxuriant sound more potent than in the Adagio of the G major concerto, or the Mozartean verve and humor more evident than in the rondo finale of the same work. These three violin concertos are, with one possible exception,[7] the last of Mozart's works in this form. The piano concerto K. 271, on the other hand, is but the first of a long series in his mature productions, a series that reaches a climax in the concertos of Mozart's Vienna period.

Vocal music

With few exceptions, Mozart's Masses, motets, and other settings of sacred texts are not to be counted among his major works. His Masses, like those of Haydn, are for the most part in the symphonic-operatic idiom of the period, intermingled with counterpoint at certain places in accordance with the current custom, the whole for chorus and soloists in free alternation, with orchestral accompaniment. An example is the *Coronation* Mass in C (K. 317), composed at Salzburg in 1779. The finest of his Masses is the one in C minor (K. 427), which Mozart wrote as fulfillment of a vow at the time of his marriage in 1782. Though the Credo and Agnus Dei were never completed, this Mass nevertheless is one of the few works of its kind in the eighteenth century worthy to be named along with the B-minor Mass of Bach. It is noteworthy that Mozart wrote it not on commission, but apparently to satisfy an inner need. Equally devout, equally profound, though brief and in simple homophonic style, is another church composition, the motet *Ave verum* (K. 618; 1791).

Mozart's last important composition before he moved to Vienna was the opera *Idomeneo*, first performed at Munich in January of 1781. *Idomeneo* is the best of Mozart's *opere serie*. The music, despite the rather clumsy libretto, is dramatic and pictorial. Numerous accompanied recitatives, conspicuous use of the chorus, and the presence of spectacular scenes show the influence of Gluck and the

---

[7] K. 271a, which, if authentic, has survived in a form that is probably not Mozart's original version.

French *tragédie lyrique;* but the ruling conception of the work, in which the music wholly dominates and embraces the dramatic movement, is Mozart's own.

The Vienna Period

When in 1781 Mozart decided, against his father's advice, to quit the service of the Archbishop of Salzburg and settle in Vienna, he was sanguine about his prospects. The first years there were, in fact, fairly prosperous. His singspiel, *Die Entführung aus dem Serail (The Abduction from the Seraglio,* 1782), was performed repeatedly; he had all the distinguished pupils he was willing to take, he was the idol of the Viennese public both as pianist and composer, and for four or five seasons he led the bustling life of a successful freelance musician. But then the fickle public deserted him, pupils fell off, commissions were few, family expenses mounted, his health declined, and, worst of all, no permanent position with a steady income came his way, except for a trifling honorary appointment in 1787 as Chamber Music Composer to the Emperor with a salary less than half that which Gluck, his predecessor in the post, had received. The most pathetic pages in Mozart's correspondence are the begging letters written between 1788 and 1791 to his friend and brother Mason, the merchant Michael Puchberg of Vienna. To Puchberg's honor, he always responded to Mozart's appeals.

Most of the works which make Mozart's name immortal were composed during the last ten years of his life, in Vienna, when the wonderful promise of his childhood and early youth came to fulfillment between the ages of twenty-five and thirty-five. The perfect synthesis of form and content, of the *galant* and the learned styles, of polish and charm on the one hand and of textural and emotional depth on the other, was finally achieved, and equally in every kind of composition. The principal influences on Mozart in this period came from his continuing study of Haydn and his discovery of the music of J. S. Bach. He became acquainted with Bach's *Art of Fugue, The Well-Tempered Clavier,* the trio sonatas, and other works. He arranged several of Bach's fugues for string trio or quartet (K. 404a, 405), and another immediate result of this new interest was his own fugue in C minor for two pianos (K. 426). The influence of Bach was deep and lasting; it is manifested in the increasing use of contrapuntal texture throughout Mozart's later works (for example, in his last piano sonata, K. 576) and in the profoundly serious moods of *The Magic Flute* and the *Requiem.*

Of the piano solo compositions of the Vienna period, the most important is the Fantasia and Sonata in C minor (K. 475 and 457). The Fantasia in its melodies and modulations foreshadows Schubert, while the sonata is clearly the model for Beethoven's *Sonate Pathétique*. Other keyboard works of this period are the Sonata in D major for two pianos (K. 448, 1781) and the finest of all Mozart's four-hand sonatas, the one in F major (K. 497, 1786). For chamber music ensembles of various kinds there is an impressive number of masterpieces, of which the following must be mentioned: the Violin Sonata in A major (K. 526), the Piano Trios in B♭ (K. 502) and E major (K. 542), the Piano Quartets in G minor (K. 478) and E♭ major (K. 493), the String Trio (K. 563), and the Clarinet Quintet (K. 581).

The *Haydn* quartets

In 1785, Mozart published six string quartets dedicated to Joseph Haydn as a token of his gratitude for all that he had learned from the older composer. These quartets were, as Mozart said in the dedicatory letter, "the fruit of a long and laborious effort"; indeed, the manuscript bears evidence of this in the unusually large number of corrections and revisions. Mozart's six *Haydn* quartets (K. 387, 421, 428, 458, 464, 465) show his mature capacity to absorb the essence of Haydn's achievement without becoming a mere imitator. Closest to Haydn in mood and themes are the opening and closing movements of the Quartet in B♭ (K. 458), while the Adagio has harmonies that may be called Romantic (Example XIV–2a). The D-minor quartet (K. 421) expresses a gloomy, fatalistic mood. The striking cross-relations in the slow introduction to the first movement of the C-major Quartet (K. 465) have given this work its name of the *Dissonance Quartet* (Example XIV–2b).

All the *Haydn* quartets are remarkably unified and concentrated. There are no merely transitional or filling passages; every measure is alive with thematic significance. Contrapuntal texture is ever present, though never obtrusive. Moreover, even in the Allegros the themes

EXAMPLE XIV–2   Themes from Quartets, Mozart

a. Mozart:. Adagio from *Quartet* K. 458

b. Mozart: Introduction of *Quartet* K. 465

always sing; the instrumental melodies have a vocal allure that reflects the Italian heritage in Mozart's training. Mozart never surpassed these six quartets in his later works for the same medium, which include the *Hoffmeister Quartet* (K. 499) and three others of a projected set of six for the King of Prussia (K. 575, 589, 590). Unlike Haydn and Beethoven, Mozart most fully revealed his genius as a chamber music composer not in his quartets, but rather in his quintets. The best of these are the string quintets in C major (K. 515) and G minor (K. 516), both composed in the spring of 1787, works comparable only with Mozart's last two symphonies, which are in the same keys. Another masterpiece is the Clarinet Quintet in A (K. 581), composed at about the same time as the *opera buffa Così fan tutte,* and similar to it in mood.

Mozart's Vienna symphonies include the *Haffner Symphony* (K. 385), the *Prague Symphony* in D major (K. 504), the charming *Linz Symphony* in C major (K. 425), and his last and greatest works in this form, the Symphonies in E♭ (K. 543), G minor (K. 550), and C major (the *Jupiter,* K. 551). These three symphonies were composed within a space of six weeks in the summer of 1788. It is not known for what occasion Mozart intended them or indeed whether he ever heard them played at all. Each has its own character; each is a complex but distinct personality, a personality which is defined perfectly by the music but which completely eludes verbal formulation. These three works must be viewed as a summation, unusually complete and clear, of three fundamental aspects of Mozart's musical being and consequently of the whole Western musical world of the late eighteenth century.

A very important place among the productions of Mozart's Vienna years must be assigned to the seventeen concertos for piano and orchestra. All were written in order to provide brand-new works for concerts, and the rise and fall of Mozart's popularity in Vienna may be roughly gauged by the number of new concertos he found it necessary to supply for each year: three in 1782–83, four in each of the next two seasons, three again in 1785–86, and only one for each of the next two seasons; after that no more until the last year of his life, when he played a new concerto (K. 595) in a concert organized by another musician.

The concertos for piano and orchestra

The first three Vienna concertos (K. 414, 413, 415) were, as Mozart wrote to his father,[8] "a happy medium between what is too easy and too difficult . . . very brilliant, pleasing to the ear, and natural, without being vapid. There are passages here and there from which connoisseurs alone can derive satisfaction; but these passages are written in such a way that the less learned cannot fail

---

[8] Letter dated December 28, 1782; pr. in *The Letters of Mozart and his Family,* Emily Anderson, ed., London, 1938, III, No. 476.

to be pleased, though without knowing why." The next concerto
(K. 449, in Eb), originally written for a pupil, was later played
by Mozart with "unusual success," as he reported. Then follow three
magnificent concertos, all completed within a month of one another
in the spring of 1784: K. 450 in Bb, K. 451 in D (both, in Mozart's
words, "concertos to make the player sweat"), and the more intimate, lovely K. 453 in G. Three of the four concertos of 1784–85
are likewise works of first rank: K. 459 in F, K. 466 in D minor (the
most dramatic and most frequently played of Mozart's concertos),
and K. 467 in C, spacious and symphonic. During the winter of
1785–86, when he was at work on *The Marriage of Figaro,* Mozart
turned out three more concertos, of which the first two (K. 482 in Eb
and K. 488 in A) are in comparatively lighter mood, while the third
(K. 491, C minor) is one of his great tragic creations, one of his most
"Beethovenish" works. The big C-major concerto of December, 1786
(K. 503) may be regarded as the triumphal counterpart of K. 491. Of
the two remaining concertos, one is the popular *Coronation Concerto* in D (K. 537), so called because Mozart played it (and probably
also K. 459) at a concert in Frankfurt in 1790 during the coronation
festivities for the Emperor Leopold II. K. 595, in Bb, Mozart's last
concerto, was completed on the fifth of January, 1791; it is a work
of serene, transcendent beauty, the testament of a musician who
must have felt himself to be already beyond the passions, the struggles, and the triumphs of this life. [9]

The concerto, particularly the piano concerto, was more important in Mozart's work than in that of any other composer of
the second half of the eighteenth century. In the realm of the
symphony and the quartet Haydn is his peer, but Mozart's concertos
are incomparable. Not even the symphonies reveal such wealth
of invention, such breadth and vigor of conception, such insight and
resource in the working out of musical ideas.

The Classical concerto, as exemplified by those of Mozart for
piano and orchestra, preserves certain schemes of the Baroque concerto. It has the three-movement sequence fast–slow–fast. The first
movement is in a modified concerto-ritornello form; the second is
a kind of aria; and the finale is generally dance-like or popular in
character.

A close look at one of the first movements, the Allegro from K.
488 in A major (NAWM/S 62) will show how the ritornello principle
of the Baroque concerto permeates the sonata form. The opening
orchestral section contains the elements of both a sonata-form
exposition and of the Baroque concerto ritornello. The ritornello
procedure affects the sonata form in quite a fundamental way:
instead of a single exposition, there are two, one orchestral and one

9 A. Einstein, *Mozart,* 314.

solo with orchestra. The orchestra presents three thematic groups. Then the pianist begins his exposition of the first theme, delicately ornamented and discreetly accompanied by the orchestra. The transitional tutti of measure 18 intervenes to start the bridge passage, completed by modulatory figuration in the piano, and arrives at the key of the second theme, E major (measure 98), which is now taken up by the soloist. The material of the orchestral closing section is then adapted to the piano (measure 114), and the exposition is closed by a restatement of the transitional tutti, now in the dominant. Instead of a development of these ideas, as is usual in such a movement, the section that follows the exposition is a dialogue based on new material between the piano and the winds, the strings acting as a "ripieno" group. In the recapitulation the transitional tutti returns once again as the head of the bridge passage. It is heard yet again—with a dramatic interruption by the new theme of the "development"—as the orchestra reaches the most suspenseful moment of the concerto, a six-four chord, upon which it pauses. The soloist now is expected to improvise an extended cadenza. The movement closes with the same tutti that ended the orchestral exposition.

The plan of this Allegro does not, of course, fit Mozart's other first movements exactly. The orchestral expositions and the recapitulations, particularly, vary, omitting one or more elements of the soloist's thematic or closing material; in some, the transitional tutti, in others the closing tutti, is de-emphasized, but in its main profile the scheme is usually observable.

Although these concertos were show pieces, intended to dazzle an audience, Mozart never allowed the element of display to get out of hand; a healthy balance of musical interest between the orchestral and the solo portions is always maintained, and Mozart's ear was infallible for the myriad combinations of colors and textures that arise from the interplay of the piano with the orchestral instruments. Moreover, the immediate public purpose of his concertos did not prevent his using the form as a vehicle for some of the most profound expressions of his musical thought.

After *Idomeneo* Mozart wrote no more *opere serie,* with the exception of *La clemenza di Tito* (*The Mercy of Titus*), which was commissioned for the coronation of Leopold II as King of Bohemia at Prague and composed in haste during the summer of 1791. The chief dramatic works of the Vienna period were the singspiel, *Die Entführung aus dem Serail* (*The Abduction from the Seraglio*, 1782), three Italian operas, *Le nozze di Figaro* (*The Marriage of Figaro,* 1786), *Don Giovanni* (*Don Juan,* Prague, 1787), and *Così fan tutte* (*Thus Do They All,* 1790)—all three on librettos by Lorenzo da Ponte (1749–1838)—and the German opera *Die Zauberflöte* (*The Magic Flute,* 1791).

Mozart's operas

Figaro is the epitome of Italian eighteenth-century comic opera, with its lively and amusing libretto, beautiful arias, and masterly ensembles. It had only moderate success in Vienna, but its enthusiastic reception at Prague led to the commission for *Don Giovanni*, which was given in that city the next year. *Don Giovanni* is a *dramma giocoso* of a very special sort. The medieval legend on which the plot is based had been treated often in literature and music since the early seventeenth century; but with Mozart, for the first time in opera, Don Juan himself was taken seriously—not as an incongruous mixture of figure of farce and horrible blasphemer, but as a romantic hero, a rebel against authority and a scorner of vulgar morality, a supreme individualist, bold and unrepentant to the last. Some of the other characters too, though they are subtly being ridiculed, must also be taken seriously—for example, the rather tragic Donna Elvira, never ceasing to complain of being jilted by the Don. And Don Giovanni's valet, Leporello, is more than a *commedia dell'arte* servant-buffoon, for he reveals deep sensitivity and intuition. The three personalities are remarkably etched in the trio of Act I, scene 5 (NAWM/S 64a). The famous "catalogue" aria of Leporello that follows (NAWM/S 64b), in which he enumerates Giovanni's conquests in various countries and the varieties of female flesh that attract him, show the care that the composer lavished on every detail of his comedies.

The second scene of Don Giovanni, *as staged by the Metropolitan Opera. Don Giovanni tries to placate Donna Elvira, while Donna Anna and Don Ottavio wonder which of the two to believe. (Photograph courtesy Louis Mélançon)*

Cosi fan tutte is an *opera buffa* in the best Italian tradition, with a brilliant libretto glorified by some of Mozart's most melodious music. The fashion of reading into Mozart's works everything from autobiography to romantic irony, neo-Freudian psychology, and crypto-revolutionary sentiments has been extended even to this sparkling opera, where all such nonsense seems to be quite superfluous.

The plot of *Die Entführung* is a romantic-comic story of adventure and rescue, set against the popular eighteenth-century oriental background; its subject had been treated by Rameau, Gluck, Haydn, and many lesser composers before Mozart. With this work, Mozart at one stroke raised the German singspiel into the realm of great art without altering any of its established features.

Die Zauberflöte is a different matter. Though outwardly a singspiel —with spoken dialogue instead of recitative, and with some characters and scenes appropriate to popular comedy—its action is full of symbolic meaning and its music so rich and profound that *Die Zauberflöte* must be regarded as the first and one of the greatest of modern German operas. The solemn mood of much of its music is probably due in part to the fact that Mozart created a relationship between the action of this opera and the teachings and ceremonies of Freemasonry. *Die Zauberflöte* gives the impression that Mozart desired to weave into new designs the threads of all the musical ideas of the eighteenth century: the vocal opulence of Italy; the folk humor of the German singspiel; the solo aria; the *buffo* ensemble, which is given new musical meaning; a new kind of accompanied recitative applicable to German words; solemn choral scenes; and even (in the duet of the two armed men in Act II) a revival of the Baroque chorale prelude technique, with contrapuntal accompaniment.

In the *Requiem*—Mozart's last work, left unfinished at his death —Baroque elements are still more prominent. The double fugue of the Kyrie has a subject that had been used by both Bach and Handel —also by Haydn in his Quartet Op. 20, No. 5—and the movement is definitely Handelian in flavor; even more so are the dramatic choral outbursts of the *Dies irae* and *Rex tremendae majestatis*. But the *Recordare* is pure Mozart, the German composer who understood and loved the musical tradition of Italy and interpreted it in his own perfect way.

XV

Ludwig van Beethoven (1770–1827)

The Man and His Music

Beethoven came on the scene at a favorable moment in history.
He inherited from Haydn and Mozart a style and certain musical

Beethoven's character

forms which were well developed but still capable of further growth.
He lived at a time when new and powerful forces were abroad in
human society, forces which strongly affected him and made themselves felt in his work. Beethoven, like Napoleon and Goethe, was a
child of the tremendous upheaval which had been fermenting all
through the eighteenth century and had burst forth in the French
Revolution. Historically, Beethoven's work is built on the achievements of the Classical period. Through external circumstances and
the force of his own genius he transformed this heritage and became
the source of much that was characteristic of the Romantic period.
But he himself is neither Classic nor Romantic; he is Beethoven,
and his figure towers like a colossus astride the two centuries.

His works include 9 symphonies, 11 overtures, incidental music
to plays, a violin concerto and 5 piano concertos, 16 string quartets,
9 piano trios and other chamber music, 10 violin sonatas and 5
violoncello sonatas, 30 large piano sonatas and many sets of variations for piano, an oratorio, an opera (*Fidelio*), and two Masses (one
the *Missa solemnis* in D), besides arias, songs, and numerous lesser
compositions of different sorts. There is an obvious disparity when

these figures are compared with the output of Haydn and Mozart: 9 symphonies, for example, to Haydn's 100 or Mozart's 50. A partial explanation, of course, is that Beethoven's symphonies are longer; but a more important reason is that Beethoven wrote music with great difficulty. Probably no other composer ever habitually subjected himself to longer or more severe criticism. Beethoven kept notebooks in which he jotted down plans and themes for compositions, and thanks to these sketchbooks we can sometimes follow the progress of a musical idea through various stages until it reaches the final form (Example XV–1).[1] The sketches for the Quartet Op. 131

EXAMPLE XV–1   Sketches for Theme of Adagio of Ninth Symphony, Beethoven

[1] See also sketches for the Fifth Symphony in the edition of that work prepared by Elliot Forbes, New York, 1971, 117–28. For a detailed study of some aspects of Beethoven's compositional processes, see Lewis Lockwood, "The Autograph Score of the First Movement of Beethoven's Sonata for Violoncello and Pianoforte, Opus 69," *The Music Forum* II (1970) 1–109 and facsimile of the autograph, with introduction by Lockwood, New York, 1970, part of which is reproduced on p. 534.

Scribbled notes by Beethoven for the third movement of the Fifth Symphony.

cover three times as many pages as the finished copy of the work.

Beethoven's music, more than that of any composer before him, gives the impression of being a direct outpouring of his personality. To understand the music, therefore, it is helpful to know something about the man himself. Sir Julius Benedict described his first sight of Beethoven (1823) in these words:

> . . . a short, stout man with a very red face, small, piercing eyes, and bushy eyebrows, dressed in a very long overcoat which reached nearly to his ankles . . . notwithstanding the high color of his cheeks and his general untidiness, there was in those small piercing eyes an expression which no painter could render. It was a feeling of sublimity and melancholy combined. . . . The wonderful impression his first appearance made on me was heightened every time I met him. When I first saw him at Baden, his white hair flowing over his mighty shoulders, with that wonderful look—sometimes contracting his brows when anything afflicted him, sometimes bursting out into a forced laughter, indescribably painful to his listeners—I was touched as if *King Lear* or one of the old Gaelic bards stood before me.[2]

The "indescribably painful" sound of Beethoven's laughter may have been due to his deafness. This most dreadful of all afflictions for a musician began to manifest itself as early as 1798, and grew steadily worse until by 1820 it was practically total. In the autumn of 1802 Beethoven wrote a letter, now known as the "Heiligenstadt testament," intended to be read by his brothers after his death; in

---

[2] Quoted in Thayer, *Life of Beethoven*, III, 138–39.

it he describes in moving terms how he suffered when he realized that his malady was incurable:

> I must live almost alone like one who has been banished, I can mix with society only as much as true necessity demands. If I approach near to people a hot terror seizes upon me and I fear being exposed to the danger that my condition might be noticed. Thus it has been during the last six months which I have spent in the country . . . what a humiliation for me when someone standing next to me heard a flute in the distance and *I heard nothing*, or someone heard a *shepherd singing* and again I heard nothing. Such incidents drove me almost to despair, a little more of that and I would have ended my life—it was only *my art* that held me back. Ah, it seemed to me impossible to leave the world until I had brought forth all that I felt was within me. . . . Oh Providence—grant me at last but one day of *pure joy*—it is so long since real joy echoed in my heart . . .[3]

—yet the same man who thus cried out of the depths had, during that same half year in the country, written the exuberantly joyful Second Symphony!

The outstanding characteristic of Beethoven's music, in comparison with that of his predecessors, is a certain daemonic energy, a quality that is felt most starkly in passages like the close of the first movement of the Fifth Symphony, the coda of the finale of the Sonata Op. 57, or the finale of the Quartet Op. 59, No. 3. The energy breaks forth also as humor—not the playfulness of Haydn nor the grace and gaiety of Mozart, but something more robust and hearty. Examples are: the anxious antics of the double basses in the trio of the Scherzo of the Fifth Symphony, the stuttering halts in the rhythm after the double bar; the metronomic Allegretto of the Eighth Symphony; the apparently premature entrance of the horn in the first movement of the Third Symphony, just before the recapitulation; or the exquisitely comic passage in the coda of the finale of the Eighth Symphony where the entire orchestra starts chasing off after the theme like a puppy after a stick in the impossibly remote key of F$\sharp$ minor—and then, once safely returned home to F, proceeds presently to reassure itself by sounding the major third F–A down and back through five octaves of the woodwinds. (Note incidentally, as an example of Beethoven's customary long-range planning, how we have been prepared for this F$\sharp$-minor episode from the very beginning of the movement: the stubborn dominant C$\sharp$ of measures 374–79—appearing first as D$\flat$ in measure 372—refers us back to the solitary, apparently totally arbitrary, and quickly abandoned *fortissimo* C$\sharp$ in measure 17.)

Beethoven's music is not always volcanic and exuberant; it may melt into tenderness (second movement of the Sonata Op. 90) or sadness (Adagio of the Quartet Op. 59, No. 1). Abrupt contrasts of

---

[3] *Thayer's Life of Beethoven*, rev. & ed., E. Forbes, Princeton, 1967, I, 304–06.

mood occur: the Sonata Op. 57 opens with an ominous theme, builds up suspense, hesitates, pauses tentatively, then bursts out in sudden fury, recedes, sighs, and finally soars into a beautiful singing melody in A♭, which is subtly akin to the first theme (Example XV–2).

EXAMPLE XV–2   First Movement from Sonata Op. 57, Beethoven

An even more striking contrast occurs in the development section of the first movement of the Third Symphony: after a long, fiercely dissonant *fortissimo* with off-beat *sforzandos,* we hear what seems to be a completely new theme, of tender melancholy, in the strangely foreign key of E minor.[4] Perhaps the most overwhelming of Beethoven's sudden changes of mood, however, is found in the finale of the Ninth Symphony, at the words "vor Gott." Full chorus and orchestra have reached a stupendous climax on a unison tonic A, to which at the last moment a strident and surprising F♮ has been added; this climax has been preparing steadily for over ninety measures, and it leaves the hearer breathless. What can possibly follow? A very strange thing indeed: after a few apparently random grunts and thumps, all the wind instruments, together with triangle, cymbals, and bass drum, go into a "Turkish March," a little 6/8 tune grotesquely caricaturing the main theme. Beethoven thus introduces a moment of comic relief, just as Shakespeare does with the entrance of the sleepy porter after Duncan's murder in *Macbeth;* but, also as with Shakespeare, the comic moment shades rapidly over into a new aspect of the prevailing mood: a heroic tenor solo followed by an intricately worked-out double fugue, all dominated by the new 6/8 rhythm, which continues to underlie the next big choral statement of the principal theme.

It is customary to divide Beethoven's works into three periods, on the basis of style and chronology. Vincent d'Indy[5] calls them the periods of Imitation, Externalization, and Reflection. Needless to say, the dividing lines are not sharp, but they run approximately as follows: the first period, of Imitation, goes to about 1802, and

[4] Neither the theme nor the key are as new and foreign as they seem. See R. B. Meikle, "Thematic Transformation in the First Movement of Beethoven's *Eroica* Symphony," *The Music Review* 32 (1971) 205–18.

[5] *Cobbett's Cyclopedic Survey of Chamber Music,* "Beethoven," London, 1926.

includes the six string quartets Op. 18, the first ten piano sonatas (through Op. 14), and the first two symphonies. The second period, of Externalization, runs to about 1816, and includes the symphonies III to VIII, the incidental music to Goethe's drama *Egmont,* the *Coriolan* overture, the opera *Fidelio,* the piano concertos in G and E♭, the violin concerto, the quartets of Opp. 59 (the *Rasumovsky* quartets), 74, and 95, and the piano sonatas through Op. 90. The last period, of Reflection, includes the last five piano sonatas, the *Diabelli* variations, the *Missa solemnis,* the Ninth Symphony, the quartets Opp. 127, 130, 131, 132, 135, and the *Grosse Fuge (Grand Fugue)* for string quartet (Op. 133, originally the finale of Op. 130).

First Style Period

The works of the first period naturally show most clearly Beethoven's dependence on the Classical tradition. The first three sonatas published at Vienna (Op. 2, 1796) contain some passages reminiscent of Haydn, to whom they are dedicated; the Adagio of No. 1, for example, is quite Haydnesque both in themes and treatment. The sonata in E♭ (Op. 7), published in 1797, is especially characteristic of Beethoven in the theme of the Largo with its eloquent pauses and in the mysterious *minore* trio of the third movement. Op. 10, No. 1, in C minor (1798) is a companion piece to the *Sonate Pathétique,* Op. 13, which was published in the following year. Each is in three movements, of which the outer two have the stormy, passionate character associated with the key of C minor, not only in Beethoven but in Haydn (particularly in the symphonies) and Mozart as well; and each has a calm, profound, and richly scored slow movement in A♭. Some of the harmonic characteristics in these early works, as well as the frequent use of octaves and the thick full texture of the piano writing, may have been suggested to Beethoven by the piano sonatas of Muzio Clementi (1752–1832) and Bohemian-born Jan Ladislav Dussek (1760–1812).

If Beethoven's piano writing may owe some stylistic features to Clementi and Dussek, his art of developing motives and animating the texture by means of counterpoint, undoubtedly built upon Haydn's example. The Quartets of Opus 18 (composed 1798–1800) demonstrate the debt; yet they are no mere imitations, for Beethoven's individuality is evident in the character of the themes, the frequent unexpected turns of phrase, the unconventional modulations, and some subtleties of formal structure. Thus the Adagio of the G-major quartet (No. 2) is a three-part *ABA* structure in C major; its middle section is an Allegro in F, consisting entirely of a development of a little motive from the closing cadence of the Adagio; and this motive, moreover, is related to conspicuous mo-

The sonatas

EXAMPLE XV–3   Related Motives from Quartet in G Major Op. 18, Beethoven

a.   Allegro

b.   Adagio cantabile   Allegro

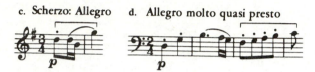

c.   Scherzo: Allegro   d.   Allegro molto quasi presto

tives in the opening themes of the other three movements (Example XV–3).

The First Symphony was composed in 1799; it was first played at a concert in April, 1800, on a program that included also a symphony of Mozart, an aria and a duet from Haydn's *Creation,* a piano concerto and the septet by Beethoven, and improvisations by Beethoven at the piano. The First is the most Classical of the nine symphonies. Its spirit and many of its technical features stem from Haydn; all four movements are so regular in form that they might serve as textbook models. Beethoven's originality is evident not in the large formal outlines but in the details of his treatment, and also in the unusual prominence given to the woodwinds, in the character of the third movement—a scherzo, though labeled a minuet—and especially in the long and important codas of the other movements. The frequent marking *cresc.* $<$ *p* is but one example of the careful attention to dynamic shading that is an essential element in Beethoven's style.

The Adagio introduction to the first movement of this symphony is especially noteworthy. The key of the symphony is C, but the introduction begins in F, modulates to G at the fourth measure, and avoids a definitive cadence in C for the next eight measures, or until the first chord of the Allegro itself; Beethoven thus converges on the tonic from two opposite sides, the subdominant and the dominant. The short introduction to the finale is a joke in the manner of Haydn: the theme is introduced, as Tovey says, by a process of "letting the cat out of the bag."

With the Second Symphony in D major (composed in 1802) we are on the verge of Beethoven's second style period. The long Adagio that introduces the first movement announces a work conceived on

The First Symphony

a scale hitherto unknown in symphonic music. The rest of the symphony has correspondingly large dimensions, with a profusion of thematic material held together in perfect formal balance. The Larghetto is especially remarkable for the large number of themes, and for its rich *cantabile* character. The scherzo and finale, like the first movement, are full of Beethovenian energy and fire. The finale is written in an enlarged sonata form, with suggestions of rondo in extra recurrences of the first theme, one at the beginning of the development section and one at the beginning of the coda; the coda itself is twice as long as the development section, and introduces a new theme.

The Second Symphony

Second Style Period

Within a dozen years after his coming to Vienna Beethoven was acknowledged throughout Europe as the foremost pianist and composer for the piano of his time, and as a symphonist who ranked equally with Haydn and Mozart. Such adverse criticisms as were uttered were directed against his eccentricity, his "frequent daring shifts from one motive to another, by which the organic connection of a gradual development of ideas was put aside. Such defects often weaken his greatest compositions, which spring from a too great exuberance of conception. . . . The singular and the original seemed to be his main object in composition." These are the words of Jan Václav Tomášek (1774–1850), pianist and composer, a slightly younger contemporary of Beethoven, who heard him improvise at Prague in 1795; they are typical of many later criticisms. Tomášek's opinions show that some of the ideas in even the early works of Beethoven, which now we accept as natural because they have become a part of our common musical language, disturbed an intelligent musician of the 1790s, for whom the ideal composers were presumably Haydn and Mozart.

The Third Symphony in E♭, composed in 1803, is one of the most important works of Beethoven's second period. This symphony bears the title *Eroica,* the "heroic symphony," and it stands as an immortal expression in music of the ideal of heroic greatness. It was a revolutionary work, of such unprecedented length and complexity that audiences at first found it difficult to grasp.

The *Eroica* Symphony

It begins, after two introductory chords, with one of the simplest imaginable themes on the notes of the E♭-major triad, but an unexpected C♯ at this point gives rise to endless variations and development in the course of the movement. Five other themes are presented in the exposition, and the development section brings in still another, which recurs in the coda. Most remarkable, however, in this movement, as in all of Beethoven's, is neither the formal pattern nor the abundance of ideas, but the way in which all the material is propelled constantly along, one theme seeming to unfold out of another in a steady dynamic growth which mounts from one climax to the next, driving with a sense of utter inevitability to the end.

In place of the usual slow movement it has a funeral march (NAWM/S 61) in C minor with a contrasting section in C major, of tragic grandeur and pathos. It is this march more than anything else in the symphony that links it with France and the republican experiment there (cf. NAWM/S 60).

The finale of the Third Symphony is a set of variations with fugally developed episodes and coda, in an extremely complex but thoroughly logical form. Beethoven's capacity to organize a large amount of contrasting material into a unified musical whole is one of the chief marks of his greatness.

Fidelio

The opera *Fidelio* was composed at about the same time as the Third Symphony and is similar to it in character. As far as the libretto is concerned, *Fidelio* is a rescue opera of the kind that was so popular at the turn of the century (its libretto, in fact, is actually borrowed from a French revolutionary-era rescue opera). Beethoven's music, however, transforms this conventional material, making of the chief character Leonore (after whom the opera was originally named) a personage of sublime courage and self-abnegation, an idealized figure. The whole last part of the opera is in effect a celebration of Leonore's heroism and the great humanitarian ideals of the Revolution. This opera gave Beethoven more trouble than any other of his works. The first performances of the original three-act version took place in November of 1805, just after the French armies had marched into Vienna; rearranged and shortened to two acts, the opera was brought out again the following March, but immediately withdrawn. Finally, in 1814, a third version, with still more extensive revisions, was successful. In the course of all these changes Beethoven wrote no fewer than four different overtures for the opera. The first was never used, being replaced at the performances of 1805 by the overture now called *Leonora No. 2;* this one in turn was replaced by *Leonora No. 3* for the revival in 1806; and for the final version of the opera in 1814 Beethoven wrote still another, now known as the *Fidelio* overture.

The Rasumovsky quartets

The three quartets of Op. 59 are dedicated to Count Rasumovsky, the Russian Ambassador to Vienna. Rasumovsky was the patron of a quartet of string players said to be the finest in Europe, in which he himself played second violin. As a compliment to the Count, Beethoven introduced a Russian melody as the principal theme of the finale of the first quartet, and another in the third movement of the second quartet. These three quartets, composed in the summer and autumn of 1806, occupy a position in Beethoven's work similar to that of the Quartets Opp. 17 and 20 in Haydn's: they are the first to exemplify the composer's mature style and characteristic manner of expression in this medium. They are indeed full of the emotional fire, boldness of formal treatment, and striking originality that characterize Beethoven's second period. So great was their novelty that musicians were slow to accept them. When Count Rasumovsky's players first tried over the Quartet in F (No. 1 of the set), they were convinced that Beethoven was playing a joke on them. Clementi, the brilliant London pianist whom Mozart had once described as a "mere mechanician," reported that he had said to Beethoven "Surely you do not consider these works to be music?" to which the composer, with unusual self-restraint, answered, "Oh, they are not for you, but for a later age." The Allegretto movement of the F-major Quartet in particular gave rise to charges of "crazy music." It took some time for musicians and audiences to realize that Beethoven's innovations were logical, that the nature of his musical ideas compelled modification of the traditional language and forms.

In the quartets of Op. 59 as well as in the *Eroica Symphony,* the sonata form is expanded to unheard-of proportions by the multitude of themes, the long and complex developments, and the extended codas which take on the dimensions and significance of a second development section. Along with this expansion, Beethoven intentionally conceals the formerly clear dividing lines between the various parts of a movement: recapitulations are disguised and varied, new themes grow imperceptibly out of previous material, and the progress of the musical thought has a dynamic, propulsive character that toys with, if not actually scorns, the neat, symmetrical patterns of the Classical era. These developments continue throughout the whole of Beethoven's second period, but the change is more radical in the quartets and piano sonatas than in the less intimate symphonies and overtures. The two quartets Op. 74 (1809) and Op. 95 (1810) show Beethoven on the way toward the dissolution of traditional form that later marked the last quartets of the third period.

Among the other chamber works of Beethoven's second period, special mention should be made of the Violin Sonatas Op. 47 (the *Kreutzer Sonata*) and Op. 96, and the Trio in B♭, Op. 97. The two Sonatas for Violoncello and Piano, Op. 102 (1815), belong stylistically to the third period.

The Fourth, Fifth, and Sixth Symphonies were all composed between 1806 and 1808, a time of exceptional productivity. Beethoven seems to have worked on the Fourth and Fifth Symphonies at the same time; the first two movements of the Fifth, in fact, were already in existence before the Fourth was completed. The two works contrast, as though Beethoven wished to express simultaneously two opposite poles of feeling. Joviality and humor mark the Fourth Symphony, while the Fifth has always been interpreted as the musical projection of Beethoven's resolution "I will grapple with

The Fourth to Eighth Symphonies

Fate; it shall not overcome me." The progress through struggle to victory, as symbolized in this symphony by the succession C minor to C major, has been an implicit subject of many symphonies since Beethoven's, but none other has so caught the popular imagination.

The Sixth (*Pastoral*) Symphony was composed immediately after the Fifth and the two were first played on the same program in December, 1808. Each of the five movements bears a descriptive title suggesting a scene from life in the country. Beethoven adapts his descriptive program to the usual Classical symphonic form, merely inserting after the scherzo (*Merrymaking of the Peasants*) an extra movement (*Storm*) which serves to introduce the finale (*Thankful feelings after the storm*). In the coda of the Andante (*Scene by the brook*), flute, oboe, and clarinet join harmoniously in imitating bird calls—the nightingale, the quail, and, of course, the cuckoo. All this programmatic apparatus is subordinate to the expansive, leisurely musical form of the symphony as a whole; the composer himself warns that the descriptions are not to be taken literally: he calls them "expression of feelings rather than depiction." The *Pastoral Symphony* is one of hundreds of works from the eighteenth and early nineteenth centuries that aimed to portray natural scenes or suggest the moods aroused by the contemplation of such scenes (*cf.* Vivaldi's *Seasons* concertos); its enduring appeal testifies not to the accuracy of its landscape painting but to the way in which the emotions of a lover of nature have been captured in great music.

The Seventh and Eighth Symphonies were both completed in 1812. The Seventh, like the Second and Fourth, opens with a long slow introduction with remote modulations, leading into an Allegro dominated throughout by the rhythmic figure ♪. ♪♪ . The second movement, in the parallel minor key of A, was encored at the first performance and has always been a favorite with audiences. The scherzo (not so labeled) is in F major, the lower submediant of the principal key of the symphony; it is unusual furthermore in that the trio (D major) recurs a second time, thus expanding this movement to a five-part form (*ABABA*). The finale, a large sonata form with coda, "remains unapproached in music as a triumph of Bacchic fury."[6] By contrast with the huge scale of the Seventh Symphony, the Eighth appears miniature—or would, if it were not for the long coda of the first movement and the still longer one of the finale. This is the most mercurial of all the nine symphonies, but its humor is sophisticated and its forms extremely condensed. The second movement is a brisk Allegretto, while the third, by way of compensation, is a deliberately archaic Minuet instead of the usual Beethoven Scherzo.

[6] D. Tovey, *Essays in Musical Analysis*, New York, 1935, I, 60.

Related in style to the symphonies are Beethoven's orchestral overtures, which usually take the form of a symphonic first movement. The *Leonore* Overtures have already been mentioned. The other most important overtures are *Coriolan* (1807), inspired by a

Mm. 36–38, in Beethoven's autograph

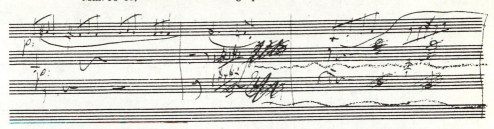

The top line is the cello part, to be read in bass clef; the second and third lines are the piano part, in treble and bass clefs, respectively; a key signature of A major is assumed.

Mm. 35–38 in the Schirmer edition

Mm. 34–37 in the Henle edition

A passage from the first movement of Beethoven's cello sonata in A major, Op. 69, as it appears in the composer's autograph and in two editions. In measure 35, Beethoven wrote a C♮ for the piano, but in measure 36 a C♯ for the cello. Until the recent Henle publication, all editions, from the first (published by Breitkopf and Härtel in 1809) have given the cello a C♮ in measure 36. The 1905 Schirmer edition shown here is one of the many (including the 19th-century Gesamtausgabe of Beethoven's works, and that edited by Donald Francis Tovey) that have perpetuated this misreading, which evidently arose from Beethoven's hurried proofreading of the first edition, in which the cello and piano parts were printed separately, rather than in score—and thus probably proofread separately by the composer.

tragedy of the same name which was performed occasionally at Vienna after 1802; and *Egmont,* composed, together with songs and incidental music, for a performance of Goethe's drama in 1810.

The sonatas and concertos

The piano sonatas of the second period show a wide range of styles and forms. Among the earliest, dating from about 1802, are the Sonata in A♭ with the funeral march, Op. 26, and the two sonatas of Op. 27, each designated as "quasi una fantasia"; the second is the one popularly known as the *Moonlight Sonata.* The first movement of the D-minor Sonata Op. 31, No. 2 has an introductory *largo* phrase which recurs at the beginning of the development section and again at the beginning of the recapitulation, each time in expanded form and with increased musical significance; its last appearance leads into an expressive instrumental recitative, of the kind that Beethoven afterward used with effect in some of his later works. The finale of this sonata is an exciting *moto perpetuo* in sonata-rondo form.

Outstanding among the sonatas of the second period are Op. 53 in C major (called the *Waldstein Sonata* after Beethoven's patron, to whom it is dedicated) and Op. 57 in F minor, commonly called the *Appassionata.* Both were composed in 1804. These two works illustrate what happened to the Classical sonata at Beethoven's hands. Each has the usual Classical three movements in the order fast–slow–fast; each exhibits the patterns of sonata form, rondo, or variations, with appropriate key-schemes. But their formal order has, as it were, been expanded from within by the resistless force of Beethoven's musical imagination, expressed in themes of elemental power that require a structure of hitherto unknown tension and concentration to support their natural development and completion. When we listen to a sonata by Mozart we rejoice in the composer's constant and willing submission to an accepted order of things musical; when we listen to one of Beethoven's sonatas we rejoice that the revolutionist submits only where he pleases, and that elsewhere he creates a new order, one growing out of the old but resembling it only in externals.

As a concert pianist Beethoven naturally composed concertos for his own use. The two largest works in this form are the Concerto in G major, Op. 58, composed in 1805–06, and the one in E♭, known as the *Emperor Concerto,* which was composed in 1808–09 and first performed at Vienna in 1812 by Carl Czerny (1791–1857). (As a young man, Czerny had studied piano with Beethoven, and subsequently had a successful teaching career at Vienna; he was the composer of many studies and other works for the piano.)

The concertos of Beethoven are related to those of Mozart much as are the symphonies of these two composers: Beethoven retained the division of the concerto into three movements and the general outline of the Classical form; but he expanded the framework, and intensified the content. The virtuosity of the solo part is more marked than in Mozart's concertos, but is not excessive in view of the expanded dimensions. In Beethoven's magnificent Violin Concerto, Op. 61 in D major (composed 1806), the solo part is ideally interwoven with the orchestra.

Third Style Period

The years up to 1815 were, on the whole, peaceful and prosperous for Beethoven. His music was much played in Vienna, and he was celebrated both at home and abroad. Thanks to the generosity of patrons and the steady demand from publishers for new works, his financial affairs were in good order, despite a ruinous devaluation of the Austrian currency in 1811; but his deafness became a more and more serious trial. As it caused him to lose contact with others, he retreated into himself, becoming morose, irascible, and morbidly suspicious even toward his friends. Family troubles, ill health, and unfounded apprehensions of poverty were also plaguing Beethoven, and it was only by a supreme effort of will that he continued composing amidst all these troubles. The last five piano sonatas were written between 1816 and 1821; the *Missa solemnis* was completed in 1822, the *Diabelli* variations in 1823, and the Ninth Symphony in 1824, each after long years of labor; and the last quartets, Beethoven's musical testament, followed in 1825 and 1826. At his death in 1827 he had plans for a tenth symphony and many other new works.

Beethoven's compositions of the third period more and more come to have a meditative character; the former urgent sense of communication is replaced by a feeling of assured tranquillity, passionate outpouring by calm affirmation. The language becomes more concentrated, more abstract. Extremes meet: the sublime and the grotesque side by side in the Mass and the Ninth Symphony, the profound and the apparently naïve side by side in the last quartets. Classical forms remain as the former features of a landscape remain after a geological upheaval—recognizable here and there under new contours, lying at strange angles underneath the new surface.

One of the characteristics—a concomitant of the meditative quality—in Beethoven's late works is the deliberate working out of themes and motives to the utmost of their potentialities. This is in part a continuation of his earlier technique of motivic development, which he now carries to its limits; more especially, it reflects a new conception of the possibilities of thematic variation.

In Beethoven's works, as in those of Haydn and Mozart, variation occurs in three kinds of situations: (1) as a technique within a larger

Characteristics
of Beethoven's
late style

formal plan, as when in a rondo each recurrence of the principal theme is varied, or in a sonata form the first theme is varied in the recapitulation; (2) a theme-and-variations as an independent composition; and (3) a theme-and-variations as one of the movements of a symphony or sonata. Examples of the first use in Beethoven's late works are the slow movements of the Sonata Op. 106, the Quartet Op. 132, and the Ninth Symphony; the finale of this symphony also begins (after the introduction) as a set of variations.

As for independent compositions in variation form, in all Beethoven wrote twenty sets of these for piano, the majority of them on favorite tunes from contemporary operas; from the last period there is only one independent set, but it is a work that surpasses anything in this form since Bach's *Goldberg Variations:* the *Thirty-three Variations on a Waltz by Diabelli,* Op. 120, which were completed and published in 1823. These differ from other variations of the late eighteenth or early nineteenth centuries in that they are made up not of comparatively straightforward alterations in the physiognomy of the theme, but of transformations in its very character. Diabelli's commonplace little waltz, taken by Beethoven as if contemptuously to show what could be made of it, surprisingly expands into a world

Beethoven's manuscript of the theme of the variation movement from the Piano Sonata Op. 109. (Library of Congress)

of variegated moods—solemn, brilliant, capricious, mysterious—
ordered with due regard for contrast, grouping, and climax. Each
variation is built on motives derived from some part of the theme,
but altered in rhythm, tempo, dynamics, or context so as to produce
a new design. Other examples of variations, like the Diabelli set but
more concentrated, are the slow movements in Beethoven's Sonata
Op. 111 and in the Quartets Opp. 127 and 131. In these, as it were,
we overhear the composer while he meditates on his theme, finding
with each meditation new depths of insight, and gradually leading
us into a realm where the music takes on a luminous and transcendent quality of mystical revelation.

Another feature of Beethoven's late style is a continuity he
achieved by intentionally blurring dividing lines: within a musical
sentence, by making cadential progressions terminate on a weak beat,
by delaying the progression of the lower voices, placing the third or
the fifth of the tonic chord in the upper voice at such a resolution,
or by otherwise concealing the cadential effect (first theme of the
slow movement of the Ninth Symphony); within a movement, by
interpenetration of Introduction and Allegro (first movements of
Sonata Op. 109 and Quartets Opp. 127, 130, 132) or making the
Introduction a part of the Allegro (first movement of the Ninth
Symphony); even within a complete work, by interpenetration of
movements (Adagio and Fuga in the Sonata Op. 110; recall of the
first movement theme after the Adagio of Op. 101). A feeling of
vastness comes also from the wide-spaced harmonic arches and the
leisurely march of the melodies in such movements as the Adagio of
the Quartet Op. 127 or the *Benedictus* of the Mass in D. At times all
motion pauses for long moments of reflection; such passages have the
character of improvisation, and may give us some idea of the actual
improvisations of Beethoven at the piano which so impressed his
hearers. (Similar examples are the slow movement of the Sonata Op.
101 and the Largo introduction to the finale of the Sonata Op. 106;
this style was forecast in the slow movement of the *Waldstein Sonata*,
Op. 53.) Sometimes these improvisatory passages culminate in instrumental recitative, as in the Adagio of the Sonata Op. 110, and also
the recitatives in the Quartets Op. 131 and Op. 132 and the finale
of the Ninth Symphony.

The abstract, suprapersonal quality of Beethoven's late style is
symbolized by the increased extent and importance of contrapuntal
textures in the compositions of the third period. This increase was
in part the fruit of his lifelong reverence for the music of J. S. Bach,
but it was also a necessary consequence of the nature of his musical
thought in the last ten years of his life. It is apparent in the numerous canonic imitations and generally contrapuntal voice-leading of
all the late works; it is evidenced specifically by fugatos incorporated
in development sections (as in the finale of Op. 101) and by complete

fugal movements, such as the finales of the Sonatas Opp. 106 and 110, the first movement of the Quartet in C♯ minor, Op. 131, the gigantic *Grosse Fuge* for String Quartet Op. 133, the fugues at the end of the Gloria and Credo of the Mass in D, and the two double fugues in the finale of the Ninth Symphony.

Another, incidental consequence of the abstract quality of Beethoven's last works was the invention of new sonorities: as the former habits of vertical tone combination were modified by the rigorous logic of contrapuntal lines, or as new ideas required new alignments of sound for their realization, he produced unaccustomed effects. The widely spaced piano sonorities at the end of the Sonata Op. 110, the partition of the theme between the two violins (on the principle of the medieval hocket) in the fourth movement of the C♯-minor Quartet, and the extraordinary dark coloring of the orchestra and chorus at the first appearance of the words "Ihr stürzt nieder" in the finale of the Ninth Symphony are instances of such new sonorities. Some critics have held that in his late works Beethoven went too far in subjugating euphony and considerations of practicability to the demands of his musical conceptions, and some attribute this alleged fault to his deafness. There are places—the finale of the Sonata Op. 106, the first section of the *Grosse Fuge,* the B-major cadenza of the four soloists in the last movement of the Ninth Symphony, the *Et vitam venturi* fugue in the Mass—that almost require a miracle to make them "sound" in performance. The ideas seem too big for human capabilities to express; but whether one approves or condemns these passages, there is not the slightest reason to suppose that Beethoven, even had his hearing been perfect, would have altered a single note, either to spare tender ears among his auditors or to make things easier for the performers.

As with Classical texture and sonority, so with Classical form in the instrumental works of Beethoven's third period: two of the last quartets and two of the last sonatas retain the external scheme of four movements, but the rest dispense with even this obeisance to tradition. The Sonata Op. 111 has only two movements, an Allegro in compact sonata form and a long set of variations, Adagio molto, so eloquent and so perfect that nothing further seems to be required. The Quartet Op. 131 has seven movements: (1) A fugue in C♯ minor, Adagio, 4/4 (see NAWM/S 57). (2) Allegretto molto vivace, D major, 6/8, in something vaguely like sonata form. (3) Eleven measures, Allegro moderato, in the spirit of a recitativo accompagnato, functioning as an introduction of the following movement and modulating from B minor to E major, which becomes the dominant of (4) Andante, A major, 2/4: theme of two double periods, with six variations and a seventh variation incomplete, merging with a coda which itself embodies still one more variation of the first and fourth periods of the theme. (5) Presto, ¢ ,

E major: four themes, rapidly chasing one another around in the *Coda* order *AbcdAbcdAbcd*A. (6) Adagio, G♯ minor, 3/4: 28 measures in the form *ABB* with coda, introducing (7) Allegro, C♯ minor, ¢, sonata form. All this could be forcibly equated with the Classical sonata scheme by calling 1 and 2 an introduction and first movement, 3 and 4 an introduction and slow movement, 5 a scherzo, and 6 and 7 an introduction and finale; a similar arbitrary adjustment would also be possible with the Quartet Op. 132, but not with Op. 130, which in the number and order of movements is more like a serenade than anything else. In any event, in all Beethoven's late sonatas and quartets both the musical material and its treatment are so different from those of Haydn and Mozart that resemblances to Classical patterns are at most incidental.

The most imposing works of the last period are the Mass in D (the *Missa solemnis*) and the Ninth Symphony. The former is, with the possible exception of Bach's Mass in B minor, the worthiest musical interpretation of this text that exists. Beethoven himself regarded it as his greatest work. It is a deeply personal and at the same time universal confession of faith. The score incorporates historic musical and liturgical symbols to an extent far greater, and in a manner far more detailed, than an uninformed listener can be aware of.[7] Like Bach's Mass, Beethoven's is too long and elaborate for ordinary liturgical use; it is rather a huge vocal and instrumental symphony using the text of the Mass as its fabric. Yet it is more than merely a "setting" of the words; one might better call it a *representation,* both pictorial and symbolic, of the whole liturgy of the Mass.

The Mass in D

The choral treatment owes something to Handel, whose music Beethoven revered equally with that of Bach; one theme of the *Dona nobis pacem* is adapted from Handel's melody to the words "And He shall reign forever and ever" in the Hallelujah Chorus, and the lofty style of the whole is quite in the spirit of Handel. The form, however, is different. Handel's oratorios and Bach's Mass were conceived, in accordance with the Baroque practice, as a series of independent numbers, without interconnecting themes or motives and usually without any very definite plan of musical unity in the work as a whole. Beethoven's Mass is a planned musical unit, a symphony in five movements, one on each of the five principal divisions of the Ordinary of the Mass. In this respect it is like the late Masses of Haydn, and like them also it freely combines and alternates solo voices and chorus in each movement.

---

[7] See the important article by Warren Kirkendale, "New Roads to Old Ideas in Beethoven's *Missa solemnis,*" MQ 56 (1970) 665–710; reprinted in P. H. Lang, ed., *The Creative World of Beethoven,* New York, 1971, 163–99; in a somewhat fuller version in *Sitzungsberichte der Oesterreichischen Akademie der Wissenschaften,* Bd. 271 (Vienna, 1971) 121–58.

Within the frame of the symphonic structure there is abundant variety of detail. Beethoven seizes every phrase, every single word that offers him a possibility for dramatic musical expression; to realize the contrast in this respect between Beethoven's treatment of the text and that of Bach, one should compare their respective settings of the words "judicare vivos et mortuos" (to judge both the quick and the dead) in the Credo. (Beethoven's effective pause after the word "et," here and elsewhere in the Credo, had been anticipated in Haydn's *Missa in tempore belli*.) The threefold interruption of the *Dona nobis pacem*—the "prayer for inward and outward peace," as Beethoven headed it—by ominous orchestral interludes with martial flourishes in the trumpets and drums is a feature likewise anticipated by Haydn as well as many earlier composers. It is a superbly theatrical touch, but neither this nor any of the other vivid details of the score is theatrical in a bad sense; all are absorbed into and made part of the vast and wonderfully organized structure of the work.

The Ninth Symphony

The Ninth Symphony was first performed on May 7, 1824, on a program with one of Beethoven's overtures and three movements of the Mass (the Kyrie, Credo, and Agnus Dei). The large and distinguished audience applauded vociferously after the symphony. Beethoven did not turn around to acknowledge the applause because he could not hear it; one of the solo singers "plucked him by the sleeve and directed his attention to the clapping hands and waving hats and handkerchiefs. . . . he turned to the audience and bowed."[8] The receipts at the concert were large, but so little remained after expenses had been paid that Beethoven accused his friends who had managed the affair of having cheated him. A repetition two weeks later before a half-full house resulted in a deficit. Thus was the Ninth Symphony launched into the world.

Its most striking novelty is the use of chorus and solo voices in the finale. Beethoven had had the thought as early as 1792 of composing a setting of Schiller's *Ode to Joy*, but his decision to make a choral finale on this text for the Ninth Symphony was not reached before the autumn of 1823. It is significant of Beethoven's ethical ideals that in choosing the stanzas to be used he selected those that emphasize two ideas: the universal brotherhood of man through joy, and its basis in the love of an eternal heavenly Father. Beethoven was troubled by the apparent incongruity of introducing voices as the climax of a long instrumental symphony. His solution of this aesthetic difficulty determined the unusual form of the last movement: a brief, tumultuous, dissonant introduction; a review and rejection (by instrumental recitatives) of the themes of the preceding movements; suggestion of the joy theme and its joyful acceptance;

---

[8] Thayer-Forbes, *op. cit.*, II, 909.

orchestral exposition of the theme in four stanzas, *crescendo,* with coda; again the tumultuous dissonant opening measures; bass recitative: "O friends, not these tones, but let us rather sing more pleasant and joyful ones"; choral-orchestral exposition of the joy theme in four stanzas, varied (including the Turkish March), and with a long orchestral interlude (double fugue) before a repetition of the first stanza; new theme, orchestra and chorus; double fugue on the two themes; and a complex, gigantic coda, in which the "heaven-descended flame" of Joy is hailed in strains of matchless sublimity. The first three movements of the symphony are on a comparably grand scale. The scherzo, in particular, is an outstanding example of Beethoven's ability to organize an entire movement in sonata form around a single rhythmic motive.

Only a few of his contemporaries understood Beethoven's late works, which in any event were so personal that they could hardly be imitated. His influence on later composers came mostly from the works of the middle period, especially the *Rasumovsky* Quartets, the Fifth, Sixth, and Seventh Symphonies, and the piano sonatas. Even in these works it was not the Classical element in Beethoven's style— not the overruling sense of form, unity, and proportion that always dominated even his most subjective creations, nor yet the painstaking craftsmanship to which the sketchbooks bear such constant witness—but rather the revolutionary element, the free, impulsive, mysterious, daemonic spirit, the underlying conception of *music as a mode of self-expression,* that chiefly fascinated the Romantic generation. As E. T. A. Hoffmann wrote, "Beethoven's music sets in motion the lever of fear, of awe, of horror, of suffering, and awakens just that infinite longing which is the essence of romanticism. He is accordingly a completely romantic composer. . . ." [9] Hoffmann was not unaware nor unappreciative of the importance of structure and control in Beethoven's music, nor in that of Haydn and Mozart— whom he also called "romantic." (One gets the impression that he used the word mainly as a general term of approbation.) Romantic or not, Beethoven was one of the great disruptive forces in the history of music. After him, nothing could ever be the same again; he had opened the gateway to a new world.

Beethoven and the Romantics

---

[9] From an essay on "Beethoven's Instrumental Music," 1813; in SR, 777 (SRRo, 37).

XVI

The Nineteenth Century:

Romanticism; Vocal Music

Classicism and Romanticism

The names of historical periods in music always have a double meaning: they denote certain styles of music and also certain segments of time during which those styles are dominant. In principle, it is always possible to define a style (or a complex of significantly related styles) in general terms and to fix more or less precisely the dates of its beginning and ending. In practice, of course, the more we learn about the music of any particular time, place, or composer, the more clearly we begin to see that the generalized style descriptions are inadequate and the period boundaries somewhat arbitrary. The terms "Classic" and "Romantic" as descriptions of style periods are especially troublesome, chiefly because the traditional antithesis Classic-Romantic is not a total antithesis. The continuity between the two styles is more fundamental than the contrast: the great bulk of the music written from about 1770 to about 1900 constitutes a single style period, with a common limited stock of usable musical sounds, a common basic vocabulary of harmonies, common basic principles of harmonic progression, rhythm, and form, and a common intention, namely to communicate meaning exclusively through music without extraneous symbolism from composer to performer to listener, starting from an exact and complete notation.

We shall now attempt to define, or suggest, the meaning of Romanticism with reference to the music of the nineteenth century. In a very general sense, all art may be said to be romantic; for, though it may take its materials from actual life, it transforms them and thus creates a new world which is necessarily to a greater or lesser degree remote from the everyday world. From this point of view, romantic art differs from classic art by its greater emphasis on the qualities of remoteness and strangeness, with all that such emphasis may imply as to choice and treatment of material. Romanticism, in this general sense, is not a phenomenon of any one period, but has occurred at various times in various forms. It is possible to see in the history of music, and of the other arts, alternations of classicism and romanticism.

Traits of Romanticism

Another fundamental trait of romanticism is boundlessness, in two different though related senses. First, romantic art aspires to transcend immediate times or occasions, to seize eternity, to reach back into the past and forward into the future, to range over the expanse of the world and outward through the cosmos. As against the classic ideals of order, equilibrium, control, and perfection within acknowledged limits, Romanticism cherishes freedom, movement, passion, and endless pursuit of the unattainable. And just because its goal can never be attained, romantic art is haunted by a spirit of longing, of yearning after an impossible fulfillment. Again, the romantic impatience of limits leads to a breaking down of distinctions. The personality of the artist tends to become merged with the work of art; classical clarity is replaced by a certain intentional obscurity, definite statement by suggestion, allusion, or symbol. The arts themselves tend to merge; poetry, for example, aims to acquire the qualities of music, and music the characteristics of poetry.

If remoteness and boundlessness are romantic, then music is the

Preliminary sketch for The Raft of the "Medusa," *by Théodore Gericault (1791–1824). Romantic art aspired to an extravagant portrayal of man's struggles and of nature in its wilder aspects.*

most romantic of the arts. Its material—ordered sound and rhythm —is almost completely detached from the concrete world of objects, and this very detachment makes music most apt at suggesting the flood of impressions, thoughts, and feelings which is the proper domain of romantic art. Only instrumental music—pure music free from the burden of words—can perfectly attain this goal of communicating emotion. Instrumental music, therefore, is the ideal romantic art. Its detachment from the world, its mystery, and its incomparable power of suggestion which works on the mind directly without the mediation of words, made it the dominant art, the one most representative, among all the arts, of the nineteenth century.

The Romantic dualities

At this point we come upon the first of several apparently opposing conditions that beset all attempts to grasp the meaning of *Romantic* as applied to the music of the nineteenth century. We shall endeavor to deal with this difficulty by summarizing the conflicting tendencies that affected the music of the time and noting in what way the musicians sought to harmonize these oppositions in their own thought and practice.

Music and words

The first opposition involves the relation between music and words. If instrumental music is the perfect Romantic art, why is it that the acknowledged great masters of the symphony, the highest form of instrumental music, were not Romantics, but were the Classical composers, Haydn, Mozart, and Beethoven? Moreover, one of the most characteristic nineteenth-century forms was the Lied, a vocal piece in which Schubert, Schumann, Brahms, and Hugo Wolf attained a new and intimate union between music and poetry. Even the instrumental music of most Romantic composers was dominated by the lyrical spirit of the Lied rather than the dramatic spirit of the symphony that was exemplified in the later works of Mozart and Haydn and above all in Beethoven. Furthermore, a large number of leading composers in the nineteenth century were extraordinarily articulate and interested in literary expression, and many leading Romantic novelists and poets wrote about music with deep love and insight.

The conflict between the ideal of pure instrumental music as the supremely Romantic mode of expression on the one hand, and the strong literary orientation of nineteenth-century music on the other, was resolved in the conception of *program music*. Program music, as the nineteenth century used the term, was instrumental music associated with poetic, descriptive, or even narrative subject matter—not by means of rhetorical-musical figures (as in the Baroque era) or by imitation of natural sounds and movements (as sometimes in the eighteenth century), but by means of imaginative suggestion. Program music aimed to absorb and transmute the imagined subject, taking it wholly into the music in such a way that the resulting composition, while it includes the "program," nevertheless transcends it and is in a certain sense independent of it. Instrumental music thus becomes a vehicle for the utterance of thoughts which, though they may be hinted in words, are ultimately beyond the power of words to express. Practically every composer of the era was, to a greater or lesser degree, writing program music, whether or not he publicly acknowledged it; and one reason why it is so easy for listeners to connect a scene or a story or a poem with a piece of Romantic music is that often the composer himself, perhaps unconsciously, was working from some such idea. Writers on music projected their own conceptions of the expressive function of music into the past, and read Romantic programs into the instrumental works not only of Beethoven but also of Mozart, Haydn, and Bach.

Another area of conflict involved the relationship between the composer and his audience. The transition from relatively small, homogeneous, and cultured audiences for music to the huge, diverse, and relatively unprepared middle-class public of the nineteenth century meant that composers, if they were to succeed, somehow had to reach the vast new audience; their struggle to be heard and understood had to occur in an incomparably larger arena than at any previous epoch in the history of music. Yet it is just this period more than any other that offers us the phenomenon of the unsociable artist, one who feels himself to be separate from his fellow-men and who is driven by isolation to seek inspiration within himself. These musicians did not compose, as did their eighteenth-century forebears, for a patron or for a particular function, but for infinity, for posterity, for some imaginable ideal audience which, they hoped, would some day understand and appreciate them; either that, or they wrote for a little circle of kindred spirits, confessing to them those inmost feelings considered too fragile and precious to be set before the crude public of the concert halls. Partly in sheer self-defense, as compensation, they were driven to the conception of the composer as an exalted combination of priest and poet, one to whom it was given to reveal to mankind the deeper meaning of life through the divine medium of music. The artist was a "genius" who wrote under "inspiration," a prophet even though his message might be rejected.

The crowd and the individual

Another contrast in the Classic-Romantic period was that between professional and amateur performers. The distinction between experts (the *Kenner*) and amateurs (the *Liebhaber*), already marked in the eighteenth century, grew sharper as professional standards of performance improved. At one extreme was the great spell-binding virtuoso before his rapt audience in the concert hall; at the other, the neighborhood instrumental or vocal ensemble or the family gathered around the parlor piano to sing favorite airs and hymns. Family music-making, almost unknown now since the coming of the phonograph and television, was a constant, if unpublicized fea-

Professional and amateur music-making

ture of the nineteenth- and early twentieth-century musical background.

Partly because of the industrial revolution, the population of Europe increased tremendously during the nineteenth century. Most of the increase occurred in cities. Consequently, the majority of **Man and** people, including the majority of musicians, no longer lived in a **nature** community, a court, or town, where everybody knew everybody else and the open countryside was never very far away; instead, they were lost in the huge impersonal huddle of a modern city. But the more man's daily life became separated from Nature, the more he became enamoured of Nature. Nature was idealized, and increasingly so in its wilder and more picturesque aspects. However, for the Romantic composer Nature was not merely a subject to be depicted. A kinship was felt between the inner life of the artist and the life of Nature, so that the latter became not only a refuge but also a source of strength, inspiration, and revelation. This mystic sense of kinship with Nature, counterbalancing the artificiality of city existence, is as prevalent in the music of the nineteenth century as it is in the contemporary literature and art.

The nineteenth century saw a rapid expansion in exact knowledge and scientific method. Simultaneously, as though in reaction, **Science and** the music of that period is constantly thrusting beyond the borders **the irrational** of the rational into the unconscious and the supernatural. It takes its subject material from the dream (the individual unconscious), as in Berlioz's *Symphonie fantastique,* or from the myth (the collective unconscious), as in Wagner's music dramas. Even Nature itself is haunted in the Romantic imagination by spirits and is fraught with mysterious significances. The effort to find a musical language capable of expressing these new and strange ideas led to extensions of harmony, melody, and orchestral color.

The nineteenth century was in the main a secular and materialistic age, though there was an important movement of revival **Materialism** in the Catholic church with musical results which we shall examine **and** later. But the essential Romantic spirit, once again in conflict with **idealism** an important trend of its time, was both idealistic and nonchurchly. The most characteristic nineteenth-century musical settings of liturgical texts were, like Beethoven's *Missa solemnis,* too personal and too big for ordinary church use: the gigantic *Requiem* and the *Te Deum* of Berlioz and the *Requiem* of Verdi. The Romantic composers also gave expression to generalized religious aspiration in nonliturgical settings, such as the *German Requiem* of Brahms, Wagner's *Parsifal,* and Mahler's Eighth Symphony. Furthermore, a great deal of Romantic music is infused with a kind of idealistic longing that might be called "religious" in a vague pantheistic sense.

Another area of conflict in the nineteenth century was political:

it was the conflict between the growth of nationalism and the beginning of supranational socialist movements outlined by the *Communist Manifesto* of Marx and Engels (1848) and Marx's *Capital* (1867). Nationalism was an important influence in Romantic music. Differences between national musical styles were accentuated and folk song came to be venerated as the spontaneous expression of the national soul. Musical Romanticism flourished especially in Germany, not only because the Romantic temper was congenial to German ways of thinking, but also because in that country national sentiment, being for a long time suppressed politically, had to find vent in music and other forms of art. Supplementary to the concentration on national music was a delight in exoticism, the sympathetic use of foreign idioms for picturesque color. The music of the great Romantic composers was not, of course, limited to any one country; what it had to say was addressed to all humanity. But its idioms were national as compared with the eighteenth-century ideal of a cosmopolitan musical language in which national peculiarities were minimized.

Nationalism and internationalism

The Romantic movement had from the beginning a revolutionary tinge, with a corresponding emphasis on the virtue of originality in art. Romanticism was seen as a revolt against the limitations of Classicism, although at the same time Beethoven and, to some extent, Mozart also were viewed by the Romantic composers as having marked out the path which they themselves were to follow. Thus arose the concept of music as an art that had a history—moreover, a history which was to be interpreted, in accord with the dominant philosophical ideas of the time, as a process of evolution.

Tradition and revolution

The past was manifested by the persistence of the Classical tradition. Composers still wrote in the Classical forms of sonata, symphony, and string quartet; the Classical system of harmony was still the basis of their music. Moreover, not all composers went the whole way in adopting Romantic innovations; there were conservatives and radicals within the general movement.

One aspect of the Romantic movement was its preoccupation with music of the distant as well as of the immediate past. Bach and Palestrina were particularly congenial to the Romantics. Bach's *Passion According to St. Matthew* was revived in a performance at Berlin under Mendelssohn's direction in 1829; this performance was one conspicuous example of a general interest in Bach's music, which led in 1850 to the beginning of the publication of the first complete edition of his works. A similar edition of Palestrina's works was begun in 1862. The rise of historical musicology in the nineteenth century was another outgrowth of the Romantic interest in the music of former ages, while the discoveries of musicologists further stimulated such interest.

Sources and Characteristics of the Romantic Style

Romantic and Classical music

Haydn's *Creation* and *Seasons,* Mozart's *Don Giovanni* and *Magic Flute,* and Beethoven's Fifth and Ninth Symphonies were the immediate sources of musical Romanticism. From Haydn came its pleasure in depicting the world of nature, from Mozart its preoccupation with the inner life of the individual human being, and from Beethoven its Faustian aspirations and storming assaults on the Ideal.

The most remarkable achievements of the nineteenth century lay in the development of harmonic technique and instrumental color. Chromatic harmonies, chromatic voice leading, distant modulations, tonal ambiguity, complex chords, freer use of nonharmonic tones, and a growing tendency to avoid distinct cadences, all operated to extend and eventually to blur the outlines of tonality. Romantic harmony as a means of expression went hand in hand with an ever-expanding palette of color. New sonorities were discovered in piano music; new instruments were added to the orchestra, and older instruments were redesigned to be more sonorous and more flexible; above all, new combinations of instruments in the ensemble were invented to produce new color effects. Harmony and color were the principal means whereby the nineteenth-century composers sought to express in music the Romantic ideals of remoteness, ardor, and boundless longing.

Franz Schubert

The pitifully short life of Franz Peter Schubert (1797–1828) illustrates the tragedy of genius overwhelmed by the petty necessities and annoyances of everyday existence. Without wide public recognition, sustained only by the love of a few friends, constantly struggling against illness and poverty, he composed ceaselessly; his works include nine symphonies, 22 piano sonatas and a multitude of short piano pieces for two and four hands, about 35 chamber compositions, six Masses, 17 operatic works, and over 600 Lieder. The songs

Schubert's Lieder

reveal Schubert's supreme gift for making beautiful melodies, a power which few even of the greatest composers have possessed so fully. Many of his melodies have the simple, artless quality of folk song; others are suffused with an indescribable romantic sweetness and melancholy; still others are declamatory, intense, and dramatic; in short, there is no mood or nuance of Romantic feeling but finds spontaneous and perfect expression in Schubert's melody. This wonderful melodic stream flows as purely and as copiously in the instrumental works as in the songs.

Along with melody went a sensitive feeling for harmonic color. Schubert's modulations, often far-flung and complex, sometimes embodying long passages in which the tonality is kept in suspense, powerfully underline the dramatic qualities of a song text. Masterly use of chromatic coloring within a prevailing diatonic sound is another characteristic of Schubert's harmony. His modulations tend characteristically to move from the tonic toward flat keys, and the mediant or submediant is a favorite relationship.

Equally diverse and ingenious are the piano accompaniments in Schubert's Lieder. Very often the piano figuration is suggested by some pictorial image of the text. Such pictorial features are never merely imitative, but are designed, in the best Romantic fashion, to contribute toward the mood of the song. Thus the accompaniment of *Gretchen am Spinnrad*—one of the earliest (1814) and best of the Lieder—suggests not only the whirr of the spinning wheel but also the agitation of Gretchen's thoughts as she sings of her lover. The pounding octave triplets of *Erlkönig* depict at the same time the galloping of the horse and the frantic anxiety of the father as he rides "through night and storm" with his frightened child clasped in his arms. This song, composed in 1815, is one of Schubert's relatively few ballads. Goethe's poem is more compact than the usual early Romantic ballad, and is all the more effective because of the speed of its action. Schubert has characterized in an unforgettable manner the three actors in the drama—the father, the wily Erlking, and the terrified child with his cries rising a tone higher at each repetition; the cessation of movement and the final line in recitative make a superbly dramatic close. An entirely different style of accompaniment is found in another of Schubert's Lieder, *Der Doppelgänger:* here are only long, somber chords, with a recurrent sinister melodic motif in low triple octaves below a declamatory voice part which rises to an awesome climax before sinking in a final despairing

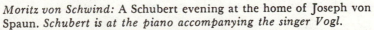

Moritz von Schwind: A Schubert evening at the home of Joseph von Spaun. *Schubert is at the piano accompanying the singer Vogl.*

phrase. Nothing could better suggest the ghostly horror of the scene than the heavy, obsessive dark chords, revolving fatally about the tonic of B minor except for one brief, lurid flash of D♯ minor near the end.

Many of Schubert's Lieder are in strophic form, with either literal repetition of the music for each stanza or repetition with slight variation. Others, particularly those on longer texts, alternate between declamatory and arioso style, the whole unified by recurring themes and evidencing a carefully planned scheme of tonalities. The form, however complex, is always suited to both poetic and musical requirements. Schubert drew on the works of many different poets for his texts; from Goethe alone he took fifty-nine poems, and he wrote five different solo settings for *Nur wer die Sehnsucht kennt* from the novel *Wilhelm Meister*. Some of the finest of Schubert's Lieder are found in the two cycles on poems by Wilhelm Müller, *Die schöne Müllerin* (1823) and *Winterreise* (1827). The *Schwanengesang* (1828), not intended as a cycle but published as such posthumously, includes six songs on poems by Heinrich Heine. On the whole, Schubert's texts are excellent material for musical treatment, though naturally uneven in literary quality; but his music is able to glorify even commonplace poetry.

Schumann's Lieder

Lieder were written by most of the Romantic composers, but the first important successor of Schubert in this field was Robert Schumann (1810–56). Schubert, though his music is Romantic in its lyrical quality and harmonic color, nevertheless always maintained a certain Classical serenity and poise. With Schumann we are in the full restless tide of Romanticism. His first collection of songs appeared in 1840, all his previously published works having been for piano. Although his melodic lines are warm and expressive, Schumann's Lieder lack the spontaneous charm of Schubert's; the accompaniments, however, are of unusual interest.

It is instructive to compare Schumann's setting of a given text with Schubert's, though, of course, no one song will illuminate all the community and disparity of their approaches. Mignon's song from Goethe's *Wilhelm Meister, Kennst du das Land? (Do you know the country where the lemon trees blossom?;* NAWM/S 71, 72) was set by both composers. Although it is a strophic poem, Schubert departs from the poetic form in the third stanza to emphasize the mystery of the mountain path shrouded in clouds. Schumann's setting is also strophic and of deceptive simplicity. It is less melody-dominated than Schubert's and the piano's commentary—in this song relying mostly on harmonic progression—contributes a great deal to the communication of the poem's inner meaning. Some of the finest of Schumann's Lieder are the love songs; in 1840, the year of his long-delayed marriage to his beloved Clara Wieck, he produced over one hundred Lieder, including the two cycles *Dichter-liebe* and *Frauenliebe und Leben*. In these works the Romantic genius of Schumann appears to perfection.

The principal successor to Schumann was Johannes Brahms (1833–97), for whom the Lied was a congenial medium and whose works in this form (over 260 altogether) come from every period of his life. Brahms declared that his ideal was the folk song, and many of his own songs, as for example the familiar *Wiegenlied*, are exactly in this style.

Brahms's Lieder

Schubert was Brahms's model in song writing, and a considerable proportion of his *Lieder* are, like Schubert's, in a more or less freely treated strophic form. Among them are *Vergebliches Ständchen*, one of the few Brahms songs of a humorous and outrightly cheerful nature. For the most part, however, Brahms's tone is serious. His music is Romantic in harmony and texture, but it has not the soaring, ardent, impulsive character of Schumann's; restraint, a certain classic gravity, an introspective, resigned, elegiac mood are predominant. Within the fundamentally reflective style of Brahms there is room for the expression of passion, expression all the more effective because it avoids excess and is felt to be always under control. Among all German Lieder there are no finer love songs than *Wie bist du meine Königin* and *Meine Liebe ist grün*.

The essential elements of Brahms's *Lieder* are the melody and bass, the tonal plan and form. The accompaniments are rarely pictorial, and there are not many of the instrumental preludes and postludes which are so important in Schumann's songs. Yet the piano parts are marvelously varied in texture, frequently using extended arpeggio figuration and syncopated rhythms. Perhaps the greatest—certainly the most typically Brahmsian—of the Lieder are those concerned with reflections on death, particularly the *Vier ernste Gesänge*, the "four serious songs" (Op. 121, 1896) on Biblical texts, the supreme achievement of Brahms's last years.

Choral Music

In considering the choral music of the nineteenth century, it is necessary to make a distinction between works in which the chorus is used as a part of a larger apparatus and those in which the choral writing is intended to be a principal focus of interest. To the former category belong the numerous and extensive choruses in operas, choral movements in symphonies, and some of the big choral-orchestral works of Berlioz and Liszt. It is significant that the two composers of the Romantic period who best understood how to write idiomatically for chorus—Mendelssohn and Brahms—were precisely the two who were most knowledgeable about the music of the past and most strongly resistant to the extreme tendencies of Romanticism. The chorus is less suited to express typically Romantic sentiments than the symphony orchestra, and indeed, many nineteenth-century composers treated the chorus primarily as a division of the orchestra, to supply picturesque touches and supplementary colors.

Nineteenth-century choral music is of three main classes: (1) part songs (that is, songs in homophonic style for a small vocal ensemble, with the melody in the topmost voice) or other short choral pieces, usually on secular words, to be sung either *a cappella* or with accompaniment of piano or organ; (2) music on liturgical texts or intended for use in church services; (3) works for chorus (often with one or more solo vocalists) and orchestra, on texts of dramatic or narrative-dramatic character, but intended for concert rather than stage performance.

Part songs and cantatas

The composition of part songs, which had begun before the end of the eighteenth century, received impetus in the Romantic period from the rise of national sentiment and the awakening of interest in folk song. The example of the popular festivals in France of the Revolutionary period, along with the multiplication of singing societies and the institution of music festivals in France and Germany during the first half of the nineteenth century were a further stimulus to choral composition. Practically every composer in Europe produced part songs and choruses for men's, women's, or mixed voices, accompanied and unaccompanied, on patriotic, sentimental, convivial, and every other imaginable kind of verse. This music served its purpose and has been for the most part forgotten. Of more permanent interest are some of the Romantic cantatas, such as Mendelssohn's *Erste Walpurgisnacht* (1832, revised 1843) and Schumann's *Paradise and the Peri* (1843) and *Scenes from Goethe's "Faust"* (1844–53). The master in this field was Johannes Brahms, whose works include many short, usually unaccompanied choral songs, as well as a number of larger compositions for chorus with orchestra. Among these are some of the most beautiful choral works, not only of the nineteenth century but of all time—the *Rhapsody* for alto solo and men's chorus (1870), the *Schicksalslied* (*Song of Fate,* 1871) and *Nänie* (song of lamentation on verses by Schiller, 1881) for mixed chorus, and *Gesang der Parzen* (*Song of the Parcae, i.e.,* the Fates; 1883), for six-part mixed chorus.

Church music

The nineteenth century was not one of the great ages of church music. Toward the middle of the century an agitation for musical reform—later called the Cecilian movement after St. Cecelia, the patron saint of music—arose within the Roman Catholic Church. The Cecilian movement was in part stimulated by Romantic interest in music of the past, and it worked to some effect for a revival of the supposed *a cappella* style of the sixteenth century and the restoration of Gregorian Chant to its pristine form; but it stimulated little significant new music from the composers who dedicated themselves to these ideals. The best Catholic church music in the early part of the century came from Luigi Cherubini at Paris and Franz Schubert at Vienna. Schubert's Masses in A♭ and E♭ (D. 678, 950)[1] are among the finest settings of this text in the nineteenth century. On the Protestant and Anglican side, the psalms of Mendelssohn and the anthems of Samuel Sebastian Wesley (1810–76) may be mentioned. In Russia, Dimitri Bortniansky (1751–1825), director of the Imperial Chapel at St. Petersburg after 1796, was the first of a long line of composers who in the nineteenth century developed a new style of church music; this derived its inspiration from the modal chants of the Orthodox liturgy, had a free rhythm, and used a wide range of unaccompanied voices in single or double choruses of four to eight or more parts, with effective octave doublings in a rich and solemn texture. The Masses and other sacred music of the Parisian Charles Gounod (1818–93) were highly regarded in their time, but his peculiar blend of piety and mild Romanticism had the misfortune to be so assiduously (though unintentionally) parodied by later composers that it has lost whatever validity it may have possessed. Gounod's most famous Mass, the *St. Cecilia* (1885), has been condemned also on liturgical grounds because of the insertion of words not normally part of the sung text in the last movement.

A dazzling conflagration was set off by the collision of Romantic musical energy with sacred themes in the *Grande Messe des Morts* (*Requiem*) and the *Te Deum* of Hector Berlioz (1803–69). These are magnificent religious works, but they are not music for the church service. Their nature is wholly original and Romantic. They are dramatic symphonies for orchestra and voices which use poetically inspiring texts that happen to be liturgical. The tradition to which they belong is not ecclesiastical but secular and patriotic; their historical forebears are the great musical festivals of the French Revolution. The *Requiem* was first performed in 1837, the Te Deum in 1855. Both works are of vast dimensions—vast not only in length and number of performers, but in grandeur of conception and brilliance of execution. Too much has been said about the orchestra of one hundred and forty players, the four brass choirs, the four tam-tams, ten pairs of cymbals, and sixteen kettledrums that Berlioz requires for the *Tuba mirum* chorus of the *Requiem*—and too little about the superb musical effect he obtains in the comparatively few

Other music on liturgical texts

[1] Schubert's works are best identified by the number assigned to them in *Schubert: Thematic catalogue of all his works in chronological order* by Otto Erich Deutsch and Donald R. Wakeling (London and New York, 1951); corrections and additions by O. E. Deutsch in *ML* XXXIV, 1953, 25–32.

places where all these are sounding. Berlioz's orchestra, like the Emperor Gordianus's twenty-two concubines,[2] is "designed for use rather than ostentation." There are a hundred other strokes of genius in the orchestration of the *Requiem:* one may take for examples the chords for flutes and trombones alternating with men's chorus in the *Hostias,* and the further development of this kind of sonority at the beginning of the Agnus Dei; the stark lines of the English horns, bassoons, and low strings in combination with unison tenor voices in the *Quid sum miser;* or the return of the wonderful long tenor melody of the Sanctus, where the five-measure responsive phrases of soloist and chorus are punctuated by *pianissimo* strokes of the bass drum and cymbals. The *Te Deum* is less replete with striking orchestral experiments than the *Requiem,* but it is in a more mature style, and its final number (*Judex crederis*) is certainly one of the most thrilling movements ever written for chorus and orchestra.

What Berlioz did outside the church Franz Liszt (1811–86) tried to do within it. His Festival Mass for the consecration of the cathedral at Gran (Esztergom), Hungary, in 1855, as well as his Mass for the coronation of the King of Hungary in 1867, are on a scale and in a style corresponding to Liszt's own ideal of Romantic sacred music, which he expressed thus in 1834:

> For want of a better term we may call the new music Humanitarian. It must be devotional, strong, and drastic, uniting on a colossal scale the theatre and the church, at once dramatic and sacred, splendid and simple, ceremonial and serious, fiery and free, stormy and calm, translucent and emotional.[3]

This duality of aim is never quite welded into unity of style in Liszt's church music. He comes closest in some shorter works, such as his setting of Psalm XIII (*How long wilt thou forget me, O Lord?*) for tenor solo, chorus, and orchestra (1855) and—in a different way, with many passages of "experimental" harmony—in the *Via Crucis (Stations of the Cross),* a large work for soloists, chorus, and organ, completed in 1879 but not published or publicly performed during Liszt's lifetime.

Two Italian composers, Gioacchino Rossini (1792–1868) and Giuseppe Verdi (1813–1901), made important contributions to church music in the nineteenth century. Rossini's *Stabat Mater* is a serious and well-made composition, containing some excellent choral writing (especially in the opening and closing numbers) along with arias in operatic style. Verdi's *Requiem* (1874) is an immense work, deeply moving, vividly dramatic, and at the same time

---

[2] E. Gibbon. *The Decline and Fall of the Roman Empire,* Book I. Ch. VII.
[3] Reprinted in Liszt, *Gesammelte Schriften,* Leipzig, 1881, II, 55–57.

thoroughly Catholic in spirit—unlike the *Requiem* of Berlioz, to which Verdi's is musically indebted in many respects.

The most important church composer of the later nineteenth century was Anton Bruckner (1824–96), whose choral and symphonic compositions are now at last beginning to be generally known outside the Germanic countries of Europe. A solitary, simple, profoundly religious soul, thoroughly schooled in counterpoint, organist of the Cathedral at Linz and from 1867 Court Organist at Vienna, Bruckner succeeded as no one before him in uniting the spiritual and technical resources of the nineteenth-century symphony with a reverent and liturgical approach to the sacred texts. The Mass in D minor was composed in 1864, that in F minor (the larger of the two) in 1867. Also in a modernized *stile antico* is the *a cappella* motet *Virga Jesse* (NAWM/S 77). The simple diatonic lines sung by the individual voices are deceiving, however, because the resultant textures, harmonies, and modulations are full of surprises that anticipate twentieth-century choral writing.

The Romantic oratorio is now remembered chiefly through Mendelssohn's *St. Paul* (1836) and *Elijah* (1846) and Liszt's *Legend of St. Elizabeth* (1857–62). Berlioz's *Enfance du Christ* (*The Childhood of Christ;* 1854) is charming and picturesque rather than churchly.

Brahms's *German Requiem* (1868), for soprano and baritone solos, chorus, and orchestra, has for its text not the liturgical words of the Latin Requiem Mass but Biblical passages of meditation and solace in German, admirably chosen by the composer himself. Brahms's music, like that of Schütz and Bach, is inspired by a deep concern with man's mortal lot and his hope of Heaven; but in the *German Requiem* these solemn thoughts are expressed with the peculiar intensity of Romantic feeling and clothed with the opulent colors of nineteenth-century harmony, regulated always by spacious formal architecture and guided by an unerring judgment for choral and orchestral effect.

XVII

The Nineteenth Century:
Instrumental Music

Music for Piano

The piano of the nineteenth century was a quite different instrument from the one for which Mozart had written. Reshaped, enlarged, and mechanically improved, it had been made capable of producing a full, firm tone at any dynamic level, of responding in every way to demands for both expressiveness and overwhelming virtuosity. The piano was the supreme Romantic instrument.

The early Romantic composers

The piano works of Carl Maria von Weber (1786–1826) include four sonatas, two concertos, and the better known *Concertstück* in F minor for piano and orchestra (1821), as well as many short pieces of which the *Invitation to the Dance* (1819) has been played by several generations of pianists. Weber's style is rhythmic, picturesque, full of contrast, and technically brilliant, but without profound content.

A distinctive school of pianists and composers flourished in Bohemia in the early nineteenth century. Jan Ladislav Dussek was known throughout Europe especially for his sonatas, some passages of which contain notable examples of early Romantic harmony. J. V. Tomášek and his pupil Jan Hugo Voříšek (1791–1825) wrote short lyrical piano pieces with titles such as *eclogue, rhapsodie,* or *impromptu.* Voříšek is also remarkable for his Piano Sonata Op. 20 and a fine Symphony in D major (1821); he lived in Vienna after 1813 and his music exerted considerable influence on Schubert.

In addition to innumerable marches, waltzes, and other dances, Schubert wrote fourteen short pieces for the piano to which his publishers gave the modest titles of *impromptu* or *moment musical*. His most important larger works for the piano are the eleven completed sonatas and a Fantasia in C major (1822) on a theme adapted from his song *Der Wanderer*. Important also are his many duets, particularly the *Grand Duo* (D. 812), the Fantasia in F minor (D. 940), and the Rondo in A major (D. 951). He wrote no concertos. The six *Moments musicaux* (D. 789) and the eight Impromptus (D. 899, 935) are for the piano what his Lieder are for the voice. Abounding in Schubertian melodies and harmonies, perfect in form and detail, each one quite distinctive in mood, these works became the model for every subsequent Romantic composer of brief, unpretentious, intimate piano pieces. The *Wanderer Fantasie* (D. 760) stands almost alone among Schubert's piano compositions in making considerable demands on the player's technique. It is in four movements like a sonata; the movements are linked together and the whole is centered around the Adagio and Variations, the theme of which also appears, variously transformed, in the other three movements of the work.

In his sonatas Schubert seems to have been influenced more by Haydn and Mozart than by Beethoven. Their external form never departs from the standard Classical patterns, but their atmosphere is more lyric than dramatic; instead of concentrated thematic development or surging Romantic emotions Schubert gives us expansive melodies and shimmering harmonic progressions. Some of the slow movements might well have been published as impromptus or *moments musicaux*—for example, those of the sonatas in B major Op. 147 (D. 575) and A major Op. 120 (D. 664). The last of his sonatas (in B♭ major; D. 960) is undoubtedly his greatest work for the piano. A long singing melody begins the first movement; hovering modulations are featured in the subsidiary theme section and the development; the sonorities are perfectly spaced throughout. The slow movement is in C♯ minor (the enharmonic lowered mediant key), with a middle section in A major; the delicately varied ostinato rhythm of this movement is typical of Schubert, as are also the expressive harmonic suspensions and the unexpected shifts between major and minor in the coda.

Felix Mendelssohn-Bartholdy (1809–47) was himself a virtuoso pianist. His piano music requires a fluent technique, but in general the style is elegant and sensitive, not given to violence or excess bravura. Mendelssohn's musical ancestors are Mozart and Domenico Scarlatti. His finest large work for piano is the *Variations sérieuses* in D minor, Op. 54 (1841). A certain elfin lightness and clarity in scherzo-like movements, a quality unique in Mendelssohn's music,

Franz
Schubert

Felix
Mendelssohn-
Bartholdy

is evident in the familiar *Andante and Rondo Capriccioso*, Op. 14. The most popular piano works of Mendelssohn were the 48 short pieces issued at intervals in six books under the collective title *Songs without Words*—a title typical of the Romantic period. Here, along with a few tunes that now seem faded and sentimental, are many distinguished examples of the Romantic short piano piece and of Mendelssohn at his best: the *Gondola Song* in A minor (Op. 62, No. 5), the delightful little Presto in C major known as the *Spinning Song* (Op. 67, No. 4), the *Duetto* in A♭ (Op. 38, No. 6), or the tenderly melancholy B-minor melody of Op. 67, No. 5. Mendelssohn's harmony has few of the delightful surprises that one encounters in Schubert, nor do his melodies, rhythms, and forms introduce many unexpected features. His music, like his life, flowed serenely and harmoniously; it is essentially Classical in outline, imbued with Romantic color and sentiment but never more than lightly touched with Romantic pathos or passion.

Mendelssohn's three preludes and fugues and six sonatas for organ are among the few distinguished contributions of the Romantic period to the literature of that instrument. Notable features in the sonatas are the frequent fugal writing and the use of Lutheran chorale melodies.

Robert Schumann

All of Robert Schumann's published compositions (Opp. 1–23) up to 1840 were for piano, and these include most of his important works for that instrument with the exception of his one concerto (1845). This concerto, the Fantasia in C major, Op. 17 (1836), and the set of variations entitled *Symphonic Études* (1834) are his chief longer works for piano, though he also wrote several other sets of variations and three sonatas. The remainder of his production consists of short character pieces, which he often grouped in loosely organized cycles with names such as *Papillons, Carnaval, Fantasiestücke, Kinderscenen, Kreisleriana, Novelletten, Nachtstücke, Faschingsschwank aus Wien*. Attractive little pieces for children are gathered in the *Album for the Young* (published 1848).

The titles of both the collections and the separate pieces suggest that Schumann intended his music not only to be considered as patterns of sound but in some manner to suggest extra-musical poetic fancies or the taking over into music of literary forms. This is a typical Romantic attitude and its significance is not at all diminished by the fact that Schumann, on his own admission, usually wrote the music before he thought of the title. His music embodies more fully than that of any other composer the depths, and the contradictions and tensions, of the Romantic spirit; it is by turns ardent and dreamy, vehement and visionary, whimsical and learned. Schumann's piano music, while far from easy to play, never aims to impress the listener by a sheer bravura. It is thoroughly idiomatic for the instrument, and the virtuoso element is always subordinate to the poetic idea.

The compositions of Frédéric Chopin (1810–49) are almost exclusively for piano. The principal works are: two concertos and a few other large pieces for piano with orchestra, three sonatas, 27 études, four scherzos, four ballades, 24 preludes, three impromptus, 19 nocturnes, numerous waltzes, mazurkas, and polonaises, a *Barcarolle* in F♯, a *Berceuse* in D♭, and a *Fantasia* in F minor.

Frédéric Chopin

Although Chopin lived in Paris from 1831, he never ceased to love his native Poland or to be afflicted by her misfortunes. His mazurkas, impregnated with the rhythms, harmonies, forms, and melodic traits of Polish popular music (though usually without any direct quotation from Polish folk themes) are among the earliest and best examples of Romantic music inspired by national idioms. In particular, the "Lydian" raised fourth, characteristic of Polish folk music, is present from the earliest works of Chopin. To some extent his polonaises may also be regarded a national manifestation. Inasmuch as this particular Polish form had come into western European music as early as the time of Bach, it had inevitably, in the course of more than a century, acquired a conventional character; but some of Chopin's polonaises blaze anew with the knightly and heroic spirit of his native land—particularly those in A♭ (Op. 53) and F♯ minor (Op. 44).

Last page of the autograph manuscript of the Chopin Barcarolle.

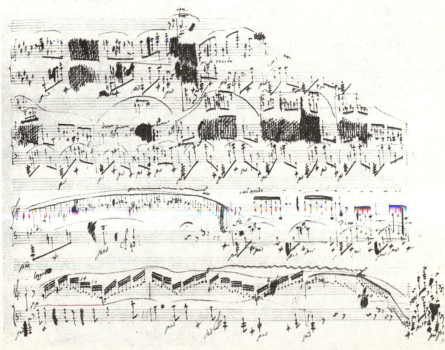

Most of Chopin's pieces have an introspective character and, within clearly defined formal outlines, contrive to suggest the quality of improvisation. Although he was a concert pianist, he was not an overwhelming, theatrical performer, and it is probable that other virtuosos have projected the heroic side of his music more emphatically than he himself was able to do, and perhaps more emphatically than he would have desired. All his works, however, demand of the player not only a flawless touch and technique but also an imaginative use of the pedals and a discreet application of *tempo rubato,* which Chopin himself described as a slight pushing or holding back within the phrase of the right-hand part while the left-hand accompaniment continues in strict time.

The nocturnes, impromptus, and preludes are Chopin's most intimate works. Both the name and the general idea of the nocturnes were taken from the Irish pianist and composer John Field (1782–1837). Although Field anticipated some of Chopin's mannerisms, he could not match the rich harmonic imagination that so powerfully supports Chopin's lyrical lines (compare Field's Nocturne No. 8 [NAWM/S 65] with the E♭ Nocturne, Op. 9, No. 2 of Chopin [NAWM/S 66]).

The preludes were composed at a time when Chopin was immersed even more deeply than usual in the music of Bach. Like the preludes in *The Well-Tempered Clavier,* these brief, sharply defined mood pictures go through all the major and minor keys, though the succession Chopin uses is by the circle of fifths (C major—A minor—G major—E minor, and so on). Chopin's music was an important source of later developments in harmony; his extraordinary genius for chromatic harmonies and modulations is evident in many of the preludes.

The fundamental traits of Chopin's style are displayed on a larger canvas in the ballades and scherzos. He was apparently the first composer to use the name *ballade* for an instrumental piece; his works in this form (especially Op. 23 in G minor and Op. 52 in F minor) capture the Romantic charm and fire of the narrative ballads of the great nineteenth-century Polish poet, Adam Mickiewicz, combining these qualities with that indefinable spontaneity, those constantly fresh turns in the harmony and form, that are a distinctive mark of Chopin. The principal scherzos are those in B minor (Op. 20) and C♯ minor (Op. 39). Chopin's scherzos have no trace of this form's original connotation of playfulness; these are wholly serious, virile, and passionate works, organized—as are the ballades—in compact forms that grow naturally out of the musical ideas. On an equally large scale but even more varied in content is the great *Fantasia* in F minor (Op. 49), a worthy companion to the like-named works of Schubert and Schumann.

Chopin's études (twelve in each of Opp. 10 and 25 and three

without opus numbers) are landmarks in the history of piano music. An *étude* is, as the name indicates, a study primarily for the development of technique. Chopin's études are transcendent studies in technique and at the same time intensely concentrated tone poems; they are all the more definite in meaning because the composer carefully avoided any clues that could serve as a pretext for attaching descriptive labels.

The life of Franz Liszt (1811–86) was one of the most brilliant of the Romantic era. His piano style was based on Chopin's, from whom he took the latter's repertoire of pianistic effects—adding new ones of his own—as well as his lyrical melodic qualities, his manner of *rubato* playing, and his harmonic innovations, which Liszt further extended. Some of the late works, in particular, contain strikingly advanced chords and modulations.

Franz Liszt

A considerable proportion of Liszt's piano music consists of transcriptions or arrangements—fantasies on operatic airs, transcriptions of Schubert's songs and Berlioz's and Beethoven's symphonies, Bach's organ fugues, excerpts from Wagner's music dramas, and the like. The usefulness these pieces had in their day should not be underrated. Related to these are the compositions which make

Joseph Dannhauser's painting of Liszt and his friends exemplifies the Romantic attitude towards the artist. Kneeling beside Liszt at the piano is Madame D'Agoult; seated behind him are George Sand and Alexandre Dumas, père. Standing in the background are Victor Hugo, Paganini and the host, Rossini. Notice the bust of Beethoven which dominates the scene.

free use of national tunes; chief among these are the nineteen *Hungarian Rhapsodies*—though by "Hungarian" Liszt and other nineteenth-century composers did not understand genuine Hungarian folk tunes, but rather the gypsy music which until recent times was thought to represent authentic folk elements.

For piano and orchestra Liszt wrote two concertos (Eb major, A major), a *Hungarian Fantasia* (expanded from the 14th Rhapsody), and the *Totentanz* (*Dance of Death*), a paraphrase on the plainsong *Dies irae*. His piano studies include the formidable 12 *Études d'exécution transcendante* published in their final version with titles in 1852; six studies transcribed from Paganini's caprices for solo violin, published in final shape in 1851 (among them *La Campanella*); and three *Études de concert* (1848).

The variety of Liszt's poetic imagination is displayed in many of his short separately published piano pieces and in several collections of tone pictures, of which the chief are *Années de pèlerinage* (three books; the first two composed before 1850 and the third in 1867–77), *Consolations* (1850), and *Harmonies poétiques et religieuses* (1852). These collections contain some of his best compositions, which negate the all too common impression of Liszt as concerned only with bravura effects. An important large work is the Sonata in B minor (1853), in which four themes are worked out in one extended movement, although with subdivisions analogous to the sections of a Classical sonata movement. The themes are transformed and combined in an apparently free rhapsodic order which, however, is perfectly suited to the thematic material and the intentions of the composer; the entire sonata, one of the outstanding piano compositions of the nineteenth century, is a successful adaptation of the principle of cyclic development characteristic of the symphonic poem.

In some of his late works Liszt experimented with harmonies that surprisingly anticipate late nineteenth-century developments in the direction of impressionism.[1] He was one of the first composers to make much use of augmented triads; the first theme of the *Faust Symphony*, for example, is derived entirely from this chord, which is also prominent in the B-minor Sonata and many other of Liszt's works. Example XVII-1 shows the ending of a short piano piece *Nuages gris* (*Gray Clouds*) composed in 1881 (the entire piece is in NAWM/S 67). The descending succession of augmented triads over the Bb–A ostinato in the bass has already been heard in the first part of the piece; now, in a broken texture it accompanies a slowly rising melody in octaves, covering fourteen steps of the chromatic

---

[1] For details see Bengt Johnsson, "Modernities in Liszt's Works," *Svensk Tidskrift för Musikforskning* 46 (1964) 83–118; late piano pieces are published in *Franz Liszt, the Final Years*, G. Schirmer Library, Vol. 1845.

EXAMPLE XVII–1   Ending, *Nuages gris*, Franz Liszt

scale in a rhythm which is an augmentation of that of the initial theme of the work. The tonality of G major is affirmed at the final cadence chiefly by the slowing down of the movement and the full-measure pause before the appoggiatura-like F♯–G in the melody. The lowest notes A–E in the penultimate chord may be said to "represent" the dominant; their effect in the closing chord is the coloristic one of an unresolved dissonance. In fact, in that chord these two notes are almost lost to hearing as distinct entities—first, because they remain unchanged from the previous measure, so that our attention is diverted to the melodic line resolving upward to the tonic; and second, because the diminuendo and the slow upward arpeggiation of the two final chords tend still further to veil, both acoustically and psychologically, the sound of these lower notes.

Johannes Brahms

The piano style of Brahms has neither the elegance of Chopin nor the brilliance and romantic rhetoric of Liszt. Its models are Schumann and Beethoven. Technically it is characterized by fullness of sonority, broken-chord figuration, frequent doubling of the melodic line in octaves, thirds, or sixths, and considerable use of cross-rhythms. It has the harmonic richness and emotional warmth of Romanticism, but the language is governed by basic conceptions that are essentially more Classical than Romantic. Brahms's works for the piano include two concertos, three sonatas, several sets of variations, and some 35 shorter pieces with titles such as ballade, rhapsody, capriccio, or intermezzo. Chief among the larger works are the concertos, the Sonata in F minor (1853), the *Variations and Fugue on a Theme of Handel* (1861), and the difficult étude-like *Variations on a Theme of Paganini* (1863). Brahms, in short, is the great conservative of the Romantic era. A direct link with the past is found in his eleven chorale preludes for the organ, written during the last years of his life—the finest compositions in this form since Bach.

Other composers

Among the piano music of Brahms's contemporaries must be noted Mussorgsky's *Pictures at an Exhibition* (1874), Balakirev's *Islamey* and *Sonata in B♭ minor,* and three works by the Belgian César Franck (1822–90), namely a *Prelude, Chorale, and Fugue* (1884), a *Prelude, Aria, and Finale* (1887) and the *Symphonic Variations* for piano and orchestra (1885). Franck studied in Paris and made his home there after 1844; like Brahms, he sought to incorporate the achievements of Romanticism in an essentially Classical framework, with a harmonic idiom influenced to some extent by the chromaticism of Liszt and Wagner. His compositions for organ include several sets of short pieces and three so-called *Chorales* (1890), which actually are richly developed fantasias on original themes.

Chamber Music

Schubert's chamber music

The style of chamber music was not congenial to many Romantic composers; on the one hand it lacked the intimate personal expressiveness of the solo piano piece or the Lied and on the other the glowing colors and overpowering sound of orchestral music. It is therefore not surprising that the best works in this medium in the nineteenth century came from those composers who had the closest affinity with the Classical tradition—Schubert and Brahms preeminently, Mendelssohn and Schumann to a lesser degree.

Schubert's first quartets, modeled after Mozart and Haydn, were written primarily for the pleasure of his circle of friends. The Quartet in E♭ (D. 87, 1813) is a work of Classical purity; in the E-major Quartet of 1816 (D. 353) Schubert's own style, combining warmth of sonority with clarity of line, is established. The most popular work from his earlier period is the *Forellen* or *Trout Quintet* for piano and strings (1819), so called because between the scherzo and the finale there is an additional movement (*andantino*) consisting of variations on his own song *Die Forelle*. Schubert's mature period in chamber music begins in 1820 with an Allegro in C minor (D. 703), intended as the first movement of a string quartet that was never completed. Three important works followed—the quartets in A minor (D. 804, 1824), D minor (D. 810, 1824–26), and G major (D. 887, 1826).

The A-minor Quartet is an outpouring of sadness, elegiac in the first movement and minuet, full of Schubertian melody and beautiful modulations. The Quartet in D minor is more grimly serious and more consistent in feeling. It is built around the second movement, a set of variations on Schubert's own song *Death and the*

Maiden. Within the sustained unity of the quartet as a whole each movement offers variety of thematic ideas, developed with great skill and contrapuntal ingenuity. The G-major Quartet is on a larger scale than either of the other two; its form is as perfect as that of the D-minor Quartet, but it is even more abundant in musical content. It opens with one of the most remarkable instances of Schubert's device of alternating major and minor forms of the triad, reversed and differently colored at the recapitulation (see Example XVII–2), and the whole is full of harmonic boldness.

Undoubtedly Schubert's masterpiece of chamber music is the String Quintet in C major (D. 956), written during the last year of his life. As in Boccherini's quintets, the added instrument is a second violoncello, and Schubert obtains from this combination some of the most exquisite sound effects in all Romantic music. The Quintet has the profound lyricism, the unobtrusive contrapuntal mastery, the long melodic lines (for example, the first fifteen measures of the

EXAMPLE XVII–2   First movement, Quartet in G major (D. 887), Franz Schubert

Adagio), and the wealth of harmonic invention that characterize the late piano sonatas. The finale, like that of the Quartet in A minor, is in a more popular style, relaxing the tension built up by the first three movements.

Mendelssohn's chamber music

Mendelssohn's published chamber music comprises six string quartets, two quintets, an octet, a sextet for piano and strings, and two piano trios, as well as a sonata for piano and violin, two sonatas for piano and violoncello, and a few lesser works and arrangements. Very few of these pieces are as interesting as his symphonic productions. Mendelssohn writes smoothly, if diffusely, in the Classical forms; but his feeling for descriptive tone color finds relatively little scope in the medium of chamber music. An exception, however, is

Mendelssohn's autograph of the second page of the scherzo from the String Octet Op. 20. (Library of Congress)

the early Octet (1825), particularly the scherzo, which is a fine example of Mendelssohn's inimitable style in this type of movement. The two piano trios (D minor, Op. 49 and C minor, Op. 66) are among the most popular of Mendelssohn's chamber works and well display both the excellences and the weaknesses of the composer in this field—tuneful, attractive themes, vigorous idiomatic writing, but occasional looseness of form and repetitiousness in the development of the material.

Schumann's string quartets reveal the influence of Beethoven not only in general aim but also in some details: developments are frequently contrapuntal, and the *Andante quasi variazoni* of the second quartet, a movement in A♭ major, is reminiscent of the Adagio of Beethoven's Op. 127. Schumann's third quartet, in A major, is a deeply Romantic work, with a particularly beautiful slow movement. The Piano Quartet, Op. 47, is less successful than the Piano Quintet, Op. 44, which is a splendid example of the mature style of this most Romantic of all the Romantic composers.

Schumann's chamber music

Brahms is the giant among composers of chamber music in the nineteenth century, the true successor of Beethoven in this field as in that of the symphony. Not only is the quantity of his production impressive—24 works in all—but it includes at least a half-dozen masterpieces of the first rank. His first published chamber work was a Piano Trio in B (Op. 8, 1854), which he issued again in a thoroughly rewritten version in 1891. Two string sextets—Op. 18 in B♭ (1862) and Op. 36 in G (1867)—make an interesting contrast. The B♭ Sextet is a hearty work of ample dimensions, combining humor and Classical poise; the slow movement is a set of variations in D minor and the finale is a Haydn-like rondo form with a big coda. The Sextet in G has a more serene mood, with widely spaced transparent sonorities in the opening Allegro and a quietly vivacious finale; the second movement, labeled Scherzo, is a semiserious moderate Allegro in 2/4 time in G minor—a type of movement that Brahms also employed, with modifications, in his symphonies—and the Adagio, in the form of a theme in E minor with five variations, may be considered an epitome of some of Brahms's most individual harmonic and rhythmic procedures.

Brahms's chamber music

Two piano quartets, Op. 25 in G minor and Op. 26 in A major, date from the late 1850s. The first is one of the most original and most popular of Brahms's chamber works, with its mysterious, romantic second movement (called Intermezzo) and lively Hungarian rondo finale on a theme of three-measure phrases. These two quartets contrast with each other much as do the first two string sextets. The third Piano Quartet (Op. 60, C minor) was given its final form in 1874; it is a grandly tragic composition, with the concentration of material characteristic of Brahms's later works.

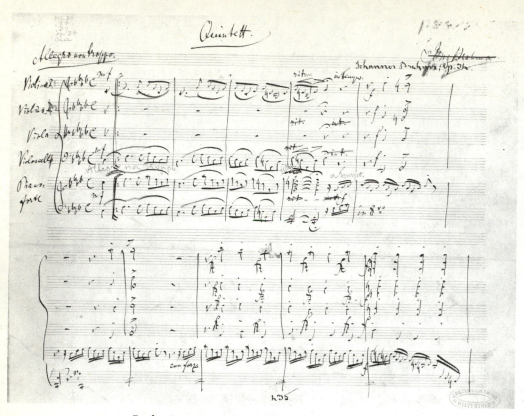

Brahms's autograph of the first page of the Piano Quintet Op. 34. (Library of Congress)

The "climax of Brahms's first maturity" is the great Piano Quintet in F minor, Op. 34A. Brahms originally composed this in 1862 as a string quintet with two violoncellos; he later arranged it effectively for two pianos, and then, still unsatisfied, combined the string and pianoforte sonorities for the final version (1864). The first movement is a powerful, closely knit Allegro in sonata form, with a second theme group in C♯ minor, a well-integrated development section, and a coda that begins *pianissimo* with a quiet contrapuntal improvisation on the principal theme above a tonic pedal and then rises to end in the stormy mood of the beginning. The slow movement (A♭) is a beautiful Schubertian three-part *Andante un poco adagio* with a middle section in E major. Both the spirit and the themes of the Scherzo (NAWM/S 70) recall those of the corresponding movement in Beethoven's Fifth Symphony. The rousing Finale is preceded by a broad *poco sostenuto* which is like a sketch for the even broader introduction to the last movement of Brahms's First Symphony.

The Trio Op. 40 for piano, violin, and Waldhorn (the natural horn, without valves) is another successful example of the union of a sonorous, expressive Romantic idiom with forms well grounded in Classical practice. The Trio was composed in 1865; it brings to an end what may be called, by analogy with Beethoven, Brahms's second period. After a pause of eight years came the two string quartets in C minor and A minor, Op. 51; then in 1876 (the year of the First Symphony) the String Quartet in B♭, Op. 67. The eloquent *Grave ed appassionato* of the String Quintet in F major, Op. 88 (1882) is combined with the scherzo in a single movement—a device used by César Franck seven years later in his Symphony.

Outstanding among Brahms's later works are the two piano trios Op. 87 in C major (1882) and Op. 101 in C minor (1886), the String Quintet in G major Op. 111 (1890), and the profound Clarinet Quintet in B minor, Op. 115 (1891). All these have something of the same character as Beethoven's late quartets and piano sonatas: the musical ideas are pure, with a purity that is sometimes thoughtlessly called abstract because it is so concretely musical as to be undefinable in any other medium; textures are smoothly contrapuntal; and forms are handled with a freedom that is the result of logic in movement and conciseness in statement.

A special category of Brahms's chamber music consists of sonatas for a single instrument with piano. There are three such sonatas for violin, two for violoncello, and two for clarinet. All except the first violoncello sonata (1862–65) are late works. The first two violin sonatas (G major, Op. 78, 1878; A major, Op. 100, 1886) contain some of Brahms's most lyric and melodious writing; the third (D minor, Op. 108, 1887) is on a more symphonic scale. The clarinet sonatas Op. 120 (F minor and E♭ major), written in 1894, may be grouped with the piano pieces Opp. 116–119, the Clarinet Quintet, the *Four Serious Songs,* and the organ chorale preludes as among the ripest achievements of the composer whose music demonstrated, more clearly than that of any other nineteenth-century composer, that the flower of Romanticism had deep roots in the Classical tradition.

The founder of modern French chamber music was César Franck; his chief works in this field are a Piano Quintet in F minor (1879), a String Quartet in D major (1889), and the well-known Violin Sonata in A major (1886). All these works employ cyclical themes— that is, themes that recur identically or transformed in two or more different movements.

Cesar Franck's chamber music

Music for Orchestra

The two main tendencies in orchestral music of the first half of the nineteenth century may be roughly designated as conservative (represented by Schubert, Mendelssohn, and Schumann) and radical (represented by Berlioz and Liszt). Generally speaking, the conservative composers were those whose musical imagination worked naturally within the formal structures, themes, harmonies, and orchestrations that had been inherited from the Classical period; if these composers gave descriptive titles to their works they did so incidentally and without emphasis. The radicals were those whose creative imagination was less apt to be stimulated by a strictly musical idea than by a literary or some other extra-musical impulse; and precisely because the impulse came from outside the conventional domain of music, the resulting composition was likely to be unconventional in some respects—in form, for instance—although in other respects it might adhere to Classical usage.

Schubert's symphonies

The most important symphonies of Schubert—the *Unfinished* in B minor of 1822 and the great C-major Symphony of 1828— exemplify the harmonic originality which has already been noted as a feature of his style. A new element, related to Schubert's harmonic sensitivity, is his feeling for orchestral tone color. The *Unfinished* may be called the first truly Romantic symphony. In the C-major Symphony Schubert has expanded his material almost to the breaking point; the "heavenly length" which Schumann admired in this work would be less heavenly if it were not for the beauty of Schubert's melodies.

Mendelssohn's symphonies

With Mendelssohn we enter the realm of Romantic landscapes. His two most important symphonies carry geographical subtitles— the *Italian* (1833) and the *Scotch* (1842). In these works Mendelssohn records some typical German Romantic impressions of the south and the north. In both works Mendelssohn's writing is, as always, impeccable, and he has skilfully fitted his melodious themes into the regular Classical forms. The four divisions of the *Scotch Symphony* are linked by the use of portions of the slow introduction to the first movement as introductions to the following two movements, as well as by subtle similarities of melodic outline among many of the themes throughout the work.

Mendelssohn's peculiar genius for musical landscapes is especially evident in his overtures *The Hebrides* (or *Fingal's Cave;* 1832) and *Calm Sea and Prosperous Voyage* (1828–32), while *Melusine* (1833) is a symphonic incarnation of the early Romantic spirit of the fairy tale. Among his incidental music for plays, the overture for Victor Hugo's *Ruy Blas* (1839) is excelled only by the incomparable *Midsummer Night's Dream* overture, written at the age of seventeen —a work that set the standard for all subsequent concert overtures of the Romantic period. Seventeen years later he wrote additional incidental music for a production of Shakespeare's play. The Scherzo (NAWM/S 68), to be played after the first act, is a brilliant example of self-renewing perpetual motion and of a heavy orchestra tamed to tiptoe like a chamber ensemble. All this music, while it may be called programmatic (in the same sense as Beethoven's *Pastoral Symphony*), and while it is certainly Romantic in the quality of its imagination and its treatment of the orchestra, is nonetheless Classical in outline (most of the overtures, for example, are in sonata form), and Classical moreover in that it avoids extremes of feeling and never allows the extra-musical inspiration to disturb the musical balance. Essentially the qualities of Mendelssohn's symphonies and overtures are not different from those of his Violin Concerto (1844), one of his masterpieces and one of the greatest of all works in this genre.

Schumann's first two published symphonies were composed in

Sketch of introduction and beginning of first movement of Schumann's First Symphony.

Schumann's symphonies

1841. The first, in B♭ major, is called the *Spring Symphony*. It was the composer's intention at one time to prefix a descriptive title to each movement—the first, for example, was to have been called "Spring's Awakening" and the Finale, "Spring's Farewell."

The Symphony in D minor was composed in 1841 but published only ten years later after extensive revisions; in consequence this symphony, though second in order of composition, was fourth in order of publication, and is so numbered. Schumann once thought of calling the revised version a symphonic fantasia. We do not know whether he had any program in mind, but the fantasia element is present in the irregular form of the first Allegro and in the fact that each movement contains themes derived from motives announced in the slow introduction to the first.

Schumann's Second Symphony (that is, the second to be published), in C major (1846), is the most severely Classical of his symphonies, but except for the Adagio its musical interest is less than that of the two earlier works. The Third or *Rhenish Symphony* in E♭ (1850) is vaguely programmatic and contains some characteristically vigorous themes, though on the whole it is less spontaneous than the First Symphony.

Apart from the symphonies and the piano concerto, Schumann's chief orchestral work is the overture from his incidental music to Byron's *Manfred* (1849). His orchestral style in general has been criticized as pianistic, and by and large he failed to achieve the long lines and the organic unity of Classical symphonic style. The beauty of Schumann's symphonies lies in their details and in the ardor of their Romantic spirit.

Berlioz's symphonies

The diffused scenic effects in the music of Mendelssohn and Schumann seem pale when compared with the feverish and circumstantial drama which is commonly supposed to constitute the story of Berlioz's *Symphonie fantastique* (1830). Because his imagination always tended to run in parallel literary and musical channels, Berlioz once subtitled this work "Episode in the Life of an Artist" and provided a program for it which was in effect a piece of romantic autobiography. In later years he conceded that if necessary, when the symphony was performed by itself in concert, the program need not be given out to the audience, since he hoped that the music would "of itself, and irrespective of any dramatic aim, offer an interest in the musical sense alone."

There is nothing revolutionary about the main formal outlines of the *Symphonie fantastique*. The principal novelty is the recurrence of the opening theme of the first Allegro (the *idée fixe*, the obsessive image of the hero's beloved, according to the program) in all the other movements. A salient aspect of Berlioz's originality is his orchestration; he had no textbooks and few models to help him, but his vivid aural imagination and his inventiveness in the realm of orchestral sonorities are evident in practically every measure of the *Symphonie fantastique*. To mention but one example: in the coda of the Adagio there is a passage for solo English horn and four kettledrums intended to suggest "distant thunder"—a marvelously poetic and evocative twenty-two measures, and no more an example of realism (if by that word is meant mere literal imitation of natural noises) than the bird songs in the slow movement of the *Pastoral Symphony*.

Berlioz's second symphony, *Harold in Italy* (1834), is a set of four scenes suggested by his reading of Lord Byron's *Childe Harold*. As with the *Symphonie fantastique*, the movements are in a conventional Classical order. There is a connecting recurrent theme, given

Berlioz's concern with the most minute details of orchestration is demonstrated on the title page of the autograph manuscript of the Symphonie fantastique. (Collection André Meyer)

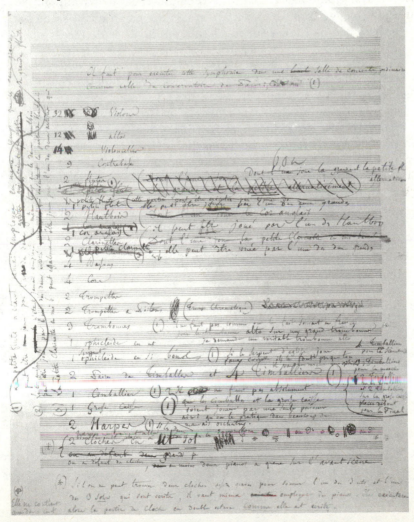

chiefly to a solo viola, and this instrument is featured throughout somewhat in the manner of a concerto; but the soloist is less dominant than in an ordinary concerto and in fact much of the symphony is scored so lightly as to suggest chamber music.

Berlioz's other symphonic works

Five years after *Harold in Italy* Berlioz produced his "dramatic symphony," *Romeo and Juliet,* for orchestra, soloists, and chorus, in seven movements. In adding voices to the symphonic orchestra, he was following the example of Beethoven; but in this work the voices enter in the first movement (after an instrumental introduction) and are used in three of the remaining ones as well, so that the entire symphony, although the scheme of the Classical order of movements can still be traced, begins to approach the form of the "dramatic legend" which the composer later perfected in his *Damnation of Faust* (1864). Nonetheless, *Romeo and Juliet* is essentially a symphonic work, and may be understood as an extension of the idea of the *Symphonie fantastique:* the program is explicitly announced in the Prologue, and words help to create the mood of the scene in the garden and of Juliet's funeral. Only the finale is decidedly operatic in character.

Among Berlioz's other symphonic works are several overtures (including the familiar *Roman Carnival,* 1844) and the *Funeral and Triumphal Symphony,* composed for a national ceremony in 1840. But his importance for the history of nineteenth-century instrumental music rests chiefly on his first three symphonies, especially the *Symphonie fantastique.* Even though his conception of the relation between music and program was widely misunderstood, these works made Berlioz the first leader of the radical wing of the Romantic movement, and all subsequent composers of program music— including Strauss and Debussy—were indebted to him. His orchestration initiated a new era: by example and precept he was the founder of modern orchestral conducting; he enriched Romantic music with new resources of harmony, color, expression, and form; and his use of a recurrent theme in different movements (as in the *Symphonie fantastique* and *Harold in Italy*) was an important impulse toward the development of the cyclical symphonic forms of the later nineteenth century.

Liszt's symphonic poems

The foremost composer of program music after Berlioz was Franz Liszt, twelve of whose symphonic poems were written between 1848 and 1858; a thirteenth was written in 1881–82. The name *symphonic poem* is significant: these works are symphonic but Liszt did not call them symphonies, presumably because they are relatively short and are not divided into separate movements in a conventional order. Instead, each is a continuous form with various sections more or less contrasting in character and tempo, and a few themes which are developed, repeated, varied, or transformed in accordance with the particular design of each work. *Les Préludes,* the only one of them that is still much played, is well designed, melodious, and effectively scored; but its idiom, like that of some of Listz's other compositions, seems rhetorical, in a bad sense. It impresses most listeners nowadays as being filled with extravagant theatrical gestures, and as lavishing excessive emotion on ideas that do not seem sufficiently important for such displays of feeling. But *Les Préludes* did not so impress its contemporaries; the Romantics did not care much for that prudent economy of the emotions which is conventional in our time, and Liszt's symphonic poems were widely influential in the nineteenth century.

Liszt's two symphonies are as programmatic as his symphonic poems. His masterpiece, the *Faust Symphony* (1854), was dedicated to Berlioz; it consists of three movements entitled respectively *Faust, Gretchen,* and *Mephistopheles,* with a finale (added later) which is a setting, for tenor soloist and chorus of men's voices, of the *chorus mysticus* which closes Goethe's drama. The first three movements correspond to the Classical plan: introduction and Allegro (in sonata form), Andante (three-part form), and Scherzo (three-part form, followed by a long additional development and coda).

It is a far journey from Liszt's seething Romanticism to the Olympian realm of Brahms's four symphonies. The Classical reaction of the second half of the nineteenth century is epitomized in these works. The First Symphony, in C minor, was finished after many years of work in 1876, when the composer was forty-three; the second, in D major, appeared in 1877, while the last two (F major and E minor) were composed in 1883 and 1885 respectively. Brahms's other works for orchestra include the masterly *Variations on a Theme of Haydn* (Op. 56A, 1873); the two piano concertos already mentioned; the Violin Concerto in D major (1878), which ranks with Beethoven's concerto in the literature of this instrument; and the Double Concerto in A minor for violin and violoncello, Op. 102 (1887).

The Brahms symphonies are Classical in several respects: they are laid out in the customary design of four movements, each of which has a form recognizably close to the Classical pattern; they make use of the Classical techniques of counterpoint and motivic development; and they have no specified program—that is, they are absolute music in the same sense as Brahms's chamber works. At the same time, the symphonies are Romantic in their harmonic idiom, in their full, multicolored orchestral sound, and in other general features of their musical language. Yet they are no mere synthesis of Classicism and Romanticism; Brahms's style is consistent and individual, and various elements may be distinguished within it—among them a profound Schubertian, lyrical breadth of

Brahms's symphonies

melodic line, a ballad-like quality of Romantic strangeness, and a fundamental respect for tradition as against the individualistic approach to music of Berlioz and Liszt. For Brahms, inspiration was not enough: ideas had to be soberly thought out and brought to a finally perfect form. He was concerned to avoid the pitfalls of Romanticism—false rhetoric, empty display of virtuosity, and above all what must have seemed to him (as it did to many of his contemporaries) the formlessness of music that apparently was held together only by an unguided stream of associated ideas in the mind of the composer. Brahms's control of his inspirations and the consequent thought-out character of all his compositions account for the feeling of repose that sets his music apart from the more impulsive, impetuous Romantic compositions of 1830 to 1860. Brahms, whether he realized it or not, was responding to a general tendency of his time. The childlike freshness and the youthful ardor of Romanticism were alike spent by the middle of the century, and the wild oats period was over; a return to discipline, a revival of order and form, is apparent in the late works of Schumann and Berlioz, and even in those of Liszt and Wagner. Brahms's symphonies illustrate the trend even more clearly.

The First is the most Romantic. In key and general construction it takes its departure from Beethoven's Fifth; it is the only one of Brahms's symphonies which uses the Romantic formula of struggle (in minor) leading to triumph (in major).

The Second Symphony, in contrast to the First, has a peaceful, pastoral character, though not without serious undertones. Its third movement (like the corresponding movement in the First and Third Symphonies) has the lyrical rhythmic grace of an intermezzo rather than the intensity of the Beethoven scherzo; it is of the type that Brahms had created in the G major Sextet of 1867.

The Third Symphony has been called Brahms's *Eroica*. Its opening measures afford a particularly good illustration of one characteristic trait in his harmonic usage, the cross-relation of the minor and major forms of the tonic triad (see Example XVII–3); the rising F–Ab–F motive of the bass is conspicuous again in the last movement

EXAMPLE XVII–3 Outline of First Theme of Third Symphony, Brahms

of this symphony, which begins in F minor and does not settle in F major until the coda.

The Andante of the Fourth Symphony is one of Brahms's balladesque movements, the mood being suggested by the modal (Phrygian) tinge of the introduction and principal theme. The finale of this work is written in a form unusual in a symphony: a passacaglia or chaconne, consisting of 32 variations and a brief coda on an ostinato eight-measure theme.

César Franck's only symphony (1888) shows some trace of Liszt in its chromatic harmonies and cyclical treatment of themes. But it is nonprogrammatic, and its stylistic elements are welded into a highly individual work, the influence of which was acknowledged by the following generation of composers in France.

Franck's symphony

Bruckner's symphonies may perhaps best be understood as the expression of a profoundly religious spirit, revealed not so much by quotation of religious themes from the Masses and the *Te Deum* as by the prevailing serious, weighty mood of the symphonies as a whole; this is especially evident in the combination of mystic ecstasy and tonal splendor of the chorale-like themes that are the climaxes of his finales (and sometimes also of the first movements). They typically begin, like Beethoven's Ninth, with a vague agitation in the strings—a *nebula*, as one writer happily describes it,[2] out of which the theme gradually condenses and then builds up in a crescendo. These first themes have what may be called an elemental character; they begin with conspicuous emphasis on the notes of the tonic triad, extended usually over an octave or more, and set the tonality of the movement in most positive terms; the favorite rhythmic formula is the pattern ($\frac{4}{4}$) ♩ ♩ ♩♩♩. The finales open in the same way and usually with the same kind of theme, which may even so closely resemble that of the first movement as to suggest cyclical recurrence. The first-theme complex is followed by the "song-theme group" (as Bruckner called it), and this in turn by a broad, closing section in which a chorale-like theme may be introduced. The movement continues with what would be called, in orthodox sonata form, development and recapitulation (sometimes merged), and a final section which often presents a grand apotheosis of the preceding themes. Both the first and last movements, though in allegro tempo, give the effect of moving slowly because of their long-breathed harmonic rhythm and spacious structure. The slow movements, usually cast in a broad sonata-like form with extended coda, are devout and solemn; those of the last three symphonies are especially impressive. The Scherzos reveal a different aspect of Bruckner's musical personality. Their energy is like Beethoven's,

Bruckner's symphonies

2 Robert Simpson, *The Essence of Bruckner*, London 1967, 20.

but the melodies and rhythms of their trios reflect the spirit of Austrian popular songs and rustic dances. Recent changes in taste, Classical clarity and easy Romantic appeal. Recent changes in taste, however, are bringing the Bruckner symphonies into deserved favor with a growing international public.

Other composers

The only remaining symphonists to be mentioned are the Bohemian Antonín Dvořák (1841–1904) and the Russian Peter Ilyich Tchaikovsky (1840–93). They have a place in this chapter because, although their music is in some respects an outgrowth of nationalist ideas, their symphonies are essentially in the line of the German Romantic tradition. Of Dvořák's nine symphonies, the best is usually said to be No. 7[3] in D minor (1885), a work copious in thematic ideas and in a prevailingly tragic mood relieved only by the G-major trio of the scherzo. More relaxed in mood, with fresh folklike melodies and rhythms and many fine touches of orchestration, are the Symphonies No. 6 in D major and No. 8 in G major (1889). Most familiar is No. 9 (*From the New World*), which Dvořák wrote in 1893 during his first sojourn in the United States. This symphony, according to the composer, uses themes suggested by American Indian melodies and especially by Negro spirituals which Dvořák had heard sung at New York by Harry T. Burleigh. Among Dvořák's other orchestral music is a fine concerto for violoncello; his string quartets are among the most attractive chamber music works of the late nineteenth century.

Tchaikovsky's principal orchestral works include his last three symphonies (No. 4, F minor, 1877; No. 5, E minor, 1888; No. 6 [*Pathétique*], B minor, 1893). The immense popularity of these symphonies is due to their tunefulness, brilliant orchestration, and somewhat theatrical exhibition of Romantic emotion. The Fourth is probably the best example of a union of programmatic features with firm symphonic construction along fairly conventional lines. Other well-known orchestral works of Tchaikovsky are the symphonic poem *Francesca da Rimini* (1877), the overture-fantasia *Romeo and Juliet* (1867, 1880), the First Piano Concerto in B♭ minor (1875), and the Violin Concerto (1878). Less pretentious, and thoroughly charming, are the ballets, particularly *Swan Lake* (1876), *The Sleeping Beauty* (1890), and *The Nutcracker* (1892).

---

[3] References are to the now standard chronological numbering of Dvořák's symphonies. Relation between old and new numbering:

New	Old
5	3
6	1
7	2
8	4
9	5

XVIII

The Nineteenth Century:
Opera and Music Drama

France

The combined influences of Gluck, the Revolution, and the Napoleonic Empire made Paris the operatic capital of Europe during the first half of the nineteenth century, and favored the rise there of a certain type of serious opera that is exemplified in *La Vestale* (1807). The composer of this work was the Empress Josephine's favorite musician, Gasparo Spontini (1774–1851), an Italian who had come to Paris in 1803 and who had a second career after 1820 as Court Music Director at Berlin. In *La Vestale* Spontini united the heroic, statuesque character of the late Gluck operas with the heightened dramatic tension of the then popular rescue plot, and clothed the whole in a grand display of solo, choral, and orchestral magnificence.

With the rise of a numerous and increasingly powerful middle class after 1820, a new kind of opera came into being, designed to appeal to the relatively uncultured audiences who thronged the theatres in search of excitement and entertainment. The leader of this school of *grand opera*, as it came to be known, was Giacomo Meyerbeer (1791–1864), whose two operas *Robert le diable* (*Robert the Devil*; 1831) and *Les Huguenots* (1836) definitely established this style. Other composers of grand opera around 1830 were Auber (*La Muette de Portici, The Mute Girl of Portici* [also known as *Masaniello*]; 1828), Rossini (*Guillaume Tell*; 1829), and Jacques

Grand opera

381

Fromental Halévy (1799–1862), whose masterpiece, *La Juive* (*The Jewess;* 1835), deservedly outlasted Meyerbeer's works. *La Juive* and *Guillaume Tell* are the best of the grand operas of this period because they best incorporate the essential grandeur of the form—grandeur of structure and of style—in music that effectively serves more than the externals of the action.

Opéra comique

Side by side with the grand opera in France, the *opéra comique* pursued its course during the Romantic period. As in the eighteenth century, the technical difference between these two was that the *opéra comique* used spoken dialogue instead of recitative. Apart from this, the principal differences were those of size and subject matter. The *opéra comique* was less pretentious than grand opera, required fewer singers and players, and was written in a much simpler musical idiom; its plots as a rule presented straightforward comedy or semiserious drama instead of the huge historical pageantry of grand opera. Two kinds of *opéra comique* may be distinguished in the early part of the nineteenth century, namely the romantic and the comic; it is not possible to maintain this distinction too rigidly, however, since many works possessed characteristics of both types. Predominantly romantic in plot, melodious, graceful, and sentimental in music, was the extremely popular *La Dame blanche* (*The White Lady*) by François Adrien Boieldieu (1775–1834), which was first performed at Paris in 1825. Similarly romantic *opéras comiques* were *Zampa* (1831) and *Le Pré aux clercs* (*The Field of Honor,* 1832) by Ferdinand Herold (1791–1833).

A more mordant Parisian style is evident in the work of Daniel François Esprit Auber (1782–1871), who in *Fra Diavolo* (1830) and his many other comic operas mingled romantic and humorous elements in tuneful music of considerable melodic originality. A new genre, the *opéra bouffe* (not to be confused with the eighteenth-century Italian *opera buffa,* despite the identity of name), which emphasized the smart, witty, and satirical elements of comic opera, appeared at Paris in the 1860s. Its founder was Jacques Offenbach (1819–80), whose *Orphée aux enfers* (*Orpheus in the Underworld;* 1858) and *La Belle Hélène* (1864) may be taken as typical. Offenbach's work influenced developments in comic opera elsewhere: the operettas of Gilbert and Sullivan in England (*The Mikado,* 1885) and those of a Viennese school whose best-known representative is Johann Strauss the Younger (*Die Fledermaus* [*The Bat*]; 1874).

Lyric opera

The Romantic type of *opéra comique* developed toward a form for which the designation "lyric opera" seems appropriate. Lyric opera lies somewhere between light *opéra comique* and grand opera. Like the *opéra comique,* its main appeal is through melody; its subject matter is romantic drama or fantasy, and its general scale is larger than that of the *opéra comique,* although still not so huge as that of the typical grand opera.

The most famous lyric opera was Gounod's *Faust,* which was

first given in 1859 as an *opéra comique* (that is, with spoken dialogue) and later arranged by the composer in its now familiar form with recitatives. Gounod wisely restricted himself to Part One of Goethe's drama, dealing chiefly with the tragic love affair of Faust and Gretchen, for which his musical gifts were adequate. The result is a work of just proportions, in an elegant lyric style, with attractive melodies, sufficiently expressive but without Romantic excess.

A landmark in the history of French opera was Georges Bizet's (1838–75) *Carmen*, first performed at Paris in 1875. Like the original version of *Faust, Carmen* was classified as an *opéra comique* because it contained spoken dialogue (later set in recitative by another composer); but the fact that this stark, realistic drama could ever be called "*comique*" is simply an indication that by this time the distinction between opera and *opéra comique* had become a mere technicality. The music of *Carmen* has an extraordinary rhythmic and melodic vitality; it is spare in texture and beautifully orchestrated, obtaining the utmost dramatic effect always with the most economical means.

Hector Berlioz contributed more than any other composer to the glory of French Romantic opera. His *Damnation of Faust* may be included here, although strictly speaking it is not an opera and is not intended for stage performance. The title page calls it a "dramatic legend." This is one of the most diversified and most inspired of Berlioz's works; the familiar orchestral excerpts (including the Hungarian *Rákóczy* March) give but a partial impression of its riches.

Hector Berlioz

The opera *Benvenuto Cellini* (1838) is another example of this composer's new way with traditional forms. Its general plan is, like that of *The Damnation of Faust,* a chain of broadly conceived episodes rather than a plot minutely developed. The score is notable for the vigor and variety of its music and for the treatment of the crowd scenes, which foreshadow those of Wagner's *Meistersinger*. The crown of Berlioz's dramatic works is the great five-act opera *Les Troyens,* composed in 1856–58. *Les Troyens* is unlike any other opera. The text, by Berlioz himself, is based on the second and fourth books of Vergil's *Aeneid;* as with *Cellini* and *Faust,* only the essential stages of the action are presented, in a series of mighty scene-complexes. The drama preserves the antique, suprapersonal, epic quality of Vergil's poem, and the music speaks in the same accents. Not a note is there for mere effect; the style is severe, almost ascetic by comparison with some of Berlioz's earlier works. At the same time every passion, every scene and incident, are brought to life intensely and on a heroic scale. *Les Troyens* is the Romantic consummation of the French opera tradition in the line of descent from Rameau and Gluck.

Italy

The history of Italian opera in the nineteenth century may be understood as the orderly evolution of an established tradition, healthily grounded in the life of the nation. Italy was less susceptible than northern countries to the seductions of the Romantic movement, and her composers were therefore less quickly tempted to try new and radical experiments. Romantic elements permeated Italian opera only gradually, and never to the same degree as in Germany and France. Moreover, opera was the only important Italian musical outlet in this period, so that the genius of the nation was largely concentrated on this one form; and such a situation also tended to encourage a conservative attitude.

Gioacchino Rossini

Gioacchino Rossini, the principal Italian composer of the early nineteenth century, was endowed with a pronounced gift for melody and a flair for stage effect that brought him quick success. Between the ages of eighteen and thirty he produced in Italy 32 operas and two oratorios, in addition to a dozen cantatas, two symphonies, and a few other instrumental works. Comic opera was congenial to Rossini, and many of his works in this genre sound as fresh today as when they were first written. His masterpiece, *Il Barbiere di Siviglia* (*The Barber of Seville,* Rome; 1816), ranks with Mozart's *Figaro* and Verdi's *Falstaff* among the supreme examples of Italian comic opera.

Rossini's style combines an inexhaustible flow of melody with pungent rhythms, clear phraseology, well-shaped and sometimes quite unconventional structure of the musical period, a spare texture, clean and discriminative orchestration, and a harmonic scheme which, though not complex, is by no means always unoriginal. The combination of beautiful melody, wit, and comic delineation is displayed in the justly famous *Una voce poco fa* (*A voice a short while ago;* NAWM/S 73) from *The Barber of Seville.* He is a master of comic delineation, both of characters and situations—comic, not merely witty, for at his best, he is able, like Mozart and Verdi, to make us feel the hint of pathos that underlies all high comedy. Rossini's ensembles, that type of scene so characteristic of comic opera, are managed with sparkle and gusto.

After the success of his masterpiece of grand opera, *Guillaume Tell,* at Paris in 1829, Rossini wrote no more operas; but his figure dominated Italian opera through the first half of the century. As far as the bulk of his work is concerned, Rossini represented the deep-rooted Italian conviction that an opera is in essence the highest manifestation of an intensely cultivated art of song, and that its primary purpose is to delight and move the hearer by music that is melodious, unsentimental, spontaneous, and, in every sense of the word, popular. This national ideal was important in the Romantic period as a counterbalance to the different conceptions of opera that were held in France and Germany.

One of the most prolific Italian composers of the second quarter of the century was Gaetano Donizetti (1797–1848), who in addition to some 70 operas composed about 100 songs, several symphonies, oratorios, cantatas, chamber music, and church music. Donizetti had some of Rossini's instinct for the theatre and his talent for melody, and in *Don Pasquale* (1843) he created a work that can well endure comparison with *Il Barbiere*. On the whole his comic operas stand the test of time better than his serious ones. The rough, primitive, impulsive character of his music is well adapted to the representation of crude, melodramatic situations, but his works —composed for the most part very rapidly and with a view to immediate success—are all too often marred by monotony of harmony, rhythm, and orchestration; yet much of *Lucia di Lammermoor* (1835) and *Linda di Chamonix* (1842), and some scenes in his other operas, must be excepted from this criticism.

Vincenzo Bellini (1801–35), by comparison, may be called the aristocrat of his period. Of his ten operas (all serious) the chief

Gaetano Donizetti

A scene from the second act of Don Pasquale *by Donizetti as it was depicted in the contemporary press of 1843 when it was first performed at the* Théâtre Italien *in Paris.*

Vincenzo Bellini

are *La Sonnambula* (*The Sleepwalker;* 1831), *Norma* (1831), and *I Puritani e i Cavalieri* (*The Puritans and the Cavaliers;* Paris, 1835). The style is one of utmost lyric refinement; the harmony is sensitive, and the intensely expressive melodies have a breadth, a flexibility of form, a certain elegance of curve, and an elegiac tinge of feeling that we associate with the nocturnes of Chopin. These qualities are exemplified in the cavatina *Casta Diva* (NAWM/S 74) from the first act of *Norma*.

Guiseppe Verdi

The career of Giuseppe Verdi practically constitutes the history of Italian music for the next fifty years after Donizetti. Except for the *Requiem* and a few other settings of sacred texts, a few songs, and a string quartet, all Verdi's published works were written for the stage. The first of his 26 operas was produced in 1839, the last in 1893. At no point did Verdi break with the past or experiment radically with new theories; his evolution was toward refinement of aim and technique, and in the end he brought Italian opera to a point of perfection never since surpassed.

The only basic Romantic issue that much affected Italian music was nationalism, and in this respect Verdi was uncompromising. He believed wholeheartedly that each nation should cultivate the kind of music that was native to it; he maintained a resolute independence in his own musical style and deplored the influence of foreign (especially German) ideas in the work of his younger compatriots. Many of his early operas contain choruses that were thinly disguised inflammatory appeals to the patriotism of his countrymen struggling for national unity and against foreign domination during the stirring years of the *Risorgimento;* and Verdi's popularity was further increased when his name became a patriotic symbol and rallying-cry: *"Viva Verdi!"* to Italian patriots stood for *"Viva Vittorio Emanuele Rè D'Italia!"*—Long live Victor Emanuel, King of Italy.

A more profoundly national trait in Verdi was his unswerving adherence to an ideal of opera as human drama—in contrast to the emphasis on romanticized Nature and mythological symbolism in Germany—to be conveyed primarily by means of simple, direct, vocal solo melody—in contrast to the orchestral and choral luxuriance of French grand opera.

Verdi's creative life may be divided into three periods, the first culminating with *Il Trovatore* and *La Traviata* (1853), the second with *Aïda* (1871), and the last comprising only *Otello* (1887) and *Falstaff* (1893). With the exception of *Falstaff* and one unsuccessful early work, all Verdi's operas are serious. His main requirements of a libretto were strong emotional situations, contrasts, and speed of action; plausibility was no object. Consequently most of the plots are violent blood-and-thunder melodramas, full of improbable characters and ridiculous coincidences, but with plenty of opportunity for the exciting, lusty, ferocious melodies and rhythms which are especially characteristic of Verdi's early style. Many features of the early period are summed up in *Il Trovatore* (*The Troubadour;* 1853), one of Verdi's most popular works. The resources that he now commanded are plainly in evidence in the first scene of Part IV of this work (NAWM/S 76). Here the gradation and progression from near-speech to higher levels of lyricism displays the versatility of Verdi's talent and at the same time his dramatic instinct to avoid the discrete "numbers," formal transitions, and ritornellos that one still finds in Bellini and Rossini.

A change in Verdi's style begins to be evident in *Luisa Miller* (1849); here and increasingly henceforward, personages are depicted with finer psychological distinction, and emotion in the music becomes less raw than in the early operas. Characterization, dramatic unity, and melodic invention unite in the masterpiece *Rigoletto* (1851). *La Traviata* (*The Lost One;* 1853) is in a more intimate vein than heretofore, and is remarkable for the appearance of a new kind of melody, a flexible, expressive, semideclamatory arioso which Verdi developed still further in *Otello*.

Two experiments in grand opera were *Les Vêpres siciliennes* (*The Sicilian Vespers;* 1855) and *Don Carlos* (1867), both of which were first performed at Paris. *Don Carlos* is the more successful of the two; its revised version (1884) contains powerful dramatic scenes, as well as some interesting orchestral and harmonic effects typical of Verdi's late style. *Un Ballo in Maschera* (*A Masked Ball;* 1859) and *La Forza del Destino* (*The Power of Destiny,* 1862; revised, 1869) make use of a device fairly common in the nineteenth century and one with which Verdi had experimented already in *Rigoletto* and elsewhere: the recurrence of one or more distinctive themes or motives at crucial points that serve to produce both dramatic and musical unity. All the advances of the second period are gathered up in *Aïda* (1871), which unites the heroic quality of grand opera with sound dramatic structure, vivid character delineation, pathos, and a wealth of melodic, harmonic, and orchestral color.

Sixteen years elapsed before Verdi came before the public with *Otello,* produced at Milan in 1887. The libretto sets forth a powerful human drama which the music penetrates, sustains, and glorifies at every turn. The harmonic language and the orchestration are fresh and vital, yet transparent, never usurping the expressive function of melody or obscuring the voices. A summary idea of these features, as well as of the evolution of Verdi's style in general, can be obtained by comparing the beautiful love duet at the end of the first act of *Otello* with some duets from his earlier operas: *Nabucco* (Act III, *Donna, chi sei?*), *Rigoletto* (end of Act II, *Piangi, fanciulla*), and *Aïda* (end of Act IV, *O terra addio*).

Otello was the consummation of Italian tragic opera, *Falstaff*

Backstage at the Paris Opera, 1894: Verdi and the baritone Victor Maurel who created the role of Iago in Otello. *(Courtesy Opera News)*

(1893) of comic opera. In both, the timeless essence of Italian opera, of the long tradition extending from Monteverdi through Steffani, Scarlatti. Hasse, Mozart, and Rossini, was fulfilled and at the same time enriched with new elements derived from Romanticism—but Romanticism purified by Verdi's clear intellect and sensitive discrimination. As *Otello* transfigured dramatic lyrical melody, so *Falstaff* transfigured that characteristic element of *opera buffa,* the ensemble. Carried along over a nimble, fine-spun, endlessly varied orchestral background, the comedy speeds to its climaxes in the great finales of the second and third acts. At times Verdi seems to be satirizing the entire Romantic century, himself included. The last scene culminates in a fugue to the words "tutto nel mondo è burla"—"all the world's a joke, all men are born fools."

Summary

In all Verdi's operas, from *Nabucco* to *Falstaff,* one trait is constant: a combination of primitive, earthy, elemental emotional force with directness, clarity, and—beneath all its refinement of detail—fundamental simplicity of utterance. Verdi is essentially more Classical than Romantic in spirit; his Classicism is attained not by triumphing over Romanticism, as Brahms did, but rather by almost ignoring it. His relation to the Romantic movement might be suggested by the contrast between his attitude and that of the northern Romantics toward Nature. The depiction of the natural background in Verdi's operas is concise, suggestive, almost formalized, like the landscapes in Renaissance Italian paintings—the storm music in *Rigoletto* and *Otello,* for example, or the exotic atmosphere in *Aïda.* His attitude toward Nature is completely unsentimental. All his interest is in humanity; Nature is there to be used, not worshiped. Verdi is the only eminent composer in history who was also a successful farmer.

German Romantic Opera

One of the distinguishing marks of the nineteenth century, as we have seen, was the strong mutual influence between music and literature. The composite art form of opera is well adapted to display the effects of such influences; and since Germany was the country in which Romanticism flourished most intensely, some of the most far-reaching developments and ramifications of the whole movement are exhibited in German opera.

The definitive work that established German Romantic opera, however, was Carl Maria von Weber's *Der Freischütz*, first performed at Berlin in 1821. There is no intelligible brief English equivalent for the title. The story revolves about a situation common in folklore and immortalized in Goethe's *Faust:* a man has sold his soul to the devil in return for earthly favors—in this instance, for some magic bullets which will enable him to win a contest of marksmanship and with it the hand of the lady he loves. As usual, the devil is cheated; the hero is redeemed by his lady's pure love from the consequences of his bargain, and all ends well. The sombre forest background is depicted idyllically by the melody for horns at the beginning of the overture and diabolically in the eerie midnight "Wolf's Glen" scene of the casting of the magic bullets (finale of Act II). Rustic choruses, marches, dances, and airs mingle in the score with full-bodied arias in Italian style. The quintessence of mysterious Romantic suggestion through orchestration and harmony is in the twelve measures at the end of the Adagio introduction to the overture; likewise, it is the orchestration and the strange harmonic scheme (contrast of F♯ minor and C minor) that chiefly contribute to the musical effectiveness of the Wolf's Glen scene, a model of Romantic depiction of supernatural horror. The overture to *Der Freischütz* is not, like so many opera overtures of the early nineteenth century, a simple medley of tunes; rather, like the overtures of Beethoven, it is a complete symphonic first movement in sonata form with a slow introduction.

Weber

The immense popular success of *Der Freischütz*—a success based on its appeal to national sentiment as well as on the beauty of the music—was not repeated either by Weber's later works or by those of his immediate followers. Most of Schubert's operas and singspiels —a half dozen of each, and several others uncompleted—never reached the stage during his lifetime, and have remained without influence, though they contain a great deal of excellent music.

German opera for twenty years after Weber was carried on by a number of estimable second-class composers, chief of whom were Heinrich Marschner (1795–1861) and Albert Lortzing (1801–51). Marschner specialized in Romantic singspiels of a semipopular sort;

Other German opera composers

his most important work, *Hans Heiling* (1833), derives from Weber and at the same time looks forward to Wagner in both its plot and its musical style. Lortzing's *Zar und Zimmermann* (*Czar and Carpenter;* 1837) is a good example of the comic genre in which he excelled.

Richard Wagner: The Music Drama

Richard Wagner

The outstanding composer of German opera, and one of the crucial figures in the history of nineteenth-century music, was Richard Wagner (1813–83). Wagner's significance is threefold: he brought German Romantic opera to its consummation, in much the same way that Verdi brought Italian opera; he created a new form, the *music drama;* and the harmonic idiom of his late works carried to the limit the Romantic tendencies toward dissolution of Classical tonality, becoming the starting point for developments that continued far into the twentieth century. In addition, Wagner's writings had considerable influence on nineteenth-century thought, not only about music, but also about literature, drama, and even political and moral issues.

For Wagner, the function of music was to serve the ends of dramatic expression; his only important compositions are those for the theatre. His first triumph came with *Rienzi,* a five-act grand opera performed at Dresden in 1842. In the following year, also at Dresden, appeared *Der fliegende Holländer* (*The Flying Dutchman*), a Romantic opera in the Weber tradition. In this opera the lines of development that Wagner was to follow in his later works are established. The libretto—written, like those of all his operas, by the composer himself—is based on a legend; the action takes place against a background of the stormy sea, and the drama is resolved with the redemption of the hero through the unselfish love of the heroine Senta. Wagner's music is most vivid in the depiction of the storm and of the contrasted ideas of curse and salvation, which are clearly set forth in the central number of the opera, Senta's ballad. The themes of the ballad are also those of the overture, and they recur elsewhere throughout the opera, although this technique was not so thoroughly and systematically applied as it was in Wagner's later works.

Tannhäuser (Dresden; 1845) is a brilliant adaptation of the substance of the German Romantic libretto to the framework of grand opera. *Lohengrin,* first performed under Liszt's direction at Weimar in 1850, is the last important German Romantic opera and at the same time embodies several changes prophetic of the music dramas of Wagner's next period. Its orchestration is at once fuller and more subdued than that of *Tannhäuser;* the music flows more con-

tinuously, with less marked traces of division into separate numbers; the well-written choruses are combined with solo singing and
orchestral background into long, unified musical scenes. Greater use
is made of the new style of declamatory, arioso melody. The technique of recurring themes is further developed and refined; tonality
becomes important in dramatic as well as musical organization. The
style on the whole is diatonic, with modulations usually toward the
mediant keys.

As a result of the political troubles of 1848–49, Wagner emigrated
to Switzerland, and this country became his home for the next ten
years. Here he found leisure to formulate his theories about opera
and to publish them in a series of essays, the most important of
which is *Opera and Drama* (1851). At the same time he was writing
the poems of a cycle of four dramas with the collective title *Der
Ring des Nibelungen* (*The Ring of the Nibelung*). The music of the
first two—*Das Rheingold* (*The Rhine Gold*) and *Die Walküre*
(*The Valkyrie*)—and part of the third, *Siegfried,* was finished by
1857; the entire cycle was completed with *Götterdämmerung* (*The
Twilight of the Gods*) in 1874, and the first complete performance
took place two years later in a theatre especially built according to
Wagner's specifications at Bayreuth. In the meantime he had composed *Tristan und Isolde* (1857–59) and *Die Meistersinger von
Nürnberg* (*The Mastersingers of Nuremberg,* 1862–67). His last
work was *Parsifal* (1882).

Wagner's conception of music drama may be illustrated through
Tristan und Isolde. The story comes from a medieval romance of
Celtic origin. (This is perhaps less typical of Wagner than the exploitation of Norse mythology in the *Ring,* but it allies him with
the mainstream of Romantic art.) The ruling ideal of Wagner's form
is the absolute oneness of drama and music; the two are organically
connected expressions of a single dramatic idea—unlike conventional
opera, in which song predominates and the libretto is mainly a
framework for the music. The action of the drama is considered to
have an inner and an outer aspect; the former is the province of
instrumental music, that is, of the orchestra, while the sung words
make clear the particular events or situations that are the outer
manifestations of the action. Consequently, the orchestral web is
the primary factor in the music and the vocal lines are part of the
polyphonic texture, not arias with accompaniment. The music is
continuous throughout each act, not formally divided into recitatives, arias, and other set numbers; in this respect Wagner carried to
its logical end a steadily growing tendency in the opera of the first
half of the nineteenth century. Even so, the continuity is not completely unbroken; broad scene divisions remain, and within the
scenes a distinction is still evident between recitative-like passages
with orchestral punctuation and others of arioso melody with con-

tinuous orchestra. Moreover, the unfolding of the drama is occasionally interrupted, or adorned, with interwoven scenes of decidedly operatic character that are not always strictly necessary to the plot.

Within the general continuity of the action and music Wagner uses two principal means for achieving articulation and formal

The leitmotif coherence. The first is the leitmotif. A leitmotif is a musical theme or motive associated with a particular person, thing, or idea in the drama. The association is established by sounding the leitmotif (usually in the orchestra) at the first appearance or mention of the object of reference. and by its repetition at each subsequent appearance or mention. Often its significance may be recognized from the words to which it is set the first time it is given to a voice. (Example XVIII–1 shows the leitmotifs in the order of their appearance in

EXAMPLE XVIII–1 Leitmotifs from *Tristan und Isolde*, Richard Wagner

the last section of Act I, scene 5, the entrance of the sailors [NAWM/S 75].The text that is sung at its most characteristic appearance is given along with the motif.) Thus the leitmotif is a sort of musical label—but it is more than that: it accumulates significance as it recurs in new contexts; it may serve to recall the thought of its object in situations where the object itself is not present; it may be varied, developed, or transformed in accord with the development of the plot; similarity of motifs may suggest an underlying connection between the objects to which they refer; motifs may be contrapuntally combined; and, finally, repetition of motifs is an effective means of musical unity, as is repetition of themes in a symphony.

Wagner's use of the leitmotif principle differs from that of such composers as Verdi and Weber. First, Wagner's motifs themselves are for the most part short, concentrated, and (in intention, at least) so designed as to characterize their object at various levels of meaning. Another difference, of course, is that Wagner's leitmotifs are the essential musical substance of the work; they are used not as an exceptional device, but constantly, in intimate alliance with every step of the action.

A system of leitmotifs, however ingeniously applied, cannot of itself produce musical coherence. To this end, Wagner wrote his acts in sections or "periods," each of which is organized in some **Formal** recognizable musical pattern, most often *AAB* (*Bar* form) or *ABA* **structure** (three-part, or *Bogen* [arch] form). This structural framework,

A contemporary production of Tristan und Isolde (*Act I*) *at the Metropolitan Opera House. (Photograph courtesy Louis Mélançon)*

Isolde's costume for the original production of Tristan und Isolde *at Munich in 1865.*

it must be said, is revealed only by analysis. The forms are not intended to be obvious to the listeners, and their essential outlines are modified by transitions, introductions, codas, varied repetitions, and many other devices. Periods are grouped and related so as to form a coherent pattern within each act, and each act in turn is a structural unit in the shape of the work as a whole. This formidable complex of forms within forms was perhaps not entirely a matter of deliberate planning on the composer's part, but it exists nevertheless.

Wagner's influence

Tristan und Isolde is in many respects the quintessence of Wagner's mature style. Few works in the history of Western music have so potently affected succeeding generations of composers. The system of leitmotifs is happily subordinated to a flow of inspiration, an unbroken intensity of emotion, that effectively conceals and transcends mere technique. In contrast to the tragic gloom and the extremely chromatic idiom of *Tristan* are the sunny human comedy and predominantly diatonic harmony of *Die Meistersinger.* Here Wagner succeeded most fully in fusing his conceptions of the music drama with the forms of Romantic opera, and in combining a healthy nationalism with universal appeal. *Parsifal,* by comparison, is somewhat less assured, less unified both in content and musical form, but abounds (as does *Die Meistersinger*) in beautiful choral scenes and instrumental numbers.

In the harmony of his later works, especially in *Tristan* and the prelude to the third act of *Parsifal,* Wagner carried out an evolution in his personal style that had been stimulated by his acquaintance in the 1850s with the chromatic idiom of Liszt's symphonic poems. The complex chromatic alterations of chords in *Tristan,* together with the constant shifting of key, the telescoping of resolutions, and the blurring of progressions by means of suspensions and other non-harmonic tones, produces a novel, ambiguous kind of tonality, one that can be explained only with difficulty in terms of the harmonic system of Bach, Handel, Mozart, and Beethoven. This departure from the Classical conception of tonality in such a conspicuous and musically successful work can today be viewed historically as the first step on the way toward new systems of harmony which marked the development of music after 1890. The evolution of harmonic style from Bruckner, Mahler, Reger, and Strauss to Schoenberg, Berg, Webern, and later twelve-tone composers can be traced back to the *Tristan* idiom.

Wagner's work affected all subsequent opera. His peculiar use of mythology and symbolism could not be successfully imitated; but his ideal of opera as a drama of significant content, with words, stage setting, visible action, and music all working in closest harmony toward the central dramatic purpose—the ideal, in short, of the *Gesamtkunstwerk* or universal art-work—was profoundly influential. Almost equally influential was his technical method of continuous music (endless melody) which minimized divisions within an act and assigned to the symphonic orchestra the function of maintaining continuity with the help of leitmotifs while the voices sang in free, arioso lines rather than in the balanced phrases of the traditional aria. As a master of orchestral color Wagner had few equals, and in this respect also his example was fruitful. Above all, his music impressed itself on the late nineteenth century because it was able, by its sheer overwhelming power, to suggest or arouse or create in its hearers that all-embracing state of ecstasy, at once sensuous and mystical, toward which all Romantic art had been striving.

XIX

The End of an Era

Post-Romanticism

Hugo Wolf

One of the foremost German composers of the late nineteenth century was Hugo Wolf (1860–1903). He is chiefly important for his 250 Lieder, which ably continue the German Romantic tradition of the solo song with piano accompaniment. Most of Wolf's songs were produced in short periods of intense creative activity during the ten years from 1887 to 1897.

Wolf's literary taste in the selection of texts was more uncompromising than that of earlier German song writers. He concentrated on one poet at a time, and placed the name of the poet above that of the composer in the titles of his collections—indicating a new conception of the relation between words and music in the Lied, derived from Wagner's music dramas, an ideal of a particular kind of equality between poetry and music, and of particular technical means for achieving such equality. Wolf adapted Wagner's methods with discrimination; the fusion of voice and instrument is achieved without sacrificing either to the other.

A good illustration of such balance is his setting of *Kennst du das Land?* (Example XIX–1; cf. NAWM/S 71 and 72), in which chromatic voice leading, appoggiaturas, anticipations, and the wandering tonality are clearly inspired by the idiom of *Tristan*. Wolf's treatment of pictorial images is always restrained but at the same time highly poetic and original; one instance among many is the suggestion of distant bells in the piano part of *St. Nepomuks Vorabend.* It is impossible to convey an adequate idea of the infinite variety of fine psychological and musical details in Wolf's songs. Study of the scores brings continuous discovery of new delights.

The last of the great German post-Romantic symphony com-

EXAMPLE XIX–1   *Kennst du das Land?*, Hugo Wolf

Do you know the mountain and the path that the muletier follows in the clouds?

posers was the Austrian Gustav Mahler (1860–1911). His works, composed for the most part in the summer between busy seasons of conducting, include nine symphonies (a tenth remained uncompleted but has since been reconstructed) and five song-cycles for solo voices with orchestra, of which the chief is *Das Lied von der Erde* (*The Song of the Earth,* composed in 1908).

Gustav Mahler

Mahler's symphonies are typical post-Romantic works: long, formally complex, programmatic in nature, and demanding enormous performing resources. Thus the Second Symphony, first performed in 1895, requires, along with a huge string section, 4 flutes (two interchangeable with piccolos), 4 oboes, 5 clarinets, 3 bassoons and a contrabassoon, 6 horns and 6 trumpets (plus four more of each, with percussion, in a separate group), 4 trombones, tuba, 6 kettle-drums and numerous other percussion instruments, 3 bells, 4 or more harps, and organ, in addition to soprano and alto soloists and a chorus. The Eighth, composed in 1906–07 and popularly known as the *Symphony of a Thousand,* calls for an even larger array of players and singers. But the size of the orchestra is not the whole story. Mahler is one of the most adventurous and most fastidious of composers in his treatment of instrumental combinations, comparable in this respect perhaps only with Berlioz; his natural genius for orchestration was reinforced by his constant activity as a conductor, which gave him opportunity to perfect details of scoring in

Mahler's symphonies

A cancelled page from the autograph orchestral score of the third movement of Mahler's Ninth Symphony, corresponding to the first 11 measures of page III/35 of the score sketch facsimile published by Universal Edition; this section does not appear in the final version. (Private collection, New York)

the light of practical experience. Instances of his felicity in orchestral effects, ranging from the most delicate to the most overwhelmingly gigantic, occur abundantly in all the symphonies (compare, for example, the ending of the third movement of the First Symphony or the beginning of the second movement of *The Song of the Earth* with the tremendous opening of the Eighth Symphony). Mahler's instrumentation, as well as his extremely detailed indications of phrasing, tempo, and dynamics and his occasional use of unusual instruments (such as the mandolins in the Seventh and Eighth Symphonies and *The Song of the Earth*), are not mere displays of ingenuity, but are intrinsically part of the composer's musical ideas. For instance, the *scordatura* solo violin—all the strings tuned one full tone higher than normally—in the scherzo of the Fourth Symphony is intended to suggest the sound of the medieval *Fiedel* (fiddle) in a musical representation of the Dance of Death, a favorite subject in old German paintings.

The programmatic content is not always expressly indicated in most of his symphonies. Mahler probably had in mind generalized extra-musical ideas similar to those illustrated in the Third and

Fifth Symphonies of Beethoven. Thus Mahler's Fifth and Seventh move steadily from funereal gloom to triumph and joy; the Sixth, on the contrary, is his "tragic" symphony, culminating in a colossal finale in which heroic struggle seems to end in defeat and death. The Ninth, Mahler's last completed symphony (composed 1909–10), flows in a mood of resignation, of indescribably strange and sad farewell to life, symbolized by deliberate reference to the *Lebe wohl* (Farewell) theme of the opening of Beethoven's Sonata Op. 81a. This motif, or reminiscences of it, pervades the first and last movement (both in slow tempo) of the Ninth Symphony, as well as that other "farewell" work of Mahler's last years, *The Song of the Earth* (Example 2d and e).

EXAMPLE XIX–2   "Farewell" Motives

a. Beethoven, *Sonata*, Op. 81a

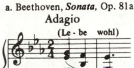

b. Mahler, *Ninth Symphony*, first movement

c. Mahler, *Ninth Symphony*, fourth movement

d. Mahler, *Song of the Earth*, No. 1

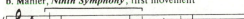

e. Mahler, *Song of the Earth*, No. 6

d. Dark is life, is death. e. The lovely earth everywhere blossoms in the new green of spring.

Mahler the symphonist cannot be separated from Mahler the song composer. Themes from his early *Lieder eines fahrenden Gesellen (Songs of a Wayfarer;* composed 1883–84) appear in the opening and closing movements of the First Symphony; the Second, Third, and Fourth Symphonies incorporate melodies from the cycle of twelve songs on folk poems from the early nineteenth-century collection *Des Knaben Wunderhorn (The Boy's Magic Horn)* which Mahler composed between 1888 and 1899. Following the example of Beethoven, Berlioz, and Liszt, Mahler uses voices as well as instruments in four of his symphonies. The last movement of the Fourth has a soprano soloist, while soprano and alto soloists join with women's and boys' choruses in the fourth and fifth movements of the Third. The most extensive use of singing, however, occurs in the Second and Eighth Symphonies.

The Second, one of Mahler's most frequently played works, is known as the *Resurrection Symphony.* Like Beethoven, Mahler brings in voices for the final climax of the work. After a long, agitated, and highly developed first movement there follows an Andante in the easy, swinging, folksong-like rhythm of an Austrian *Ländler,* or slow waltz. The third movement is a symphonic adaptation of one of the *Wunderhorn* songs, and the brief fourth movement is a new setting, for contralto solo, of still another poem from this collection. This serves to introduce the finale which, after a vivid and dramatic orchestral section depicting the day of Resurrection, leads to a monumental setting for soloists and chorus beginning with the text of a Resurrection ode by the eighteenth-century German poet Klopstock. The Eighth Symphony consists of two huge choral movements, on the texts respectively of the plainsong hymn *Veni creator spiritus* and the whole closing scene of Part II of Goethe's *Faust.* The second movement is practically a complete secular oratorio in itself, resembling in many ways Liszt's *Faust Symphony* and *St. Elizabeth,* or Wagner's *Parsifal.*

The Song of the Earth

The Song of the Earth is based on a cycle of six poems translated from the Chinese by Hans Bethge under the title *The Chinese Flute.* The texts alternate between a frenzied grasping at the fleeting dream-like whirl of life and a resigned sadness at imminent parting from all its joys and beauties. As Mahler called on the human voice in the symphonies to complete his musical thought with the language of words, so here he calls on the orchestra to sustain and supplement the tenor and contralto solos with all its resources, both in accompaniment and in extensive connecting interludes. The exotic atmosphere of the words is lightly suggested by details of instrumental color and the use of the pentatonic scale. *The Song of the Earth* is deservedly Mahler's best-known work, one that epitomizes all the traits of his genius. Nowhere else did he so perfectly define and bring into balance that peculiar dualism of feeling, that ambivalence of ecstatic pleasure underlaid with deadly foreboding, that seems to characterize not only the composer himself but also the whole autumnal mood of late Romanticism. At no other time in history, perhaps, could the insistently recurring phrase "Dark is life, dark is death" (Example XIX–2d) have been given such poignant musical expression.

The most general clue to Mahler's style is just this dualism, which extends to every feature of his work. In his symphonies he attempted—not always with success—to join sophistication with simplicity, to juxtapose the most lofty, wide-ranging cosmic conceptions and struggles with lyricism, Austrian folk song, nature painting, popular dance rhythms, chorale themes, marches, elements of parody, the spooky, and the grotesque. In his own phrase, each symphony was to be "a world." In this Faustian striving to be all-inclusive, Mahler was at one with the Romantic spirit, which he embodied most clearly in the Second Symphony. The Third, on the other hand, suffers from a too apparent dichotomy of styles. A vast, full-blown symphonic first movement is followed by five relatively short ones, diverse in character: a minuet with trio, a *scherzando* based on one of Mahler's early songs and featuring a posthorn, a contralto solo on a text from Nietzsche's *Zarathustra*, a soprano solo with boys' and women's chorus on a merry song from *Des Knaben Wunderhorn*, and, for conclusion, a broadly expressive orchestral adagio. The Fourth Symphony likewise mirrors a variegated "world," but one better unified in musical form, shorter, more lightly orchestrated, and altogether more easily accessible; this symphony and the Second have always been more popular than any of Mahler's works except *The Song of the Earth*.

With the *Kindertotenlieder* of 1901–04 for solo voice and orchestra on poems of Friedrich Rückert, Mahler forecast the change of style which is evident in his Ninth and (unfinished) Tenth Symphonies and the *Song of the Earth*. The typically full, crowded textures of the earlier works were often replaced by a more austere idiom thus achieving a transparent chamber-like sound that with its sparse use of instruments allows the delicate counterpoint to shine through. At the same time, some of Mahler's techniques contributed to the steadily weakening sense of traditional tonal organization and furnished suggestions of procedure which later composers took up and developed. Mahler was thus, in a way to which there seems to be no real parallel in previous musical history, a transitional composer. He fell heir to the whole Romantic tradition —Berlioz, Liszt, Wagner—and particularly to the Viennese branch— Beethoven, Schubert, Brahms, and above all Bruckner. Restlessly experimenting, all-devouring in his interests, he expanded the Romantic symphony and symphony-oratorio to their point of final dissolution; still experimenting, he foreshadowed a new age and became a prime influence on the later Viennese composers, Schoenberg, Berg, and Webern.

Richard Strauss

A quite different historical significance must be assigned to the most famous of the German post-Romantic composers, Richard Strauss (1864–1949). He wrote some 150 Lieder, of which not more than a dozen or so—mostly from his early period—are commonly known outside Germany and Austria; but he is important mainly for his symphonic poems and operas. Most of the symphonic poems were produced before 1900, while all but one of the operas came after that date.

There are two kinds of program for a symphonic poem: one, which we may call the "philosophical," lies in the realm of general ideas and emotions, unattached to particular incidents; the other, which we may call the "descriptive," requires the composer to render or attempt to illustrate in music particular nonmusical events. The two types cannot be strictly set apart, since philosophical programs often include descriptive elements and descriptive programs usually have also a more general significance; the distinction rests only on the relative conspicuousness of the descriptive details.

Strauss wrote symphonic poems to both philosophical and descriptive programs. His best works of the former type are *Tod und Verklärung* (*Death and Transfiguration;* 1889) and *Also sprach Zarathustra* (*Thus Spake Zarathustra;* 1896); of the latter, *Till Eulenspiegels lustige Streiche* (*Till Eulenspiegel's Merry Pranks;* 1895) and *Don Quixote* (1897). Among his other orchestral works are the symphonic poems *Don Juan* (1889) and *Ein Heldenleben* (*A Hero's Life;* 1898) and the *Sinfonia domestica* (1903).

Tod und Verklärung embodies a program similar to that of many symphonies and operas of the nineteenth century: the progress of the soul through suffering to self-fulfillment. This is a general, philosophical program, though Strauss later admitted that he had had in mind certain descriptive details. The music is worked out with genuine warmth of emotion in themes and harmonies of spontaneous power, with strong dramatic contrasts. Its musical form can best be understood as an Allegro in free sonata form with a slow introduction and a hymnlike epilogue; the principal themes occur in cyclical fashion in all three parts.

The program of *Zarathustra* is philosophical in a double sense: the work is a musical commentary on the celebrated prose-poem by the brilliant, erratic Friedrich Nietzsche, whose doctrine of the superman was agitating all Europe at the end of the century (a choice of subject typical of Strauss's highly developed sense for the value of

Strauss's symphonic poems

publicity). Although a part of Nietzsche's prologue stands at the head of the score and the various divisions are furnished with titles from the book, the music cannot be regarded as an attempt to depict a philosophical system in tones; Nietzsche's ideas served merely as a stimulus to Strauss's musical imagination. The only obviously artificial touch is the construction of a fugue theme which uses all twelve notes of the chromatic scale (Example XIX–3) to symbolize the all-embracing but dark and cloudy realm of *Wissenschaft* (science, learning, knowledge)—the symbolism being reinforced by the low-lying thick sound of the fugal exposition, which is given to the double-basses and violoncellos, each divided in four parts.

EXAMPLE XIX–3   Fugue subject from *Also sprach Zarathustra,*
Richard Strauss

In *Till Eulenspiegel,* the popular favorite among his symphonic poems, Strauss developed a comic program in music of unfading freshness and melodic attractiveness. The realistic details of Till's adventures (specified by a few marginal notes that the composer added to the printed score) are so thoroughly blended with the musical flow that the work could easily be heard simply as a character sketch of a particularly appealing rascal, or even more simply as a piece of unmeditated musical humor, reminiscent of Haydn. A further suggestion of Haydn lies in Strauss's indication that *Till* is "in rondo form." Rondo it is not in the Classical sense, but rondo-like by reason of the many recurrences of the two *Till* themes, which appear in an endless variety of guises, enlivened by shrewd touches of instrumentation. In no other work does Strauss seem so unconstrained, so spontaneously himself, as in this merry musical tale.

Strauss leaped into fame as an opera composer first in 1905 with *Salome* and from that time on the powers of depiction and characterization that had formerly gone into symphonic poems were utilized almost exclusively in opera. He accepted the Wagnerian principles of continuous music, the primacy of the polyphonic orchestra, and the systematic use of leitmotifs. *Salome* is a setting of Oscar Wilde's one-act play in German translation. The music by its orchestral splendor, novel rhythms, and keenly descriptive harmonies captures the macabre tone and atmosphere of the drama with such expressive force as to lift it to a plane where artistry prevails over perversion. *Elektra* (1909) began the long and fruitful

Strauss's operas

collaboration between Strauss and the Viennese dramatist Hugo von Hofmannsthal (1874–1929). For Hofmannsthal's rather one-sided version of Sophocles's play, which dwells throughout its long single act on the emotions of insane hatred and revenge, Strauss conceived music that in sharpness of dissonance and apparent harmonic anarchy outdid anything previously known.

Salome and *Elektra* scandalized the respectable public of the 1900s, the former chiefly by its subject and the latter by its music. Time has tempered the criticisms, and the once fearful dissonances sound common enough. What remains, and is to be esteemed, is Strauss's amazing virtuosity in the invention of musical ideas and instrumental sonorities to characterize both persons and actions.

Der Rosenkavalier (*The Rose Cavalier*, 1911), on an excellent libretto in three acts by von Hofmannsthal, takes us into a sunnier world, a world of elegant, stylized eroticism and tender feeling, the aristocratic wig-and-powder milieu of eighteenth-century Vienna. *Der Rosenkavalier* is Strauss's operatic masterpiece. The sultry harmonies of *Salome* and the cacophonies of *Elektra* are softened to a mature synthesis of the elements in the earlier operas and symphonic poems. The ultra-Romantic, sensuous melodic curves, the sophisticated chromatic harmonies (see Example XIX–4), the magical orchestral colors, tumultuous rhythms, lively sense of comedy, and speciously simple diatonic style derived from South German dances and folk songs, are held together in poise and given depth of meaning by an overruling humane sympathy that never quite slips over the verge into irony. Consistent with this turn toward Classicism, in *Der Rosenkavalier* the human voice once again becomes prominent; woven into the orchestral background and alternating with much cleverly wrought *parlando* dialogue are melodious arias, duets, trios—not really separate numbers as in the Classical opera,

Alfred Roller's design for the original 1911 Vienna production of Strauss's Der Rosenkavalier. *The caption reads: "Stage setting for the 3rd Act: Private room in a small inn." (Reproduced by permission of Boosey & Hawkes, Inc.)*

EXAMPLE XIX–4   Introduction, measures 69–74, *Der Rosenkavalier,* Strauss

but still significant as departing from the Wagnerian (and earlier Straussian) rule of purely declamatory or, at most, arioso singing subordinated to the orchestra. The whole score, with its mingling of sentiment and comedy, is pervaded with the lighthearted rhythms and melodies of Viennese waltzes.

Ariadne auf Naxos (Ariadne at Naxos, 1912) was originally set, with other incidental music, in the framework of von Hofmanns-thal's adaptation of Molière's *Le Bourgeois Gentilhomme.* It has survived in revised form (1916) as an independent work, half *opera buffa* and half mythological drama. Its delightful music, in a modernized Mozartean idiom and using a small orchestra, includes recitatives, ensembles, and arias in Classical forms; it is, in short, a model of neo-Classical chamber opera.

In his subsequent operas, Strauss remained comparatively unaffected by the progressive currents of his time, preferring to continue along the lines he had laid down in *Der Rosenkavalier* and *Ariadne.* Of special interest are the comic opera *Intermezzo* (1924) and the lyrical comedy *Arabella* (1933), the last of Strauss's seven operas on librettos by von Hofmannsthal.

Nationalism, Old and New: Russia

Nationalism was a potent force in nineteenth-century music. A distinction must be made, however, between early Romantic nationalism and the nationalism which appeared after 1860. The results of the early nineteenth-century German folk-song revival were so thoroughly absorbed into the fabric of German music as to become an integral part of its style, which in that period was the nearest thing to an international European musical style. The new nationalism, in contrast to the old, flourished largely in countries that had no great or unbroken musical tradition of their own but had long been musically dependent on other nations, chiefly Germany. Nationalism was one of the weapons by which composers in those countries sought to free themselves from the domination of foreign music. As a movement, it was self-conscious, and sometimes aggressive. It underlies such externals as the choice of national subjects for operas and symphonic poems, the collecting and publishing of folk songs, and the occasional quoting of folk tunes in compositions; but a more important consequence was the rise of new styles through fertilization of orthodox Germanic music by tonal, melodic, harmonic, rhythmic, and formal characteristics of the national idioms. This development took place earliest in Russia.

The first well-known landmark of Russian nationalism was the patriotic opera *A Life for the Tsar* by Michael Glinka (1804–57). This work gave impetus to a movement that culminated with a group of composers known as "the mighty handful": Mily Balakirev (1837–1910), Alexander Borodin (1833–87), Modest Mussorgsky (1839–81), and Nicolas Rimsky-Korsakov (1844–1908).

All these men save Balakirev were amateurs—a fact important in the growth of Russian music. The nationalist composers' comparative ignorance of conventional harmony and counterpoint became a positive asset: it forced them to discover their own ways of doing things, and in the process they used the materials nearest at hand, namely folk songs.

Balakirev made effective use of folk-song melodies in his symphonic poem *Russia* (1887) and his piano fantasia *Islamey* (1869). Borodin's principal works are the Second Symphony in B minor (1876), the second String Quartet in D major (1885), a symphonic sketch *In Central Asia* (1880), and the four-act opera *Prince Igor*, completed after his death by Rimsky-Korsakov and Glazunov and first performed in 1890. Borodin seldom quotes folk tunes but his melodies are permeated with their spirit. His talent, like Mendelssohn's, was primarily lyrical and descriptive, and *Prince Igor* is less a drama than a series of picturesque tableaus. The familiar *Polovetsian Dances,* which occur in Act II of the opera, illustrate the iridescent harmonies, bright colors, graceful melodic lines, and the refined, exotic oriental flavor that characterize much Russian music in this period.

Modest Mussorgsky

Mussorgsky, the greatest of the "mighty handful," was also the one least well-equipped with the techniques of composition. A militant nationalist, he earned a painful living as a clerk in the civil service, and received most of his musical training from Balakirev. His principal works were: a symphonic fantasy *Night on Bald Mountain* (1867); the set of piano pieces *Pictures at an Exhibition* (1874); the song cycles *Sunless* (1874), *Songs and Dances of Death* (1875), and *The Nursery* (1872); and the operas *Boris Godunov* (first performed in 1874) and *Khovanshchina,* which was completed by Rimsky-Korsakov and privately performed in 1886, but not produced publicly till 1892. Mussorgsky's individuality is evident in every aspect of his music. His treatment of texts aims at the closest possible adherence to the accents of natural speech; hence in his vocal music he generally avoids lyrical melodic lines and symmetrical phrasing. His songs are among the finest of the nineteenth century. Although Mussorgsky only occasionally quotes actual folk tunes (as in the Coronation Scene of *Boris*), it is evident that Russian folk song is rooted in his musical nature even more deeply than in Borodin's.

Russian folk tunes tend to move within a narrow range and to be made up either of obsessive repetition of one or two rhythmic motives or of phrases in irregular rhythm constantly sinking to a cadence, often by the interval of a descending fourth. Another prominent feature of Russian folk songs, and of Mussorgsky's melodies, is their modal character, and this modality affected Mussorgsky's harmonic style, as well as that of all the Russian nationalists. It was the Russians first of all who were responsible for introducing modality into the general musical language of Europe, and their influence in this respect on the music of the early twentieth century is important. Mussorgsky's use of nonfunctional harmonic

The Coronation Scene from Boris Godunov, *as staged by the Bolshoi Opera in Moscow. George London appears in the title role.*

EXAMPLE XIX–5

a. Folk Song from the collection 30 Chants populaires russes *harmonized by Mily Balakirev.*

Oï, u-tu-shka mo-ía lu-go-va-ía oï, u-tu-shka mo-ía lu-go-va-ía

oï_____ lu-go-va-ía oï_____ lu-go-va-ía.

a. Oh, duckling my meadow, oh, duckling my meadow, oh, meadow, oh meadow!

b. Folk Song, idem.

Kak pod le-som, pod__ le-soch-kom, shel-ko-va tra-va,____ Oï-li,*

Oï-li, oï-li, oï liu-shen-ki shel-ko-va tra-va!

* Oili is a stock folk song syllable, like fa la la or tra la la.
Liushën′ki is a diminutive of another stock syllable: liuli.

b. Now near the wood, near the wood, silky grass.

c. Melody from the Prologue of Boris Godunov, *Modeste Mussorgsky.*

Na ko-go ty nas po-ki-da-esh, o-tets nash!

Na ko-go, da ty__ o-sta-vlia-esh′, ro-di-my ï!

My te-bía, si-ro-ty, pro-sim, mo-lim, so_____ slë-za-mi,

so go-riü-chi-mi!

c. To whom do you leave us, our father! To whom do you abandon us, dear ones! We are orphans, we beg you, we implore you with tears, with scalding tears.

progressions in *Les Jours de fête sont finis* (*The festive days are over;* NAWM/S 86) from the cycle *Sans Soleil* (*Sunless*) attracted the attention of Debussy, who borrowed an accompaniment pattern from it for his *Nuages* (NAWM/S 78) (see Example XIX–9). *Les Jours* is remarkable for its harmonic successions, as for example a G♭-major triad going directly to a seventh chord on G. Other such juxtapositions and simultaneous combinations appear to be chosen for their color rather than for their direction. (Mussorgsky's music was one of the main sources for Debussy's style.) In his harmony the Russian was one of the most original and indeed revolutionary of all composers. Unfettered by traditional habits of thought and unpracticed in the manipulation of standard formulas, he was obliged to work out laboriously at the piano his "bold, new, crude,

EXAMPLE XIX–6   End of Act II, *Boris Godunov*, Mussorgsky

Lord! You do not wish the death of a sinner. Forgive the soul of guilty Tsar Boris!

but curiously 'right' harmonies"[1]—for which, as well as for his rhythms, he may have been indebted to his memories of polyphonic folk singing. His harmonic vocabulary is seldom advanced, but his apparently simple progressions convey precisely the effect he wants, and often resist any attempt to explain them by analysis on normal textbook principles (see Examples XIX–5, 6).

The realism that is such a prominent trait in nineteenth-century Russian literature is exemplified in the music of Alexander Dargomizhsky's (1813–69) opera *The Stone Guest* (first performed in 1872) and also finds some echo in Mussorgsky—not only in the sense of imitating the spoken word, but in the lifelike musical depiction of gestures (*Boris,* end of Act II), the sound and stir of people in crowds (choral scenes in *Boris* and *Khovanshchina*), and even paintings (*Pictures at an Exhibition*).

Rimsky-Korsakov

The work of Rimsky-Korsakov forms a link between the first generation of nationalists and the Russian composers of the early twentieth century. His compositions include symphonies, chamber music, choruses, and songs, but his principal works are symphonic poems and operas. Rimsky's music, in contrast to the intense dramatic realism of Mussorgsky's, is distinguished by lively fantasy and bright orchestral colors. The *Capriccio espagnol* (1887), the symphonic suite *Scheherazade* (1888), and the *Russian Easter Overture* (1888) are outstanding manifestations of his genius for orchestration; his teachings on this subject were systematized in a treatise published in 1913. In the two most important of his fifteen operas—*Sadko* (1897) and *The Golden Cockerel* (first performed in 1909)—he alternates a diatonic, often modal style with one lightly chromatic, fanciful, and most apt at suggesting the fairytale world in which the action of these pieces takes place.

Alexander Scriabin

The coloristic employment of harmony observed in Mussorgsky reached a high point in the music of Alexander Scriabin (1872–1915), an unclassifiable Russian composer of the post-Romantic period whose music had no connection with the nationalistic movement. A concert pianist, Scriabin began by writing nocturnes, preludes, études, and mazurkas in the manner of Chopin. Influenced by the chromaticism of Liszt and Wagner, and to some extent also by the methods of impressionism, he gradually evolved a complex harmonic vocabulary peculiar to himself; the growth of this language can be followed step by step in his ten piano sonatas, of which the last five, composed 1912–13, dispense with key signatures and attain a harmonic vagueness amounting at times to atonality. Traditional tonal structures were replaced by a system of chords built on unusual intervals (particularly fourths, with chromatic altera-

---

[1] G. Abraham, *A Hundred Years of Music,* 151.

tions; see Example XIX–7); traditional formal articulations were dissolved in a stream of strange, colorful, and sometimes magnificent sound. All this was intended to express vast conceptions of an extraordinary, mysterious, theosophical cast; Scriabin eventually developed a theory of an ultimate synthesis of all the arts for the sake of inducing states of unutterable mystic rapture. His most typical compositions, apart from the late sonatas, are two orchestral works, the *Poem of Ecstasy* (1908) and *Prometheus* (1910); for the latter the composer wished the concert hall to be flooded with colored light during the playing of the music.

EXAMPLE XIX–7   Chord Forms, Alexander Scriabin

Other Nations

Bedřich Smetana (1824–84) and Antonín Dvořák were the two principal Czech composers of the nineteenth century. (Dvořák has already been mentioned in connection with the symphonic and chamber music of the Romantic period.) Bohemia had for centuries been an Austrian crown land, and thus, unlike Russia, had always been in contact with the main stream of European music; her folk songs do not differ from those of Western nations nearly so much as do the Russian. Nor was the Czech nationalist movement marked from the outset, as was the Russian, by self-conscious efforts to avoid Western influence. The nationalism of Smetana and Dvořák is chiefly apparent in the choice of national subjects for program music and operas, and in the infusion of their basic musical language (Smetana's derived from Liszt, Dvořák's more like Brahms's) with a melodic freshness and spontaneity, a harmonic and formal nonchalance, together with occasional traces of folklike tunes and popular dance rhythms. The most prominent national traits of both composers are found in some of their operas—Smetana's *Bartered Bride* (1866) above all, but also in his later opera *The Kiss* (1876)—and in some works in small forms, such as Dvořák's *Slavonic Dances*.

A Czech composer with thoroughly national tendencies was Leoš Janáček (1854–1928), a more important figure in early twentieth century music than his as yet limited fame would indicate. Unlike Smetana and Dvořák, Janáček after 1890 consciously renounced the

Czech composers

styles of western Europe. Like Bartók but even earlier, he was a diligent scientific collector of folk music, and his own mature style grew out of the rhythms and inflections of Moravian peasant speech and song. Recognition came late, beginning only with the performance of his opera *Jenufa* (1903) at Prague in 1916. Janáček's creative power continued unabated to the end of his life. Later operas were *Kát'a Kabanová* (1921), *The Cunning Little Vixen* (1924), *The Makropulos Case* (1925), and *From a House of the Dead* (1928). Janáček composed much choral music, among which the *Glagolitic Mass* of 1926, on a text in Old Slavic, is an outstanding work. His chamber music includes two quartets and a violin sonata; for orchestra the chief works are the symphonic rhapsody *Taras Bulba* (1918) and a *Sinfonietta* (1926).

NORWAY

Nationalism in Norway is represented by Edvard Hagerup Grieg (1843–1907), whose best works are his short piano pieces, songs, and incidental orchestral music to plays. Among his larger compositions are the well-known Piano Concerto in A minor (1868, revised 1907), a piano sonata, three violin sonatas, a violoncello sonata, and a string quartet (1878) that apparently provided Debussy with a model for his own work in the same form fifteen years later.

The weaknesses in these works arise from Grieg's tendency to think always in two- or four-measure phrases and his inability to achieve rhythmic continuity and formal unity in long movements; such national characteristics as they possess are superimposed on an orthodox style which Grieg learned in youthful studies at the Leipzig Conservatory. His essential nationalism is more clearly apparent in the songs on Norwegian texts, the choruses for men's voices Op. 30, the four Psalms for mixed chorus Op. 74, many of his *Lyric Pieces* for piano (ten collections), the four sets of piano arrangements of folk songs, and especially the *Slåtter* (Norwegian peasant dances arranged by Grieg for the piano from transcripts of country fiddle playing). His piano style, with its delicate grace notes and mordents, owes something to Chopin, but the all-pervading influence in his music is that of Norwegian folk songs and dances; this is evidenced particularly in modal turns of melody and harmony (Lydian raised fourth, Aeolian lowered seventh, alternative major-minor third), frequent drone basses (suggested by old Norwegian stringed instruments), and such details as the fascinating combination of 3/4 and 6/8 rhythm in the *Slåtter*. These national characteristics blend with Grieg's sensitive feeling for harmony in a personal, poetic music that has not lost its freshness.

UNITED STATES

Musical nationalism in the European countries could be defined as the rise of an important body of art music under the impetus of patriotic feeling, in a style whose distinctive features result from the composers' more or less conscious use of folk elements as material or inspiration for compositions. In this sense there was no continuity of musical nationalism in the United States of America in the nineteenth century. The material, to be sure, lay ready in profusion—old New England hymnody, rural revival-meeting songs, tunes from the urban popular minstrelsy of Stephen Foster (1820–94) and James Bland (1854–1911), Indian tribal melodies, above all the great body of black folk spirituals with their unique fusion of African and Anglo-American elements—but to no avail. All the "serious" music the American public could take was imported—Italian opera, English oratorio, German symphony—while the piano pieces in Creole rhythms by Louis Moreau Gottschalk (1829–69) were dismissed as claptrap. Dvořák's enthusiastic interest in the American musical heritage suggested to a few composers the possibility of using national materials in symphonic works; but the composers of this group, who were chiefly active in the first two decades of the twentieth century, lacked both the genius and the social encouragement to do for the United States what Glinka, Balakirev, and Mussorgsky had done for Russia.

Specific national traits are not prominent in the music of the two most celebrated American composers of the post-Romantic era. Horatio Parker (1863–1919), whose output included songs, choruses, and two prize-winning operas, is best known for his cantatas and oratorios, especially the oratorio *Hora novissima* (1893). Edward MacDowell (1860–1908) lived and studied for ten years in Germany, where he became known as a pianist and where many of his compositions were first played and published. From 1896 to 1903 he held the first professorship of music at Columbia University. His compositions include songs, choruses, symphonic poems, orchestral suites, many piano pieces and studies, four piano sonatas, and two piano concertos.

MacDowell's melodies have a peculiar charm; his harmony, late Romantic in color but without modality, is handled in a distinctly personal way. A fine sensitiveness for the sonorous effects of spacing and doubling is evident in his short piano pieces, which are his most characteristic works. Most of them were issued in collections—*Woodland Sketches,* the *Sea Pieces,* the *New England Idyls*—and the individual pieces are furnished with titles or poems suggesting musical moods and pictures of the sort common in Grieg, to whose general style MacDowell's bears some resemblance. One of his finest works, and the only one that uses American folk material (Indian melodies), is the second (*Indian*) suite for orchestra. The fourth movement, called *Dirge* (NAWM/S 69), demonstrates a powerful orchestral imagination and successful assimilation of European musical styles.

The first important distinctively American composer was Charles Ives (1874–1954), a pupil of his father and of Horatio Parker. Like the early Russian nationalists, Ives was not a musician by profession. Public recognition of his achievements came only in the 1930s, many years after he had, in isolation and without models, created works that anticipated some of the most radical developments of twentieth-century music (dissonance, polytonality, polyrhythm, and experimental form). His compositions, most of which were written between 1890 and 1922, include some 200 songs, five violin sonatas and other chamber music, two piano sonatas, five symphonies, and other orchestral music. Conventional and unconventional elements stand side by side in his works, or are mingled—in John Kirkpatrick's phrase—"with a transcendentalist's faith in the unity behind all diversity"; fragments of folk songs, dance tunes, or gospel hymns emerge from a complex, rhapsodic, uniquely ordered flow of sound. The many movements based on hymn tunes offer a parallel to the use of Lutheran chorales by German composers.

Ives's technical procedures, which he would have scorned to designate as a system, were dictated by an uncompromising idealism in the pursuit of his artistic aims, coupled with an extraordinary musical imagination and a mordant sense of humor. His work has been of incalculable importance to younger generations of American musicians.

FINLAND

The great Finnish composer Jean Sibelius (1865–1957) is nationalistic only in a limited sense. His mind was steeped in the literature of his country, particularly the *Kalevala,* the Finnish national epic, from which he chose texts for vocal works and subjects for symphonic poems; and it is easy to imagine much of his music—"somber," "bleak," and "elemental" are favorite adjectives for it—as having been inspired by his love of nature and the particular aspects of nature characteristic of northern countries. On the other hand, he does not quote or imitate folk songs and there is small evidence of direct folk song influence in his works, the best of which depend little, if at all, on qualities that can be concretely defined as national.

Although Sibelius lived until 1957, he published no important works after 1925. The first of his seven symphonies appeared in 1899, the last in 1924. Three symphonic poems—*En Saga, The Swan of Tuonela,* and the familiar *Finlandia*—were works of the 1890s (all revised about 1900); the principal later symphonic poems were *Pohjola's Daughter* (1906) and *Tapiola* (1925). The programs of these poems, except for *Pohjola's Daughter,* are very general; the symphonies have no expressed programmatic suggestions.

Sibelius's originality is not of a sensational order. Except in the Fourth Symphony, his conception of tonality and his harmonic vocabulary are close to common practice; he makes no conspicuous use of chromaticism or dissonances, though modality is a basic factor. Sibelius remained aloof from the disturbing experimental movements in European music in the first quarter of the century, and in his late works, particularly the Seventh Symphony and *Tapiola,* he arrived at a final synthesis in a style of Classical tranquillity.

Nationalism in English music came comparatively late. Sir Edward Elgar (1857–1934) was the first English composer in more than two hundred years to obtain wide international recognition; but his music is not in the least touched by folk song nor has it any technical characteristics that seem to derive from the national musical tradition. His oratorio *The Dream of Gerontius* (1900) and the *Enigma Variations* (1899) for orchestra are his most important works.

The English musical renaissance signalized by Elgar took a nationalist turn in the twentieth century. Folksong collections by Cecil Sharp (1859–1924), Ralph Vaughan Williams (1872–1958), and others led to the use of these melodies in compositions such as Vaughan Williams's *Norfolk Rhapsodies* for orchestra (1907) and the *Somerset Rhapsody* by Gustav Holst (1874–1934). These two composers became the leaders of a new English school which will be dealt with in the following chapter.

ENGLAND

In Spain a nationalist revival somewhat like the English was initiated by Felipe Pedrell (1841–1922) with his editions of sixteenth-century Spanish composers. Further nationalist impetus came from the works of Isaac Albéniz (1860–1909), whose piano suite *Iberia* (1909) used Spanish dance rhythms in a colorful virtuoso style. The principal Spanish composer of the early twentieth century, Manuel de Falla (1876–1946), collected and arranged national folk songs, and his earlier works—for example, the opera *La Vida breve* (*Life is Short;* composed 1905) and the ballet *El Amor Brujo* (*Love, the Sorcerer;* 1915)—are imbued with the melodic and rhythmic qualities of Spanish popular music. *Nights in the Gardens of Spain,* three "symphonic impressions" for piano and orchestra (1916), testify both to national sources and the influence of Debussy. Falla's finest mature works are the concerto for harpsichord with five solo instruments (1926) and the little stage piece *Master Peter's Puppet Show* (1923), based on an episode from *Don Quixote.*

SPAIN

New Currents in France

Three main lines of development—interdependent, naturally—may be traced in the history of French music from 1871 to the early years of the twentieth century. Two of these are best defined by their historical background: first, the cosmopolitan tradition, transmitted through César Franck and carried on by his pupils, especially d'Indy; and second, the specifically French tradition, transmitted through Saint-Saëns and continued by his pupils, especially Fauré. The third development, later in inception but more fundamental and far-reaching in its influence, was rooted in the French tradition and was carried to unforeseen consequences in the music of Debussy.

The cosmopolitan tradition

The principal compositions of Vincent d'Indy (1851–1931) are the First Symphony, "on a French mountain air" (1886), the Second Symphony, in B♭ (1903), the symphonic variations *Istar* (1896), the symphonic poem *Summer Day on the Mountain* (1905), the Violin Sonata (1904), and the opera *Fervaal* (1897). The First Symphony is exceptional for a French work because it uses a folk song as its principal subject; both this and the Second Symphony exhibit to the highest degree the process of cyclical transformation of themes that d'Indy learned from Franck. The quasi-programmatic *Istar* variations are remarkable as an inversion of the usual plan: the set begins with the most complex variation and progresses to the simple statement of the theme at the end. *Istar* and the First Symphony are the most spontaneous and attractive of d'Indy's compositions.

The French tradition

The specifically French tradition is something essentially Classical: it rests on a conception of music as sonorous form, in contrast to the Romantic conception of music as expression. Order and restraint are fundamental. Emotion and depiction are conveyed only as they have been entirely transmuted into music. That music may be anything from the simplest melody to the most subtle pattern of tones, rhythms, and colors; but it tends always to be lyric or dance-like rather than epic or dramatic, economical rather than profuse, reserved rather than grandiloquent; above all, it is not concerned with delivering a Message, whether about the fate of the cosmos or the state of the composer's soul. A listener will fail to comprehend such music unless he is sensible to quiet statement, nuance, and exquisite detail, able to distinguish calmness from dullness, wit from jollity, gravity from portentousness, lucidity from emptiness. This kind of music was written by two French composers as remote in time and temperament as Couperin and Gounod. Berlioz did not write such music; and Berlioz was not a success in France.

In Camille Saint-Saëns this French inheritance was coupled with high craftsmanship, facility in managing Classical forms, and the ability to adopt at will any of the fashionable tricks of Romanticism. This eclectic, hedonistic trait also runs through the many successful operas of Jules Massenet (1842–1912), which exhibit the composer's talent for suave, sensuous, charming, and often sentimental melody. The music of Gustave Charpentier's (1860–1956) operá *Louise* (1900) is in a style not greatly different from Massenet's.

Gabriel Fauré

Gabriel Fauré (1845–1924) was one of the founders of the National Society for French Music and first president of the Independent Musical Society, which branched off from the parent association in 1909. His refined, highly civilized music embodies the aristocratic qualities of the French tradition. Except for a few songs,[2] his works

[2] He is not the composer of *The Palms*. That song was perpetrated by Jean-Baptiste Faure (1830–1914).

have never become widely popular, and many foreigners, even musicians, cannot understand why he is so highly regarded in France. Primarily a composer of lyric pieces and chamber music, his few compositions in larger form include the *Requiem* (1887), incidental music to Maeterlinck's *Pelléas et Mélisande* (1898), and the operas *Prométhée* (1900) and *Pénélope* (1913). His music is not remarkable for color; he was not skilled at orchestration, and published no symphonies or concertos. His characteristics are most fully revealed in his nearly one hundred songs and piano pieces, which were written during all periods of his creative life. The principal chamber compositions are three late works: the second Violin Sonata (1917), the second Piano Quintet (1921), and the String Quartet (1924).

Fauré began with songs in the manner of Gounod, and piano salon pieces deriving from Mendelssohn and Chopin. In some respects he never changed: lyrical melody, with no display of virtuosity, remained always the basis of his style, and small dimensions were always congenial to him. But in his maturity, from about 1885, these small forms began to be filled with a language that was new. Aside from a steadily growing power to create living, plastic melody, there were innovations in harmony. *Avant que tu ne t'en ailles* (*Before you go*) from the cycle *La Bonne Chanson* (NAWM/S 85) illustrates some of his melodic and harmonic idiosyncrasies. The fragmentary phrases of melody, one for each verse, decline to commit their al-

EXAMPLE XIX–8   *Avant que tu ne t'en ailles,* Gabriel Fauré

What joy in the fields of ripe wheat

legiance to any major or minor scale. The equivocal tonality, which has been attributed to Fauré's being imbued with the modal idiom of plainchant in his schooling, is owed partly to the lowering of the leading tone. The harmony, thus shielded from the pull of the tonic, and further deprived of tension and resolution by the introduction of foreign notes that neutralize the chords' tendencies, achieves an equilibrium and repose that is the antithesis of the emotional unrest of Wagner's. In Example XIX–8 the chords consist mainly of dominant sevenths and ninths, as in Wagner, but the tension melts as one chord fades into another and the seventh or ninth that demanded resolution becomes a wayward member of another chord. Fauré's music has often been described as "Hellenic" in recognition of the qualities of clarity, balance, and serenity that recall the spirit of ancient Greek art.

One of the greatest of French composers, and one of the most potent influences on the course of music in the twentieth century, was Claude-Achille Debussy (1862–1918). One aspect of his style—an aspect which sometimes is over-emphasized—is summed up in the term "impressionism." This word was first applied to a school of French painting which flourished from about 1880 to the end of the century; its chief representative is Claude Monet (1840–1926). In relation to music, the word is thus defined in Webster's Dictionary: "A style of composition designed to create descriptive impressions by evoking moods through rich and varied harmonies and timbres."

Claude Debussy

Impressionism is thus a kind of program music. It differs from most Romantic program music in that, first, it does not seek to express feeling or tell a story, but to evoke a mood, an "atmosphere," with the help of suggestive titles and occasional reminiscences of natural sounds, dance rhythms, characteristic bits of melody, and the like; second, impressionism relies on allusion and understatement instead of the more forthright or strenuous methods of the Romantics; and third, it employs melodies, harmonies, colors, rhythms, and formal principles which, in one way and another, contribute to making a musical language radically different from that of the German Romantic tradition.

Some of the ingredients of this new language may be observed in the first of the orchestral *Nocturnes* (1899), entitled *Nuages (Clouds;* NAWM/S 78). Also evident are some of the sources of his style. The piece begins with a chordal pattern borrowed from Mussorgsky's song *Les Jours de fête sont finis* (NAWM/S 86), but whereas Mussorgsky alternates sixths and thirds, Debussy alternates the starker sounding fifths and thirds (see Example XIX–9). As in Mussorgsky there is an impression of movement but no harmonic direction, a perfect analogy for slowly moving clouds. Debussy maintains tonality in this piece by pedal points or frequent returns to the pri-

EXAMPLE XIX–9   Chord progressions in *Nuages* (Debussy), and *Les Jours de fête* (Mussorgsky)

mary chords of the key.

The middle section of *Nuages*—for it is in the *ABA* form Debussy favored—has a more exotic source, the Javanese *gamelan,* an orchestra made up mainly of gongs and percussion, that Debussy heard at the Paris exposition in 1889. In his simulation of the *gamelan* texture Debussy gives the flute and harp a simple pentatonic tune, analogous to the Javanese nuclear theme, while the other instruments supply a static background, only occasionally approaching, however, the colotomic method of the Javanese players who enter in a predetermined staggered order. The return of the *A* section is fragmentary, like a dream recollected imperfectly.

The *Nocturnes* were preceded by Debussy's most celebrated orchestral work, the *Prélude à l'après-midi d'un faune* (1894), based on a poem of Mallarmé. Later followed the symphonic sketches, *La Mer* (1905). Debussy's orchestration is admirably suited to the musical ideas. A large orchestra is required, but it is seldom used to make a loud sound. Strings are frequently divided and muted; harps add a distinctive touch; among the woodwinds, the flute (especially in the low register), oboe, and English horn are featured in solos; horns and trumpets, also often muted, are heard in short *pianissimo* phrases; percussion of many types—kettledrums, large and small drums, large and small cymbals, tamtams, celesta, glockenspiel, xylophone—is still another source of color.

Instances of all these devices may easily be found in Debussy's piano music, which—along with Ravel's—constitutes the most important addition made to the literature of that instrument in the early twentieth century. The structure of chords is often veiled by abundance of figuration and by the blending of sounds with the use of the damper pedal. No mere listing of technical features can suggest the coruscating play of color, the ravishing pianistic effects, the subtle poetic fancy these pieces reveal. The principal impressionistic piano works of Debussy occur in collections published between 1903 and 1913: *Estampes,* two books of *Images,* and two books of *Préludes.*

As we have already indicated, "impressionism" is only one aspect of Debussy's style; in many of his compositions there is little or no trace of it—for example (among the piano music), the early *Suite Bergamasque* (1893), the suite *Pour le piano* (1901), and the delight-

The first page of the original manuscript of Prélude à l'après-midi d'un faune. *The dedication in the upper right-hand corner is to Gaby Dupont, to whom Debussy gave the manuscript in 1899.*

ful *Children's Corner* (1908), which in the midst of the *Golliwog's Cake Walk* introduces a satirical quotation from Wagner's *Tristan* and with *Dr. Gradus ad Parnassum* pokes fun at Czerny. The String Quartet (1893) fuses Debussy's harmonic and coloristic traits with Classical forms and cyclic treatment of themes. Far from "impressionistic" are his late works, in particular the ballet *Jeux* (1912), the four-hand piano *Epigraphes antiques* (1914), the piano *Études* (two books, 1915), the suite *En blanc et noir* for two pianos (1915), and the *Sonates pour divers instruments* (violoncello and piano; flute, viola, and harp; piano and violin) of 1915–17.

Debussy's only completed opera is his setting of Maeterlinck's symbolist play *Pelléas et Mélisande* (1902). The veiled allusions and images of the text are perfectly matched by the strange (often modal) harmonies, subdued colors, and restrained expressiveness of the music. The voices, in plastic recitative, are supported but never dominated by a continuous orchestral background, while the instrumental interludes connecting the scenes carry on the mysterious inner course of the drama.

Pelléas et Mélisande

From the French tradition Debussy inherited his fine sensibilities, his aristocratic taste, and his anti-Romantic conception of the function of music; and in his last works he turned with renewed conviction to the heritage of Couperin and Rameau. The changes that Debussy introduced, especially those in the harmonic system, made him one of the great seminal forces in the history of music. To name the composers who at one time or another came under his influence would be to name nearly every distinguished composer of the early and middle twentieth century.

An anti-impressionist (not altogether anti-Debussy) movement in France was spearheaded on the literary and theatrical side by Jean Cocteau and on the musical side by the eccentric genius Erik Satie (1866–1925). Some of Satie's early piano pieces (for example the three *Gymnopédies* of 1888) anticipated the unresolved chords and quasi-modal harmonies of impressionism in an ostentatiously plain texture. His piano works between 1900 and 1915 specialized in caricature, which took the outward form of surrealistic titles, with a running commentary and directions to the player in the same style,

Erik Satie

Among Satie's works for other media than the piano are the stylized "realistic ballet" *Parade* (1917) on a scenario by Cocteau with scenery and costumes by Picasso; and the "symphonic drama" *Socrate* (1920)—three songs for soprano voice and a small orchestra on texts translated from Plato—which, particularly in the last scene, *The Death of Socrates*, attains a poignancy which is intensified by the very monotony of the style and the studied avoidance of direct emotional appeal.

The next important French composer after Debussy was Maurice Ravel (1875–1937); the titles of his first two and last compositions

The curtain painted by Pablo Picasso for the Diaghilev production of Parade *in Paris, 1917. The ballet, with music by Satie, is a satire on the activities of a small French touring company. The instrumentation includes sirens and typewriters.*

Maurice Ravel

for piano—*Menuet antique* (1895), *Pavane pour une Infante défunte* (*Pavane for a Deceased Infanta;* 1899), and *Le Tombeau de Couperin* (1917)—give a hint of the direction in which his work diverged from that of Debussy. Although Ravel adopted some of the impressionist technique, this never overcame his basic affinity for the clean melodic contours, distinct rhythms, and firm structures of Classicism. Moreover, his harmonies, while complex and sophisticated, are functional. Thus, in the *Menuet* (NAWM/S 79) of *Le Tombeau de Couperin* the melody is clearly phrased in groups of four measures, with a tonic cadence at the end of the first phrase and a mediant cadence with raised third at the end of the second. Ravel's Classical orientation is most clearly apparent, of course, in such works as the piano *Sonatine* (1905) and the chamber music. His most markedly impressionistic works for piano are the *Jeux d'eau* (1901), the five pieces entitled *Miroirs* (1905), and the three entitled *Gaspard de la nuit* (1908). Impressionist also to some extent are the orchestral suite *Rapsodie espagnole* (1907) and the ballet *Daphnis et Chloé* (1909–11).

Ravel was able to absorb ideas from everywhere, adapting them to his own use. He used jazz elements in the piano *Concerto for the Left Hand* (1930), and Spanish idioms in the *Rapsodie,* the comic opera *L'Heure espagnole* (1910), and the rousing *Bolero* (1928), which became the musical equivalent of a best-seller. One of his most charming works is *Ma Mère l'Oye* (*Mother Goose*), a set of five little piano duets written in 1908, children's music comparable to Mussorgsky's *Nursery* songs and Debussy's *Children's Corner.*

Among Ravel's songs are many settings of folk melodies from various countries; his important original songs are the five humorous and realistic characterizations of animal life in the *Histoires naturelles* (1906) and the *Chansons madécasses* (*Songs of Madagascar;* 1926), for voice, flute, violoncello, and piano.

A composer whose significance extends beyond the first decade of the century is Albert Roussel (1869–1937) whose three symphonic *Évocations* (1911) and the opera-ballet *Padmâvatî* (composed 1914, first performed 1923) carried to new heights the French Romantic musical treatment of exotic subjects. His later works show the contemporary trend toward neo-Classicism, evident particularly in the orchestral *Suite in F* (1926), the Third Symphony, in G minor (1930), and the *Sinfonietta* for string orchestra (1934).

Peripheries

One of the lesser musical "isms" of the late nineteenth century was *verism* (*verismo*) in Italian opera. The word means literally "truthism"; it is sometimes translated as "realism" or "naturalism." Its first sign is the choice of a libretto that presents everyday people in familiar situations acting violently under the impulse of primitive emotions. Its second sign is a musical style appropriate to such a libretto. The veristic opera is the innocent grandfather of the television and cinema shock drama. It was just as typical of the post-Romantic period as dissonance, hugeness, and the other musical devices which were used to titillate jaded sensibilities. The veristic operas par excellence are *Cavalleria rusticana* (*Rustic Chivalry;* 1890) by Pietro Mascagni (1863–1945) and *I Pagliacci* (*The Clowns;* 1892) by Ruggiero Leoncavallo (1858–1919). Verism was shortlived, though it had some parallels or repercussions in France and Germany.

Italian opera

The most important Italian opera composer of the late nineteenth and early twentieth centuries was Giacomo Puccini (1858–1924), like Massenet a successful eclectic whose works reflect in turn the late Romantic taste for sentiment (*Manon Lescaut;* 1893), sentiment with realism (*La Bohème;* 1896), verism (*Tosca;* 1900), and exoticism (*Madama Butterfly,* 1904; *Turandot,* first performance 1926) in music of lyric intensity, discreetly incorporating modern touches of harmony, and managed with a marvelous flair for theatrical effect.

Running through all the later nineteenth century was the steady trend toward the dissolution of Classical tonality, a trend already perceptible in Schubert and Chopin, continued in Liszt and Wagner, accentuated with the harmonic experiments of Mussorgsky,

Summary

Theatrical poster created by Adolfo Hohenstein for the opera Tosca *by Giacomo Puccini, 1899.*

Mahler, Strauss, Fauré, Debussy, and Ravel, and climaxed to a certain point in the prewar works of Scriabin, Ives, Schoenberg, Bartók, and Stravinsky. Chromaticism, complex and unorthodox chords, national folk song, exoticism, modality, the use of pentatonic, whole-tone, or other non-Classical scales, chord-streams, polytonality—all had a part. To a large extent composers in the first half of the twentieth century were occupied with endeavors to work out new concepts of, or find an adequate substitute for, tonality and to reconcile with new harmonic idioms the other musical elements of instrumentation, counterpoint, rhythm, and form.

XX

The Twentieth Century

Introduction

In this final chapter we shall survey the work of a few composers who were leading figures in music from about 1910 to 1970 and give some account of various movements that have arisen since the latter date. Some of the composers to be mentioned were already active before 1910, others rose to prominence only after the Second World War; the career of one, Stravinsky, spanned the entire period 1910 to 1970. We shall still be concerned in this chapter with the momentous first decade of the century—not, now, in its aspects as the end of the Classic-Romantic age but as the beginning of a new era.

Three main directions or tendencies may be traced in the music of the first half of the twentieth century, which correspond roughly to the three main lines of development in the preceding period: first, the continuing growth of musical styles which employed significant elements from national folk idioms; second, the rise of various movements, including neo-Classicism, in the interwar years, which aimed at incorporating the new discoveries of the early part of the century into musical styles having more or less overt connection with principles, forms, and techniques of the past (especially, in some cases, the pre-nineteenth-century past); and third, the transformation of the German post-Romantic idiom into the *dodecaphonic* or twelve-tone styles of Schoenberg, Berg, and Webern. Cutting across all these tendencies, participating to some extent in one or more of

General features

them but not classifiable under any one of them, is the work of two extraordinary composers, Messiaen and Stravinsky, whom we must consider independently.

The three directions or tendencies mentioned are not "schools": except for the group around Schoenberg, none of these movements acknowledged a single central authority; all overlapped in time; each included many diverse practices, and more than one of them often were evident in a single composer or even a single composition; moreover, traces of Romanticism, exoticism, impressionism, and other influences were often mingled with them in one way or another.

Musical Styles Related to Folk Idioms

Consistent with the diversity of the musical scene in the first half of the twentieth century, national differences continued to be emphasized; indeed, speedier communication at first only accentuated contrasts between cultures. The nationalist musical activities of the twentieth century differed in several respects from those of the nineteenth. The study of folk material was undertaken on a much wider scale than previously, and with rigorous scientific method. Folk music was collected not by the clumsy process of seeking to transcribe it in conventional notation but with the accuracy made possible by the use of the phonograph; and collected specimens were analyzed objectively, by techniques developed in the new discipline of ethnomusicology, so as to discover the actual character of folk music instead of ignoring its "irregularities" or trying to adjust them to the rules of art music, as the Romantics had often done. More realistic knowledge led to greater respect for the unique qualities of folk music. Composers, instead of trying to absorb folk idioms into more or less traditional styles, used them to create new styles, and especially to extend the realm of tonality.

Central Europe was the scene of some of the earliest extensive scientific study of folk music. Janáček's pioneer work in the Czecho-Slovak region was soon followed by that of two Hungarian scholar-composers, Zoltán Kodály (1882–1967) and Béla Bartók (1881–1945).

Béla Bartók

Bartók's importance is threefold. He published nearly two thousand folk tunes, chiefly from Hungary and Rumania, these being only a part of all that he had collected in expeditions ranging over Central Europe, Turkey, and North Africa. He wrote five books and innumerable articles on folk music, made settings of or based compositions on folk tunes, and developed a style in which he fused folk elements with highly developed techniques of art music more intimately than had ever been done. Second, he was a virtuoso pianist and a teacher of piano at the Budapest Academy of Music from 1907 to 1934; his *Mikrokosmos* (1926–37)—153 piano pieces in six books of graded difficulty—is not only a work of great pedagogical value but also a summary of Bartók's own style and of many aspects of the development of European music in the first half of the twentieth century. Third and finally, he was one of the four or five composers active between 1910 and 1945 whose music is likely to endure for several generations to come.

The earliest works that begin to manifest Bartók's individual style were composed about 1908, shortly after he had become interested in Hungarian, Rumanian, and other folk songs. Compositions of this period include the First Quartet (1908), the one-act opera *Duke Bluebeard's Castle* (1911), and the *Allegro barbaro* for piano. The last is frequently cited as an example of "primitivism," that is, the stylized imitation of primitive music by means of pounding, frenetic rhythms, limited melodic range with much repetition of motives, and pungent percussive harmonies. Bartók, like many

Autograph manuscript of the first page of the Finale of Bartók's Concerto for Orchestra. (*Library of Congress*)

twentieth-century composers, often treats the piano more as an instrument of percussion, in a class with the celesta or xylophone, than as a producer of cantabile melodies and arpeggiated chords, as the Romantics had conceived it. By 1917, the influences from late Romanticism and impressionism had been thoroughly absorbed into the characteristic rhythmic vigor, exuberant imagination, and elemental folk qualities of Bartók's style; in that year he wrote the Second Quartet. Compositions of the next ten years show him pushing toward the limits of dissonance and tonal ambiguity, reaching the furthest point with the two violin sonatas of 1922 and 1923. Other works of this decade were the pantomime *The Miraculous Mandarin* (1919), the *Dance Suite* for orchestra (1923), the Piano Sonata (1926), the first Piano Concerto (1926), and the Third Quartet (1927).

The later works of Bartók are the most widely known. In the *Cantata profana* (1930), for tenor and baritone soloists, double chorus, and orchestra, is distilled the spirit of all Bartók's many vocal and instrumental works specifically based on folk songs or folklike themes. A second Piano Concerto dates from 1931. The Violin Concerto (1938) and the *Concerto for Orchestra* (1943) are masterpieces in large form. Other works of the late period are the Fifth and Sixth Quartets (1934, 1939), the *Divertimento* for string orchestra (1939), the *Mikrokosmos,* the *Music for String Instruments, Percussion, and Celesta* (1936), the *Sonata for Two Pianos and Percussion* (1937), and the Third Piano Concerto (1945; his last completed composition).

Bartók's ideal was to express, in twentieth-century terms, Bach's texture of contrapuntal fullness, Beethoven's art of thematic development, and Debussy's discovery of the sonorous (as distinct from the functional) value of chords. The elements of his style are: melodic lines derived or sublimated from east European folk music; powerful "motoristic" rhythms, characteristically subtilized by irregular meters and offbeat accents; an intense expressionistic drive, regulated by strong formal control embracing everything from the generation of themes to the comprehensive design of an entire work. His textures may be prevailingly homophonic or be made up of contrapuntal lines carried on with secondary regard for vertical sonorities (*linear* counterpoint). The polyphony may include free use of imitative, fugal, and canonic techniques (No. 145 of the *Mikrokosmos,* the first movement of the *Music for String Instruments, Percussion, and Celesta,* or the two outer movements of the *Concerto for Orchestra*); and frequently one or more of the interweaving lines will be enriched by parallel-moving voices in chord streams.

Bartók's harmony is in part an incidental result of the contrapuntal movement; it grows out of the character of the melodies, which may be based on pentatonic, whole-tone, modal, or irregular scales (including those found in folk music) as well as the regular diatonic and chromatic scales. All kinds of chords appear, from triads to combinations built on fourths (quite frequent) and other constructions more complex. Bartók often gives pungency to a chord by adding dissonant major or minor seconds (as in the final Ab triad of the *Allegretto pizzicato* movement of the Fourth Quartet: see Example XX–1a); sometimes seconds are piled up in tone clusters (as in the Piano Sonata, the first Piano Concerto [Example

Bartók's harmony

EXAMPLE XX–1   Examples of Chords with Seconds and Tone Clusters, Béla Bartók

XX–1b], or the slow movement of the Second Concerto). But on the whole, especially in the quartets, both the construction and the progressions of chords are extremely complex and difficult to analyze. Bartók's music, although it is essentially Western, not exotic, nonetheless has a great deal of the strange, unpredictable violence of barbaric impulses in its harmonies as well as in its rhythms.

Most of his music is tonal in the sense that a fundamental key center is recurrently present, though it may be effectually obscured for considerable stretches either by modal or chromatic means, or both at once. Occasionally, and especially in the works of the nineteen-twenties, Bartók writes on two or more simultaneous harmonic planes (so-called *polytonality*), but he does not aim systematically at negating tonality. Moreover, though he sometimes writes a theme that includes up to twelve different tones in a row (as in the first movement of the Violin Concerto, measures 73–75 and finale at 129–34), or otherwise uses all the notes of the chromatic scale in a single phrase (opening of the Third and Fourth Quartets), he never uses a technique systematically based on this device. In some of Bartók's late works tonality is defined by relatively familiar procedures—particularly so in the Third Piano Concerto, the *Concerto for Orchestra,* and the Second Violin Concerto. More commonly, however, the tonal field is less definite and the relations within it harder to grasp.

In the Adagio movement of the *Music for String Instruments, Percussion, and Celesta* (NAWM/S 83) Bartók experiments with mirror form both on a minute and large scale. In microcosm it is seen in the xylophone solo, which, taking the drum roll as a starting point, is identical going in either direction. On a large scale the midpoint of the piece, at measures 47–50, is itself in mirror canon, that is, measures 47–48 are identical to 49–50 played backwards. This is formally the midpoint in the sense that the piece is approximately symmetrical in the distribution of material around this point: Prologue *ABCDC/BA* Epilogue. Several diverse styles may be discerned. The *A* sections are in the *parlando-rubato* idiom of Serbo-Croatian folk song. The *B* section, which recurs in combination with the *C* section, represents another folk technique, that of heterophony, in which instruments play in octaves against drones and a chordal tapestry of sound produced by plucked instruments, as in the Bulgarian dance orchestras. In the *C* sections, two mutually exclusive pentatonic scales are juxtaposed in the celesta and piano figurations. The *D* section, which includes the mirror writing, is again heterophonic. In this Adagio, then, Bartók has fully assimilated styles of improvised folk music into one of his most original and thoroughly deliberated works of art music.

Brilliant, imaginative sonorities are amply evident in any of Bartók's scores: examples are the colorful orchestration of *The Miraculous Mandarin,* the *Dance Suite,* and the *Concerto for Orchestra.* Virtuosity in the treatment of percussion is especially notable in the *Sonata for Two Pianos and Percussion.* The quartets are full of arresting sonorities, in some of which multiple stops, glissandos, different types of pizzicato, *col legno,* and the like play a part.

The range of Bartók's style is summarized not only in the *Mikrokosmos* but also—and even more thoroughly—in the quartets, which constitute the most important large addition to the repertoire of this medium since Beethoven. The guiding thread through all Bartók's work is the variety and skill with which he integrated the essence of folk music with the highest forms of Western art music. Bartók was not primarily an innovator; rather, like Handel, he gathered up the achievements of the past and present in an individual synthesis and expressed them eloquently. It is a sign of the difference between their worlds—and particularly of the changed relationship between composer and public—that, unlike Handel, Bartók was very little understood during his lifetime.

Russian folk songs, textures, and rhythms appear to some extent in the early compositions of Stravinsky. National influences of various sorts are of course prominent in much Soviet music, as for example the cantata *Alexander Nevsky* (1938: originally a film score) and the opera *War and Peace* (1941) by Sergei Prokofiev (1891–1953), the folk song quotations in the opera *Lady Macbeth* (1934) by Dmitri Shostakovich (1906–76), and the same composer's Seventh Symphony, inspired by the heroic defense of Leningrad against the German armies in 1941.

Other composers

Neither Prokofiev nor Shostakovich, however, is a nationalist in the narrower meaning of the word. Prokofiev lived outside Russia from 1918 to 1934, and his compositions of these years are only sporadically touched by national influences. The *Scythian Suite* for orchestra (1916) represents an early nationalistic stage in his music. The *Classical Symphony* (1918), the Third Piano Concerto (1921), and some of the music from the opera *The Love of Three Oranges* (1921) are the best known of his early works; the symphonic suite *Lieutenant Kije* (1934; arranged from music for a film), the "symphonic fairy tale" *Peter and the Wolf,* for narrator and orchestra (1936), and the ballet *Romeo and Juliet* (1938) have become widely popular. Prokofiev's other works include chamber music, piano sonatas and other piano pieces, operas, ballets, concertos, and symphonies, among which the second Violin Concerto (1935) and the Fifth Symphony (1944) are outstanding. In general, Prokofiev's style is spiced by a sufficient admixture of national and modern features to save it from banality without endangering its chances for wide popular acceptance. The music of Shostakovich, whose principal compositions, in addition to those already noted, are the Fifth Symphony (1937), the Piano Quintet (1940), and the astringent, lightly scored Fourteenth Symphony (1969), assimilates the national heritage (coming largely through Tchaikovsky) to the main European tradition, with particular influences from Mahler and Hindemith; but although it is undeniably Russian in sound, it shows few traces of specific folk-song elements.

England

The foremost English composer in the first half of the twentieth century was Ralph Vaughan Williams, whose productions include nine symphonies and other orchestral pieces, songs, operas, and a great many choral works. Amid all the variety of dimensions and forms, Vaughan Williams's music was constantly motivated from sources both national and cosmopolitan: English folk song, hymnody—he even created new hymn tunes, such as the *Sine nomine*

Vaughan Williams

EXAMPLE XX–2   Examples of Themes by Ralph Vaughan Williams

a. Hymn tune, *Sine nomine*

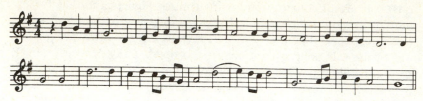

b. *Pastoral Symphony*, 4th movement

c. *Pastoral Symphony*, 3rd movement

d. *Pastoral Symphony*, 1st movement

Molto moderato

(Example XX–2a)—and literature on the one hand, and the European tradition of Bach and Handel, Debussy and Ravel on the other. But the essential quality of his music is deeper than any enumeration of influences can suggest; his works exemplify his own saying that "the composer must not shut himself up and think about art, he must live with his fellows and make his art an expression of the whole life of the community"[1]—meaning here not only the English nation but the whole community of English-speaking peoples on both sides of the Atlantic.

[1] From an essay, "Who Wants the English Composer?", 1912, pr. in Hubert Foss, *Ralph Vaughan Williams,* 200.

The *London Symphony* (1914; revised 1920), is a loving evocation of the sounds and atmosphere of the city, a program symphony in the same sense as Mendelssohn's *Italian* or Schumann's *Rhenish*. It has the regular four movements—the third is called *Scherzo (Nocturne)*—and dies away at the end in an Epilogue on the theme of the lento introduction to the first movement. Similar epilogues are found in the later symphonies, and many of Vaughan Williams's large compositions end *pianissimo*. The *London* was his second symphony. The first, the *Sea Symphony* (1910) for orchestra and voices on texts from Walt Whitman, is less important than another early work, the *Fantasia on a Theme of Thomas Tallis* (1909) for double string orchestra and string quartet, in which are heard the antiphonal sonorities and the rich texture of ascetic triads in parallel motion within a modal framework that also characterized many of his later compositions.

The *Pastoral Symphony* (1922) is less definitely programmatic than the *London*. A single mood prevails throughout; there are few strong contrasts of melodic character, dynamics, or tempo among the four movements, but many changing instrumental colors. A wordless melisma in unbarred free rhythm for solo soprano is heard at the beginning and (in shortened form) the close of the last movement (Example XX–2b); it exemplifies a type of melody with gapped scales (here of pentatonic character) that often occurs in Vaughan Williams's music. Equally characteristic and folk-song-like is the trumpet tune in the trio of the third movement (Example XX–2c). Especially effective use is made of the chord-stream texture in this symphony (Example XX–2d).

Vaughan Williams was on the whole a conservative composer, sharing the Englishman's typical distrust of theories, especially theories pushed to extremes in practice. Even his most dissonant passages never outrage the national instinct for euphonious sound present also in the *Sumer* canon and the works of Dunstable and Byrd; and although his field of tonality is broad, as befits a composer of the twentieth century, it does not extend to regions of obscurity. Fundamental simplicity, a sense of humor, and a horror of Romantic rhetoric are compatible with strong ethical, even mystical, emotions.

The principal English contemporary, as well as close friend, of Vaughan Williams was Gustav Holst (1874–1934), whose music was influenced not only by English folk song but also by Hindu mysticism. His best-known work is an orchestral suite *The Planets* (1916). Outstanding among Holst's later music is an orchestral piece *Egdon Heath* (1927), which the composer considered to be his best work.

Benjamin Britten (1913–76), the most prolific and most famous English composer of the mid-twentieth century, is distinguished

Vaughan Williams's style

Other English composers

especially for his choral works (*A Boy Was Born,* 1935; *A Ceremony of Carols,* 1942; *Spring Symphony,* 1947), songs, and operas, of which the most important are *Peter Grimes* (1945) and *The Turn of the Screw* (1954). The closing pages of *Peter Grimes* (NAWM/S 88) are an eloquent example of the remarkable dramatic effects Britten creates out of very simple means, orchestrally dressed up. His *War Requiem* (1962) received worldwide acclaim following its first performance at Coventry Cathedral. It is an impressive, large work for soloists, chorus, boys' choir, and orchestra on the Latin text of the Requiem Mass alternating with verses by Wilfred Owen, a young English soldier who was killed in France in 1918. The music, while incorporating many modern features in a very individual way, is not essentially radical in its language. The work takes its place in the long European musical tradition and particularly—like Britten's other vocal works—in the great English tradition of choral music.

The United States

Nationalism has played only a subsidiary part in the musical scene of twentieth-century United States of America. The composer who hoped to bridge the gulf between popular music and the concert hall audience in the 1920s was George Gershwin (1898–1937), whose *Rhapsody in Blue* (1924) was an attempt to combine the languages of jazz and Lisztian Romanticism. More spontaneous expression of his natural gifts came in the musical comedies (*Of Thee I Sing;* 1931) and especially in the "folk opera" *Porgy and Bess* (1935).

Aaron Copland

An example of integration of national American idioms in the music of a composer of high endowment and thorough technical training is found in the work of Aaron Copland (born 1900). Copland was the first of many American composers of his generation who studied at Paris under the famous teacher Nadia Boulanger (1887–1979). Jazz idioms and dissonance are prominent in some of his earlier works, such as the *Music for the Theater* (1925) and the Piano Concerto (1927). These were followed by a number of compositions of a more reserved and harmonically complex style, represented by the Piano Variations of 1930. The felt need to appeal to a larger audience motivated a turn toward simplicity, diatonic harmonies, and the use of folk-song material—Mexican folk songs in the brilliant orchestral suite *El Salón México* (1936), cowboy songs in the ballets *Billy the Kid* (1938) and *Rodeo* (1942). The apex of this trend was reached in *Appalachian Spring* (1944), first written as a ballet with an orchestra of thirteen instruments but better known in the arrangement as a suite for symphony orchestra. *Appalachian Spring* is in Copland's work what the *Pastoral* Symphony is in Vaughan Williams's. Unlike the English composer, Copland incorporates an actual folk tune (the Shaker hymn *The Gift to Be Simple*) as well as suggestions of folk dance music; but the material is subtly transfigured and its essence absorbed in a work that sincerely and simply expresses the pastoral spirit in authentically American terms.

On the technical side, Copland sometimes uses any or all notes of the diatonic scale for vertical combinations: the opening chord of *Appalachian Spring*, with its derivations and amplifications, serves as a unifying device, a characteristic sonority with divided strings and soft woodwinds that returns from time to time throughout the work (see Example XX–3).

EXAMPLE XX–3   Chord Forms in *Appalachian Spring*, Aaron Copland

A new synthesis on a large scale appeared with the Third Symphony (1946), which has no overt programmatic significance (though some of its tunes are suggestive of folk songs), and well exemplifies Copland's characteristic combination of "leanness and grandiosity."[2] A more finely-wrought chamber music idiom, a further evolution from the style of the Piano Variations, is found in the Piano Sonata (1941). In the songs on *Twelve Poems of Emily Dickinson* (1950), and more markedly in the Piano Quartet (1950), the Piano Fantasy (1957), and the orchestral *Inscape* (1967), Copland adopts some features of the twelve-tone technique. Despite the various influences reflected in the range of styles in his works, Copland retains an unmistakable personal quality. His music preserves the sense of tonality, though not always by traditional means; his rhythms are live and flexible, and he is adept at obtaining new sounds from simple chords by instrumental color and spacing. His work and counsel have influenced many younger American composers.

A more self-conscious nationalist was Roy Harris (1898–1979), whose music at its best (as in the Third Symphony, 1939) suggests something of the rugged simplicity of Walt Whitman; some of his works embody actual folk themes, as for example the choral *Folk Song Symphony* (1941). Likewise incorporating specifically

Other American composers

2 Arthur Berger, *Aaron Copland*, 40.

American idioms (blues) is the *Afro-American Symphony* (1931) of William Grant Still (1895–1978).

The genuinely national element in this country's music is not easily isolated or defined, blended as it is with cosmopolitan style features which it shares with European music of the period. It may be detected, perhaps, in a certain forthright, optimistic character, or in a feeling for flowing, unconstrained color and melody as in Ulysses Kay's (born 1917) *Serenade for Orchestra* (1954) and *Umbrian Scene* (1964)—or again, in a fast-driving rhythmic energy, such as that of Robert Palmer's (born 1915) Piano Quartet (1947). Some eminent American composers wrote habitually in a language that cannot be called national in any limiting sense of the word. Howard Hanson (1896–1981) was an avowed neo-Romantic with a style influenced by Sibelius; the chamber music and symphonies of Walter Piston (1894–1976) are in a sturdy and sophisticated neo-Classical idiom. The music of Roger Sessions (born 1896) is more intense, dissonant, and chromatic, receptive to influences from his teacher Ernest Bloch and, to a lesser degree, from Arnold Schoenberg, but nonetheless stoutly individual (Third Symphony, 1957; the opera *Montezuma,* 1962; the cantata *When lilacs last,* 1971). An equally personal style, with notable innovations in the treatment of rhythm and form, is evident in the compositions of Elliott Carter (born 1908), particularly the *Variations for Orchestra* (1955), the Second String Quartet (1959), and the Double Concerto for piano and harpsichord (1961); still further innovations characterize his more recent Piano Concerto and *Concerto for Orchestra.*

The principal representatives of nationalism in Latin American music were Heitor Villa-Lobos (1887–1959) of Brazil and Silvestre Revueltas (1898–1940) and Carlos Chávez (1899–1978) of Mexico. Significant among more recent Latin-American composers is the Argentinian Alberto Ginastera (1916–1983), whose opera *Bomarzo* made a strong impression at its first performances in 1967.

Neo-Classicism and Related Movements

The effects of experiments begun in the earlier part of the century continued to be felt in the interwar decades. Many composers (including most of those mentioned in the foregoing section) endeavored, in various ways and to varying extents, to absorb the new discoveries without losing continuity with tradition; they held to some recognizably familiar features of the past—tonal centers (defined or alluded to often in quite new ways), melodic shape, goal-oriented movement of musical ideas, for example—while incorporating fresh and unfamiliar elements. Two composers of this era in France were Arthur Honegger and Darius Milhaud.

Honegger (1892–1955), of Swiss parentage but born in France and resident in Paris after 1913, excelled in music of dynamic action and graphic gesture, expressed in short-breathed melodies, strong ostinato rhythms, bold colors, and dissonant harmonies. Honegger became world famous after the appearance in concert form (1923) of his oratorio *King David,* which had been first presented in an original stage version two years before. On a grander scale—with five speaking parts, five soloists, mixed chorus (which both sings and speaks), children's chorus, and large orchestra—is *Jeanne d'Arc au Bûcher (Joan of Arc at the Stake;* 1938), an elaborate oratorio-drama by Paul Claudel, with music in which Gregorian Chant, dance tunes, and modern and medieval folk-songs are mingled with Honegger's dissonant, highly colored idiom; this work is held together more by dramatic power than by musical architecture.

Darius Milhaud (1894–1974) was a native of Aix in Provence. He created a gracious memorial of his native region in the *Suite Provençale* for orchestra (1937), which incorporates melodies of the early eighteenth-century composer André Campra. Milhaud produced an immense quantity of music. He was an artist of Classical temperament, not given to theories or systems, but infinitely receptive to many kinds of stimuli which are spontaneously converted to musical expression: Brazilian folk melodies and rhythms, for example, in the orchestral dances (later arranged for piano) *Saudades do Brasil (Souvenirs of Brazil;* 1920–21); saxophones, ragtime syncopations, and the blues third in the ballet *La Création du monde (The Creation of the World;* 1924). Milhaud's music is essentially lyrical in inspiration, blended of ingenuousness and ingenuity, clear and logical in form, and addressed to the listener as objective statement, not personal confession.

One technical device which appears recurrently in Milhaud as well as in many other composers contemporary with him (for example, the Netherlander Willem Pijper, 1894–1927) is *polytonality* —one of those terms that are easier to use than to define. Of course we can say that polytonality is the property of music written in two or more keys at once. But is it really possible to *hear* more than one tonality at a time? If it is not, we must conclude that "polytonal" music means no more than music in which one can discern by analysis (usually visual) that two or more lines of melody or planes of harmony, each in a distinct and different key, are sounding simultaneously. A simple instance is given in Example XX–4.

Extension of the polytonal principle produced the complex dissonances of *Christophe Colomb* and of the closing scene of the opera *Les Euménides* (1924); in the latter Milhaud builds up to six simultaneous different keys, reduces them gradually to two, and finally resolves on the single key of C major. A similar piling up

Darius Milhaud

EXAMPLE XX–4 Polytonality in *Saudades do Brasil,* I, No. 4
("Copacabana"), Milhaud

a. *Saudades do Brasil,* I, No. 4 ("Copacabaña")

Saudades do Brasil, © 1922, renewed 1950 by Editions Max Eschig. Used by permission of Associated Music Publishers, Inc.

of tonalities occurs in the first movement of the Fourth Symphony (1948). Of course no listener hears the two tonalities B major and G major in Example XX–4. What he hears is G major with a few dissonant notes which he probably interprets as passing tones or nonresolving appoggiaturas; in *Les Euménides* and similar passages, he hears a mass of undifferentiated dissonance in which the direction of the musical movement is defined by rhythms and melodic lines, while the arrival at the final goal is made climactic by the resolution of dissonance into consonance. Milhaud offers a simple explanation of his use of polytonal chords: "The sound of them satisfied my ear; a polytonal chord when soft is more subtly sweet and when forceful is more violent than the normal kind." And he adds that he used such chords "only to support a diatonic melody" —an important qualification, to which another may be added, namely that the various polytonal planes are distinguished by different instrumental timbres in orchestral writing, and this incidentally diminishes their dissonant effect.

The gamut of Milhaud's style is disclosed in his operas. In addition to the music for Claudel's translations of three plays from Aeschylus (composed between 1913 and 1924), these include *Les Malheurs d'Orphée* (*The Misfortunes of Orpheus,* 1924), *Le Pauvre Matelot* (*The Poor Sailor,* 1926) on a libretto by Jean Cocteau; three *opéras minutes,* running about ten minutes each, on parodies of classical myths (1927); the huge oratorio-opera *Christophe Colomb* (1928); and the Biblical opera *David,* commissioned to celebrate the 3,000th anniversary of Jerusalem as the capital of David's kingdom, and first performed in concert version at Jerusalem in 1954. All Milhaud's operas, in contrast to the symphonic music dramas of Wagner, are organized in distinct scene complexes with arias and choruses, and the singing voices are the center of interest rather than the orchestra.

The compositions of Francis Poulenc (1899–1963) are for the

most part in small forms. He combined the grace and wit of the Parisian popular *chansons* with a gift for satirical mimicry—of Puccini, Massenet, and Debussy in his comic opera *Les Mamelles de Tirésias* (*The Breasts of Tiresias;* 1940), for example—and natural fluent melody with an ingratiating harmonic idiom. By no means were all his works frivolous. His *Concert champêtre* (*Pastoral Concerto*) for harpsichord or piano and small orchestra (1928) is neo-Classical in the spirit of Rameau and Domenico Scarlatti; among his compositions are a Mass in G for chorus *a cappella* (1937), several motets, and other choral works. He is very highly regarded as a composer of songs. His three-act serious opera *Dialogues des Carmélites* (*Dialogues of the Carmelites;* 1956) is a most effective setting of an unusually fine libretto by Georges Bernanos.

Francis Poulenc

Hindemith

The leading German composer of the first half of the twentieth century was Paul Hindemith (1895–1963). He is notable not only as a composer but also as a theorist who undertook to formulate a general system of composition, hoping to establish a basis on which the divergent practices of the time might find common ground for further progress. His work as a teacher—at the Berlin School of Music 1927–37, Yale University 1940–53, and the University of Zurich after 1953—was also important.

Hindemith was first of all a practical musician. An experienced solo, orchestral, and ensemble player on the violin and viola, he learned to play many other instruments as well. Younger than Schoenberg, Bartók, and Stravinsky, he did not go through any early important Romantic or impressionist stage but plunged at once with his first published compositions into the confused and confusing world of the new music in Germany of the 1920s. It is noteworthy that in the light of changed conceptions of tonality the composer some twenty-five years later revised the three principal large works of this decade. These were a song cycle for soprano voice and piano on poems of R. M. Rilke, *Das Marienleben* (*The Life of Mary,* 1923), the tragic expressionist opera *Cardillac* (1926), and the comic opera *Neues vom Tage* (*News of the Day;* 1929). Four string quartets and a large quantity of other chamber music are also among Hindemith's works of this period.

In the late 1920s and early 1930s, Hindemith, disturbed by the cleavage between composers and an increasingly passive public, undertook the works that caused his name to be associated with *Gebrauchsmusik*—that is, music for use, as distinguished from music for music's sake. Among such works were a musical playlet for children entitled *Wir bauen eine Stadt* (*Let's Build a Town;* 1930) and a number of pieces of the sort known in Germany as *Sing- und Spielmusik,* a term for which there is no convenient English equivalent. It means "music for singing and playing" by amateurs who do it for fun; it is "play" music in a double sense of the word. It is of necessity not too difficult, and must be attractive for the performers without being vulgar. *Spielmusik* occupies an important place both in Hindemith's works and in his teachings about the social obligations of a composer.

Less dissonant linear counterpoint, more systematic tonal organization, and a new quality of almost Romantic warmth became evident in the 1930s (compare Example XX–5a and b). Compositions of this decade include the opera *Mathis der Maler (Matthias the Painter;* 1934), based on the life and works of the sixteenth-century German artist Matthias Grünewald; the symphony composed of excerpts from this opera is probably the best known of all Hindemith's works. Also from this time come the three piano sonatas

EXAMPLE XX–5   Examples of Hindemith's Harmony

a. *Quartet No. 4*, slow movement

b. *Mathis der Maler*, Scene 6

(1936); a sonata for piano four hands (1938); the ballets *Nobilissima visione* (1938; on St. Francis of Assisi) and *The Four Temperaments* (1940); and the Symphony in E♭ (1940).

Much of Hindemith's music was composed for use in the sense that it was written for particular players, or to add to the repertoire of certain instruments for which little literature existed: among his numerous sonatas are some for such comparatively neglected solo instruments as the viola d'amore, horn, trumpet, English horn, double bass, and tuba, as well as the more usual ones (flute, oboe, clarinet, viola, violin, organ). There are concertos for orchestra and various instrumental groups (string quartet with piano, brass, and two harps; woodwinds and harp; trumpet, bassoon, and strings) and for solo instruments (piano, violin, violoncello, clarinet, organ); and there is a *Symphony for Concert Band* (1951).

Another kind of music for use was written for teaching purposes. The title *Klaviermusik: Übung in drei Stücken* (*Piano Music: Three Practice Pieces;* 1925) is reminiscent of Bach's *Clavier Übung.* Analogous to *The Well-Tempered Clavier* is Hindemith's *Ludus tonalis* (*Game of Tonalities;* 1942) for piano: subtitled "Studies in Counterpoint, Tonal Organization, and Piano Playing," it consists of twelve fugues (one in each key) with modulating interludes, a Prelude (C → F♯), and Postlude (F♯ → C).

Compositions after 1940 include the Fifth and Sixth Quartets (1943, 1945), the *Symphonic Metamorphoses* on themes of Weber (1943), a "requiem" on words of Whitman (*When lilacs last in the dooryard bloom'd*), and other choral works; and the opera *Die*

Harmonie der Welt (*The Harmony of the Universe*). Hindemith had begun writing this opera in the 1930s, but laid it aside when he came to the United States because there seemed no chance of getting such a work performed at that time. In 1952 he made a three-movement orchestral symphony out of some of the music and then continued work on the opera, which was finally presented at Munich in 1957. Among Hindemith's last works were an Octet for clarinet, bassoon, horn, violin, two violas, violoncello, and double bass; several fine madrigals;[3] an unpretentious one-act opera, *The Long Christmas Dinner* (after Thornton Wilder; 1961), and a Mass for chorus a *cappella,* first sung in Vienna in November of 1963.

Hindemith's work was as versatile and nearly as large in amount as Milhaud's. He was a mid-twentieth-century representative of the German cosmopolitan line of Schumann, Brahms, and Reger; additional influences in his work came from Debussy as well as from Bach, Handel, Schütz, and the German sixteenth-century Lied composers. Hindemith was a "natural musician" like Bach, producing music as a tree produces fruit. Although his efforts to establish a common basis for all musical composition in the twentieth century were not successful, his music retains its vitality. Several of his compositions—*Mathis der Maler,* the Violin Concerto of 1939, the *Nobilissima visione,* the *Symphonic Metamorphoses*—are still among the most frequently performed works in concerts, while his numerous sonatas for brass and other wind instruments are staples in the repertoire of players.

Messiaen

An influential, unique, and quite unclassifiable figure in music around the middle of the twentieth century was Olivier Messiaen. Born at Avignon in 1908, Messiaen studied organ and composition at Paris and became professor in the Conservatoire there in 1942. His many distinguished pupils included Pierre Boulez and Karlheinz Stockhausen, who became leaders among the new musical movements of the 1950s and '60s, as well as the Italian Luigi Nono (b. 1924), the Netherlander Ton de Leeuw (b. 1926), and many other important composers of that generation.

It is a tribute to the quality of Messiaen's teaching that not one of his pupils has merely imitated his style; each, while acknowledging a debt to the instruction received, has gone his own way. Thus Messiaen was not the founder of a school of composition in the ordinary sense of the word. His own compositions of the 1930s, especially those for the organ, attracted favorable attention every-

[3] See the score and analysis of one of these madrigals in Austin, *Music in the Twentieth Century,* 408–16.

where; his works of the '40s and '50s are less widely known. In his music after 1960 he continued to cultivate a highly personal idiom, which diverged more and more from the main "progressive" currents of the second half of the century. An intricate system of verbal and grammatical equivalences pervades his *Meditations on the Mystery of the Holy Trinity* for organ, composed in 1969.

Characteristic of Messiaen's music from the beginning is a complete integration of wide-ranging emotional expressiveness, deeply religious in tone, with minutely organized means of intellectual control. To these he brings continuous discoveries of new sounds, new rhythms and harmonies, and new modes of relation between music and life—life in both the natural and the spiritual (supernatural) realms, which Messiaen views as wholly continuous or interlocked. His musical language shows traits of such diverse ancestors as Debussy, Scriabin, Wagner, Rimsky-Korsakov, Monteverdi, Josquin, and Perotin. In addition, he is a poet (writing his own texts for vocal works), a student of Greek poetry, and an accomplished amateur ornithologist.

Besides numerous works for piano and his own instrument, the organ, Messiaen's principal compositions include a *Quatuor pour la fin du temps* (*Quartet for the End of Time*) for violin, clarinet, violoncello, and piano, first performed by the composer and three fellow-prisoners at a German military prison camp in 1941; *Trois petites liturgies pour la présence divine* (*Three Short Liturgies of the Divine Presence*) for unison chorus of women's voices and small orchestra (1944); a symphony *Turangalîla* in ten movements for large orchestra (1948); *Cinq rechants* (*Five Refrains*) for unaccompanied chorus of mixed voices (1949); and *Chronochromie* (literally, *Time-Color*) for orchestra (1960).

Bird songs and other natural sounds always interested Messiaen; decorative bird-like figurations appear in the *Quatuor* of 1941 and increasingly in subsequent compositions. The *Oiseaux exotiques* for piano (1958) are entirely devoted to them, and they make up practically the entire melodic-harmonic substance of *Chronochromie*. This devotion exemplifies one way in which Messiaen conceived music as related most intimately to Nature and, through Nature, to all of life. In this sense, all his music is programmatic—not only imitative or descriptive but also symbolical. One can best comprehend this from reading some of his explanatory "program notes" to his own works.

Stravinsky

We come now to a composer whose works exemplify nearly every significant musical tendency of the first half of the twentieth century,

Early works

whose career might almost by itself serve as an epitome of that changeful epoch, and whose influence on three generations of composers has been as great as, if not greater than, Wagner's influence between 1870 and 1910: Igor Stravinsky. Born in Russia in 1882, he came to Paris in 1911, lived in Switzerland after 1914, in Paris again after 1920, in California after 1940, and in New York from 1969 until his death in 1971. Stravinsky's principal early compositions were three ballets commissioned by Sergei Diaghilev (1872–1929), the founder and director of the Russian Ballet, which for twenty years after its first season at Paris in 1909 was a European institution that attracted the services of the leading artists of the time. For Diaghilev and Paris, Stravinsky wrote *The Fire Bird* (1910), *Petrushka* (1911), and *Le Sacre du printemps* (*The Rite of Spring,* subtitled *Pictures of Pagan Russia;* 1913). *The Fire Bird* stems from the Russian nationalist tradition, and has the exotic orientalism and rich sensuous orchestration of Stravinsky's teacher, Rimsky-Korsakov. *Petrushka* brings a touch of *verismo* in its circus scenes and characters, while the alert rhythms, bright raw orchestral colors, and leaner contrapuntal texture indicate realms that later were further explored by Stravinsky. The *Sacre* is undoubtedly the most famous composition of the early twentieth century; it had the effect of an explosion that so scattered the elements of musical language that they could never again be put together as before. Its first performance provoked a famous riot at Paris, though in the long run this work, along with *The Fire Bird* and *Petrushka,* has enjoyed more public favor than Stravinsky's later compositions.

1913–1923

The forced economy of wartime, together with Stravinsky's inner impulsion toward new goals, led to a change of style that became evident in the years 1913 to 1923. Compositions of this period include chamber music, short piano pieces, and songs; the ballets *L'Histoire du Soldat* (*The Soldier's Tale;* 1918), *Les Noces* (*The Wedding;* 1917–23), and *Pulcinella* (1919); and the Octet for Wind Instruments (1923). The first feature of the new style which strikes one is the replacement of a large orchestra by small combinations: for *L'Histoire,* solo instruments in pairs (violin and double bass, clarinet and bassoon, cornet and trombone) and a battery of percussion played by one person; for *Les Noces,* four pianos and percussion; for *Pulcinella,* a small orchestra with strings divided into concertino and ripieno groups. The *Ragtime* and *Piano Rag Music* were early examples (followed by some others, such as the *Ebony Concerto* of 1945) of his interest in jazz, an interest reflected also in the instrumentation and rhythms of *L'Histoire. Pulcinella* is a prelude to Stravinsky's neo-Classical period, of which the Octet is an example convenient for study. The Octet was followed by a Concerto for Piano and Wind Instruments (1924), a Piano Sonata (1924), and the *Serenade in A* for piano (1925).

The title page of Stravinsky's piano arrangement of Ragtime (*J. & W. Chester, London, 1919*), designed by Picasso.

Neo-Classical is the tag usually attached to Stravinsky's style from the time of the Octet to that of the opera *The Rake's Progress* (1951). The word may more broadly also designate a general tendency of this period, one best exemplified perhaps in Stravinsky and largely inspired by him, but evident also to a greater or lesser degree in the majority of other contemporary composers (including Schoenberg). In this sense neo-Classicism may be defined as adherence to the Classical principles of balance, coolness, objectivity, and absolute (as against Romantic program) music, with the corollary characteristics of economy, predominantly contrapuntal texture, and diatonic as well as chromatic harmonies; it sometimes involves also imitation or quotation of, or allusion to, specific melodies or style traits of older composers—as in Stravinsky's *Pulcinella,* which is built on themes supposedly from Pergolesi, or the ballet *Le Baiser de la Fée* (*The Fairy's Kiss;* 1928), based on themes from Tchaikovsky.

Of course the idea of renewing an art by turning to principles and models of an earlier time was not new; it was one of the basic ideas of the Renaissance, and composers of all periods have on occasion deliberately made use of older styles. But the neo-Classicism of the twentieth century had two special features: first, it was a symptom of a search for principles of order, for some way other than Schoenberg's out of the pitfalls of Romanticism and the seeming chaos of the years between 1910 and 1920; and second, composers as never before had a detailed knowledge of many past styles and were aware of the uses they were making of them. The aim was not to revive archaic idioms, but to acknowledge tradition in the sense that Stravinsky defined it: "a living force that animates and informs the present. . . . Far from implying the repetition of what has been, tradition presupposes the reality of what endures. It appears as an heirloom, a heritage that one receives on condition of making it bear fruit before passing it on to one's descendants." [4]

It was difficult for critics and the public, who thought of Stravinsky as the revolutionary composer of the *Sacre,* to comprehend the apparent reversal implied by *L'Histoire, Pulcinella,* and the Octet. With our perspective we can see that the change was not so radical as it at first seemed. However, each new work by Stravinsky continued to cause some reaction of surprise, because in each he elaborated a particular generative idea in forms, timbres, and harmonies appropriate to that idea and to no other. Merely to label all of his compositions written between 1923 and 1951 as neo-Classical would be—as always with classifications but especially so here—to overlook the variety in these productions, the individuality of each composition, and the continuity that underlies not only this period but the whole of his work from *The Fire Bird* on.

Stravinsky contributed two large compositions to choral literature: the opera-oratorio *Oedipus rex (Oedipus the King;* 1927) on a Latin translation of Cocteau's adaptation of Sophocles, for soloists, narrator, men's chorus, and orchestra; and the *Symphony of Psalms* (1930) for mixed chorus and orchestra on Latin texts from the Vulgate. Stravinsky used Latin because the language's being conventionalized, like a ritual, left him free to concentrate, as he said, on its "phonetic" qualities. *Oedipus* is statuesque, static, blocklike, intense within its stylized form. The *Symphony of Psalms* is one of the great works of the twentieth century, a masterpiece of invention, musical architecture, and religious devotion.

The subject of the opera *The Rake's Progress* (1951) was suggested by Hogarth's engravings; the libretto is by W. H. Auden and Chester Kallman. In this work Stravinsky adopts the eighteenth-century division into recitatives, arias, and ensembles, organizes the entire opera on the basis of key relationships, and achieves in the final scenes a climax of pathos without sentimentality.

Stravinsky's late works

A setting of the Mass (1948) for mixed chorus with double wood-wind quintet and brasses exhibits an austere "neo-Gothic" style that places this work transitionally between the *Symphony of Psalms* and the *Canticum sacrum* for tenor and baritone soloists, chorus, and orchestra, composed "in honor of St. Mark" and first sung in St. Mark's basilica at Venice in 1956. In parts of the *Canticum sacrum* and other compositions of the 1950s (including the Septet, 1953; the

---

[4] Stravinsky, *Poetics of Music,* 58–59.

song *In memoriam Dylan Thomas,* 1954; the ballet *Agon,* 1954–57; and *Threni,* 1958, for voices and orchestra on texts from the Lamentations of Jeremiah), Stravinsky, very gradually and judiciously but most effectively, adapted for his own purposes the techniques of the Schoenberg-Webern school—techniques that he explored still further in *Movements* (1959) and the *Orchestra Variations* (1964).

An analysis of Stravinsky's style that would do justice to both the diversity of its manifestations and the unity that underlies it throughout would require a book. Here we can only call attention to a few characteristic features, emphasizing as we do that Stravinsky's rhythms, harmonies, colors, and all other details are inseparate from a living body of music; the student should hear and study these features in their context, in the works themselves, and in so doing he will sharpen his perception for all the details in Stravinsky's music.

Stravinsky's style

Rhythm: One of the steps of the present century was the liberation of rhythm from the "tyranny of the barline," that is, from the regularity of constant two- or three-unit groups of strong and weak accents in which the strong accents regularly coincide with changes of harmony. Stravinsky often denies the barline by introducing an irregular pattern of rhythm after a regular one has been established, and by returning to the regular pattern from time to time (Example XX–6a). The regular beat may be maintained in one part against a conflicting irregular pattern in another (Example XX–6b); or two different rhythms may be combined (Example XX–6c). A rhythmic motive may be shifted from place to place in the measure (Example XX–6d). The rhythm at the beginning of the last movement of *Sacre* looks very irregular but sounds orderly; as a matter of fact it is organized rather symmetrically around the motive ♪ ♫♫ which appears eight times (Example XX–6e). Patterns of the subtlety of Example XX–6f may be found in practically any of Stravinsky's compositions of the neo-Classical period. Particularly fascinating is the way in which he thickens and then opens out the harmonies, dislocates and relocates the rhythms, in a long pulsation of tension and release before an important cadence: the endings of the Octet, the third and fourth movements of the Symphony in C, and the Sanctus in the Mass.

Another detail in Stravinsky's rhythm is his use of silences—sometimes merely a lift between chords, sometimes a breath on the downbeat before the beginning of a phrase, sometimes a rhetorical pause that accumulates tension in the progress toward a climax, for example in the second movement and the Interlude between the second and third movements of the *Symphony in Three Movements* (the second movement is in NAWM/S 80).

Harmony: Stravinsky's music is organized around tonal centers. Ambiguous chords like the one in the second movement of *Sacre*

EXAMPLE XX–6   Examples of Stravinsky's Rhythms

a. *Sacre du printemps* (Augures printaniers)

b. *Histoire du soldat*, Scene 1

osti-
nato:G d   A   g etc.

c. *Petrushka*, Part I

d. *Symphony of Psalms*, last movement

e. *Sacre du printemps* (Danse sacrale)

f. *Symphony in C*, second movement

(Example XX–7a) and the notorious bitonal C–F♯ in *Petrushka*
(Example XX–7b), however they may be explained, are certainly
not to be interpreted in their context as atonal. One type of ambiguity common in Stravinsky's work results from his use of both
the major and minor third of a triad either simultaneously or in
close juxtaposition (Examples XX–7c and d; in the latter example,
other degrees of the scale are also present in simultaneously conflicting forms).

A more subtle use of the major-minor third relationship is shown
in Example XX–7e: here the conflict between the keys of C and E♭

EXAMPLE XX–7   Examples of Stravinsky's Harmony

Symphony of Psalms, © 1931 by Russischer Musikverlag; renewed 1958. © and renewal assigned 1947 to Boosey & Hawkes, Inc. Revised version © 1948 by Boosey & Hawkes, Inc, renewed 1975. Reprinted by permission.

major (the minor third of C) is resolved to C major at measure seven. This chord marks at the same time a resolution of the tonal tendencies of the two preceding movements which centered respectively on the notes E and E♭, the major and minor thirds of C.

The diatonic passage in A major (with a chromatic F♮) of Example XX–8a contrasts with the more linear texture of Example XX—8b (notice the motive marked by brackets). This passage is in D and predominantly modal (Dorian). It is an instrumental phrase that recurs identically twice as a ritornello; at the end (Example XX–8c) Stravinsky takes B♯ = C♮ as a pivot note for a modulation back from the dominant A, then recapitulates in condensed form the harmonies

EXAMPLE XX–8   Further Examples of Stravinsky's Harmony

a. *Symphony in Three Movements*

b. **Agnus Dei** from *Mass:* beginning

c. **Agnus Dei** from *Mass:* conclusion

Symphony in Three Movements, copyright 1946 by Schott & Co., London. Copyright renewed. Used by permission of European American Music Distributors Corp. Sole U.S. agent for Schott & Co., London. *Mass*, © 1948 by Boosey & Hawkes, Inc.; renewed 1975. Reprinted by permission.

of the ritornello and adds a cadential echo, using only modal tones and leaving the seventh of the mode (C♮) with its fifth (G) unresolved in the final chord.

Orchestration: A high proportion of Stravinsky's works is written for unusual groups of instruments. This is another respect in which each new composition is a law to itself; the particular color is part of the particular musical conception in each instance. The odd combination of *L'Histoire* is ideally suited to—is inseparable from—the kind of music that the piece is; so equally are the serene strings of *Apollon musagète,* the dark solo woodwinds at the opening of the *Sacre,* and the Mozartean clarity of the orchestra of the Symphony in C.

The piano is used conspicuously and effectively in *Petrushka;* it contributes to the orchestral color (usually in conjunction with the harp) in many later works, notably *Oedipus,* the *Symphony of Psalms, Perséphone,* and the *Symphony in Three Movements.* Several works of the years around 1920 use no stringed instruments (*Ragtime, Les Noces,* Octet, Piano Concerto, *Symphonies of Wind Instruments*); it is as though Stravinsky distrusted their color as associated with sentimentality. The warm tones of the violins, violas, and clarinets are avoided in the *Symphony of Psalms.* In some of the late works the instruments are grouped antiphonally. In the Mass two oboes, English horn, and two bassoons are balanced against two trumpets and three trombones; the instrumentation of the *Canticum sacrum* is similar though somewhat larger (seven woodwinds and eight brasses), and harp, organ, violas, and double basses are also added to the antiphony. The tenor voice in the Dylan Thomas song is accompanied sparely by solo strings with short ritornellos for string quartet, and the song is framed by a prelude and postlude in which the strings alternate with a quartet of trombones in chorale-like dirge canons.

Stravinsky's esthetic

Stravinsky clearly defined his attitude toward composition in the *Poetics of Music* as the acceptance of limits as a means to freedom:

> The creator's function is to sift the elements he receives from [imagination], for human activity must impose limits on itself. The more art is controlled, limited, worked over, the more it is free.
>
> As for myself, I experience a sort of terror when, at the moment of setting to work and finding myself before the infinitude of possibilities that present themselves, I have the feeling that everything is permissible to me. . . .
>
> Will I then have to lose myself in this abyss of freedom? To what shall I cling in order to escape the dizziness that seizes me before the virtuality of this infinitude? . . . Fully convinced that combinations which have at their disposal twelve sounds in each octave and all possible rhythmic varieties promise me riches that all the activity of human genius will never exhaust . . . I am always able to turn immediately to the concrete things that are here in question. I have no use for a theoretic freedom. Let me have something finite, definite—matter that can lend itself to my operation only insofar as it is commensurate with my possibilities. And such matter presents itself to me together with its limitations. I must in turn impose mine upon it. . . .
>
> My freedom thus consists in my moving about within the narrow frame that I have assigned myself for each one of my undertakings.
>
> I shall go even farther: my freedom will be so much the greater and more meaningful the more narrowly I limit my field of action and the more I surround myself with obstacles. Whatever diminishes constraint diminishes strength. The more constraints one imposes, the more one frees oneself of the chains that shackle the spirit.[5]

---

[5] *Ibid.,* Lesson Three: "The Composition of Music". Quoted by permission of the publisher, Harvard University Press.

Schoenberg and His Followers

The movement which because of its radical nature attracted most attention in the first half of the twentieth century grew out of the music of post-Romanticism in Germany. The earliest important work of Arnold Schoenberg (1874–1951), the string sextet *Verklärte Nacht* (1899), is in a chromatic idiom clearly derived from that of *Tristan*, while the symphonic poem *Pelleas und Melisande* (1903) is reminiscent of Strauss. With the huge symphonic cantata *Gurre-Lieder* (*Songs of Gurre*) for five soloists, narrator, four choruses, and large orchestra (1901, orchestration finished 1911) Schoenberg outdid even Mahler and Strauss in size and complexity of the score and Wagner in Romantic violence of expression.

A new direction is evident in the works of Schoenberg's second period, which include the first two Quartets (D minor and F♯ minor, 1905 and 1908), the first *Kammersymphonie* (*Chamber Symphony;* 1906) for fifteen instruments, the *Five Orchestral Pieces,* Op. 16 (1909), two sets of short piano pieces (Op. 11, 1908 and Op. 19, 1911), a cycle of songs with piano accompaniment, *Das Buch der hängenden Gärten* (*Book of the Hanging Gardens;* 1908), a mono-drama for soloist and orchestra *Erwartung* (*Expectation;* 1909), and a dramatic pantomime *Die glückliche Hand* (*The Lucky Hand;* 1911–13). In these works Schoenberg turns away from post-Romantic gigantism either to small instrumental combinations or, if he uses a large orchestra, to soloistic treatment of instruments or swift alternation of colors (as in the *Five Orchestral Pieces* and *Erwartung*) rather than massive blocks of sound. Concurrent with this is an increasing rhythmic and contrapuntal complexity and fragmentation of the melodic line, together with greater concentration: for example, the First Quartet, which is in a one-movement cyclical form, evolves all its themes from variations and combinations of a few germinal motives and uses hardly any material, even in the subsidiary voices, that is not derived from the same motives. Historically significant also is the fact that between 1905 and 1912 Schoenberg moved from a chromatic style on a tonal basis to something that is commonly called *atonality*.

Atonal means literally "not tonal." Roughly speaking, atonal music is music in which the person who is using the word cannot hear tonal centers. More precisely, atonal music is that in which the composer systematically avoids reference to tonal centers by avoiding harmonic and melodic formulas—for instance, dominant-tonic progressions and melodic phrases implying such progressions, or diatonic scales and triads or even voice-leading from other intervals to octaves—which suggest the traditional system of chords

Atonality

organized about a fundamental tonic or key note. It is unfortunate that the negative term has become fixed in usage instead of Schoenberg's own word *pantonal,* meaning "inclusive of all tonalities." In recent years a distinction is being made between atonal music and twelve-tone or serial music. From 1908 to 1923 Schoenberg wrote atonal music in the sense that it is not bound by the traditional tonalities. After 1923 he wrote music based on sets, series, or rows of twelve tones. Twelve-tone music need not be atonal, and conversely atonal music is not necessarily based on the twelve-tone technique.

Much late Romantic music, especially in Germany, had been unconsciously tending toward atonality. Chromatic melody lines and chord progressions, even in Wagner, had resulted in passages in which no tonal center could be perceived; but these passages had been exceptional, relatively short, and anchored within a tonal context. Schoenberg explored the extreme possibilities of chromaticism within the limits of tonality in the *Gurre-Lieder* and *Pelleas.* After that, it was a natural move to cut loose altogether from a key center and treat all twelve notes of the octave as of equal rank instead of regarding some of them as chromatically altered tones of a diatonic scale. Corollary to this was another step—already foreshadowed by the nonfunctional harmonies of Debussy—which Schoenberg called "the emancipation of the dissonance," meaning the freedom to use any combination of tones whatever as a chord not requiring resolution. The change from tonality obscured by extreme chromaticism to atonality with free dissonance was a gradual process with Schoenberg. The piano pieces of Op. 11 are in a transitional style; the last movement of the Second Quartet (except for the final cadence in F♯) and the piano pieces of Op. 19 are more nearly atonal.

Pierrot Lunaire (Moonstruck Pierrot; 1912), Schoenberg's best-known composition of the prewar era, is a cycle of twenty-one songs drawn from a larger cycle published in 1884 by the Belgian symbolist poet Albert Giraud and later translated into German. It is for a woman's voice with a chamber ensemble of five players and eight instruments: flute (interchangeable with piccolo), clarinet (bass clarinet), violin (viola), violoncello, and piano. The voice throughout the cycle declaims the text in a so-called *Sprechstimme* (speaking voice), approximating the written pitches but keeping closely to the notated rhythm. For this effect Schoenberg used the sign ♩ . Some of the pieces use constructive devices such as canons to assure unity, since they cannot depend on chord relationships within a tonality for this purpose. Schoenberg calls No. 8, entitled *Nacht (Night;* NAWM/S 82a), a passacaglia, but it is an unusual one, because the unifying motive, a rising minor third followed by a descending major third, appears constantly in various note-values throughout the parts of the texture. No. 13, *Enthauptung (Beheading;* NAWM/S 82b), shows another side of Schoenberg's music at this time. Thematic development is abandoned for what appears to the listener as anarchic improvisation subject to the changing message of the text. As certain painters belonging to a movement called expressionism depicted real objects in distorted representations to reflect their feelings about their surroundings and themselves, so here Schoenberg used exaggerated graphic images and speech inflections to express the poet's inner feelings.

Schoenberg and his pupil Alban Berg are the chief representatives in music of *expressionism.* This word, like *impressionism,* was first used in connection with painting. Expressionism emphasized a contrasting approach, however; whereas impressionism sought to represent objects of the external world as perceived at a given moment, expressionism, proceeding in the opposite direction, sought to represent *inner* experience, using whatever means seemed best suited to the purpose. By virtue of its subjective starting point expressionism is an outgrowth of Romanticism; it differs from Romanticism in the kind of inner experience it aims to portray, and in the means chosen to portray it. The subject matter of expressionism is

Expressionism

In Street, Berlin *(1913) by Ernst Ludwig Kirchner, the jagged and geometric structure within a tightly confined space combines with cubist pattern and Gothic distortion to create the emotionally charged atmosphere characteristic of German Expressionism. (Collection, The Museum of Modern Art, New York)*

man as he exists in the modern world and is described by twentieth-century psychology: isolated, helpless in the grip of forces he does not understand, prey to inner conflict, tension, anxiety, fear, and all the elemental irrational drives of the subconscious, and in irritated rebellion against established order and accepted forms.

Hence, expressionistic art is characterized both by desperate intensity of feeling and revolutionary modes of utterance: both characteristics are illustrated by Schoenberg's *Erwartung,* which has tremendous emotional force and is written in a dissonant, rhythmically atomistic, melodically fragmentary, strangely orchestrated, nonthematic musical idiom. *Erwartung, Die glückliche Hand,* and *Pierrot Lunaire* are all expressionist works. They are devoted, down to the last detail, not to being either pretty or realistic, but to using the most penetrating means imaginable, no matter how unusual—subject, text, scene design and lighting (in the operas), as well as music—to communicate the particular complex of thought and emotion which Schoenberg wanted to express. Form, of course, they must have. At this period of his development Schoenberg was depending mostly on the text to establish unity in long works; the early atonal piano pieces of Op. 19 are so short—models of concise, epigrammatic style—that the difficulties of formal unity inherent in long instrumental compositions are avoided.

Dodecaphony By 1923, after six years during which he published no music, Schoenberg had formulated a "method of composing with twelve tones which are related only with one another." The essential points of the theory of this twelve-tone (dodecaphonic) technique may be summarized as follows. The basis of each composition is a *row* or *series* consisting of the twelve tones of the octave arranged in any order the composer decides. The tones of the series are used either successively (as melody) or simultaneously (as harmony or counterpoint), in any octave and with any desired rhythm. The row may also be used in inverted, retrograde, or retrograde inverted form, and in transpositions of any of the four forms. The style is thus chromatic —not like Wagner's, in which chromatic passages are always to be understood with reference to a diatonic basis, but chromatic in a new and radical way.

In practice, all sorts of modifications, refinements, complications, and compromises are made. Stated baldly, the theory may sound like a recipe for turning out music by machine. Actually, when applied mechanically it will not work; and moreover, it no more necessarily inhibits a composer's spontaneity than do the rules for composing a tonal fugue, provided the technique has been mastered. Using the same tone row for an entire composition is a means of unity analogous to using one main key for a composition in tonal style; at the same time the technique permits and indeed requires much variety of rhythm, texture, dynamics, and timbre. In a sense, a work using this method may be called a perpetual variation of the basic row.

The first works in which Schoenberg deliberately used tone rows were the five piano pieces Op. 23 (1923), of which however only the last has a complete row of twelve tones. The technique was perfected over the next few years in some works which are often designated as neo-Classic (Serenade, Op. 24; Suite for Piano, Op. 25; Wind Quintet, Op. 26) and the twelve-tone method appears completely developed in the Third Quartet (1926) and the *Variations for Orchestra* (1928). It is employed also for most of the works Schoenberg wrote after coming to America in 1933, particularly the Violin Concerto (1936) and the Fourth Quartet (1937). "In olden [and tonal] style" he wrote a Suite for String Orchestra (1934). In the *Ode to Napoleon* and the Piano Concerto (both 1942), he approached a synthesis of his own system with some elements of orthodox tonality; but these works are less characteristic than the String Trio (1946) and the *Fantasy for Violin and Piano* (1949).

In 1931–32 Schoenberg composed the first two acts of a three-act opera for which he had written his own libretto, entitled *Moses and Aaron*. The music was never completed, and the score remains a magnificent torso. Against the Old Testament background Schoenberg presents the tragic conflict between Moses as mediator of the word of God and Aaron as Moses's interpreter to the people: conflict, because Moses is unable himself to communicate his vision, and Aaron, who can communicate, cannot rightly understand; tragic, because the flaw of separation is intrinsic and not to be overcome by good will, being rooted in the nature of the philosopher-mystic on the one hand and the statesman-educator on the other. (Aaron says to Moses [Act III, Scene 1], "I was to discourse in images, you in concepts; I to the heart, you to the mind.") Symbolically, Moses speaks (*Sprechstimme*) but does not sing: the Word is not incarnate in music save for one moment only (Act I, Scene 2) as Moses warns Aaron, "Purify your thought: set it free from earthly things, dedicate it to Truth." The solemn alliteration of the German text is reminiscent of Wagner (see Example XX–9) and throughout Schoenberg employs vowel and consonant sounds in symbolic connection with the music and the dramatic ideas.

Moses and Aaron

EXAMPLE XX–9   *Moses and Aaron, Act I, Scene 2, Schoenberg*

Rei-ni-ge dein Denk-en,   lös es von Wert-los-em,   wei-he es   Wahr - em:

The first page of the autograph score of Schoenberg's Moses and Aaron.
(The Arnold Schoenberg Institute Archives, Los Angeles, Cal.)

The work of Schoenberg is on the boundary of the Western musical tradition. The continuity of his thought (and, in many respects, his practice) with that of Bach, Mozart, Beethoven, Brahms, and Wagner is genuine, but the radical break is equally a fact: what Schoenberg did in music could not be repealed—any more than could the achievements of James Joyce in literature. Expressionism, and atonalism as a musical style closely associated with it, were in tune with a state of mind prevalent in western Europe in the 1920s, and are therefore significant as a social phenomenon of the period. The Schoenberg followers must be regarded, as far as the first half of the twentieth century is concerned, as a school existing side by side with others which still maintain an allegiance to Classical tonal principles. The music of Berg, some of the late works of Schoenberg, and experiments by other composers with serial methods indicate a potential synthesis which, however, could be only individual, not communal.

Schoenberg's famous pupil Alban Berg (1885–1935) adopted most of his master's methods of construction, but he used them with freedom and often chose tone rows that allowed for tonal-sounding chords and progressions in the harmony. Moreover, Berg combined the technique with a warmth of Romantic feeling so that his music is more readily accessible than that of many twelve-tone composers. His chief works are a *Lyric Suite* for string quartet (1926); a Violin Concerto (1935); and two operas, *Wozzeck* (composed 1917–21, first performed 1925) and *Lulu* (composed 1928–35, the orchestration not quite completed at Berg's death).

Alban Berg

Wozzeck is the outstanding example of expressionist opera as well as an impressive historical document. The libretto, arranged by Berg from fragments of a drama by Georg Büchner (1813–37), presents the soldier Wozzeck as a symbol of "wir arme Leut' " ("we poor people"), a hapless victim of his environment, despised, betrayed in love, driven finally to murder and suicide. The music is continuous throughout each of the three acts, the changing scenes (five in each act) being connected by orchestral interludes as in Debussy's *Pelléas*. Berg's music is unified partly by the use of a few leitmotifs but chiefly by being organized in closed forms adapted from those of Classical music (suite, rhapsody, song, march, passacaglia, rondo, symphony, inventions) and by other subtle means. Thus, the third act contains five so-called inventions: on a theme (six variations and fugue); on a note (the pitch B); on a rhythm; on a chord; and on a duration (the eighth note). Scene 3 (NAWM/S 87), the invention on a rhythm, is a wild polka.

In the vocal parts Berg flexibly alternates ordinary speech and *Sprechgesang* with conventional singing. The many passages of stylized realism (snoring chorus, gurgling of water, a tavern orchestra with an out-of-tune piano caricaturing a waltz motive from Strauss's *Rosenkavalier*) are skilfully employed for expressionistic purposes. The grim, ironical, symbolical action, the wealth of musical invention, the ever-varied, ingenious, and appropriate orchestration, the formal clarity and concentration, the pictorial quality and dramatic force of the music cumulate in an effect of unforgettable poignancy.

Lulu is a more abstract, complex opera, equally expressionistic but with more involved symbolism than *Wozzeck;* its music is organized more strictly on twelve-tone lines, though not without some tonal implications. The *Lyric Suite* and the Violin Concerto, like the two operas, are typical of Berg's constant tendency to show the connection between the new style and that of the past. Both the

Suite and the Concerto are partially written according to the twelve-tone method; both display Berg's inventive genius and his easy mastery of contrapuntal technique. The basic row of the Concerto is designed in such a way that tonal combinations become practically inevitable (Example XX–10); in the finale also the tone row forms a link to introduce the melody of a chorale that Bach had harmonized to the words of the hymn *It is Enough* (Cantata No. 60)—an allusion to the death of Manon Gropius, to whose memory the Concerto is dedicated.

EXAMPLE XX–10   Tone Row in Alban Berg's Violin Concerto

Berg represents the Romantic potential of Schoenberg's teaching; Schoenberg's other celebrated pupil, Anton Webern (1883–1945) represents the Classical potential—atonality without Romanticism. Webern wrote no opera and he never used the device of *Sprechstimme*. The ruling principles in his work are economy and extreme concentration. In his mature style each composition is evolved by imitative counterpoint (often strictly canonic); he uses devices such as inversion and rhythmic shifts, but avoids sequences and (for the most part) repetitions. The melodic outline of the generating "cells" usually involves intervals like major sevenths and minor ninths which exclude tonal implications. Textures are stripped to bare essentials; rhythmic patterns are complex, often based on simultaneous duple and triple divisions of all or a part of the measure; and the sound, with all its fine gradation of dynamics, seldom rises above the level of a forte.

Anton Webern

Most remarkable is Webern's instrumentation. A melodic line may be distributed among different instruments somewhat in the manner of medieval hocket, so that sometimes only one or two—seldom more than four or five—successive tones will be heard in the same timbre. The result is a texture made up of sparks and flashes of sound blending in a unique balance of color (see Example XX–11). A good illustration of this kind of orchestration applied to a more familiar kind of music is Webern's arrangement of the

Ricercare from Bach's *Musical Offering*. Special effects—pizzicato, harmonics, tremolo, muting, and the like—are common in all of Webern's music. His sensitiveness for color and clarity often leads him to choose unusual combinations, as in the Quartet Op. 22 for violin, clarinet, tenor saxophone, and piano, or the three songs Op. 18 for soprano, E♭ clarinet, and guitar.

It is natural that in a style of such concentration the compositions should be short. Not all are so brief as the *Six Bagatelles* for string quartet, Op. 9, or the Five Pieces for Orchestra, Op. 10 (both 1913), which average respectively about 36 and 49 seconds for each movement (No. 5 of Op. 10 runs only 19 seconds); but even "larger" works like the Symphony (1928) and the String Quartet (1938) take only eight or nine minutes' playing time, so intensely compressed is the language. This compression, together with the unfamiliarity of the idiom, requires an unusual degree of attention from the listener. With respect to dissonance (the effect of which is largely mitigated by skilful use of contrasting timbres) and harmonic complexity in general, Webern's music is considerably easier to hear than that of Schoenberg, Berg, and many other twentieth-century composers.

In his development, Webern, like Schoenberg, passed through the stages of late Romantic chromaticism, free atonality, and organization by tone rows, the last beginning with the three songs of Op. 17 (1924). With few exceptions his works are in chamber style; they are about equally divided between instrumental and vocal compositions. The principal instrumental works are the Symphony Op. 21, the String Quartet Op. 28, the Concerto for nine instruments Op. 24 (1934), and the Piano Variations Op. 27 (1936). For voices there are numerous collections of solo songs—some with piano, others with different small ensembles—and a few choral pieces, notably *Das Augenlicht* (*Light of the Eyes;* 1935) and two cantatas (1939, 1943) for soloists, chorus, and orchestra. These cantatas, and also the Variations for Orchestra Op. 30 (1940), are in a somewhat more relaxed and expressive style than Webern's previous works; in them he applied the serial technique but included homophonic as well as contrapuntal texture.

The Symphony Op. 21 is for nine solo instruments. It is in two movements, the first in sonata form and the second a theme with seven variations. Some idea of Webern's use of the serial technique may be obtained from Example XX–11, the beginning of the first movement. (The entire movement is in NAWM/S 81). What may be called the "original" form of the tone row[6] is designated by the numbers 1, 2, etc. (note that the second half of the row is the retrograde of the first half and that consequently the retrograde form of

---

6 See W. Kolneder, *Anton Webern* (1968), p. 115.

EXAMPLE XX–11   First Movement, Symphony Op. 21, Anton Webern

the entire row is a duplicate of its original form); the numbers 1′, 2′, etc. designate an inversion (or a retrograde inversion) of the original form, beginning a major third lower; 1″, 2″, etc. designate an inversion (or retrograde inversion) beginning at the original

pitch. The C♯ in measure four begins a statement of the original form of the row (or its retrograde) transposed a major third upward. To be noted also in this example is the characteristically spare, open texture, the numerous rests in all the parts; thus every single note counts, and the ensemble becomes a succession of tiny points or wisps of sound.

Webern's output was small: his complete works (excepting the recently discovered early music) have been recorded on eight long-playing record sides. Though his achievement received hardly any acclaim during his lifetime, recognition of his work grew steadily in the years after the Second World War, and his music launched important new developments in Italy, Germany, France, and the United States.

After Webern

The first half of the twentieth century witnessed a progressive breakup of the system of music which had prevailed over the preceding two hundred years, roughly from Bach to Richard Strauss. Schoenberg, at first intuitively and later methodically with his twelve-tone rows, had introduced a new conception of musical structure and with his "emancipation of the dissonance" had in effect simply abolished the traditional distinction between consonance and dissonance. Stravinsky had participated, in turn, in all the movements of the time, arriving in the 1950s as his own version of dodecaphony. Many other composers had by 1950 accepted in principle the twelve-tone system, modifying it in details and adapting it to their own purposes. It was Webern, however, who more than anyone else anticipated and stimulated a movement which came to be associated with a group of young composers centered about the "holiday courses for new music" at Darmstadt. These courses had begun immediately after the end of the war, in 1946. At a memorial concert of his works at Darmstadt in 1953, Webern was hailed as the father of the new movement. The two principal composers of the Darmstadt group, both pupils of Messiaen, were Pierre Boulez (born 1925) of Paris and Karlheinz Stockhausen (born 1928) of Cologne. Darmstadt was important in that many of the ideas fostered there spread through the world and stimulated experiments on the part of composers everywhere, including eventually the countries of eastern Europe. But every composer worked independently, striking out in new directions, cultivating his own language, his own style, his own special techniques. There was no allegiance to one consistent body of principles, no well-defined "common practice" as in the eighteenth and nineteenth centuries.

We shall not attempt to deal with the work of every composer individually, but rather try to summarize the most general common features and mention a few of the most notable individual achievements of the period since 1945. It is essential to remember that all the features we are about to discuss came into prominence almost simultaneously; all were evident, to different extents and in varying degrees and combinations, in the new music of the third quarter of the present century.

One of the first developments, beginning even before 1950, was the rise of "total serialism," that is, the extension of the principle of Schoenberg's rows to elements of music other than pitch. If the twelve tones of the chromatic scale could be serialized, as Schoenberg had done, so also could the factors of duration, intensity, timbre, texture, silences, and so on. But whereas in the eighteenth and nineteenth centuries all these elements—particularly those involving melody, rhythm, and harmony—had been conventionally interdependent (being combined in certain accepted ways), now all could be regarded as simply interchangeable. Thus a series of pitches could be combined with a series of one or more of the other factors—as Messiaen had shown with his *Mode de valeurs et d'intensités* and Milton Babbitt (born 1916), in a different formulation, with his *Three Compositions for Piano* (1948). The different series might be conceived independently, or all might be derived in one way or another from a single arithmetical series; in either case the various series could intersect, all proceeding simultaneously, to a point of "total control" over every detail of a composition. Naturally this could not be done just by arbitrarily or mechanically selecting the various series and their combinations. Their relationship had to be a musically rational, not merely a mathematical one; otherwise the application of total control in this sense would produce music which gave the effect of total randomness. Especially for an unaccustomed ear, that impression could not easily be avoided even in works constructed by the most musically sensitive composers working with the technique.

Serialism

One reason for such an impression was that music based on these principles was typically *athematic:* that is, it had no themes in the classical sense of readily perceived melodic-rhythmic-harmonic entities and recognizable extensions, derivations, and developments of those. Concomitant with this was the typical absence of a distinct rhythmic pulse and—even more important—the absence of any sense of progression, of movement toward definite foreseeable points of climax culminating toward the end of the work, such as had been characteristic of the symphony, for example, from the time of Haydn through the nineteenth century. Instead, one was aware only of successive, unrepeated, and unpredictable musical "events." Such events might take the form of minute "points" of sound—color, melody, rhythm—intertwining, dissolving into one another in an apparently random fashion. Of course, when a work was well constructed the totality of the events would form a logical pattern, but it might be a very complex one which only became perceptible after much study and repeated hearings.

The rigidities of total serialism were soon relaxed. The pointillist style is fused with sensitive musical realization of a text in one of the most famous avant-garde pieces, Boulez's *Le Marteau sans maître* (*The Masterless Hammer;* 1954, revised 1957). This is a setting of verses from a cycle of surrealist poems by René Char, interspersed with instrumental "commentaries," in nine short movements. The ensemble (a different grouping in each movement) comprises alto flute, xylorimba, vibraphone, guitar, viola, and a variety of light percussion instruments; it produces a translucent tissue of sound, all in the middle and high registers, with effects often suggestive of Balinese music. The contralto vocal line, with wide melodic intervals, glissandos, and occasional use of *Sprechstimme,* is often the lowest voice in the texture, and is related in a quasi-systematic way to particular instruments in the ensemble.

New timbres   One of the most conspicuous features of the new music was the immense number of new sounds that were found acceptable for use. Earlier examples of such new sounds were the "tone clusters" on the piano, introduced by the American Henry Cowell (1897–1965) in the 1920s, and the "prepared piano" of John Cage (born 1912) in the 1940s. Other examples include a great many hitherto unexploited uses of conventional instruments: for example, new harmonics and increased use of the flutter-tongue technique and other special effects on wind instruments; glissandos; dense chromatic clusters or "bands" of sound for strings or voices, a frequent recourse of the Greek composer Yannis Xenakis (born 1922), the Polish Krzysztof Penderecki (born 1933), and the Italian Luigi Nono (born 1924); spoken and whispered sounds (words, syllables, letters, noises) in vocal pieces—and required also occasionally of instrumentalists. New instruments, such as the vibraphone and the *Ondes Martenot,* appeared in the orchestra. Especially noteworthy throughout the whole period was the tremendously expanded percussion group (often including instruments borrowed from or suggested by Asian or African musics) and the greatly increased importance of percussive sounds in ensembles of all kinds.

Decisive for recognition of the importance of timbre in the new music was the work of Edgard Varèse (1883–1965). For Varèse, sounds as such were the essential structural components of music, more basic than melody, harmony, or rhythm. In his *Ionisation* (1933), written for a huge battery of percussion instruments (including piano and bells) along with chains, anvils, and sirens, Varèse created a form which could be said to be defined by contrasting blocks and masses of sound. Some of his late works (*Déserts,* 1954; *Poème électronique,* 1958) utilized new sound resources that became available soon after the middle of the century.

Electronic resources   No development after 1950 attracted more public attention or held greater potential for new structural and other far-reaching changes in the world of music than the use of electronically produced or manipulated sounds. This began with the *musique con-*

The Philips Pavilion, Brussels World Fair, 1958. Composer Edgard Varèse collaborated with architect Le Corbusier when he wrote his Poème électronique, commissioned for performance in this building. (Photo courtesy of The Museum of Modern Art, New York)

crète of the early 1950s; the raw material consisted of musical tones or other natural sounds which after being transformed in various ways by electronic means were assembled on tape to be played back. The next step was to replace or supplement sounds of natural origin by sounds generated electronically in a studio. One of the most familiar early electronic compositions, Stockhausen's *Gesang der Jünglinge (Song of the Young Men; 1956),*[7] as well as many of his later works in this medium, used sounds from both sources.

The consequences of the new discovery were immense, and have not yet been anywhere near completely explored. In the first place, it freed the composer from all dependence on a performer, enabling him to exercise complete, unmediated control over the sound of his compositions (except for unavoidable uncertainties about acoustical conditions in the place where the music was to be heard). Already much of the new music demanded minute shadings of pitch, intensity, and timbre which could be only approximately notated in a score, as well as complexities of "irrational" rhythms which were hardly realizable by performers; and since absolute accuracy of performance was necessary, the practical requirements of specially qualified personnel and lengthy rehearsal time [8] were additional

7 The reference is to Dan. III: 12 and the aprocryphal insertion after v. 23.

8 With experienced conductor and performers "less than a dozen rehearsals" would be needed for Boulez's *Marteau sans maître,* "a very modest figure" (Hodeir, *Since Debussy,* p. 154); but the expense, even with only eight musicians involved, would hardly be a "modest figure."

obstacles. But in the electronic studio every detail could be accurately calculated and recorded. Moreover, a whole new realm of possible sounds now became available—including an infinitude of sounds not producible by any "natural" means. Different acoustical effects could be attained by placing the loudspeakers in various positions relative to the audience. Composers in Europe, America, and Japan industriously exploited all these advantages. Further possibilities (and problems) were revealed by the use of tape recordings in combination with live performers. One ingenious example of such combination was Milton Babbitt's *Philomel* (1964), for soprano soloist with tape which incorporates an altered recording of the voice together with electronic sounds.

Electronics did not by any means supersede live music. A good many of the new composers, among them Boulez, did not work at all, or to any important extent, with electronic media. Undoubtedly, however, the electronic sounds stimulated the invention of new sound effects to be obtained from voices and conventional instruments; this is especially noticeable in the music of the Hungarian György Ligeti (born 1923).

One of the contributions that *musique concrète* and electronic music have made is to gain acceptance as music of sounds not produced by voices or instruments. George Crumb (b. 1929) has been one of the most imaginative in seeking new sounds, often out of ordinary objects. In *Ancient Voices of Children* (1970), a cycle of four songs and two instrumental interludes based on texts by Federico García Lorca, some unusual sound-sources are employed: a toy piano, a musical saw, and a number of instruments rarely heard Japanese temple bells, and electric piano. The third song, subtitled *Dance of the Sacred Life-Cycle*, on the text *¿De dónde vienes, amor, mi niño?* (NAWM/S 84), has in the background a constant bolero rhythm in the drums that increases and decreases slightly in dynamics in the course of each statement.

In both electronic and live music many composers worked with the idea of dispersing the various sound sources and thereby incorporating space as, so to speak, an additional dimension of music. In the latter half of the century, composers began to use space with more calculation and inventiveness than ever before. Thus, two or more groups of instruments might be placed on different parts of the stage; loudspeakers or performers might be located at the sides or back of the hall, above or below the level of the audience, or even in the midst of the audience. Varèse's *Poème électronique*, featured at the Brussels Exposition in 1958, was projected by 425 loudspeakers ranged all about the interior space of Le Corbusier's pavilion while moving colored lights and projected images accompanied the music. By such means as these, direction in space became a potential factor for defining the form of a work.

From the end of the seventeenth century, all Western music had utilized a set of twelve equidistant semitones systematically controlling the space of an octave. Proposals at one time or another for including more tones in the octave came to no practical result. Now, however, the very conception of distinct pitches and intervals (including the octave itself) came to be supplemented by the conception of pitch as a *continuum,* an unbroken range of sound from the lowest to the highest audible frequencies, without distinguishing separate tones of fixed pitch. Of course in practice some sounds of shifting pitch had always been used, for example glissandos in singing and on stringed instruments; also sounds outside the twelve semitones of the tempered scale, as in minute adjustments by string players or specified quarter-tones (or other microtones) such as Berg required in his *Chamber Concerto* (1925). Unspecified shifting pitch characterized the *Sprechstimme* of Schoenberg and Berg. The sirens in Varèse's *Ionisation* and similar electronic sounds in his later works, the glissandos of the *Ondes Martenot* in Messiaen's *Turangalîla,* the frequent glissando effects on traditional instruments in the music of Penderecki and others, are striking examples of use of the pitch continuum. Related to this is the use of complex or unpitched nonmusical sounds, from whatever source, as elements in composition.

The pitch continuum

Throughout the history of Western music since the Middle Ages, there has been continual interaction between composer and performer, between those factors (such as pitch and relative duration) which the composer could specify by notation and those which were left to the performer, either by convention or of necessity through lack of adequate notational signs. In the twentieth century, multiplication of detailed indications for dynamics, manner of attack, tempo (frequent metronome marks), pauses, and rhythms (changing time signatures, minute and complex subdivisions of the beat) evidenced the aim of composers to exercise total control over performance; but total control became possible, or nearly possible, only in the case of all-electronic works, where the performer was totally eliminated. Roughly contemporary with this step (though not as a consequence of it) arose the characteristic twentieth-century forms of the control-freedom polarity.

Indeterminacy

Basic to all these is the fact that the limits of control (determinacy) and freedom (indeterminacy[9]) are planned and can hence be planned differently for each composition. The indeterminate features do not originate either from established conventions of choice,

[9] Indeterminacy (John Cage's term) is used here in preference to the more restricted term "aleatory" (from the Latin *alea* = dice), to cover everything from improvisation within a fixed framework to situations where the composer gives only the minimum of directions to the performer or exercises only the minimum of choice in composition.

as in the sixteenth century, or accidentally out of imprecision of notation, as in the nineteenth century. In practice, indeterminacy operates primarily in the area of performance; it is applicable to either live or electronic performances or to combinations of the two. It may occur as indeterminate sections (somewhat like improvisation) within a composition otherwise fixed by the score; or it may occur as a series of distinct musical "events," each one of which the composer specifies more or less exactly while leaving the order in which they are to occur partly or wholly indeterminate, thus making what is sometimes called "open" form. In such works the performer (soloist, member of a group, or conductor) may either determine the order of the events simply by his own choice, or be led by means of certain devices into an apparently chance or random order. Or he may also, both within an event and in choosing the order of events, be guided by his reactions to what others in the group (or even members of the audience) are doing. In short, the possibilities of indeterminacy—the possible modes of interaction between freedom and authority, the extent to which "chance" can be "controlled"—are limitless.

The composer who has worked most consistently in this domain is Stockhausen. Reference to two of his compositions may help to clarify some of the procedures. The score of *Klavierstück* (piano piece) *XI* (1956) consists of nineteen short segments of notation displayed on a large sheet (about 37 by 21 inches); these segments can be put together in various ways as the player's eye happens to light on one after another; certain directions are given as to the manner of linking the segments played; not all need be played, and any may be repeated. When in the course of his performance the pianist finds he has repeated any one segment twice, the piece ends.

The setup in Stockhausen's *Opus 1970* is a little more complicated. This piece is performed by four players (piano, electric viola, electronium, and tam-tam) and four loudspeakers.

> Material is obtained from a regulating system (radio short waves), selected freely by the player and immediately developed . . . spread, condensed, extended, shortened, differently colored, more or less articulated, transposed, modulated, multiplied, synchronized. . . . The players imitate and vary, adhering to the sequence of development specified by the score. . . . As regulating system each of the four players has a magnetophone [tape recorder] on which, for the whole of the recording period, a tape, prepared differently for each of the players, continuously reproduces fragments of music by Beethoven. The player opens and shuts the loudspeaker control whenever he wishes.[10]

A new element here is the incorporation of fragments (transformed but immediately recognizable) from Beethoven. Stockhausen had al-

[10] Wilfried Daenicke: from the record jacket DGG 139–461–SLPM.

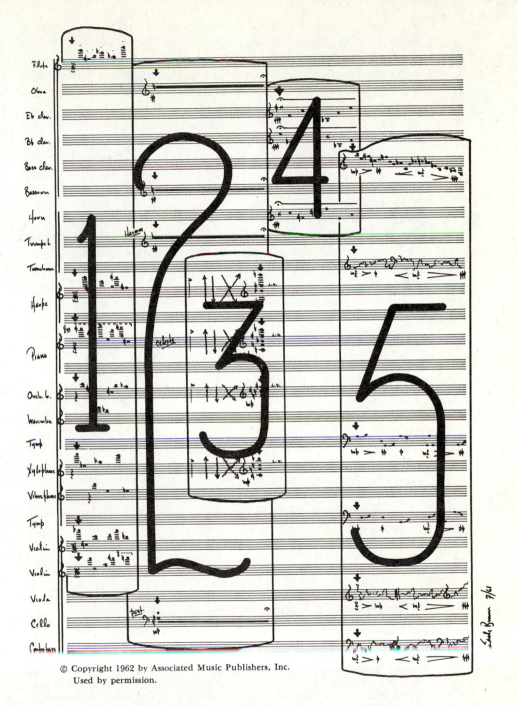

A page from Earle Brown's Available Forms I *(1961). The five numbered areas, or "events" may be played in any succession specified by the conductor, whose downbeat also implies the relative speed and intensity.*

ready used borrowed material in similar ways in some of his earlier works, notably the *Gesang der Jünglinge,* the *Telemusik* (1966), and the *Hymnen* (1967). *Hymnen* incorporates words and melodies of many different national anthems in a performance combining electronic sounds with voices and instruments. The intention in every instance is, in Stockhausen's words, "not to interpret, but to hear familiar, old, preformed musical material with new ears, to penetrate and transform it with a musical consciousness of today." This represents a quite new mode of relating music of the present to that of the past. "Quotation" music is exemplified also in the works of George Rochberg (b. 1918) in America and of Peter Maxwell-Davies (b. 1934) in England.[11]

One by-product of indeterminacy is the variety of new kinds of notation. "Scores" range all the way from fragments of conventional staff-notes through purely graphic suggestions of melodic curves, dynamic ranges, rhythms, and the like to even more impressionistic and meager directives.

Naturally, one main consequence of indeterminacy is that no two performances of the "same" piece will be the same. The difference, whether small or great, between one performance and another will not be merely a matter of interpretation but a substantive difference in musical content and order of presentation. (Recordings of such works can be only of one particular performance.) The meaning of "a composition" thus becomes quite unlike the traditional meaning. In effect, a composition does not exist as such, but only as a performance, or as the inconceivable totality of possible performances.

Indeterminacy may be applied to the act of composition as well as to performance; this is the case when some or all of the pitches, durations, intensities, timbres, and so on of the notated score have been decided by chance—by casting dice, tossing coins, using tables of random numbers, and similar means. And finally, indeterminacy in composition may be combined with indeterminacy in performance. When the indeterminacy is practically total on both sides the result evidently is no longer a work of art in the normal sense of the word, that is, something *made.*

[11]The psychology of quotation in literature is analogous to that in music: "Even if a text is wholly quotation, the condition of quotation itself qualifies the text and makes it so far unique. Thus a quotation from Marvell by Eliot has a force slightly different from what it had when Marvell wrote it. Though the combination of words is unique it is read, if the reader knows his words either by usage or dictionary, with a shock like that of recognition. The recognition is not limited, however, to what was already known in the words; there is a perception of something previously unknown, something new which is a result of the combination of the words, something which is literally an access of knowledge. Upon the poet's skill in combining words as much as upon his private feelings, depends the importance or the value of the knowledge." (R. P. Blackmur, *Form and Value in Modern Poetry,* 184; quoted in Leonard B. Meyer, *Music, the Arts, and Ideas,* 201.)

Indeterminacy, random techniques of all kinds, tended to focus attention on radically new ideas about the nature and purposes of music, ideas which came into prominence especially in America around the middle of the century. As we have already noted, the music of total serialism and its offshoots, and even more the music of indeterminacy, is heard as a succession of discrete musical events, no one of which apparently grows out of its predecessors nor apparently sets up any situation from which the hearer can anticipate (let alone predict) what is to follow. Nevertheless, throughout all this the composer maintains some degree of control, even if only the slightest; both he and the performer make choices, and the consequent result is a musical form, even though (with indeterminacy) that form may be different every time the music is heard. The principle of cause (the choices) and effect (the form) is still operative.

"Anti-art"

Now, however, let us suppose that one extends spontaneity to a point where all choice is voluntarily abandoned. Whether as composer, performer, or listener, one decides to accept what happens without regard to his own preferences as to what *ought* to happen. As listener, he simply hears sounds as sounds, enjoying each as it comes, not trying to connect one sound with preceding or following ones, not expecting the music to communicate feelings or meanings of any kind. The sounds may not even be only intentional ones; any mistake, any accidental noise from anywhere that happens in the course of a performance, is perfectly acceptable. Value judgments are therefore irrelevant and musical time becomes simply duration, something that can be measured by a clock.

However strange such an aesthetic may seem—and however vulnerable in practice to sheer dilettantism—it has a tenable philosophic basis; but the philosophy in question, though familiar in the Orient and to some Western mystics, is fundamentally different from the main line of Western philosophy which has come down unbroken from the time of ancient Greece and whose ideas are so ingrained in our thinking that most of us never imagine it possible to question them. The chief proponent of this "new" philosophy is the enigmatic John Cage, who has been in the forefront of most new musical developments in both America and Europe since the late 1930s. His influence in Europe has been greater than that of any other American composer. Since 1956 he has worked more and more toward total openness in every aspect of composition and performance, constructing his scores by wholly random methods and offering to performers such options as in his *Variations IV* (1963): "for any number of players, any sounds or combinations of sounds produced by any means, with or without other activities." The "other activities" might well include dance and theater. All this is consonant with Cage's personal interest in Zen Buddhism. More important, it is consonant with what is probably a growing tendency for Western artists—and for Western civilization generally—to become more open to the ideas and beliefs of other great world cultures.

Conclusion

If we recall the four basic characteristics of Western music which began to take shape in the eleventh century (see Ch. III, pp. 79-80), we can see that some developments in the twentieth century have altered three of them almost out of recognition. *Composition,* in the sense of existence of a work of music apart from any particular performance, has in some quarters given way to controlled improvisation (which was the practice in antiquity and the early Middle Ages). As to *notation,* the score in many cases is now no longer a definitive set of directions; the performer, instead being only a mediator between composer and audience, has become himself to a great extent the composer (again, as in the early Middle Ages). *Principles of order* have changed—arguably, the change is greater than any within the whole previous eight hundred years; and, if we think of total indeterminacy, principles of order have simply ceased to exist. Only *polyphony* remains. In view of all this, it seems not too much to say

Composer-conductor Pierre Boulez during a discussion period at a New York Philharmonic "Encounter" concert in the New York Shakespeare Festival Theatre. In the background, the American composer Charles Wuorinen. (Whitestone Photo)

that the twentieth century has witnessed a musical revolution in the full sense of the word.

It is a revolution, however, that has affected only a few people. This is not to say that those few are unimportant. Even the total audience for all "serious" music (that is, art music of a certain complexity which requires some effort to understand) has never at any time been more than a minute fraction of the population. Now that audience is still relatively small, and within it the audience for the new and experimental is even smaller. This too is normal. Composers who write in a difficult, unfamiliar idiom cannot expect a large popular following. Meanwhile, who cares if they listen?[12] The revolution may go on; if it does, no one knows what directions it may take.

We have been concerned in this section exclusively with the new techniques and ideas in recent Western music, but we should keep in mind that a good deal of the music of the past—and more of it all the time—is still very much alive and meaningful to many people. So also—though some advocates of "new" styles do not accept it—is a great deal of music written by composers of the present (Britten, for example) who deliberately refuse to go all the way with the new discoveries. Efforts in this century toward reconciling old and new in one common great musical culture have come to naught. What of the future?

Let us resist the temptation to prophesy, and leave the last word with Schoenberg: "Contemporaries are not final judges, but are generally overruled by history."[13]

---

12 Distortion (non-electronic) of the provocative title of a wise essay "Who Cares if You Listen?" by Milton Babbitt in *High Fidelity* VIII, 2 (February 1958), reprinted in E. Schwartz and B. Childs, *Contemporary Composers on Contemporary Music,* 243–50.

13 From "Composition with Twelve Tones" (1941), in *Style and Idea,* 103.

Glossary

Accidental. A sign used to change the pitch of a note by raising it one semitone (sharp, ♯), lowering it one semitone (flat, ♭), or cancelling the effect of a previous sharp or flat (natural, ♮).

Aleatory, see *Indeterminacy.*

Alteration. Changing the pitch of a note by means of an accidental (♯, ♭, or ♮) to raise or lower it by one semitone from its normal pitch in the scale.

Appoggiatura. A nonharmonic tone, sounded on a strong beat and resolved (regularly by step) to a harmonic tone on a following weaker beat (see also *suspension*).

Athematic. Property of music which does not use themes as structural units of composition.

Atonality (atonal). The absence of tonality.

Bar. (1) A vertical line (barline) through the staff(s) marking the division into measures; (2) a measure (not used in this sense in this book); (3) a form, *AAB*, common in medieval monophonic music, polyphonic ballads of the four-teenth century, Lutheran chorales, and other music.

Cadence. The melodic and/or harmonic formula that marks the end of a musical phrase, section, or composition. The most common harmonic final cadence is the progression Dominant-Tonic (V-I).

Canon, canonic imitation. (1) Exact imitation, continued for more than one phrase, of the melody of one voice by another voice or voices: the imitating voice(s) may begin on the same note as the leading voice (canon at the unison), or on another note (canon at the fifth above, at the fourth below, etc.); (2) a rule or direction specifying the way in which such imitation is to be carried out; (3) a composition in which two or more voices proceed throughout in canonic imitation (see also *round*).

Chord. A simultaneous combination of three or more notes of different pitch forming an entity that can be used for the analysis of harmony (see also *triad*).

Chromaticism (chromatic). (1) The use of tones not in the regular diatonic scale of the composition or passage in which such tones occur; (2) a quality of harmonic style marked by the frequent use of such tones (see also *Twelve-tone music*).

Circle of fifths. The arrangement of keys by ascending fifths (C–G–D, etc.), each key having one more sharp or one less flat in its signature; or by descending fifths (C–F–B♭, etc.), each key having one more flat or one less sharp in its signature. *Circle* refers to the fact that at the twelfth step the series returns to its point of beginning: in the equal-tempered tuning B♯ or D♭♭ = C.

Cluster (tone cluster). On the piano, the effect obtained by striking a number of adjacent keys with the flat of the hand or with the forearm; also, similar effects by other instruments.

Coda. A concluding section of a composition, particularly of a fugue or a movement of a sonata or symphony.

Codetta. Literally, a "small coda"; particularly, the closing passage of one section of a piece, for example, of the exposition of a movement in sonata form.

Color. (1) The quality of a musical sound (as the color of the clarinet tone) or of sounds in combination (as the color of Debussy's orchestration); (2) the quality of the sound of a composition or passage (see also *texture, timbre*).

Consonance (consonant). An interval or chord which produces an agreeable or satisfactory effect, or an effect of repose.

Contrary motion. Movement of two simultaneous voices in opposite directions, one upward and the other downward.

Counterpoint (contrapuntal). A musical texture consisting predominantly of two or more simultaneous melodic lines, with or without additional material.

Cross-relation. The use of a note and its chromatic alteration in different voices, either simultaneously or in immediate or close juxtaposition.

Diatonic. (1) Pertaining to a major, minor, or modal scale of eight tones to the octave; (2) the quality of music marked by infrequent use of chromatic tones.

Dissonance (dissonant). An interval or chord which produces a disagreeable ("discordant") or unsatisfactory effect, or an effect which requires completion (see also *resolution*).

Dodecaphonic (dodecaphony), see *Twelve-tone music.*

Dominant. In harmonic practice, the fifth degree or note of the scale (see also *cadence*).

Drone. (1) A note or notes, usually in the bass, sustained throughout an entire piece or section; (2) a string, pipe, or mechanism for producing such notes (see also *ostinato*).

Duet, duo. A composition, or section of a composition, having two equally important melodic lines, with or without accompaniment; or a composition written for two performers of equal importance, on the same or different instruments.

Enharmonic. In Greek music, intervals less than a semitone; in

Western music, notes which are identical in sound in the equal-tempered scale (as F♯-G♭).

Equal temperament. A method of tuning in which the octave is divided into twelve equal semitones.

Form patterns. The arrangement of material within a composition. In this book form patterns are designated by italic letters thus: *aba, ABA,* etc. The mark ′ after a letter (*A′*) indicates a modified repetition of the formal unit.

Free rhythm. Rhythm in which the durations of the notes and rests are not fixed fractions or multiples of a common unit of duration (see *metrical rhythm*).

Fuga (Latin, "flight"). In medieval and renaissance usage, a canon; after 1600, the meaning is usually the same as *fugue.*

Fugato. A short fugal passage or fugal exposition.

Fughetta. A short fugue.

Fugue (fugal). A type or style of contrapuntal composition based on the development of (usually) a single short theme or *subject* in imitation.

Harmonic. (1; adj.) A musical texture consisting predominantly of chords or of melody accompanied by chords; (2; noun) a high flute-like tone produced by lightly touching the string of a violin at 1/2, 1/3, etc. of its length. (3) sounds produced by analogous means on other instruments.

Harmonic rhythm. The movement of music as marked by the succession of changing harmonies.

Harmony. (1) Any simultaneous combination of sounds; a chord; (2) the chordal or "vertical" aspect of a musical composition as contrasted with melodic, contra-

puntal, rhythmic, coloristic, or other aspects; (3) the style of a composition considered with respect to the chords employed and the principles governing their succession (see also *harmonic*).

Hemiola (literally, "one and one-half"). A mensural device in the notation of the fifteenth and sixteenth centuries which in effect alters the movement from | ♩.♩. | to | ♩ ♩ ♩ |. Hence, in Baroque music, a common cadential formula in triple meter, by which two measures of 3/4 time are made to sound like one measure of 3/2 time: | ♩ ♩ | ♩ ♩ |.

Heterophony. The sounding of a melody simultaneously in a simple and an ornamented form.

Homophony. A texture in which all the voice parts move in the same or nearly the same rhythm.

Imitation. The closely following restatement of a melody or phrase by another voice or voices in a contrapuntal texture. If the restatement is exact, it is called *strict* imitation; if similar, but not exact, *free* imitation.

Indeterminacy. Method of composition in which certain factors (e.g., pitches, duration, rhythms, textures, order of succession) are not, or not wholly, specified by the composer. Also called *aleatory.*

Interval. The distance in pitch between two tones, simultaneous or successive. Intervals are measured (usually upward) by scale degrees or steps, counting both the first and last tones; thus, C–E is a third, D–G is a fourth, and so on.

Inversion. Substitution of a higher for a lower note. An interval is inverted when its higher note is placed below its originally lower note: a chord is inverted (or *in inversion*) when any of its notes other than the root is in the bass; a melody is inverted when an equal descending interval is substituted for every ascending interval and *vice versa;* two or more melodic lines in counterpoint are inverted when one of them, originally higher, is placed below the other.

Key, keynote. A tone (including its duplication in any octave) to which the other tones of the octave stand in subordinate relation.

Key signature. Sharp(s) ♯ or flat(s) ♭ placed on line(s) or spaces(s) at the beginning of each staff; all notes on the lines or spaces so indicated are to be raised or lowered respectively one semitone (unless the effect of the sharp or flat is cancelled by a natural ♮). A particular combination of sharps or flats may indicate the key of a composition.

Keyboard music. Music for a keyboard instrument (organ, harpsichord, clavichord, piano).

Line. A melody or part of a melody, considered either by itself or as a constituent in a polyphonic (especially a contrapuntal) texture.

Measure. (1) A unit of time, usually comprising two to six smaller units (*beats*); (2) the space between two bar lines.

Melody. A succession of tones perceived as an entity.

Metrical rhythm. Rhythm in which the duration of every note and rest is a fixed multiple or fraction of a common unit of duration.

Microtone. Any interval smaller than a semitone.

Mixture. An organ stop by which certain higher tones ("harmon-

ics") are artificially made to sound along with the fundamental tone.

Modality. The quality of music written more or less definitely in accordance with the system of the modes of medieval music instead of the major or minor scales.

Modulation. Harmonic movement from one key to a different key in the course of a composition.

Monophony (monophonic). A musical texture consisting of a single line of melody without accompaniment; opposite of *polyphony.*

Motive, motif. The smallest unit of a musical idea (see also *phrase, theme*).

Nonharmonic tone. A tone foreign to, and therefore dissonant with, the basic harmony or chord with which it is sounding.

Note. (1) A graphic sign directing a performer to produce a tone of a certain pitch and duration; (2) the tone represented by such a sign.

Note designation. In this book, a note referred to without regard to its octave register is designated by a capital letter (A). A note in a particular octave is designated by a letter according to the following scheme:

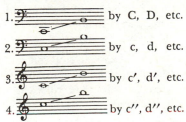

1. by C, D, etc.
2. by c, d, etc.
3. by c′, d′, etc.
4. by c″, d″, etc.

Oblique motion. Movement of two voices in which one remains at the same pitch while the other moves to a different pitch.

Ornament, ornamentation. Decorative notes added to a melodic line.

Ostinato. (1) A short melodic figure persistently repeated, usually in the same voice and at the same pitch, throughout a composition or section of a composition; (2) a persistently repeated pattern of rhythm, not necessarily coinciding with any repeated melodic or harmonic pattern.

Parallel motion. Two or more voices moving constantly at the same interval from one another.

Part. (1) A section of a composition; (2) a voice in contrapuntal texture.

Partial signature. A signature applied to fewer than all the voices of a polyphonic composition.

Phrase. A musical unit made up of one or more motives, and corresponding to a sentence in speech.

Pivot chord. In modulation, the chord which is heard as common to both the initial key and the new key.

Polyphony (polyphonic). "Many-voiced"; a musical texture consisting of two or more lines of melody (see *counterpoint*), or melody and accompaniment, or chords. In this book *polyphonic* is used in contrast to *monophonic*, as a general term including both contrapuntal and harmonic textures (see also *monophonic, counterpoint, harmony*).

Principal. An organ stop controlling the pipes which produce the basic, characteristic tone color of the instrument.

Recitative. A style of vocal writing based on imitating the rhythms and inflections of speech, with a minimum of musical structure.

Resolution. The movement of a dissonant interval or chord to a more consonant one, producing an ef-

fect of completion or of comparative repose.

Root. The lowest note of a chord considered as a combination of tones built up by successive thirds (see also *root position, triad, inversion*).

Root position. A chord is in root position when its root is the lowest sounding note (compare *inversion*).

Round. A canon, usually vocal, in which each voice continues to repeat its part as many times as desired (see *canon*).

Rubato. A slight modification of the regularity of the beat, introduced by the performer for the purpose of musical expression.

Serial, serialism. Technique of composition in which the principle of ordered pitches of twelve-tone music is extended to other parameters such as duration, intensity, timbre, etc.

Signature, see *key signature, time signature.*

Stop. A mechanism of the organ enabling the player to bring on or shut off different ranks of pipes at will.

Stretto. (1) A portion of a fugal composition in which imitations of the subject occur at closer time intervals than in the original presentation of the subject; (2) a closing portion, in quicker time, of a movement in fast tempo.

Subject. The theme of a fugue.

Suspension. A nonharmonic tone held over (*suspended*) on a strong beat from a previous harmony in which it was a harmonic tone, and then resolved (regularly by step downward) to a harmonic tone on a weaker beat (compare *appoggiatura*).

Syncopation. Displacement of the normal accent by transferring it from a strong to a weak beat, or from a strong to a weak part of a beat.

Tempered, see *equal temperament*.

Texture. The character of a musical composition in terms of its density, tone colors, and relative levels of activity in the different voice parts. With regard to the last criterion, textures range from those in which the level of activity is the same in all voices (*homophony*) to those in which the levels of activity are markedly distinct while the voices retain equal melodic importance (*counterpoint*).

Theme. A characteristic musical idea which serves as the basis for development of a composition or section of a composition.

Thirds, see *interval*.

Timbre. The characteristic color or quality of a musical sound as produced by various instruments—as the timbre of the clarinet, oboe, and so on (see also *color*).

Time signature. A sign placed at the beginning of a composition to indicate either (a) the proportion according to which longer time values are to be divided into shorter ones; or (b) the number of beats in each measure and the kind of note that represents a single beat: a time signature of 3/4 means three beats in a measure, a quarter note representing one beat.

Tonality (*tonal*). (1) The quality by virtue of which a musical composition, or a part of a composition, is organized harmonically around a constant central tone (compare *atonality, modality*); (2) the central tone or key of a composition.

Tone. A musical sound of definite pitch.

Tonic. The first note of the scale; the key note.

Triad. A chord consisting of three notes: one, the root, and two others respectively a third and a fifth above the root (see also *root position, inversion*).

Trio. (1) A composition, or section of a composition, in three voices; (2) a composition for three performers; (3) in Classical sonatas and symphonies, a second two-part section following a minuet or scherzo, and followed by a repetion of the minuet or scherzo.

Tritone. The interval of the augmented fourth, which contains three whole tones, as F–B♮, C–F♯, B♭–E. In strict contrapuntal writing this interval may not occur harmonically between the bass and an upper voice, or melodically as two successive notes in any voice.

Twelve-tone music. Music in which a certain order of the twelve tones of the chromatic scale, and derivations of that order, are systematically adhered to throughout a composition.

Vibrato. A slight fluctuation of pitch, used especially by singers and by players of bowed string instruments to make the tone more expressive.

Voice. A melodic line, especially in contrapuntal texture.

Abbreviations

AIM	*American Institute of Musicology;* publications include CEKM, CMM, CSM, MD, MSD. For lists, see MD 25 (1971), 229–51.
AMM	Richard H. Hoppin, ed., *Anthology of Medieval Music*, New York, 1978.
CDMI	*I Classici della Musica Italiana,* Milan, 1918–20 (36 vols.).
CEKM	*Corpus of Early Keyboard Music,* AIM, 1963–
CM	*Collegium Musicum,* New Haven, 1955– ; second series, New Haven and Madison, 1969–
CMI	*I Classici Musicali Italiani,* Milan, 1941–43, 1956 (15 vols.).
CMM	*Corpus mensurabilis musicae,* AIM, 1948–
CSM	*Corpus scriptorum de musica,* AIM, 1950–
DdT	*Denkmäler deutscher Tonkunst,* Leipzig, 1892–1931 (65 vols.); reprinted, Wiesbaden, 1957–61.
DTB	*Denkmäler deutscher Tonkunst, 2. Folge: Denkmäler der Tonkunst in Bayern,* Braunschweig, 1900–38 (38 vols., many of which are subdivided).
DTOe	*Denkmäler der Tonkunst in Oesterreich,* Vienna, 1894–19– . Numbers by volumes and also, up to Vol. 83, by years (*Jahrgänge*); many of the yearly volumes are subdivided: for example, Vol. 39 is Jahrgang 19/2; reprinted, Graz, 1959–
EE	Alfred Einstein, Appendix to *A Short History of Music,* New York, 1947. Contains notes, some translations, and many musical examples.
EM	*Early Music,* Oxford University Press, 1973–
EMW	*Early Musical Masterworks,* University of North Carolina Press, 1977–
EP	R. Eitner, ed., *Publikationen älterer praktischer und theoretischer Musikwerke, vorzugsweise des XV. und XVI. Jahrhunderts,* Berlin, 1873–1905 (29 vols., in 33 *Jahrgänge*).
GMB	Arnold Schering, ed., *Geschichte der Musik in Beispielen* [*History of Music in Examples*], Leipzig, 1931. Notes and translations in German; indications for performances frequently arbitrary.
HAM	Archibald T. Davison and Willi Apel, eds., *Historical Anthology of Music,* Cambridge, 1950. Vol. I: Oriental, Medieval, and Renais-

	sance Music; Vol. II: Baroque, Rococo, and Pre-Classical Music. Notes and translations.
JAMS	*Journal of the American Musicological Society,* 1948–
JMT	*Journal of Music Theory,* 1957–
LSS	Edward R. Lerner, ed., *Study Scores of Musical Styles,* New York, 1968.
MB	*Musica Britannica,* London, 1951–
MD	*Musica Disciplina,* 1946–
MM	Carl Parrish and John F. Ohl, eds., *Masterpieces of Music Before 1750,* New York, 1951. Translations, good editorial notes.
MMA	Gustave Reese, *Music in the Middle Ages,* New York, 1940.
MQ	*The Musical Quarterly,* 1915–
MR	Gustave Reese, *Music in the Renaissance,* 2nd ed., New York, 1959.
MRM	Edward Lowinsky, ed., *Monuments of Renaissance Music,* Chicago, 1964–
MSD	*Musicological Studies and Documents,* AIM, 1951–
NOHM	*New Oxford History of Music,* London and New York, 1954– Vol. I, *Ancient and Oriental Music,* 1957; Vol. II, *Early Medieval Music up to 1300,* 1954; Vol. III, *Ars Nova and the Renaissance, 1300–1540,* 1960; Vol. IV, *The Age of Humanism, 1540–1630,* 1968; Vol. V, *Opera and Church Music, 1630–1750,* 1975; Vol. VII, *The Age of Enlightenment, 1745–1790,* 1973; Vol. X, *The Modern Age, 1890–1960,* 1974; (other volumes in preparation).
NS	Roger Kamien, ed., *The Norton Scores,* 3rd ed., New York, 1977. Vol. I, Machaut to Beethoven; Vol. II, Schubert to Copland.
OMM	Thomas Marrocco and Nicholas Sandon, eds., *Oxford Anthology of Medieval Music,* New York, 1977.
PAM	*Publikationen älterer Musik . . . bei der deutschen Musikgesellschaft,* Leipzig, 1926–40.
PMM	Thomas Marrocco, ed., *Polyphonic Music of the XIVth Century,* Monaco, 1956–
PMMM	*Publications of Medieval Music Manuscripts,* Brooklyn, 1957–
PMS	L. Schrade, ed., *Polyphonic Music of the Fourteenth Century,* Monaco, 1956–
RMAW	Curt Sachs, *The Rise of Music in the Ancient World,* New York, 1943.
RTP	William Waite, ed., *The Rhythm of Twelfth-Century Polyphony,* New Haven, 1954.
SR	Oliver Strunk, *Source Readings in Music History,* New York, 1950. Also published as separate paperbacks, which are indicated as follows:
SRA	—— *Source Readings in Music History: Antiquity and the Middle Ages.*
SRRe	—— *Source Readings in Music History: The Renaissance.*
SRB	—— *Source Readings in Music History: The Baroque Era.*
SRC	—— *Source Readings in Music History: The Classic Era.*
SRRo	—— *Source Readings in Music History: The Romantic Era.*
TEM	Carl Parrish, ed., *A Treasury of Early Music,* New York, 1958.
WM	Johannes Wolf, *Music of Earlier Times;* the American edition of Wolf's *Sing- und Spielmusik aus älterer Zeit,* 1926. No notes or translations.

Note: Throughout the bibliographies, "Cambridge" as place of publication means Cambridge, Massachusetts, unless otherwise specified. Not all modern reprints are mentioned; see current catalogues.

Bibliography

General Bibliography

Music Anthologies

In addition to the anthologies of music examples listed below by chapters, the following series will be found useful: *Anthology of Music,* ed. K. G. Fellerer, vols. 1–47, Cologne, 1955–75, with Index, 1976; each volume is devoted to examples of music in a particular form or from a particular period, edited by a specialist, with introduction and notes. See also the series *Monuments of Music and Music Literature in Facsimile,* New York, 1978–

Composers and compositions can be located with the help of *Historical Sets, Collected Editions, and Monuments of Music,* compiled by Anna Harriet Heyer, 2nd ed., Chicago, 1969. Many older editions of music are available in reprints: see current catalogues of Broude Bros., Dover Publications, Da Capo Press (all in New York). Gregg Press, and others

Reference Works

The leading encyclopedias are: *Die Musik in Geschichte und Gegenwart* (MGG), Friedrich Blume, ed., Kassel, 1949–68, 14 vols., with Supplements, 1968– ; *The New Grove Dictionary of Music and Musicians,* Stanley Sadie, ed., 6th ed., 20 vols., London, 1980; *New Oxford History of Music,* London and New York, 1954– ; W. W. Cobbett, *Cyclopedic Survey of Chamber Music,* 2nd ed., 1963, 3 vols. (third vol., Colin Mason, ed.). Most convenient, indeed indispensable, are: Willi Apel, *Harvard Dictionary of Music,* 2nd ed., Cambridge, 1970; Don Michael Randel, *Harvard Concise Dictionary of Music,* Cambridge, 1978; and *Baker's Biographical Dictionary of Musicians,* 6th ed., New York, 1978.

Chapter I (Pp. 1–15)

Music

Transcriptions of the extant Greek melodies and fragments are given in Théodore Reinach, *La Musique grècque,* Paris, 1926. Examples also in HAM, Nos. 7, 8; GMB, No. 1; EE, No. 2.

Examples of Hebrew and Byzantine music are given in HAM, Nos. 6 and 8.

For the music of Gregorian Chant, see Bibliography for Chapter II. Examples of chants from other Western liturgies are given in TEM, Nos. 1–3; HAM, Nos. 9 and 10.

Books and articles listed under this heading are not offered as bibliography, but are simply suggested readings (mostly in English) which will be profitable to a student beginning the study of music history. Under no circumstances should this reading be regarded as a substitute for the listening or playing experience, or for the study of the music itself.

A basic book is SR (also SRA). For Chapter I, read the selections in the first chapter, "The Greek View of Music," and in the second chapter, "The Early Christian View of Music."

Also see RMAW; and MMA, Chapters 1 through 4.

On Greek music: Plato, *Timaeus; Republic,* Book III, 395–403; Aristotle, *Politics,* Book VIII.

On Hebrew music: A. Z. Idelsohn, *Jewish Music in Its Historical Development,* New York, 1967.

On Byzantine music: see Oliver Strunk, *Essays on Music in the Byzantine World,* New York, 1977; Egon Wellesz, *A History of Byzantine Music and Hymnody,* 2nd ed., Oxford, 1961.

For better acquaintance with Boethius—and he is well worth knowing—one should read his famous *Consolation of Philosophy,* which is available in many editions and translations. The best short introduction to Boethius is ch. 5 of E. K. Rand's *Founders of the Middle Ages,* Cambridge, 1929.

A fascinating book dealing with the influence of ancient and early medieval writings on art and literature is Kathi Meyer-Baer, *Music of the Spheres and the Dance of Death,* Princeton, 1970. Also useful is Edgar de Bruyne, *The Esthetics of the Middle Ages,* New York, 1969.

For Further Reading

Chapter II (Pp. 16–42)

Antiphonale Sacrosanctae Romanae Ecclesiae pro diurnis horis, Paris, 1949.
Graduale Sacrosanctae Romanae Ecclesiae, Paris, 1948.
The Liber Usualis with Introduction and Rubrics in English, New York, 1956.

Syllabic Chant: MM, No. 3; LSS, Nos. 4, 5, 9; AMM, No. 13; OMM, No. 3a, 3b.

Melismatic Chant: MM, No. 2; HAM, Nos. 12, 13; AMM, No. 11.

Psalm Tones, with antiphons: MM, No. 1; HAM, No. 11; AMM, No. 2; OMM, No. 7.

Tracts: *Graduale,* 208, 232; OMM, No. 9.

Graduals: HAM, No. 12; LSS, No. 6; AMM, No. 10.

Alleluias: MM, No. 2; HAM, No. 13; EE, No. 2; LSS, No. 7.

Kyrie: HAM, No. 15a; LSS, No. 2; AMM, No. 6.

Gloria and Sanctus: GMB, No. 2; OMM, No. 11c, 11n.

Other chants of the Ordinary of the Mass: *Liber Usualis,* 16–94; LSS, No. 3.

Sequences and proses: HAM, No. 16; MM, No. 3; GMB, Nos. 4–6; EE, No. 5; LSS, No. 9; AMM, No. 12.

Hymn: LSS, No. 8; OMM, No. 10a.

Liturgical dramas: TEM, No. 5; GMB, No. 8; OMM, No. 12.

Monophonic conductus: HAM, No. 17; AMM, No. 17.

Troubador songs: TEM, No. 6; HAM, No. 18; GMB, Nos. 11, 13; EE, No. 7; LSS, No. 12; AMM, No. 41.

Trouvère songs: MM, No. 4; HAM, No. 19; GMB, No. 14; LSS, Nos. 13–15; AMM, No. 45.

Minnesongs: MM, No. 5; HAM, No. 20; GMB, Nos. 12, 21; OMM, Nos. 31, 32.

Meistersongs: TEM, No. 22; HAM, No. 24; GMB, Nos. 78, 79; EE, No. 8.

Other monophonic songs: TEM, Nos. 7, 8; HAM, Nos. 21–23; GMB, No. 25; LSS, Nos. 17–21.

Music

Additional Examples in Other Anthologies

Instrumental pieces: MM, No. 12; HAM, Nos. 40, 41, 58, 59; GMB, No. 28; AMM, No. 57, 58.

For Further Reading

For a comprehensive account of the chant (not primarily historical) see Willi Apel, *Gregorian Chant*, Bloomington, 1958.

Rev. Dom Dominic Johner, *A New School of Gregorian Chant*, New York, 1925. A practical introduction to the subject of Gregorian Chant, with much historical and liturgical information.

J. R. Bryden and D. Hughes, *An Index of Gregorian Chant*, Cambridge, 1969, 2 vols.

Richard H. Hoppin, *Medieval Music*, New York, 1978.

Richard Crocker, *The Early Medieval Sequence*, Berkeley, 1977.

Chapter III (Pp. 43–69)

Additional Examples in Other Anthologies

Early organum: MM, No. 6; HAM, No. 25; OMM, No. 37.

Eleventh-century counterpoint: MM, No. 7; HAM, No. 26; GMB, No. 9; OMM, No. 38.

St. Martial organum: MM, No. 8; HAM, No. 27; AMM, No. 29.

Notre Dame organum (period of Perotin): MM, No. 9; HAM, No. 31; LSS, No. 23; AMM, No. 35.

Conductus: MM, No. 11; HAM, Nos. 38, 39; GMB, No. 16; EE, No. 6; LSS, No. 24; OMM, No. 54.

Conductus style: HAM, No. 32c.

Interchanged voices (*Stimmtausch*): MM, No. 10; HAM, Nos. 32c, 33a; OMM, No. 48.

Motet: TEM, Nos. 10, 12; MM, No. 10; HAM, Nos. 28f–i, 32–35; GMB, Nos. 18–20; EE, No. 9; WM, No. 3; NS, Vol. I, No. 2.

Miscellaneous cantilena types: HAM, No. 36.

Hocket: TEM, No. 11; LSS, No. 25.

Rota (*Sumer* canon): HAM, No. 42; GMB, No. 17.

Dance: LSS, No. 26.

For Further Reading

Music Theory Translations Series, published by Yale University Press, New Haven: Vol. 1, Gasparini, trans. F. Stillings, 1963; Vol. 2, Zarlino, trans. C. Palisca and G. Marco, 1969; Vol. 3, medieval treatises by Hucbald, Guido, and John, trans. W. Babb, 1979.

For details of the notation of twelfth- and thirteenth-century polyphonic music, see Willi Apel, *The Notation of Polyphonic Music*, Cambridge, 1961, 5th ed.; Carl Parrish, *The Notation of Medieval Music*, New York, 1978 (repr.); William Waite, *The Rhythm of Twelfth-Century Polyphony*, New Haven, 1954.

Chapter IV (Pp. 70–88)

Additional Examples in Other Anthologies

Motets from the *Roman de Fauvel*: HAM, No. 43.

Works of Guillaume de Machaut:

Chansons balladeés: HAM, No. 46; GMB, No. 26b.

Motets: HAM, No. 44; GMB, No. 27; WM, No. 5; LSS, No. 27.

Ballades: HAM, No. 45; GMB, No. 26a; AMM, No. 62.

Mass: MM, No. 13 (Agnus Dei); NS, Vol. I, No. 3 (Kyrie).

Church music of the fourteenth and early fifteenth centuries: TEM, Nos. 13, 14; HAM, Nos. 55, 56; GMB, No. 29.

Late fourteenth-century secular French music: TEM, No. 17; HAM, Nos. 47, 48; GMB, No. 24; LSS, No. 30; AMM, No. 68.

Italian music of the fourteenth century:

  Madrigals: HAM, Nos. 49, 50; GMB, No. 22; LSS, No. 28.

  Cacce: TEM, No. 16; HAM, No. 52; AMM, No. 66; LSS, No. 29.

  Ballata: HAM, No. 51; AMM, No. 67; OMM, Nos. 74, 77.

Instrumental music: TEM, No. 15; HAM, Nos. 58, 59; OMM, No. 105.

Selections from fourteenth-century treatises in SR (also, SRA): Marchetto da Padua, 160–71; Jean de Muris, 172–79; and Jacob of Liège, 180–90; translation of Philippe de Vitry's *Ars nova* by Leon Plantinga in JMT 5 (1961), 204–23; see also CSM 8.

GUILLAUME DE MACHAUT: For a short but excellent survey, see G. Reaney, *Guillaume de Machaut,* Oxford Studies of Composers, 9, London, 1971. Articles dealing with various aspects of Machaut's work: G. Reaney, "The Ballades, Rondeaux and Virelais of Guillaume de Machaut: Melody, Rhythm and Form," *Acta musicologica* 27 (1955), 40–58; *id.,* "Voices and Instruments in the Music of Guillaume de Machault," *Revue Belge de Musicologie* 10 (1956), 3–17, 93–104; George Perle, "Integrative Devices in the Music of Machaut," MQ 24 (1948), 169–76; Otto Gombosi, "Machaut's *Messe Notre-Dame,*" MQ 36 (1950), 204–24.

MARCHETTO DA PADUA: Nino Pirrotta, in MD 9 (1955), 57–73.

The original Latin text of Pope John XXII's decree of 1324 concerning church music is in Vol. I of the old *Oxford History of Music,* London, 1929, 294–95. For some other pronouncements on this subject see MMA, 321, 390; and P. H. Lang, *Music in Western Civilization,* New York, 1941, 140, 163.

On instruments in the music of this period, see essays by E. A. Bowles, F. Ll. Harrison, and G. Reaney in Jan LaRue, ed., *Aspects of Medieval and Renaissance Music,* New York, 1978 (repr).

Chapter V (Pp. 89–106)

English music of the fourteenth and early fifteenth centuries, other than Dunstable: HAM, Nos. 57, 63, 64 (compare also HAM, Nos. 25c, 33a, 37, 42 and EE, No. 6); AMM, 71; OMM, 102, 103.

  Dunstable: TEM, No. 18; HAM, Nos. 61, 62; GMB, No. 35; WM, No. 11; LSS, No. 31; OMM, No. 97. (The transcriptions of GMB, Nos. 32 and 34 are not reliable.)

  The Burgundian School: *Chansons:* MM, No. 16; HAM, Nos. 67–72; GMB, Nos. 40, 41, 42; LSS, No. 35; OMM, Nos. 98, 99, 100. *Motets:* HAM, No. 65; GMB, Nos. 38, 43; WM, No. 12; LSS, No. 33, NS. Vol. I, No. 4 *Masses:* MM, No. 15; HAM, No. 66 (and compare Nos. 73, 92); GMB, No. 39; EE, No. 12; LSS, No. 34; OMM, Nos. 89–93.

E. A. Bowles, *Musikleben im 15. Jahrhundert,* Leipzig, 1977.

Howard M. Brown, *Music in the French Secular Theatre, 1400–1550* and the companion volume, *Theatrical Chansons of the Fifteenth and Early Sixteenth Centuries,* Cambridge, 1963; *id.,* "Instruments and Voices in the 15th-century Chanson," *Current Thought in Musicology,* ed. J. W. Grubbe, Austin, 1976, 89–138.

Manfred F. Bukofzer, *Studies in Medieval and Renaissance Music,* New York, 1950. The first four essays in this volume are concerned with English music of the fourteenth and early fifteenth centuries. The seventh essay ("*Caput:* a Liturgico-Musical Study") deals with the origins of the cyclic Mass and contains an analysis of three Masses based on the "*Caput*" *cantus firmus; id.,* "John Dunstable: A Quincentenary Report," MQ 10 (1954), 29–49. Biography, musical sources, style, and significance, in brief and attractive form.

Richard Leighton Greene, *The Early English Carols,* Oxford, 1935. The fundamental work on the form of the carol; includes a collection of all extant carol texts to 1550.

Charles Hamm, *A Chronology of the Works of Guillaume Dufay,* Princeton, 1964.

Frank Ll. Harrison, *Music in Medieval Britain,* London, 1958. An excellent study of the period from the eleventh century to the Reformation; it deals not only with musical style but also with the institutions under whose patronage the music was composed and performed.

Nino Pirrotta, "Music and Cultural Tendencies in 15th Century Italy," JAMS 19 (1966), 127–61.

Chapter VI (Pp. 107–29)

Additional Examples in Other Anthologies

Josquin des Prez: MM, No. 19; HAM, Nos. 90, 91; NS, Vol. I, Nos. 6, 7, 8; LSS, No. 37. The motet *Absalon fili* is in the *Oxford History of Music,* Vol. II, 77–83. The Mass *Pange lingua* is Vol. I of Blume, *Das Chorwerk.*

Obrecht: MM, No. 18; HAM, Nos. 77, 78.

Ockeghem: MM, No. 17; HAM, Nos. 73 (the very strict treatment of the *cantus firmus* in this example is exceptional in Ockeghem), 74, 75; LSS, No. 36.

Canonic devices in Netherlands music: MM, No. 17, with introductory commentary; HAM, Nos. 66c, 89, 91, 92, with commentary on pages 223, 225–26.

The Netherlands chanson in the early sixteenth century: HAM, Nos. 68, 69, 70, 72, 74, 75, 79 (an exceptional type, the motet chanson), 91; GMB, No. 53. For instrumental pieces in vocal collections dated around 1500, see HAM, Nos. 78, 83; GMB, Nos. 56, 62b, 67, 68.

Contemporaries of Obrecht and Josquin: HAM, Nos. 88, 92.

For Further Reading

The indispensable starting point for any detailed study of this period is Gustave Reese, *Music in the Renaissance,* New York, 1959, a comprehensive, concrete, and very accurate account of every phase of musical activity from 1400–1600. Very full bibliographic references are included. A very appealing introduction to the styles and practices of the period is Howard M. Brown, *Music in the Renaissance,* Englewood Cliffs, 1976.

An excellent survey of this and the following era is Friedrich Blume, *Renaissance and Baroque Music,* New York, 1967. See also Edward Lowinsky, *Tonality and Atonality in Sixteenth-Century Music,* Berkeley, 1961.

JOSQUIN DES PREZ: Helmuth Osthoff, *Josquin Desprez,* 2 vols., Tutzing, 1962–65, is the standard work on this composer. See also Edward E. Lowinsky, ed., *Josquin des Prez,* London, 1976; id., *Proceedings of the International Josquin Festival-Conference,* London, 1975; Leeman Perkins, "Mode and Structure in the Masses of Josquin," JAMS 26 (1973).

Chapters V, VI, and VII of Manfred Bukofzer's *Studies in Medieval and Renaissance Music* deal chiefly with the period 1450–1550.

A good succinct account, with illustrations, is A. Hyatt King's *Four Hundred Years of Music Printing,* 2nd ed., London, 1968.

Howard M. Brown, *Instrumental Music Printed before 1600,* Cambridge, 1965.

Chapter VII (Pp. 130–56)

Netherlands composers 1520–*ca.* 1550: HAM, Nos. 106, 109, 113, 114, 125; EE, No. 15; WM, No. 27; GMB, No. 118.

National schools of the early sixteenth century: *Italy:* TEM, Nos. 20, 21; HAM,

Nos. 94 (the use of an antiphon melody [see MM, p. 63] in this lauda is exceptional, as are likewise the antiphonal two-voice phrases and, to a lesser degree, the imitations in measures 29 to 37), 95; WM, Nos. 20–23; GMB, Nos. 69–72. *France:* HAM, No. 107; EE, No. 16. *Germany:* TEM, No. 32; HAM, Nos. 81, 82, 87, 93, 110; GMB, No. 87; Quodlibets: TEM, No. 31; HAM, No. 82; GMB, No. 111; Ode, GMB, No. 73. *Spain:* HAM, Nos. 97, 98, 128; TEM, Nos. 19,23; GMB, No. 96. *England:* HAM, Nos. 86, 112, 127.

Instrumental music:

Organ pieces on a *cantus firmus:* HAM, Nos. 100, 101, 120, 133.

Vocal compositions transcribed: GMB, Nos. 62b, 63a; from a later date, but illustrative of the technique of transcription, are the compositions in MM, Nos. 20, 21; HAM, No. 145.

Ricercare (imitative): HAM, Nos. 115, 116; GMB, Nos. 105, 113; EE, No. 22.

Ricercare (non-imitative): GMB, Nos. 94, 115.

Canzona: HAM, No. 118 (also compare No. 91).

Dances: HAM, No. 137; MM, No. 22; GMB, Nos. 90, 91; LSS, Nos. 46, 48.

Improvisatory pieces: HAM, Nos. 84, 99, 121; GMB, Nos. 63b, 93.

Variations: HAM, Nos. 122, 124, 134; compare No. 103 (ostinato pattern).

Secular vocal music of the late sixteenth century:

Italy: TEM, No. 33; MM, No. 27; HAM, Nos. 129–131, 155, 158, 161, 188; GMB, Nos. 98, 100, 101, 106, 140, 165 (the lower voices arbitrarily edited for instruments), 167; EE, Nos. 18, 20; WM, Nos. 38, 46, 47; LSS, Nos. 38, 39, 47, 60.

Spain: LSS, No. 40.

Germany and France: HAM, Nos. 138, 142, 145a, 146a, 147, 165, 168; GMB, Nos. 124, 125, 139, 141, 144, 152; LSS, Nos. 41–42, 45, 49.

England: TEM, No. 34; MM, No. 28; HAM, Nos. 159, 162, 163, 170; GMB, Nos. 145, 146; LSS, Nos. 56, 57.

G. GABRIELI: Denis Arnold, *Giovanni Gabrieli,* London, 1979.

GESUALDO: Glenn Watkins, *Gesualdo, The Man and His Music,* London, 1973; Cecil Gray and Philip Heseltine, *Carlo Gesualdo, Prince of Venosa, Musician and Murderer,* London, 1926.

MARENZIO: Denis Arnold, *Marenzio,* London, 1965.

MONTEVERDI: Leo Schrade, *Monteverdi, Creator of Modern Music,* New York, 1969.

Edward Lowinsky, *Secret Chromatic Art in the Netherlands Motet* brilliantly presents a theory which, although controversial in some details, is well established in essentials. A related article is Lowinsky's "The Goddess Fortuna in Music," MQ 29 (1943), 45–77.

Alfred Einstein, *The Italian Madrigal,* Princeton, 1949 (3 vols.) is the definitive work on this subject, a rare combination of scholarly accuracy, wide knowledge, and attractive presentation. Chapter I deals with the frottola and other forerunners of the madrigal in Italy. On the interrelationship of various forms of secular vocal music in this period see James Haar, ed., *Chanson and Madrigal 1480–1530,* Cambridge, 1964.

For examples of Italian madrigal poetry in accurate but inelegant translation, see HAM, Vol. I, 251ff and MM, No. 27. On madrigal poetry in general, see Walter Rubsamen, *Literary Sources of Secular Music in Italy (ca. 1500),* Berkeley, 1943; Einstein, *The Italian Madrigal,* Vol. I, 166–212; and E. H. Fellowes, *English Madrigal Verse,* Oxford, 1929; Dean T. Mace, "Pietro Bembo and the Literary Origins of the Italian Madrigal," MQ 55 (1969).

Willi Apel, *The History of Keyboard Music to 1700,* trans. Hans Tischler, Bloomington, 1972.

On improvisation in Renaissance music, see E. Ferand, " 'Sodaine and Unexpected' Music in the Renaissance," MQ 37 (1951), 10–27.

For information about English music of the early sixteenth century: John Stevens, *Music & Poetry in the Early Tudor Court*, Lincoln, Neb., 1961; and Paul Doe, *Tallis*, London and New York, 1968; of the Elizabethan age: E. H. Fellowes, *The English Madrigal Composers*, Oxford, 1921; Peter Warlock (pseudonym for Philip Heseltine). *The English Ayre*, London, 1926; Ernest Walker, *A History of Music in England*, Oxford, 1952, Ch. IV; Walter L. Woodfill, *Musicians in English Society*, New York, 1969. Charles Kennedy Scott, *Madrigal Singing*, London, 1931; Joseph Kerman, *The Elizabethan Madrigal*, New York, 1962.

Morley's *A Plaine and Easie Introduction to Practicall Musicke* (1597) has been published in a modern edition, with the spelling brought up to date and the musical examples transcribed in modern notation, by R. Alec Harman, New York, 1952. See also SR Nos. 29 and 37 (SRRe Nos. 8 and 16) by Morley and Henry Peacham, respectively.

Gioseffo Zarlino, *The Art of Counterpoint, Part III of Le Istitutioni harmoniche*, trans. Guy A. Marco and Claude V. Palisca, New Haven, 1968; reprinted, New York, 1976.

Chapter VIII (Pp. 157–80)

Additional Examples in Other Anthologies

Protestant church music: *Lutheran:* TEM, No. 24; HAM, Nos. 108, 111, 167a; GMB, Nos. 77, 80, 84, 108–110, 123, 143, 159–162; WM, No. 35; LSS, Nos. 43–44. *Calvinist:* TEM, Nos. 25, 26; HAM, Nos. 126, 132; GMB, No. 142. *Anglican:* TEM, No. 27; HAM, Nos. 151, 169, 171, 172; LSS, No. 58.

Catholic church music of the late Renaissance: MM, Nos., 23–25; HAM, Nos. 139–141, 143, 144, 146b, 148–150, 152, 156, 164, 166; GMB, Nos. 120–122, 126–129, 131, 179; WM, No. 41; LSS, Nos. 50, 51–52.

Instrumental music of the late Renaissance: TEM, Nos. 29, 30, 35, 36; MM, No. 29; HAM, Nos. 135–137, 145b, 153, 154, 160b, 167b, 173–180; GMB, Nos. 134–138, 147–151, 153, 155–157, 174; EE, Nos. 22, 25, 26; WM, Nos. 39, 40, 43, 56, 57; LSS, No. 55.

The Venetian School: TEM, No. 28; HAM, Nos. 157, 173; GMB, Nos. 130, 148; EE, No. 19; LSS, Nos. 53, 54.

For Further Reading

SR, Nos. 28, 29, 34–36, 38, 40, 43–45. (SRRe 7, 8, 13–15, 17, 19, 22–24.)

The basic work on Lutheran church music is Friedrich Blume, *Protestant Church Music*, New York, 1974.

Waldo S. Pratt, *The Music of the Pilgrims*, Boston, 1921, contains a description of the Ainsworth Psalter: see also Irving Lowens, "The Bay Psalm Book in 17th-Century New England," JAMS 8 (1955), 22–29.

Palestrina's music is subjected to detailed analysis in Knud Jeppesen's *The Style of Palestrina and the Dissonance*, London, 1927. Some counterpoint textbooks based on the Palestrina style are: R. O. Morris, *Contrapuntal Technique in the Sixteenth Century*, Oxford, 1922; K. Jeppesen, *Counterpoint*, tr. G. Haydon, New York, 1929; A. T. Merritt, *Sixteenth Century Polyphony*, Cambridge, 1939. On the legend of the *Pope Marcellus Mass*, see the edition of this work in the Norton Critical Scores.

English translation of Thoinot-Arbeau's *Orchésographie* (1588): Jehan Tabourot, *Orchesography by Thoinot-Arbeau*, tr. M. S. Evans, New York, 1948; reprinted 1967.

On English music of the late sixteenth and early seventeenth centuries: Peter LeHuray, *Music and the Reformation in England, 1549–1660*, New York, 1967.

M. C. Boyd, *Elizabethan Music and Musical Criticism,* 2nd ed., Philadelphia, 1962. Joseph Kerman, "On William Byrd's *Emendemus in melius,*" MQ 49 (1963), 431–49 (a model of musical analysis); E. H. Fellowes, *William Byrd,* London, 1948; *id., English Cathedral Music,* new ed., rev. J. A. Westrup, New York, 1969; D. Stevens, *Thomas Tomkins,* New York, 1967; see also W. Mellers, "John Bull and English Keyboard Music," MQ 40 (1954), 364–83, 548–71.

Chapter IX (Pp. 181–210)

The opera and its forerunners: MM, No. 31; HAM, Nos. 182, 186, 187, 206, 208, 209, 221, 230; GMB, Nos. 164, 166, 171, 175–178, 199–204; EE, No. 24; WM, No. 48; LSS, Nos. 59, 62, 63; NS, Vol. I, No. 14.

Vocal chamber music: MM, No. 30; HAM, Nos. 184, 189, 203–205; GMB, Nos. 170, 172, 173, 187, 193, 194, 197; WM, Nos. 49, 53, 65, 66.

Catholic church music and oratorio: TEM, No. 37; MM, No. 32; HAM, Nos. 183, 185, 207; GMB, Nos. 168, 169, 180, 198; WM, No. 52; LSS, Nos. 61, 68.

Lutheran church music in Germany: TEM, No. 38; MM, No. 33; HAM, Nos. 201, 202, 213; GMB, Nos. 188–192; EE, No. 27; LSS, No. 64; NS, Vol. I, No. 17.

Instrumental music: TEM, No. 39; MM, Nos. 26, 34, 35; HAM, Nos. 190a, 191–199, 210–212, 215–217, 229, 230, 256; GMB, Nos. 153, 155–158, 182–185, 196, 205, 207 (compare 206), 215, 216, 218; EE, No. 26; WM, Nos. 54–56, 63, 64; LSS, Nos. 65, 66, 67.

Additional Examples in Other Anthologies

SR, Nos. 46–56 (SRB 1–11).

Manfred F. Bukofzer, *Music in the Baroque Era,* New York, 1947. A comprehensive survey of the entire Baroque, with music examples and bibliographies.

On the interrelation of music and the other arts in general, see Curt Sachs, *The Commonwealth of Art,* New York, 1946.

Frank Arnold's *The Art of Accompaniment from a Thorough-Bass as Practiced in the XVIIth and XVIIIth Centuries,* New York, 1965, is the basic work on this subject, with copious quotations and examples from the sources. A very useful introduction, both scholarly and practical, is Peter F. Williams, *Figured Bass Accompaniment,* Edinburgh and Chicago, 1970, 2 vols.

On the opera, in the Baroque and later periods, see D. J. Grout, *A Short History of Opera,* New York, 1965, 2nd edition; Joseph Kerman, *Opera as Drama,* New York, 1956. Egon Wellesz, *Essays on Opera,* London, 1950, deals for the most part with seventeenth-century works.

On the Florentine Camerata and Italian vocal chamber music, see Claude V. Palisca, *Mei,* 2nd ed., 1977; *idem.,* "The 'Camerata' Fiorentina; a Reappraisal," *Studi musicali* I (1972), 203–34; Nino Pirrotta, "Temperaments and Tendencies in the Florentine Camerata," MQ 40 (1954), 169–89; Nigel Fortune, "Italian Secular Monody from 1600 to 1635; An Introductory Survey," MQ 39 (1953), 171–95; see also articles by H. Wiley Hitchcock in MQ 56 (1970), 387–404; JAMS 25 (1972), 58–78; 26 (1973), 438–60; 27 (1974), 145–47. Putnam Aldrich, *Rhythm in Seventeenth-Century Monody,* New York, 1966.

MONTEVERDI: Denis Arnold, *Monteverdi,* London and New York, 1963; Leo Schrade, *Monteverdi,* New York, 1950; D. Arnold and N. Fortune, eds., *The Monteverdi Companion,* New York, 1968.

Other aspects of Baroque music are treated in Curt Sachs, *A World History of the Dance,* New York, 1937; William S. Newman, *The Sonata in the Baroque Era,* 3rd ed., New York, 1972; Alan Curtis, *Sweelinck's Keyboard Music,* Leiden, 1969; Howard E. Smither, *A History of the Oratorio,* 2 vols., Chapel Hill, 1977.

For Further Reading

Chapter X (Pp. 211–29)

Music Collections

Examples of French opera overtures may be found in MM, No. 36 and HAM, Nos. 223 and 224; examples of the same form in other contexts are EE, No. 30 and GMB, Nos. 278 and 292. Some other examples are: J. S. Bach, the four Suites (*Ouvertures*) for orchestra, and the opening movements of the cantatas Nos. 61, 97, 119; Handel, Overture to *Messiah* and first movements of the *Concerti Grossi* Nos. 10 and 12.

The following examples of the passacaglia form in Baroque music may be compared with Purcell's aria "When I am laid in earth" from *Dido and Aeneas*: HAM, Nos. 222, 238; GMB, Nos. 230, 231, 233; and the "Crucifixus" from Bach's *Mass in B Minor*.

Some modern editions of Italian vocal chamber music of the seventeenth and eighteenth centuries are: CDMI, Vols. 2 (G. B. Bassani), 17 (Marcello), 30 (A. Scarlatti); CMI, Vol. 2 (Marcello); K. Jeppeson, ed., *La Flora*; H. Riemann, ed., *Kantaten Frühling, 1633–1682*, Leipzig, no date (2 vols.); H. Riemann, ed., *Ausgewählte Kammer-Kantaten der Zeit um 1700*, Leipzig, no date, 6 numbers. For others, see Bukofzer, *Music in the Baroque Era*, 462–63.

Additional Examples in Other Anthologies

Opera: TEM, Nos. 44, 46; MM, No. 36; HAM, Nos. 222–225, 241, 243, 244, 255, 267, 281; GMB, Nos. 195, 222–224, 226, 227, 231, 232, 233, 234, 236, 247, 250, 258, 259, 261, 266, 268–270, 272, 274, 293; EE, No. 30; LSS, Nos. 69, 71, 72, 78–79; NS, Vol. I, No. 19.

Cantata and song: TEM, No. 49; HAM, Nos. 228, 254, 258, 273 (by Francesco Durante, 1684–1755; a *tour de force* of chromatic harmonies and remote modulations; compare also GMB, No. 197 and TEM, No. 49); GMB, Nos. 209, 210, 217, 235, 242, 248, 254, 256, 260, 262, 287; EE, No. 28; LSS, No. 73.

Roman Catholic and Anglican church music: TEM, Nos. 42, 43; HAM, Nos. 218, 226, 242, 257, 266, 268; GMB, Nos. 225, 230, 246, 271, 273, 275, 310; LSS, Nos. 70, 74.

Lutheran church music: HAM, Nos. 213, 214, 235, 272; GMB, Nos. 208, 211, 212, 267, 290.

For Further Reading

SR, Nos. 57–64 (SRB, Nos. 12–19).

Beekman C. Cannon, *Johann Mattheson, Spectator in Music*, New Haven, 1947, an account of the famous theorist of the early eighteenth century, a contemporary of Bach and Handel. Mattheson's *Der vollkommene Capellmeister* [*The Perfect Music Director*] of 1739 has been published in a facsimile edition, Kassel, 1954.

For an invaluable overview, see James R. Anthony, *French Baroque Music from Beaujoyeulx to Rameau*, rev. ed., New York, 1978.

On English opera of this period the basic work is E. J. Dent, *Foundations of English Opera*, New York, 1965. On Venetian opera in the second half of the seventeenth century, see Simon Towneley Worsthorne, *Venetian Opera in the Seventeenth Century*, Oxford, 1954.

The books listed in the Appendix to Chapter IX should also be consulted for supplementary reading for the material in Chapter X.

Chapter XI (Pp. 230–47)

Additional Examples in Other Anthologies

Music for organ: TEM, No. 41; MM, No. 37; HAM, Nos. 190b,c,d, 215, 231, 234, 237, 239, 247, 249a,b, 251; GMB, Nos. 243, 249, 263, 265, 291; EE, No. 35.

Music for lute, harpsichord, and clavichord: TEM, No. 40; MM, Nos. 38, 40; HAM, Nos. 212, 232, 233, 236, 240, 248, 250, 261, 265a, 265b, 280; GMB, Nos. 215, 216, 218, 244, 253, 264; LSS, Nos. 82, 83. The keyboard suite by J. K. F. Fischer in HAM, No. 248 has for its second movement a "passacaille"; in this passacaglia the theme, instead of being continuously repeated, recurs like a refrain, with contrasting interludes. The movement thus assumes the form of a rondeau (compare HAM, No. 265b). The French clavecinists used the terms *chaconne* or *passacaglia* for pieces of this kind (compare HAM, No. 212; HAM, No. 240 combines the regular passacaglia with the rondeau form).

Solo sonatas with basso continuo: HAM, Nos. 219, 238, 252, 253, 275, 278; GMB, Nos. 238, 245, 294, 295; EE, No. 32; LSS, No. 75.

Trio sonatas: MM, No. 39; HAM, Nos. 245, 263, 269; GMB, Nos. 240, 241; EE, No. 29; LSS, No. 76; NS, Vol. I, No. 18.

Works for larger ensembles: TEM, No. 45 (chaconne); HAM, Nos. 220, 223; GMB, Nos. 214, 220, 221, 224, 233, 252.

Orchestral suites and concertos: HAM, Nos. 246, 260; GMB, Nos. 251, 257, 277.

J. J. Fux, *Gradus ad Parnassum* (facsimile), New York, 1966 (Monuments of Music and Music Literature in Facsimile, Ser. 2, No. 24); *The Study of Counterpoint from Johann Joseph Fux's Gradus ad Parnassum*, rev. ed., tr. and ed. A. Mann and J. Edmunds, New York, 1965.

Francesco Geminiani, *Art of Playing on the Violin* (facsimile), D. Boyden, ed., London, 1952; *id., A Treatise of Good Taste in the Art of Musick* (facsimile), with introd. by R. Donington, New York, 1969.

Ernst H. Meyer, *English Chamber Music*, 2nd ed., London, 1951.

William S. Newman, *The Sonata in the Baroque Era*, 3rd ed., New York, 1972.

Marc Pincherle, *Corelli et son temps*, Paris, 1954; H. E. M. Russell, tr., *Corelli, His Life, His Music*, New York, 1968.

(margin note) For Further Reading

Chapter XII (Pp. 248–77)

(margin note) Music Collection

Wolfgang Schmieder, ed., *Thematisch-systematisches Verzeichnis der musikalischen Werke von Johann Sebastian Bach (BWV)*, 6th ed., reprinted, 1976. A complete systematic-thematic index of Bach's works, with references to the Bach Society edition and also to other standard modern editions.

(margin note) Additional Examples in Other Anthologies

Bach: MM, Nos. 46–50; HAM, No. 190d; GMB, Nos. 283–85; EE, No. 33; LSS, Nos. 84, 85, 86; NS, Vol. I, Nos. 23–26.

Handel: MM, Nos. 43–45; GMB, Nos. 278–80; LSS, Nos. 80, 81; NS, Vol. I, Nos. 21, 22.

Rameau: MM, No. 41; HAM, Nos. 276, 277; GMB, Nos. 296, 297.

Vivaldi: TEM, No. 47; HAM, No. 270; GMB, No. 276; LSS, No. 77; NS, Vol. I, No. 20.

(margin note) For Further Reading

BACH: The standard work is Philipp Spitta, *Johann Sebastian Bach*, 4th ed., Leipzig, 1930 (2 vols.). An English translation in three volumes, published at London in 1889, has been reissued: *Johann Sebastian Bach, His Work and Influence on the Music of Germany*, New York, 1951. A good general study is Karl Geiringer, *Johann Sebastian Bach; the Culmination of an Epoch*, New York, 1966.

An invaluable book is Hans David and Arthur Mendel, *The Bach Reader*, New York, 1966; it contains (in English translation) "all the surviving sources of any importance from which our knowledge of Bach's life and reputation has been drawn," as well as essays on Bach's life and music and on the history of his fame.

A detailed account of Bach's life is given in Charles Sanford Terry, *Bach, a Biography*, London, 1928; the same author's *Bach, the Historical Approach* is semipopular in style but sound in substance. Albert Schweitzer, *J. S. Bach*, first published in 1908 (English translation, New York, 1966) has been an influential book, but its historical conclusions and treatment of Bach's musical symbolism can no longer be accepted uncritically.

Johann Nikolaus Forkel, *Johann Sebastian Bach: His Life, Art, and Work,* tr. C. S. Terry, New York, 1974.

Barbara Schwendowius and Wolfgang Dömling, eds., *J. S. Bach, Life, Times, Influence,* Kassel, 1976.

Robert C. Marshall, *The Compositional Process of J. S. Bach: A Study of the Autograph Scores of the Vocal Works,* Princeton, 1972.

Frederick Neumann, *Ornamentation in Baroque and Post-Baroque Music, with Special Emphasis on J. S. Bach,* Princeton, 1978.

HANDEL: The essential books are: P. H. Lang, *George Frideric Handel,* New York, 1966; and O. E. Deutsch, *Handel, a Documentary Biography,* New York, 1954, a "collection of all known and many hitherto unknown or overlooked documents referring to Handel's life"; it contains also a large bibliography.

The long chapter entitled "Origin of the Italian Opera in England and its Progress There during the Present Century" in Burney's *General History of Music* (Book IV, Ch. 6) includes a detailed account of Handel's operas in London and many observations on the music. This chapter is found in the second edition of Burney's work, F. Mercer, ed., New York, 1935 (2 vols.), II, 651–904.

On *Messiah,* see Robert Manson Myers, *Handel's* Messiah, *a Touchstone of Taste,* New York, 1948; and Jens Peter Larsen, *Handel's Messiah; Origins, Composition, Sources,* New York, 1972. See also Winton Dean, *Handel's Dramatic Oratorios and Masques,* London, 1959; id., *Handel and the Opera Seria,* Berkeley, 1969.

RAMEAU: The best comprehensive study in English is Cuthbert Girdlestone, *Jean-Philippe Rameau, His Life and Work,* New York, 1969.

VIVALDI: The best comprehensive study is Walter Kolneder, *Vivaldi,* B. Hopkins, tr., Berkeley, 1971. The general structure of the Vivaldi concerto is so clearly reflected in J. J. Quantz's *Essay on How to Play the Flute* of 1752 (see SR, 583–88 or SRC, 9–14) that we may suppose the author to have had Vivaldi's works in mind as a model.

Chapter XIII (Pp. 278–97)

Additional Examples in Other Anthologies

Sonatas by Domenico Scarlatti are in MM, No. 42; HAM, No. 274; GMB, No. 282; NS, Vol. I, No. 27. The sonata movement in F-sharp minor by Manuel Blasco de Nebra, HAM, No. 308, has some of the qualities of rhythmic alertness, coloristic dissonances, and use of repeated phrases characteristic of Scarlatti.

The *empfindsamer Stil;* C. P. E. Bach: HAM, Nos. 288, 289, 296, 297; GMB, Nos. 303, 304 (Pt. 1).

Symphony and chamber music: HAM, Nos. 271, 283, 294, 295, 304, 307; GMB, Nos. 305–307; EE, No. 31. (*Note:* the edition from which HAM No. 283 is taken has added a second violin part to Sammartini's original score and rewritten the recapitulation so as to make it conform to the exposition.)

Italian *opera seria:* HAM, Nos. 262, 282; GMB, No. 298.

Gluck: HAM, Nos. 292, 293; GMB, No. 313; EE, No. 39; NS, Vol. I, No. 28.

Comic opera: TEM, No. 50; HAM, Nos. 264, 285–287, 291, 300, 301, 305, 306; GMB, Nos. 281, 309; EE, No. 36.

The Lied: GMB, Nos. 287, 289, 299–301.

Church music and oratorio: HAM, Nos. 272, 279, 281, 298, 299; GMB, Nos. 308, 310.

For Further Reading

SR, Nos. 65–77 (SRC)

C. P. E. Bach's *Versuch über die wahre Art, das Clavier zu spielen* was first published in 1753 (Part One) and 1762 (Part Two); a facsimile of the first edition, ed. L. Hoffmann-Erbrecht, was published at Leipzig in 1957. An English translation by William J. Mitchell, *Essay on the True Art of Playing Keyboard Instruments*, New York, 1949, combines the original and revised editions of the eighteenth century. Excerpt in SR, No. 67 (SRC, No. 3). Bach's autobiography (1773) is available in a facsimile edition with critical annotations by William S. Newman, Hilversum, 1967.

The *Versuch einer Anweisung, die Flöte traversiere zu spielen* [*Essay on the Method of Playing the Transverse Flute*] by Johann Joachim Quantz (1697–1773), another important treatise of this period, was first published in 1752. There is a facsimile of the third edition of 1789, Kassel, 1953; English translation by E. R. Reilly, New York, 1966. Excerpts in SR, No. 65 (SRC, No. 1).

On the sonata, see William S. Newman, *The Sonata in the Classic Era*, New York, 1972.

Important sources of information about eighteenth-century musical life are Dr. Charles Burney's *General History of Music* and his two travel books: *The present State of Music in France and Italy*, London, 1771, and *The Present State of Music in Germany, The Netherlands, and the United Provinces*, London, 1775 (2 vols.), as well as his *Memoirs of the Life and Writings of the Abate Metastasio, in Which Are Incorporated Translations of His Principal Letters*, London, 1796 (3 vols.). Excerpts from *The Present State of Music In France and Italy* are in SR, No. 74 (SRC, No. 10); a new edition, under the title *Music, Men and Manners in France and Italy, 1770*, H. E. Poole, ed., London, 1969. Brief excerpts from the travel books and Burney's journals, with connecting summaries by the editor, are found in Cedric Howard Glover, *Dr. Charles Burney's Continental Travels 1700–1772*, London, 1927. See also Percy A. Scholes, *The Great Dr. Burney; His Life, His Travels, His Works, His Family and His Friends*, London, 1948 (2 vols.). Scholes also edited Burney's two travel books under the titles *An Eighteenth-Century Musical Tour in France and Italy* and *An Eighteenth-Century Musical Tour in Central Europe and the Netherlands*, both London and New York, 1959.

On the *symphonie concertante*, see Barry S. Brook, *La Symphonie française dans la seconde moitié du XVIIIe siècle*, Paris, 1962 (3 vols., including one volume of music).

BACH SONS: For an account of the life and music of J. S. Bach's sons, see Karl Geiringer, *The Bach Family*, New York, 1954; P. M. Young, *The Bachs, 1500–1850*, New York, 1970.

GLUCK: Martin Cooper, *Gluck*, New York, 1935, and Alfred Einstein, *Gluck*, London and New York, 1954, are comprehensive studies of the life, works, and musical environment of this composer.; *Collected Correspondence*, H. and E. H. Mueller von Asow, eds., S. Thomson, tr., London 1962; Ernest Newman, *Gluck and the Opera*, London, 1967.

D. SCARLATTI: The best book about D. Scarlatti is Ralph Kirkpatrick, *Domenico Scarlatti*, New York, 1968, a model of scholarly authority and musical insight.

Chapter XIV (Pp. 298–323)

General Reading

Friedrich Blume, *Classic and Romantic Music*, New York, 1970, is a comprehensive survey of all aspects of music in the period *ca.* 1770–1910. Charles Rosen, *The Classical Style: Haydn, Mozart, Beethoven*, New York, 1971, is strongly recommended. His most recent book, *Sonata Forms*, New York, 1980, provides stimulating insights into the development of the genre.

Haydn

The definitive edition of his works is in course of publication by the Haydn Institute of Cologne under the direction of J. P. Larsen and G. Feder, Munich-Duisberg, 1958– ; thematic catalogue by A. van Hoboken, Mainz, 1957–78, 3 vols.

Haydn Studies, the proceedings of the International Haydn Conference held in Washington, D.C. in 1975, edited by J. P. Larsen, James Webster, and Howard Serwer, New York, 1981.

A definitive study is H. C. Robbins Landon's five-volume *Haydn's Chronicle and Works,* Bloomington, 1976– , of which vols. 2, 3, 4, and 5 have so far appeared. The best short general biographies are: Karl Geiringer, *Haydn, a Creative Life in Music,* Berkeley, 1968; and Rosemary Hughes, *Haydn,* London, 1946. On the symphonies: H. C. Robbins Landon, *The Symphonies of Joseph Haydn,* London, 1955, with *Supplement,* New York, 1961; D. F. Tovey, *Essays in Musical Analysis,* vol. i, London, 1935, is a mine of entertainment, information, and enlightenment about the late Haydn symphonies as well as symphonies of Mozart, Beethoven, Schubert, and Brahms. On the quartets, see Tovey's article "Haydn" in *Cobbett's Cyclopedic Survey of Chamber Music,* London, 1963.

Mozart

The standard collected edition is *W. A. Mozart's Sämtliche Werke,* Leipzig, 1876–1907; 14 séries including supplementary volumes; reprinted, Ann Arbor, 1951–56, and New York, 1968 in miniature format. Eventually this edition will be superseded by the *Neue Ausgabe sämtlicher Werke* (Salzburg, International Mozart Foundation, 1956–), now at about Vol. 65 of the planned 110 volumes.

Ludwig Köchel, *Chronologisch-thematisches Verzeichnis,* 6th ed., Wiesbaden, 1964.

The standard book about Mozart's life and music is Hermann Abert, *W. A. Mozart,* Leipzig, 1956 (2 vols.). This is a revision of Otto Jahn's *Mozart,* which was first published in four volumes in 1856–59; an English translation in three volumes appeared at London in 1882; reprinted, New York, 1969. A. Hyatt King's *Mozart,* Hamden, Conn., 1970, is a convenient short biography; it includes useful annotated lists of books about Mozart in English and a bibliography of Mozart editions.

Useful books about Mozart in English are: Alfred Einstein, *Mozart: His Character, His Work,* tr. A. Mendel and N. Broder, New York, 1962; A. Hyatt King, *Mozart in Retrospect,* 3rd ed., London, 1970; H. C. Robbins Landon and D. Mitchell, eds., *The Mozart Companion,* New York, 1969; Arthur Hutchings, *Mozart: The Man, the Musician,* New York, 1976.

Important and interesting source material is found in *The Letters of Mozart and His Family,* Emily Anderson, ed., London and New York, 1966 (2 vols.).

Chapter XV (Pp. 324–43)

Beethoven

Collected edition: *Ludwig van Beethovens Werke,* Leipzig, 1864–90 (24 series and supplementary volume; reprinted, Ann Arbor, 1949 and New York, 1967 (also in miniature format). *Supplemente zur Gesamtausgabe,* W. Hess, ed., Wiesbaden, 1959– *Sämtliche Werke,* Schmidt-Görg, ed., Munich, 1960–

Thematic index: Georg Kinsky and Hans Halm, *Das Werk Beethovens; Verzeichnis seiner sämtlich vollendeten Kompositionen,* Munich, 1955; additional material in Kurt Dorfmüller, ed., *Studien und Materialien zum Werkverzeichnis von Kinsky-Halm,* Munich, 1979.

The Letters of Beethoven, tr. and ed. Emily Anderson, New York, 1961 (3 vols.).

The standard biography is *Thayer's Life of Beethoven,* rev. and ed. Elliot Forbes, Princeton, 1969, 2 vols. (available in paper, 1 vol., Princeton, 1970). Special insights into Beethoven's life and personality may be gained from Anton Schindler's *Beethoven as I Knew Him* (1840), D. W. MacArdle, ed., C. S. Jolly, tr., New York, 1966; and O. G. Sonneck, ed., *Beethoven: Impressions by His Contemporaries,* New York, 1967. See especially Maynard Solomon, *Beethoven,* New York, 1977, for new light on the identity of Beethoven's "Immortal Beloved."

Of the innumerable books about Beethoven's music, only a few can be cited: D. F. Tovey, *Beethoven*, London, 1945, the unfinished last work of one of the most perceptive musicians of the present century; J. Kerman, *The Beethoven Quartets*, New York, 1971; the classic *Beethoven and His Nine Symphonies* by Sir George Grove, first published in 1896 and republished (from the third edition) New York, 1962.

Chapters XVI and XVII (Pp. 344–80)

Logan Pearsall Smith, in his fascinating short essay *Four Words: Romantic, Originality, Creative, Genius*, London, 1924, traces the history of the ideas that have been denoted by these words at various periods. On "romantic" see also the valuable chapters viii–xii in Arthur Lovejoy, *Essays in the History of Ideas*, New York, 1955, and the same author's "The Meaning of Romanticism for the History of Ideas," *Journal of the History of Ideas* (June 1941), 257–78; for an interesting personal interpretation, see Preface to the third edition of C. S. Lewis, *The Pilgrim's Regress*, London, 1943. A general survey is H. G. Schenk, *The Mind of the European Romantics*, New York, 1969.

For Further Reading: General

On nineteenth-century music in general: SR, Nos. 78–82, 85, 86 (SRRo, Nos. 1–5, 8, 9); Alfred Einstein, *Music in the Romantic Era*, New York, 1947; Gerald Abraham, *A Hundred Years of Music*, 3rd ed., Chicago, 1964; W. S. Newman, *The Sonata Since Beethoven*, New York, 1972.

On the social history of the piano, see Arthur Loesser, *Men, Women, and Pianos*, New York, 1954; on its mechanical history, R. E. M. Harding, *The Piano-Forte; Its History to the Great Exhibition of 1851*, Cambridge, England, 1933.

Composers

BERLIOZ: His *Treatise on Instrumentation* (1843), rev. and enl. by Richard Strauss (1905), is published in English translation, New York, 1948; his *Memoirs*, tr. and ed. D. Cairns, New York, 1969. See also Jacques Barzun, *Berlioz and the Romantic Century*, 3rd ed., New York, 1969, 2 vols.

BRAHMS: Karl Geiringer, *Brahms: His Life and Work*, rev. ed., London, 1961; B. Jacobson, *The Music of Johannes Brahms*, London, 1977.

BRUCKNER: A helpful introduction is Robert Simpson, *The Essence of Bruckner*, London, 1967; see also Erwin Doernberg, *The Life and Symphonies of Anton Bruckner*, London, 1960.

CHOPIN: The standard study is G. Abraham, *Chopin's Musical Style*, London, 1960; see also A. Walker, ed., *The Chopin Companion: Profiles of the Man and the Musician*, New York, 1973.

DVOŘÁK: The best book in English is John Clapham, *Antonin Dvořák*, Rev. ed., New York, 1979. See also *Letters and Reminiscences*, O. Sourek, ed., Prague, 1954.

FRANCK: Vincent d'Indy, *César Franck*, New York, 1910; Laurence Davies, *César Franck and His Circle*, Boston, 1970.

LISZT: Alan Walker, comp., *Franz Liszt: The Man and His Music*, New York, 1970; Sacheverell Sitwell, *Liszt*, New York, 1967; E. Perenyi, *Liszt: The Artist as Romantic Hero*, New York, 1974.

MENDELSSOHN: Philip Radcliffe, *Mendelssohn*, London, 1954; rev. ed., Totowa, New Jersey, 1976; Wilfred Blunt, *On Wings of Song: A Biography of Felix Mendelssohn*, New York, 1974. Mendelssohn's letters are available in various English editions.

PAGANINI: G. I. C. de Courcy, *Paganini*, Norman, Oklahoma, 1957; reprinted, New York, 1977, 2 vols.

SCHUBERT: O. E. Deutsch, *Schubert: A Documentary Biography*, New York, 1977; id., ed., *The Schubert Reader*, New York, 1947; id., *Schubert: Memoirs by His Friends*, New York, 1958; M. J. E. Brown, *Schubert: a Critical Biography*,

New York, 1958; *id.*, *Essays on Schubert*, London and New York, 1966; John Reed, *Schubert: the Final Years*, New York, 1972; R. Capell, *Schubert's Songs*, New York, 1957.

SCHUMANN: G. Abraham, ed., *Schumann, a Symposium*, New York, 1952; Marcel Brion, *Schumann and the Romantic Age*, New York, 1956; L. Plantinga, *Schumann as Critic*, New Haven, 1967.

TCHAIKOVSKY: G. Abraham, ed., *The Music of Tchaikovsky*, New York, 1974; David Brown, *Tchaikovsky: The Early Years*, New York, 1978.

Chapter XVIII (Pp. 381–95)

For Further Reading: Composers

SR, Nos. 83, 84, 87 (SRRo, Nos. 6, 7, 10).

BIZET: Mina Curtiss, *Bizet and His World*, New York, 1958; Winton Dean, *Georges Bizet, His Life and Work*, 3rd ed., London, 1975.

DONIZETTI: see works on this composer by H. Weinstock, New York, 1963, and W. Ashbrook, London, 1965.

ROSSINI: biography by Herbert Weinstock, New York, 1968. Stendhal's *Life of Rossini* (1824), New York, 1957, gives delightful insights into the way the composer was regarded by a hero-worshipping contemporary who evidently regarded factual accuracy as a negligible requirement.

VERDI: The best biography is Frank Walker, *The Man Verdi*, New York, 1962; for an excellent introduction, see Francis Toye, *Giuseppi Verdi, His Life and Works*, New York, 1946, and, for a fuller treatment, George Martin, *Verdi, His Music, Life, and Times*, New York, 1963. *The Verdi Companion*, New York, 1979, edited by William Weaver and Martin Chusid, contains articles by Sir Isaiah Berlin, Rodolfo Celletti, Julian Budden, Luigi Dallapiccola, Andrew Porter, and others. See also Julian Budden, *The Operas of Verdi*, New York, 1973; William Weaver, *Verdi: A Documentary Study*, New York, 1977.

WAGNER: The standard biography is Ernest Newman's *Life of Richard Wagner*, 4 vols., New York, 1933–46 (reprinted paper, 1976). Other recent Wagner studies include C. von Westernhagen, *Wagner: A Biography* (2 vols.), Cambridge, Eng., 1979; R. Taylor, *Richard Wagner*, New York, 1979; P. Burbridge and R. Sutton, eds., *The Wagner Companion*, Cambridge, Eng., 1979.

WEBER: J. H. Warrack, *Carl Maria von Weber*, London and New York, 1968, is the best book about this composer, his works, and his position in the history of nineteenth-century music. Weber's biography by his son, Max von Weber, was published in an English adaptation at London in 1865 (2 vols.) and has been reprinted, New York, 1969.

Chapter XIX (Pp. 396–424)

For Further Reading

An excellent survey of the period covered in this chapter will be found in Gerald Abraham, *A Hundred Years of Music*; Neville Cardus, *A Composers Eleven*, London, 1958, contains good nontechnical essays on Schubert, Wagner, Brahms, Bruckner, Mahler, Richard Strauss, César Franck, Debussy, Elgar, Delius, and Sibelius.

MAHLER: D. Mitchell, *Gustav Mahler*, 2 vols., London, 1958 and 1976; Henry-Louis de La Grange, *Mahler*, vol. 1, New York, 1973; Kurt Blaukopf, *Mahler: A Documentary Study*, New York, 1976; N. Cardus, *Gustav Mahler, His Mind and His Music*, London, 1965; Alma Mahler Werfel, *Mahler: Memories and Letters*, D. Mitchell, ed., B. Creighton, tr., New York, 1969.

Late Romanticism

STRAUSS: Norman Del Mar, *Richard Strauss; a Critical Commentary on His Life and Work*, 3 vols., London, 1963, 1969, 1972; Ernst Krause, *Richard Strauss, The Man and His Work*, Boston, 1969; W. Mann, *Richard Strauss: a Critical Study of his Operas*, London, 1964. The composer's own *Recollections and Reflections*, London, 1953. Of the published correspondence, the following volumes are available in translation; with von Hoffmansthal, under the title *A Working Friendship*, New York, 1961, reprint, 1974; with von Bülow, London, 1953; with Romain Rolland, Berkeley, 1968.

On Russian music in general, see Gerald Abraham, *Studies in Russian Music*, New York, 1968; *id.*, *On Russian Music*, London, 1939; *id.*, *Slavonic and Romantic Music*, New York, 1968; M. D. Calvocoressi and G. Abraham, *Masters of Russian Music*, New York, 1971.

National-ism Old and New

GLINKA: *Memoirs*, R. B. Mudge, tr., Norman, Oklahoma, 1963.

MUSSORGSKY: Jay Leyda and S. Bertensson, eds., *The Mussorgsky Reader*, New York, 1947; reprint, 1970; M. D. Calvocoressi, *Mussorgsky*, New York, 1962.

RIMSKY-KORSAKOV: *My Musical Life*, New York, 1923, reprint, 1974. His *Principles of Orchestration*, with music examples from his own works, in English translation, New York, 1933.

JANÁČEK: J. Vogel, *Leoš Janáček; his Life and Works*, Rev. ed., New York, 1981.

Other Nations

GRIEG: G. Abraham, ed., *Grieg: a Symposium*, Norman, Oklahoma, 1950.

SIBELIUS: G. Abraham, ed., *The Music of Sibelius*, London, 1947; E. Tawaststjerna, *Sibelius*, English tr. London, vol. i, 1975.

For general survey of music of the United States of America, see Gilbert Chase, *America's Music*, New York, 1955; H. Wiley Hitchcock, *Music in the United States: a Historical Introduction*, Englewood Cliffs, 1969; Wilfred Mellers, *Music in a New Found Land*, London, 1965; Eileen Southern, *The Music of Black Americans*, New York, 1971; *id.*, *Readings in Black American Music*, New York, 1971. For more specialized studies: Robert Stevenson, *Protestant Church Music in America*, New York, 1966; Irving Lowens, *Music and Musicians in Early America*, New York, 1964; Thomas Marrocco and Harold Gleason, eds., *Music in America: an Anthology . . . 1620–1865*, New York, 1964; Edward MacDowell, *Critical and Historical Essays*, W. J. Baltzell, ed., New York, 1969.

United States

IVES: His *Essays Before a Sonata and Other Writings*, H. Boatwright, ed., New York, 1962; his *Memos*, J. Kirkpatrick, ed., New York, 1972; H. and S. Cowell, *Charles Ives and His Music*, New York, 1955. See also Vivian Perlis, *Charles Ives Remembered: An Oral History*, New Haven, 1974.

For English musical nationalism in the early twentieth century, see Ch. 13 of Ernest Walker, *History of Music in England*, Oxford, 1952.

England and Spain

ELGAR: Diana McVeagh, *Edward Elgar: His Life and Music*, London, 1955; Percy Young, ed., *Letters of Elgar and Other Writings*, London, 1956; Michael Kennedy, *Portrait of Elgar*, London and New York, 1968.

FALLA: Jaime Pahissa, *Manuel de Falla: His Life and Works*, London, 1954.

For an overview of new currents in France see Martin Cooper, *French Music from the Death of Berlioz to the Death of Fauré*, London, 1961: Paul Collaer, *A History of Modern Music*, New York, 1961, chs. 4–7.

France

DEBUSSY: Debussy's essays were published at Paris in 1923 under the title *Monsieur Croche, anti-dilettante;* in translation, *Debussy on Music*, ed. F. Lesure and R. L. Smith, New York, 1977. The best biography is E. Lockspeiser, *Debussy: His Life and Mind*, London, 1965–66, 2 vols. F. Lesure, *Catalogue de l'oeuvre de Claude Debussy*, Paris, 1977.

FAURÉ: Norman Suckling, *Fauré*, London, 1946.

D'INDY: Norman Demuth, *Vincent d'Indy*, London, 1951.

RAVEL: Norman Demuth, *Ravel*, New York, 1962; reprint, 1978; A. Orenstein, *Ravel, Man and Musician*, New York, 1975; Rollo Myers, *Ravel: His Life and Works*, London, 1960, reprint, 1973.

Books about other French composers: Rollo Myers, *Emanuel Chabrier and His Circle*, London, 1969; Laurence Davies, *César Franck and His Circle*, Boston, 1970; Basil Deane, *Albert Roussel,* London, 1961; Rollo Myers, *Eric Satie*, New York, 1968; see also the two chapters on Satie in Roger Shattuck, *The Banquet Years,* New York, 1958.

Chapter XX (Pp. 425–75)

For Further Reading

1900–1979 in general: William W. Austin, *Music in the Twentieth Century from Debussy through Stravinsky*, New York, 1966 (includes copious annotated bibliographies); Eric Salzman, *Twentieth-Century Music; an Introduction,* Englewood Cliffs, 2nd ed., 1974 (complements Austin, with more information on American music and the period since 1950); Nicolas Slonimsky, *Music since 1900*, 4th ed., New York, 1971; Elliott Schwarz and Barney Childs, eds., *Contemporary Composers on Contemporary Music,* New York, 1967; Paul Collaer, *A History of Modern Music,* New York, 1961; P. H. Lang and N. Broder, eds., *Contemporary Music in Europe,* New York, 1965; Leonard B. Meyer, *Music, the Arts, and Ideas; Patterns and Predictions in Twentieth-Century Culture*, Chicago, 1967; Allen Forte, *Contemporary Tone Structures,* New York, 1955; André Hodeir, *Since Debussy; a View of Contemporary Music*, N. Burch, tr., New York, 1961 (a stimulating book, strongly French-oriented and very sure of the future); J. Samson, *Music in Transition: A Study of Tonal Expansion and Atonality, 1900–1920,* New York, 1977; A. Whittall, *Music since the First World War,* London, 1977.

Composers

Soviet Composers: Gerald Abraham, *Eight Soviet Composers*, New York, 1943; I. V. Nestyev, *Prokofiev*, F. Jonas, tr., Stanford, 1960 (3rd ed. in preparation); D. Shostakovich, *The Power of Music*, New York, 1968; B. Schwarz, *Music and Musical Life in Soviet Russia, 1917–1970,* New York, 1972.

BARTÓK: Halsey Stevens, *The Life and Music of Béla Bartók*, 2nd ed., New York, 1964.

BERG: Willi Reich, *Alban Berg*, tr. Cornelius Cardew, London, 1965; Douglas Jarman, *The Music of Alban Berg*, Berkeley, 1978.

BOULEZ: His *Notes of an Apprenticeship*, H. Weinstock, tr., New York, 1968; *Boulez on Music Today*, S. Bradshaw and R. R. Bennett, trs., Cambridge, 1971; P. Griffiths, *Boulez*, Oxford Studies of Composers, London, 1979.

BRITTEN: Eric W. White, *Benjamin Britten, His Life and Operas*, Berkeley, 1970.

CAGE: His own writings, particularly *Silence*, London, 1968, which gives the best idea of his work and theories; *A Year from Monday*, Middletown, 1967; R. Kostelanetz, ed., *John Cage*, New York, 1970.

CARTER: Allen Edwards, ed., *Flawed Words and Stubborn Sounds; a Conversation with Elliott Carter*, New York, 1971; K. and E. Stone, eds., *The Writings of Elliott Carter*, Bloomington, 1977.

COPLAND: His own writings, including *Music and Imagination*, New York, 1959; *The New Music 1900–1960*, rev. ed., New York, 1968; *Copland on Music*, New York, 1963; A. Berger, *Aaron Copland*, New York, 1953.

HINDEMITH: His *The Craft of Musical Composition*, New York, 1945, and *A Composer's World; Horizons and Limitations*, New York, 1961.

HOLST: Imogen Holst, *The Music of Gustav Holst*, 2nd ed., London and New York, 1968; id., *Holst*, London, 1974..d.

MESSIAEN: His *The Technique of My Musical Language*, Paris, 1956; R. Nichols, *Messiaen*, Oxford Studies of Composers, London, 1975; R. S. Johnson, *Messiaen*, Berkeley, 1975.

MILHAUD: His autobiography, *Notes Without Music*, D. Evans, tr., New York, 1970; G. Beck, *Darius Milhaud*, Paris, 1949.

POULENC: Pierre Bernac, *Francis Poulenc: The Man and His Songs,* New York, 1977; Henri Hell, *Francis Poulenc,* Paris, 1958, Eng. tr., London, 1959.

SCHOENBERG: Willi Reich, *Schoenberg, a Critical Biography,* New York, 1972; René Leibowitz, *Schoenberg and His School,* Eng. tr. 1949, reprint, 1975; Dika Newlin, *Bruckner-Mahler-Schoenberg,* rev. ed., New York, 1978; *id., Schoenberg Remembered,* New York, 1980; G. Perle, *Serial Composition and Atonality,* 4th ed., Berkeley, 1977; Alban Berg, "Why Is Schoenberg's Music So Hard to Understand?" in *The Music Review* 13 (1952), 187–96; the composer's *Letters,* E. Stein, ed., New York, 1965, and essays, *Style and Idea,* enlarged edition, ed. L. Black, London, 1975.

SESSIONS: Oliver Daniel and others, *Roger Sessions,* New York, 1965; Sessions, *The Musical Experience of Composer, Performer, Listener,* New York, 1962, and *Questions about Music,* New York, 1970.

STOCKHAUSEN: J. Cott, *Stockhausen: Conversations with the Composer,* London, 1974; R. Maconie, *The Works of Karlheinz Stockhausen,* London, 1976; Karl H. Wörner, *Stockhausen,* London, 1973.

STRAVINSKY: His *Autobiography,* Eng. tr., reprinted, 1966, and *Poetics of Music,* New York, 1956. Stravinsky's numerous books in collaboration with Robert Craft, 1959–69, contain many wise and penetrating observations on music and musicians in the twentieth century. See also Lillian Libman, *And Music at the Close: Stravinsky's Last Years,* New York, 1972; Vera Stravinsky, *Stravinsky: In Pictures and Documents,* New York, 1978; Eric W. White, *Stravinsky: The Composer and His Works,* Berkeley, 1966.

VARÈSE: Louise Varèse, *Varèse: a Looking-Glass Diary,* Vol. 1 (1883–1928), New York, 1972; Sherman Van Solkema, ed., *The New Worlds of Edgard Varèse,* Institute for Studies in American Music, Brooklyn, New York, 1979.

VAUGHAN WILLIAMS: A. E. F. Dickinson, *Vaughan Williams,* London, 1963; Ursula Vaughan Williams, *R. V. W., a Biography,* London, 1964; M. Kennedy, *The Works of Ralph Vaughan Williams,* London, 1964; and the composer's own writings, including *National Music,* New York, 1964.

WEBERN: H. Moldenhauer, *Anton von Webern,* New York, 1979; Webern's *Letters,* ed. J. Polnauer, tr. C. Cardew, Bryn Mawr, 1967, and *The Path to New Music,* tr. L. Black, Bryn Mawr, 1963; W. Kolneder, *Anton Webern; an Introduction to His Works,* tr. H. Searle, Berkeley, 1968.

Chronology

This chronology is intended to provide a background for the history of music, and to enable the reader to see the individual works and composers in relation to their times.

Entries fall into three categories, each listed in a separate paragraph under the given date:

(M) Significant musical events.
(H) Concurrent events in political, social, and intellectual history.
(A) Representative works and events in the other arts.

The first time a writer's or artist's name appears it is given in full, together with dates of birth and death. Thereafter, unless there is a chance of confusion, it appears in the surname form alone.

800–461 B.C.
(H) Rise of city states in Greece.

753 B.C.
(H) Traditional date of founding of Rome.

586 B.C.
(M) Sakadas of Argos wins Pythian Games with *Nomos Pythicos*.

500 B.C.
(M) Pythagoras (d. *ca.* 497).
(A) Pindar (522–443), *Odes*.
(H) Establishment of early Roman Republic.

461–429 B.C.
(H) Age of Pericles.

458 B.C.
(A) Aeschylus (525–456), *Agamemnon*.

432 B.C.
(A) Parthenon completed.

431–404 B.C.
(H) Peloponnesian War.

429 B.C.
(H) Death of Pericles.
(A) Sophocles (446–406), *Oedipus Rex*.

414 B.C.
(A) Euripides (480–406), *Iphigenia in Tauris*.

401 B.C.
(A) Xenophon (434–255), *Anabasis*.

400 B.C.
(H) Athens defeated by Sparta; decline of democracy in Greece.

399 B.C.
(H) Death of Socrates.

380 B.C.
(A) Plato (427?–347), *Republic*.

502

350 B.C.
(A) Aristotle (384–322), *Politics*, Praxiteles. (4th c. B.C.), *Hermes with Infant Dionysos.*

338–337 B.C.
(H) Macedonian conquest of Greece.

336–323 B.C.
(H) Conquests of Alexander the Great and subsequent division of his Empire.

330 B.C.
(M) Aristoxenus (b. *ca.* 354), *Harmonic Elements.*

323 B.C.
(H) Hellenistic Age.

306 B.C.
(A) Nike of Samothrace.

286 B.C.
(H) Library at Alexandria founded.

175 B.C.
(A) Frieze from Altar of Zeus at Pergamon.

150 B.C.
(M) Delphic *Hymn to Apollo.*

146 B.C.
(H) Greece under Roman rule.

60 B.C.
(A) Lucretius (*ca.* 96–55), *De Rerum Natura.*

58–51 B.C.
(H) Julius Caesar (100–44) invades Gaul and Britain.

46 B.C.
(H) Julius Caesar becomes dictator.

27 B.C.
(H) Augustus Caesar (63 B.C.–14 A.D.) first Emperor of Rome; Principate or Early Empire (27 B.C.–284 A.D.).
(A) Vergil (70–19), *Aeneid;* Horace (65–3), *Ars Poetica;* Ovid (43 B.C.–17 A.D.), *Metamorphoses.*

4 B.C.
(H) Birth of Jesus.

Ca. 33 A.D.
(H) The Crucifixion.

50
(H) Rise of the Papacy (to *ca.* 300).

54
(H) Nero (37–68) Emperor of Rome.

65
(H) First persecution of Christians in Rome.

70
(H) Temple at Jerusalem destroyed.
(A) Colosseum begun at Rome.

81
(A) Arch of Titus completed.

100
(M) Plutarch (50–120), *On Music.*
(H) Germanic migrations and invasions begin (to *ca.* 600).

112
(M) Pliny the Younger (62–113) reports hymn singing by Christians.

118
(A) Pantheon begun (till 126).

150
(M) Ptolemy, *Harmonics.*

211
(A) Baths of Caracalla started (till 217).

284
(H) Diocletian becomes Emperor; beginning of Late Roman Empire (284–476).

285
(M) Oxyrhynchos hymn fragment.

313
(H) Constantine I (306–337) issues Edict of Milan.

325
(H) Council of Nicea.

330
(H) Constantinople established as new capital of Roman Empire.

374
(H) St. Ambrose (340–397) consecrated as Bishop of Milan.

395
(H) Separation of Eastern and Western Roman Empires.

410
(H) Sack of Rome by Alaric the Visigoth; invasion of Britain by Angles and Saxons.

413
(A) St. Augustine (354–430), *City of God.*

Ca. 450
(A) Establishment of seven liberal arts as course of study.

452
(H) Invasion of Italy by Attila the Hun; Venice founded.

455
(H) Rome sacked by Vandals.

476
(H) Romulus Augustulus deposed; traditional date of end of Roman Empire.

481
(H) Merovingian dynasty in France established (till 751).

493
(H) Ostrogothic rule in Italy established (till 552).

500
(M) Boethius (480–524), *De institutione musica*.

527
(H) Justinian becomes Emperor of Eastern Roman Empire.
(A) Construction started on Hagia Sophia, Constantinople (finished 565).

529
(H) Benedictine order founded.

568
(H) Lombard invasion of northern Italy.

590
(H) Election of Pope Gregory the Great (*ca.* 540–604).

622
(M) Isidore of Seville (*ca.* 560–636), treatise on the arts.
(H) Hegira of Mohammed (*ca.* 570–632).

630
(H) Capture of Mecca.

633
(H) Council of Toledo.

650
(H) Rise of monasteries (to *ca.* 700); Arab conquests in Asia and North Africa.

700
(H) Irish and Anglo-Saxon missionaries on Continent; monastic schools flourish.

735
(H) Death of the Venerable Bede (673–735).

750
(H) Arabic science brought to Europe.

768
(H) Charlemagne (742–814) King of the Franks.

800
(M) Cultivation of music in the monasteries.
(H) Charlemagne crowned Emperor by Pope at Rome; Arabic culture appears in Europe; Viking raids and conquests begin.

805
(A) Minster of Aix-la-Chapelle dedicated.

830
(A) The Utrecht Psalter.

850
(H) University of Constantinople opened.

871
(H) Alfred the Great (849–899) King of England.

900
(M) Arabic musical instruments introduced into Europe; tropes and sequences; *Musica enchiriadis*.

962
(H) Otto the Great (912–973) crowned first Emperor of the Holy Roman Empire.

987
(H) Hugh Capet (*ca.* 940–996) elected King of France.

1025
(M) Guido of Arezzo's (*ca.* 955–1050) first writings on music.

1050
(A) *Chanson de Roland.*

1054
(H) Final separation of Eastern and Western Churches.

1066
(H) Norman invasion of England; Battle of Hastings.

1073
(M) Winchester Tropes.

1080
(A) The Bayeux Tapestry.

1086
(H) Domesday Book compiled.

1094
(A) St. Mark's Cathedral, Venice, begun.

1096
(H) First Crusade (till 1099).

1100
(M) Beginnings of St.-Martial organum.

1145
(A) Chartres Cathedral begun.

1150
(M) Troubadours flourish in Provence; Notre Dame School assumes musical leadership; liturgical dramas appear.
(A) Cathedrals at Sens, Senlis, and Noyen begun.
(H) Rise of universities throughout Europe; high point of Scholasticism.

1160
(A) Laon Cathedral begun (till 1205).

1163
(A) Cornerstone of Notre Dame at Paris laid.

1167
(H) Beginning of Oxford University.

1170
(H) Beginning of the University of Paris. Murder of Thomas Becket at Canterbury.

1175
(M) Leonin, master of Notre Dame School (fl. after 1150), *Magnus liber organi.*
(A) Canterbury Cathedral begun.

1183
(M) Perotin active at Notre Dame.

1189
(H) Richard Coeur de Lion (1157–99) King of England.

1200
(M) Trouvères flourish in France, Minnesingers in Germany.
(A) Reims Cathedral begun.

1209
(H) St. Francis of Assisi (1182–1226) founds the Franciscan Order; Cambridge University founded.

1213
(A) The Alhambra begun (completed 1388).

1215
(H) Magna Carta signed by King John.

1240
(M) Motet becomes important type of polyphonic composition *Sumer* canon.
(A) Chartres Cathedral rebuilt.

1248
(M) Sequence *Dies irae*, attributed to Thomas of Celano.
(A) Cologne Cathedral begun; Sainte-Chapelle, Paris, built.

1250
(M) Period of *ars antiqua.*

1260
(M) Franco of Cologne (active 1250–80), *Ars cantus mensurabilis.*
(A) Nicola Pisano (*ca.* 1225–*ca.* 1278), pulpit of baptistry, Pisa.

1270
(M) English musicians in Paris; Cantigas de Santa Maria; Petrus de Cruce active; Motets of Bamberg Codex.
(A) Roger Bacon (*ca.* 1214–94), *Opus maius*; St. Thomas Aquinas (1225–74), *Summa theologica.*
(H) Start of Louis' Second Crusade; Sicilian Vespers.

1284
(M) Adam de la Hale (*ca.* 1230–88), *Robin et Marion.*

1297
(A) Marco Polo (*ca.* 1254–*ca.* 1324), *Book of Various Experiences.*

1300
(M) Beginning of French *Ars nova* (to *ca.* 1370); Treatises of Walter Odington and Johannes de Grocheo.
(H) Papal jubilee in Rome; feudalism declines.

1305
(A) Arena chapel frescoes by Giotto (1266–1337).
(H) The papacy in exile at Avignon.

1307
(A) Dante (1265–1321), *The Divine Comedy.*

1308
(A) Duccio (1268–1319) begins painting Siena panels.

1316
(M) Illuminated manuscript of *Roman de Fauvel*; Philippe de Vitry (1291–1361), *Ars nova.*
(H) Pope John XXII elected (till 1334).

1318
(M) Marchetto da Padua, *Pomerium artis musicae mensurabilis.*

1319
(M) Jean de Muris (*ca.* 1290–*ca.* 1351), *Ars novae musicae.*

1325
(M) Robertsbridge Codex.

1327
(A) Petrarch (1304–74) meets Laura.

1330
(M) Italian *Ars nova* (till 1410); Jacob of Liège (fl. 14th c.), *Speculum musicae.*

1337
(H) Outbreak of the Hundred Years' War.

1348
(H) The Black Death.

1353
(A) Boccaccio (1313–75), *Decameron.*

1360
(M) Guillaume de Machaut (*ca.* 1300–77), *Messe de Notre Dame.*

1362
(A) William Langland, *The Vision of Piers Plowman.*

1376
(A) Wycliffe's (*ca.* 1320–84) translation of the Bible.

1378
(H) Start of Papal schism.

1385

(H) Heidelberg University chartered.

1386

(A) Chaucer (*ca.* 1340–1400), *The Canterbury Tales*.

1405

(H) Duchy of Burgundy (till 1477).

1415

(H) Battle of Agincourt; Council of Constance.

1416

(A) *Très riches heures* of the Duc de Berry.

1417

(H) End of Papal schism.

1420

(M) Squarcialupi Codex; Old Hall Manuscript; Trent Codices (to 1480).
(A) Thomas à Kempis, *Imitatio Christi*.

1425

(M) White notation introduced in England.
(A) Giovanni da Prato, *Paradiso degli Alberti*. Ghiberti (1378–1455) begins *Gates of Paradise* for Baptistry at Florence.

1426

(A) Jan (*ca.* 1366–1426) and Hubert (*ca.* 1370–*ca.* 1440) Van Eyck begin the Ghent Altarpiece.

1431

(A) Lucca della Robbia (*ca.* 1400–82) starts work on *Cantoria*.
(H) Jeanne d'Arc executed.

1434

(H) Medici powerful at Florence (till 1494).

1435

(A) Donatello (*ca.* 1386–1466), *David*.

1436

(M) Guillaume Dufay (*ca.* 1400–74), *Nuper rosarum flores*.

1439

(H) Great Church Council of Florence.

1440

(M) Meistersinger in Germany; Canonici Manuscript.

1447

(H) Pope Nicholas V elected (till 1455); Vatican Library founded.
(A) Humanism rises in Italy.

1452

(H) Emperor Frederic III (till 1493), last Holy Roman Emperor to be crowned at Rome.

(A) Fouquet (*ca.* 1420–81), *Book of Hours of Etienne Chevalier*.

1453

(H) End of Hundred Years' War; Constantinople conquered.

1454

(H) Gutenberg (1398–1468) invents printing from movable metal type.
(A) Andrea Mantegna (1431–1506), *St. James Led to Martyrdom*.

1455

(M) Lochamer *Liederbuch*.
(H) Beginning of War of the Roses (till 1485).

1456

(H) Gutenberg prints the Mazarin Bible.

1460

(M) Dufay, Mass *Se la face ay pale*; first Doctor of Music degree awarded at Oxford.

1471

(A) Poliziano, *Orfeo*.

1478

(H) Lorenzo de' Medici (1449–92; the "Magnificent") ruler in Florence.
(A) Sandro Botticelli (*ca.* 1444–1510), *La Primavera*.

1480

(M) Jacob Obrecht (*ca.* 1452–1505), first Masses.

1481

(A) Andrea del Verrocchio (1435–1488), *Colleoni*.

1484

(A) Sir Thomas Malory, *Morte d'Arthur*, printed by Caxton.

1485

(H) Tudor dynasty in England (till 1603).

1486

(M) Josquin des Prez (*ca.* 1440–1521) at Rome, Papal Chapel.

1487

(A) Giovanni Bellini (*ca.* 1430–1516), San Giobbe Altarpiece.

1492

(M) Obrecht at Antwerp (till 1504).
(H) Unification of Spain; first voyage of Columbus; Alexander VI (Borgia) elected Pope.

1495

(A) Hieronymus Bosch (*ca.* 1450–1516), *Temptation of St. Anthony;* Leonardo da Vinci (1452–1519), *Last Supper*.

1496

(M) Franchino Gafori (1451–1522), *Practica musicae*.

1497

(H) Voyage of John Cabot (1450–98) to Canada; Vasco da Gama (ca. 1469–1524), voyage to India; first voyage of Amerigo Vespucci.

1498

(M) License to print music granted to Ottaviano dei Petrucci, Venetian music publisher; first to print complete song collections from movable type.
(H) Execution of Savonarola (1452–98) at Florence.

1501

(M) Petrucci publishes Odhecaton, first book of Josquin's Masses, first book of frottole.

1502

(A) Donato Bramante (1444–1514) Tempietto, Rome.

1503

(M) Obrecht Masses printed by Petrucci.
(A) Henry VII's chapel, Westminster; Leonardo da Vinci (1452–1519), Mona Lisa.

1504

(M) Josquin leaves Italy for France.
(A) Michelangelo Buonarotti (1475–1564), David.

1505

(A) Giorgione (ca. 1475-1510), Fête Champêtre.

1506

(A) St. Peter's begun at Rome, under Bramante's direction.

1507

(A) Albrecht Dürer (1471–1528), Adam and Eve.
(M) Petrucci issues first printed lute tablature.

1508

(A) Michelangelo begins Sistine Chapel ceiling.

1509

(A) Raphael (1483–1520), School of Athens.
(H) Henry VIII King of England (till 1547).

1511

(M) Sebastian Virdung, Musica getutscht.
(A) Desiderius Erasmus (1466–1536), The Praise of Folly.

1512

(M) Oeglin's Liederbuch.

1513

(H) Balboa (1475–1517) discovers the Pacific Ocean; election of Pope Leo X (Giovanni de' Medici).
(A) Matthias Grünewald (1485–1530), Isenheim Altarpiece.

1514

(A) Dürer, St. Jerome in His Study; Niccolò Machiavelli (1469–1527), The Prince.

1516

(A) Raphael, Sistine Madonna; Sir Thomas More (1478–1535), Utopia; Lodovico Ariosto (1474–1533), Orlando Furioso.

1517

(H) Martin Luther (1483–1546), ninety-five theses.

1518

(H) Conquest of Mexico by Cortes.
(A) Pontormo (1494–1557), Joseph in Egypt.

1519

(H) Ferdinand Magellan (ca. 1480–1521) circumnavigates the globe; Charles V (1500–58), Holy Roman Emperor (till 1556).

1520

(A) Michelangelo, sculpture for Medici tombs.
(H) Field of the Cloth of Gold.

1524

(M) Johann Walter (1496–1570), Geystliche Gesangk Buchleyn.

1525

(A) Titian, Deposition.

1526

(A) Luther, Deudsche Messe.

1527

(M) Pierre Attaingnant's (d. 1552) first publication, Brevarium noviomense.
(H) Sack of Rome.

1528

(A) Conte Baldassare Castighone (1478–1529), The Courtier.

1530

(A) Nicolaus Copernicus (1473–1543), De Revolutionibus Orbium Coelesticum.

1532

(A) François Rabelais (1494?–1553), Gargantua.

1533

(M) First Italian madrigals.
(A) Hans Holbein the Younger (1497–1543), The Ambassadors.

1534

(H) Act of Supremacy separates Church of England from the Papacy.

1535

(A) Angelo Bronzino (1503–72), Portrait of a Young Man. Il Parmigianino (1503–1540), Madonna del Collo Lungo.

1536
(M) First music publications of Gardano (Venice) and Petreius (Nuremberg).
(A) Library at Venice founded.

1538
(A) Titian, *Venus of Urbino*.

1539
(M) Jacob Arcadelt (*ca.* 1505–*ca.* 1560), first book of five-part madrigals.
(H) Statute of the Six Articles.

1540
(H) Society of Jesus founded.

1541
(H) Hernando de Soto (1500–42) discovers Mississippi River.
(A) Michelangelo, *Last Judgment* in Sistine Chapel.

1542
(M) Cipriano de Rore (1516–65), first book of madrigals.
(H) Ireland made a kingdom.

1545
(H) Council of Trent (till 1563).

1547
(M) Glareanus (1488–1563), *Dodecachordon*.
(A) Benevenuto Cellini (1500–71), *Perseus*.
(H) Edward VI King of England (till 1553).

1549
(M) Adrian Willaert (*ca.* 1490–1562), *ricercari*.
(H) Book of Common Prayer authorized by Edward VI.

1551
(M) Claude Goudimel (1505–72), *First Book of Psalms*.

1553
(H) Catholicism restored in England under Queen Mary (till 1558).

1554
(M) Giovanni Palestrina (*ca.* 1526–94), first book of Masses; Philippe de Monte (1521–1603), first book of madrigals.

1555
(M) Orlando di Lasso (*ca.* 1532–94), first book of madrigals.
(H) Peace of Augsburg.

1557
(M) Claudio Merulo (1533–1604) at San Marco.

1558
(M) Gioseffo Zarlino (1517–1590), *Istitutioni harmoniche;* Willaert, *Musica nova*.
(H) Elizabeth I, Queen of England (till 1603).

1561
(M) Palestrina, *Improperia*.

1562
(H) Religious wars of the French Huguenots.

1563
(H) Establishment of the Church of England.

1565
(M) Lasso, *Penitential Psalms*.

1566
(A) Pieter Brueghel the Elder (*ca.* 1525–69), *The Wedding Dance*.

1568
(H) Revolt of the Netherlands.

1569
(M) Palestrina, first book of motets.

1571
(H) Naval battle of Lepanto.

1572
(H) Massacre of Protestants in Paris.
(A) Giovanni da Bologna (*ca.* 1529–1608), *Mercury*.

1575
(M) William Byrd (1543–1623) and Thomas Tallis (*ca.* 1505–85), *Cantiones sacrae*.

1576
(A) Tintoretto (1518–94), *Ascension of Christ*.

1577
(M) Monte at Prague.
(H) Sir Francis Drake (1540–96) starts voyage around the world.

1580
(A) Michel Eyquem de Montaigne (1533–92), *Essays*.

1581
(M) Vincenzo Galileo (*ca.* 1520–91), *Dialogo della musica antica e della moderna*.

1582
(H) Calendar reform by Pope Gregory XIII.

1586
(M) Jakob Handl (Gallus; 1550–91), *Opus musicum*.

1587
(M) Claudio Monteverdi (*ca.* 1567–1643), first book of madrigals.

1588
(M) Nicholas Yonge (d. 1619) issues *Musica transalpina*.
(H) War between Spain and England; defeat of the Spanish Armada.

(A) Christopher Marlowe (1564–93), *Doctor Faustus.*

1589

(M) Byrd, *Cantiones sacrae, Songs of Sundrie Natures.*

1590

(A) Edmund Spenser (1552–99), *The Faerie Queene.*

1592

(A) Tintoretto, *The Last Supper.*

1594

(M) Thomas Morley (1557–1602) *The First Book of Ballets for Five Voices;* Orazio Vecchi (1540–1603), *Amfiparnaso;* Carlo Gesualdo (*ca.* 1560–1613), first book of madrigals.
(A) William Shakespeare (1564–1616), *Romeo and Juliet.*

1597

(M) Morley, *A Plaine and Easie Introduction to Practicall Musicke;* Jacopo Peri (1561–1633), *Dafne;* John Dowland (1562–1626), *First Book of Songs or Ayres;* Giovanni Gabrieli (*ca.* 1554–1612), *Symphoniae sacrae.*

1600

(M) Peri, *Euridice;* Giulio Caccini (1546–1618), *Euridice;* Emilio de' Cavalieri (1550–1602), *La Rappresentazione di anima e di corpo.*
(H) Henry IV marries Marie de' Medici; Giordano Bruno (1548–1600) burned at stake.
(A) Annibale Carracci (1560–1609), *Polyphemus Hurling Rocks at Acis.*

1601

(M) Caccini, *Le Nuove Musiche.*
(A) Shakespeare, *Hamlet.*

1602

(M) Lodovico Viadana (1564–1645), *Cento concerti ecclesiastici.*
(H) Galileo Galilei (1564–1642) discovers law of falling bodies; Dutch East India Company founded.

1603

(H) James I of England (James VI of Scotland) crowned (till 1625).

1604

(A) Shakespeare, *Othello.*

1605

(M) Monteverdi, *Fifth Book of Madrigals;* Michael Praetorius (1571–1621), *Musae Sioniae;* Thomas Luis de Victoria (*ca.* 1549–1611), *Requiem;* John Dowland (1562–1626), *Lachrymae.*
(H) Gunpowder plot; Pope Paul V crowned (till 1621).
(A) Miguel de Cervantes (1547–1616), Part I of *Don Quixote;* Francis Bacon (1561–1626), *On the Advancement of*

Learning; Ben Jonson (*ca.* 1573–1637), *Volpone.*

1606

(A) Shakespeare, *Macbeth.*

1607

(M) Monteverdi, *Orfeo;* Marco da Gagliano (*ca.* 1575–1642), *Dafne;* Agostino Agazzari (1578–1640), *Del sonare sopra il basso.*
(H) Founding of Jamestown Colony.

1608

(M) Monteverdi, *Arianna;* Girolamo Frescobaldi (1583–1643), organist at St. Peter's.
(H) Quebec founded by Champlain.

1609

(M) Heinrich Schütz (1585–1672) and G. Gabrieli at Venice; Peri, *Le varie musiche.*
(H) Henry Hudson (d. 1611) explores Hudson River; Johannes Kepler (1571–1630), *Astronomia nova.*

1610

(H) Louis XIII crowned (till 1643).
(A) Honoré d' Urfé (1568–1625), *L'Astrée.*

1611

(M) *Parthenia* published.
(A) King James version of Bible.

1612

(A) Bacon, *Novum organum.*
(H) Louvre begun (till 1690).

1613

(M) Domenico Cerone (*ca.* 1560–1626), *The Art of Music and Instructor;* Monteverdi at San Marco.

1614

(M) *Medicean Gradual* published at Rome.
(A) Peter Paul Rubens (1577–1646), *The Descent from the Cross.*

1615

(M) G. Gabrieli, *Canzoni e sonate, Symphoniae sacrae II.*

1617

(M) Biagio Marini (1595–1665), *Affetti musicali;* J. H. Schein (1586–1630), *Banchetto musicale;* Schütz at Dresden.

1618

(M) Schein, *Opella nova.*
(H) Start of Thirty Years' War.

1619

(M) Praetorius, *Syntagma musicum.*
(H) Ferdinand II Holy Roman Emperor (till 1637).

1620

(H) Pilgrims arrive at Cape Cod; Mayflower Compact.

1621

(M) Schein, *Musica Boscareccia.*
(H) Gregory XV Pope (till 1623); Philip IV King of Spain (till 1665).

1623

(M) Schütz, *Historia der fröhlichen und siegreichen Auferstehung.*
(A) Shakespeare first folio; Marino, *Adone.*

1624

(M) Monteverdi, *Il Combattimento di Tancredi e Clorinda;* Samuel Scheidt (1587–1654), *Tabulatura nova.*
(H) Cardinal Richelieu in power in France (till 1642).
(A) Franz Hals (*ca.* 1580–1666), *The Laughing Cavalier;* Jakob Böhme (1572–1624), *Der Weg zu Christo.*

1625

(M) Schütz, *Cantiones sacrae.*
(H) Charles I crowned King of England (till 1649).

1626

(M) Domenico Mazzocchi (1592–1655), *La Catena d' Adone.*
(H) Manhattan Island bought by Peter Minuit.

1627

(M) Schein, *Leipziger Kantional;* Schütz, *Dafne.*

1628

(M) Orazio Benevoli (1605–72), *Salzburg Festival Mass.* Gagliano and Peri, *La Flora;* Schütz, *Psalms of David;* Carissimi (1605–74) at San Apollinare in Rome.
(A) William Harvey (1578–1657), *Essay on the Motion of the Heart and the Blood.*
(H) La Rochelle captured; end of Huguenot power in France.

1629

(M) Schütz, *Symphoniae Sacrae I.*

1630

(H) Puritans establish Boston.

1631

(H) Battle of Lützen; Galilei, *Dialogo dei due massimi sistemi del mondo.*
(A) Rembrandt van Rijn (1606–1669), *The Anatomy Lesson.*

1633

(M) Schütz at Copenhagen; Dresden Chapel closed.

1634

(M) Stefano Landi (*ca.* 1590–1655), *Il Sant' Alessio;* Henry Lawes (1596–1662), *Comus.*
(A) Taj Mahal begun (till 1653).

1635

(H) Académie Française founded.
(A) Diego Velasquez (1599–1660), *Surrender of Breda.*

1636

(M) Marin Mersenne (1588–1648), *Harmonie Universelle.*

(H) Founding of Harvard College; Roger Williams' first settlement in Rhode Island.
(A) Pierre Corneille (1606–1684), *Le Cid.*

1637

(M) Johann Froberger (1616–67), organist at court chapel, Vienna; Giovanni Doni (1594–1647), *Della musica scenica;* first public opera theatre (Venice).
(A) René Descartes (1596–1650), *Discourse on Method;* Anthony van Dycke (1599–1641), *The Children of Charles I.*
(H) Ferdinand III Holy Roman Emperor (till 1657).

1638

(M) Heinrich Albert (1604–51), first arias; Mazzocchi, *Madrigali a 5 voci in partitura;* Monteverdi, *Madrigali guerrieri et amorosi;* Pier Francesco Cavalli (1602–76), second organist at San Marco.

1639

(M) Virgilio Mazzocchi (1597–1646) and Marco Marazzoli (1600–62) compose first comic opera, *Chi soffre, speri;* Loreto Vittori (1604–70), *La Galatea.*
(A) Nicolas Poussin (1594–1665), *Shepherds in Arcadia.*

1640

(H) Frederick William becomes Elector of Brandenburg. *The Bay Psalm Book,* first book printed in English colonies.

1642

(M) Monteverdi, *L'incoronazione di Poppea.*
(A) Rembrandt, *The Night Watch.*

1643

(H) Louis XIV King of France at age of five (till 1715).

1644

(A) Giovanni Lorenzo Bernini (1598–1680), *The Ecstasy of St. Teresa.*

1645

(M) Andreas Hammerschmidt (1612–75), *Dialogues;* Schütz, *Seven Last Words.*

1647

(M) Luigi Rossi's (1597–1653) *Orfeo* staged in Paris; Johann Crüger (1598–1662), *Praxis pietatis melica.*

1648

(M) Schütz, *Geistliche Chormusik.*
(H) Treaty of Westphalia; end of Thirty Years' War.

1649

(M) Cavalli, *Giasone;* Marc' Antonio Cesti (1623–69), *Orontea.*
(H) King Charles I beheaded; Commonwealth established (till 1660).

1650

(M) Carissimi, *Jephtha;* Samuel Scheidt (1587–1654), chorales for organ; Schütz,

Symphoniae sacrae, Part III; Athanasius Kircher (1602–80), *Musurgia universalis.*
(A) Descartes, *Musicae compendium.*

1651

(A) Thomas Hobbes (1588–1679), *Leviathan.*

1653

(M) Jean-Baptiste Lully (1632–87) court composer at Paris.
(H) Oliver Cromwell (1599–1658) dissolves Parliament.

1656

(A) Velasquez, *The Maids of Honor.*

1660

(M) Cavalli, *Serse.*
(H) Restoration of Charles II in England (till 1685).
(A) Samuel Pepys (1633–1703), *Diary.*

1661

(M) Marc' Antonio Cesti, *Dori.*
(H) Absolute reign of Louis XIV (till 1715).

1662

(M) Cavalli, *Ercole amante.*
(A) Molière (1622–73), *Ecole des Femmes.*

1664

(M) Schütz, *Christmas Oratorio.*
(H) New Amsterdam becomes New York.

1665

(M) Schütz, *St. John Passion.*
(H) Charles II of Spain crowned (till 1700); plague in London.
(A) Baruch Spinoza (1632–77), *Ethics.*

1666

(M) Schütz, *St. Matthew Passion.*
(H) Great fire of London.

1667

(M) Johann Rosenmüller (*ca.* 1620–84), *12 Sonate da camera a 5 stromenti;* M. A. Cesti (1623–69), *Il pomo d'Oro.*
(A) John Milton (1608–74), *Paradise Lost;* Bernini, colonnade of St. Peter's.

1668

(A) La Fontaine (1621–95), *Fables.*

1669

(M) Paris Academy of Music founded.
(A) Claude Gellée Lorrain (1600–82), *Egeria.*

1670

(M) Jacques Chambonnières (*ca.* 1602–72), clavecin pieces.
(A) Blaise Pascal (1623–62), *Pensées;* Molière, *Le Bourgeois Gentilhomme.*

1674

(A) Nicolas Boileau-Despréaux (1636–1711), *L'Art Poétique.*

1675

(M) Lully, *Thésée.*
(A) Sir Christopher Wren (1632–1723) begins St. Paul's Cathedral.

1677

(A) Jean Baptiste Racine (1639–99), *Phèdre.*

1678

(A) Bartolomé Murillo (1617–82), *Mystery of the Immaculate Conception;* John Bunyan (1628–88), *Pilgrim's Progress.*

1681

(M) Arcangelo Corelli (1653–1713), first trio sonatas.

1682

(H) Reign of Peter the Great (till 1725); La Salle explores the Mississippi; Philadelphia founded by William Penn.

1685

(M) Giovanni Legrenzi (1626–90) at San Marco; John Playford (1623–86), *The Division Violist.*
(H) James II of England crowned (till 1688); revocation of the Edict of Nantes.

1686

(M) Lully, *Armide.*

1687

(A) Isaac Newton (1642–1727), *Principia mathematica.*

1689

(M) Agostino Steffani (1654–1728), *Enrico detto il Leone;* Henry Purcell (*ca.* 1659–95), *Dido and Aeneas;* Johann Kuhnau (1660–1722), Clavier Sonatas.
(H) William III and Mary (d. 1694) rulers of England (till 1702).
(A) Thomas Burnet, *The Sacred Theory of the Earth.*

1690

(M) Georg Muffat (1653–1704), *Apparatus musico-organisticus.*
(A) John Locke (1632–1704), *An Essay Concerning Human Understanding.*

1692

(H) Salem witchcraft trials; College of William and Mary chartered.

1695

(M) Muffat, *Florilegium I;* Reinhard Keiser (1674–1739) director of Hamburg opera.

1696

(M) Kuhnau, *Frische Klavier Früchte.*

1697

(M) André Campra (1660–1744), *L'Europe galante.*
(A) John Dryden (1631–1700), *Alexander's Feast.*

1698

(M) Giuseppe Torelli (1658–1709), Violin Concertos Op. 6; *Bay Psalm Book*, first edition with music.

1700

(M) Johann Sebastian Bach (1685–1750) at Lüneburg.
(H) Philip V of Spain crowned (till 1746).

1701

(M) Muffat, *12 Concerti Grossi*.
(H) Frederick I of Prussia crowned; war of the Spanish Succession (till 1714); Detroit founded; Yale College founded.

1702

(H) Queen Anne of England crowned.

1703

(M) George Frideric Handel (1685–1759) at Hamburg.
(H) St. Petersburg founded.

1704

(M) Handel, *St. John Passion*. Georg Telemann (1681–1761) founds Collegium musicum at Leipzig.

1706

(M) Jean-Philippe Rameau (1683–1764), first book of clavecin pieces; Handel in Italy.

1707

(M) Alessandro Scarlatti (1660–1725), *Mitridate eupatore;* first Bach cantatas.

1708

(M) Bach at Weimar.

1709

(M) First pianoforte built; *opera buffa* in Italy.
(A) *The Tatler* and *The Spectator* founded.

1710

(M) Campra, *Fêtes Vénitiennes;* Handel in England; Academy of Ancient Music founded at London.
(A) George Berkeley (1685–1753), *A Treatise Concerning the Principles of Human Knowledge.*

1711

(M) Keiser, *Croesus;* Handel, *Rinaldo.*
(H) Charles VI crowned Holy Roman Emperor (till 1740).
(A) Alexander Pope (1688–1744), *Essay on Criticism.*

1712

(M) Antonio Vivaldi (1678–1741), Concertos, Op. 3. Handel settles in London.
(H) Toleration Act, London.
(A) Pope, *Rape of the Lock.*

1713

(M) François Couperin (1668–1733), *Pièces de Clavecin*, I; Bach, *Ich hatte viel Bekümmernis.*
(H) Peace of Utrecht.

1714

(M) Silbermann's organ at Freiburg.
(H) George I of England (Handel's patron).
(A) Gottfried Leibnitz (1646–1716), *Monadologie.*

1715

(M) First *opéra comique* founded; A. Scarlatti, *Tigrane.*
(H) Louis XV of France crowned (till 1774).
(A) Alain Lesage (1668–1747), *L'Histoire de Gil Blas de Santillane.*

1716

(M) Handel, *Passion;* Couperin, *L'Art de Toucher le Clavecin* and *Pièces de Clavecin, II.*

1717

(M) Bach at Cöthen—*Orgelbüchlein.*
(H) Triple Alliance.
(A) Jean Watteau (1684–1721), *Embarkation for Cythera.*

1719

(H) Herculaneum and Pompeii rediscovered.
(A) Daniel Defoe (*ca.* 1659–ca. 1731), *Robinson Crusoe.*

1720

(M) Benedetto Marcello (1686–1739), *Il teatro alla moda.*
(H) South Sea and Mississippi bubbles.

1721

(M) Bach: *Brandenburg Concertos; French* and *English Suites.*
(A) Baron de Montesquieu (1689–1755), *Lettres Persanes.*

1722

(M) Bach, *The Well-Tempered Clavier*, I; Rameau, *Traité de l'Harmonie.*

1723

(A) François Voltaire (1694–1778), *Henriade.*

1724

(M) Handel, *Giulio Cesare;* Bach, *St. John Passion;* cantata, *Ein' feste Burg.*

1725

(M) *Concerts spirituels* at Paris; Johann Fux (1660–1741), *Gradus ad Parnassum.*

1726

(M) Vivaldi, *The Seasons;* Rameau, *Nouveau système de musique théorique.*
(A) Jonathan Swift (1667–1745), *Gulliver's Travels.*

1727

(M) Handel, *Coronation Anthem.*
(H) George II of England crowned.

1728

(M) John Gay (1685–1732), *Beggar's Opera.*

1729
(M) Bach, *St. Matthew Passion.*

1730
(M) Johann Hasse (1699–1783), *Artaserse.*

1731
(M) Bach, *Klavierübung, I.*
(H) Treaty of Vienna.
(A) Abbé Prévost (1697–1763), *Manon Lescaut.*

1732
(A) Voltaire, *Zaïre;* William Hogarth (1697–1764), *A Harlot's Progress.*

1733
(M) Giovanni Pergolesi (1710–36), *La Serva padrona.*
(H) Founding of Georgia; War of Polish Succession.

1734
(M) Bach, *Christmas Oratorio;* Giuseppe Tartini (1692–1770), Sonatas, Op. 1.
(A) François Boucher (1703–70), *Rinaldo and Armida.*

1735
(M) Rameau, *Les Indes Galantes.*
(H) Carolus Linnaeus (1707–78), *Systema naturae.*
(A) Hogarth, *A Rake's Progress.*

1736
(M) Handel, *Alexander's Feast.*

1737
(M) Rameau, *Castor et Pollux;* Domenico Scarlatti (1685–1757), first published sonatas; San Carlo Opera opens, Naples.
(H) First lodge of Freemasons in Germany.

1738
(M) D. Scarlatti, *Essercizi;* Bach *Mass in B minor;* Handel, *Saul, Israel in Egypt, Serse.*
(H) Methodist church founded by Wesley and Whitefield.

1739
(M) Handel, *Concerti grossi;* Johann Mattheson (1681–1764), *Der vollkommene Capellmeister.*
(A) David Hume (1711–76), *A Treatise of Human Nature.*

1740
(H) Age of enlightened despots (till 1796); Frederick the Great of Prussia (till 1786).
(A) Giovanni Tiepolo (1696–1770), *Triumph of Amphitrite;* Samuel Richardson (1689–1761), *Pamela.*

1741
(M) Christoph Gluck (1714–87), *Artaserse.*

1742
(M) Bach, *Goldberg Variations;* Handel, *Messiah* performed at Dublin; C. P. E. Bach (1714–88), *Prussian Sonatas.*

(H) Charles VII Holy Roman Emperor (till 1745).

1743
(M) Handel, *Samson.*
(H) Treaty of Fontainebleau.
(A) Voltaire, *Mérope.*

1744
(M) C. P. E. Bach, *Württemberg Sonatas.*

1745
(M) Gluck in England; Johann Stamitz (1717–57) at Mannheim.

1746
(M) Handel, *Judas Maccabaeus.*
(H) Ferdinand I of Spain crowned (till 1759).
(A) Boucher, *Toilet of Venus.*

1747
(M) Handel, *Joshua.* J. S. Bach, *Musical Offering.*
(A) Sans Souci castle at Potsdam.

1748
(H) End of war of Austrian Succession.
(A) Montesquieu, *Esprit des lois;* Voltaire, *Zadig;* Gottlieb Klopstock (1724–1803), *Der Messias.*

1749
(M) Rameau, *Zoroastre;* J. S. Bach, *Die Kunst der Fuge.*
(A) Henry Fielding (1707–54), *Tom Jones.*

1750
(M) Johann Quantz (1697–1773), Flute Concertos.
(A) George Buffon (1707–88), *Histoire Naturelle.*

1751
(M) Handel, *Jephtha.*
(H) First volumes of *Encyclopédie;* Benjamin Franklin (1706–90), *Experiments and Observation on Electricity.*
(A) Thomas Gray (1716–71), *Elegy Written in a Country Churchyard;* Voltaire, *Le Siècle de Louis XIV.*

1752
(M) Quantz, *Versuch einer Anweisung die Flöte traversiere zu spielen;* War of the Buffons in Paris; first German *Singspiele.*

1753
(M) C. P. E. Bach, *Versuch über die Wahre Art.* Jean-Jacques Rousseau (1712–78), *Lettre sur la musique française.*

1754
(M) Rameau, *Observations sur notre instinct pour la musique.*
(A) Samuel Johnson (1709–84), *Dictionary;* Thomas Chippendale manufacturing furniture.

1755
(M) Franz Joseph Haydn (1732–1809),

first quartets. Karl Graun (1701–59), *Der Tod Jesu*.
(H) Lisbon earthquake; Moscow University founded.
(A) Gotthold Lessing (1729–81), *Miss Sara Sampson*.

1756
(H) French and Indian Wars.
(A) Voltaire, *Essai sur les moeurs;* Piranesi's engravings of ancient Roman ruins.

1759
(H) Wolfe captures Quebec.
(A) Voltaire, *Candide;* Laurence Sterne (1713–1768), *Tristram Shandy*.

1760
(H) George III of England crowned (till 1820).
(A) Jean Fragonard (1732–1806), Park of the Villa D'Este in Tivoli, James Macpherson (1736–96), *Ossian*.

1761
(M) Haydn at Eisenstadt; Gluck, *Le Cadi dupé; Don Juan*.

1762
(M) Gluck, *Orfeo ed Euridice*.
(A) Rousseau, *Le Contrat Social, Emile, Pygmalion*.

1763
(H) Beginnings of excavations at Pompeii and Herculaneum; Treaty of Paris; Canada ceded to England.

1764
(M) Gluck, *La Rencontre imprévue;* Mozart (1756–91) in London.
(A) Voltaire, *Dictionnaire philosophique;* Johann Winckelmann (1717–68), *Geschichte der Kunst des Altertums*.

1766
(M) Haydn, Quartets, Op. 9.
(A) Petit Trianon built. Lessing, *Laokoon;* Oliver Goldsmith (1728–74), *The Vicar of Wakefield*.

1767
(M) Haydn, Symphonies 35–38; Gluck, *Alceste;* Rousseau, *Dictionnaire de musique*.

1768
(M) Mozart, *Bastien und Bastienne*.
(A) Leonhard Euler (1707–83), *Lettres à une princesse d'Allemagne;* Sterne, *Sentimental Journey*.

1769
(M) Mozart in Italy.
(H) Watt's steam engine patented.

1770
(M) Mozart, first quartets; William Billings (1746–1800) *The New England Psalm Singer*.

(H) Beginning of the factory system; James Hargreaves (d. 1778), spinning jenny patented.
(A) Thomas Gainsborough (1727–88), *The Blue Boy*.

1771
(H) First edition of *Encyclopedia Britannica*.

1772
(M) Haydn, *Sun* Quartets, Op. 20.
(H) First partition of Poland.

1773
(M) Mozart, Symphonies K. 183, 201.
(H) Dissolution of Jesuit order by Clement XIV.

1774
(M) Gluck, *Iphigénie en Aulide, Orphée et Euridice*.
(H) First Continental Congress assembled at Philadelphia; Louis XVI King of France (till 1792); Joseph Priestley discovers oxygen.

1775
(H) Volta's electric battery invented; American Revolution (till 1783).
(A) Pierre Beaumarchais (1732–99), *Le Barbière de Séville*.

1776
(M) Sir John Hawkins (1719–89) and Charles Burney (1726–1814), general histories of music; Gluck, *Alceste*.
(H) Declaration of Independence; discovery of hydrogen.
(A) Thomas Paine, *Common Sense;* Adam Smith (1732–90), *The Wealth of Nations*.

1777
(M) Gluck, *Armide*.
(H) Articles of Confederation.
(A) Richard Sheridan (1751–1816), *The School for Scandal*.

1778
(M) Mozart, Piano Sonatas K. 310, 330–333, Violin Sonatas K. 296, 301–306; La Scala Opera opens in Milan.

1779
(M) Gluck, *Iphigénie en Tauride*.
(A) Lessing, *Nathan der Weise;* Sheridan, *The Critic*.

1780
(M) Haydn, Quartets, Op. 33.
(H) Cornwallis surrenders at Yorktown.

1781
(M) Haydn, *Jungfrau* Quartets; Mozart, *Idomeneo*.
(A) Immanuel Kant (1724–1804), *Critique of Pure Reason;* Jean Houdon (1741–1828), *Voltaire*.

1782

(M) Mozart, *Die Entführung*.
(A) Johann Schiller (1759–1805) *Die Räuber;* Rousseau, *Confessions*.

1784

(M) Andre Grétry (1741–1813), *Richard Coeur de Lion;* Martin Gerbert (1720–93), *Scriptores ecclesiastici*.
(A) Beaumarchais, *Le Mariage de Figaro*.

1785

(M) Haydn, *Seven Last Words;* Mozart, Haydn Quartets.
(A) Thomas Jefferson (1743–1826), design for Virginia State Capitol.

1786

(M) Mozart, *Le nozze di Figaro;* Haydn, *Paris Symphonies*.
(H) Frederick Wilhelm II of Prussia (till 1797).
(A) Robert Burns (1759–96), first edition of poetry; Joshua Reynolds (1723–92), *The Duchess of Devonshire*.

1787

(M) Mozart, *Don Giovanni*, Quintets K. 515, 516.
(H) American Constitutional Convention.
(A) Schiller, *Don Carlo;* Johann Goethe (1749–1832), *Iphigenia*.

1788

(M) Mozart, last three symphonies.
(H) John Fitch's steamboat invented; American constitution ratified.
(A) Edward Gibbon (1737–94), *The History of the Decline and Fall of the Roman Empire;* Goethe, *Egmont;* Jacques David (1748–1825), *Paris and Helen*.

1789

(M) Haydn, Quartets, Opp. 54, 55.
(H) French Revolution (till 1794); George Washington first president of United States.
(A) Goethe, *Torquato Tasso*.

1790

(M) Mozart, *Così fan tutte;* Haydn in London.
(A) Kant, *Critique of Judgment*.

1791

(M) Mozart, *The Magic Flute, Requiem;* Haydn, first *London* Symphonies.
(H) Bill of Rights.
(A) James Boswell (1740–95), *Life of Samuel Johnson*.

1792

(M) Domenico Cimarosa (1749–1801), *Il Matrimonio segreto;* Ludwig van Beethoven (1770–1827) at Vienna.
(H) France declared a republic.

1793

(H) Reign of Terror; Eli Whitney invents cotton gin.

(A) David, *Death of Marat;* William Blake (1757–1827), *Marriage of Heaven and Hell*.

1794

(M) Haydn, second trip to London.
(A) J. G. Fichte (1762–1814), *Uber den Begriff der Wissenschaftslehre*.

1795

(M) Beethoven, Trios Op. 1; Paris Conservatory founded.

1796

(M) Haydn, *Missa in tempore belli*.
(H) Jenner's first vaccination; Paul I of Russia (till 1801); Napoleon in Italy; Battle of Lodi.

1797

(M) Luigi Cherubini (1760–1842), *Médée*.
(A) Wilhelm Wackenroder (1773–98), *Herzensergiessungen*. François Gérard (1770–1837), *Cupid and Psyche*.

1798

(M) Haydn, *The Creation, Imperial Mass*.
(H) Napoleon in Egypt.
(A) Samuel Coleridge (1772–1834) and William Wordsworth (1770–1850), *Lyrical Ballads;* Thomas Malthus (1766–1834), *Essay on the Principle of Population;* Charles Bulfinch (1763–1844) designs the Massachusetts State House.

1799

(M) Beethoven, First Symphony, *Sonata Pathétique*.
(H) Napoleon becomes First Consul.
(A) Schiller, *Wallenstein;* Friedrich Hölderlin (1770–1843), *Hyperion*

1800

(M) Haydn, *The Seasons*.
(H) Discovery of ultraviolet rays; Volta invents voltaic pile.
(A) David, *Madame Recamier;* Schiller, *Die Jungfrau von Orleans*.

1802

(M) Beethoven, Second Symphony.
(H) Napoleon made Consul for life.
(A) Chateaubriand, *Génie du Christianisme*.

1803

(M) Haydn, Quartets, Op. 103; Beethoven, *Eroica Symphony, Kreutzer Sonata*.
(H) Louisiana Purchase.

1804

(M) Beethoven, Sonata, Op. 53.
(H) Napoleon crowned Emperor; Lewis and Clark expedition.
(A) Schiller, *Wilhelm Tell;* Jean Paul Richter (1763–1825), *Die Flegeljahre;* Jean Ingres (1780–1867), *Mme. Rivière*.

1805

(M) Beethoven, *Fidelio*, Sonata, Op. 54.
(H) Battle of Trafalgar.

(A) Ludwig Arnim (1781–1831) and Clemens Brentano (1778–1842), *Des Knaben Wunderhorn.*

1806

(M) Beethoven, Fourth Symphony, Violin Concerto, Sonata, Op. 57.
(H) Formal dissolution of the Holy Roman Empire; Lewis and Clark reach Pacific.

1807

(M) Beethoven, Fifth Symphony, *Coriolanus Overture.*
(H) Fulton builds the first commercial steamboat; London streets lighted by gas; Hegel, *Phenomenology of the Spirit.*
(A) Wordsworth, *Intimations of Immortality.*

1808

(A) Goethe, *Faust, Part I.*

1810

(M) John Wyeth (1770–1858), *Repository of Sacred Music.*
(A) Sir Walter Scott (1771–1832), *The Lady of the Lake.*

1811

(M) Franz Schubert (1797–1828), first *Lieder.*
(A) Goethe, *Dichtung und Wahrheit.*

1812

(M) Beethoven, Seventh and Eighth Symphonies, Violin Sonata, Op. 96.
(H) Napoleon retreats from Moscow.
(A) George Byron (1788–1824), *Childe Harold's Pilgrimage;* Jacob (1785–1863) and Wilhelm (1786–1859) Grimm, *Kinder- und Hausmärchen.*

1813

(M) London Philharmonic Society founded.
(H) Napoleon abdicates.
(A) Jane Austen (1775–1817), *Pride and Prejudice.*

1814

(M) Schubert, *Gretchen am Spinnrad.*
(H) Napoleon to Elba; Congress of Vienna.
(A) Scott, *Waverly;* Francisco Goya (1746–1828), *King Ferdinand VII.*

1815

(M) Invention of the metronome; Schubert, *Der Erlkönig,* Third Symphony.
(H) Battle of Waterloo; the Holy Alliance.
(A) Goya, *Witch's Sabbath.*

1816

(M) Schubert, Fourth and Fifth Symphonies, Third Piano Sonata, Mass in C; Gioacchino Rossini (1792–1868), *The Barber of Seville, Otello.*
(A) Percy Bysshe Shelley (1792–1822), *Alastor, or the Spirit of Solitude.*

1817

(M) Muzio Clementi (1752–1832), *Gradus ad Parnassum.*

1818

(A) David Ricardo (1772–1823), *Principles of Political Economy and Taxation;* John Keats (1795–1821), *Endymion;* Byron, *Manfred.*

1818

(M) Beethoven, Sonata, Op. 106; Schubert, Sixth Symphony, Quartet in E.

1819

(M) Schubert, *Forellen* Quintet, Piano Sonata No. 13.
(H) First steamship crosses Atlantic; Florida purchased from Spain.
(A) Scott, *Ivanhoe.*

1820

(M) Anthony Philip Heinrich (1781–1861), *Dawning of Music in Kentucky.*
(A) Shelley, *Prometheus Unbound;* Blake, *Jerusalem.* Alphonse Lamartine (1790–1869), *Méditations Poétiques.*

1821

(M) Carl Maria von Weber (1786–1826), *Der Freischütz;* Beethoven, Sonatas, Opp. 110, 111.
(H) Faraday's electric motor and generator.
(A) John Constable (1776–1837), *The Hay Wain.*

1822

(M) Beethoven, *Missa solemnis;* Schubert, *Unfinished Symphony.*

1823

(M) Weber, *Euryanthe;* Beethoven, Ninth Symphony, *Diabelli Variations;* Schubert, *Die schöne Müllerin.*
(H) Monroe Doctrine.

1824

(H) Charles X of France crowned.

1825

(M) Beethoven, Quartets, Opp. 127, 132; Felix Mendelssohn (1809–1847), String Octet.
(H) Erie Canal opened; Ludwig I of Bavaria crowned.
(A) Alessandro Manzoni (1785–1873), *I Promessi Sposi;* Alexander Pushkin (1799–1837), *Boris Godunov.*

1826

(M) Beethoven, Quartets, Opp. 130, 135; Schubert, *Die Winterreise;* Mendelssohn, *Midsummer Night's Dream Overture.*
(A) James Fenimore Cooper (1789–1851), *The Last of the Mohicans.*

1827

(M) Beethoven, Quartet, Op. 131.
(H) Mormon church founded.
(A) Heinrich Heine (1797–1856), *Buch der Lieder.*

1828

(M) Rossini, *Le Comte Ory;* Schubert,

Symphony in C, last three piano sonatas, string quintet; Paganini concerts.
(A) First performance of Goethe's *Faust.*

1829

(M) Hector Berlioz (1803–69), *Symphonie Fantastique;* Rossini, *Guillaume Tell.*
(H) Independence of Greece.
(A) Honoré de Balzac (1799–1850), *La Comédie Humaine.* Victor Hugo (1802–85), *Les Orientales;* James Mill (1773–1836), *Analysis of the Mind.*

1830

(M) Daniel Auber (1782–1871), *Fra Diavolo;* Robert Schumann (1810–56), *Abegg Variations,* Op. 1; Mendelssohn's first *Songs Without Words.*
(H) First railroad, Liverpool to Manchester; July Revolution in France.
(A) Lamartine, *Harmonies poétiques et religieuses;* Hugo, *Hernani;* Stendhal (1783–1842), *Le Rouge et le Noir.*

1831

(M) Vincenzo Bellini (1801–35), *Norma;* Schumann, *Papillons.*
(H) William Lloyd Garrison founds the *Liberator;* beginning of anti-slavery movement.
(A) Hugo, *Notre Dame de Paris.*

1832

(M) Frédéric Chopin (1810–49), *Etudes,* Op. 10, *Mazurkas,* Op. 6; Mendelssohn, *Hebrides Overture;* Rossini, *Stabat Mater;* G. Donizetti (1797–1848), *L'Elisir d'Amore;* *Concerts historiques* founded at Paris.

1833

(M) Wagner, *Die Feen.*
(H) Slavery outlawed in British Empire.
(A) Thomas Carlyle (1795–1881), *Sartor Resartus.*

1834

(M) Berlioz, *Harold in Italy; Neue Zeitschrift für Musik* founded by Schumann.
(H) McCormick patents mechanical reaper.
(A) Edward Lytton (1803–73), *The Last Days of Pompeii.*

1835

(M) Donizetti, *Lucia di Lammermoor;* Schumann, Symphonic Etudes, Op. 13, *Carnaval,* Op. 9; Bellini, *I Puritani.*

1836

(M) Giacomo Meyerbeer (1791–1864), *Les Huguenots;* Michael Glinka (1803–57), *A Life for the Tsar.* Chopin, *Ballades,* Op. 23.
(A) Charles Dickens (1812–70), *The Pickwick Papers;* Sir Charles Barry designs Houses of Parliament, London.
(H) Independence of Texas.

1837

(M) Berlioz, *Requiem;* Franz Liszt (1811–86), *Années de Pèlerinage.*
(H) Morse's telegraph; Queen Victoria crowned; Mount Holyoke College founded.
(A) Carlyle, *The French Revolution.*

1838

(M) Schumann, *Kinderszenen, Kreisleriana;* Berlioz, *Benvenuto Cellini;* first public school instruction in music (Boston).
(H) Daguerre (1789–1851) takes first photographs.
(A) Ferdinand Delacroix (1798–1863), *The Capture of Constantinople.*

1839

(M) Chopin, Préludes, Op. 28; New York Philharmonic Society founded; Vienna Philharmonic founded; Berlioz, *Romeo and Juliet;* Schumann, *Nachtstücke.*
(A) Joseph Turner (1775–1851), *The Fighting Temeraire;* Edgar Allan Poe (1809–49), *Tales of the Grotesque and Arabesque;* Stendhal, *The Charterhouse of Parma.*

1840

(M) Schumann, *Lieder;* Donizetti, *The Daughter of the Regiment.*
(H) First incandescent electric bulb.

1841

(M) Schumann, First and Fourth Symphonies.
(H) Invention of the saxophone.
(A) *Punch* founded.

1842

(M) Wagner, *Rienzi;* Glinka, *Russlan and Ludmilla;* Giuseppe Verdi (1813–1901), *Nabucco;* Third New York Philharmonic Society founded.

1843

(M) Wagner, *Der fliegende Holländer;* Donizetti, *Don Pasquale.*
(A) Sören Kierkegaard (1813–55), *Fear and Trembling.*

1844

(M) Verdi, *Ernani;* Mendelssohn, Violin Concerto; B. F. White (1800–79), *The Sacred Harp.*
(H) First telegraph message transmitted.
(A) Alexandre Dumas (1824–95), *The Three Musketeers.*

1845

(M) Liszt, *Les Préludes;* Wagner, *Tannhäuser;* Louis Moreau Gottschalk (1829–69), *La Bamboula.*
(A) Dumas, *The Count of Monte Cristo.*

1846

(M) Berlioz, *The Damnation of Faust;* Mendelssohn, *Elijah.*
(H) First use of ether as an anesthetic; Howe's sewing machine patented; Smithsonian Institution founded.

1847

(M) Verdi, *Macbeth;* Friedrich von Flotow (1812–83), *Martha.*

1848

(H) Potato famine in Ireland; gold rush in California; first Women's Rights Convention; revolutionary uprisings in Europe.
(A) Thomas Macaulay (1800–59), *History of England;* William Thackeray (1811–63), *Vanity Fair;* Alexandre Dumas *fils, La Dame aux Camélias;* Karl Marx (1818–83) and Friedrich Engels (1820–95), *Communist Manifesto.*

1849

(M) Wagner, *Die Kunst und die Revolution;* Meyerbeer, *Le Prophète;* Anton Bruckner (1824–96), *Requiem.*
(A) Gustave Courbet (1819–77), *The Stone Breaker;* Dickens, *David Copperfield.*

1850

(M) Bachgesellschaft founded; Wagner, *Lohengrin.*
(A) Nathaniel Hawthorne (1804–64), *The Scarlet Letter;* Dante Rossetti (1828–82), *The Annunciation;* Theodor Storm (1817–88), *Immensee;* Henry Wadsworth Longfellow (1807–82), *Evangeline.*

1851

(M) Wagner, *Oper und Drama;* Schumann, Third Symphony; Verdi, *Rigoletto;* Stephen Foster (1826–64), *Old Folks at Home.*
(H) First submarine telegraph cable.
(A) Herman Melville (1819–91), *Moby Dick;* Jean Millet (1814–75), *The Gleaners.*

1852

(H) Second Empire under Napoleon III.
(A) Harriet Beecher Stowe (1811–96), *Uncle Tom's Cabin.*

1853

(M) Verdi, *Il Trovatore, La Traviata.*
(H) Crimean War; Commodore Perry opens Japan to the West; first rail connection New York-Chicago.

1854

(M) Liszt, Sonata in B minor.
(A) Henry David Thoreau (1817–62), *Walden.*

1855

(M) Liszt, *Faust* Symphony; Verdi, *Vespri siciliani.*
(H) Charge of the Light Brigade.
(A) Walt Whitman (1819–92), *Leaves of Grass.*

1856

(M) Liszt, *Hungarian Rhapsodies.*

1857

(H) Dred Scott decision.
(A) Gustave Flaubert (1821–80), *Madame Bovary;* Currier and Ives publish prints; Pierre Baudelaire (1821–67), *Les Fleurs du Mal.*

1858

(M) Berlioz, *Les Troyens;* Verdi, *Un Ballo*

in Maschera; Jacques Offenbach (1819–80), *Orphée aux enfers.*
(H) Covent Garden opera house opens.

1859

(M) Charles Gounod (1818–93), *Faust;* Wagner, *Tristan und Isolde.*
(H) Charles Darwin (1809–82), *Origin of Species;* John Brown raids Harper's Ferry.
(A) Millet, *The Angelus;* Alfred Lord Tennyson (1809–92), *Idylls of the King.*

1861

(M) *Tannhäuser* performed at Paris.
(H) Serfs emancipated in Russia; unification of Italy; Civil War in America (till 1865).
(A) George Eliot (1819–80), *Silas Marner.*

1862

(M) Verdi, *La Forza del Destino;* Köchel's Mozart catalogue begun.
(H) Bismarck chancellor of Prussia.
(A) Ivan Turgenev (1818–83), *Fathers and Sons;* Honoré Daumier (1808–79), *Third Class Carriage.*

1863

(M) Berlioz, *Les Troyens* (first performance).
(H) Gettysburg Address; Emancipation Proclamation.
(A) Edouard Manet (1832–83), *Olympia.*

1864

(M) Johannes Brahms (1833–97), Piano Quintet in F minor, *Lieder,* Op. 33; Bruckner, First Symphony; Offenbach, *La Belle Hélène.*
(H) First International founded by Karl Marx; first ascent of the Matterhorn; first successful transatlantic cable.
(A) Lewis Carroll (1832–98), *Alice in Wonderland;* Leo Tolstoy (1828–1910), *War and Peace.*

1865

(H) Lincoln assassinated; Thirteenth Amendment ratified, outlawing slavery.

1866

(M) Ambroise Thomas (1811–96), *Mignon;* Bedřich Smetana (1824–84), *The Bartered Bride.*
(H) Christian Science founded by Mary Baker Eddy.
(A) Feodor Dostoyevsky (1821–81), *Crime and Punishment.*

1867

(M) Verdi, *Don Carlo;* Johann Strauss (1825–99), *On the Beautiful Blue Danube;* first collection of Negro spirituals.
(H) Purchase of Alaska; Franz Joseph I of Austria-Hungary (till 1916).
(A) Henrik Ibsen (1828–1906), *Peer Gynt;* Marx, *Das Kapital.*

1868

(M) Brahms, *A German Requiem;* Mage-

lone songs, Op. 33; Gesellschaft für Musik-
forschung founded at Berlin.
(A) Robert Browning (1812–89), *The
Ring and the Book;* Dostoyevsky, *The Idiot.*

1869

(H) Suez Canal opened; first American
transcontinental railroad.
(A) Jules Verne (1828–1905), *Twenty
Thousand Leagues Under the Sea.*

1870

(M) Wagner, *Die Walküre* performed.
(H) Heinrich Schliemann (1822–90) ex-
cavates the site of Troy; Rome becomes the
capital of Italy; Franco-Prussian War; Vatican Council proclaims papal infallibility.

1871

(M) Verdi, *Aïda;* Brahms, *Schicksalslied;*
Edvard Grieg (1843–1907), first lyric pieces
for piano.
(H) Bismarck chancellor of Germany;
Paris Commune, Third Republic.
(A) Ralph Waldo Emerson (1860–1927),
Essays; Darwin, *The Descent of Man.*

1872

(M) Georges Bizet (1838–75), *L'Arlési-
enne;* Bruckner, Mass in F minor.
(A) Eliot, *Middlemarch;* James Whistler
(1834–1903), *Portrait of Miss Alexander;*
Alphonse Daudet (1840–97), *Tartarin de
Tarascon;* Friedrich Nietzsche (1844–1900),
The Birth of Tragedy.

1873

(M) Bruckner, Third Symphony; Brahms,
Quartet, Op. 51.
(A) Edgar Degas (1834–1917), *Place de la
Concorde.*

1874

(M) Modest Mussorgsky (1839–81), *Boris
Godunov, Pictures at an Exhibition;* Verdi,
Requiem; J. Strauss, *Die Fledermaus.*

1875

(M) New Paris opera house opened; Bizet,
Carmen; Smetana, *My Fatherland.*
(A) Mary Baker Eddy (1821–1910), *Sci-
ence and Health;* Tolstoy, *Anna Karenina.*

1876

(M) First Wagner festival at Bayreuth.
(H) Telephone invented by Bell.
(A) Stéphane Mallarmé (1842–98), *L'-
Après-midi d'un Faune;* Mark Twain
(1835–1910), *Tom Sawyer;* Pierre Renoir
(1841–1919), *Le Bal du Moulin de la
Galette.*

1877

(M) Wagner, *Parsifal;* Brahms, First and
Second Symphonies; Camille Saint-Saëns
(1835–1921), *Samson and Delilah.*
(H) Edison invents the phonograph.
(A) Claude Monet (1840–1926), *Gare
Saint-Lazare.*

1878

(M) Brahms, Violin Concerto; James
Bland's (1854–1911) song "Carry Me Back
to Old Virginny" published.

1879

(M) Tchaikovsky, *Eugen Onegin;* Sir
George Grove (1820–1900), *Dictionary of
Music and Musicians.*
(H) Edison invents an improved incan-
descent electric light.
(A) Henry George (1839–97), *Progress and
Poverty;* Ibsen, *The Doll's House;* Dos-
toyevsky, *The Brothers Karamazov.*

1880

(H) Irish insurrection; Pavlov's experiments on conditioned reflexes.
(A) Emile Zola (1840–1902), *Nana.*

1881

(M) Offenbach, *Tales of Hoffmann;* Bos-
ton Symphony founded; John Knowles
Paine (1839–1906), music for *Oedipus
Tyrannus.*
(H) Tsar Alexander II assassinated; Presi-
dent Garfield shot; Panama Canal built.
(A) Renoir, *Luncheon of the Boating
Party;* Henry James (1843–1916), *Portrait
of a Lady.*

1882

(M) Berlin Philharmonia founded.
(H) Koch discovers tuberculosis germs;
Triple Alliance.
(A) Manet, *The Bar at the Folies Ber-
gères.*

1883

(M) Brahms, Third Symphony; Metropolitan Opera opened; Amsterdam Concertge-
bouw founded.
(H) Gottlieb Daimler (1834–1900) patents
automobile motor.
(A) Nietzsche, *Also sprach Zarathustra;*
Robert Louis Stevenson (1850–94), *Treasure Island.*

1884

(M) Jules Massenet (1842–1912), *Manon.*
(H) Pasteur innoculates against rabies;
mean solar day adopted as unit of universal
time.
(A) Auguste Rodin (1840–1917), *The
Burghers of Calais;* Georges Seurat (1859–
91), *Sunday Afternoon on Grande Jatte;*
Twain, *Huckleberry Finn.*

1885

(M) Bruckner, *Te Deum;* J. Strauss, *Der
Zigeunerbaron;* Brahms, Fourth Symphony;
Sir William Gilbert (1836–1911) and Sir
Arthur Sullivan (1842–1900), *The Mikado.*
(H) First American electric street railway;
Brooklyn Bridge built.
(A) Henry Richardson (1838–86) designs
Marshall Field warehouse; Guy de Mau-
passant (1850–93), *Contes et Nouvelles;*

Paul Cézanne (1839–1906), *Mont St. Victoire;* William Dean Howells (1839–1920), *The Rise of Silas Lapham.*

1886

(M) César Franck (1822–90), *Violin Sonata.*
(H) American Federation of Labor organized; Statue of Liberty unveiled in New York Harbor.
(A) Nietzsche, *Jenseits von Gut und Böse;* Pierre Loti (1850–1923), *Pêcheur d'Islande;* Henri Rousseau (1844–1910), *Un Soir de carnaval.*

1887

(M) Verdi, *Otello.*
(A) A. Strindberg (1849–1912), *Der Vater.*

1888

(M) Franck, *Symphony in D minor;* Nikolas Rimsky-Korsakov (1844–1908), *Scheherazade;* Erik Satie (1866–1925), *Gymnopédies;* Hugo Wolf (1860–1903), *Mörike Lieder;* Tchaikovsky, Fifth Symphony.
(H) Kaiser Wilhelm II crowned (till 1918).
(A) Vincent van Gogh (1853–1900), *The Sunflowers.*

1889

(M) Richard Strauss (1864–1949), *Don Juan;* Wolf, *Spanisches Liederbuch;* Mahler, First Symphony.
(H) Paris World's Fair opened; Brazil expels emperor, becomes republic.
(A) Eiffel Tower completed; Henry Adams (1838–1918), *History of the United States* (1889–91); Auguste Rodin (1840–1917), *The Thinker.*

1890

(M) Pietro Mascagni (1863–1945), *Cavalleria Rusticana;* R. Strauss, *Death and Transfiguration;* Tchaikovsky, *Pique Dame.* Alexander Borodin (1833–87), *Prince Igor* (first performance).
(A) Ibsen, *Hedda Gabler.*

1891

(M) Wolf, *Italienisches Liederbuch.*
(A) Sir Arthur Conan Doyle (1859–1930), *Adventures of Sherlock Holmes;* Augustus Saint-Gaudens (1848–1907), Adams Memorial.

1892

(M) Gabriel Fauré (1845–1924), *La Bonne Chanson;* Bruckner, Eighth Symphony; Ruggiero Leoncavallo (1858–1919), *I Pagliacci.*
(A) Cézanne, *The Card Players;* Maurice Maeterlinck (1862–1949), *Pelléas et Mélisande;* Henri de Toulouse-Lautrec (1864–1901), *At the Moulin Rouge.*

1893

(M) Engelbert Humperdinck (1854–1921), *Hansel und Gretel;* Giacomo Puccini (1858–1924), *Manon Lescaut;* Verdi, *Falstaff;*

Tchaikovsky, Sixth Symphony; Horatio Parker (1863–1919), *Hora Novissima.*
(A) Stephen Crane (1871–1900), *The Red Badge of Courage;* Oscar Wilde (1856–1900), *Salome;* Louis Sullivan (1856–1924), Transportation Building at World's Columbian Exposition.

1894

(M) Anton Dvořák (1841–1904,) *New World Symphony;* Debussy, *Prélude à l'après-midi d'un faune.*
(H) Nicholas II crowned; last Czar of Russia; Dreyfus Affair (till 1905).
(A) Rudyard Kipling (1865–1936), *Jungle Book;* George Bernard Shaw (1856–1950), *Candida.*

1895

(M) Strauss, *Till Eulenspiegel.*
(H) Wilhelm Roentgen (1845–1923) discovers X-rays.
(A) Winslow Homer (1836–1910), *Northeaster.*

1896

(M) Brahms, *Vier ernste Gesänge;* Vincent d'Indy (1851–1931), *Istar;* Edward MacDowell (1861–1908), *Indian Suite;* Puccini, *La Bohème;* Wolf, *Der Corregidor.*
(A) Paul Gauguin (1843–1903), *Maternity;* A. E. Housman (1859–1936), *A Shropshire Lad.*

1897

(M) d'Indy, *Fervaal;* Strauss, *Don Quixote;* John Philip Sousa (1845–1932), *The Stars and Stripes Forever.*

1898

(M) Rimsky-Korsakov, *Sadko;* MacDowell, *Sea Pieces;* R. Strauss, *Ein Heldenleben.*
(H) Spanish-American War.
(A) Edmond Rostand (1868–1918), *Cyrano de Bergerac.*

1899

(M) Maurice Ravel (1875–1937), *Pavane pour une infante défunte;* Arnold Schoenberg (1874–1950), *Verklärte Nacht;* Jean Sibelius (1865–1957), *Finlandia;* Scott Joplin (1868–1917), *Maple Leaf Rag.* Internationale Musikgesellschaft founded at Leipzig.
(H) Boer War.

1900

(M) Edward Elgar (1857–1934), *The Dream of Gerontius;* Puccini, *Tosca;* Debussy, *Nocturnes;* Gustave Charpentier (1860–1956), *Louise.* Philadelphia Orchestra founded.
(H) Boxer Rebellion; Count Ferdinand Zeppelin constructs first dirigible; Sigmund Freud (1856–1939) *The Interpretation of Dreams;* Hopkins, first studies of vitamins.
(A) Joseph Conrad (1857–1924), *Lord Jim;* John Singer Sargent (1856–1925), *The Wyndham Sisters;* Tolstoy, *Resurrection.*

1901

(M) Gustav Mahler (1860–1911), Fourth Symphony; Schoenberg, *Gurrelieder;* Sergei Rachmaninov (1873–1943), Second Piano Concerto; Charles Martin Loeffler (1861–1935), *A Pagan Poem.*
(H) Edward VII King of England (till 1910); Guglielmo Marconi transmits wireless telegraph signals across the Atlantic; Max Planck develops quantum theory.
(A) Shaw, *Caesar and Cleopatra;* Aristide Maillol (1861–1944), *Mediterranean;* Thomas Mann (1875–1955), *Buddenbrooks.*

1902

(M) Sibelius, Second Symphony; Debussy, *Pelléas et Mélisande.*
(H) Discovery of radium by Pierre (1859–1906) and Marie (1867–1934) Curie.
(A) Maxim Gorky (1868–1936), *Tales;* Claude Monet (1840–1926), *Waterloo Bridge.*

1903

(M) Leos Janáček (1854–1928), *Její Pastorkyna (Jenufa)* composed; Strauss, *Sinfonia domestica.*
(H) Wilbur (1867–1912) and Orville (1871–1948) Wright, first successful airplane flight; Encyclical *Motu proprio* of Pope Pius X; Twsett, studies in adsorption chromatography.
(A) Shaw, *Man and Superman.*

1904

(M) Puccini, *Madama Butterfly;* Ravel, *Quartet in F.* London Symphony founded.
(H) Russo-Japanese War.
(A) Anton Chekhov (1860–1904), *The Cherry Orchard;* James Barrie (1860–1937), *Peter Pan;* Romain Rolland (1866–1943), *Jean Christophe.*

1905

(M) Debussy, *La Mer;* Strauss, *Salome;* Franz Lehár (1870–1948), *The Merry Widow.*
(H) Norway separates from Sweden; First Russian Revolution. Albert Einstein (1879–1955), special relativity theory; Wilstätter, first chemical investigations in photosynthesis.

1906

(M) First Mozart festival at Salzburg. Schoenberg, *Kammersymphonie,* First Quartet.
(H) San Francisco earthquake and fire.
(A) André Derain (1880–1954), *London Bridge.*

1907

(M) Alexander Scriabin (1872–1915), *Poem of Ecstasy;* Rimsky-Korsakov, *The Golden Cockerel.* First music broadcast.
(H) Second Hague Conference; Triple Entente.
(A) J. M. Synge (1871–1909), *The Playboy of the Western World;* William James

(1842–1910), *Pragmatism;* Pablo Picasso (1881–1973), *Les Demoiselles d'Avignon.*

1908

(M) Ravel, *Rapsodie Espagnole;* Debussy, *Children's Corner;* Béla Bartók (1881–1945), First Quartet.
(H) Model "T" Ford produced.
(A) Rainer Maria Rilke (1875–1926), *Neue Gedichte.*

1909

(M) Schoenberg, Piano Pieces Op. 11; Ralph Vaughan Williams (1872–1958), *Fantasia on a Theme of Thomas Tallis;* Strauss, *Elektra.*
(H) Robert Peary (1856–1920) reaches North Pole.
(A) Frank Lloyd Wright (1869–1959), Robie House, Chicago; Ferenc Molnár (1878–1952), *Liliom.*

1910

(M) Ravel, *Daphnis et Chloé, Ma Mère l'Oye;* Bartók, *Allegro Barbaro;* Igor Stravinsky (1882–1971), *The Fire Bird;* Vaughan Williams, *Sea Symphony;* Mahler's Eighth Symphony performed; Debussy, *Préludes,* Book I.
(H) Discovery of protons and electrons; George V King of England (till 1936).
(A) Bertrand Russell (1872–1970) and Alfred North Whitehead (1861–1947), *Principia Mathematica;* John Masefield (1878–1959), *The Tragedy of Pompey the Great.*

1911

(M) Mahler, *Das Lied von der Erde;* Strauss, *Der Rosenkavalier;* Sibelius, Fourth Symphony; Bartók, *Duke Bluebeard's Castle;* Stravinsky, *Petrushka;* Ravel, *L'Heure espagnole;* Scott Joplin's opera *Treemonisha* performed at New York.
(H) Roald Amundsen (1872–1928) reaches the South Pole.
(A) Edith Wharton (1862–1937), *Ethan Frome;* Giorgio de Chirico (1888–), *La Nostalgie de l'infini.*

1912

(M) Schoenberg, *Pierrot Lunaire;* Strauss, *Ariadne auf Naxos.*
(H) Titanic disaster; Balkan wars.
(A) Marcel Duchamp (1887–1968), *Nude Descending a Staircase;* Wassily Kandinsky (1866–1944), *Improvisation.*

1913

(M) Anton Webern (1883–1945), *Six Orchestral Pieces;* Stravinsky, *Sacre du Printemps;* Manuel de Falla (1876–1946), *La vida breve;* Satie, *Descriptions automatiques.*
(A) D. H. Lawrence (1885–1930), *Sons and Lovers;* Thomas Mann, *Death in Venice;* John Sloane (1871–1955), *Sunday, Women Drying their Hair;* Georges Braque (1881–1963), *Musical Forms;* Marcel Proust (1871–1922), *Remembrance of Things Past.*

1914

(M) Vaughan Williams, *A London Symphony;* W. C. Handy (1873–1958), *St. Louis Blues.*

(H) First World War (till 1918); Panama Canal opened.

(A) Robert Frost (1876–1963), *North of Boston;* Vachel Lindsay (1879–1940), *The Congo and Other Poems;* D. W. Griffith (1875–1948), *The Birth of a Nation;* G. de Chirico (1888–1978), *Mystery and Melancholy of a Street.*

1915

(M) Bartók, *Piano Sonatina;* Debussy, *Etudes;* Max Reger (1873–1916), *Mozart Variations for Orchestra;* Charles Ives (1874–1954), *Concord Sonata;* Ferdinand Morton (1885–1942), *Jelly Roll Blues* published.

(H) Bragg, *X-Rays and Crystal Structure;* T. H. Morgan, *Mechanism of Mendelian Heredity* (theory of the gene).

(A) W. Somerset Maugham (1874–1965), *Of Human Bondage.*

1916

(M) Ernest Bloch (1880–1959), *Schelomo;* Enrique Granados (1894–1928), *Goyescas;* Ives, *Fourth Symphony* composed.

(H) Einstein, general relativity theory; Bolshevik revolution in Russia; Battle of Verdun.

(A) Wright, Imperial Hotel in Tokio.

1917

(M) Ottorino Respighi (1879–1936), *Fountains of Rome;* Schoenberg, *Four Songs for Voice and Orchestra,* Op. 22; Hans Pfitzner (1869–1949), *Palestrina.*

(H) U.S. enters World War I.

(A) Georges Rouault (1871–1958), *Three Clowns;* W. B. Yeats (1865–1939), *Wild Swans at Coole.*

1918

(M) Puccini, *Il Tabarro, Gianni Schicchi;* Stravinsky, *L'Histoire du Soldat;* Sergei Prokofiev (1891–1952), *Classical Symphony.*

(A) Willa Cather (1873–1916), *My Antonia;* Oswald Spengler (1880–1936), *Decline of the West.*

1919

(M) Falla, *The Three-Cornered Hat;* Strauss, *Die Frau ohne Schatten.*

(H) Treaty of Versailles; League of Nations; first Atlantic airplane crossing.

(A) André Gide (1869–1951), *La Symphonie Pastorale;* Fernand Léger (1881–1955), *The City;* Paul Claudel (1868–1955), *Le Père Humilié.*

1920

(M) Gustav Holst (1874–1934), *The Planets;* Ravel, *Le Tombeau de Couperin, La Valse;* Satie, *Socrate.*

(H) First commercial radio broadcast.

(A) Sinclair Lewis (1885–1951), *Main Street.*

1921

(M) Arthur Honegger (1892–1955), *King David;* Prokofiev, *The Love for Three Oranges;* Vaughan Williams, *Pastoral Symphony;* Stravinsky, *Symphony for Wind Instruments;* Janácek, *Katya Kabanova;* Darius Milhaud (1892–1974),*Saudades do Brasil.*

(A) Picasso, *Three Musicians;* Piet Mondriaan (1872–1944), *Painting No. 1;* Charlie Chaplin, *The Kid.*

1922

(M) Schoenberg, method of composing with twelve tones; Carl Nielsen (1865–1931), *Fifth Symphony.*

(H) Fascist revolution in Italy; discovery of insulin.

(A) John Galsworthy (1867–1933), *The Forsyte Saga;* T. S. Eliot (1888–1965), *The Waste Land;* James Joyce (1882–1941), *Ulysses;* Rilke, *Duino Elegies, Sonnets to Orpheus.*

1923

(M) Stravinsky, *Les Noces, Octet;* Sibelius, *Sixth Symphony;* Paul Hindemith (1895–1963), *Das Marienleben;* Honegger, *Pacific 231.*

(H) Hitler-Ludendorff Putsch in Munich.

(A) Paul Klee (1879–1940), *At the Mountain of the Bull.*

1924

(M) George Gershwin (1898–1937), *Rhapsody in Blue;* Schoenberg, *Serenade, Woodwind Quintet;* Puccini, *Turandot.*

(H) Stalin becomes dictator in Russia.

(A) Shaw, *Saint Joan;* Mann, *The Magic Mountain;* Franz Kafka (1883–1924), *The Trial.*

1925

(M) Alban Berg (1885–1935), *Wozzeck;* Bloch, *Concerto Grosso.*

(H) Keilin, discovery of cytochromes and beginning of molecular biology.

(A) Theodore Dreiser (1871–1945), *An American Tragedy;* F. Scott Fitzgerald (1896–1940), *The Great Gatsby.*

1926

(M) Zoltán Kodály (1882–1967), *Háry János;* Dimitri Shostakovich (1906–), *First Symphony.*

(A) Ernest Hemingway (1899–1961), *The Sun Also Rises.* First all-sound films.

1927

(M) Stravinsky, *Oedipus Rex;* Ernest Krenek (1900–), *Jonny spielt auf;* Kurt Weill (1900–50), *Aufstieg und Fall der Stadt Mahaganny.* International Musicological Society founded at Basle.

(H) Charles Lindbergh, solo flight across the Atlantic; first television transmission; W. Heisenberg and others propound "uncertainty principle" in quantum physics.
(A) Sir Jacob Epstein (1880–1959), *Madonna and Child;* Ole Rölvaag (1876–1931), *Giants in the Earth;* Virginia Woolf (1882–1945), *To the Lighthouse;* Eugene O'Neill (1888–1953), *Strange Interlude.*

1928

(M) Kurt Weill (1900–1950), *Threepenny Opera;* Ravel, *Bolero;* Webern, Symphony, Op. 21.
(H) Dirigible Graf Zeppelin crosses Atlantic; first radio broadcast of New York Philharmonic.
(A) Lawrence, *Lady Chatterly's Lover;* Aldous Huxley (1894–1963), *Point Counter Point;* Stephen Vincent Benét (1898–1943), *John Brown's Body.*

1929

(M) Hindemith, *Neues vom Tage.*
(H) New York stock market crash; beginning of world-wide depression.
(A) Mies Van der Rohe (1886–1969), German pavilion; Jean Giraudoux (1882–1944), *Amphitryon 38;* Thomas Wolfe (1900–1938), *Look Homeward, Angel;* William Faulkner (1897–1962), *The Sound and the Fury.*

1930

(M) Milhaud, *Christophe Colomb;* Stravinsky, *Symphony of Psalms;* Prokofiev, Fourth Symphony.
(A) Mondriaan, *Fox Trot;* Edward Hopper (1882–1967), *Early Sunday Morning;* Grant Wood (1892–1942), *American Gothic;* José Ortega y Gasset (1883–1954), *The Revolt of the Masses;* Hart Crane (1899–1932), *The Bridge.*

1931

(M) William Walton (1902–1983), *Belshazzar's Feast;* Gershwin, *Of Thee I Sing;* Edgard Varèse (1885–1965), *Ionisation.*
(H) Japan invades Manchuria.
(A) O'Neill, *Mourning Becomes Electra.*

1932

(M) Prokofiev, Fifth Piano Concerto; Ravel, two piano concertos.
(H) Discovery of the neutron.
(A) Gertrude Stein (1874–1946), *Matisse, Picasso and Gertrude Stein.*

1933

(M) Hindemith, *Mathis der Maler;* Strauss, *Arabella;* Stravinsky, *Perséphone;* Shostakovich, First Piano Concerto.
(H) Franklin D. Roosevelt (1882–1945) President of the United States; Adolf Hitler (1889–1945) Chancellor of Germany.
(A) Joan Miró (1893–1983), *Composition;* Arnold Toynbee (1899–), *A Study of History;* André Malraux (1901–76), *La Condition humaine.*

1934

(M) Virgil Thomson (1898–), *Four Saints in Three Acts.* American Musicological Society founded at New York.
(H) Adrian, studies in the electric nature of nerve impulses; Joliot, discovery of induced radioactivity.
(A) Mann, *Joseph and His Brothers.*

1935

(M) Berg, *Violin Concerto;* Gershwin, *Porgy and Bess;* Honegger, *Joan of Arc at the Stake.*
(H) Italy invades Ethiopia.
(A) Eliot, *Murder in the Cathedral;* José Orozco (1883–1949), *Man in Four Aspects.*

1936

(M) Prokofiev, *Peter and the Wolf.* 440 adopted as standard pitch.
(H) Spanish Civil War.
(A) John Dos Passos (1896–1970), *U. S. A.*

1937

(M) Carl Orff (1895–1982),*Carmina Burana;* Berg, *Lulu;* Shostakovich, Fifth Symphony.
(H) Japan invades China. Andersson, discovery of positive electrons and mesons; Krebs, metabolic pathways; Hill, demonstration of chloroplast reaction in plants.
(A) Picasso, *Guernica;* John Marquand (1893–1960), *The Late George Apley.*

1938

(M) Walter Piston (1894–), *The Incredible Flutist;* Bartók, *Violin Concerto.*
(H) Hans Bethe, *Energy Production in Stars;* discovery of nuclear fission; development of penicillin.
(A) Raoul Dufy (1879–1953), *Regatta.*

1939

(M) Bartók, Sixth Quartet; Prokofiev, *Alexander Nevsky;* Roy Harris (1898–1979), Third Symphony.
(H) World War II (till 1945).
(A) Joyce, *Finnegans Wake;* C. S. Forester (1899–1966), *Captain Horatio Hornblower;* John Steinbeck (1902–1968), *The Grapes of Wrath.*

1940

(M) Stravinsky, *Symphony in C Major.*
(H) First radio broadcast of the Metropolitan Opera; Roosevelt elected to third term; first commercial electron microscope; microwave radar.
(A) Hemingway, *For Whom the Bell Tolls.*

1941

(M) Aaron Copland (1900–), *Piano Sonata.*
(H) United States enters war; Atlantic Charter.

1942

(M) Shostakovich, Seventh Symphony; Heitor Villa-Lobos (1887–1959), *Choros No. 11.*
(H) United Nations Alliance.

1943
(M) Vaughan Williams, Fifth Symphony.
(A) Marc Chagall (1887–), *Crucifixion*.

1944
(M) Copland, *Appalachian Spring*; Bartók, *Concerto for Orchestra*; Hindemith, *Ludus Tonalis*; Michael Tippett (1905–), *A Child of Our Time*.
(H) Roosevelt elected to fourth term; Allied armies invade Germany.

1945
(M) Benjamin Britten (1913–), *Peter Grimes*; Bartók, Third Piano Concerto; Strauss, *Metamorphosen*.
(H) Surrender of Germany; atomic bomb used against Japan; New York chosen as seat of United Nations. Radio astronomy; jet planes and rockets.

1946
(M) Shostakovich, Ninth Symphony; Britten, *The Rape of Lucretia*; Copland, Third Symphony.
(H) First Assembly of United Nations; Nuremberg trials.
(A) Le Corbusier (1887–1965), Unité d'Habitation, Marseilles; Dylan Thomas (1914–1953), *Deaths and Entrances*.

1947
(M) Prokofiev, *War and Peace*; Piston, Third Quartet.
(H) Marshall Plan; independence of India. Perutz, X-ray studies on crystalline proteins.
(A) Tennessee Williams (1914–1983), *A Streetcar Named Desire*.

1948
(M) Piston, Third Symphony; Stravinsky, *Mass*; Vaughan Williams, Sixth Symphony; John Cage, *Sonatas and Interludes* for prepared piano.

1949
(M) Orff, *Antigonae*; Samuel Barber (1910–1981), *Knoxville: Summer of 1915*; Olivier Messaien (1908–), *Turangalila Symphony*.
(H) North Atlantic Defense Pact; Communist government in China.
(A) George Orwell (1903–1950), *1984*; Arthur Miller (1916–), *Death of a Salesman*.

1950
(M) Honegger, Fifth Symphony; Gian Carlo Menotti (1911–), *The Consul*; Luigi Dallapiccola (1904–75), *Il Prigioniero*.
(H) Korean War; hydrogen bomb.
(A) Eliot, *The Cocktail Party*.

1951
(M) Menotti, *Amahl and the Night Visitors*; Stravinsky, *The Rake's Progress*; Pierre Boulez (1925–), *Polyphonie X*.
(H) NATO formed from North Atlantic Pact.

(A) Jacques Lipchitz (1891–), *Birth of Venus*.

1952
(M) Columbia University Electronic Studio founded.
(A) Alexander Calder (1898–), *Giraffe*; Albert Camus (1913–1960), *L'Homme revolté*; Eliot, *Complete Plays and Poems*; André Maurois (1885–1967), *Lélia, ou la vie de George San*; Helen Frankenthaler (1928–), *Mountains and Sea*.

1953
(M) Karlheinz Stockhausen (1928–), *Kontra-Punkte*.
(H) Malenkov succeeds Stalin in Russia. Watson-Crick model of DNA molecule.
(A) Reg Butler (1917–), *The Unknown Political Prisoner*; Churchill, *History of the Second World War*; Samuel Beckett (1906–), *En attendant Godot*.

1954
(H) Gordon, Zeiger, and Townes, molecular amplification by stimulated emission of radiation (Maser); U. S. Supreme Court decision outlawing school segregation.
(A) e. e. cummings (1894–1962), *Poems 1923–1954*; Thomas, *Under Milk Wood*; Morris Lewis (1912–62), *First Veil*.

1955
(M) Luigi Nono (1924–), *Incontri*; Boulez, *Le Marteau sans maitre*.
(H) E. R. Andrew, *Nuclear Magnetic Resonance*.
(A) W. H. Auden (1907–1973), *The Shield of Achilles*.

1956
(M) Stravinsky, *Canticum sacrum*; Ernst Pepping (1901–), *Te Deum*; Stockhausen, *Gesang der Jünglinge*.
(H) Revolt in Hungary.

1957
(M) Stravinsky, *Agon*; Wolfgang Fortner, (1907–), *Bluthochzeit*; Francis Poulenc (1899–1963), *Dialogues des Carmélites*; Hindemith, *Die Harmonie der Welt*; Leonard Bernstein (1918–), *West Side Story*.
(H) First Sputnik launched; International Geophysical Year begins; T. D. Lee and C. N. Yang awarded Nobel Prize for discovery of principle of non-conservation of parity.

1958
(M) Stravinsky, *Threni*; Witold Lutoslawski (1913–), *Funeral Music*; Messiaen, *Catalogue des oiseaux*.
(H) Explorer I (U.S. satellite); voyage of the *Nautilus*; Khrushchev becomes Premier of U.S.S.R.

1959
(M) Orff, *Oedipus der Tyrann*.

(H) First moon rockets; studies in the structure of viruses.

1960

(M) Copland, *Nonet for Strings;* Messiaen, *Chronochromie;* Boulez, *Pli selon pli;* Frank Martin (1890–), *Mystère de la Nativité;* Niccolo Castiglione (1932–), *Aprèsludes.*
(H) 25 artificial satellites now in orbit; first working laser.
(A) Jean Tinguely (1925–), *Homage to New York.*

1961

(M) Elliott Carter (1908–), *Double Concerto;* Nono, *Intolleranza 1960;* Krzysztof Penderecki (1933–), *Lament for the Victims of Hiroshima;* Hans Werner Henze (1926–), *Elegy for Young Lovers.*
(H) Peace Corps established; Berlin Wall erected; first manned space flights.
(A) Claes Oldenburg's (1929–) "Store" opens in New York; "Art of Assemblage" show at Museum of Modern Art; David Smith (1906–1965), "Cubi" sculptures.

1962

(M) Britten, *War Requiem;* Stravinsky, *A Sermon, a Narrative and a Prayer;* Yannis Xenakis, (1922–), *Stratégie.*
(H) Vatican Council II convenes; Cuban missile crisis.
(A) Edward Albee (1928–), *Who's Afraid of Virginia Woolf?*

1963

(M) Witold Lutoslawski, *Trois Poèmes d'Henri Michaux.*
(H) President J. F. Kennedy assassinated; increasing U. S. involvement in Vietnam.
(A) Rachel Carson (1917–1964), *Silent Spring.*

1964

(M) Roger Sessions (1896–), *Montezuma;* Yannis Xenakis (1922–), *Strategy;* György Ligeti (1923–), *Requiem;* Britten, *Curlew River.*
(H) Kosygin becomes Premier of U.S.S.R.

1965

(M) First performance of Ives's Fourth Symphony.
(H) Gemini space vehicles; Civil Rights march in Alabama.
(A) *The Autobiography of Malcolm X;* Peter Weiss (1916–), *The Persecution and Assassination of Jean-Paul Marat* (Marat-Sade); Hans Hofmann (1880–1966) paints *Renate* series.

1966

(M) Penderecki, *St. Luke Passion;* Gunther Schuller (1925–), *The Visitation;* Britten, *The Burning Fiery Furnace.*
(A) Harold Pinter (1930–), *The Homecoming.*

1967

(M) Alberto Ginastera (1916–1983), *Bomarzo* (opera); Copland, *Inscape;* Stockhausen *Hymnen;* the Beatles, *Sergeant Pepper's Lonely Hearts Club Band.*
(H) Israeli-Arab Six-Day War. Development of astrophysics; G. and M. Burbidge, *Quasi-Stellar Objects* ("quasars"); J. C. Lilly, *The Mind of the Dolphin.* Length of one second of time now determinable within limit of error of 1-2 parts in 10^{10}.

1968

(M) Luciano Berio (1925–), *Sinfonia;* Orff, *Prometheus;* Britten, *The Prodigal Son.*
(H) Soviet invasion of Czechoslovakia; student uprisings in France; massive anti-war protests in U.S.A.; assassinations of Martin Luther King and Robert F. Kennedy.

1969

(M) Karlheinz Stockhausen (1928–), *Stimmung.*
(H) First men on the moon.

1970

(M) Roger Sessions, *When Lilacs last in the Dooryard Bloomed;* Peter Maxwell Davies (1934–), *Taverner.*
(A) Alvin Toffler (1928–), *Future Shock;* Charles Reich (1928–), *The Greening of America.*

1971

(M) International Josquin Congress at New York.
(H) Indo-Pakistan war; independence of Bangladesh.

1972

(M) Complete Works of Scott Joplin published at New York.
(H) Watergate; Black September terrorist killings at Munich Olympics; Pioneer 10 launched.

1973

(M) Opening of Sydney Opera House; Xenakis, *Polytope de Cluny.*
(H) End of U.S. involvement in Viet Nam.
(A) Aleksandr Solzhenitsyn (1918–), *The Gulag Archipelago;* Thomas Pynchon (1937–), *Gravity's Rainbow.*

1974

(M) Arnold Schoenberg Institute established; Ives and Schoenberg centennial celebrations.
(H) Hearst kidnapping; USSR deports Solzhenitsyn; President Nixon resigns.
(A) Opening of Hirshhorn Museum, Washington, D.C.

1975

(M) International Haydn Conference held in Washington, D.C.

(H) War in Cambodia ends; International Women's Year; Suez Canal reopens.

1976

(M) Elliott Carter, *Brass Quintet;* Britten, *String Quartet No. 3.*

(H) U.S. Bicentennial celebrations; earthquake in Guatemala kills an estimated 23,000 people; death of Mao-Tse Tung; Carter elected president.

1977

(M) Elliott Carter, *Symphony of Three Orchestras;* opening of the Centre National d'Art et de Culture Georges Pompidou; Paris: Boulez founds IRCAM (Institut de Recherche et de Coordination Acoustique/ Musique).

(H) Detection of rings around the planet Uranus; blackouts in New York City; atrocities in Uganda under Amin regime; Orient Express makes last run between Paris and Istanbul; Panama Canal Treaty signed.

(A) Televised dramatization of Alex Haley's *Roots* sets new records; tomb of Alexander the Great's father uncovered.

1978

(M) Penderecki, *Paradise Lost;* Druckman, Viola Concerto.

(H) First test-tube baby; discovery of Pluto's moon "Charon;" Pope John Paul II elected.

(A) Opening of the East Wing of the Nattional Gallery, Washington, D.C.

1979

(M) Premiere of completed *Lulu;* Dominick Argento, *Miss Havisham's Fire.*

(H) Khomeini leads revolution in Iran; U.S. hostages taken.

1980

(M) Eugene Ormandy retires; Metropolitan Opera Season cancelled; John Williams leads Boston Pops.

(H) Polish workers strike; Russia invades Afghanistan.

(A) Major retrospective Picasso exhibit at Museum of Modern Art, New York.

Index

Page numbers in **boldface** refer to examples.
Those in *italics* refer to illustrations.
Abgesang, 39
Absalon fili mi, Josquin des Prez, 126, **126**
Absolute musicality, 311
Académie de Poésie et de Musique, 152
Accidentals, *musica ficta* and, 84, 110, 131–32, 167
Ach, susse Seel', Hassler, 150
Ach Schatz, Hassler, 150
Adam de la Halle, 37, *37*
Adam of St. Victor, 29
Adelaide, Sartorio, 211
Adieu ces bons vins de Lannoys, Dufay, 101
Affections, in Baroque music, 182
Afro-American Symphony, Still, 436
Agnus Dei, 21, 26–27
Agréments, 208, 235, 244
Agricola, Alexander, 120, 123
Ahime, dov'é 'l bel viso, Arcadelt, 144–45, **144**
Aïda, Verdi, 387
Air, French, 314
Albéniz, Isaac, 415
Album for the Young, Schumann, 360
Alceste, Lully, *213*
Alceste (Calzabigi), Gluck, *292*, 293
Alcina, Handel, 291
Alexander Nevsky, Prokofiev, 431
Alexander's Feast, Handel, 274
Allegro barbaro, Bartók, 427
Alleluia, 10, 20, 25, 26, 28
Alleluia Pascha nostrum, 51–54, *51*, **52**, **53–54**
Allemande (*alman*), 209
Alle psallite—Alleluia, 90
Allgemeine musikalische Zeitung, 270
Alma Redemptoris Mater, 18
Alma Redemptoris Mater, Dufay, 102
Almira, Handel, 270
Also sprach Zarathustra, Nietzsche, 401
Also sprach Zarathustra, Strauss, 402, *403*
Amadis, Lully, 215, **215**
Amati, Niccolò, 238
Ambrose, Saint, 9, 10
Ambrosian Chant and liturgy, 9
Amor Brujo, El, Falla, 415
Ancient Voices of Children (García Lorca), Crumb, 468
Andante and Rondo Capriccioso, Mendelssohn, 360
Anerio, Felice, 168
Anglebert, Jean Henri d', 208
Anglican music, 163
Animuccia, Giovanni, 168
Années de pélerinage, Liszt, 364

Anthems, 163–64
Anti-art, 473
Antiphona ad introitum, *20*
Antiphonale (Antiphonal), 17, 25
Antiphonal psalmody, 7, 12
Antiphons, 10–11, 25
Apollo, worship of, *3*, 4, 10
Appalachian Spring, Copland, 435, **435**
Appassionata Sonata, Beethoven, 336
Appoggiaturas, 242
Aquinas, Saint Thomas, 29
Aquitanian organum, 46–49
Arabella (von Hofmannsthal), Strauss, 405
Arcadelt, Jacob, 144, 164
Aria di Ruggiero, 206
Ariadne auf Naxos (von Hofmannsthal), Strauss, 405
Arias:
  eighteenth-century, 290–91, 296, 297
  recitative vs., 186, 196
Ariettes, 295
Arioso, 213, 214
Ariosti, Attilio, 206
Armide, Lully, 214, 215
Arne, Thomas Augustine, *279*, 295
Ars antiqua, 58–69
Ars cantus mensurabilis, Franco of Cologne, 65
Ars nova, 70–77
Ars nova, Philippe de Vitry, 70
Ars novae musicae, Jean de Muris, 70
Art of Fugue, The, Bach, 259, 264
Art of Playing on the Violin, The, Geminiani, 244
Astronomy, music and, 15
Athematic music, 465
Atonality, 453–54, 460
Attaingnant, Pierre, 133, *135*, 140
Auber, Daniel François Esprit, operas of, 381, 382
Aucun vont—Amor qui cor—Kyrie, 63–64, **63–64**
Auden, W. H., 446
Augenlicht, Das, Webern, 461
Augustine, Saint, 10n
Aulos, 3, *3*, 4, 8, *8*, 10
Aus Italien, Strauss, 402
Available Forms, Brown, *471*
Ave Maria, Josquin des Prez, 127
Ave Sanctissima Mass, la Rue, 129
Ave verum, Mozart, 316
Ayres, 156, 204

Babbitt, Milton, 465, 468
Bach, Carl Philipp Emanuel, 285, 288, 296

Bach, Carl Philipp Emanuel (*continued*)
  Haydn influenced by, 304
  oratorios of, 285, 297
  sonatas of, 285
Bach, Johann Christian, 312
Bach, Johann Sebastian, 253, 256–70, 281,
    342, 357, 361
  cantatas of, 264–67
  chorale preludes of, 234, 259–60
  clavier music of, 260–63
  influence and significance of, 297, 317, 331
  Mass of, 268
  motets of, 267
  organ music of, 257–60
  Passions of, 159, **159**, 227, 270
Bach, Wilhelm Friedemann, 258
Bagpipe, 42
Baïf, Jean-Antoine de, 152
Baiser de la Fée, Le, Stravinsky, 445
Balakirev, Mily, 406
Ballades:
  of Chopin, 362
  of Machaut, 74–75
Ballades notées, 74
Ballad opera, 295
Ballads:
  medieval, 37
  of Romantic period, 361
Ballate, 78
Ballet:
  in post-Romantic period, 415, 422
  of Tchaikovsky, 380
  in twentieth century, 431, 434, 441, 444,
    446
Balleti, 150, 152, 153
Balletts (fa-la's), 153
Balli, 195
Ballo in Maschera, Un, Verdi, 387
Bamberg Codex, *67*
Banchetto musicale, Schein, 207
Barbiere di Siviglia, Il, Paisiello, 294
Barbiere di Siviglia, Il, Rossini, 384, 385
Barcarolle, Chopin, 361, *361*
Baroque music, 181–247
  affections in, 182
  cantata in, 196, 201, 218–21, 227–28, 264–
    67
  church music in, 196–202, 221–29, 259–60,
    264–69
  Classical period compared to, 281, 285
  concerto in, 250–53, 263
  counterpoint in, 185, 196
  dualism in, 183
  historical background of, 181
  instrumental music in, 202–10, 230–47,
    250–53, 257–64, 271
  opera in, 186–92, 211–18, 249, 272
  oratorios in, 198–99, 201, 222–23
  Passions in, 159, **159**, 201, 228–29, 268
  vocal chamber music in, 192–96
Baros, de mon dan covit, 38
Bartered Bride, The, Smetana, 411
Bartók, Bela, 412, 426–30
  chords of, 428–29, **429**
Basse fondamentale, 253
Basso continuo, 183–84, 192, 195, 202, 239
Bassoon, 184
Bastien und Bastienne, Mozart, 312
Bay Psalm Book, 161

Beethoven, Ludwig van, 280, 288, 311, 324–
    43
  church music of, 269, 324, 341–43
  concertos of, 324, 336–37
  deafness of, 326–27
  Haydn's influence on, 310, 324
  influence on other composers of, 379, 398–
    99
  opera of, 295, 332
  quartets of, 327, 332–33
  sonatas of, 284, 324, 327, 336, 338, 359, **399**
  style periods of, 328
  symphonies of, 289, 324, 327, 328, 342, 373,
    402
  use of variation in work of, 337–38
Beggar's Opera, The, 295
Bélanger, François-Joseph, *292*
Belle bonne, Baude Cordier, 81*n*
Bellini, Vincenzo, 385–86
Bells, 28, 87
Benedicamus Domino, 21, 48, 62
Benedict, Saint, Order of, 11–12
Benedict, Sir Julius, 326
Benedictus, 20
Benevoli, Orazio, 197
Benvenuto Cellini, Berlioz, 383
Berceuse, Chopin, 361
Berg, Alban, 395, 402, 425, 455, 459–60, 469
  operas of, 459
  Violin Concerto of, 460, **460**
Berlin school, 288
Berlioz, Hector, 311, 397, 416
  choral works of, 353
  operas of, 293, 383
  symphonies of, 371, 374–6
Bethge, Hans, 400
Billy the Kid, Copland, 434
Binchois, Gilles, *98*, 101–2, 106, 119
Bird quartet, Haydn, 304
Bizet, George, 383
Black folk spirituals, 380, 413
Bland, James, 413
Blow, John, 216, 217
B-minor Mass, 268
Boccaccio, Giovanni, 78
Boccherini, Luigi, 289–90
Boethius, 14–15, 107
Bohème, La, Puccini, 423
Bohemian music:
  medieval and Renaissance, 162
  of nineteenth century, 411
Böhm, Georg, 234
Boieldieu, François Adrien, 382
Bomarzo, Ginastera, 436
Bononcini, Giovanni, 291
Bordoni, Faustina, 291
Boris Godunov, Mussorgsky, 407, *407*, **408**,
    409
Borodin, Alexander, 406
Bortniansky, Dimitri, 355
Boulez, Pierre, 442, 464, 466, *474*
Bourgeois, Loys, 161
Boy Was Born, A, Britten, 434
Brahms, Johannes, 401
  chamber music of, 369–71
  choral works of, 354
  clarinet music of, 371
  Lieder of, 353
  piano music of, 365

symphonies of, 377–79, **378**
Breviary (*Breviarium*), 21
Britten, Benjamin, 433–34
Brockes, B. H., 268
Brown, Earle, *Available Forms,* **471**
Bruck, Arnold von, 160
Bruckner, Anton, 395
  choral works of, 357
  Mahler influenced by, 401
  symphonies of, 379–80
Buch der Hängenden Gärten, Das, Schoenberg, 453
Büchner, Georg, 469
Bull, John, 172
Burden, 96
Burgundian School, 97–106
  cadence formulas of, 100, **101**
  chansons, of, 101, 118–20
  masses of, 102–6
  motets of, 102
  voice combination in, 100, 103
Burnacini, Ludovico, *191*
Burney, Charles, 288
  on definition of music, 280
Buti, Francesco, 190
Buus, Jacques, 178
Buxtehude, Dietrich, 210, 225, 231, 232
Byrd, William, 156, 170, 176
Byron, George Gordon, Lord, 375
Byzantine music, 8

Cabezón, Antonio de, 143
Caccia, trecento, 77, 79
Caccini, Giulio, 186–87
Cadences:
  Burgundian, 100, **101**
  chromatically altered, 84, **84**
  double leading-tone, 84, **84**
  Landini, 78–80, 100
  open (*ouvert*) and closed (*clos*), 40
  thirteenth-century, 64
Cadenzas, Baroque, 242–43
Cage, John, 466, 473
Caldara, Antonio, 222
Calisto, Cavalli, 190
Calm Sea and Prosperous Voyage, Mendelssohn, 372
Calvin, Jean, 161
Calzabigi, Raniero, 292
Cambert, Robert, 214
Campion, Thomas, 156
Campra, André, 437
Cancrizans (crab) canon, 115
Canon, 78, 90, 114–16, 221
  cancrizans (crab), 115
  double, 115
  of the Mass, 21
  mensuration, 115
  retrograde, 115
Canonical Hours, 17–18, 23–25
Cantata profana, Bartók, 428
Cantatas:
  Baroque, 196, 201, 218–21, 227–28, 264–67
  of J. S. Bach, 228, 264–67
  in Lutheran church music, 228
Canti B, 120
Canti C, 120
Canti carnascialeschi, 128, 133
Canticum sacrum, Stravinsky, 446, 452

Cantilena, 67–68, 92
Cantiones sacrae, Byrd, 170
Cantiones sacrae, Schütz, 200, **200**
Cantor, 11–12
Cantus firmus:
  in discanting, 92
  instrumental, 60, 171
  in Masses, 103–6, 118, 136
  migrant, 93
  in motets, 59, 96
  in organum, 57
Cantus planus, see Chant, Gregorian
Cantus prius factus, 58, 92
Canzona, Macque, **173**
Canzona, Trabaci, **205**
Canzonas, 140, 172–74, 202, 204, 205, 206, 239
Canzonette, 150, 153
Capella, Martianus, 14
Capriccio espagnol, Rimsky-Korsakov, 410
Capriccios, 174, 202
Caput Mass, Obrecht, 118, **119**
Caput Mass, Ockeghem, 113, 114
Caput Mass, pseudo-Dufay, 104
Cardillac, Hindemith, 439
Carissimi, Giacomo, 196, 198, 219, 222
Carmen, Bizet, 383
Carnaval, Schumann, 360
Carols, English, 95–96
Carter, Elliott, 436
Caserta, Anthonello da, 81
Castor et Pollux, Rameau, 255
Castrati, 291
Cavalieri, Emilio de', 198
Cavalleria rusticana, Mascagni, 423
Cavalli, Pier Francesco, 190, 212
Cavata, 266
Cecilian movement, 354
Cello, *see* Violoncello
Cento concerti ecclesiastici, Viadana, 197
Ceremony of Carols, A, Britten, 434
Certon, Pierre, 133
Cesti, Antonio, 191, 219
Chabanon, Michel Paul Gui de, 278
Chaconne, 193, **194**, 202, 214, 236, 261
Chamber Concerto, Berg, 469
Chamber music:
  Baroque, 238–47
  of Classical period, 289–90
  see also Instrumental music; *specific musical forms*
Chambonnières, Jacques Champion de, 208
Champion des Dames, Le, 98
Chandos anthems, Handel, 274
Chanson balladées, 73
Chanson de geste, 36
Chansonniers, 37
Chansons:
  Burgundian, 101
  French sixteenth-century, 133–34, 152
  Netherlands School, 119–20, 152
  troubadour and trouvère, 37–39
Chansons madécasses, Ravel, 423
Chant, Ambrosian, 9
Chant, Gregorian, 12–13, 16–36
  classifications of, 23–30
  liturgical books of, 21
  manuscript sources of, 21–22, 34–35
  for Masses, 20–21, 23
  modern status of, 16–17

Chant, Gregorian (continued)
  music theory and, 30–34
  notation of, 34
  for Offices, 17–20, 23–25
  St. Gregory and, 12
  text-setting in, 23
  tropes and sequences in, 27–28
Chantilly manuscript, 81n
Char, René, 466
Charlemagne, 21
Charpentier, Gustave, 416
Charpentier, Marc-Antoine, 220
Chasse, La, Haydn, 304
Chávez, Carlos, 436
Cherubini, Luigi, 293, 355
Chest, of instruments, 138
Children's Corner, Debussy, 420–21, 423
Chodowiecki, Daniel Nikolaus, 281
Choirbooks, 67
Chopin, Frederic, 311, 410
  piano music of, 361–63
Chorale fantasias, 233
Chorale motets, 160
Chorale partitas, 202, 233, 235
Chorale preludes, 202, 234, 259–60
Chorales (Chorals), 158–60, 227, 234, 266–67
Chorales, Franck, 366
Chorale settings, polyphonic, 159–60
Chorale variations, 255
Choralis Constantinus, Isaac and Senfl, 128
Choral music, nineteenth-century, 353–57
Christ lag in Todesbanden, 158
Christ lag in Todesbanden (Cantata No. 4),
  Bach, 266
Christmas Oratorio, Bach, 267
Christmas Oratorio, Schütz, 201
Christophe Columb, Milhaud, 438
Chromaticism:
  fourteenth-century, 84–85, 84
  sixteenth-century, 148, 176
  seventeenth-century, 203
Chronochromie, Messiaen, 443
Church modes, 30–34, 31
Church music, Baroque, 196–202, 221–29,
  259–60, 264–69
  Anglican, 223
  Lutheran, 259–60, 264–69
  Roman Catholic, 196–98, 221–23
Church music, Classical, 296–97
Church music, early Christian, 6–15
  anti-pagan attitude of, 6–7
  Byzantine, 8
  hymns in, 9–10
  Jewish liturgical influence in, 6–7, 8, 10
  Roman dominance of, 11–12
  trained choirs in, 10, 13–14
  see also Chant, Gregorian; Liturgy, Ro-
  man; Masses; Offices, liturgical
Church music, Lutheran, 157–60, 198–202,
  264–69
Church music, nineteenth-century, 353–57
Church music, Reformation, 157–64
  Anglican, 162, 163
  Counter-Reformation and, 164–71
  French (Calvinist), 161
  Lutheran, 157–60
Church music, twentieth-century, 446
Ciacona, see Chaconne
Cimarosa, Domenico, 294
Cinq rechants, Messiaen, 443

Classical music, eighteenth-century, see
  Eighteenth-century Classical music
Classical Symphony, Prokofiev, 431
Classicism:
  neo-Classicism and, 436–42
  Romantic, 377
  Romanticism compared with, 344–49
Claudel, Paul, 437, 438
Clausulae, 54, 58–59
Clavecin, 139, 208, 256
Clavicembalo, 139
Clavichord, 286
Clavier, 139, 184, 235
Clavier music, 235–38, 260–63, 285–86, 296,
  308–9
Clavier Übung, Bach, 258, 260, 261, 269, 441
Clemens, Jacobus (Clemens non Papa), 131,
  161
Clementi, Muzio, 329
Clemenza di Tito, La, Mozart, 321
Clérambault, Louis Nicolas, 220
Cocteau, Jean, 421, 438, 446
Coffee Cantata, Bach, 267
Collects, 20
Color, in isorhythm, 71–72
Coloratura, 211
Combattimento di Tancredi e Colorinda,
  Monteverdi, 195
Comic opera, 284, 293
Commercial composer, defined, 315
Communion, 21, 25, 27
Compère, Loyset, 120
Concertato style, 192, 194, 195, 196, 197–98,
  212, 244
Concert champêtre, Poulenc, 439
Concerted church music, 225, 227
Concerto for Orchestra, Bartók, 427, 428,
  430
Concerto for Orchestra, Carter, 436
Concerto for the Left Hand, Ravel, 422
Concerto grosso, 246
Concertos:
  Baroque, 246–47, 250–53, 263, 271
  Classical vs. Baroque, 320
  of Mozart, 316, 319–21
  sacred, 199, 200–1
  sonata distinguished from, 285
  symphonies influenced by, 285
  twentieth-century, 428, 434, 452, 469
Concerts, public, rise of, 279, 279
Concertstück, Weber, 358
Conditor alme siderum, Dufay, 102
Conductus:
  monophonic, 35–36
  polyphonic, 58, 90
Consolations, Liszt, 364
Consonanze stravaganti, Macque, 175, 176
Consort, of instruments, 138, 204
Consort songs, 156, 164
Constantine, Emperor, 1, 8
Contenance angloise, 93
Continuum, pitch as, 469
Contrafacta, 157, 158
Copland, Aaron, 434–35
Coprario (Cooper), John, 204
Cordier, Baude, 81n
Corelli, Arcangelo, 240–41, 246, 257, 271
Coriolan overture, Beethoven, 329, 335
Cori spezzati, 178
Coronation Concerto, Mozart, 320

Coronation Mass in C, Mozart, 316
Così fan tutte, Mozart, 319, 321, 322
Costeley, Guillame, 152
Council of Trent (1545–1563), 29, 164
Counterpoint:
  Baroque, 185, 196
  in Beethoven, 329
  in Brahms, 377
  in Mozart, 313
Counter-Reformation music, 164–71
Couperin, François, 235–36, 243, 416, 421
Couperin, Louis, 208
Courante, 209, 235
Cowell, Henry, 466
Crab (cancrizans) canon, 115
Creation, The, Haydn, 309, 350
Création du monde, La, Milhaud, 437
Crécquillon, Thomas, 135
Credo, 20, 26
Cromornes, 138
Crucifixus, Bach, 269
Cruda Amarilli, Monteverdi, 148, **149**
Crumb, George, 468
Cunning Little Vixen, The, Janáček, 412
Cymbals, 87
Czayner Thancz, John of Lublin, **142**
Czech Brethren (Moravian Brethren), 162–63
Czech music, nationalism in, 411–12, 426
Czerny, Carl, 336

Dame blanche, La, Boieldieu, 382
Dame gentil, Anthonello da Caserta, 82, **82–83**
Damnation of Faust, The, Berlioz, 376, 383
Dance music:
  Baroque, 202, 208, 214, 235–38
  early ballate as, 78
  fourteenth- and fifteenth-century, 87
  of Lully, 214
  medieval, 40
  Renaissance, 140–41, *141,* 174–75
Dances, paired, *141,* 174
Dance Suite, Bartók, 428, 430
Danican-Philidor, François André, 295
Danket dem Herrn, denn er ist sehr freundlich, Buxtehude, 233
Dannhauser, Joseph, *363*
Dante, 15, 69
Daphnis et Chloé, Ravel, 422
Da Ponte, Lorenzo, 321
Dargomizhsky, Alexander, 410
Darmstadt group, 464
Datemi pace, 146
David, King, *41*
Death and the Maiden, Schubert, 366–67
Debussy, Claude-Achille, 376, 419, 418–21
  influence of, 415, 454
  Mussorgsky as influence on, 409, 418, 419–20
  opera of, 421
  piano music of, 419–20
Decameron, Boccaccio, 78
De institutione musica, Boethius, 15
Delalande, Michel-Richard, 222
Déserts, Varèse, 466
Des Knaben Wunderhorn, Mahler, 400, 401
Des Prez, Josquin, 118, 119, 120–28, 130, 157
  chansons of, 120–21

Masses of, 122–23
motets of, 122
Determinacy, 469
Deudsche Messe, Luther, 157
Diabelli variations, Beethoven, 329, 336, 338
Diaghilev, Sergei, *422,* 444
Dialogues between God and a Believing Soul, Hammerschmidt, 225, **226**
Dialogues des Carmélites (Bernanos) Poulenc, 439
Dichterliebe (Heine), Schumann, 353
Dido and Aeneas (Tate), Purcell, 216–17
Die mit Tränen säen, Weckmann, 225
Dietrich, Sixtus, 160
Dioclesian, Purcell, 217
Discant, 47, 54, 58–59
Dissonance, 464
Dissonance Quartet, Mozart, 318
Ditters von Dittersdorf, Karl, 296
Divertimento, Bartók, 428
Divine Comedy, Dante, 15, 69
Dodecachordon, Glarean, 109n
Dodecaphony, 425, 426, 464
Donati, Baldassare, 178
Don Carlos, Verdi, 387
Don Giovanni (da Ponte), Mozart, 308, 321, *322,* 350
Donizetti, Gaetano, 385
Don Juan, Strauss, 402
Don Pasquale, Donizetti, 385
Don Quixote, Strauss, 402
Doppelgänger, Der, Schubert, 351
Double ballades, 74
Double canon, 115
Dowland, John, 156
Doxology, 24
Dramma giocoso, 294, 296
  of Mozart, 322
Dream of Gerontius, The, Elgar, 415
Dr. Gradus ad Parnassum, Debussy, 421
Drum Roll Symphony, Haydn, 306
Drums, 42, 87
Ducis, Benedictus, 160
Duetto, Mendelssohn, 360
Dufay, Guillaume, 98, 100, 101, 102, 103–6, 112
Duke Bluebeard's Castle, Bartók, 427
Dunstable, John, 93–95, 97, 106
Dupont, Gaby, *420*
Durch Adams Fall, Bach, 259, **260**
Dussek, Jan Ladislav, 329, 358
Dvořák, Antonín, 380, 411, 413

Eastern European music, *see* Bohemian music; Hungarian music; Polish music
Eccard, Johannes, 160
Egdon Heath, Holst, 433
Egisto, Cavalli, 190–91
Egmont, Beethoven, 329, 336
Ego dormio et cor meum vigilat, Schütz, 200, **200**
Eighteenth-century Classical music, 278–323
  Baroque period compared, 281–83, 288–90
  chamber music in, *281*
  church music in, 296–97
  instrumental music of, 281–90
  national styles in, 294
  opera in, 281, 290–95
  sonatas in, 283, 286–87

Eighteenth-century Classical music (cont.)
  songs in, 296
  symphonies in, 281, 288–90, 313
Electronic music, 468
Elektra (Hofmannsthal), Strauss, 403–4
Elgar, Sir Edward, 415
Elijah, Mendelssohn, 357
Emperor Concerto, Beethoven, 336
Empfindsamer Stil (expressive style), 281,
  285, 286
En blanc et noir, Debussy, 421
Enfance du Christ, L', Berlioz, 357
English music:
  Baroque, 216–17, 221, 243
  of Classical period, 279, 295
  fifteenth-century, 92–96
  medieval, 40, 89–92
  nationalism in, 415
  Notre Dame school and, 90
  opera, 216-17, 295, 434
  Renaissance, 136, 153–56, 161, 163, 170–71,
    176–77
  twentieth-century, 431–34
English Suites, Bach, 261
Enigma Variations, Elgar, 415
Enlightenment, see Eighteenth-century
  Classical music
En non Diu—Quant roi—Eius in oriente,
  66–67, 67
En Saga, Sibelius, 414
Ensemble music:
  Baroque, 238–47
  opera finale, 294
Entführung aus dem Serail, Die, Mozart,
  315, 321, 322
Épigraphes antiques, Debussy, 421
Epistle, 20
Erlkönig, Schubert, 351
Eroica Symphony, Beethoven, 289, 331–32,
  333
Erste Walpurgisnacht, Mendelssohn, 354
Erwartung, Schoenberg, 453, 456
Essay on the True Art of Playing Keyboard
  Instruments, C. P. E. Bach, 287
Estampes, Debussy, 420
Estampies, 40
Esterházy, Nicholas (the Magnificent), 298,
  304
Esterházy, Nicholas II, 299
Esterházy, Paul Anton, 298–99
Et in terra pax, 20
Eton College choirbook, 95
Études:
  of Chopin, 361, 362–63
  of Debussy, 421
  of Liszt, 364
Euménides, Les, Milhaud, 438
Euouae, 24
Euridice (Rinuccini), Caccini, 187
Euridice (Rinuccini), Peri, 187
Évocations, Roussel, 423
Expressionism, 455–56, 459
Expressive style, 280, 281, 285, 291
Eyck, Jan van, 99

Fairy Queen, The, Purcell, 217
Falla, Manuel de, 415
Falsobordone, 124
Falstaff, Verdi, 384, 386, 387

Fancies, 174, 202, 204
Fantasia, Chopin, 362
Fantasia, Haydn, 307
Fantasia a 4, Sweelinck, 203
Fantasia on a Theme of Thomas Tallis,
  Vaughan Williams, 433
Fantasias, 142, 174, 202, 203, 204, 258, 361
  of Mozart, 317
  of Schubert, 359, 362
  of Schumann, 360, 362
Fantasiestücke, Schumann, 360
Fantasy for Violin and Piano, Stravinsky,
  457
Farnaby, Giles, 177
Faschingsschwank aus Wien, Schumann, 360
Fashionable Theatre, The, Marcello, 291
Faulte d'argent, Josquin des Prez, 120
Fauré, Gabriel, 415, 416–18
Faure, Jean-Baptiste, 416n
Faust, Goethe, 377, 389, 400
Faust, Gounod, 382–83
Faust Symphony, Liszt, 364, 377
Fauxbourdon, 92, 96
Faysans regres Mass, Josquin des Prez, 123,
  124
Fedeltà premiata, La, Haydn, 304
Fenice fù, Jacopo da Bologna, 77
Ferrabosco, Alfonso, the Younger, 204
Fervaal, d'Indy, 416
Festa, Costanzo, 144, 164
Feste Burg, Ein,' Luther, 158
Feste Burg, Ein' (Cantata No. 80), Bach, 266
Fevin, Antoine de, 120
Ficta, see Musica ficta
Fidelio, Beethoven, 295, 324, 329, 332
Fiedel (vielle), 40–41
Field, John, 362
Figured bass, see Basso continuo
Filles à marier, Binchois, 119
Finck, Heinrich, 134
Fingal's Cave, Mendelssohn, 372
Finlandia, Sibelius, 414
Finta semplice, La, Mozart, 312
Fiori musicali, Frescobaldi, 203
Fire Bird, The, Stravinsky, 444, 446
Fireworks Music, Handel, 271
Fischer, J. K. F., 244
Fitzwilliam Virginal Book, 172, 176
Five Orchestral Pieces, Schoenberg, 453
Five Pieces for Orchestra, Webern, 461
Fliegende Holländer, Der, Wagner, 390
Florentine opera, 186–89
Florid organum, 46–49
Florilegium, Muffat, 244
Flute, 42, 87, 287
Folk music, 415
  Grieg influenced by, 412
  Janáček's use of, 412
  medieval vernacular lyrics and, 39–40
  Romantic music and, 361, 405–6
  in Russian music, 406, 408, 431
  trouvère songs and, 38
  in twentieth-century music, 426–36
  virginalists and, 176
Folk Song Symphony, Harris, 435
Fontegara, Ganassi, 110
For all the Saints, Vaughan Williams, 432
Forbes, Elliot, 325n
Forelle, Die, Schubert, 366
Forellen Quintet, Schubert, 366

Forkel, J. N., 270
Formes fixes, 73, 88, 119, 143
Fortspinnung, 300
Forza del Destino, La, Verdi, 387
Foster, Stephen, 413
Four Temperaments, The, Hindemith, 441
Fra Diavolo, Auber, 382
Francesca da Rimini, Tchaikovsky, 380
Franck, César, 366, 371, 415
    symphonies of, 379
Franconian motets, 62, 68
Franconian notation, 64–67
Franco of Cologne, 62, 65
Frauenliebe und Leben (Chamisso), Schumann, 353
Frederick the Great, king of Prussia, 285
Freischütz, Der, Weber, 389
French music:
    ars nova, 70–77
    Baroque, 208, 213–16, 220, 234–35, 253–56
    chamber music in, 371
    in Classical period, 288, 295
    impressionism in, 418–23
    late fourteenth-century, 80–84, 87
    medieval, 36–38, 46–68
    neo-Classical movement in, 436–39
    opéra comique in, 295
    operas in, 213–16, 295, 381–83, 416, 417, 421, 423, 437–38
    Renaissance, 133–34, 152
    of Romantic period, 381–83
    see also Burgundian School; Netherlands School
French overture, 215–16, 255, 265
French Revolution, 295, 311, 324, 381
French Suites, Bach, 261
Frescobaldi, Girolamo, 203, 206, 209–10
Frische Klavierfrüchte, Kuhnau, 238
Froberger, Johann Jakob, 204, 209, 210
From a House of the Dead, Janáček, 412
From the New World, Dvořák, 380
Frottole, 133
Frye, Walter, 95, 123
Fuga, 202
Fugues, 202, 210, 231, 232–33, 258, 261, 403
Fulget coelestis curia—O Petre flos—Roma gaudet, 90, 91
Funeral and triumphal Symphony, Berlioz, 376
Fuseli, Henry, *303*
Fux, Johann Joseph, 221, 244, 288

Gabrieli, Andrea, 174, 178, 179
Gabrieli, Giovanni, 178, 199
Gaillarde, 141, 174
Gallican liturgy, 22
Galuppi, Baldassare, 294
Gamba, bass, 184
Gamelan, 419
García Lorca, Federico, 468
Gaspard de la nuit, Ravel, 422
Gassmann, Florian Leopold, 288
Gastoldi, Giacomo, 150, 153
Gaultier, Denis, 208
Gebrauchsmusik, 439
Geistliche Chormusik, Schütz, 201
Geistliche Konzerte, Schein, 199
Geminiani, Francesco, 244
Genere rappresentativo, 195

Genus, in Greek music, 107
German Mass, Luther, 157
German music:
    Baroque, 199–202, 217–18, 220–21, 231–34, 238, 256–70
    of Classical period, 295–97
    Lieder in, 296
    operas in, 217–18, 402–5, 439, 442
    post-Romantic, 406
    Renaissance, 134, 157–60
    of Romantic period, 349, 389–94
German Requiem, Brahms, 348, 357
Gershwin, George, 434
Gesamtkunstwerk, Wagner's ideal of, 395
Gesang der Jünglinge, Stockhausen, 467, 472
Gesang der Parzen, Brahms, 354
Gesualdo, Carlo, 148
Giasone, Cavalli, 190
Gibbons, Orlando, 156, 163, 176
Gigues, 207, 209, 235, 238
Ginastera, Alberto, 436
Giraud, Albert, 454
Giulio Cesare, Handel, 272
Giustino, Legrenzi, 212
Glagolitic Mass, Janáček, 412
Glarean, 32, 109*n*, 128, 129
Glazunov, Alexander, 406
Glinka, Michael, 406
Gli Scherzi quartets, Haydn, 308
Gloria, 20, 26, 27
Gloria in excelsis Deo, 20
Gloria patri, 24, 25
Gluck, Christoph Willibald, 280, 316, 317
    operas of, 292–93, 381
Glückliche Hand, Die, Schoenberg, 453, 456
Goe from my window, Munday, 176, 177
Goethe, Johann Wolfgang von, 324
    dramas of, 329, 336, 377, 389, 400
Goldberg Variations, Bach, 261, 338
Golden Cockerel, The, Rimsky-Korsakov, 410
Goldoni, Carlo, 294
Goliard songs, 35
Golias, Bishop, 35
Gombert, Nicolas, 130–31, 135, 198
Gondola Song, Mendelssohn, 360
Gospel, 21
Gossec, François Joseph, 289
Götterdammerung, Wagner, 391
Gottschalk, Louis Moreau, 413
Goudimel, Claude, 161
Gounod, Charles, 355, 416
    operas of, 382–83
Graces, 242
Gradual, 20, 25–26
Graduale, 21
Grand Duo, Schubert, 359
Grande Messe des Morts, Berlioz, 348, 355
Grandi Alessandro, 198
Grand opera, 381
Graun, Johann Gottlieb, 288
Graun, Karl Heinrich, 291, 296, 297
Graupner, Christoph, 228
Great Service, Byrd, 163
Greek music, ancient, 1–6, 86
    characteristics of, 4, 5–6
    church music and, 2, 4, 5–6
    drama and, 3–4
    education and, 4, 8–9
    improvisation in, 4–5

Greek music, ancient (*continued*)
  instruments in, 3, 4
  medieval music and, 5–6
  in mythology, 4–5
  poetry and, 3, 4–6
  religious ceremonies and, 3, 4–5
  theory, 5–6
Greene, Maurice, 297
Gregorian Chant, *see* Chant, Gregorian
Gregory I, Pope, 12, *13*, 22
Gretchen am Spinnrad, Schubert, 351
Grétry, André Ernest Modeste, 295
Grieg, Edvard Hagerup, 412, 413
Griselda, Scarlatti, 213
Grosse Fuge, Beethoven, 329, 340
Ground bass, 191, 192, 236
Guarneri, Giuseppe Bartolomeo, 238
Guerre, La, Janequin, 133
Guido of Arezzo, *31*, 32, 34
Guillaume Tell, Rossini, 382, 384
Gurre-Lieder, Schoenberg, 453, 454
Gymnopedies, Satie, 421

Haec dies quam fecit Dominus, **56–57**
Haffner Serenade, Mozart, 315
Haffner Symphony, Mozart, 315
Halévy, Jacques Fromenthal, 382
Hammerschmidt, Andreas, 225
Handel, George Frideric, 270–77, 281, 295
  Beethoven influenced by, 341
  choral style of, 275–76
  Haydn influenced by, 309
  operas of, 291, 295
  oratorios of, 273–74, 309, 341
Handl, Jacob, 136, 179
Hans Heiling, Marschner, 90
Hanson, Howard, 436
Harmonice Musices Odhecaton A, 119–20
Harmonie der Welt, Die, Hindemith, 442
Harmonies poétiques et religieuses, Liszt, 364
Harmonious Blacksmith, The, Handel, 271
Harmony, in Baroque vs. Classical period, 282–83
Harold in Italy, Berlioz, 375, 376
Harp, 40, 87
Harpsichord, 139, *209*, 212, 235, 283, 289, 301
Harris, Roy, 435–36
Hasse, Johann Adolf, 222
Hassler, Hans Leo, 150, 159, 160, 179, 200
Haydn, (Franz) Joseph, 280, 281, 288, 298–310, 313
  Beethoven influenced by, 310, 329
  church music of, 309–10
  C. P. E. Bach's influence on, 304
  Handel's influence on, 309
  Mozart compared with, 304, 311, 318, 320
  operas of, 308
  oratorios of, 299, 309–10
  orchestra of, 289, 300, 306
  patrons of, 298–99
  significance to Romantic music, 306, 309–10, 343, 346
  sonatas of, 284, 304, 359
  songs of, 308
  string quartets of, 299, 302–3, 304, 305, 307, 318, 366
  symphonies of, 299, 304, 306
  use of variation in, 337

Haydn, Michael, 288
Haydn quartets, Mozart, 318
Hebrew music, 7, 10
Hebrides, The, Mendelssohn, 372
"Heiligenstadt testament," Beethoven, 326–27
Heldenleben, Ein, Strauss, 402
Hellinck, Lupus, 160
Henrici, C. F., 268
Henry, Roy, 93
Hercules, Handel, 274
Hercules auf dem Scheidewege, Bach, 267
Hercules dux Ferrariae Mass, Josquin des Prez, 122
Herold, Ferdinand, 382
Herzlich thut mich verlangen, 159
Heterophony, 44, 87
Heure espagnole, L', Ravel, 422
Hexachords, 32–34, **33**, 171–72
Hilary, Bishop of Poitiers, 9
Hiller, Johann Adam, 296
Hindemith, Paul, 431, 439–42
  harmonic method of, 440–41, **440**
Hippolyte et Aricie (Pellegrin), Rameau, 254–55, **255**
Histoire du Soldat, L', Stravinsky, 444, 446
Histoires naturelles, Ravel, 423
Historia, 228
Hocket, 68, 73
Hoffmann, E. T. A., 343
Hoffmeister Quartet, Mozart, 320
Hofhaimer, Paul, 134
Hofmannsthal, Hugo von, 404
Hohenstein, Adolfo, *423*
Holst, Gustav, 415, 433
Homme armé, L', 104, **104**
Homme armé, L' Mass, Dufay, 104, **105–6**
Homme armé, L' Mass, Morton, 104
Honegger, Arthur, 436–37
Hora novissima, Parker, 413
Horn, 42, 87
Hothby, John, 95, 103
Hugo, Victor, *363*, 372
Huguenots, Les, Meyerbeer, 381
Hungarian Fantasia, Liszt, 304
Hungarian music, 426
Hungarian Rhapsodies, Liszt, 364
Hurdy-gurdy, 41
Hymnen, Stockhausen, 472
Hymns:
  definition of, 9–10
  fauxbourdon settings of, 92
  Roman rite and, 9–10, 58
  secular origins of, 9–10
  see also Chorales
Hymn to St. Magnus, 89

Iberia, Albéniz, 415
Ich armer Mann, Lasso, 150, **151**
Idiomatic writing, Baroque, 182, 230
Idomeneo, Mozart, 316, 321
Images, Debussy, 420
Impressionism, 364
Improvisation:
  composition vs., 43–44
  in early Greek music, 4–5
  instrumental forms and, 175–76
  organum and, 47
  Renaissance instrumental, 137, 140–42

In Central Asia, Borodin, 406
Incoronazione di Poppea, L' (Busenello), Monteverdi, 190
Independent Musical Society, 416
Indes galantes, Les, Rameau, 254, 255, 256
Indeterminacy, 469–70
Indian Queen, The, Purcell, 217
Indian Suite, MacDowell, 413
In dulci jubilo, 158
Indy, Vincent d', 328, 415, 416
In ecclesiis, Gabrieli, 178
Ingegneri, Marc' Antonio, 148
In illo tempore Mass, Monteverdi, 198
Inscape, Copland, 435
Instrumental music:
    Baroque, 202–10, 230–47, 250–53, 257–64, 271
    fourteenth- and fifteenth-century, 86–87
    improvisation in, 137, 140
    in liturgical dramas, 29
    medieval, 40–42
    medieval vocal music and, 28
    in motets, 59, 60
    Renaissance, 136–43, 171–77, 178
    Renaissance vocal music and, 156, 171–72, 178
    of Romantic period, 358–80
    Venetian, 178
    see also specific forms
Instruments:
    continuo, 184
    equal temperament in, 233
    fourteenth- and fifteenth-century, 79–80, 86–87
    haut and *bas*, 87, *138*
    medieval, 40–42
    Renaissance, 137–39, *138*, 178
    see also specific instruments
Intermezzo, Strauss, 405
Introit, 20, 25, 27
Invitation to the Dance, Weber, 358
Ionisation, Varèse, 466, 469
"*Io parto*" *e non più dissi*, Gesualdo, **147**
Iphigénie en Aulide, Gluck, 293
Iphigénie en Tauride, Gluck, 293
Isaac, Henricus, 118, 119, 128–29, 134, 158
Isbruck, ich muss dich lassen, Isaac, 128, 158
Islamey, Balakirev, 365, 406
Isorhythmic motets, 55, 71–72, 93, 97, 104
Israel in Egypt, Handel, 273, 275–76
Istar, d'Indy, 416
Istitutioni, Zarlino, 109*n*
Italian music:
    ancient, 10
    Baroque, 186–92, 194–95, 196–98, 211–14, 218–20, 248–53
    of Classical period, 285
    influence on Josquin des Prez, 123–24
    medieval, 40
    Renaissance, 132–33, 143–50, 164–68, 277–79
    trecento, 77–80, 88
Italian opera:
    Baroque, 186–92, 211–14, 238–42
    of Classical period, 290–95
    dramma giocoso, 294, 308, 322–23
    nationalism in, 386
    opera buffa, 294, 322–23
    opera seria, 290–91

overture of, as forerunner of symphony, 285, 300
    of Romantic period, 384–88
    verismo in, 423
Italian Symphony, Mendelssohn, 372
Ite, missa est, 20, 21
Ives, Charles, 413–14

Jacob of Liège, 70
Jacopo da Bologna, 77
Jacopo da Todi, 29
Janáček, Leoš, 411–12, 426
Janequin, Clément, 133
Jazz, 434
Jean de Muris, 70
Jeanne d'Arc au Bûcher (Claudel), Honegger, 437
Jenkins, John, 202
Jenufa, Janáček, 412
Jesu meine Freude, Bach, 267
Jeu de Robin et de Marion, Adam de la Halle, 37
Jeux d'eau, Ravel, 422
Johannes de Grocheo, 68
John of Lublin, *142*
Johnson, Samuel, 295
Jongleurs, 36–37, 41
Joseph, Handel, 274
Joshua, Handel, 273
Josquin des Prez, *see* Des Prez, Josquin
Journal de Printemps, Fischer, 244
Jours de fête sont finis, Les, Mussorgsky, 409, 418, **419**
Judas Maccabaeus, Handel, 273
Juive, La, Halévy, 382
Jupiter Symphony, Mozart, 319

Kallman, Chester, 446
Kammersymphonie, Schoenberg, 453
Kát'a Kabanová, Janáček, 412
Kay, Ulysses, 436
Keiser, Reinhard, 218, 220
Keyboard music:
    fourteenth-century manuscripts of, 80
    tablatures for, 139
    see also Clavier music; Piano sonatas; Organ music
Khovanshchina, Mussorgsky, 407, 410
Kinderscenen, Schumann, 360
Kindertotenlieder (Rückert), Mahler, 401
King Arthur, Purcell, 217
King David, Honegger, 437
Kirchenlied, see Chorales
Kirkpatrick, John, 414
Kirkpatrick, Ralph, 283
Kiss, The, Smetana, 411
Kithara, 3, 4, 5
Klaviermusik: Übung in drei Stücken, Hindemith, 441
Klavierstück, Stockhausen, 470
Kleine geistliche Konzerte, Schütz, 200–1
Kleine Nachtmusik, Eine, Mozart, 315
Köchel, L. von, 311
Kodály, Zoltán, 426
Kreisleriana, Schumann, 360
Kreutzer Sonata, Beethoven, 333
Krieger, Adam, 220
Krieger, Johann, 228, 233

Krummhorn, 138
Kuhnau, Johann, 228, 238
Kunst der Fuge, Die, Bach, 259, 264, 269, 317
Kyrie, 20, 26–7, 28

Lady Macbeth, Shostakovich, 431
Lais, 73
Lamentations, 97, 301
Lamentations, Tallis, 136
Landi, Stefano, 189
Langue d'oc, 36
Langue d'oil, 37
La Rue, Pierre de, 129
Lascia, deh lascia, Scarlatti, 219, **219**
Lasso, Orlando di, 146, 150, 152, 169–70
Lauda Sion, Aquinas, 29
Laudate pueri dominum, Byrd, **170–71**
Laude:
  monophonic, 39
  polyphonic, 133, 168, 198
Lauds, 17
Lechner, Leonhard, 160
Leeuw, Ton de, 442
Legend of St. Elizabeth, Liszt, 357
Legrenzi, Giovanni, 212, 219, 222, 257
Leitmotifs:
  defined, 392
  Wagner's use of, 392
Le Jeune, Claude, 152, 161
Leoncavallo, Ruggiero, 423
Leonin, 51–54, 58
Leonore Overtures, Beethoven, 335
Lesser Doxology, 24
Liber Usualis, 21
Libro de musica de vihuela de mano intitulado El Maestro, Milán, 142
Lieder:
  eighteenth-century, 296
  of Mahler, 399, 400, 401
  Renaissance, 134
  of Wolf, 259
Lieder eines fahrenden Gesellen, Mahler, 400
Lied von der Erde, Das, Mahler, 397, 399, **399,** 400, 401
Lieutenant Kije, Prokofiev, 431
Life for the Tsar, A, Glinka, 406
Ligatures, 50, **50,** 67
Ligeti, György, 468
Linda di Chamounix, Donizetti, 385
Linz Symphony, Mozart, 319
Liszt, Franz, *363,* 410
  choral works of, 353, 356
  piano music of, 363, 365
  psalms of, 356
  on Romantic sacred music, 356
  symphonic poems of, 376–77, 394
  symphonies of, 371, 400
Liturgical dramas, 29–30, 36
Liturgical year, seasons of, 18n
Liturgies:
  Ambrosian, 9
  Byzantine, 8
  Gallican, 22
  Jewish, 6–7, 10
  Roman ascendancy in, 11–12
  Sarum, 90

Liturgy, Roman, 16–30
  Masses in, 20–21, 23
  Notre Dame polyphony in, 51–58
  Offices (Canonical Hours) in, 17–20, 23–25
  seasons of year in, 18n
Locke, Matthew, 204
Logroscina, Nicola, 294
Lohengrin, Wagner, 390
London Symphonies, Haydn, 299, 301, 306
London Symphony, Vaughan Williams, 433
Long Christmas Dinner, The, Hindemith, 442
Longo, A., 283
Lord Nelson (Imperial) Mass, Haydn, 309
Lortzing, Albert, 389
Loth to depart, Farnaby, 177
Lotti, Antonio, 222
Louise, Charpentier, 416
Love of Three Oranges, The, Prokofiev, 431
Love songs, medieval, 36–39
Ludus tonalis, Hindemith, 441
Luisa Miller, Verdi, 387
Lully, Jean-Baptiste, 214–16, 236, 254, 255
Lulu, Berg, 459
Lute, 41, 139, 184, 208, 233
Lute songs, 87, 156
Luther, Martin, 157, 158, 159, 161
Lutheran church music, 157–60, 223–29, 264–69, 297
Lyric opera, 382–83
Lyric Pieces, Grieg, 412
Lyric Suite, Berg, 459

MacDowell, Edward, 413
Machaut, Guillaume de, 72–77, *73,* 78
  Messe de Notre Dame of, 75–76
  monophonic songs of, 73
  motets of, 72–73
  polyphonic songs of, 73–74
Macque, Jean de, 173
Madama Butterfly, Puccini, 423
Madrigali spirituali, 146, 169
Madrigals:
  English, 153–55, 156
  sixteenth-century Italian, 143–49
  trecento, 77–78, 80, 143
Maeterlinck, Maurice, 417, 421
Magic Flute, The, Mozart, 279, 317, 321, 328, 350
Magnificat, 18, 97, 103
Magnificat, Bach, 267
Magnum opus musicum, Lasso, 169
Magnus liber organi, 51
Mahler, Gustav, 431
  Lieder of, 395, 397, 399, 400, 401
  symphonies of, 397–402, *398,* **399,** 401
Major-minor tonality, 186, 253–54
Makropulos Case, The, Janáček, 412
Malheur me bat Mass, Josquin des Prez, 122–23
Malheurs d'Orphée, Les, Milhaud, 438
Mamelles de Tirésias, Les, Poulenc, 439
Ma Mère l'Oye, Ravel, 422
Manchicourt, Pierre de, 135
Manfred (Byron), Schumann's incidental music to, 374
Mannheim school, 288
Manon, Massenet, 423

Marcello, Benedetto, 291
Marche lugubre, Gossec, 289
Marchetto da Padua, 84
Marenzio, Luca, 146, 148
Marian antiphons, 11, 18–19, 23
Mariazeller Mass, Haydn, 309
Marienleben, Das (Rilke), Hindemith, 439
Marriage of Figaro, The (da Ponte), Mozart, 308, 320, 322, 384
Marschner, Heinrich, 389
Marteau sans maître, Le, Boulez, 466
Martianus Cappella, 14
Martini, Padre Giambattista, 313
Mascagni, Pietro, 423
Massenet, Jules, 416
Masses:
  Baroque, 221–22
  Burgundian, 102–6
  cantus firmus (cyclical), 103–6, 118, 136
  chants for, 23
  French organ, 235
  Lutheran, 157
  motto, 103
  in Old Hall ms., 93
  Ordinary of (*Ordinarium missae*), 21, 26–27, 75–76, 102–3
  paraphrase, 123
  parody, 122–23
  Plainsong (*missa choralis*), 103
  Proper of (*Proprium missae*), 21, 75
  texts of, 20–21
  see also Liturgy, Roman; Offices, liturgical; *specific composers and works*
Mass in B Minor, Bach, 268–69, 341
Mass of Mariazell, Haydn, 309
Master Peter's Puppet Show, Falla, 415
Mathis der Maler, Hindemith, 440, **441**, 442
Matins, 17
Matrimonio Segreto, Cimarosa, 294
Mattheson, Johann, 228
Mauduit, Jacques, 152
Maxwell-Davies, Peter, 472
Measured music, 152–53
Meditations on the Mystery of the Holy Trinity, Messiaen, 443
Meine Liebe ist grün, Brahms, 353
Mein Gmüth ist mir verwirret, Hassler, 159, **159**
Meistersinger von Nürnberg, Die, Wagner, 39, 383, 391, 394
Melismatic organum, 46–49
Melodia Germanica, La, No. 3, Stamitz, 288
Melody, in Baroque vs. Classical period, 282
Melusine, Mendelssohn, 372
Mendelssohn-Bartholdy, Felix, 270, 354
  chamber music of, 368
  choral works of, 357
  concertos of, 378
  piano music of, 359–60
  symphonies of, 371, 372–73
Ménestrels, 36–37
Mensuration canon, 115
Menuet antique, Ravel, 422
Mer, La, Debussy, 419
Merula, Tarquinio, 205
Merulo, Claudio, 175, 178
Mesomedes of Crete, hymns of, 4
Messe de Notre Dame, Machaut, 75–76
Messiaen, Olivier, 442–43, 464
Messiah, Handel, 273, 274, 275

Metastasio, Pietro, 291
Meyerbeer, Giacomo, 381
  operas of, 381–82
Mickiewicz, Adam, 362
Middle Ages, 16–106
  ars antiqua in, 58–69
  ars nova in, 70–77
  Burgundian School in, 97–106
  early polyphony in, 43–50
  instrumental music in, 40–42
  late, style evolution, 96–97
  music theory in, 30–34
  secular songs (monody) in, 35–40
middle class, influence on music of, 279, 281, 291, 381
Midsummer Night's Dream, Mendelssohn's incidental music for, 372
"Mighty handful, the," 406–10
Mikrokosmos, Bartók, 427, 428, 430
Milan, Ambrosian liturgy in, 9
Milán, Luis, 142
Milhaud, Darius, 437–38
  operas of, 437
  polytonality in, 437
Mille regretz, Josquin des Prez, 120, **121**
Milton, John, 309
Minnelieder, 39
Minnesingers, 39
Minstrels, 36–37
Miraculous Mandarin, The, Bartók, 428, 430
Miroirs, Ravel, 422
Missa canonica, Fux, 221
Missa caput, see Caput Mass
Missa della Madonna, Frescobaldi, 203
Missa di San Carlo, Fux, 221
Missa in angustiis, Haydn, 309
Missa in tempore belli, Haydn, 342
Missal (*Missale*), 21
Missa prolationum, Ockeghem, 115, **116**
Missa solemnis, Beethoven, 269, 324, 329, 336, 341, 348
Misterieuse, La, Couperin, 235
Mitridate, Scarlatti, 213
Mode de valeurs et d'intensité, Messiaen, 465
Modes, church (medieval), 24, 30–32, **31**
  accidentals in, 32
  authentic and plagal, 30
  musica ficta and, 131–32
  in nineteenth-century Russian music, 407
  reciting tone (dominant) in, 31
  tenor in, 31
  in troubadour and trouvère songs, 38
Modes, rhythmic, 49–50, **50**
Moments musicaux, Schubert, 359
Monflambert, La, Couperin, 235
Monn, Georg Matthias, 288
Monochord, 31
Monody, 186
Monophony:
  medieval forms of, 44
  see also specific forms
Monsigny, Pierre-Alexandre, 295
Monteverdi, Claudio, 146, 148, 181, 194–95, 196
  church music of, 198
  madrigals of, 148
  operas of, 187–89, 190, 192
Montezuma, Sessions, 436
Montpellier Codex, *67,* 90

Mood, 85
Moonlight Sonata, Beethoven, 336
Morales, Cristóbal de, 135, 164
Morley, Thomas, 153, 154
Morton, Robert, 104
Moses and Aaron, Schoenberg, 457, **457**, 458
Motet Passion, 229
Motets:
  of Bach, 267
  Burgundian, 102
  chorale, 160
  English, 90
  Franconian, 62
  harmonic vocabulary of, 64
  instruments in, 59, 60
  isorhythmic, 55, 71–72, 93, 97, 104
  performance of, 64–67
  Petronian, 63–64
  rhythmic development in, 62–64
  of Schütz, 199–200
  seventeenth-century, 222–23
  Venetian polychoral, 178, 194
Motets, thirteenth-century, 58–64
  origins of, 58–59
  rhythm of, 59–60
  sacred vs. secular in, 61–62, 69
  tenors of, 59–60
  texts of, 59–60
Mourn for thy Servant, Blow, 216
Mouton, Jean, 129
Mozart, Leopold, 310, 311, 313
Mozart, Wolfgang Amadeus, 270, 280, 287, 310–23
  church music of, 316–17
  concertos of, 316, 319–21
  Haydn compared with, 304, 309, 313–14, 320
  influences on, 288, 316, 317, 323, 324
  melody in, 288
  operas of, 279, 294, 296, 316, 321–22, 384
  serenades of, 315–16, *315*
  significance to Romantic music, 343, 359
  sonatas of, 284, 315, 316, 359
  string quartets of, 314, 316, 318–19, **318**, 366
  symphonies of, 281
  use of variation in, 337
Muette de Portici, La, Auber, 381
Muffat, Georg, 216, 244
Munday, 176, 177
Musica enchiriadis, 44
Musica falsa, 84
Musica ficta, 84, 109–10, 131–32, 167, 167n
Musica getutscht und ausgezogen, Virdung, 137
Musica humana, 15
Musica instrumentalis, 14
Musical Offering, Bach, 68, 259, 269, 461
Musica mundana, 15
Musica reservata, 125–26, 180
Musica transalpina, Yonge, 153
Music festivals, growth of, in nineteenth century, 354
Music for Strings, Percussion and Celesta, Bartók, 428, 430
Music for the Theater, Copland, 434
Music printing, *see* Printing, music
Music theory:
  early Greek, 5–6
  medieval, 30–34, 64–67

Musikalische Exequien, Schütz, 201
Musikalisches Opfer, Bach, 68, 259, 269, 461
Musique concrète, 467, 468
Musique mesurée, 152–53
Mussorgsky, Modest, 365, 406–9, 423
  Debussy influenced by, 407–9, 418, 419–20
Mythology, Greek, 3, 4

Nachdem David war redlich, Sachs, 39
Nachstücke, Schumann, 360
Nänie (Schiller), Brahms, 354
Nanino, Giovanni Maria, 168
Napoleon I (Bonaparte), 324
Nationalism:
  French music revival and, 415–23
  in post-Romanticism, 405–23
  in Renaissance, 132–36
  in Romantic period, 348, 361, 386
  Romantic vs. post-Romantic, 405–6
  in twentieth-century music, 626–36
National Society for French Music, 416
Nations, Les, Couperin, 243
Native American music, 380, 412–13
Nature, in Romantic music, 240, 348
Neapolitan opera, 212–13
Neo-Classicism, 425, 436–42, 447
  of Stravinsky, 445–46
Neri, Filippo, 168, 198
Netherlands School, 112–32
  canons of, 114–16
  chansons of, 152
  choral performance in, 117
  concealed technique in, 116
  cosmopolitan character of, 112, 118
  musica reservata in, 125–26
  see also specific composers
Neue Arien, Krieger, 220
Neues vom Tage, Hindemith, 439
Neumeister, Erdmann, 227, 265
Neumes, 34, 50
New England Idyls, MacDowell, 413
Nietzsche, Friedrich, 401, 402–3
Night on Bald Mountain, Mussorgsky, 406
Nights in the Gardens of Spain, Falla, 415
Nina, Paisiello, 294
Nobilissima visione, Hindemith, 441, 442
Noces, Les, Stravinsky, 444, 452
Nocturnes, Debussy, 418–19
Non avrà ma' pietà, Landini, *78*
Nones, 17
Nono, Luigi, 442, 466
Norfolk Rhapsodies, Vaughan Williams, 415
Norma, Bellini, 386
Norwegian music, nationalism in, 412
Notation:
  choirbook, 67
  of early polyphony, 44, 46
  fourteenth-century (Italian and French), 84–85
  of Gregorian Chant, 34
  motet (Franconian), 64–67
  of rhythmic modes, 50, 52
  score, 49, 66–67
  tablature, 136, *155*
  twentieth-century, 472, 474
Notker Balbulus, 28
Notre Dame organum, 50–59
Nouvelle Suites de Pièces de clavecin, Rameau, 256

Novelletten, Schumann, 360
Nozze di Figaro, Le (da Ponte), Mozart, 302, 320, 321, 322
Nuages, Debussy, 409, 418–19, **419**
Nuages gris, Liszt, 364–65, **365**
Nun komm' der Heiden Heiland, 158
Nun komm, der Heiden Heiland (Cantata No. 61), Bach, 261
Nuove musiche, Le, Caccini, *184*, **185**, 186, 187
Nursery, The, Mussorgsky, 407, 423
Nutcracker, The, Tchaikovsky, 380

Obrecht, Jacob, 118, 119
O Care, thou wilt despatch me, Weelkes, 153, **154**
Ockeghem, Johannes, 112–18, *115*
  canons of, 114–15, 122
  masses of, 113, 114, 115–18
  musical style of, 113
O crux, splendidior, Willaert, 131, **132**
Octets:
  of Mendelssohn, 368
  of Stravinsky, 444, 445, 446, 452
Ode for St. Cecilia's Day, Handel, 274
Ode to Joy, Schiller, 279, 342
Ode to Napoleon, Schoenberg, 457
Odhecaton, 119–20
O Domine Jesu Christe, Viadana, 197
Oedipus rex, Stravinsky, 446, 452
Offertory, 20, 25, 26, 27
Offices, liturgical, 17–20, 23–25
Of Thee I Sing, Gershwin, 434
O gladsome light, 9
O Haupt voll Blut und Wunden, 159
Oiseaux exotiques, Messiaen, 443
Old Hall manuscript, 92–93
"Old Hundredth," 162
Old Roman Chant, 11–12
O Mensch, bewein' dein' Sünde gross, Bach, 259–60
Ondes Martenot, Messiaen, 466, 469
Opella nova, Schein, 199
Opera:
  Baroque, 186–92, 211–18, 249
  church music influenced by, 296–97
  of Classical period, 290–95, 296–97
  English, 295, 434
  French, 213–16, 295, 381–83, 417, 420, 423, 437–38
  German, 217–18, 389–94, 402–5, 439–42
  grand opera, 381–95
  Italian, *see* Italian opera
  overtures in, 285, 300
  in Romantic period, 295, 381–95
  Russian, 431
  twentieth-century, 427, 431, 434, 442, 457, 459
  see also specific composers
Opera and Drama, Wagner, 390
Opéra bouffe, 382
Opera buffa, 294, 388
  of Mozart, 312, 319, 322–23, 388
Opéra comique, 282, 294
Opera seria, 293
  of Mozart, 313, 316
Opus 1970, Stockhausen, 470
O quam tu pulchra es, Grandi, 201
O quam tu pulchra es, Schütz, 198

Oral transmission of early liturgical melodies, 8, 44
Oratorio Passion, 229
Oratorios:
  Baroque, 198–99, 201, 273–74
  nineteenth-century, 413
  twentieth-century, 434, 437
Oratorio volgare, 222
Orchestra:
  of Gabrieli, 179
  of Haydn, 289
  of La Pouplinière, 288
  of Lully, 216
  of Monteverdi, 189
  of Rameau, 256
  Romantic music for, 371–80
Orchestral music, Baroque, 244–47
Orchestral suites, 244, 263
Ordres, 235–36
Orfeo, Monteverdi, 187–88, *188*, 190, 192
Orfeo (Buti), Rossi, 190
Orfeo ed Euridice (Calzabigi), Gluck, 292, 293
Organ:
  Baroque, 206–7, 231–35, 257–60
  as continuo, 184
  with Gregorian Chant, 28
  pedals for, 87, 139
  portative, 78, 87, 139
  positive, 87, 139
  regal, 139
Organ chorales, 231, 233, 234
Organetto, 78, 87
Organistrum, 41
Organ music, twentieth-century, 443
Organum, 44–58
  chant in, 51
  early, 44–46, **45**, **46**
  florid (St. Martial), 46–49, *47*
  meaning of, 47–48, 58–59
  Notre Dame, 50–58
  rhythmic modes and, 49–50
Organum duplum, 47
Organum purum, 47, 54
Organum quadruplum, 55, 58
Organum triplum, 55, 58
Orgelbüchlein, Bach, 259
Ormindo, Cavalli, 190
Ornamentation, Baroque, 208, 235, **236–37**, 242
  see also Coloration
O rosa bella, Dunstable, 94
Ostinato bass, 193, 269
Otello, Verdi, 386, 387
Ottave rime, 206
Ottone, Handel, 272
Ouverture, see French overture
Ouvertures, Bach, 263
O vos omnes, Victoria, 169
O Welt, ich muss dich lassen, 128, 158

Pachelbel, Johann, 227, 231, 234
Padmâvatî, Roussel, 423
Padovano, Annibale, 178
Paganini, Niccolò, *363*
Pagliacci, I, Leoncavallo, 423
Paien, Thomas, 74
Paisiello, Giovanni, 294
Palamento, 40

Palestrina, Giovanni Pierluigi da, 164, *165*, 178, 221, 297, 349
Pallavicino, Carlo, 212
Palmer, Robert, 436
Palms, The, Fauré, 446*n*
Pantonality, 454
Papacy, influence on music of, 11–12, 80
Papillons, Schumann, 360
Parade (Cocteau), Satie, 421, *422*
Paradise and the Peri, Schumann, 354
Paradise Lost, Milton, 309
Parker, Horatio, 413
Parodies, 157, 158
Parsifal, Wagner, 348, 391, 394, 400
Partial signatures, 82
Partitas, 202, 238
Part songs, nineteenth-century, 354
Passacaglia (*passecaile*), 193, **193**, 202, 236, 261
Passacaille ou Chaconne, Couperin, 236, **236**– 37
Passamezzo, 174
Passio et lamentatio, Haydn, 301
Passion according to St. John, Bach, 268
Passion according to St. Matthew, Bach, 159, **159**, 227, 229, 268, 270, 349
Passions, Baroque, 159, 201, 228–29, 268
Pastoral Symphony, Beethoven, 334
Pastoral Symphony, Vaughan Williams, 373, *432*, 433
Pastourelles, 37
Pater noster, 21
Pathétique Symphony, Tchaikovsky, 380
Patrem omnipotentem, 20
Patronage, 279, 298–99
Pauvre Matelot, Le (Cocteau), Milhaud, 438
Pavane, 141, 174
Pavane pour une Infante défunte, Ravel, 422
Peasant Cantata, 267
Pedrell, Felipe, 415
Pelléas et Mélisande (Maeterlinck), Debussy, 427
Pelléas et Mélisande (Maeterlinck), Fauré's incidental music to, 417
Pelleas und Melisande, Schoenberg, 453, 454
Penderecki, Krzysztof, 466, 469
Pénélope, Fauré, 417
Performance practice:
    of chorales, 158
    of fourteenth-century (trecento) music, 79– 80
    of Machaut's Mass, 74
    of motets, 59, 60
    of sixteenth-century madrigals, 154
    of troubadour and trouvère songs, 38–39
Pergolesi, Giovanni Battista, 222
    operas of, 294
Peri, Jacopo, 187
Peronne, 74
Perotin, 50, 54–58
Perséphone, Stravinsky, 452
Peter and the Wolf, Prokofiev, 431
Peter Grimes, Britten, 434
Petrarch, 146
Petronian motets, 63–64, 68
Petrucci, Ottaviano de, 108, 132, 140
Petrus de Cruce (Pierre de la Croix), 66
Petrushka, Stravinsky, 444, 451

Philippe de Vitry, 70, 71, 78
Philip the Good, 98–99
Philomel, Babbit, 468
Phoebus and Pan, Bach, 267
Piano, changes in, nineteenth-century, 358– 59
Pianoforte, 286
Piano music, of Romantic period, 358–66
Piano quartets:
    of Copland, 435
    of Mozart, 318
    of Palmer, 436
    see also Quartets
Piano quintets, of Fauré, 417
    see also Quintets
Piano Rag Music, Stravinsky, 444
Piano sonatas:
    of Beethoven, 317, 324, **328**, 329, 335, 338
    of Mozart, 317
    in post-Romantic music, 414
    of Romantic period, 359
    twentieth-century, 435, 441, 444
    see also Sonatas
Piano trios:
    of Beethoven, 324
    of Brahms, 369
    of Mendelssohn, 368–69
    of Mozart, 318
Picasso, Pablo, 421, *422, 445*
Piccinni, Niccolò, 294
Pictures at an Exhibition, Mussorgsky, 366, 406, 410
Pictures of a Pagan Russia, Stravinsky, 444
Pièces de clavecin en concerts, Rameau, 256
Pierrot Lunaire, Schoenberg, 454, 456
Pietism, 225, 227
Piston, Walter, 436
Plainsong, *see* Chant, Gregorian
Planets, The, Holst, 433
Plato, 14, 421
Pliny the Younger, on Christian singing, 7
Poème électronique, Varèse, 466, 467, *467*, 468
Poem of Ecstasy, Scriabin, 411
Poetics of Music, Stravinsky, 452
Poetry, music, and:
    of ayres, 156
    early Greek, 3, 5–6
    English madrigal, 154–55
    of Machaut, 72–74
    Renaissance, 110–11, 180
    sixteenth-century Italian madrigal, 143– 44
    troubadour and trouvère, 37–39
Pohjola's Daughter, Sibelius, 414
Pointillist style, 465
Polish music, of Chopin, 361
Polovetsian Dances, Borodin, 406
Polyphony, early, historical background of, 43–44
Polytonality, 429, 438
Pomerium, Marchetto da Padua, 84
Pomo d'oro, Il, Cesti, 191, *191*
Pope Marcellus Mass, Palestrina, 165–66, **166**
Porgy and Bess, Gershwin, 434
Porpora, Nicola, 291
Portuguese music, 283
Post-Communion, 21
Post-Romantic music:

nationalism in, 405–23
    Schoenberg and, 454
    verism in, 423
Poulenc, Francis, 438–39
Pouplinière, La, 289
Pour le piano, Debussy, 420
Power, Leonel, 93
Praetorious, Michael, 137, 160, 179
Prague Symphony, Mozart, 319
Preambulum, 142
Pré aux clercs, Le, Herold, 382
Preface, 20
Prélude à l'après-midi d'un faune, Debussy, 419, 420
Preludes, 142, 202, 232, 258, 361, 362, 365, 371
Préludes, Debussy, 420
Préludes, Les, Liszt, 377
"Prepared piano," 466
Prima prattica, 181
Prime, 17
Prince Igor, Borodin, 406
Printing, music, 108
    in Classical period, 279
Program music:
    post-Romantic, 397, 398
    Romantic, 346, 373, 376–77, 380
    use of term, 346
Prokofiev, Sergei, 431
Prolation, 85
Prométhée, Fauré, 417
Prometheus, Scriabin, 411, 411
Proportio (proportz), 175
Prosa (prosula), 28–29
Provenzale, Francesco, 212
Prussian quartets, Haydn, 305
Prussian sonatas, C. P. E. Bach, 285
Psalmen Davids, Schütz, 200
Psalms:
    fauxbourdon settings of, 92
    in Jewish services, 7
    in Offices, 24
    see also Psalters
Psalm tones, 31
Psalters:
    American, 161
    Dutch, 161
    English (Sternhold and Hopkins), 161
    French (Marot and de Bèze), 161
    German, 199
    Scottish, 161
Psaltery, 41, 87
Puccini, Giacomo, 423, 423
Pucelete—Je languis—Domino, 60–61, 62
Puchberg, Michael, 317
Puisque m'amour, Dunstable, 94
Pulcinella, Stravinsky, 444, 445, 446
Purcell, Henry, 204, 216–17, 221
Puritani e i Cavalieri, I, Bellini, 386
Pythagoras, 14

Quadrivium, 15
Quam pulchra es, Dunstable, 94, 95, 96, 97
Quant Theseus—Ne quier veoir (Paien), Machaut, 74–75
Quantz, J. J., 278, 280, 287, 296
Quartets:
    of Beethoven, 324, 325, 327, 329, 340–41

of Mozart, 318–19, 318, 366
    in post-Romantic music, 366, 371, 406, 411
    in Romantic period, 428, 443, 453
    see also Piano quartets; String quartets
Quatuor pour la fin du temps, Messiaen, 443
Quintets:
    of Brahms, 370, 371
    of Schoenberg, 457
    see also Piano quintets; String quintets
Quodlibet, 262
"Quotation" music, 472

Ragtime, Stravinsky, 444, 445, 446, 452
Rake's Progress, The (Auden and Kallman), Stravinsky, 445
Rameau, Jean-Philippe, 186, 253–56, 421
Rappresentazione di anima e di corpo, La, Cavalieri, 198
Rasumovsky, Count, 332, 343
Rasumovsky quartets, 329
Ravel, Maurice, 419, 421–23
Recitative:
    accompanied, 212
    aria vs., 189, 196
    Baroque, 214
    dry, 212, 214, 271
Recitativo accompagnato, 212
Recitativo secco, 212, 214, 272
Reciting tones, 31
Reformation, see Church music, Reformation
Refrains:
    in ballate (ripresa), 78
    in balletts, 153
    English (burden), 96
    liturgical, 10, 26
    in troubadour and trouvère songs, 39
Reger, Max, 395
Reinken, Jan Adam, 206, 234
Renaissance, 107–80
    Eastern European music in, 136, 162–63
    English music in, 136, 153–56, 161, 163, 170–71, 176–77
    French music in, 133–34, 152–53
    German music in, 157–60
    historical background of, 107–8
    Italian music in, 132–33, 143–50, 164–68, 277–79
    meaning of, 107
    musical style in, 109
    Netherlands School in, 112–32
    Spanish music in, 134–35, 168–69
Requiem, Berlioz, 348
Requiem, Fauré, 417
Requiem, Mozart, 317, 323
Requiem, Verdi, 348, 356, 386
Requiem Mass for the Empress Maria Victoria, 168
Respond, 26
Responsorial psalmody, 7, 12
Responsory (respond), 11
Resurrection Symphony, Mahler, 400, 401
Retrograde canon, 115
Revueltes, Silvestre, 436
Rhapsody, Brahms, 354
Rhapsody in Blue, Gershwin, 434
Rhaw, Georg, 159
Rheingold, Das, Wagner, 390

Rhenish Symphony, Schumann, 374
Rhétorique des dieux, La, Gaultier, 208, 208
Rhythm:
  in Baroque music, 183
  in Burgundian School music, 101
  in Greek music, 5–6
  in late fourteenth-century French music, 81–82
  modal, 49–50, 53
  in motets, 59, 62–64
  in Renaissance music, 110, 180
  in troubadour and trouvère songs, 38
Ricercar dopo il Credo, Frescobaldi, 203
Ricercare, Gabrieli, 174
Ricercari, 140, 142, 172, 174, 202, 204, 231, 233
Richard Coeur-de-Lion, Grétry, 295
Richter, Franz Xaver, 290
Rienzi, Wagner, 390
Rigoletto, Verdi, 387
Rilke, Rainer Maria, 439
Rimsky-Korsakov, Nicolas, 406, 407, 410
Rinaldo, Handel, 272
Ring des Nibelungen, Der, Wagner, 390
Rinuccini, Ottavio, 187
Ripieno, 244
Ritornello, in trecento madrigals, 77, 143
Ritorno d'Ulisse, Il, Monteverdi, 190
Robert le diable, Meyerbeer, 381
Rochberg, George, 472
Rococo style, 281–83, 317
Rodeo, Copland, 434
Roland, Lully, 214
Roller, Alfred, 404
Roman Carnival Overture, Berlioz, 376
Roman Catholic Church, see Liturgy, Roman
Romances, 142
Roman de Fauvel, 71, 72
Roman Empire:
  decline and fall of, 1–2, 11–12
  Papal power and, 2, 11
Romanesca bass, 193, 206
Roman opera, 189–90
Romanticism:
  Classicism compared with, 344–49, 350, 377
  dualities of, 346–47
  in Germany, 348, 389–94
  meaning of term, 344, 350
  traits of, 249, 345
Romantic music, 358–95
  chamber music in, 366–71
  characteristics of style of, 350
  choral music, 353–57
  instrumental, 346, 358–80
  nationalism in, 361, 380
  opera in, 295, 381–95
  for piano, 358–66
  program music, 346, 373, 376–77, 380
  variations in, 365
  vocal, 344–57
  see also Post-Romantic music
Romeo and Juliet, Berlioz, 376
Romeo and Juliet, Prokofiev, 431
Romeo and Juliet, Tchaikovsky, 380
Rondeaux:
  of Machaut, 74
  of troubadours and trouvères, 38
Rondellus, 90

Rore, Cipriano de, 145–46, 178
Rosenkavalier, Der, Strauss, 404–5, 404, 405
Rosenmüller, Johann, 244
Rospigliosi, Giulio, 189
Rossi, Luigi, 190, 196, 219
Rossini, Gioacchino, 356, 363
  operas of, 381, 384
Rota, 90
Roussel, Albert, 423
Rowlandson, Thomas, 279
Roy Henry, 93
Rückert, Friedrich, 401
Russia, Balakirev, 406
Russian Easter Overture, Rimsky-Korsakov, 410
Russian music:
  nineteenth-century, 406–11
  opera in, 406, 407, 431
Russian quartets, Haydn, 304
Ruy Blas overture, Mendelssohn, 372

Sachs, Hans, 39
Sackbut, 87
Sacre du printemps, Le, Stravinsky, 444
Sadko, Rimsky-Korsakov, 410
St. Cecilia, Gounod, 355
St. Gall, monastery of, 77
St. Mark's Cathedral, 131, 145, 148, 178, 250
St. Martial organum, 46–49
St. Paul, Mendelssohn, 357
Saint-Saëns, Camille, 415, 416
Salome, Strauss, 403, 404
Salomon, Johann Peter, 299, 306
Salon México, El, Copland, 434
Salve Regina, 18, 19, 20
Salzburg Mass, Benevoli, 197
Sammartini, G. B. (San Martini), 285, 292, 313
Sanctus, 20, 26, 93
Sans Soleil, Mussorgsky, 407, 409
Sant' Alessio, Landi, 189
Sarabande, 207, 209, 235, 261
Sartorio, M. A., 211
Sarum liturgy, 90
Satie, Erik, 421, 422
Saudades do Brasil, Milhaud, 437, 438
Saul, Handel, 273
Scarlatti, Alessandro, 212, 213, 219, 220, 283
Scarlatti, Domenico, 283, 285, 359
Scenes from Goethe's "Faust," Schumann, 354
Scheherazade, Rimsky-Korsakov, 440
Scheidemann, Heinrich, 203
Scheidt, Samuel, 203, 206, 224, 234
Schein, Johann Hermann, 150, 199, 224
Schenk, Johann, 160
Scherzi, Walther, 243
Schicksalslied, Brahms, 354
Schiller, Johann von, 279, 342
Schleicht, spielende Wellen, Bach, 267
Schoenberg, Arnold, 395, 402, 425, 436, 453–59, 464, 469, 475
  symphonies of, 453
Schola Cantorum (Rome, eighth century), 12
Scholia enchiriadis, 44
Schöne Müllerin, Die, Schubert, 352
Schubert, Franz Peter, 296, 317, 350, 351, 401

chamber music of, 366–68
choral works of, 355
Lieder of, 350–52
piano music of, 359
quartets of, **367**
sonatas of, 359
symphonies of, 372
Schübler chorales, Bach, 260, 269
Schumann, Robert:
　chamber music of, 369
　choral works of, 354
　Lieder of, 346, 352
　piano music of, 360
　symphonies of, 371, 373–74
Schütz, Heinrich, 150, 179, 198, 199–202, 224, 225, 229, 259, 357
Schwanengesang, Schubert, 352
Schwind, Moritz von, *351*
Scordatura, 244
Scotch Symphony, Mendelssohn, 372
Scriabin, Alexander, 410–11, **411**
Scythian Suite, Prokofiev, 431
Sea Pieces, MacDowell, 413
Seasons, The, Haydn, 309, 350
Seasons, The, Vivaldi, 252
Sea Symphony, Vaughan Williams, 433
Secular songs (monody), of Middle Ages, 35–40
Secunda prattica, 181
Se la face ay pale Mass, Dufay, 104, 106
Semele and Hercules, Handel, 274
Senescente mundano filio, 48, **48**
Senfl, Ludwig, 128, 134, 160
Sequences (*sequentia*), 28–29, 58
Serenade for Orchestra, Kay, 436
Serenade in A, Stravinsky, 444
Serialism, total, 464, 473
Serial music, 456
Sermisy, Claudin de, 133
Serse, Handel, 291
Serva padrona, La, Pergolesi, 294
Sessions, Roger, 436
Seven Last Words, The, Haydn, 309
Seven Last Words, The, Schütz, 201, 229
Sext, 17
Sextets:
　of Brahms, 367
　of Mendelssohn, 368
Sfogava con le stelle, Caccini, *184*, **185**
Shakespeare, William, 372
Sharp, Cecil, 415
Shawms, 42, 87, 138
Shostakovich, Dmitri, 431
Sibelius, Jean, 414–15
Siciliano, 266
Siegfried, Wagner, 390
Sinfonia, 238–39, 300
Sinfonia a 8, Stamitz, 288
Sinfonia domestica, Strauss, 402
Sinfonietta, Janáček, 412
Sinfonietta, Roussel, 423
Singspiels, 295–96
　of Mozart, 312, 315, 321, 323
Sing- und Spielmusik, 440
Six Bagatelles, Webern, 461
Slåtter, Grieg, 412
Slavonic Dances, Dvořák, 411
Sleeping Beauty, The, Tchaikovsky, 380
Smetana, Bedřich, 411
Socrate (Plato), Satie, 421

Soggetto cavato, 122
Solo sonatas, Baroque, 239, 243–44, 263
Solo songs:
　Baroque, 220–21
　Renaissance, 180
　see also Chansons; Lieder
Somerset Rhapsody, Holst, 415
Sonata da camera, 230, 239, 244
Sonata da chiesa, 172, 202, 206, 239, 263, 271, 300
Sonata for Two Pianos and Percussion, Bartók, 428, 430
Sonata pian' e forte, Gabrieli, 179
Sonatas:
　Baroque, 205–6, 238–40, 243–44, 263
　of Classical period, 283, 286–87
　form of, outlined, 284–85
　in Romantic period, 361, 368
　sixteenth-century, 179, 196
　twentieth-century, 441
　see also Piano sonatas; Violin sonatas; Violoncello sonatas; *specific composers*
Sonatas for Connoisseurs and Amateurs, C. P. E. Bach, 286, **286**, 287
Sonate Pathétique, Beethoven, 329
Sonates pour divers instruments, Debussy, 421
Sonatine, Ravel, 422
Sonato-rondo form, 304, 305
Sonetos, 142
Song of Roland, 36
Songs and Dances of Death, Mussorgsky, 407
Songs without Words, Mendelssohn, 360
Sonnambula, La, Bellini, 386
Souterliedeken, Clemens, 161
Spanish music, 283
　medieval, 39, 46
　nationalism in, 415
　Renaissance, 134–35, 168–69
Spanish Paven, Bull, 176
Speculum musicae, Jacob of Liège, 70
Spinet, 139, 177
Spinning Song, Mendelssohn, 360
Spontini, Gasparo, 293, 381
Sprechstimme, 460, 466
Spring Symphony, Britten, 434
Spring Symphony, Schumann, 374
Stabat Mater, Jacopo da Todi, 29
Stabat Mater, Palestrina, 178
Stabat Mater, Pergolesi, 222
Stabat Mater, Rossini, 356
Stamitz, Johann, 281, 288
Stay Corydon thou swain, Wilbye, 155
Steffani, Agostino, 212
Stile antico, 181
Stile concertato, *see Concertato* style
Stile concitato, 195, 196
Stile moderno, 181, 196
Still, William Grant, 436
Stimmtausch, 90
Stockhausen, Karlheinz, 442, 464, 467, 470
Stoltzer, Thomas, 160
Stone Guest, The, Dargomizhsky, 410
Stradella, Alessandro, 212, 219, 221
Stradivari, Antonio, 238, *238*
Strauss, Richard, 376, 395, 402–5
　harmony of, **405**
Stravinsky, Igor, 425, 443–521
　ballets of, 444
　on composition, 452

Stravinsky, Igor (continued)
    style of, 447–51, **451**
Striggio, Alessandro, 187
String quartets:
    of Fauré, 417
    of Grieg, 412
    of Haydn, 302, 303, 304, 305, 307, **307**
    of Mozart, 318–19, **318**, 366
    in Romantic period, 366
    twentieth-century, 436, 459, 460
    see also Quartets
String quintets:
    of Mozart, 319
    of Schubert, 369
    see also Quintets
Strophic variation, 192
Sturm und Drang (storm and stress), 287,
    301, *303*, 310, 313
Style bourgeois, 281
Style brisé, 208
Style galant (rococo), 281
Stylus gravus, 181
Stylus luxurians, 181
Substitute clausulae, 55, 58–59
Suite Bergamasque, Debussy, 420
Suite in F, Roussel, 423
Suite Provençale, Milhaud, 437
Suites, Baroque, 202, 207, 209, 214, 235, 243,
    261, 263, 271, 290
Sumer is icumen in, 90
Summer Day on the Mountain, d'Indy, 416
Sunless, Mussorgsky, 407, 409
Super flumina Babilonis, Gombert, 130
Surprises de l'Amour, Les, Rameau, 256
Susanna, Handel, 274
Swan Lake, Tchaikovsky, 380
Swan of Tuonela, The, Sibelius, 414
Sweelinck, Jan, 152, 161, 203
Symphoniae sacrae, Schütz, 201
Symphonic Etudes, Schumann, 360
Symphonic Metamorphoses, Hindemith, 441,
    442
Symphonic poems:
    of Liszt, 376–77
    in post-Romantic music, 402–3, 406, 414
    types of program for, 402
Symphonic Variations, Franck, 365
Symphonie concertante, 289
Symphonie fantastique, Berlioz, *326*, 327,
    348, 374–75, *375*, 376
Symphonies:
    of Classical period, 281, 285, 288–90, 297,
    313, **325**
    origin of, 285
    in post-Romantic music, 397–402, 406, 414,
    423
    in Romantic period, 371–80
    twentieth-century, 431, 433, 434, 446, 453,
    461
    see also specific composers
Symphonies of Wind Instruments, Stravin-
    sky, 452
Symphony for Concert Band, Hindemith,
    441
Symphony in Three Movements, Stravinsky,
    447
Symphony of a Thousand, Mahler, 397
Symphony of Psalms, Stravinsky, 446, 450
Syntagma musicum, Praetorius, 137, *138*
Syrian music, 7–8

Tablatures, lute, 136, 139, *155*
Talea, in isorhythm, 71–72
Tallis, Thomas, 136, 163
Tannhaüser, Wagner, 390
Tapiola, Sibelius, 414
Taras Bulba, Janáček, 412
Tartini, Giuseppe, 244
Taverner, John, 136
Tchaikovsky, Peter Ilyich, 380, 431, 445
    concertos of, 380
Te Deum, Berlioz, 348, 355
Te Deum, Bruckner, 379
Te Deum laudamus, 10, 23, 30
Telemann, Georg Phillip, 220, 228, 244
Telemusik, Stockhausen, 472
Tempest, The, Purcell, 217
Terce, 17
Terradellas, Domingo, 291
Theme and variations:
    Baroque, 192, 202, 206, 227, 235
    Renaissance, 143, 146–47
Theodora, Handel, 274
Thoroughbass, see Basso continuo
Three Compositions for Piano, Babbitt, 465
Tigrane, Scarlatti, 213
Ti lascio l'alma impegno, Legrenzi, 212
Till Eulenspiegels lustige Streiche, Strauss,
    402, 403
Time, in French notation, 85
Toccata in E minor, Pachelbel, 231
Toccatas, 175, 202, 209–10, 231–32, **232**, 258
Tod Jesu, Der, K. H. Graun, 297
Tod und Verklärung, Strauss, 402
Tomášek, Jan Václav, 331, 358
Tombeau, 209
Tombeau de Couperin, Le, Ravel, 422
Tomkins, Thomas, 163, 176
Tonality, major-minor, 186, 253–54
Tone clusters, 466
Torelli, Giuseppe, 246–47, 251
Tosca, Puccini, 423, *423*
Total serialism, 464, 473
Totentanz, Liszt, 363
Tract, 20, 25
Tragédies lyriques, 254, 290, 293, 317
Trauersinfonie, Haydn, 302
Traviata, La, Verdi, 386, 387
Treatise on Harmony, Rameau, 186
Trecento (fourteenth century), 78–80
Trills, 242
Trionfo di Dori, Il, 154
Trio sonatas, 204, 206, 239, 240–41, 256, 258–
    59, 263
Tristan und Isolde, Wagner, 391, **392**, *393–
    94*
Triumphes of Oriana, The, Morley, 154
Triumph of Time and Truth, The, Handel,
    274
Trois petites liturgies pour la presence di-
    vine, Messiaen, 443
Trombone, 87, 139, 225
Tropes, 48
Troubadours, 36–39
Trout Quintet, Schubert, 366
Trouvères, 36–39, 73, 82
Trovatore, Il, Verdi, 386, 387
Troyens à Carthage, Les, Berlioz, 293, 383
Trumpet, 42, 87, 139
Turandot, Puccini, 423
Turangalila, Messiaen, 443, 469

Turba, 228
Turn of the Screw, The, Britten, 434
Turnovský, Jan Trajan, 136
Tu solus, qua facis mirabilia, Josquin des Prez, 123, 125
Tutti, 246
Twelve Poems of Emily Dickinson, Copland, 435
Twelve-tone technique, 454, 456, 464
Twentieth-century music, 425–75
  composer-performer interaction in, 469
  expressionism in, 455–56, 459
  influences on, 425–26
  nationalism in, 426–36
  Schoenberg group in, 453–64
  space as element in, 468
  in United States, 434–36
  unusual sound-sources in, 468
  after Webern, 464–75
Tye, Christopher, 163

Umbrian Scene, Kay, 436
Unfinished Symphony, Schubert, 372
United States:
  Dvořák influenced by music of, 380
  post-Romantic music in, 412–14
  twentieth-century music in, 434–36
Ut queant laxis, 32, 33

Varèse, Edgard, 466, 468
Variation canzona, 205
Variations, see Theme and variations
Variations for Orchestra, Carter, 436
Variations IV, Cage, 473
Variations on a Theme of Haydn, Brahms, 365, 377
Variations of a Theme of Paganini, Brahms, 365
Variations sérieuses, Mendelssohn, 359
Vatican Council (1962–1965), 16, 17
Vaudevilles, 152, 295
Vaughan Williams, Ralph, 415
Venetian opera, 190, 192, 211–12, 249, 290
Venetian school, 131, 177–79, 197
Veni Creator Spiritus, 94, 400
Veni Creator Spiritus, Dufay, 102
Veni Redemptor gentium, 158
Veni Sancte Spiritus, 29, 94
Veni sponsa Christi Mass, Palestrina, 165
Venus and Adonis, Blow, 216, 217
Vêpres siciliennes, Les, Verdi, 387
Verdelot, Philippe, 129, 144
Verdi, Giuseppe, 356
  operas of, 384, 386–88
Verism, 423, 444
Verklärte Nacht, Schoenberg, 453
"Verse" anthems, 163
Verses (versets), 202
Vers la flamme, Scriabin, 411
Versus, 48, 58
Vespers, 17
Vespers, Monteverdi, 197
Vestale, La, Spontini, 381
Via Crucis, Liszt, 356
Viadana, Lodovico, 197
Vicentino, Nicola, 107, 109n

Victimae paschali laudes, 29, 30
Victoria, Tomás Luis de, 168–69
Vida breve, La, Falla, 415
Vielle (Fiedel), 40–41, 87
Vienna school, 288, 289
Viennese serenade, 290
Vier ernste Gesänge, Brahms, 353, 371
Vihuela de mano, 139, 142
Villancicos, 142
Villanella, 149, 152
Viol, 155, 182, 233
Violin, 41, 182, 263
Violin concertos:
  of Beethoven, 324, 329, 336
  of Romantic period, 373, 380
  twentieth-century, 428, 429, 431, 457
  see also Concertos
Violin sonatas:
  of Beethoven, 324, 333
  of d'Indy, 416
  of Fauré, 417
  of Ives, 414
  of Janáček, 412
  of Mozart, 318
  see also Sonatas
Violoncello, 184, 263
Virelais, of Machaut, 73–74
Virga Jesse, Bruckner, 357
Virginalists, 176–77, 206
Virginals, 139, 176–77, 177
Visionaire, La, Couperin, 235
Vitry, Philippe de, 70, 71, 78
Vittrici schieri, Sartorio, 211
Vivaldi, Antonio, 249–53, 257
  instrumental music of, 251
Vivray je tousjours en soucy, Sermisy, 134
Vocal ranges, late fifteenth-century, 113
Vom Himmel hoch, Bach, 269
Vořísek, Jan Hugo, 358
Votive antiphons, 95
Vox organalis, 45–46
Vox principalis, 45–46

Wachet auf, Buxtehude, 225
Wacław of Szamotuł, 136
Wagenseil, Georg Christoph, 288
Wagner, Richard, 39, 454
  influence on other composers of, 366, 410
  music dramas of, 348, 383, 390–95
Waldstein Sonata, Beethoven, 336
Walküre, Die, Wagner, 390
Walter, Johann, 159, 229, 243
Wanderer Fantasie, Schubert, 359
War and Peace, Prokofiev, 431
War Requiem, Britten, 434
Water Music, Handel, 271
Weber, Carl Maria von, 358, 389
Webern, Anton von, 395, 402, 425, 460–61
  influence of, 464
  symphonies of, 461, 462
Weckmann, Matthias, 225
Weelkes, Thomas, 153, 163
Well-Tempered Clavier, The, Bach, 259, 260–61, 262, 270, 317, 362
Wende dich, Herr, Hammerschmidt, 226
Wenn der Herr die Gefangenen, Weckmann, 224
Wert, Giaches de, 146

Wesley, Samuel, 297, 355
Western Wynde Mass, Taverner, 136
When David Heard, Tomkins, 163
Whitman, Walt, 435, 441
Wie bist du meine Königin, Brahms, 353
Wiegenlied, Brahms, 353
Wilbye, John, 153, 155
Wilde, Oscar, 403
Wilhelm Meister (Goethe), 352
Willaert, Adrian, 131–32, 144, 178
Winchester Troper, *35*
Winterreise, Schubert, 352
Wipo, 29
Wir bauen eine Stadt, Hindemith, 439
With drooping wings, Purcell, 217
Without Sun, Mussorgsky, 407, 409
Wizlau von Rügen, Prince, 39
Wolf, Hugo, 396
  Lieder of, 346, 396
Wolfenbüttel 677 (W₁), 90
Woodland Sketches, MacDowell, 413

Wozzeck, Berg, 459
Wuorinen, Charles, *474*
Württemberg sonatas, C. P. E. Bach, 285

Xenakis, Yannis, 466

Yonge, Nicholas, 153

Zachow, Friedrich Wilhelm, 228
Zampa, Herold, 382
Zarlino, 132, 178
Zar und Zimmermann, Lortzing, 390
Zauberflöte, Die, Mozart, 279, 317, 321, 323, 350
Zelter, Carl Friedrich, 270
Zielenski, Mikolaj, 179
Zither, 41
Zoroastre, Rameau, 255